T0379804

SICILY AND THE HELLENISTIC MEDITERRANEAN WORLD

In *Sicily and the Hellenistic Mediterranean World,* D. Alex Walthall investigates the royal administration of Hieron II (r. 269–215 BCE), the Syracusan monarch who leveraged Sicily's agricultural resources to build a flourishing kingdom that, at one time, played an outsized role in the political and cultural affairs of the Western Mediterranean. Walthall's study combines a historical overview with the rich archaeological evidence that traditionally has not been considered in studies of Hellenistic kingdoms. Exploring the Hieronian system of agricultural taxation, he recasts the traditional narrative of the island's role as a Roman imperial "grain basket" via analysis of monumental granaries, patterns of rural land-use, standardized grain measures, and the circulation of bronze coinage – the material elements of an agricultural administration that have emerged from recent excavations and intensive landscape survey on the island. Combining material and documentary evidence, Walthall's multidisciplinary approach offers a new model for the writing of economic and social history of ancient societies.

D. ALEX WALTHALL is an associate professor in the Department of Classics at the University of Texas at Austin. He has worked for more than two decades in Sicily, much of which has been spent directing archaeological campaigns for the American Excavations at Morgantina. His research has been sponsored by the Archaeological Institute of America, the Council of American Overseas Research Centers, the American Academy in Rome, and the Loeb Classical Library Foundation.

SICILY AND THE HELLENISTIC MEDITERRANEAN WORLD

ECONOMY AND ADMINISTRATION DURING THE REIGN OF HIERON II

D. ALEX WALTHALL

University of Texas at Austin

CAMBRIDGE
UNIVERSITY PRESS

CAMBRIDGE
UNIVERSITY PRESS

Shaftesbury Road, Cambridge CB2 8EA, United Kingdom

One Liberty Plaza, 20th Floor, New York, NY 10006, USA

477 Williamstown Road, Port Melbourne, VIC 3207, Australia

314–321, 3rd Floor, Plot 3, Splendor Forum, Jasola District Centre, New Delhi – 110025, India

103 Penang Road, #05-06/07, Visioncrest Commercial, Singapore 238467

Cambridge University Press is part of Cambridge University Press & Assessment, a department of the University of Cambridge.

We share the University's mission to contribute to society through the pursuit of education, learning and research at the highest international levels of excellence.

www.cambridge.org
Information on this title: www.cambridge.org/9781316511053

DOI: 10.1017/9781009036474

First published 2024

Printed in the United Kingdom by CPI Group Ltd, Croydon CR0 4YY

A catalogue record for this publication is available from the British Library.

Library of Congress Cataloging-in-Publication Data
NAMES: Walthall, D. Alex, 1982- author.
TITLE: Sicily and the Hellenistic Mediterranean world : economy and administration during the reign of Hieron II / D. Alex Walthall, University of Texas, Austin.
DESCRIPTION: Cambridge ; New York, NY : Cambridge University Press, 2024. | Includes bibliographical references and indexes.
IDENTIFIERS: LCCN 2023020303 (print) | LCCN 2023020304 (ebook) | ISBN 9781316511053 (hardback) | ISBN 9781009005234 (paperback) | ISBN 9781009036474 (epub)
SUBJECTS: LCSH: Hieron II, Tyrant of Syracuse, -215 B.C.? | Hellenism. | Agriculture, Ancient–Italy–Syracuse. | Syracuse (Italy)–Kings and rulers. | Syracuse (Italy)–Politics and government. | Syracuse (Italy)–Economic conditions. | Sicily (Italy)–Civilization–Greek influences | Sicily (Italy)–History–To 800.
CLASSIFICATION: LCC DG55.S9 W35 2024 (print) | LCC DG55.S9 (ebook) | DDC 937/.801–dc23/eng/20230516
LC record available at https://lccn.loc.gov/2023020303
LC ebook record available at https://lccn.loc.gov/2023020304

ISBN 978-1-316-51105-3 Hardback

This publication is made possible in part from the Barr Ferree Foundation Fund for Publications, Department of Art and Archaeology, Princeton University.

For Poppy and Sloop

CONTENTS

FIGURES

ACKNOWLEDGMENTS

This is a book long in the making and along the way I have benefited immensely from the guidance and support of many individuals and institutions.

My colleagues with the American Excavations at Morgantina (AEM) have certainly provided the greatest source of inspiration. I owe my deepest gratitude to Malcolm Bell III, who first gave me the opportunity to take part in the Morgantina excavations – an experience that changed the course of my life – and who has fostered my growth as an archaeologist ever since. Carla Antonaccio, Shelley Stone, Barbara Tsakirgis, Hal Sharp, Sandra Lucore, Lars Karlsson, Ingrid Edlund-Berry, Monika Trümper, and Holger Baitinger have all shared generously of their time and unmatched knowledge of Morgantina, its history and archaeology. Many of the ideas that appear in the following pages were refined in conversation with friends and colleagues from the AEM: Contrada Agnese Project, who have long humored my ardent enthusiasm for ceramic measuring vessels and corroded bronze coins. Most of all, I am grateful to Jared Benton, Nicole Berlin, Caroline Cheung, Ben Crowther, Steve Gavel, Ben Gorham, Luke Hollis, James Huemoeller, Katharine Potts-Dupre Huemoeller, Leigh Lieberman, Christy Schirmer, China Shelton, Mali Skotheim, Randall Souza, Andrew Tharler, Annie Truetzel, and Elizabeth Wueste. I have benefited immensely from our conversations on site, in the magazzino, and around the dinner table at the Expedition House in Aidone. For nearly two decades now, the town of Aidone has been a second home to me; I have cherished the relationships built with the entire community, especially those with Angelo Minacapilli, Emilia Trovato, Serena Raffiotta, Filippo La Tora, Bruno Cristiano, and Filippo Campanella.

In the storerooms and archaeological museums around Sicily, my research was supported by Paola Pelagatti, Giovanni Di Stefano, Beatrice Basile, Concetta Cuircina, Maria Musumeci, Maria Costanza Lentini, Laura Maniscalco, Rosario Patané, Henri Tréziny, Enrico Caruso, Brian McConnell, Liborio Calascibetta, Carlo Staffile, Federica Barbarino, Giancarlo Filantropi, and Raffaella Greca, among many others. The *custodi* of the Museo Archeologico di Aidone kept my spirits high with coffee, camaraderie, and the occasional admonition in dialect. I owe a special debt of gratitude to Angela Maria Manenti at the Museo Archeologico Regionale "Paolo Orsi" of Syracuse, who helped me time and again with gaining access to all manner of material essential to my research.

In matters of advice, guidance, and constructive feedback, I am first and foremost indebted to Nino Luraghi, who has been a wellspring of inspiration and encouragement over the years. Even long after my time at Princeton, Michael Koortbojian, William A. P. Childs, Michael Flower, Harriet Flower, Alan Stahl, and Michael Padgett remained brilliant advisors and interlocutors. In its final form, this book profited from the expertise and insights freely shared by a great number of individuals, including Carmen Arnold-Biucchi, Hayley Barnett, Deborah Beck, Emma Blake, Jesper Blid, Sophie Bouffier, Kim Bowes, Greg Butler, Lorenzo Campagna, Kathleen Coleman, Steven Ellis, Paul Kosmin, Kevin Lee, Leigh Lieberman, Neil MacDougall, Clemente Marconi, Catharine McNall, Simon Oswald, Jonathan Prag, Adam Rabinowitz, Timm Radt, Sam Ross, Christy Schirmer, Rob Schon, Richard Thomas, Annie Truetzel, John Tully, Caroline Veit, Héctor Vera, Dan Wolf, and two anonymous reviewers. Above all, I wish to express my utmost gratitude to my colleague Rabun Taylor, who offered valuable comments on most every chapter and who, along with Beatrice Rehl, helped me to see the light at the end of the tunnel.

My research was made possible thanks to the financial support of numerous institutions, including the Archaeological Institute of America, the Center for Hellenic Studies, the John Anson Kittredge Educational Fund, and the Center for European Studies at the University of Texas at Austin. Additionally, subvention funding for this publication was made in part from the Barr Ferree Foundation Fund for Publications, Department of Art and Archaeology, Princeton University, and from the College of Liberal Arts, University of Texas at Austin.

Last but certainly not least, the support of friends and family was paramount from start to finish. My parents, Christina and Denton, and brother, Nick Danger, have been an unwavering source of support and encouragement. Finishing this book would not have been possible without the help of our incredible and indefatigable childcare providers, especially Giuseppa DiDomenico. None of this would be possible without the incomparable Lauren Dearing Russo.

INTRODUCTION

Σικελία πασῶν τῶν νήσων καλλίστη ὑπάρχει, ὡς μεγάλα δυναμένη συμβάλλεσθαι πρὸς
αὔξησιν ἡγεμονίας.
—Diod. 23.1–2

In the opening lines of the twenty-third book of his universal history, Diodorus Siculus praises his native Sicily as "the fairest of all islands, since it can contribute greatly to the growth of an empire."[1] Sitting at the intersection of prevailing maritime routes, the island served as a natural landing for ships plying their way between the Mediterranean's Eastern and Western Basins. Its broad coastal plains supported large urban centers and entrepôts that opened onto the Tyrrhenian Sea to the north, the Ionian Sea to the east, and the vast Libyan Sea to the south and west, inviting contacts from the Italian Peninsula, the Greek mainland, and North Africa. Indeed, located at the heart of the Mediterranean basin, Sicily has occupied an equally central place in the geopolitics of the region across much of the last three millennia.

By the time Diodorus composed his sweeping historical account in the late first century BCE, Sicily had certainly played host to its share of settlers, would-be rulers, and occupying forces eager to boost their political fortunes. Not surprisingly, the island factors with some regularity in ancient narratives of empire.[2] The disastrous invasion by Athenian forces in the 410s, as reported by Thucydides, was stoked by the Athenians' desire to leverage the island's vast wealth to defeat their Lacedaemonian adversaries.[3] Two centuries later, Sicily would become Rome's first overseas province, a proving ground for the imperial expansion that swiftly followed. From that point forward, the island was habitually extolled in Roman narratives that traced and legitimated the growth and development of their imperial power. Nowhere are such sentiments more clearly expressed than in the prosecutorial speeches written by Marcus Tullius Cicero for the trial of Gaius Verres, whose governorship of Sicily (73–71) was characterized by storied brutality and corruption. Throughout his speeches, Cicero asks that the jurors consider Verres' crimes against the backdrop of Rome's centuries-long relationship with the island and its residents. In doing so, he recapitulates the view that Sicily played an instrumental role in bolstering Rome's imperial efforts around the Mediterranean. The orator's second speech against Verres opens with a crystallization of the *mythos* that had developed around the island by the time of the Late Republic, nostalgically locating Sicily as fertile ground that bore the fruit of Roman imperial ambition. His remarks bear transcription in full:

> atque antequam de incommodis Siciliae dico, pauca mihi videntur esse de provinciae dignitate, vetustate, utilitate dicenda. nam cum omnium sociorum provinciarumque rationem diligenter habere debetis, tum praecipue Siciliae, iudices, plurimis iustissimisque de causis, primum quod omnium nationum exterarum princeps Sicilia se ad amicitiam fidemque populi Romani adplicavit. prima omnium, id quod ornamentum imperi est, provincia est appellata; prima docuit maiores nostros quam praeclarum esset exteris gentibus imperare.... itaque maioribus nostris in Africam ex hac provincia gradus imperi factus est; neque enim tam facile opes Carthaginis tantae concidissent nisi illud et rei frumentariae subsidium et receptaculum classibus nostris pateret.

> And before I begin to speak of the distresses of Sicily, it seems to me that I ought to say a little of the dignity and antiquity of that province, and of the advantage which it is to us. For as you ought to have a careful regard for all the allies and provinces, so especially ought you to have a regard for Sicily, Jurors, for many, and those the greatest, reasons: First, because of all foreign nations Sicily was the first who joined herself to the friendship and alliance of the Roman people. She was the first to be called a province; and the provinces are a great ornament to the empire. She was the first who taught our ancestors how glorious a thing it was to rule over foreign nations.... From this province therefore it was that our forefathers took that great step in their imperial career, the invasion of Africa: for the great power of Carthage would never have been crushed so readily had not Sicily been at our disposal, both as a granary to supply us with grain and as a harbor for our fleets.[4]

Cicero's words lay bare exactly the quality that made Sicily so *kallistē* in the eyes of Diodorus and would-be hegemonic powers and that which drew the Athenians to risk ruinous defeat so far from home. It was the island's renowned agricultural wealth, the capacity of its fertile soils to produce grains and agricultural goods in remarkable abundance. The Roman orator leaves no room for doubt, as he further elaborates what made Sicily so instrumental to the growth of the Romans' own overseas empire:

> ad omnis res sic illa provincia semper usi sumus ut, quicquid ex sese posset efferre, id non apud nos nasci, sed domi nostrae conditum iam putaremus. deberet non ad diem dedit? quando id quod opus esse putaret non ultro pollicita est? quando id quod imperaretur recusavit? itaque ille M. Cato sapiens cellam penariam rei publicae nostrae, nutricem plebis Romanae Siciliam nominabat. nos vero experti sumus Italico maximo difficillimoque bello Siciliam nobis non pro penaria cella, sed pro aerario illo maiorum vetere ac referto fuisse; nam sine ullo sumptu nostro, coriis, tunicis, frumentoque suppeditando, maximos exercitus nostros vestivit, aluit, armavit.

> [W]e have always so esteemed the island of Sicily for every purpose, as to think that whatever she could produce was not so much raised among the Sicilians as stored up in our own homes. When did she not deliver the grain which she was bound to deliver, by the proper day? When did she fail to promise us, of her own accord, whatever she thought we stood in need of? When did she ever refuse anything which was exacted of her? It is for this reason that Marcus Cato the wise called Sicily a storehouse of provisions for our republic – the nurse of the Roman people. Indeed, we ourselves experienced, in that long and difficult Italian war, that Sicily was not only a storehouse of provisions to us, but was also an old and well-filled treasury left to us by our ancestors; for, supplying us with hides, with tunics, and with grain, the island clothed, armed, and fed our great armies, without any expense to us at all.[5]

With its mild, wet winters and long, arid summers, Sicily was climatically disposed to intensive agricultural production, particularly cereals crops like wheat and barley, which thrived in the rich volcanic soils of the island's eastern lowlands.[6] Throughout much of antiquity, the island's productive landscapes generated surpluses well in excess of what its resident population consumed. This capacity for consistent and abundant harvests allowed the island to become a major exporter of grain and other agricultural goods from as early as the sixth century BCE.[7] Sicily's reputation as a perennial source of plentiful grain was so well established that the island regularly figured in etiological myths that traced the origins of agricultural practice. By some accounts, the inhabitants of Sicily were the first to receive the gift of grain from the goddesses Demeter and Persephone, who were said to count the island as their earthly home.[8] In the ancient Mediterranean world, where food shortage was prevalent and arable land in high demand, ensuring a reliable source of grain took on immeasurable significance for the island's political and military leaders.[9]

The confluence of political authority and control over the island's agricultural wealth found ample expression in antiquity to the point where it had reached the status of a rhetorical *topos*.[10] Decades before the Athenians attempted to annex the island into their overseas empire, the Deinomenid tyrant, Gelon of Syracuse, reportedly offered them an object lesson in the vast wealth and military power that flowed from command of the island's natural resources. According to Herodotus, the Athenians and Spartans sent envoys to the court of Gelon in the months leading up to Xerxes' invasion of Greece with a request that the Syracusan ruler send troops and aid in support of the unified Hellenic effort to stymie the Persian king's advance.[11] After giving audience to their request, Gelon replied with what was ultimately an unacceptable proposition for the Athenians and Spartans: the Syracusan ruler offered to send no fewer than 30,000 men together with 200 triremes and, most significantly, food and provisions to sustain the entire Hellenic force for the duration of the war (an enormous amount by any estimate) but only if he was made the supreme commander of the united Greek forces. Gelon's proposal is instructive, regardless of its historicity, for the underlying message it conveyed: Sicily's agricultural base could be effectively harnessed to achieve considerable political and military power. Was this not, after all, what ultimately brought the Athenians back to the island some 65 years later as would-be conquerors?

AGRICULTURE AND POWER IN THE KINGDOM OF HIERON II

While the association between control of Sicily's agricultural resources and the ambitions of foreign powers is a well-established theme in both ancient and modern narratives, the role of agriculture as a currency of political power on the island itself has attracted far less attention. This book aims to redress the deficit by exploring what was arguably the most vibrant expression of this relationship, namely, the manifestation of autocratic rule in the person of Hieron son of Hierokles, better known to us as Hieron II (r. 269–215), who exercised political authority over much of southeastern Sicily for the greater part of the third century BCE. Although comparatively small when measured against the vast territorial kingdoms of the Seleucid and Ptolemaic dynasts, the Hellenistic kingdom of Hieron II nevertheless constituted a major economic and cultural force in the western Mediterranean at the time. Not coincidentally, it was during the period of Hieron's kingship that the island's famed agricultural resources were for the first time comprehensively taxed and mobilized through a sophisticated administrative system designed to extract an annual tithe on agricultural production from the cities of eastern Sicily. Hieron's remarkable success and longevity as a monarch hinged on exploiting agricultural resources to consolidate and maintain sovereign authority over his kingdom.

This is not the first book to take the kingdom of Hieron II as its principal subject. My own work builds on early studies such as Alexander Schenk Graf von Stauffenberg's *König Hieron der Zweite von Syrakus* (1933) and Helmut Berve's *König Hieron II* (1959), which were among the first to systematically review the ancient literary sources that relay aspects of Hieron's rule and, in effect, write political biographies of the king. Although rather limited in their scope, especially by today's standards, both von Stauffenberg's and Berve's works dealt with issues that remain subject to ongoing academic debate, issues such as Hieron's political status vis-à-vis Rome and the nature of his rule with respect to his contemporaries who ruled over the larger Successor kingdoms in the eastern Mediterranean. The publication of Giovanna De Sensi Sestito's *Gerone II: Un monarca ellenistico in Sicilia* (1977) broke new ground in its expansive approach to the Hieronian kingdom, particularly in the amount of consideration given to discussion of the royal economy and Hieron's foreign relations. Moreover, De Sensi Sestito would be the first to broadly engage with material culture and incorporate archaeological evidence in her study of Hieron II. Nearly three decades later, Caroline Lehmler's *Syrakus unter Agathokles und Hieron II: Die Verbindung von Kultur und Macht in einer hellenistischen Metropole* (2005) took up the baton from De Sensi Sestito and brought Hieronian Sicily into conversation with more recent academic discourse, particularly in arguing that Hieron's cultural policies are best understood when viewed within the mainstream practices of Hellenistic kingship.

My book keeps with Lehmler's views about the cultural politics of Hieron, but goes on to break new ground in two ways. First, my approach centers on illuminating aspects of royal administration that have long been omitted from discussions of the Hieronian kingdom. The blossoming of art, literature, and science at the Hieronian court has long attracted the attention of scholars, many of whom count Syracuse among the major cultural centers of the Early Hellenistic world, a rival even to Alexandria and Athens. Few, however, have attempted to grapple with the underlying roots that sustained Hieron's political power and made this cultural florescence possible. This is no minor omission as the mundane demands of administration (e.g., the payment of tithe grain to a tax-collector, the reporting of harvest data to a royal official) arguably held far greater relevance to the vast majority of Hieron's subjects than did the bucolic idylls of Theokritos or mathematical treatises of Archimedes. For this reason alone, the royal administration of the Hieronian court and its manifestation in the material world deserve our consideration. More so even as improving our knowledge of Hieron's administrative infrastructure promises to yield new modes for viewing how other Hellenistic kingdoms were run. Just as a growing number of scholars in recent decades have increasingly directed their attention to the royal economy and administration of Hellenistic kingdoms, the time has come to bring Hieron's Sicilian kingdom into the conversation.[12]

Second, I foreground archaeological evidence in my discussion to a far greater degree than previous scholars. From the rich volcanic soil of eastern Sicily, a veritable bounty of archaeological material has come to light over the past century, evidence that demands greater attention for what it reveals about the character and scope of Hieron's political authority. Doing so brings greater clarity to our view of the Hieronian kingdom, which should be appraised not only by the spectacular and museum-worthy monuments that have long captured our attention but in equal, if not greater, measure by artifacts of quotidian bearing, which have traditionally received far more limited consideration. When placed in conversation, the monumental and the mundane can reveal much about the manifestation of political power in the Hellenistic world. In Chapter 5, for instance, the analysis of ceramic measuring vessels found at several sites around southeastern Sicily sheds light on efforts taken by the Hieronian court to establish a unified system of volumetric measurement throughout the kingdom. This opens a window onto one of the more subtle mechanisms by which royal authority came to infiltrate the daily lives of those who lived in areas controlled by Hellenistic kings.

Today, as in antiquity, the kingdom of Hieron II is overshadowed by the Attalids, Ptolemies, and Seleucids. Wider surveys of the Hellenistic Mediterranean rarely deal with the Sicilian monarch, and those that do usually treat him as a minor figure obscured in the penumbra of the Successor kingdoms.[13] The Hieronian kingdom was, after all, relatively slight on the scale by which Hellenistic empires are commonly measured – the size of one's army, territorial possessions, and cash reserves. Moreover, the surviving literary and documentary sources that touch on Hieron's political activities are rather limited, thwarting the kind of in-depth study that can be achieved for the royal court of the Seleucids or epistolary practices of the Attalids.[14] And yet there can be no doubt that Hieron himself behaved as an equal to the kings of the eastern Mediterranean and, accordingly, fashioned his *basileia* (kingship) after that of contemporary cultural and political models. The time has come for a wider reappraisal of the Hieronian kingdom, one that brings the kingship of Hieron II into dialog with recent scholarship concerning the nature of Hellenistic monarchy. Doing so may also help to shine a brighter light on Sicily, which has itself been largely omitted from general historical treatments of the Hellenistic period.[15]

THE STRUCTURE OF THE BOOK

In its broad structure, this book is divided into two parts, each of which seeks to advance one of two interconnected aims. I discuss these aims below along with a brief summary of the chapters in each part of the book.

The three chapters that form Part I ("Fashioning a Kingdom") of this book aim to situate the *basileia* of Hieron II within mainstream discussions of

Hellenistic monarchy, with regard to both political ideology and actual state-craft. As I argue throughout, Hieron's fashioning of autocratic rule is best understood when viewed through the lens of contemporary developments taking place in the larger Hellenistic kingdoms of the eastern Mediterranean. In this point of view I am not alone, as a growing chorus of voices has emerged in recent decades to express this same idea.[16] Nevertheless, a fundamental ambiguity persists in scholarship surrounding the nature of Hieron's rule.[17] Establishing Hieron's bona fides as a Hellenistic monarch requires first confronting the fact that scholars have long diverged in their characterization of the king's political standing and the nature of his rule.[18] Unsurprisingly, these diverse opinions tend to reflect the historical lens through which one views Hieron, who – with rare exception – generally appears as only a minor character in much larger historical narratives.

One such lens, often encountered in works focusing on Sicilian history, situates Hieron's political authority within the ambit of autocratic rule characterized by the Syracusan tyrants of the fifth and fourth centuries BCE. It is not only that these individuals wielded vast power over large swaths of the island as Hieron would later come to do, but that the manifestation of autocratic rule persisted on Sicily for far longer than elsewhere in the Greek world. It is partially on account of this proximity in space and time that some scholars have found it preferable to classify Hieron as a "tyrant" or even "tyrant king," presenting him as a successor to the Classical tyrannies of the Deinomenids and Dionysii.[19] Hieron, after all, followed a long line of Syracusan strongmen in his rise to autocratic rule by first seizing power through established institutional structures, initially as *stratēgos* (military general) and then later as *stratēgos autokrator* (military general with broad powers) of the Syracusans. He would even come to magnify his own, presumably fictitious, hereditary connection to the Deinomenid clan.[20] But such details should not distract from the very nontraditional foundations behind his claim to legitimate rule as a sovereign *basileus*, a claim that found no immediate basis in Syracusan institution or custom but instead rested squarely with contemporary forms of autocratic rule that could be found within the Successor kingdoms of the eastern Mediterranean. While not to wholly dismiss the potential influence that these earlier, Sicilian expressions of autocratic rule might have had on Hieron's approach to kingship, they do not ultimately provide a compelling model for the self-styled monarchy of Hieron II.[21] Failure to acknowledge those typically Hellenistic qualities of his rule only serves to prolong the tendency to relegate Hieron and, by extension, the Hieronian kingdom to parochial or, at best, peripheral status on the wider Mediterranean stage.

Histories of the Roman Republic, both ancient and modern, provide the second lens through which we have come to commonly view Hieron's rule. Framed within the larger narrative of Roman hegemony, Hieron helps set in motion a series of events that would precipitate the decades-long conflict with Carthage and eventually Rome's rise to power throughout the Mediterranean. In this role, Hieron is generally cast as a "client king," a faithful and loyal ally of the Republic whose political authority was principally defined by his relationship to Rome.[22] This is an attitude shared by many of our surviving historical and literary accounts composed in the second and first centuries BCE, which tend to characterize Hieron as being nothing less than the archetypal client king. Yet this should be understood for what it truly was, an anachronistic characterization made for the benefit of a contemporary Roman audience of the first century, who were familiar with a much different species of foreign king than the Romans of the mid-third century BCE. That Hieron acted in a fashion that later Romans would come to expect from their royal clientele cannot be taken as evidence that either Hieron or, for that matter, his Roman contemporaries would have viewed their relationship in such terms. This is not to suggest that Rome did not loom large in shaping Hieron's behavior, but simply to challenge attitudes like that expressed by Peter Green in his influential work on the Hellenistic period, wherein the Sicilian king's political authority is described as wholly circumscribed by Roman policy.[23] While Rome's growing intervention in Sicily from the time of the First Punic War certainly had a hand in shaping the political character and territorial expression of Hieron's rule, simply labeling him as a client king misconstrues the relationship between the monarch and Rome as one of political dependency, falsely stripping Hieron of agency. Moreover, it projects a teleological view of a situation for which there was yet no precedent.[24]

To be sure, the character of Hieron's rule was not fashioned *ex nihilo*; it was influenced by Sicily's historical relationship with autocratic rule no less than by the growing political and military presence of Rome in Sicily over the course of the third century BCE. The island had long been a middle ground for cultural syncretism, and there is no reason to believe that the conditions inside the sociopolitical cauldron from which Hieron's kingship had emerged were in any sense different. Yet neither lens offers truly sufficient or convincing grounds to serve as the basis of Hieron's style of monarchic rule. Instead, we should be looking to the Successor kingdoms, where Hieron himself clearly looked when establishing the grounds for his rule.

Chapter 1 ("From General to King") sketches the events that transpired in eastern Sicily during the turbulent years leading up to Hieron's ascension to power, as would-be tyrants and bellicose kings grappled for political and military control of the island. We first meet Hieron in the year 276 when he emerges in our historical sources as a *stratēgos* of the Syracusan army; there follows a selective narrative of his long reign as a *basileus* (king) from 269 until his death in 215. I begin this account *in medias res*, so to speak, with the death of Agathokles in 289 and the political turmoil that erupted across eastern Sicily in the following decades. Doing so foregrounds the immediate political and social context of Hieron's rise to power, while intentionally omitting a lengthy historical narrative geared toward outlining the broader arc of Sicilian history. Readers who wish to gain a more comprehensive understanding of the island's rich history can avail themselves of several excellent books that have appeared in recent years.[25]

In Chapter 2 ("Fashioning Kingship"), I place Hieron's kingship in conversation with the Hellenistic monarchies of the eastern Mediterranean and go on to explore the qualities of his rule that set Hieron's *basileia* ahead of its time – as, for example, in his diplomatic dealings with Rome. I argue that Hieron fashioned his brand of autocratic rule in conformance with contemporary modes of legitimate monarchy that germinated within the Successor kingdoms, while also displaying a degree of creative adaptation. To demonstrate this point, I follow Hieron through three periods of his political career, three acts in which our protagonist successively establishes and refashions the ideological grounds upon which he founds his autocratic authority. Each act unfolds in the wake of a momentous political event: his victory over the Mamertines in the year 269, the conclusion of a peace treaty with Rome in 263, and the elevation of his son, Gelon, to the position of co-regent around the year 240. Following each of these episodes, we can observe – by way of the surviving literary, epigraphic, and archaeological evidence – the steps taken by the king to redefine the terms of his autocratic authority, often in ways that simultaneously show an embrace for contemporary practices deployed by the Ptolemaic and Seleucid kings and a flexibility shaped by geopolitical events taking place in the western Mediterranean.

Discussion shifts in Chapter 3 ("Cities in the Kingdom") to the broader political landscape of the kingdom and to the nature of Hieron's relationship with the cities of southeastern Sicily that recognized his political authority as a *basileus*. Although well-defined in antiquity, the borders of the Hieronian kingdom are today the subject of ongoing discussion, and so I begin by addressing the varying scholarly positions on the subject. Both textual and material evidence offer valuable insight into the size of the territory under Hieron's control, which I argue was considerably larger than has been previously recognized. Recognizing the contours of the kingdom is a necessary starting point for appreciating the material resources that Hieron stood to exploit through taxation, a topic explored in depth in Chapter 4. I next consider the legal status of cities vis-à-vis the king, asking what limitations were placed on their civic autonomy and what benefits were accrued by acknowledging Hieron as a king. As emerged in Chapter 2, there is ample evidence to suggest that Hieron's interactions with the cities of southeastern Sicily followed closely on the model set by the rulers of the Successor kingdoms. This is abundantly clear thanks to the survival of a partially intact inscription that is believed to transcribe a letter written by Hieron to the Syracusan *polis*.

Ultimately, my aim in the first part of the book is to highlight the qualities of Hieron's kingship that made his rule much like that of contemporary Hellenistic monarchs while also drawing attention to those aspects that set him apart. In documenting Hieron's own dynamic and evolutionary approach to establishing the legitimacy of his rule, we can draw valuable conclusions about the nature of Hellenistic kingship and the inherent elasticity in the political rationale used to justify autocratic power at the time. Such elasticity, or resilience, is especially evident in Hieron's early interactions with Rome, and, in many ways, his actions foreshadowed those taken later on by monarchs of the Successor kingdoms whose own military might would eventually come to be challenged and diminished by the growth of Roman power in the eastern Mediterranean.[26]

Building on the foundations of Part I, the chapters that form Part II ("Measuring a Kingdom") center on the administration of the Hieronian state with a particular focus on the taxation of agricultural goods. Like most Hellenistic monarchs, Hieron relied on the revenue generated from taxation to maintain the mechanisms of state that served to reinforce his status as king. While the tax laws of Hieron have been the subject of academic interest for over a century, scholarship has largely focused on their Roman afterlife as the *lex Hieronica*, the details of which come to us almost exclusively from the courtroom speeches of Cicero. This is chiefly due to the paucity of contemporary third-century sources that preserve details about the operation of the tax system in Hieronian Sicily. We lack, for instance, the rich documentary record that is available to us from the territories subject to the Attalid, Ptolemaic, and Seleucid kings. I expand our frame to include a wide spectrum of material evidence (i.e., standardized grain measures, coins, monumental granaries) that pertain to the original, third-century operation of Hieron's administrative armature. Such instruments of fiscal administration have long been treated in isolation or simply overlooked within the broader context of the king's political authority and the governance of his kingdom, yet they surely played an essential role in sustaining the Hieronian state. In addition to addressing the role of these instruments from a top-down perspective of the royal state, I also explore the broader social repercussions stemming from the introduction of the royal tax administration in southeastern Sicily and, in particular, the widespread availability of new, standardized tools of exchange.

Chapter 4 ("Seeing the Hieronian State") focuses on an institution central to the administration of the Hieronian state: the agricultural tithe collected annually from the *poleis* subject to Hieron's authority. After a brief overview of the evidence related to agricultural taxation in Sicily during the fifth and fourth centuries BCE, I turn to the tax laws established during Hieron's reign.

Drawing on a variety of source material, I examine the chief institutional structures of the tithe system (e.g., proportional taxation, reliance on tax farmers, etc.), addressing each in light of Margaret Levi's theory of predatory rule, which seeks to explain how a ruler's desire to extract maximum revenue from their subjects was balanced against the constraints placed upon their power. I next turn our attention to the operational stages of the tithe, considering each step that brought agricultural goods from productive farmlands around southeastern Sicily to the royal granaries at Syracuse.

Chapter 5 ("Standards and the State") builds the case that the Hieronian state brought about the standardization of volumetric measurement throughout southeastern Sicily during the course of the third century BCE. Upon seizing power in the year 269, Hieron found himself the new sovereign over a patchwork of communities ranging from large *poleis* to smaller satellite towns and agrarian villages. In consolidating his rule over this mosaic of polities, the king and his court would have benefited from the establishment of kingdom-wide metrological standards that served as the common units of measurement for all royal transactions (e.g., payments, taxes in kind, etc.). As established in Chapter 4, the fiscal administration of the Hieronian kingdom relied on the extensive collection and dissemination of information, particularly in furtherance of the agricultural tithe operation, the principal source of Hieron's wealth. Without a common set of standards – a shared language of measurement by which royal officials, tax farmers, and cultivators could communicate – the administration of the agricultural tithe would have been costly and inefficient. Drawing on firsthand research in archaeological collections across Sicily, I present evidence in Chapter 5 for the introduction and adoption of a new class of ceramic measuring vessel in the areas subject to Hieronian control that share a standard typology and were produced according to a uniform volumetric system. I argue that the rapid adoption of these standard measures, as viewed through the archaeological record, was the result of royal mandate aimed at facilitating the oversight and operation of royal taxation.

Trading the handheld for the monumental, Chapter 6 ("Monumental Granaries") takes as its focus the remains of two above-ground granaries that once stood in the agora of Morgantina, one of the cities that recognized Hieron's authority as a *basileus*. After a brief discussion of the buildings' architectural form and function, I explore where the Morgantina granaries fit within the corpus of known Hellenistic granary buildings. Following on the conclusions of Chapters 4 and 5, I argue that the granaries at Morgantina likely served an essential role in the operation of the Hieronian tithe. Here, I draw on the wealth of papyrological evidence from the Ptolemaic kingdom, which attests to the importance of royally controlled regional granaries for the collection of agricultural taxes in Egypt during the third century BCE. By comparison, the granary buildings at Morgantina can be considered reliable indices of Hieron's political control over the city and its agricultural resources. Like the standardized volumetric measures of Chapter 5, the granary buildings at Morgantina offer material witness to the reach of Hieron's royal authority. In this respect, I suggest that they were more than simply administrative warehouses, but also served an important ideological role in projecting Hieron's authority to the western edge of his kingdom.

Chapter 7 ("The Hieronian Mint"), examines the ways in which coinage was employed by the king to bolster his rule. The chapter begins with an introductory survey of the coinage struck by the royal mint during Hieron's reign. I address how variations in the style and types of coins struck at different points in his reign elucidate how Hieron employed coinage to promote an ideology of legitimate kingship. From there, I examine three circumstances in which it might be said that Hieron pursued "monetary policy" to benefit the state. First, I discuss a major currency reform of the 260s that ushered in the exclusive production of bronze coinage by the royal mint for upward of three decades. Second, I consider Hieron's decision to renew the minting of silver coinage after ca. 240 and the rationale behind striking this coinage on the Sicilian litra standard, resulting in coins that were substantially lighter than many of their contemporary counterparts. Third, I address the question of whether Hieron actively sought to curb the production of local, civic coinages by the cities subject to his political authority. The available numismatic evidence appears to reflect a total abeyance of civic minting by the cities of the kingdom throughout the five decades of the king's reign. I consider whether this inactivity was the result of royal interference aimed at suppressing the operation of civic mints or simply the consequence of cities voluntarily interrupting their local mint operations due to the widespread availability of Hieron's own state-sanctioned coinage.

I switch perspectives with Chapter 8 ("Institutions and Markets in Hieronian Sicily") and consider how the consolidation of royal authority impacted the agricultural and economic landscapes of southeastern Sicily, paying particular attention to the ways in which the tithe administration may have fostered trade and economic prosperity for the cities of the kingdom. Drawing on work in the field of new institutional economics, this chapter builds the case that the annual tithe owed to the king created the appropriate conditions and stimuli for economic growth based on the sale of surplus grain and other agricultural goods. I argue that the tax administration brought interior communities into increased economic contact with Syracuse and, by extension, Mediterranean-wide trade networks. Several factors enabled this market integration, including the advent of long-term peace and stability within the territories subject to Hieron; the kingdom-wide unification of coinage and volumetric measures under a single, royal standard; and the

implementation of an administrative infrastructure designed to move agricultural produce from the interior to the coast. While not to suggest that the
Hieronian tithe administration ushered in an era of affluence for all inhabitants
of the kingdom, the archaeological record does support the thesis that, on the
whole, the communities of southeastern Sicily enjoyed marked prosperity
during the reign of Hieron II.

NOTES

[1] Diod., 23.1–2; Greek in chapter epigram.

[2] All dates given are BCE unless otherwise stated.

[3] Thuc., 3.86.4; 6.1.1; and see discussion by Rutter (1986).

[4] Cic., 2.*Verr*.2.2–3. Trans., Yonge (1903) with modifications.

[5] Cic., 2.*Verr*. 2.2.5. Trans., Yonge (1903) with modifications.

[6] De Angelis (2000).

[7] That cultivation and trade of surplus grains may have begun as early as the eighth century
BCE, see De Angelis (2002), discussing evidence from Megara Hyblaia.

[8] For Sicily as home of Demeter and Persephone, Pin. *Nem.* 1.11–16; Diod., 5.2.3–5.5.1;
Cic. 2.*Verr*.4.48; Ovid, *Fasti* 4.417. Worship of the goddesses is attested in the archaeological
record at sites around the island, dating from at least the first half of the sixth century BCE
with notable cult centers constructed early on at Gela, Selinus, and Akragas; see Hinz
(1998). And see White (1964), who highlights the manipulation of the cult by the island's
political leaders.

[9] Garnsey (1988).

[10] For excellent discussion of this relationship between control of Sicily's agricultural resources
and the expression of political authority, see De Angelis (2006).

[11] Hdt. 7.157–61.

[12] Among others, Manning (2003); von Reden (2007); Aperghis (2004).

[13] As the single reference to Hieron by Walbank (1981: 75) typifies. Shipley (2000: 52)
mentions Hieron only in a parenthetical aside embedded within a brief discussion of
Agathokles' career. Similarly, Morkholm (1991) does not include Hieron II or his royal
portrait coinage in his survey of Early Hellenistic coinage.

[14] Diodorus' *Bibliotheke*, for instance, survives in only a fragmentary state after Book 20, which
leaves off at the year 302; for the impact that this loss has had on the historiography of
Hellenistic and Republican Sicily, see Prag (2007: 69). So too do we lack the portions of
Timaeus' *Histories*, as well as the now lost *Pyrrhus*, which surely touched on the early career
of Hieron II; Baron (2013: 38–42).

[15] Events taking place in Sicily, for instance, receive little more than passing mention in
"standard" histories like Walbank's *The Hellenistic World* (1981) or Shipley's *The Greek World
after Alexander (323–30 BC)* (2000). Nor are Sicilian events commonly taken up in edited
handbooks, such as Erskine's *A Companion to the Hellenistic World* (2003) – with the notable
exception of the chapter by Dench (2003: 294–310), or Bugh's *The Cambridge Companion to
the Hellenistic World* (2006). The roots of this failure to incorporate Sicily and the western
Mediterranean into the mainstream of general Hellenistic historiography are explored by
Prag and Quinn (2013: 1–13), who offer a salutary contribution with *The Hellenistic West:
Rethinking the Ancient Mediterranean*. See also, in the same volume, Wilson (2013: 80–83),
with specific discussion of Hellenistic Sicily.

[16] Haake (2005). Lehmler (2005) remains the most systematic effort to date. In particular,
Lehmler's work elaborates on arguments advanced by, among others, Berve (1959), Finley
(1968: 121), and De Sensi Sestito (1977) that Hieron's rule owed more to contemporary

Ptolemaic and Seleucid models of autocracy than to the tyrannical mode of rule of Classical Sicily. Along these lines, see Veit (2013).

[17]   A very clear case of this ambiguity is found by comparing how Hieron II is characterized in two recent museum exhibition catalogs, *Sicily: Art and Invention between Greece and Rome* (2013) and *Sicily: Culture and Conquest* (2016). In the former, Veit (2013: 31–5) considers Hieron's *basileia* as having been very closely modeled on the cultural politics of the Hellenistic kingdoms of the eastern Mediterranean. In the latter, Higgs (2016: 119) characterizes Hieron as a "tyrant king," whose rule emerged at the end of a long Sicilian tradition of autocratic rulers.

[18]   We see an evolution of perspective in the work of F. W. Walbank, whose early take on the king that "Hiero's monarchy was in the simple 'democratic' Syracusan tradition, and . . . it owed little to Hellenistic ideas" (1957: I.57) was later emended to say that "[the] rule of Hiero II . . . displays many of the characteristics of Hellenistic monarchy" (1981: 75).

[19]   Along these lines, see Schenck von Stauffenberg (1933: 22–3); Higgs (2016: 119). Taking a different angle, Oost (1976) argues, rather unconvincingly, that the Deinomenids and Dionysii formally used the title *basileus* themselves. For the Classical tyrannies of Sicily, Luraghi (1994) remains the standard reference.

[20]   Rutter (1993); Lewis (2009: 117–18); and see discussion *infra* 65–67.

[21]   In many respects, Hieron's nearest political prototype was Agathokles, whose own form of kingship drew as heavily on the behavior of the Successor kings as it had on precedents of autocratic power in Sicily. For an updated approach to the kingship of Agathokles, see De Lisle (2021), who convincingly argues that the Syracusan king drew on traditions of both Classical tyranny and contemporary political ideology of Hellenistic monarchy in fashioning his own approach to autocratic rule.

[22]   On Hieron as a client king, see Serrati (2000: 118–19; 2007: 487); Booms (2016: 119). Wilson (2013: 83) calls into question whether Hieron would have viewed his position vis-à-vis Rome in terms of political dependency, underscoring the anachronism of applying the term "client king" to Hieron's situation.

[23]   Green (1990: 225–6).

[24]   A position epitomized by Green (1990: 225–6). In his detailed analysis of the legal grounds underpinning Hieron's relationship with Rome, Eckstein (1980; 1987: 115–31) affords Hieron a greater degree of political agency, while still situating the king's ambit firmly within the Roman sphere.

[25]   For Archaic and Classical Sicily, De Angelis (2016) is now essential; and, for the reign of Agathokles, see De Lisle (2021). Excellent surveys of the island's Roman phases have been written by Wilson (1990) and Pfuntner (2019).

[26]   Along these lines, Haake (2013: 116) notes that Hieron's relationship with Rome made him a prototype for the "friendly" kings who ruled on the edges of Rome's expanding empire. For "friendly" kings, see Braund (1984). Gotter (2013) recasts these "friendly" monarchs as "castrated" kings.

PART I

FASHIONING A KINGDOM

ONE

FROM GENERAL TO KING

His upbringing as a child virtually presaged the sovereignty that lay in store for him. His father was Hieroclitus, a nobleman whose lineage derived from Gelon, former tyrant of Sicily, but on his mother's side his family was lowly, even shameful. Born of a slave-girl, he had been exposed by his father as a disgrace to his family. But the baby, deprived of any human succor, was for many days fed by bees who heaped their honey round him where he lay. And so, on the advice of the soothsayers, who predicted the child was marked out for kingship, the father took back the infant and made every effort to train him for prospective sovereignty which he was promised. Furthermore, when Hieron was at his lessons in school with his schoolmates, a wolf suddenly appeared amongst the crowd of boys and seized his writing-tablet. Also, when he was a young man and beginning his first military campaigns, an eagle settled on his shield and an owl on his spear, a portent which signified that he would be a prudent politician, a courageous fighter and a king. Finally, he often fought against men who challenged him to single combat, and he always emerged the winner. He was given many military awards by King Pyrrhus. He was possessed of extraordinary good looks as well as strength that was amazing for a mere mortal. He had an engaging way of speaking, was fair in his business dealings and prudent in his exercise of authority, so that the only regal attribute he seemed to lack was a kingdom.
—Just. *Epit.* 23.4.3–15[1]

The historical details of Hieron's life can best be described as sketchy, deriving in large part from only a handful of minor references found scattered among literary sources written long after his death.[2] As a result, documenting his rise to power can be accomplished with only the broadest of brushstrokes. Despite such limitations, this chapter sets forth a historical narrative of Hieron's life and career that may serve as a foundation for the discussions that follow in subsequent chapters. Little can be said about Hieron's youth, except that he may not have been born to high status.[3] Only the brief passage in Justin's *Epitome*, which introduces this chapter, remarks on his formative years. This, however, is almost mockingly credulous, retailing a conventional fable of kingly omens and portents.[4] Even for his exceptionally long reign of 54 years, historical references are uniformly brief; moreover, they come to us primarily in the work of later Roman authors, who tend to cast Hieron in overly flattering light. One such eulogistic sketch is found in Polybius' *Histories*:

> Ἱέρων μὲν γὰρ πρῶτον μὲν δι' αὑτοῦ κατεκτήσατο τὴν Συρακοσίων καὶ τῶν συμμάχων ἀρχήν, οὐ πλοῦτον, οὐ δόξαν, οὐχ ἕτερον οὐδὲν ἐκ τῆς τύχης ἕτοιμον παραλαβών. Καὶ μὴν οὐκ ἀποκτείνας, οὐ φυγαδεύσας, οὐ λυπήσας οὐδένα τῶν πολιτῶν, δι' αὑτοῦ βασιλεὺς κατέστη τῶν Συρακοσίων, ὃ πάντων ἐστὶ παραδοξότατον, ἔτι δὲ τὸ μὴ μόνον κτήσασθαι τὴν ἀρχὴν οὕτως, ἀλλὰ καὶ διαφυλάξαι τὸν αὐτὸν τρόπον. Ἔτη γὰρ πεντήκοντα καὶ τέτταρα βασιλεύσας διετήρησε μὲν τῇ πατρίδι τὴν εἰρήνην, διεφύλαξε δ' αὑτῷ τὴν ἀρχὴν ἀνεπιβούλευτον, διέφυγε δὲ τὸν ταῖς ὑπεροχαῖς παρεπόμενον φθόνον· ὅς γε πολλάκις ἐπιβαλόμενος ἀποθέσθαι τὴν δυναστείαν ἐκωλύθη κατὰ κοινὸν ὑπὸ τῶν πολιτῶν.

> For Hieron, in the first place, acquired the sovereignty of Syracuse and her allies by his own merit, having found ready provided for him by fortune neither wealth, fame, nor anything else. And, what is more, he made himself king of Syracuse without killing, exiling, or injuring a single citizen, which indeed is the most remarkable thing of all; and not only did he acquire his sovereignty so, but maintained it in the same manner. For during a reign of fifty-four years he kept his country at peace and his own power undisturbed by plots, and he avoided the envy which typically follows greatness. Actually, on several occasions when he wished to lay down his authority, he was prevented from doing so by the common action of the citizens.[5]

Here, as elsewhere in the works of Livy and Polybius, Hieron is presented in such a fashion as to caricature the "good" king, whose behavior toward Rome in the third century served as a foil for the historians' treatment of later political leaders considered to have acted in opposition to Rome's interests.[6] The pro-Roman bias that encapsulates our view of the Syracusan monarch in the majority of these accounts should evince skepticism, not wholesale dismissal, of the reported facts when reconstructing the actions of the king. Material evidence can help to round out this narrative in far greater detail, and Chapter 2 will take a closer look at the archaeological, epigraphic, and numismatic evidence related to Hieron's kingship. For the moment, let us focus on the basic timeline of events as they are transmitted by our surviving historical sources, beginning with the political and military turmoil that unfolded following the death of the monarch Agathokles.

SETTING THE STAGE

The death of Agathokles in the year 289 brought about renewed instability throughout eastern Sicily (Figure 1.1). For nearly two decades, the king had exercised sovereign control over a territory that stretched across much of the island, from Syracuse to the Halykos (modern Platani) River, and even extended up to southern Italy and into the Adriatic Sea.[7] Agathokles' reign was not without its share of bloodshed, incitement, and turmoil.[8] Yet we hear little of the violence that characterized his rise to power and self-proclamation as king (*basileus*) in 304.[9] His suppression of minor tyrants and appointment of loyal overseers (*epistatai*) to govern cities within his realm did have the effect of limiting political instability on a local level. Moreover, the peace he brokered with Carthage in 306 had produced its own form of cautious stability in the region after more than a decade of vicious warfare, as both sides agreed to refrain from aggression outside the bounds of their respective *epikrateiai*, the relatively flexible zones of territorial dominion claimed by the island's two main "super powers."[10] But in the wake of his passing, with no appointed successor and no central authority to fill the political vacuum, Agathokles' kingdom rapidly fragmented and devolved into chaos, as old and new threats to peace soon emerged. Many cities found themselves embroiled in flaring tensions between oligarchic and democratic factions, a situation exploited by those seeking to hold absolute rule.[11] In 288/7, Hiketas seized autocratic power at Syracuse, having secured the office of *stratēgos autokrator* amid the political turmoil that racked the *polis*. For much of the next decade, Hiketas would lead the Syracusans in a series of profitless conflicts against their enemies. At Akragas, tyrannical rule emerged in the person of Phintias, who rose to power immediately following Agathokles' death, taking for himself the title of *basileus*.[12] Phintias soon embarked on an irredentist campaign to recapture lands lost to Agathokles in the 290s, ultimately setting his sights on attacking Syracuse itself.

To make matters worse, Agathokles' demise had awakened a slumbering threat in the Mamertines, a group of South Italian mercenaries formerly employed by the king.[13] The failure to enfranchise these men into the Syracusan civic body resulted in violent conflict between the mercenaries and the *dēmos*, which ultimately left the Mamertines in search of a new home.[14] They eventually settled at Messana on the north coast, where they reportedly massacred the male population, betraying those who had welcomed them into the city.[15] Once established at Messana, the Mamertines strengthened their position through alliances with both the Romans and a group of fellow Campanian mercenaries occupying Rhegion.[16] Emboldened by their position, the Mamertines began to expand their control over many of the smaller *poleis* north of Mount Etna, installing a number of garrisons and

I.I Map of Sicily showing locations mentioned in the text (base map: © Sémhur/Wikimedia Commons/CC-BY-SA-3.0).

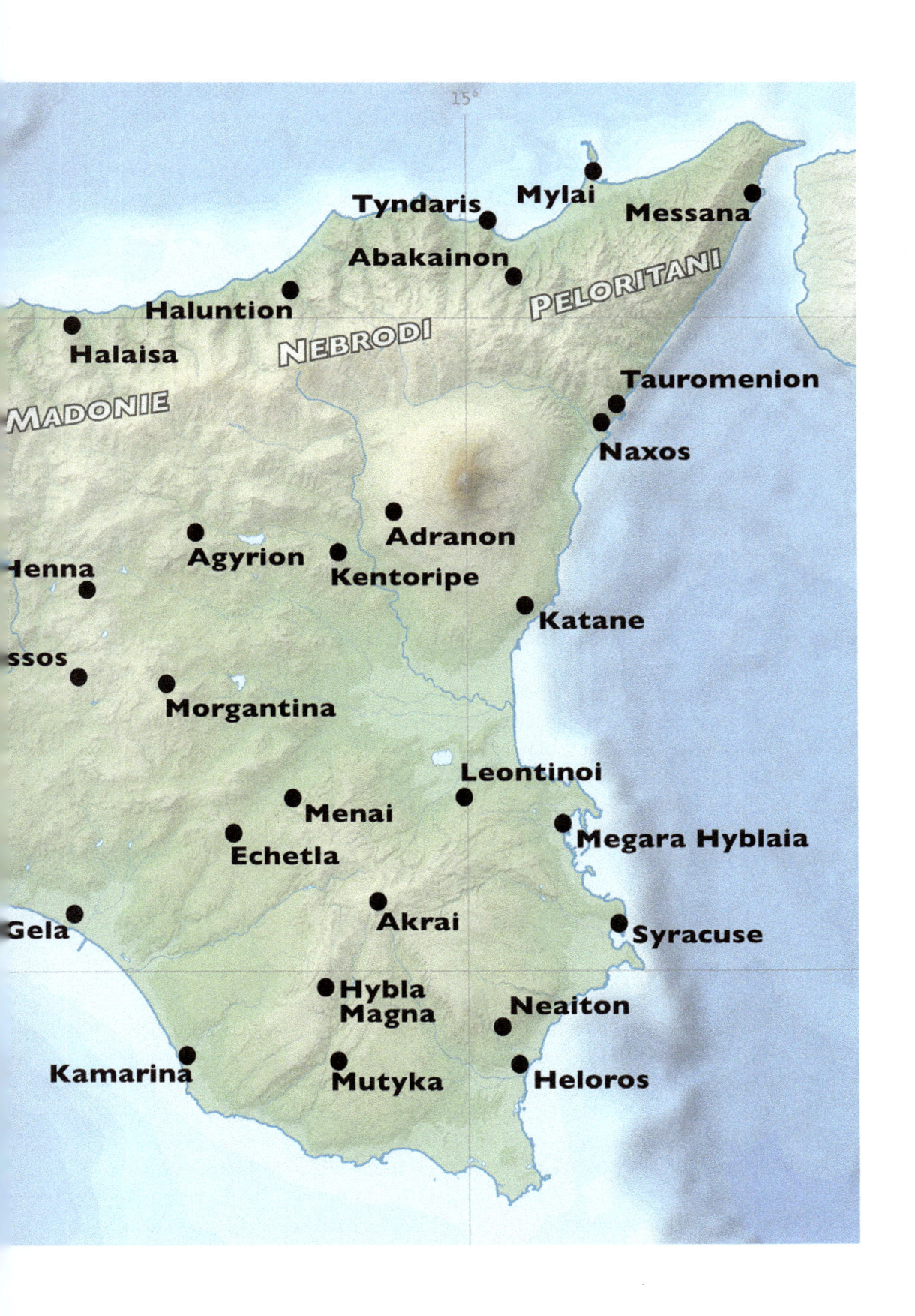

forts in the area.[17] South of the volcano, they marauded the region widely. Even cities on the island's southern coast, including Gela and Kamarina, were held to be among the victims of Mamertine aggression, an assertion that may have some foundation in the archaeological record.[18] It would not be long before the Mamertines found themselves in renewed conflict with the Syracusans. Not to be left out, the Carthaginians seized on the opportunity to expand their military presence east of the Himera and Salsus Rivers, the former boundary of their *epikrateia*; only months after Agathokles' death, Punic forces were already reportedly in the Catania plain.[19] By 288, they were aiding Menon, erstwhile slave of Agathokles and reputed tyrannicide, in his struggle against Hiketas and his allies at Syracuse.[20]

The rise of Phintias at Akragas and Hiketas at Syracuse, the establishment of the Mamertines at Messana, and the increasing presence of Carthaginian troops east of the Himera and Salsus Rivers left four major players vying for territory in Agathokles' former kingdom. The ensuing conflicts embroiled eastern Sicily for the greater part of the next decade. Smaller communities were left vulnerable to attack and found themselves and their territories frequent victims of the overwhelming military force of these much larger players contending for control over the island.

Phintias and Hiketas were the first to square off, each vying for command of the fertile coastal plain that lies between Akragas and Syracuse. Light skirmishing between the two sides came to a head in 285 when both armies finally met at the River Hyblaeus (modern Dirillo) in the territory of Kamarina.[21] There, the Syracusan army defeated the Akragantines in a decisive battle. The loss forced Phintias into retreat, but it did not dislodge him from his position at Akragas, where he continued to rule until 279. Although he avoided future conflict with the Syracusans, he continued to exercise violent control closer to home, including, most notably, the forced depopulation of Gela in 282 and the resettlement of the Geloans at an eponymous city (Phintias) that he founded some 30 kilometers to the west.[22] Ruthlessly suppressing revolts, Phintias extended his control over nearly thirty *poleis* to form a heavily garrisoned territorial state that extended as far north as Agyrion.[23] Hiketas turned his attentions northward toward the Punic forces that had embedded themselves in the territory around Leontinoi, only 40 kilometers from Syracuse. In 284, Carthaginian and Syracusan armies met outside Leontinoi at the River Terias; the Syracusans were routed and forced to retreat behind their city walls, leaving southeastern Sicily and their own territory open to Carthaginian occupation.[24]

Following his defeat, Hiketas managed to hold on to power for several more years until he was eventually ousted by political rivals in 279. Violent civil strife once again gripped Syracuse.[25] Capitalizing on the crisis, Carthaginian forces marched into Syracusan territory and laid siege to the city. By the spring of 278, the Syracusans found themselves beset by Punic forces both on land and at sea.[26] As conditions in the city worsened and Carthaginian occupation seemed imminent, the Syracusans sought assistance from Pyrrhus of Epirus, who was campaigning in southern Italy at the time.[27] They managed to convince the Epirote king to set aside his operations against the Romans and take the lead in the fight against the Carthaginians.[28] Pyrrhus arrived in Sicily with his army in the autumn of 278, landing first at Tauromenion, where he was welcomed by the local tyrant, Tyndarion, and given troops to supplement his ranks.[29] At least initially, Pyrrhus' presence on the island appears to have been warmly embraced by the Greek *poleis* of eastern Sicily.[30]

Wasting little time, Pyrrhus and his forces swept west across the southern coast in the spring of 277. Within months he had captured the Punic strongholds at Azones and Heraklea, taken possession of Akragas from the tyrant Sosistratus, and received the peaceful submission of Selinus, Halicyae, and Segesta.[31] He next marched to the north coast, where he seized Panormus, Eryx, and several smaller Punic garrisons, never once meeting the Carthaginian army in open battle.[32] By the autumn of 277, only the Punic stronghold of Lilybaeum lay between Pyrrhus and complete control of the island. Here, however, the king was checked in his progress by the city's exceptional fortifications.[33] After two months of stalemate and without sign of an imminent victory, Pyrrhus raised the siege and began his march back to Syracuse, where he began planning an invasion of North Africa.[34] On his way back east, Pyrrhus advanced his army into Mamertine-controlled territories, where he reportedly destroyed several fortresses and expelled garrisons.[35]

The decision to raise the siege of Lilybaeum was a turning point for Pyrrhus. Tensions between the king and the Greek *poleis* had developed not long after his arrival, largely due to conflicting attitudes about the nature and scope of his authority on the island.[36] The islanders had grown increasingly frustrated by Pyrrhus' demands for tribute, his confiscation of private lands, and his encroachment on the autonomy of individual *poleis* through the personal appointment of civic magistrates.[37] The failure to capture Lilybaeum, coupled with the compulsory military enlistments that followed, only further stoked their resentment.[38] The situation grew so bad, Plutarch reports, that some *poleis* switched allegiance to the Carthaginians or Mamertines.[39] With support for the king fading as quickly as it had arisen, Pyrrhus found a ready excuse to quit the island and resume his military exploits in southern Italy. In the summer of 276, just two years after their arrival, Pyrrhus and his remaining troops boarded ships at Syracuse and set sail for Tarentum on the south coast of Italy.[40]

Pyrrhus' failure to maintain the support of the Greek *poleis* of Sicily has been ascribed to a fundamental misunderstanding regarding the source of his authority vis-à-vis the communities that had initially welcomed his arrival to the island.[41] For his part, Pyrrhus clearly had ambitions of establishing his own personal monarchy in the west, a territorial kingdom to rival the monarchies of the eastern Mediterranean. Whether the Syracusans and other Greek *poleis* had initially shared a similar perspective when making their appeals to the Epirote ruler is another matter altogether. According to Polybius, the Greek *poleis* had indeed recognized Pyrrhus as both *hegemon* and *basileus*.[42] This has led some scholars, notably Pierre Lévêque, to argue that Pyrrhus' Sikeliote allies recognized him as the "King of Sicily."[43] There is, however, no convincing evidence to suggest that Pyrrhus' *basileia* in Sicily was of the same "national" character as that which he held among the Molossians.[44] Rather, the weight of the evidence suggests that those Sicilian cities considered his position and authority a temporary reflection of his personal exploits and charismatic behavior, much in the same way that Agathokles had claimed the title and authority of king following his invasion of North Africa. Functionally, Pyrrhus' authority in Sicily derived from his position as *hegemon* of the allied forces, which itself was offered by the Sikeliote *poleis* on account of his military exploits, most notably in his encounters with the Romans in southern Italy. The titulature *hegemon* and *basileus* could be read as shorthand for "*hegemon* of the allied Greek *poleis* in their war against the Carthaginians and King (of the Molossians)," but certainly not "King of Sicily." Forced conscription, exaction of tribute, and harsh taxation smelled of tyranny, not collaborative relief. That Pyrrhus operated on Sicily in the mode of a charismatic king would explain why the Sicilian Greeks turned against him so quickly after his failure to capture Lilybaeum. In turn, his failure to capture this prize may have resolved him to be quit of his erstwhile allies. Had Pyrrhus successfully captured Lilybaeum and driven the Carthaginians from their last foothold on Sicily, the outcome might have been very different, but the humiliation of lifting a siege, even if technically not a loss, threatened a charismatic leader's legitimacy to rule, if only because charisma was needed to supplement a finite store of military strength. Understanding Pyrrhus' failure to win over the Greek *poleis* of Sicily is important for what it can tell us about Hieron's success less than a decade later.

What territorial gains Pyrrhus had made against the Carthaginians and Mamertines were fleeting. Eastern Sicily was again left open to encroachment of the Carthaginians and, increasingly, of the Mamertines, who were showing a greater presence in the area south of Mount Etna and the Nebrodi range.[45] Emboldened by Pyrrhus' sudden departure, the Carthaginians swiftly reestablished control over their former possessions west of the Himera River. Syracuse itself was again thrust back into divisive contention among rival political factions for control of the city. It is at this moment that our protagonist, Hieron, son of Hierokles, made his entrance onto the main stage of Sicilian history.

HIERON II: FROM *STRATĒGOS* TO *BASILEUS*

Hieron's first appearance on the historical stage comes in the year 276; Pyrrhus has retreated from Sicily and the Syracusan army has gathered at a place called Mergane with Hieron in command.[46] Polybius does not tell us why the soldiers have left the city, but most scholars believe their withdrawal was related to the renewal of unrest within Syracuse itself following the departure of Pyrrhus. The assembled troops, likely displeased with the political maneuverings of the oligarchic factions within the city, held their own election at Mergane, choosing Hieron and an otherwise unknown individual, Artemidoros, as their leaders (ἄρχοντες; *archontes*).[47] Hieron had served under Pyrrhus during the Epirote king's Sicilian campaign, distinguishing himself as a soldier and earning the reputation of a capable military commander.[48] An election held by the Syracusan army was unusual and, very likely, unconstitutional, since under normal conditions military leadership was delegated to a *stratēgos*, a civic magistrate elected by the Syracusan *dēmos*.[49] What occurred at Mergane, thus, looks very much like the first step in a coup d'état orchestrated by Hieron and his supporters.[50]

Hieron returned to Syracuse, where he accomplished his coup by relying on the backing of the army to secure his election as *stratēgos autokrator* in 276/5.[51] That nothing more is heard of his co-archon, Artemidoros, may lend credence to the belief that Hieron seized autocratic power at the time. Following the precedent set by Agathokles and other Syracusan leaders before him, Hieron appears to have used the declaration of war against the Carthaginians as pretense or justification for extending this authority to himself.[52] Whether the Carthaginians actually posed an imminent threat to the Syracusans is not clear, and of Hieron's initial war with Carthage we hear no word.[53] Rather, he soon turned his attention north to the Mamertines, who by that point had extended their control across a sizable portion of northeastern Sicily, stretching from Messana to Halaisa on the Tyrrhenian coast and as far south as the Symaithos (mod. Simeto) River. Hieron spent much of the next decade attempting to dislodge the Mamertines from their fortified positions around Etna and along the Tyrrhenian coast. In 274, he led an army of Syracusan citizens and mercenaries into the territory of Kentoripe, where they met a Mamertine force near the Kyamosoros River (mod. Salso Cimarosa). Here, Hieron suffered a major defeat and returned to Syracuse, having lost the greater part of his mercenary contingent in the battle. Polybius, our only ancient source to discuss the battle at the Kyamosoros in detail, frames this loss as part of a clever stratagem carried out by Hieron to rid the Syracusan army of seditious mercenaries.[54] Although the Syracusans were no strangers to the perils of mercenary warfare and thus might have considered sacrificing these men on the battlefield, the account reads more like a whitewashing than accurate war reporting.[55] Strategically, this made no sense; for regardless of the intention, the Syracusans were rebuffed and weakened, and the Mamertines, emboldened by their victory at the Kyamosoros, continued to expand their hold over the territories south of the Nebrodi by garrisoning locations like Ameselon (mod. Regalbuto), which lie between the cities of Agyrion and Kentoripe.[56]

Once back in Syracuse, Hieron moved to secure his undoubtedly precarious position. Among his first steps was to recruit a new mercenary force, a measure

likely to aim as much at replacing the soldiers lost at Kyamosoros as at
surrounding himself with troops that owed their loyalty to him above the
Syracusan *dēmos*. Polybius (1.9.6) specifies that Hieron personally hired the
mercenaries (ξενολογήσας δι' αὑτοῦ πλῆθος ἱκανὸν μισθοφόρων), and afterward
ruled in safety (ἀσφαλῶς ἤδη τὰ κατὰ τὴν ἀρχὴν διεξῆγεν), implying a degree
of causality between one process and the other.[57] If the phrase δι' αὑτοῦ can be
taken as indication that Hieron used personal funds to hire these men, it
follows that, in standard fashion for the day, he struck coins to pay the
mercenaries. It may be around this time that he began to issue coinage in his
own name, including a series of gold hemistaters and silver octobols.[58] The
hemistaters employed the same obverse and reverse types and the same Attic-
Euboic weight standard as those struck by Hiketas and Pyrrhus (Figure 1.2).[59]
Likewise, Hieron's silver octobols (Figure 1.3) were issued at an identical
weight as the silver coinage minted by Pyrrhus during his campaigns in
Sicily and, moreover, employed obverse and reverse types remarkably similar
to those of Agathokles' silver staters.[60] The iconographic choices made for this
earliest period of coinage point to an interest in maintaining continuity with
the high-value denominations struck by his predecessors. So similar, in fact, are
Hieron's hemistaters and those of Hiketas that the only easily distinguishable
feature is the addition of Hieron's name in the genitive, ΙΕΡΩΝΟΣ, on the
reverse type. Such familiar, high-value coinage was surely meant to pay for his
military campaigns against the Mamertines. The same motive would also
account for the decision to continue minting coinage on the Attic-Euboic
standard. Accepted more widely than coinage struck on the local Sicilian
litra standard, it enjoyed greater circulation thus was of greater appeal
to mercenaries.

Hiring mercenaries as a personal bodyguard was not Hieron's only move to
shore up his position at Syracuse. In fact, prior to the battle at the Kyamosoros,
he courted the support of the city's powerful oligarchic factions by marrying
Philistis, the daughter of a leading Syracusan named Leptines.[61] By co-opting
oligarchic support through marriage, Hieron seems to have learned from the
mistakes of Agathokles and Pyrrhus, who were reportedly swift to answer
political resistance with violence.[62] In fact, ancient commentators remark on
the largely peaceful means by which Hieron seized and held power, reportedly
avoiding the violence and expulsions that had been characteristic of previous
autocratic regimes.[63] So secure was Hieron in this arrangement that he reportedly left Leptines in charge of the city while he was away on campaign.[64] With
the support of the powerful oligarchic factions and a large mercenary force at
his command, Hieron was in firm possession of power at Syracuse, where he
continued to hold the office of *stratēgos autokrator*.

Little is known about his activities between 274 and 270. Efforts were made
to strengthen the Syracusan military by acquiring new arms and training the
citizen-levies drawn both from Syracuse and its allied *poleis*.[65] During this

1.2 Top: Gold hemistater of Hicetas, ca. 288–279 BCE (ANS 1954.237.408; courtesy of the American Numismatic Society). Bottom: Gold hemistater of Hieron II, ca. 276–269 BCE (ANS 1997.9.102; courtesy of the American Numismatic Society).

period, Hieron also began reaching out to foreign powers, including Rome. Presaging many such future gifts, he reportedly sent grain and soldiers to support the Roman army besieging Rhegion in 270.[66] In the same year, Hieron and his army marched north along the Ionian coast toward Messana. Along the way, he received requests for alliance from Tauromenion and Katane, two cities increasingly threated by the growing Mamertine presence south of Etna.[67] Finding the Mamertines safely ensconced behind their fortifications at Messana, he advanced against Mylae (mod. Milazzo), a small city located roughly 25 kilometers west of the Mamertine stronghold. He captured the city and reportedly enrolled some 1,500 soldiers, who were garrisoning the

1.3 Top: Silver stater of Agathokles, ca. 317–289 BCE (ANS 1944.100.57007; courtesy of the American Numismatic Society). Bottom: Silver octobol of Hieron II, ca. 276–269 BCE (BM G1874,0715.116. © The Trustees of the British Museum).

city for the Mamertines, into his own army. From Mylae, he crossed over the Nebrodi range and moved south against the Mamertine fortress at Ameselon. As at Mylae, he pardoned the soldiers garrisoning the fort and enrolled them into his army. Hieron divided the territory formerly controlled by Ameselon and gave it to Agyrion and Kentoripe, two cities whose alliance he had already secured.

In the following year (269), Hieron and his army again crossed the Nebrodi range, this time approaching the Mamertine-controlled territories from the west. As in the previous year, he welcomed the voluntary surrender of cities under Mamertine control, including Halaisa (mod. Tusa), Tyndaris, and

Abakainon.[68] Continuing east with his army he met the Mamertines at the Longanus River (mod. Patrì), which ran between the territories of Tyndaris and Mylae. Here, the Syracusans dealt a crushing blow to the Mamertines, forcing their retreat to Messana. According to Diodorus, the demoralized Mamertines were prepared to hand over the city to Hieron, but a Carthaginian naval commander forestalled their surrender by sending a small contingent of soldiers from the nearby island of Lipari to garrison the city.[69] Presumably not wishing to risk war with Carthage, Hieron halted his campaign and returned to Syracuse.

It was a momentous homecoming. According to Polybius, all the allies hailed Hieron as king (αὐτὸς δὲ παραγενόμενος εἰς τὰς Συρακούσας βασιλεὺς ὑπὸ πάντων προσηγορεύθη τῶν συμμάχων).[70] We are not told precisely who numbered among these *symmachoi*, but they surely represented the roughly two dozen *poleis* that had fought alongside Hieron or sought alliance during his campaigns against the Mamertines.[71] One wishes that Polybius had offered more details. Still, reasonable inferences may be drawn, based on the fact that this seemingly impromptu acclamation finds clear precedent in the manner that the Successor kings first laid claim to the title of *basileus*. First and foremost, the initial claim to kingship rested on an acclamation by the army. The situation for Hieron, we may conjecture, was likely no different, especially given that such an act was extraconstitutional and had no basis in Syracusan political custom. The acclamation attributed to the *symmachoi* alone (i.e., the allied contingents who had fought alongside Hieron) probably issued from the whole assembled army – including Syracusan citizens and the mercenaries paid directly by Hieron himself.

Like the event itself, the timing of this very public spectacle cannot have been left to chance either; it fits too neatly with the established practices of the Successor kings, who engineered their seemingly spontaneous acclamations to occur after a major military victory.[72] Hieron's victory at Longanus was tantamount to that won by Antigonos Monophthalmos and Demetrios Poliorketes over Ptolemy I at Salamis in 306.[73] In both instances, success on the battlefield served to ground viable claims of kingship.[74] By assuming the title and authority of *basileus*, Hieron removed himself from any remaining constitutional limits on his authority as *stratēgos autokrator*. He was the third king recognized by the Syracusans in as many decades, but unlike Agathokles and Pyrrhus, his rule would extend for more than half a century.

Although these events are described here as having taken place in the year 269, it is important to note that scholars remain divided over the actual date of the battle at the Longanus River.[75] Disagreements have arisen due to perceived discrepancies in the narratives of Polybius and Diodorus concerning the circumstances and outcomes of this battle. By Polybius' account, for instance, Hieron's victory at Longanus was the catalyst for his acclamation as *basileus* at Syracuse. The two events are intimately related. Later, in his obituary for the

Syracusan ruler, Polybius states that he ruled as king (βασιλεύσας) for 54 years.[76] Since we are quite certain that Hieron died in 215, this should place the battle and subsequent proclamation of kingship in the year 269. This would be consistent with Polybius' statement that the Mamertine defeat at Longanus came "on the heels" (παρὰ πόδας) of the Roman expulsion of Campanian mercenaries from Rhegion in 270.[77] Yet there appears to be a problem in reconciling the date of 269 for the battle at the Longanus with another famous episode in the Polybian narrative. After their defeat, the Mamertines sent an embassy to Rome, prompting the Romans to dispatch soldiers to Sicily, a move that will spark the outbreak of the First Punic War. As Polybius narrates it, the Mamertine embassy also followed closely on Hieron's victory at Longanus, yet the episode is firmly fixed in the year 264, five years later. Vexed by this interval, some scholars have argued that the battle at Longanus took place in 265, closer to the start of the First Punic War.

The surviving passage from Diodorus' history offers little clarity on the question of absolute chronology.[78] In fact, while Diodorus offers a more detailed account of the battle at Longanus and the Carthaginian intervention to garrison Messana afterward, there is no mention of the Mamertine embassy to Rome in the surviving portion of his history. Nor does Diodorus mention Hieron's coronation following his victory. Rather, he refers somewhat problematically to Hieron as a king from the start of his narrative. This has led some scholars to posit further that Hieron assumed the title of *basileus* even before his victory at Longanus.[79]

Various solutions have been put forward to reconcile these divergent threads, while also shifting the date of the battle closer to the start of the First Punic War. None, so far, has found universal favor. Dexter Hoyos has offered the strongest case for dating the battle to 265, the year before the Roman intervention, arguing that details of the Polybian narrative that seem to imply the battle followed shortly after the Roman seizure of Rhegion in 270 are better understood as stylistic license rather than a precise chronological sequence.[80] He and others have circumvented Polybius' declaration that Hieron ruled for 54 years by various means, including Gaetano De Sanctis's bold (if unconvincing) choice to emend the text to render Hieron's reign to only 51 years.[81]

Yet Polybius' statement that Hieron ruled for 54 years (ἔτη γὰρ πεντήκοντα καὶ τέτταρα βασιλεύσας) remains stubbornly resistant to challenge.[82] It is perhaps not an insignificant detail that the author used the term βασιλεύειν, rather than ἄρχειν or κυριεύειν, which strongly suggests that he was not counting Hieron's years as *stratēgos autokrator* among those of his "kingship."[83] The proponents of the 265 date must accommodate not just Polybius but also Diodorus, who implies that Hieron had already claimed the title of *basileus* by the time of the battle. Thus, they propose a scenario in which Hieron was twice declared king, first by the Syracusans (an event that goes unattested) and then later by the *symmachoi*, as Polybius reports. According to this scenario, the battle at the Kyamosoros River took place in 269 (not 274) and was followed by the acclamation of Hieron as king by the Syracusans alone. Thus, Hieron ruled as king of the Syracusans from 269, a title the *symmachoi* only ratified with their own acclamation after his victory at Longanus in 265. This explanation is clever; nevertheless, it fails to convince on the grounds that Hieron's loss at Kyamosoros (whether it took place in 274 or 269) could not have been easily translated into legitimacy as a charismatic monarch.[84] Furthermore, the idea that Hieron ruled as "king of the Syracusans" had no foundation in contemporary political practice at Syracuse. Hieron's loss at Kyamosoros, however, could have served as grounds for prolonging his position as *stratēgos autokrator*, as Agathokles appears to have done following his loss to the Carthaginians at the battle of the Himera River in 311. Although consensus on this issue will likely remains out of reach for some time to come, the weight of the evidence favors the year 269 for the battle of Longanus and the beginning of Hieron's *basileia*. The relationship between Hieron's victory at Longanus and his adoption of the royal title is significant for it reveals an awareness of the precedents set by the Successor kings, who had established that military success was a prerequisite to the legitimacy of autocratic rule in the generations following the death of Alexander III.

Historical sources are silent on Hieron's activities in the period between 269 and 265. With the Mamertine threat temporarily at bay, Hieron likely turned his attention toward consolidating control over his newly formed kingdom, which at the time stretched north from Syracuse to Halaisa on the Tyrrhenian coast and west into the Heraian range as far as Morgantina and Herbessos. Foremost in importance among the undertakings at hand for the king and his court was to put in place administrative policies designed to extract resources from the territories now under his control. The cornerstone of this administrative system – a tithe collected on agricultural production – will be discussed at length in Chapter 4. Drawing on the bountiful revenue generated by the tithe, Hieron continued to strengthen his military forces in anticipation of what at the time surely seemed like inevitable conflict with the Carthaginians and Mamertines. The construction of fortification walls at Tyndaris, Troina, and Halaisa around this time seems to confirm Hieron's intent to strengthen allied cities and, in the process, to hem in the Mamertines.[85]

Hieron's third recorded campaign against the Mamertines began in 264. According to Polybius, the Carthaginian garrison had been recently expelled from Messana and Hieron saw an opportunity to drive the Mamertines from their stronghold once and for all. He sought an alliance with Carthage, and in 264 a joint Syracusan-Carthaginian force laid siege to Messana.[86] This was the moment the Mamertines appealed to Rome, leading to a debate in the Roman Senate over the wisdom of committing troops to Sicily.[87] Once the decision was made to aid the Mamertines, the Romans dispatched Appius Claudius with two legions to Messana. Before leaving Rhegion, Appius sent envoys to

Hieron and the Carthaginians – perhaps the first of two attempts – proposing a peaceful settlement if the Syracusans would raise their siege of Messana.[88] In response, Diodorus reports, Hieron himself harshly rejected the terms set forth by the Roman commander, articulating his justification for war against the Mamertines.[89] On arriving in Sicily, Appius promptly drove off both armies from Messana and then marched on Syracuse, which he besieged.[90] Skirmishing outside the walls continued for several months, but the tide eventually turned in favor of the Syracusans, who forced Appius' retreat back to Messana and, ultimately, back across the Straits to Rhegion. Stung by this setback, the Romans responded by dispatching both of their consular armies to Sicily in the following year.[91]

In 263, the consuls Manius Valerius Maximus and Manius Otacilius Crassus landed on Sicily with four consular legions, totaling approximately 40,000 men and cavalry. They immediately moved against Hieron's allies at Adranon and Kentoripe. While besieging Kentoripe, the consuls received envoys from many cities suing for peace and offering to deliver their cities into Roman hands.[92] With their troop numbers augmented by contributions from these new allies, Valerius and Otacilius marched on Syracuse. Confronted with the Roman army outside the city and reportedly faced with unrest from aristocratic factions within, Hieron quickly came to terms with the consuls.[93]

The terms of this treaty are recorded by several ancient authors, who are in general agreement about the details.[94] For his part, Hieron was to return without ransom all Roman prisoners of war and pay a small indemnity to the Romans.[95] Our sources diverge only on the total sum to be paid, which ranges from 25 to 200 talents of silver.[96] For their part, the Romans recognized Hieron's *basileia* and his sovereignty over a kingdom comprising several *poleis* in southeastern Sicily. Diodorus names six *poleis*, in addition to Syracuse, that remained subject to Hieron by the terms of the treaty: Akrai, Leontinoi, Neaiton, Megara Hyblaia, Heloros, and Tauromenion.[97] Several more cities – namely, Morgantina, Kamarina, and Herbessos – also fell under Hieron's political hegemony.[98] While Hieron retained control over a sizable portion of the island, his kingdom was now far smaller than the territory he had controlled between 269 and 263. There is no indication that he regained control over those cities north of the Chrysas River (mod. Dittaino), like Kentoripe or Adranon, which had gone over to Rome in 264. The precise legal relationship between Hieron and Rome entailed by the treaty is unclear, leaving open the question of whether they entered into a formal *foedus sociale*, or were simply bound by a more informal relationship of *amicitia* or *philia*.[99] Arthur Eckstein has argued persuasively for the latter interpretation, noting that at no point in his long reign does Hieron appear to act under legal obligation in his dealings with Rome.[100] The significant effect that this treaty had on the definition of Hieron's *basileia* and the organization of his kingdom will be discussed further in Chapter 2.

For the next 48 years, Hieron ruled as a sovereign monarch over his Sicilian kingdom, a remarkable feat given that the average lifespan of a Hellenistic monarch was not exceptionally long. In that time, Hieron was never again to lead an army on campaign or distinguish himself in battle, as he had done for the greater part of the previous two decades. On several occasions, he did send aid in the form of grain, money, soldiers, and military supplies to the Romans during both the First and Second Punic Wars.[101] His peace with Rome was renewed in 248, some 15 years after the initial treaty of 263.[102] Even amid the violence of the First Punic War, the territories under Hieron's protection remained sheltered from the destruction meted out by the Romans and Carthaginians during their long struggle for control of the island. While western Sicily was awash in violence, Hieron's kingdom remained stable and secure.[103] At the conclusion of the First Punic War, the king and his territories both were specifically protected under the terms of Rome's accord with Carthage that brought hostilities to a close in 241.[104]

Peace brought prosperity to Hieron and to his kingdom. In a world where agricultural productivity formed the basis of wealth, the fortunes of both individuals and communities were directly tied to agrarian stability. Largely exempted from the violence of the Punic Wars, the cities under Hieron's protection enjoyed a period of cultural and economic affluence sustained by extraordinary agricultural productivity. Syracuse, above all, flourished as a center of innovation and art, standing alongside Alexandria and Athens as one of the great urban centers and intellectual capitals of the Hellenistic Mediterranean.[105] For the smaller cities of the kingdom (e.g., Heloros, Morgantina, Tauromenion) this was equally a moment of economic florescence, judging from the archaeological remains of monumental construction projects and lavish displays of private wealth.[106] Such prosperity in eastern Sicily stands in stark relief against the lack of similar large-scale civic investment taking place in the western part of the island at this time – the result, no doubt, of the crisis brought about by the First Punic War.[107]

Hieron maintained a flourishing Hellenistic kingdom in the growing shadow of Rome. And while he cultivated good standing with the Senate and Roman people, Hieron also forged relations in the Aegean with kings and cities alike through trade, euergetism, and lavish displays of wealth familiar to the Hellenistic monarchies of the eastern Mediterranean. His actions, as Polybius notes, earned Hieron an unimpeachable reputation among the Greeks:

> εὐεργετικώτατος δὲ καὶ φιλοδοξότατος γενόμενος εἰς τοὺς Ἕλληνας μεγάλην μὲν αὐτῷ δόξαν, οὐ μικρὰν δὲ Συρακοσίοις εὔνοιαν παρὰ πᾶσιν ἀπέλιπε.

> And having shown himself most beneficent to the Greeks, and most anxious to earn their good opinion, he [Hieron] left behind him not

merely a great personal reputation but also a universal feeling of goodwill toward the Syracusans.

For the Romans, as well, Hieron was a model (if not *the* model) of the ideal king, whose fidelity and wartime aid to Rome's civilians and military were benchmarks against which Rome would come to measure its interactions with other kings.[108] Livy (22.37.10) similarly elaborates on this ideal, noting Hieron's many virtues:

> ab senatu ita responsum regi est: uirum bonum egregiumque socium Hieronem esse atque uno tenore, ex quo in amicitiam populi Romani uenerit, fidem coluisse ac rem Romanam omni tempore ac loco munifice adiuuisse. id perinde ac deberet gratum populo Romano esse.

> The Senate, in replying to the royal emissaries, said that Hieron was a good man and a rare ally, who from the time when he became a friend of the Roman People had maintained an unswerving loyalty, and always and in every place had given generous assistance to the Roman cause. For this the Romans were grateful, as in duty-bound.

In some ways, Hieron's kingship was an experiment before its time – a brief glimpse at what was to come once Roman power would grow to eclipse even that of the Seleucids and Ptolemies, the Hellenistic leviathans of the eastern Mediterranean, by stripping them of their prerogative for regular military aggression, which had long formed the foundation of their royal authority.[109] Hieron styled himself a friend to the Roman people too; he traded on euergetism to maintain an international profile before the Attalids would claim center stage. In 237, he traveled to Rome to witness the *ludi Romani*, possibly at the invitation of the Roman Senate as thanks for his support during the First Punic War. He was the first Hellenistic king to visit Rome, but he would certainly not be the last.[110]

Neither Hieron's kingdom nor the Sicilian experiment with Hellenistic *basileia* would long outlast his death in 215 at the age of 91 or 92.[111] Hieron's son and co-regent from 241, Gelon, had died suddenly in 216, leaving Gelon's 15-year-old son, Hieronymos, next in line for succession.[112] Hieronymos assumed his grandfather's *basileia* amid the turbulence of the Second Punic War, as Carthage had once again made Sicily a battleground for its war with Rome. Flush with the intemperance of an adolescent boy, Hieronymos abandoned his grandfather's longstanding alliance with Rome, choosing to side instead with the Carthaginians.[113] At the time, this decision may have been looked upon favorably by many Syracusans, but it was of no use to Hieronymos. As the young king's behavior began to verge on the tyrannical, it was not long before an assassin's dagger found his heart, only 13 months into his reign.[114]

The assassination could not save the Syracusans and their allies from Hieronymos' fateful decision to abandon Rome. By that time, according to

Livy, too many in Syracuse supported the Carthaginian alliance and were resolved to seek war with Rome.[115] Roman forces, led by Marcus Claudius Marcellus, besieged Syracuse for the greater part of a year. Although they were long held at bay by the inventions of Archimedes, the Romans would eventually breach the city's fortifications. Even as Syracuse fell, many of the *poleis* formerly allied with Hieron continued to hold out resistance against Rome, bolstered by support from Carthaginian troops. Yet within a matter of months they too ultimately capitulated or were captured with overwhelming military force. With the fall of the last remaining Carthaginian stronghold at Akragas in 210, Rome came into total possession of Sicily.

In his *Life of Marcellus*, Plutarch writes that when Syracuse fell to Roman forces in 212, the general is said to have looked over the city and wept, lamenting the fate of the once great capital, which now stood open to the depredations of his soldiers.[116] What Marcellus saw was the royal capital of Hieron's kingdom — a thriving metropolis of some 200,000 residents that rivaled Alexandria as one of the great urban centers of its day.[117] He saw a city ornamented with grand stoa buildings, public fountains and bath complexes, monumental granaries, and one of the largest stone theaters of the Greek world. He saw the court that had fostered the likes of Archimedes, Theokritos, the sculptor Mikon, and countless other intellectuals and artists whose names are lost to time. He saw a city whose temples, public monuments, and private households were so richly adorned with artwork and sculpture that the booty hauled back to Rome by his soldiers would forever alter the Romans' taste for Greek art and culture.[118]

For a brief time, Hieron's kingdom lived on as an assignment (*provincia*) given to Roman generals operating against the Carthaginians in the final years of the war.[119] Hieron's fidelity to Rome during his lifetime had earned him an impeccable reputation among the Roman cognoscenti, judging from the praise heaped upon the king by first-century authors like Cicero and Livy. Yet all the gold and grain that Hieron had delivered up to the Romans during his lifetime was no match for the untold bounty they would come to harvest in the generations following his death, thanks in no small part to the adoption of the king's system of agricultural taxation as part of their new provincial administration. By coopting the Hieronian tax system and expanding it to cover the whole of Sicily, Rome tapped into the agricultural wealth of its first province and used it to fuel the expansion of an overseas empire. For their part, the Romans gave credit where it was due, referring to this system of taxation as the *lex Hieronica*.

NOTES

[1] Translation by Yardley (1994).

[2] The primary historical sources for Hieron's rise to power are the histories of Polybius and Livy, both of whom relied on the work of Timaeus of Tauromenion, the only Sicilian

historian writing around Hieron's lifetime for whom a substantial amount of text survives. Consensus holds that Timaeus' now lost work, the *Pyrrhus*, almost certainly took the outbreak of the First Punic War as its end point. If correct, the author must have documented Hieron's rise to power. On the chronological range and subject matter of the *Pyrrhus*, see Baron (2013: 38–42); Polyb. 1.5.1, 39.8.4. Giovanna De Sensi Sestito's *Gerone II* (1977) remains the principal treatment of Hieron's kingship with emphasis on the political, economic, and cultural facets of his reign. De Sensi Sestito's treatment is comprehensive with respect to available documentary sources, but must now be supplemented by fresh archaeological discoveries, as well as more recent contributions to the study of Hellenistic monarchy. In this respect, Caroline Lehmler's *Syrakus unter Agathokles und Hieron II* (2005) is an essential resource for the study of Hieron II.

3   On Hieron's parents, see also Zonaras (8.6), who echoes Justin (*Epit.* 23.4.3–15) on the servile status of his mother, but goes out of his way to note that Hieron's father as well bore no special distinction.

4   Lewis (2000: 105–6) sets this passage within the broader tradition of Sicilian tyrants, who promoted stories of natural omens that foretold and justified their rise to power. It is also worth noting that in an earlier chapter of the *Epitome*, Justin (*Epit.* 15.4.13–18) employed a similar set of royal portents in his historical narrative regarding the rise of the Indian king Chandragupta Maurya.

5   Polyb. 7.8.1. Translation by Paton (1923) with adaptations.

6   Eckstein (1985: 267–73) explores this idea with respect to Polybius' treatment of the king, going on to suggest areas of the text (e.g., 1.16.10–11) where Polybius may have diverged from his source texts (e.g., Fabius Pictor) to add personal reflection on Hieron's virtues as a pro-Roman ally; cf. Gelzer (1933: 138).

7   On Agathokles' career, see Consolo Langher (2000); Meister (1984).

8   As, for instance, the violence instigated by Agathokles in 319/318 against members of the Six Hundred, the oligarchic faction that controlled Syracuse, which reportedly resulted in the murder of 4,000 partisans: Diod. 19.5.4–8; Meister (1984: 388–9). Zambon (2006: 78) observes that some ancient accounts, including the *Universal History* of Diodorus Siculus, appear at times to incorporate elements of pro-Agathoklean propaganda, which surely aimed at whitewashing some of the worst elements of his rule. Zambon gives the example of the title taken by Agathokles when he first seized power at Syracuse, noting the disparity between the *Marmor Parium* (*FgrHist* 239 F 12), where Agathokles is described as the *stratēgos autokrator* of the Syracusans, and that of Diodorus (19.5.4–5), which sets Agathokles in a more favorable light as simply holding the office of *stratēgos* and protector of the peace (στρατηγὸς κατεστάθη καὶ φύλαξ τῆς εἰρήνης). While there is much to Zambon's interpretation, it should be noted that the example taken from Diodorus was set within a larger narrative about how Agathokles had used deception to win the support of the *dēmos*.

9   Regarding Agathokles' decision to take the title of *basileus* in 306, Diodorus (20.54.1) relates that he did so in emulation of the Diadochoi, who had only recently begun to adopt the title themselves. For discussion of Agathokles' rise to power and the underlying principles/political contours of his kingship, see Zambon (2006: 78–85).

10   The conflict between Agathokles and Carthage is detailed by Diodorus (19.106–10; 20.1–79). Ameling (2011: 50–1) discusses the fluidity of the Syracusan and Carthaginian *epikrateiai*.

11   At Tauromenion, Leontinoi, and possibly Katane, tyrants used the outbreak of *stasis* to seize power: Diod. 22.2.1–3; Zambon (2008: 53–5).

12   On Phintias' rise to power and rule, see La Bua (1960: 98–109); Berve (1967: II.458–62); and, more recently, Zambon (2008: 56–63). Phintias is often described as a tyrant in surviving historical narratives (e.g., Diod. 22.2.1), although he clearly acted in a manner that followed precedents set by Hellenistic monarchs of the East, such as by minting coins with the legend ΒΑΣΙΛΕΟΣ ΦΙΝΤΙΑΣ and founding a new city that bore his name. The negative portrayal of the Akragantine leader found in most historical accounts was

undoubtedly influenced by the violence he perpetrated against the Sicilian communities under his control, including Diodorus' hometown of Agyrion; Diod. 22.2.2–4. Diodorus himself was likely relying on the work of the third-century historian Philinus of Akragas, who certainly held no positive views of Phintias; for Philinus, see Jacoby *FGrH* 174.

[13] On the multi-ethnic composition of the Mamertines, see Zambon (2008: 40–5).

[14] On the departure of the Mamertines from Syracuse: Mafodda (1979: 203); Zambon (2000: 305); Prestianni Giallombardo (2006: 123).

[15] The accounts of Polybius (1.7.1–4) and Diodorus (21.18.3, 22.1.2–3, 22.7.4, 23.1.4) portray this unfavorable narrative of the Mamertine settlement at Messana. On their sources, see La Bua (1966: 203–4). A more positive account of the episode is preserved in the *lexicon* of Festus (150 L) under the entry "Mamertini," which preserves a passage from the *Bellum Carthaginiense* of the poet Alfius; for discussion, see Dench (1995: 56), who notes that the Oscan origins of this otherwise unknown Alfius, judging from his name, may account for the pro-Mamertine perspective of his account. The archaeological evidence emerging from excavations within the ancient city does not appear to support the narrative of a dramatic shift in the settlement's demographics, resulting from the mass expulsions and murder that followed the Mamertine capture of Messana, as preserved in Roman historical accounts; on this subject, see Zambon (2008: 51–2); Crawford (2007). Rather, the arrival of the Mamertines at Messana is marked in the material record most notably by the production of bronze coinage with the legend MAMEPTINΩN; see Särström (1940).

[16] On the alliances, Polyb. 1.8.1. Yet Polybius also asserts at an earlier point in his history (1.7.8) that the Mamertines offered some form of assistance to this group of 4,000 Campanian mercenaries in their massacre of the citizens of Rhegion, an act that drew the ire of Rome; cf. Diod. 22.1.2. Leaving aside the possibility of a formal alliance with Rhegion, there was certainly active trade across the Straits, evidenced by among other things the presence of terracotta bricks stamped MAMEPTINOYM at Rhegion and PHΓINΩN at Messana; Spadea (1986); Zambon (2008: 48).

[17] For Mamertine forts in the area around Mount Etna, see Diod. 22.13.1.

[18] Mamertine assaults against Gela and Kamarina, which reportedly left both cities depopulated (ἀναστάτοι), are mentioned by Diodorus (23.1.4). The passage in question purports to paraphrase Hieron II's response to the Roman consul Appius Claudius, who in 264 sent an envoy to the king urging that he raise his siege of Messana and return to Syracuse. Here, Hieron justifies his assault on Messana and refusal to stop his war against the Mamertines by recalling the violence wrought by the mercenaries at Gela and Kamarina, as well as the impious means by which they seized Messana. The impact of Mamertine violence elsewhere in eastern Sicily is discussed by Bell (2011: 194), who invites us to contemplate the destruction of agricultural lands, and by Di Stefano (1987: 159–61), with specific reference to violence at Kamarina and Scornavacche. Zambon (2000) contends that the Mamertine assaults on Gela and Kamarina preceded the settlement of Messana.

[19] Following the narrative of Diodorus (20.78–9), it appears the treaty of 306, concluded between Carthage and Agathokles, established the boundary of the respective *epikrateia* at the Himera and Salsus Rivers.

[20] On Punic expansion to the east, see Just. 23.2.13, who states that the Carthaginians sent troops to the island upon receiving news of Agathokles' imminent death; cf. Goldsberry (1973: 83, n. 4). For the Carthaginian support of Menon, see Diod. 21.18.1.

[21] The battle is described by Diodorus (22.2.1). On the identification of the Hyblaeus as the modern Dirillo River, see Uggeri (2015: 22–3, 221–2).

[22] On forced depopulation of Gela and foundation of Phintias, see Diod. 22.2.2–3; Zambon (2000). Archaeological remains of the settlement at Phintias have been identified near modern Licata, where recent excavations have revealed portions of a residential quarter; for excavations, see La Torre and Mollo (2013) and Toscano Raffa et al. (2015). The destruction that accompanied the forced depopulation of Gela in 282 has been documented in the archaeological record, most notably in a pair of articles by Adamesteanu and Orlandini (1956; 1960),

which publish the excavations conducted at the site in the 1950s. It bears reiterating that even following the forced relocation to Phintias (Licata), the settlement at Gela was never fully abandoned. As the archaeological record confirms, occupation continued to persist at the site.

23 Phintias' dealings with Agyrion are mentioned by Diodorus (22.3–4), who states that his proclivity for violence and murder garnered the hatred of those subject to his rule. That upward of thirty cities came under his control is an inference made, again, on the testimony of Diodorus (22.8.4, 22.10.1), who states that in 278, Pyrrhus took over the thirty cities ruled by the tyrant Sosistratus, who had himself seized power at Akragas upon the death of Phintias; on this, see Berve (1967: II.733).

24 La Bua (1968: 154–5); De Sensi Sestito (1980: II.1.347).

25 For the expulsion of Hiketas, see Diod. 22.7.2–3. According to Diodorus (22.7.6), violence soon broke out between partisans loyal to Thoinon, the Syracusan leader responsible for expelling Hiketas, and Sosistratus, the tyrant of Akragas, who seems to have been invited by the Syracusans to help overthrow Thoinon. At the time of Pyrrhus' arrival, the city was politically and physically divided between the faction of Thoinon, who occupied the island of Ortygia, and that of Sosistratus, who controlled Achradina, the mainland portion of Syracuse. On the complicated political situation in Syracuse, see Zambon (2008: 69–74).

26 Diodorus (22.8.1) gives the total number of Carthaginian troops at 50,000 infantry (undoubtedly exaggerated) and 100 ships.

27 On the Syracusans' envoy to Pyrrhus, Plut., *Pyrrh.* 22.1–2.

28 Pyrrhus' rationale for accepting the Syracusans' request for assistance remains subject of speculation. Zambon (2006: 85–7) considers it of the Epirote king's ambition to establish a personal kingdom in the model of the Successor kingdoms. According to Diodorus (22.8.2), the Syracusans, for their part, had hoped Pyrrhus would respond positively to their request on account of the fact that he had once been married to Agathokles' daughter, Lanassa, with whom he had a son.

29 For Pyrrhus's arrival in Sicily, Diod. 22.8.2–5 and Plut. *Pyrrh.* 22.3. According to Diodorus (22.7.4–5), the Mamertines and Carthaginians made a joint effort to prevent Pyrrhus' crossing from south Italy.

30 Polyb. 7.4.5. Diodorus (22.8.5) reports that while in Syracuse preparing for his campaign, Pyrrhus received envoys from a number of Sikeliote *poleis*, who came with offers to turn over their cities to the king and provide soldiers to aid him in his fight against the Carthaginians.

31 Diod. 22.10.1–2.

32 Diod. 22.10.3–4.

33 For discussion of the archaeological remains for Punic fortifications at Lilybaeum, see Caruso (2006).

34 Diod. 22.10.7; Plut. *Pyrrh.* 23.3–4.

35 Plut. *Pyrrh.* 23.1. Following Plutarch's narrative, Lévêque (1957: 477–9) and Vartsos (1970: 95–6) put this incursion into Mamertine territory between the siege of Eryx and the siege of Lilybaeum. Opting for the period after Lilybaeum (in 276), La Bua (1980: 241) and Zambon (2008: 175).

36 On the monarchical ambitions of Pyrrhus in Sicily, see Zambon (2008: 118–21).

37 Lévêque (1957: 489–91); Zambon (2008: 169–70). Both Zonaras (8.5) and Appian (*Samn.*, Frag. 12) allude to the growing frustrations that the Sikeliote communities held for Pyrrhus, whom they saw as acting with increasing tyrannical ambitions.

38 Plut. *Pyrrh.* 23.3.

39 Plut. *Pyrrh.* 23.5.

40 According to Plutarch (*Pyrrh.* 23.5–6), Pyrrhus used requests by Samnites and Tarentines as an excuse to withdraw from Sicily.

41 Scholars have long struggled to define the nature of Pyrrhus' political authority in Sicily during his brief tenure on the island; for a summary of the various positions taken on this subject, see Zambon (2008: 118–21).

42 Polyb. 7.4.5.

43 Lévêque (1957: 205ff.). In the *Epitome* of Justin (23.3.2), Pyrrhus is said to have been hailed by the Syracusans as *rex Sicliae*, as well as *rex Epiri*, yet these titles are surely anachronistic and best understood as exogenous labels deriving from later Roman sources.

44 Both Will (1966: 113) and Zambon (2008: 118–21) argue against the idea that Pyrrhus' *basileia* in Sicily was conceived of as being somehow "national" in character.

45 Polyb. 1.8.3.

46 Mergane (Μεργάνη) is otherwise unattested in surviving sources. Various theories have been put forward for the identification of Mergane, with the two most popular options being Morgantina and Megara Hyblaia; for overview, Berve (1959: 9); favoring Morgantina, De Sanctis (1967: 91); favoring Megara, Manni (1981: 203). Given its proximity to Syracuse, Megara Hyblaia is the more plausible choice here.

47 Polyb. 1.8.3; see also Hoyos (1985: 45, n. 47). This is the sole attestation to the position of a military *archon* in Sicily during this period.

48 Justin 23.4.12.

49 For the role of the Syracusan *dēmos* in selecting and overseeing the actions of their generals, see Robinson (2011: 84–6). Although not a precise parallel, the army assembly has been recognized as playing a central role in conferring sovereignty to Hellenistic kings. Even from the time of Alexander III, the army assembly was a source of political legitimacy that could have direct involvement in policy decisions; for analysis, see Zancan (1934: 35–47).

50 Roussel (1970: 22); Eckstein (1985: 267).

51 Polyb. 1.8.4; Paus. 6.12.2; Berve (1959: 8–10); Zambon (2008: 182–4).

52 The Syracusans reportedly made similar charges against Dion, who they claimed had unnecessarily prolonged his war with Dionysius I in order to maintain the powers of *stratēgos autokrator*; Plut. *Dion* 33.5, 49.1. While much of Hieron's reported military action was taken against the Mamertines, the initial focus of his attention appears to have been Carthaginian forces in Sicily. Theokritos refers to expelling the Carthaginians from Sicily in his *Idyll* 16 (ll. 76–87), which he wrote for Hieron around 275/4. This is echoed in the work of Zonaras (8.6) and Justin (23.4.1), where Hieron is described as coming to power as *dux adversus Karthaginienses*.

53 Judging from historical accounts, it does appear that the Carthaginians continued to extend their influence and presence east of the Himera River in the decade following Pyrrhus' departure from Sicily. For example, Polybius (1.15.10) states that, by 264, the *polis* Echetla (mod. Grammichele) was situated between the *epikrateiai* of the Carthaginians and that of the Syracusans.

54 Polyb. 1.9.4–6.

55 Berve (1959: 12–13) takes Polybius at his word. Following De Sanctis (1916: 94, n. 8), Walbank (1957: 56) holds that Timaeus of Tauromenion may have been Polybius' source if this was indeed an attempt to exculpate Hieron for a battlefield loss. Vallone (1955: 53) suggests this could have been a version disseminated by Hieron himself in an effort to mitigate the political fallout from his defeat.

56 Diod. 22.13.

57 Polyb. 1.9.6. For the recent suggestion that the mercenaries may have been sent by Ptolemy II, see Wolf and Lorber (2011: 33), who have convincingly argued that the series of large bronze denominations bearing Ptolemaic types of Zeus/Eagle, which regularly turn up in third-century contexts around eastern Sicily, are in fact the products of a Ptolemaic mint operating on the island.

58 Here, Hieron followed precedent set by Agathokles, who struck coins in his own name while occupying the positon of *stratēgos autokrator*; Armagrande (2000); De Lisle (2017: 11). Some scholars, including Maria Caccamo Caltabiano, have argued that Hieron could not have struck coins in his name prior to becoming king in 269, citing that constitutional limits placed on his authority, even as *stratēgos autokrator*, would have precluded him from doing so; Caccamo Caltabiano et al. (1995: 198–9). Yet these objections raised by Caccamo Caltabiano fail to consider the precedent set by Agathokles, focusing instead on the issues

of Hiketas, on which the personal name is preceded by ΕΠΙ, which is taken to be an indication of the constitutional limits to his authority.

59 Regarding the weight standards of the hemistaters, see Caccamo Caltabiano et al. (1995: 200–1).

60 On the date of these coins, see Franke (1958) and Caccamo Caltabiano et al. (1995: 204–7). For the silver coinage of Agathokles in question, see *SNG ANS*, 554–7; Castrizio (1995: 295–302).

61 This Leptines, Hieron's father-in-law, might have been a descendant of the fourth-century Syracusan historian and statesman Philistus, who married the daughter of another Leptines, the eldest brother of the tyrant Dionysius I. For genealogy and discussion, see Just. *Epit.*, 23.4.3–15; Walbank (1957: 55–6). Hieron's two daughters also married into Syracusan aristocratic families.

62 As, for example, the murder of Syracusan oligarchs and confiscation of their property by partisans of Agathokles; Diod. 19.5.4–8; or Pyrrhus' treatment of rival Syracusan leaders, Thoinon and Sosistratus; Plut., *Pyrrh.* 23.4–5; Dionys. Hal. 20.8.3–4.

63 Polyb. 7.8.1–7.

64 Polyb. 1.9.2.

65 Polyb. 1.9.7–8.

66 Zonaras, 8.6.14; accepted by Berve (1959: 13–14) and De Sensi Sestito (1995: 29–30). This was certainly a strategic move aimed at winning favor with the Romans, but there was very likely a more immediate rationale for Hieron, namely, to weaken the Mamertines, who had relied on the support of the Campanians at Rhegion in the past; see Polyb. 1.7.6; Diod. 22.1.

67 For the advance on Messana and narrative of the campaigns of 270, see Diod. 22.13.1.

68 Diod. 22.13.2. Although not mentioned in surviving historical sources, it is likely that other Greek cities along the Tyrrhenian coast, including Kale Akte, Apollonia, and Haluntion, also freely surrendered to Hieron at this time; see Berve (1959: 16) and Goldsberry (1973: 114).

69 Diod. 22.13.6–8.

70 Polyb. 1.9.8: "and upon his return to Syracuse, he was proclaimed king by all the allies."

71 This number would include cities long in the orbit of Syracuse (e.g., Akrai, Heloros, Leontinoi), as well as those who more recently allied themselves with Hieron (e.g., Tauromenion, Kentoripe, Halaisa).

72 On the theatricality surrounding the coronation of Antigonos Monophthalmos, see Billows (1990: 157–8); Plut., *Demtr.* 17.2–18.1. Contrary to the impression given by Diodorus' account (20.53–4) that Ptolemy and the other Successors simply followed Antigonos' lead and spontaneously declared themselves kings in 306, Gruen (1985: 255–9) has demonstrated that Ptolemy, Seleucus, and others deferred for up to two years before laying claim to the title of king, as each waited until the opportunity arose to ground their claims on a justifiable military victory.

73 For Antigonos: Plut. *Demetr.* 17.2ff. Similarly, Attalos I took on the title of *basileus* following his victory against the Galatians at the Kaïkos River in 241; see Polyb. 18.41.7; *OGIS* 269.

74 Gehrke (2013) explores the relationship between claims to legitimacy and military success for Hellenistic monarchs. That Hieron was tapping into this well-established precedent of Hellenistic monarchy is a subject further explored in Chapter 2.

75 For detailed discussion of the "high" (269) and "low" (265) dates for the battle of the Longanus, see Hoyos (1985), who strongly favors the low date. In favor of 269, most notably, see Berve (1959: 14–15); De Sensi Sestito (1977: 223–32); Zambon (2008: 197–200); Braccesi and Millino (2000: 186–7); Bell (2011: 195). In favor of 265, among others, see Schenck von Stauffenberg (1933: 92–5); Walbank (1957: 54–5); Hoyos (2011).

76 Polyb. 7.8.4.

77 Polyb. 1.8.2.

78 Diod. 22.13.1–8.

79 Hoyos (2011: 137).

[80] Hoyos (2011: 138), who further argues that the phrase "παρὰ πόδας" was used by Polybius to add dramatic effect to his narrative, and thus should not be taken literally.

[81] De Sanctis (1967: 93–5).

[82] Polyb. 7.8.4.

[83] Pace Hoyos (2011: 138).

[84] It was not the habit of would-be monarchs to claim legitimacy for autocratic rule following a military defeat, but precisely the opposite. On this, see note 73 and Gruen (1985: 258), who observes, with regard to the acclamation of Ptolemy I, "the new ruler claimed his prerogatives to underscore success, not to mitigate defeat."

[85] For discussion of fortifications, see Karlsson (1992; 1993).

[86] Diod. 23.1.2–3; Polyb. 1.11.4. For discussion of the sequence of events leading up to and including Hieron's siege of Messana, see Goldsberry (1973: 116–20).

[87] For the appeal and subsequent debate: Hoyos (2011: 138–43); Bellomo (2013).

[88] Appius appears to have dispatched envoys to both Hieron and the Carthaginians in an attempt to forestall war. Diodorus (23.1.4), drawing on Philinus' account (Polyb. 1.15.5), puts Appius in Rhegion when he sends the envoys, while Polybius's account (1.11.10–12) has Appius send the envoys only after arriving in Messana. For further discussion, see Walbank (1957: 62–3). Most scholars seem to favor the account given by Philinus, as Berve (1959: 23–4); De Sanctis (1967: 105–6). However, Hoyos (2011: 144–5) accepts that the Roman consul might have, in fact, made two attempts at securing a peaceful settlement.

[89] Diodorus (23.1.4) paraphrases Hieron's response: "Hieron replied that the Mamertines, who had laid waste Kamarina and Gela and had seized Messana in so impious a manner, were besieged with just cause, and that the Romans, harping as they did on the word fides, certainly ought not to protect assassins who had shown the greatest contempt for good faith; but if, on behalf of men so utterly godless, they should enter upon a war of such magnitude, it would be clear to all mankind that they were using pity for the imperiled as a cloak for their own advantage, and that in reality they coveted Sicily" (trans. Walton 1957).

[90] Two versions of Appius' initial successes and failures in Sicily are recorded by Polybius, reflecting the divergent accounts given by Fabius Pictor (1.12.4) and Philinius (1.15.5). Nonetheless, both agree that Appius Claudius advanced against Syracuse and besieged the city. For discussion of sources, see Walbank (1957: 66–7).

[91] Hoyos (2011: 142–3) offers a persuasive argument that the Roman Senate actually declared war on Hieron and Syracuse in 264, not the Carthaginians.

[92] Diodorus (23.4.1) puts the number of cities that sent embassies to the Romans at sixty-seven and Eutropius (2.19) at fifty-two, figures that most scholars consider exaggerated, e.g., Berve (1959: 33–4); De Sensi Sestito (1977: 221). La Bua (1966: 39–40), however, accepts Diodorus' number as accurate.

[93] Diodorus (23.4.1) comments on the Syracusans' desire to come to terms with the Romans, so as to avoid a prolonged siege; see also Eutrop., 2.19; Polyb. 1.16.4. For further discussion of Hieron's motivations for seeking peace without resistance, see Berve (1959: 35) and Goldsberry (1973: 122).

[94] The provisions of the treaty are mentioned by various authors, including Diod. 23.4.1; Polyb. 1.16.3; Zonaras 8.9. Polybius (1.17.1) relates that the treaty was ratified by the Roman people. For detailed discussions of Hieron's treaty with Rome, see Eckstein (1980: 183–203) and Zambon (2008: 211–20). This episode is itself a prelude to Rome's diplomatic handling of Hellenistic monarchs during the period of their expansion into the Greek East in the late third and second centuries.

[95] According to Diodorus (23.4.1), Hieron was expected to make payments over a 15-year period; cf. Walbank (1957: 69), who asserts that Diodorus was incorrect in stating that the treaty had a 15-year term from the outset on the grounds that Romans did not conclude treaties with circumscribed durations.

[96] Diodorus (23.4.1) records the amount at 25 talents (the equivalent of 150,000 drachmas). Polybius (1.16.9) puts the figure at 100 talents of silver, which Walbank (1957: 69) suggests was the amount given by Fabius Pictor. Eutropius (2.19) and Orosius (4.7.3) each give the amount of 200 talents. Most scholars have accepted Polybius' account as the most reliable of the lot. Even an indemnity of 200 talents of silver would be a rather paltry sum for Hieron, and comparatively small considering the Carthaginians were required to pay the Romans roughly 3,200 talents over 10 years according to the terms of the peace treaty that brought to end the First Punic War; Polyb. 1.62.7–63.3. For discussion of how Hieron may have gone about repaying the indemnity, see Goldsberry (1973: 174, n. 88).

[97] Diod. 23.3.4.

[98] The case for the political subordination of these three cities to Hieron, which rests largely on archaeological evidence, will be presented in Chapter 3.

[99] The legal relationship stipulated by the treaty of 263 has been the subject of much discussion, with most Roman historians coming down on the side of informal *amicitia* rather than a legally binding *foedus* that left the king in the position of *clientele*; here, see Burton (2003: 352–3); Goldsberry (1973: 123).

[100] Eckstein (1980; 1987: 115–31). Walbank (1957: 69) expressed similar sentiment, noting that Hieron enjoyed "much greater independence than the Italian *socii*, and during the first two Punic Wars Roman control was barely noticeable."

[101] Hieron sends grain and soldiers to support the Roman legion besieging Rhegion in 270. Additional provisioning of Roman troops is reported for the year 262, during the siege of Akragas, and again in 258, during the Roman assault on Kamarina.

[102] See Zonaras 8.16, where it is mentioned that the treaty was renewed and the outstanding indemnity owed to Rome was cancelled; Naev. *Poen.* Fr. 41–3. Similarly, Diodorus (23.4.1) mentions that the terms of the treaty specified the length of 15 years.

[103] Wilson (2013: 99ff.) effectively draws attention to the disparity between the Hieronian kingdom and the rest of Sicily by focusing on the marked imbalance in the number and scale of public building projects accomplished at the time in either part of the island. Citing his early scholarship (Wilson 1985: 314–19), Wilson also emphasizes the decline in the number of hill towns in central and western Sicily between the end of the fourth and end of the third century. Among the victims of the war, Kamarina and Myttistraton were reportedly sacked in 258, and half of the population of Akragas was sold into slavery. At the site of Monte Adranone in southwestern Sicily, archaeologists have discovered the remains of a fortified settlement or garrison with clear evidence for destruction dating to the first half of the third century BCE; Diod. 23.4.1–2; Serrati (2000: 128–30); Fiorentini (1988–9: 18).

[104] Polybius (1.62.8) quotes the preliminary treaty proposed by the consul Gaius Lutatius, which ran along the lines of "There shall be friendship between the Carthaginians and Romans on the following terms if approved by the Roman people. The Carthaginians to evacuate the whole of Sicily and not to make war on Hieron or bear arms against the Syracusans or the allies of the Syracusans. The Carthaginians to give up to the Romans all prisoners without ransom. The Carthaginians to pay to the Romans by instalments in twenty years two thousand two hundred Euboean talents." Polybius notes that while the Roman people did not initially accept the terms of the treaty, the only significant changes in the final version were an increase in the indemnity owed to Rome and the stipulation that the Carthaginians evacuate the Aeolian islands. It is unclear whether Hieron and the Carthaginians concluded a separate treaty at this time, but Polybius' (1.83.1–4) comment that Hieron assisted the Carthaginians during the Mercenary War may indicate that there may have been at least an informal agreement in place; see also Serrati (2000: 118). Hieron's support of the Carthaginians during the Mercenary War has received a great deal of attention, often characterized in terms of modern political theory; e.g., balance of power theory, Schmitt (1974: 81–3); or Realpolitik, Eckstein (1987: 129–30).

[105] On the cultural efflorescence of Syracuse during the Hieronian period, see Wescoat (1989); Lehmler (2005); Campagna (2004); Bell (1999; 2013); Veit (2008). Beloch (1886: 281) estimated that by the year 300, the population of Syracuse had reached 200,000. The expansion and development of the Achradina district at Syracuse during Hieron's reign was surely to accommodate further growth in the city's urban demographics.

[106] For an overview of monumental building at sites within the kingdom of Hieron, see Wilson (2013: 80–99). Wolf (2016: 57–72) offers a recent study of the two-story stoa building at Heloros. For the monumental building program in the agora at Morgantina, see Bell (1988), and for the architectural transformation at Hellenistic Tauromenion, see Campagna (2008; 2019).

[107] For further commentary on this disparity in the material culture of the eastern and western portions of the island during the third century, see Wilson (2013).

[108] On numerous occasions, Livy remarks on Hieron's unwavering fidelity to Rome (23.21.5, 25.28.8, 25.29.7, 26.32.4), and later contrasts the king's actions to those of his grandson and successor, Hieronymos. Praise for Hieron's loyalty toward Rome also found poetic expression, as in Sil. *Pun.*, 14.79–93, where again Hieron's virtue, expressed in his loyalty to Rome (*socialia iura Ausoniis multos servarat casta per annos*) is contrasted with Hieronymos' ignoble crime of switching sides to ally himself with Carthage.

[109] Austin (1986); Gehrke (2013).

[110] Eutrop., 3.1; Zevi (1991).

[111] On Hieron's age at death: Polyb. 7.8.7.

[112] Liv. 24.4.

[113] The young king had neither institutional support nor responsible regents and so was doomed from the start. See Haake (2013) for Hieronymos and the issue of dynastic transition; cf. Zahrnt (2000). The Carthaginians, aware of the growing discord among the Syracusans, actively sought to influence the situation, sending Epikides and Hippokrates, two Carthaginian citizens of Syracusan descent, to Sicily with the task of stirring up anti-Roman sentiment at Syracuse and advocate on the Carthaginians' behalf; Liv. 24.6.1–3; Polyb. 7.5.1–9. On Gelon's support for Carthage, see Liv. 23.30.11–12.

[114] Liv. 24.7; Paus. 6.12.4.

[115] Liv. 24.21, 26.31.

[116] Plut. *Marc.* 19.1–3; cf. Liv. 25.31 for a far less affecting account of the fall of Syracuse.

[117] Bonacasa (2004: 37).

[118] According to Livy (25.40), Marcellus and his troops marched off with the lion's share of these great works, bringing them back to Rome and, in doing so, sparking a passion for Greek art among the Roman elite. Back in Rome, Marcellus was forced to defend his actions before the Senate, after Sicilian legates pleaded with the senators not to allow Marcellus to once again take Sicily as his appointed consular assignment. After both sides were heard, Livy (26.32.4) reports that long debate followed among the senators, with the majority ultimately siding with Titus Manlius Torquatus, who reportedly advocated for the censure of Marcellus after asking his fellow senators how Hieron might react if risen from the grave to see Syracuse despoiled and Rome adorned with the plundered art.

[119] After the capture of Syracuse, the island was temporarily divided into two administrative zones, the "old province" and the "former kingdom." For the year 213, for instance, Livy (24.44.4) reports that Marcellus was assigned *Sicilia finibus eis, quibus regnum Hieronis fuisset* ("Sicily with the boundaries which Hieron's kingdom had had"), while the propraetor Publius Lentulus was assigned the *provincia vetus*, which amounted to the remainder of the island that Rome had exercised authority over since the conclusion of the First Punic War in 241 BCE; and, similarly, Liv. 24.7.9, 25.111.6.

TWO

FASHIONING KINGSHIP

Βασιλεία. οὔτε φύσις οὔτε τὸ δίκαιον ἀποδιδοῦσι τοῖς ἀνθρώποις τὰς βασιλείας, ἀλλὰ τοῖς δυναμένοις ἡγεῖσθαι στρατοπέδου καὶ χειρίζειν πράγματα νουνεχῶς· οἷος ἦν Φίλιππος καὶ οἱ διάδοχοι Ἀλεξάνδρου. τὸν γὰρ υἱὸν κατὰ φύσιν οὐδὲν ὠφέλησεν ἡ συγγένεια διὰ τὴν τῆς ψυχῆς δυναμίαν. τοὺς δὲ μηδὲν προσήκοντας βασιλεῖς γενέσθαι σχεδὸν ἁπάσης τῆς οἰκουμένης.

Kingship. It is neither descent nor law that gives monarchies to men, but the ability to command an army and to handle affairs competently. Such was the case with Philip and the Successors of Alexander. For Alexander's natural son was in no way helped by his kinship with him, because of his weakness of spirit, while those who had no connection with Alexander became kings of almost the whole inhabited world.[1]

HIERON II: A HELLENISTIC KING?

In this chapter, we step back from the chronological narrative of Chapter 1 to consider the nature of Hieron's kingship, placing it in conversation with the Hellenistic monarchies of the eastern Mediterranean. There is much in the way of surviving literary, epigraphic, and archaeological evidence to suggest that Hieron modeled his rule on principles and practices that by the early third century had come to exemplify the type of autocratic rule embraced by Successor kings who came to power in the years following the death of Alexander III. Situating Hieron's political resume in terms of contemporary models of Hellenistic kingship offers an instructive framework for contextualizing much of what we know about the Syracusan ruler's behavior, particularly with respect to his efforts to establish and maintain political legitimacy. By the same token, centering the Hieronian kingdom within mainstream discussions of Hellenistic monarchy promises to open new vantage points for understanding the greater spectrum of political conventions, actions, and philosophies that evolved to justify autocratic rule in the Mediterranean world at this time. Indeed, the blossoming of a kingdom beyond the borders of Alexander's former empire offers valuable insights on the nature of Hellenistic *basileia* and on the reception of those elements deemed essential to the acquisition and perpetuation of monarchic power in the middle decades of the third century BCE.

While Hieron himself would rule over his island kingdom for 54 years (a reign rarely matched for longevity by his counterparts in the eastern Mediterranean), his political dynasty collapsed barely a year after his death. Compared with the generations of Seleucid and Ptolemaic rulers that shaped the political landscape of the eastern Mediterranean for more than two centuries, the Hieronian "dynasty" might be better classified as an experiment. Yet it is precisely for this reason that the Hieronian kingdom – neatly bounded in time and space – offers an ideal landscape in which to explore the role that Hellenistic kingship and its related institutions (such as the royal tax administration) played in shaping the political, economic, and social conditions of the wider Mediterranean world.

In what follows, I trace the development of Hieron's approach toward legitimizing his rule throughout three different periods (or "acts") of his 54-year reign. At each stage, I situate the king's behavior with respect to political developments taking place within the Successor kingdoms of the eastern Mediterranean in order to demonstrate that Hieron's *basileia* was neither unresponsive to local circumstances nor static in the face of changing concepts of kingship in the wider Mediterranean world. Drawing on a range of literary and material evidence, I highlight the king's cultural and political policies that most readily show the influence of contemporary ideas and practices associated with autocratic rule. Ultimately, this chapter aims to reveal the inherent flexibility of Hellenistic kingship, a quality evident enough in Hieron's own behavior at various points throughout his reign to justify a significant reassessment of his importance in the third-century Mediterranean.

ACT I: A WINNING KING

In his influential article, "Der siegreiche König," Hans-Joachim Gehrke argued that Early Hellenistic monarchy is best understood in terms of Max Weber's concept of charismatic authority.[2] For Weber, charismatic authority manifested in a single individual who typically rose to prominence in moments of political or economic instability and who claimed the legitimacy to rule on the grounds of extraordinary deeds and exceptional qualities – what Weber calls "supernatural" gifts – of the mind and body.[3] Charismatic authority fell outside legal frameworks that had traditionally granted one the power to rule; it was thus fundamentally unstable, requiring the charismatic leader to consistently maintain legitimacy by reinforcing the exceptional force of character that had first distinguished them in the eyes of their subjects.[4] Unsurprisingly, charismatic leaders often claimed association with divine powers in order to further bolster their legitimacy to rule. It is not difficult to see how Weber's model – with its emphasis on this exceptional, unstable, and very personal form of rule – grafts neatly onto the type of autocratic rule that developed in the eastern Mediterranean following the death of Alexander III.[5]

In Gehrke's estimation, the exceptional quality that distinguished Hellenistic kings and set them apart as charismatic rulers was their ability to wage war and, more importantly, to achieve victory on the battlefield. Drawing on a wealth of documentary evidence, Gehrke emphatically underscores the instrumental role that military success played in the construction of political legitimacy for Early Hellenistic kings. He concludes that the projection of one's image as a *siegreicher König*, or victorious king, was fundamental both to the initial claim to regal authority and to the maintenance of autocratic legitimacy. Warfare provided the ideal medium through which the Successor kings could display the exceptional qualities that distinguished them, whether it was through sound leadership on the battlefield, remarkable skill in combat, or even divine patronage.[6]

Reflecting on the intimate connection that developed between military achievement and Hellenistic kingship, Gehrke states, "Als Sieger hatte man also eine gute Chance, getragen von der Zustimmung der Untertanen, insbesondere des Heeres, seine Herrschaft mit der Würde des Königtums zu versehen und zu legitimieren."[7] Hieron undoubtedly grasped this very concept and promoted his militaristic image as a victorious general both on and off the battlefield throughout his early career, which is here defined as the period between his acclamation as king in 269 and the conclusion of his treaty with Rome in 263. As we saw in Chapter 1, Hieron claimed the title of *basileus* immediately after his victory over the Mamertines at Longanus and, in doing so, followed a model set by the Successor kings.[8] So far as we can tell, Hieron took the title of king without geographic distinction, indicating that he viewed himself not as "King of the Syracusans" or even "King of Sicily," but as sovereign over all the spear-won territory that he had already conquered or would come to conquer throughout his lifetime.[9] While Hieron would soon find his authority confined to southeastern Sicily, there is no reason to discount the possibility that he held ambitions of ruling a far larger kingdom.

After securing his acclamation by the Syracusan army and his allies, Hieron continued to accompany his troops into battle, as was customary for kings of his day.[10] He even reportedly distinguished himself in hand-to-hand combat on multiple occasions.[11] Such behavior certainly burnished his persona as a warrior king, an image he took care to amplify in a variety of media. For example, Hieron's martial character found contemporary expression in the sixteenth idyll of the Syracusan poet Theokritos, who sought the ruler's patronage in the 270s. Although *Idyll* 16 was probably composed around 275 while Hieron still held power as *stratēgos autokrator* of the Syracusans, Theokritos was clearly working within the genre of the Hellenistic *encomium* written by court poets on behalf of kings.[12] The poem casts Hieron in the guise of a Homeric hero, the champion of the island's Sikeliote *poleis*, who will restore peace and prosperity to the island once he has driven the Carthaginians from Sicily. Employing epic language, Theokritos describes Hieron not just as a warrior (ll. 103: αἰχμητὴν Ἱέρωνα), but even as a peer of Ajax and Achilles:

ἔσσεται οὗτος ἀνὴρ ὃς ἐμεῦ κεχρήσετ' ἀοιδοῦ,
ῥέξας ἢ Ἀχιλεὺς ὅσσον μέγας ἢ βαρὺς Αἴας
ἐν πεδίῳ Σιμόεντος, ὅθι Φρυγὸς ἠρίον Ἴλου.
ἤδη νῦν Φοίνικες ὑπ' ἠελίῳ δύνοντι
οἰκεῦντες Λιβύας ἄκρον σφυρὸν ἐρρίγασιν·
ἤδη βαστάζουσι Συρακόσιοι μέσα δοῦρα,
ἀχθόμενοι σακέεσσι βραχίονας ἰτεΐνοισιν·τὲν δ' αὐτοῖς Ἱέρων προτέροις
    ἴσος ἡρώεσσι
ζώννυται, ἵππειαι δὲ κόρυν σκιάουσιν ἔθειραι.

there shall be a man who shall have need of me as his
poet, when he has achieved as much as great Achilles or grim Ajax
on the plain of Simois where the tomb of Phrygian Ilus stands.
Already the Phoenicians beneath the setting sun, who inhabit the
farthest edge of Libya, tremble with fear; already the Syracusans
grasp their spears by the middle and load their arms with their
wicker shields; and among them Hieron prepares himself like the
    warriors
of old, a horsehair crest shadowing his helmet.[13]

In an allusion to a Homeric arming scene (ll. 80–1), Hieron prepares for battle alongside his soldiers and is distinguished among their ranks by his armor and the horsehair crest of his helmet (ἐν δ' αὐτοῖς Ἱέρων προτέροις ἴσος ἡρώεσσι ζώννυται, ἵππειαι δὲ κόρυν σκεπάουσιν ἔθειραι).[14] The term αἰχμητής ("spearman") not only carries epic connotations, but plays up the symbolic connotations of the spear as the weapon par excellence of Macedonian-style kingship.[15] The poet would later revive the image of the spear-bearing king in his encomium to Ptolemy II, where he refers to both Ptolemy II (17.56) and his father (17.57) as αἰχμητής and later praises Ptolemy II for his skill at wielding a spear (17.103: ἐπιστάμενος δόρυ πάλλειν).[16]

At several points in the poem (ll. 76–7, 85–7), Theokritos portrays the Carthaginians as foreign invaders on Sicilian soil who must be driven back across the sea before peace and prosperity can be restored on the island. We see this, for instance, in lines 85ff.:

ἐχθροὺς ἐκ νάσοιο κακαὶ πέμψειαν ἀνάγκαι
Σαρδόνιον κατὰ κῦμα φίλων μόρον ἀγγέλλοντας
τέκνοις ἠδ' ἀλόχοισιν, ἀριθμητοὺς ἀπὸ πολλῶν.
ἄστεα δὲ προτέροισι πάλιν ναίοιτο πολίταις,
δυσμενέων ὅσα χεῖρες ἐλωβήσαντο κατ' ἄκρας.

May harsh compulsion drive our enemies from this island
Over the Sardinian sea, to bring hard news to wives
And children about their loved ones' deaths, and may
These messengers be but a fraction left from the invading army.
May the cities which enemy hands have cruelly razed
Be once again peopled by their former inhabitants.[17]

As a well-educated Syracusan, Theokritos would have surely recognized the great antiquity of many Punic settlements on the island, and yet he sets Hieron's impending showdown with the Carthaginians within the rhetorical frame of the Greek struggle against a barbarian enemy.[18] As a political message, the Greek struggle against barbarians had gained popularity among the Hellenistic kings of the eastern Mediterranean, as it allowed them to cast themselves as champions of the Greek *poleis* and protectors of their political freedom.[19] In *Idyll* 16, Theokritos does no less, casting Hieron as the savior of the Sikeliote *poleis* that have long suffered at the hands of a foreign army.

Efforts to project this martial image were not limited to the literary sphere, but also found expression in the material record. While court poetry reinforced its message at a local level, Hieron pursued other strategies aimed at disseminating his image as victorious king throughout the Mediterranean. This was undoubtedly the motivation behind his dedication of weapons at the sanctuary of Athena Lindia on Rhodes. The king's offering was recorded in the temple's inventory, which includes the decidedly charismatic detail that Hieron had personally used the weapons in battle (XLI.122: Βα[σ]ιλεὺ[ς Ἱ]έρω[ν] ὅπλα, οἶς αὐτὸς ἐχρε[ῖτ]ο).[20] The inventory does not give a precise date for the dedication, but sometime shortly after the battle at Longanus (269) seems the ideal moment both to commemorate his victory over the Mamertines and to highlight his recent ascension to kingship on the international stage.[21] The choice of the Rhodian sanctuary was certainly not arbitrary. By the third century BCE, the sanctuary had become a favored location for kings to commemorate their military victories.[22] Hieron's dedication thus visibly positioned him in the company of kings like Pyrrhus and Alexander, who had themselves offered up arms and armor to the goddess.[23] Hieron's choice of the Rhodian sanctuary may have further served to foster connections with the Rhodians themselves, whose merchants acted as one of the principal agents in the market for Sicilian grain.[24]

Engagement with a wider audience also found material expression in the dedication of honorific statues of the king, both in Sicily and in the Panhellenic sanctuary of Zeus at Olympia. Pausanias mentions seeing at least five statues of Hieron at Olympia, specifying that three were dedicated by the king's children and two by the Syracusans.[25] Whether these were of a martial cast, Pausanias does not say, but his observation that one was equestrian in nature urges that conclusion.[26] In 1954, archaeologists discovered the base of an honorific statue dedicated to Hieron in the sanctuary (Figure 2.1). The fragmentary inscription reads:

[Βασιλέα Ἱέρωνα] Ἱεροκλέος
[ἀνέθηκε ἁ πό]λις τῶν Ταυρο-
[μενιτᾶν Διὶ Ὀ]λυμπίωι
          Μίκιων Νικητρ[άτ]ου Συρακόσιος
          ἐποήσ[εν].

(This statue of) King Hieron, son of Hierokles.
The *polis* of the Tauromenitans dedicated (it) to Zeus Olympios.
Mikion, son of Nikeratos, of Syracuse made (it).[27]

Since Pausanias does not mention a dedication made by the *dēmos* of Tauromenion, some scholars have speculated that this may belong to a sixth honorific statue of the king at the sanctuary.[28] If Pausanias' numbers can be trusted, statues of Hieron at Olympia might have outnumbered those dedicated to any other single Hellenistic king.[29]

Closer to home, honorific dedications for Hieron have also been found at Syracuse, including a base for either a statue or tripod discovered during the eighteenth century in the Achradina district of the city. The dedicatory inscription reads:

Βασιλέος ἀγε[ομένου] | Ἱέρωνος Ἱεροκλέος | Συρακόσιοι θεοῖς πᾶσι

When Hieron, son of Hierokles, was king and *hegemon*,
the Syracusans [dedicated this] to all the gods.[30]

2.1 Inscribed base for an honorific statue dedicated by the citizens of Tauromenion to Hieron II in the panhellenic sanctuary of Zeus at Olympia (photo: E.-M. Czakó, D-DAI-ATH-Olympia 3917; courtesy of the German Archaeological Institute).

2.2 Bronze coin of Hieron II, ca. 269–215 BCE, with portrait of the king wearing a laurel crown (ANS 1944.100.57129; courtesy of the American Numismatic Society).

The language of the inscription clearly marks this as a dedication made by the Syracusans following a military victory achieved under Hieron's leadership. Opinions diverge on the event that precipitated the dedication, although a majority of scholars consider this part of a monument commemorating Hieron's victory over the Mamertines at Longanus.[31] The title of *hegemon* hints at the militaristic nature of the dedication and may also refer to Hieron's position as leader of a *koinon* formed by the *poleis* within his kingdom.[32]

Perhaps the clearest expression of Hieron's efforts to promote his image as victorious general can be found on the bronze coinage minted after his victory at Longanus (Figure 2.2). These were large coins weighing roughly 17 grams, struck on flans averaging 27 millimeters in diameter. The obverse type bears a portrait of the king, who is shown clean-shaven with the idealized facial features and stylized hair common to contemporary portraiture of eastern monarchs.[33] In his portrait, Hieron wears a laurel wreath, not the cloth diadem that had emerged as the standard headgear worn by Hellenistic kings to symbolize their sovereignty.[34] The significance of the laurel wreath remains subject to speculation, and has been variously interpreted as a reference to Hieron's recent military victory at Longanus or even as the emblem of a priesthood.[35] On the coin's reverse, a heavily armored cavalryman charges to the right with a spear in his hand above the legend ΙΕΡΩΝΟΣ. Here, the visual association between kingship and military success is reduced to the very essentials so as to be inescapable.

In issuing these coins, Hieron became the first Sicilian ruler to strike coinage bearing his own portrait. While both Agathokles and Pyrrhus had minted coins with their regal title and name, neither had issued portrait coins. The significance of this move cannot be overstated, as it undoubtedly situated Hieron's *basileia* within the mainstream practice of the day. Among the first generation of the Successor kings, the ruler portrait – including that of the posthumous Alexander III himself – became a potent symbol of kingship.[36] Unsurprisingly, portraiture and militaristic iconography found frequent expression in the coinage struck by the freshly minted Successors.[37] Circulation of coins bearing a ruler's image facilitated the widespread dissemination of visual propaganda, arguably more so than even the dedication of honorific statues or ostentatious architectural monuments. The impact of this new mentality toward the utility of portrait coinage and its role in legitimating royal authority is perhaps nowhere more clearly expressed than in the adoption of the practice by fledgling monarchs, like Hieron, whose decision to strike portrait coinage underscores the belief that the king's image was intimately associated with legitimate rule.[38]

The charging cavalryman on the coin's reverse type bore a straightforward militaristic message, possibly referring to the concept of a king's spear-won territory (δορίκτητος χώρα; *doriktētos chōra*), which Hieron himself likely claimed across much of eastern Sicily at the time.[39] The image of the king fighting on horseback was popularized by Alexander III, who was renowned for his daring cavalry charges.[40] The figure of the charging cavalryman, while not particularly common, did appear on coinage struck by other Hellenistic kings.[41] Whether or not the horseman on Hieron's coin was intended to represent the king himself, the proximity of Hieron's name in the exergue below and his portrait on the obverse conveyed an unmistakable message aimed at reinforcing the connection between legitimate rule and military accomplishment.

Hieron's commitment to maintaining his image as a victorious general during the early phase of his reign supports Gehrke's theory about Hellenistic kingship as a form of charismatic rule. It also goes to substantiate Gehrke's argument that the projection of militarism was an indispensable aspect of all foundational claims of regal legitimacy and was not simply confined to the generation of the Successor kings. Yet even in Gehrke's estimation, maintaining legitimacy as a ruler in the eyes of one's subjects necessarily involved more than just exhibiting success on the battlefield; it required projecting one's image as a competent statesman capable of protecting his subjects from external threats. The surviving literary and material evidence shows that Hieron took steps in the second phase of his reign to expand the basis of his claims to legitimacy.

ACT II: *EUERGETES* AND *SŌTĒR*

The treaty of 263 marked an important transition in the development of Hieron's *basileia* only six years after he initially took the title of king. The terms of the peace with Rome removed the opportunity for military aggression against his longtime target, the Mamertines, thus eliminating the hallmark of regal legitimacy as contemporary Hellenistic monarchs perceived it. At first glance, Hieron's strategic quiescence presented a serious threat to him personally, for his authority rested on the projection of martial prowess and the concept of unconditional sovereignty.[42] Ulrich Gotter, exploring the impact of Roman military expansion on the freedom of Late Hellenistic monarchs to wage unfettered warfare, notes that "[t]he principal source of legitimacy for the Hellenistic king was thus simple success, or more specifically, his victory in war ... Under these circumstances, a king without the opportunity to triumph was inconceivable – something that neither should nor could be: a monstrum."[43] The resolution of the treaty, which effectively forbade expansionary military operations on the part of Hieron, might have looked at the time like the end of the line for the king. Hieron's capitulation to the Romans in 263, however, did not fatally undermine his claims to legitimacy. Arguably, it even strengthened his position in unexpected ways, as the ground of regal legitimacy shifted beneath him, impelling him to embrace a wider framework of cultural politics and redefine the terms of his authority.

The second act of Hieron's kingship – here roughly defined as the period between the conclusion of the treaty of 263 and the elevation of his son, Gelon, as co-regent in the early 230s – was characterized by the adoption of a new set of legitimacy-building practices aimed at promoting the king's image as a benefactor and protector of his kingdom. In many respects, Hieron's situation revealed an inherent flexibility in the concept of kingship, one that augured the ideological changes that would occur more widely in the following century, as Rome's interests expanded into the eastern Mediterranean and Roman armies began to challenge the primacy of the Seleucid and Antigonid kings on the battlefield. Indeed, as Mattias Haake has aptly noted, Hieron's rapid transformation from "victorious king" to "friendly king" presaged the refashioning of kingship in the growing shadow of Rome.[44]

This did not mean that after 263 Hieron completely abandoned the trappings of a victorious king. After all, he maintained his charismatic military persona through coinage, continuing to strike portrait coins with the charging cavalryman throughout his lifetime. A subtle, but important, change occurred in the king's portrait around this time, as Hieron was now shown wearing a cloth diadem in place of the laurel wreath (Figure 2.3). This relatively minor modification brought his portraiture in line with contemporary practice of all living kings. Nor did the treaty of 263 require Hieron to reduce the size of his army, so far as we know; consequently, at least within his kingdom, he could project military power through the deployment of troops.[45] That he maintained some form of standing military force is further suggested by his

2.3 Bronze coin of Hieron II, ca. 269–215 BCE, with portrait of the king wearing a broad cloth diadem (ANS 1944.100.57134; courtesy of the American Numismatic Society).

promotion of civic *gymnasia* throughout his kingdom, which Giuseppe Cordiano has argued was a means of training a citizen military reserve that could be levied in the event of war.[46]

Remarkably, Hieron now laid claim to military achievement as a Roman ally. His support for Rome's war against Carthage allowed him to maintain certain aspects of the martial image that he had cultivated during the first decade of his reign. On several occasions, he sent aid in the form of men, weapons, and grain to support Roman forces fighting in Sicily or abroad.[47] In return, the Roman Senate recognized him for his contributions, bolstering his image as an ally both in the ongoing contest with Carthage and in their conflicts with other enemies. According to Plutarch, after the Roman consul Marcus Claudius Marcellus defeated a Gallic army at Clastidium in 222, he sent a share of the spoils to Hieron in recognition of the king's support during Rome's campaigns against the Insubres of Cisalpine Gaul.[48] This might have consisted of bullion and coinage, but could very well have included weapons taken from the defeated enemy; in fact, Livy reports that such *spolia*, captured in Rome's wars against the Gauls and Illyrians, hung on the walls of the Temple of Olympian Zeus in Syracuse.[49] These were a gift of the Roman people to Hieron, who presumably displayed them on the temple's walls as a statement of his own continued involvement (and continued success) in military affairs.[50]

If Hieron could not actively seek out military success through expansionary campaigns, the next best thing was to suppress external threats against the safety or autonomy of the *poleis* within his kingdom. Many of the Sicilian *poleis* that initially pursued an alliance with Hieron in the 260s likely did so seeking protection from Mamertine aggression. Ensuring the safety of one's kingdom was central to the legitimacy of a Hellenistic king.[51] A king who could not defend his subjects and allies from external threats risked losing their support and the mandate for his right to rule, not to mention critical sources of revenue. John Serrati has noted the discernable proliferation of the epithet *sōtēr* ("savior") during the Hellenistic period, as the term that had been previously reserved for divinities was now applied to living monarchs.[52] Angelos Chaniotis has convincingly argued that a king's ability to offer protection to entire cities and regions was considered an essential quality of his "mortal divinity," making him the likely recipient of divine honors from the *poleis* under his dominion.[53] The extant literary and material sources are largely silent on the issue of whether or not Hieron received divine honors as did so many Hellenistic monarchs. The single piece of evidence in favor of a ruler cult is a small limestone altar bearing the inscription Διὸς Σωτῆρος Ἱέρωνος, which archaeologists discovered in 1949 while conducting excavations in the Achradina district of Syracuse (Figure 2.4).[54] This portable altar has naturally captured the attention of scholars interested in settling the question of whether Hieron and his family received divine honors, yet the altar alone is not dispositive evidence for state-sponsored honors carried out by the Syracusans. It may represent a private manifestation of worship for the king, judging from its miniature scale and the rather desultory manner of the inscription.[55] Certainly, the assimilation of Hieron with Zeus Soter is noteworthy given the king's promotion of his image as a protector of his kingdom. As we will see below, this is not the only material attestation of efforts on the part of Hieron to associate his rule with the divine patronage of Zeus.

Setting aside the question of whether Hieron or his family developed a ruler cult, there is every reason to believe that the First Punic War created enough peripheral violence in Sicily that Hieron could credibly establish himself as a defender (perhaps even savior) of the *poleis* within his kingdom. This could have taken place through visible expressions of "hard power," like the mobilization and garrisoning of troops to protect the cities that recognized his sovereignty. Yet one cannot underestimate the role that the treaty of 263 played in providing security to the territories under his control. By establishing the political boundaries of his kingdom and recognizing his sovereignty over it, Hieron's treaty with Rome provided a largely inviolate barrier against the military violence that devastated much of western Sicily during the long decades of the Punic Wars. After 263, one reason that *poleis* continued to recognize Hieron's sovereignty was surely for the security that their political subordination guaranteed. This benefit was no abstraction; surely the devastation wrought by Mamertine soldiers in previous decades lay well within the living memory of those who had suffered from it. Even the Syracusans themselves had endured successive sieges by the Carthaginians and Romans

2.4 Inscribed limestone miniature altar found in 1948 during excavations in the area of the Giardino Spagna, Syracuse (Museo Archeologico Regionale Paolo Orsi, inv. 51593; courtesy of the Parco Archeologico e paesaggistico di Siracusa, Eloro, Villa del Tellaro e Akrai).

within a single generation. The First Punic War brought with it far greater atrocities, like mass enslavements at Akragas, the utter destruction of Myttistraton, and the deportation of citizens from Selinus, reports of which certainly would have reached those *poleis* of eastern Sicily under Hieron's protection.[56] Protections were made still more explicit in the terms of Rome's peace treaty with Carthage that bought an end to war in 241. From the text of the treaty reported by Polybius, the Carthaginians were "to evacuate the whole of Sicily and were not to make war on Hieron or bear arms against the Syracusans or the allies of the Syracusans."[57] The peace and security that accompanied a city's political subordination to Hieron must have far outweighed the limits placed on their civic autonomy.

Protection alone was not enough. With expenditure on warfare largely removed from the equation, Hieron mobilized his immense wealth to pursue what Caroline Lehmler has defined as a program of *Kulturpolitik*, cultural policies intended to bolster his claims to legitimate rule both at home and abroad.[58] As an element of their charismatic authority, Hellenistic kings regularly applied their unparalleled resources toward extending material benefactions to the *poleis* that recognized the legitimacy of their rule.[59] As with the epithet *sōtēr*, Hellenistic kings were increasingly identified as an *euergetes* in honorific dedications and civic decrees. Royal munificence often found material expression through the financing and construction of large-scale architectural monuments and infrastructure projects. Hieron appears to have embraced this policy with relish.

As the de facto capital of his kingdom, Syracuse benefited most visibly from Hieron's benefactions. Today, the city preserves the most striking examples of the monumental construction undertaken during his reign. Much of this work was done in transforming the city's Neapolis district, which had developed into a bustling residential quarter of the city over the course of the late fourth and early third century (Figure 2.5).[60] Here, Hieron's grandest architectural project found its expression during the 230s, which began with the wholesale reorganization of the urban plan and the creation of a new orthogonal grid of city streets and residential blocks. Large swaths of land were set aside for a monumental complex that spread over more than 1.2 square kilometers.

The centerpiece of this new complex was the massive 14,000-person stone theater carved into the Temenite hill, overlooking the city's Great Harbor (Figure 2.6).[61] This was one of the largest stone theaters ever built in the ancient Mediterranean.[62] Hieron used the *cavea* of the theater as a vehicle to promote his sponsorship of the project and as a means of furthering his political ideology by inscribing the seats of the upper *diazoma* with the names of the royal family alongside those of divinities, including Zeus Olympios (Figure 2.7). The significance of the theater's epigraphic program for Hieron's dynastic claims will be explored later in this chapter.[63] The theater was surmounted by a massive pi-shaped stoa complex, which measured 110 meters × 90 meters and may have framed an older temple of Apollo.[64] Located just to the southeast of the theater was the so-called Great Altar, which most scholars now believe was dedicated to Zeus Olympios.[65] Measuring nearly 200 meters long and well over 6 meters in elevation, it is the largest surviving stone altar from the ancient Mediterranean world.[66] Together with the new urban grid plan, the monumental altar, theater, and pi-shaped stoa complex radically reshaped the landscape of Neapolis and stood as an unmistakable expression of Hieron's wealth and power (Figure 2.8). They were just the type of outsized expression of grandeur that Hellenistic kings were fond of making.

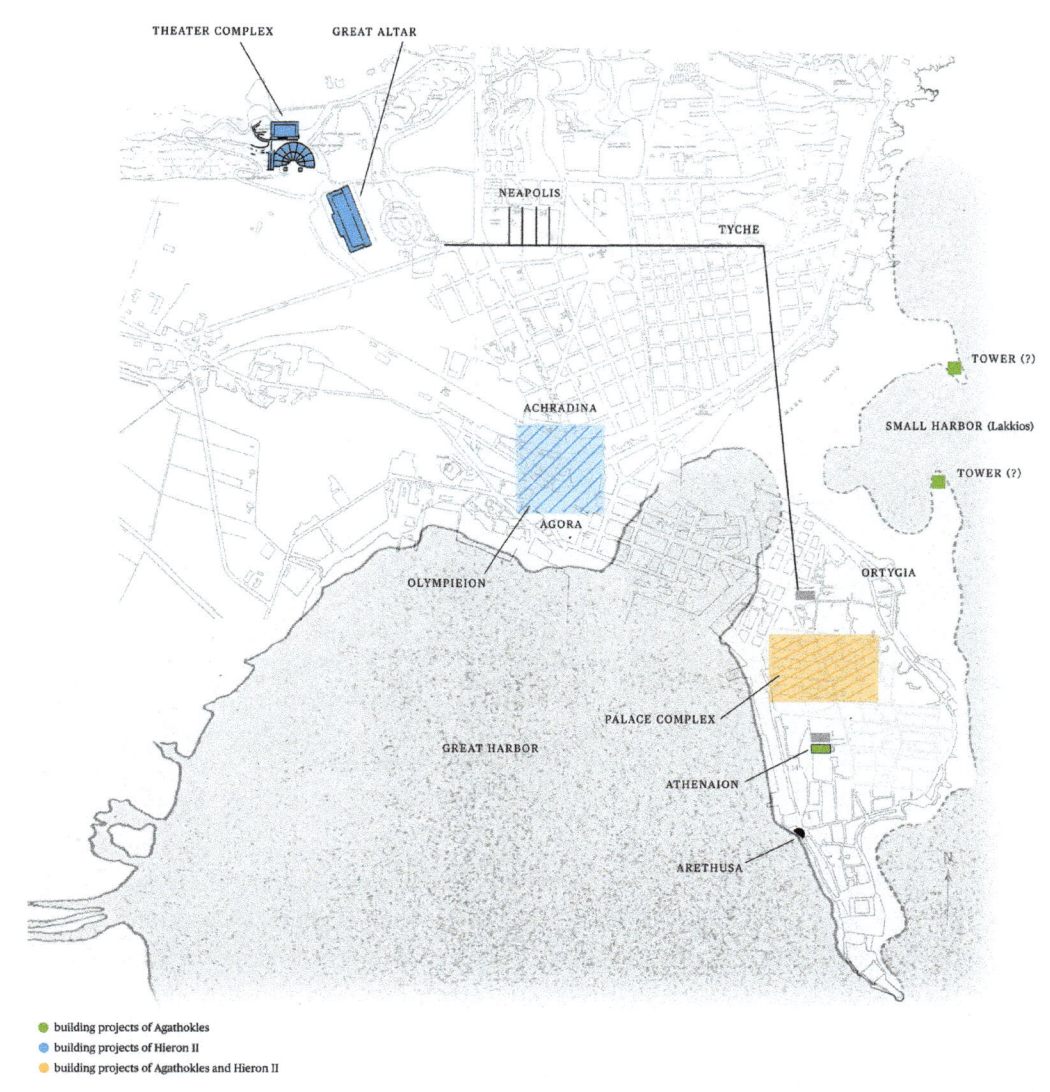

THEATER COMPLEX

GREAT ALTAR

NEAPOLIS

TYCHE

TOWER (?)

ACHRADINA

SMALL HARBOR (Lakkios)

TOWER (?)

AGORA

OLYMPIEION

ORTYGIA

PALACE COMPLEX

GREAT HARBOR

ATHENAION

ARETHUSA

● building projects of Agathokles
● building projects of Hieron II
● building projects of Agathokles and Hieron II

2.5 Plan of Syracuse showing location of Hieronian interventions in the urban layout of the city (after Veit 2013; courtesy of Getty Publications, J. Paul Getty Museum).

Hieron's monumental intervention was not limited to the Neapolis district. He is also credited with the completion of a temple for Zeus Olympios in the city's agora, which today lies buried under the Achradina district of modern Syracuse (see Figure 2.5).[67] The consecration of this massive temple served to reinforce Hieron's association with Zeus Olympios, who was likely cast as the divine patron of the Hieronian dynasty. Hieron appears to have chosen the island of Ortygia as the site of his residence.[68] While details of the location and organization of Hieron's palace complex remain a mystery, there is good reason to believe that the complex included fortified granaries, which held the proceeds of the agricultural tithe collected by Hieron from all the cities

2.6 Aerial view of the Hieronian theater at Syracuse (photo: M. Ponzio).

within his kingdom.[69] Hieron is also credited with several other major construction projects at Syracuse, including the strategic renovations to the Euryalos Fortress, which stood at the northwestern edge of the Epipolai plateau, guarding over the principal western approach to the city.[70] So too, the king may have been responsible for financing the construction or expansion of an extensive network of underground galleries that supplied fresh water to the city by tapping aquifers located in the Epipolai hills. Today, the efficacy of the system can still be appreciated: fresh water from the Galermi gallery continues to rush forth, filling the large tanks of the rock-cut nymphaeum above the Hieronian theater.[71]

Syracuse was almost certainly not alone in benefiting from Hieron's euergetism. While we lack explicit evidence for direct intervention by Hieron at the other cities of his kingdom, there is strong circumstantial evidence that his allies enjoyed the king's benefactions, such as through the sponsorship of civic *gymnasia* and the completion of large architectural projects.[72] Of the latter, royal patronage has been posited for a handful of surviving monuments found throughout eastern Sicily, monuments that at times have been viewed in terms of a coherent Hieronian *Baupolitik*.[73] The most noteworthy candidate for such royal intervention is the monumental building program that transformed the

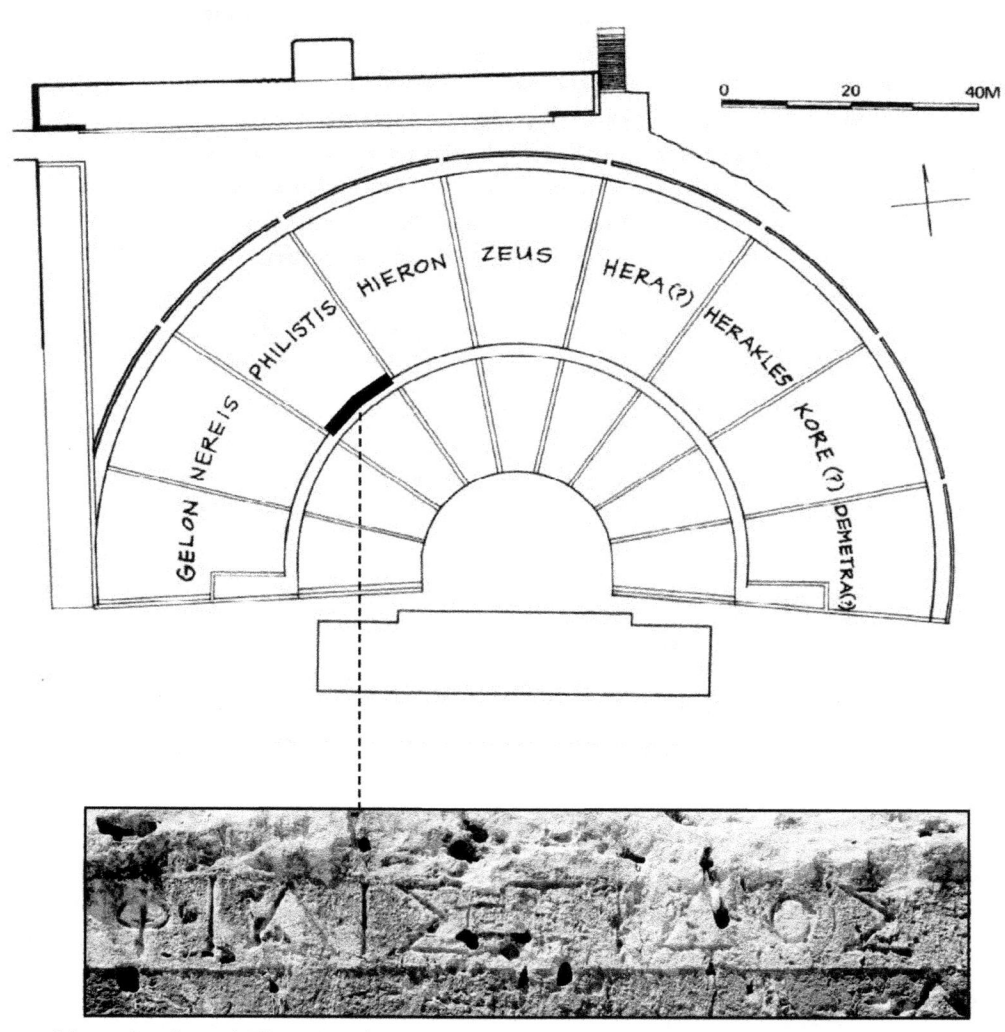

2.7 Schematic plan of Hieronian theater at Syracuse, showing the names (known and hypothesized) inscribed on the nine *cunei* of the *diazoma*. Photograph shows a portion of the preserved inscription for Queen Philistis, which reads [ΒΑΣΙΛΙ]ΣΑΣ ΦΙΛΙΣΤΙΔΟΣ (plan after Bell 1999; photograph after Wilson 2013).

agora of Morgantina. Over the course of the several decades in the mid-third century, the city's agora was almost wholly refashioned by the construction of three new stoa buildings, a fountain house, a stone theater, and two monumental granaries (Figure 2.9). The massive scale of the project, together with the coordinated siting of the buildings, certainly speaks to a unified plan, which Malcolm Bell has ascribed to the intervention of a Syracusan architect from the court of Hieron II.[74]

Beyond Morgantina, Markus Wolf has recently argued that Hieronian patronage can be found in the construction of several additional monuments located elsewhere in the kingdom. In particular, Wolf focuses on a stoa and

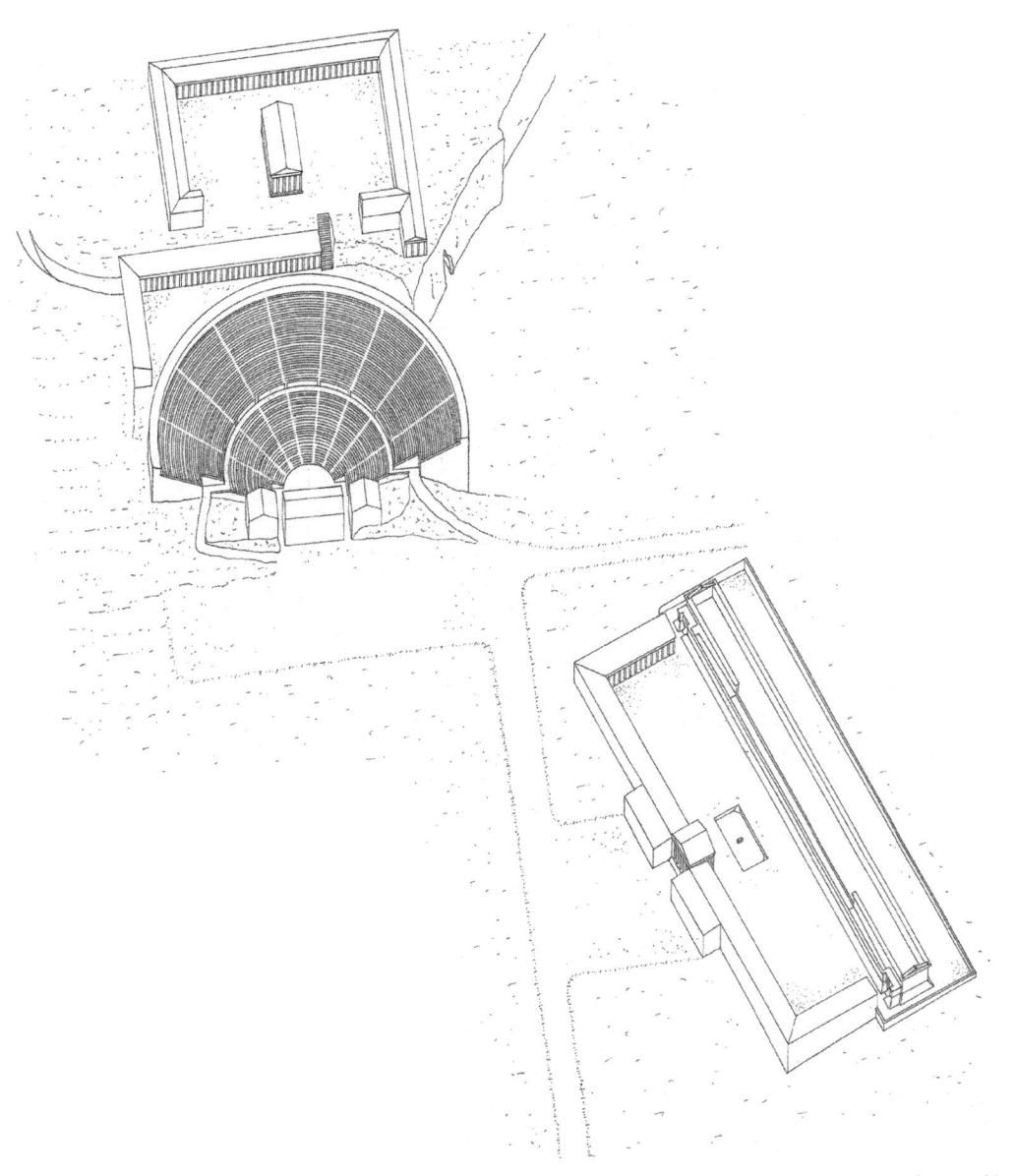

2.8 Axonometric projection of the Hieronian theater and altar complex at Syracuse (after Wolf 2016; drawing: M. Wolf).

temple complex in the agora at Heloros, one of the cities reportedly left under Hieronian control by the treaty of 263.[75] This complex consisted of a small, Doric prostyle temple that is believed to have been dedicated to the goddess Demeter and a larger, two-story stoa of mixed orders.[76] Wolf argues that the stylistic affinities shared by these two buildings suggests they were designed as a unified group during the second half of the third century BCE.[77] He goes on to posit that the Hieronian court was behind the construction of these

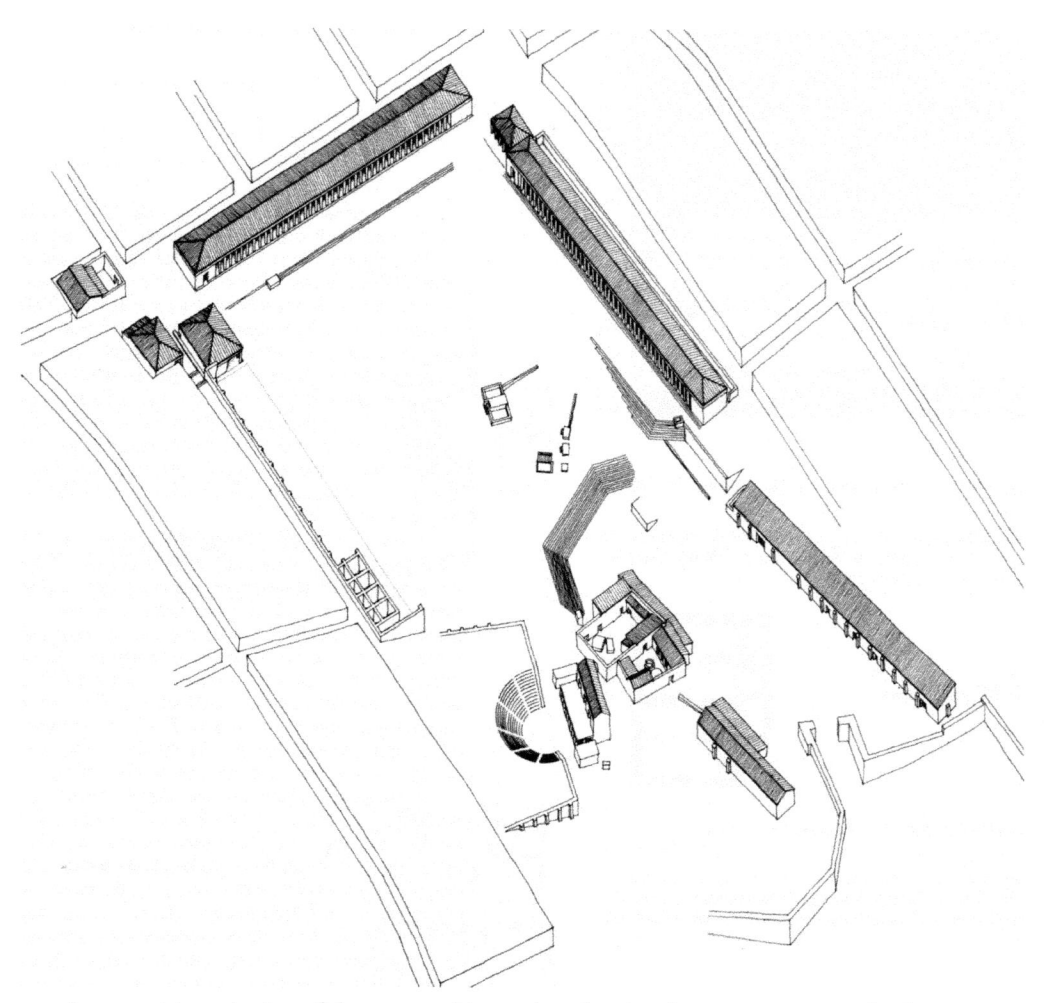

2.9 Axonometric projection of the agora at Morgantina, showing the monuments associated with the public building program of the third century BCE (drawing: E. Thorkildsen; courtesy of the American Excavations at Morgantina).

buildings at Heloros, noting parallels with the scenographic arrangement of the king's Syracusan theater-altar complex. Along similar lines, Wolf ascribes Hieronian influence to the construction of a mixed-order temple at Megara Hyblaia as well as the temple that lies under the church of Santa Caterina at Tauromenion, both of which, he hypothesizes, were dedicated to Zeus Olympios.[78] Taking up the notion of a Hieronian *Baupolitik*, Wolf goes on to argue that these building projects, in both their execution and design, were part of a coordinated effort to promote Hieronian propaganda throughout the cities of his kingdom. While the idea that these monuments reflect a unified Hieronian building policy has not found universal acceptance, the buildings themselves nonetheless attest to the stability and prosperity enjoyed by the communities under Hieron's protection.[79]

Royal patronage, of course, was not mutually exclusive with the vital role that civic elites would have continued to play within the *poleis* subject to Hieron's authority, and benefaction by the king could have very well engendered similar acts of euergetism by local leaders. Lorenzo Campagna has persuasively argued that this was the case at Tauromenion, where civic agency might have driven many of the most substantial transformations to the city's urban center during the Hieronian period.[80] Even at Morgantina, where benefaction by the Hieronian court may offer the most likely explanation for the swift and rather dramatic monumentalization of the agora, there is evidence to suggest that local elites also may have had a hand in sponsoring new public architecture.[81] As we will discuss later on in Chapters 4 and 8, the system of agricultural taxation established by Hieron relied on the involvement of local elites, opening new avenues for enrichment and fostering economic growth even in the smaller communities of the Sicilian *mesogeia*.

Hieron also directed his attention beyond the confines of his kingdom, using his material resources to export his image as *basileus* and *euergetes* to the wider Mediterranean world.[82] A well-known instance of this international self-promotion followed the earthquake of 227 that inflicted great damage to the island of Rhodes. Polybius' account makes clear that this disaster presented an opportunity for kings to compete among themselves in gift-giving. Hieron was not to be left out, as Polybius recounts:

> Ἱέρων γὰρ καὶ Γέλων οὐ μόνον ἔδωκαν ἑβδομήκοντα καὶ πέντ' ἀργυρίου τάλαντα πρὸς τὴν εἰς τὸ ἔλαιον τοῖς ἐν τῷ γυμνασίῳ χορηγίαν, τὰ μὲν παραχρῆμα, τὰ δ' ἐν χρόνῳ βραχεῖ παντελῶς, ἀλλὰ καὶ λέβητας ἀργυροῦς καὶ βάσεις τούτων καί τινας ὑδρίας ἀνέθεσαν, πρὸς δὲ τούτοις εἰς τὰς θυσίας δέκα τάλαντα καὶ τὴν ἐπαύξησιν τῶν πολιτῶν ἄλλα δέκα, χάριν τοῦ τὴν πᾶσαν εἰς ἑκατὸν τάλαντα γενέσθαι δωρεάν. καὶ μὴν ἀτέλειαν τοῖς πρὸς αὑτοὺς πλοϊζομένοις ἔδοσαν καὶ πεντήκοντα καταπέλτας τριπήχεις. καὶ τελευταῖον τοσαῦτα δόντες, ὡς προσοφείλοντες χάριν, ἔστησαν ἀνδριάντας ἐν τῷ τῶν Ῥοδίων δείγματι, στεφανούμενον τὸν δῆμον τῶν Ῥοδίων ὑπὸ τοῦ δήμου τοῦ.

> Hieron and Gelon [his son], for instance, presented [the Rhodians] with seventy-five talents of silver, part at once, and the rest at a very short interval, as a contribution toward the expenses of the gymnasium; gave them for religious purposes some silver cauldrons and their stands, and some water vessels; and in addition to this ten talents for their sacrifices, and ten more to attract new citizens: their intention being that the whole present should amount to a hundred talents. Not only so, but they gave immunity from customs to Rhodian merchants coming to their ports; and presented them besides with fifty catapults of three cubits length. In spite too of these large gifts, they regarded themselves as under an obligation to the Rhodians, and accordingly erected statues in the *Deigma*, or market, of Rhodes, representing the community of Rhodes crowned by that of Syracuse.[83]

That Polybius discusses Hieron's gifts to the Rhodians in the same breath as those made by Ptolemy III, Antigonos II, and Seleucus II certainly suggests that the king's strategy was effective. Hieron's lavish gifts to the Rhodians may have been just one of many such benefactions that have gone unrecorded by our surviving literary sources. Polybius (7.8.6) certainly suggests as much when noting that Hieron had earned a glowing reputation as a great benefactor (εὐεργετικώτατος δὲ καὶ φιλοδοξότατος) among the Greek *poleis* of the Aegean.[84]

At the same time as he cultivated the image as a *euergetes* for Greek cities around the Mediterranean, Hieron was also actively working to insert himself into the more rarified arenas of competitive display, generally reserved for Hellenistic monarchs. Tipping the scales toward sheer ostentation, Hieron commissioned the construction of a massive merchant vessel, the *Syrakosia*, which he reportedly sent to Alexandria as a gift to Ptolemy III. The ship, as described in the *Deipnosophistai* of Athenaeus, was nothing short of a floating city with eight defensive towers, a bath and gymnasium complex, a temple to Aphrodite, well-watered gardens, mosaic pavements, and even a tribunal of judges.[85] That the description of the ship itself may be more exaggeration than sober fact only underscores the truth of Hieron's talent for mythic self-representation: he clearly engaged in the boastful extravagance that characterized nonmartial competition between Hellenistic sovereigns. Moreover, the story attests to a policy of sophisticated exchange – commercial, cultural, and intellectual – between the two kingdoms that is certainly visible in the material record.[86] Although our surviving documentary sources reveal no formal, legally codified relationship between the Ptolemies and Hieron, many historians and archaeologists have seen Ptolemaic influence behind certain aspects of the Hieronian *basileia*, including the promotion of the royal family through various media and the organization of Hieron's famed agricultural tithe.[87] The reliance of the Hieronian tax system on that of the Ptolemaic model is a question that will be considered at greater length in Chapter 4.[88]

Closer to home, Hieron used his bountiful agricultural resources to secure his position with Rome and Carthage, the two external powers whose disposition held the most immediate consequences for his political stability. This often took the form of grain shipments sent to both the Romans and Carthaginians in times of need.[89] Modern commentators have suggested such gifts were part of the king's broader political strategy aimed at strengthening his position amid two geopolitical giants, Rome and Carthage, characterizing him as "a master practitioner of *Realpolitik*" and his actions as "grain diplomacy."[90] But Hieron's shrewd actions were recognized by ancient observers as well, most notably by Polybius, who commends the king for his "wholly sound and prudent" (πάνυ φρονίμως καὶ νουνεχῶς) decision to send aid to the Carthaginians at the outbreak of the Mercenary War in 241:

Ἱέρων δ' ἀεὶ μέν ποτε κατὰ τὸν ἐνεστῶτα πόλεμον μεγάλην ἐποιεῖτο σπουδὴν εἰς πᾶν τὸ παρακαλούμενον ὑπ' αὐτῶν, τότε δὲ καὶ μᾶλλον ἐφιλοτιμεῖτο, πεπεισμένος συμφέρειν ἑαυτῷ καὶ πρὸς τὴν ἐν Σικελίᾳ δυναστείαν καὶ πρὸς τὴν Ῥωμαίων φιλίαν τὸ σῴζεσθαι Καρχηδονίους, ἵνα μὴ παντάπασιν ἐξῇ τὸ προτεθὲν ἀκονιτὶ συντελεῖσθαι τοῖς ἰσχύουσι, πάνυ φρονίμως καὶ νουνεχῶς λογιζόμενος. οὐδέποτε γὰρ χρὴ τὰ τοιαῦτα παρορᾶν οὐδὲ τηλικαύτην οὐδενὶ συγκατασκευάζειν δυναστείαν, πρὸς ἣν οὐδὲ περὶ τῶν ὁμολογουμένων ἐξέσται δικαίων ἀμφισβητεῖν.

Now Hieron, of Syracuse, during this war had been all along exceedingly anxious to do everything that the Carthaginians asked him; and at this point of it was more forward to do so than ever, from a conviction that it was for his interest, with a view alike to his own sovereignty and to his friendship with Rome, that Carthage should not perish, and so leave the superior power to work its own will without resistance. And his reasoning was entirely sound and prudent. It is never right to permit such a state of things, nor to help anyone to build up so preponderating a power as to make resistance to it impossible, however just the cause.[91]

Hieron's gifts could be quite substantial; the largest recorded shipment followed the Roman defeat at Cannae in 216 when, as Livy reports, he sent his fleet of transport ships to Ostia carrying roughly 3,500 metric tons of grain.[92] In the following year, just before his death, he sent another convoy of grain ships carrying over 2,000 metric tons of wheat and barley to Tarentum, where the Roman fleet was preparing for war with Philip V.[93] As will be discussed in Chapter 6, even these enormous consignments of grain were well within the limits of what Hieron might have expected to accrue annually from the agricultural taxes collected from the cities of his kingdom.

After 263, Hieron was undoubtedly successful in shifting the basis of his political legitimacy so that it was no longer predicated on military victory alone. To achieve this, he mobilized his wealth and resources to carry out a sweeping program of cultural investments, successfully reframing his legitimacy in terms of euergetism and protection from external threats. In doing so, he showed himself both receptive to contemporary ideas of Hellenistic kingship and innovative in his approach to deploying them to his own advantage.

ACT III: FOUNDER AND DYNAST

Secure in his position at Syracuse, Hieron next turned to one of the most difficult tasks facing a charismatic ruler, namely, the challenge of establishing hereditary succession and institutional norms as the basis for legitimate autocrat rule with an eye toward transferring one's exceptional powers onto a chosen successor.[94] Many of the Successor kings had wrestled with the same challenge as they sought to preserve their spear-won kingdoms after death by passing along their *basileia* to young sons. Viewed within the framework of Weber's model of charismatic authority, this was a potentially fraught venture for a group of men whose own rise to power had negated the very principle of rule by birthright. In this last act of Hieron's reign, which ran roughly from the elevation of Gelon to co-regent around the year 240 to Hieron's death in 215, we see greater attention paid to securing his dynastic ambitions.

For Hieron, ensuring a smooth transfer of power to his son involved shaping the past as much as it required planning for the future. One step in this process appears to have involved a refashioning of his own genealogical line. From what little is known about Hieron's origins, his lineage seems to have been rather undistinguished. Polybius relates that he rose to power "without wealth, without reputation, and without any other advantage from fortune" (οὐ πλοῦτον, οὐ δόξαν, οὐχ ἕτερον οὐδὲν ἐκ τῆς τύχης ἕτοιμον παραλαβών).[95] The brief biographical sketch preserved in the text of Justin's *Epitome* identifies his mother as a slave.[96] In the same text, however, his father, Hierokles, is identified as a descendent of the fifth-century Deinomenid tyrant Gelon.[97] Many scholars have observed that this convenient genealogical detail bears all the hallmarks of a later fabrication designed to bolster Hieron's claims to legitimate rule.[98] The Deinomenids, as unsavory as they may now seem today, might have presented an attractive Syracusan dynastic model in Hieron's day. It would certainly seem this way, judging from the fact that Hieron chose to name his children after the tyrant (Gelon) and his wife (Damarete).[99] And this alone does not appear to have been Hieron's only effort to establish a connection with the fifth-century ruler and, in the process, reconstrue the Deinomenid dynasty within the contemporary norms and behavior of the third-century Syracusan court.[100]

There is good reason to believe that the elder Gelon's legacy enjoyed a vigorous rehabilitation in the third century by way of Hieronian court propaganda. Among the most persuasive arguments reinforcing this perspective is Keith Rutter's thesis that the court of Hieron II was the source of the now well-known legend of the *Damareteion* coinage.[101] The story, first preserved in the text of Diodorus, relates how in the year 480 Gelon's wife, Damarete, was honored by the Carthaginians with a gold crown worth 100 talents for her role in helping to secure peace between Carthage and Syracuse.[102] As the story goes, Damarete subsequently used the gold to strike a series of *dekadrachm* coins that came to be known, in the singular, as the *Damareteion*. Rutter explores the underlying expression of authority involved in Damarete's reportedly singular decision to mint coins, noting that the account finds close parallels with the appearance of queens on regal coinage of the Hellenistic period, including that of Queen Philistis, the wife of Hieron II. Provocatively, Rutter concludes that the whole story explaining the origins of the *Damareteion* was an apocryphal tale concocted by the Hieronian court, which served as a convenient

2.10 Obverse type of silver coin struck by Hieron II, ca. 240/230–215 BCE, showing portrait of Queen Philistis wearing royal diadem (ANS 1964.79.53; courtesy of the American Numismatic Society).

etiological model for the so-called *Philistideion* coinage, which was struck with the regal portrait and title of Queen Philistis, presumably to punctuate an act of royal munificence (Figure 2.10).[103]

Further evidence for a rehabilitation of Gelon's image can be gleaned from Diodorus' presentation of the Syracusan ruler throughout Book 11 of his *Universal History*. Rutter notes that many of the qualities ascribed to the Classical tyrant were stereotypical characteristics attributed to "good kings" of the Hellenistic period; these included success in military action (11.21.3; 11.22.5), fairness (*epeikeia*: 11.26.1–4), and generosity or beneficence (*philanthrōpia*: 11.67.2; *euergesia*: 11.26.4–6, 11.67.4).[104] More telling still is Diodorus' description of Gelon's acclamation as king by the Syracusan army following his victory over the Carthaginians in 480. In Diodorus' narrative, Gelon, on arriving back to Syracuse, called his soldiers into assembly where they acclaimed him as their king, benefactor, and savior (ὥστε μιᾷ φωνῇ πάντας ἀποκαλεῖν εὐεργέτην καὶ σωτῆρα καὶ βασιλέα). These clearly anachronistic epithets are those belonging to Hellenistic kings, not Classical tyrants. While some scholars have argued that Diodorus drew inspiration from Ptolemaic titulature of the later fourth and third centuries (i.e., Ptolemy I *Sōtēr*, Ptolemy III *Euergetes*) in framing his account of Gelon's status as king, it overlooks the more likely explanation that the narrative of Gelon's soldiers acclaiming him their king and the regal qualities ascribed to him are a product of the Hieronian court, much as Rutter has argued for the origins of the *Damareteion* myth.[105] This would explain why the story so closely resembles that of Hieron's own acclamation to kingship following his victory at Longanus as well as the transmission of two central virtues animating Hieron's own legitimacy – benefaction (*euergesia*) and security (*sōtēria*) – to Gelon's biography.

Looking not just to the past but to the future, Hieron took a necessary step toward securing the survival of his *basileia* around the year 240 by elevating his son, Gelon, to the status of co-regent. From that point forward, Gelon shared the title of *basileus* with his father and was publicly acknowledged as Hieron's successor.[106] By the later third century, co-regency had become common practice, particularly among the Ptolemaic kings, as a means of anticipating potential power struggles upon the death of a king.[107] The policy had many merits, among them the opportunity to introduce and acclimate one's subjects to their future monarch. There is ample evidence to suggest that Gelon's planned succession of his father was widely advertised in the kingdom as well as throughout the Mediterranean. Polybius, as we have seen, credited both men with the aid sent to Rhodes following the earthquake of 227. Closer to home, at least two monuments survive from Syracuse that highlight the co-regency. The first, an inscribed marble base found on Ortygia, records the dedication of a bronze statue of Gelon (and perhaps Hieron as well) to Zeus Hellanios by the Syracusan *dēmos*.[108] The inscription clearly identifies Gelon as king:

> ὁ δᾶμος τῶν Συρακοσίων
> βασιλέα Γέλωνα βασιλέος Ἱέρωνος
> Διὶ Ἑλλανίωι

> The *dēmos* of the Syracusans [dedicates this statue of]
> King Gelon, son of King Hieron
> To Zeus Hellenios

The second monument, a fragmentary block of gray limestone discovered in the Neapolis district of the city, appears to be related to a dedication made by Gelon to the goddesses Demeter and Persephone. The inscribed stone is severely damaged, such that only the leftmost letters can be read. What does survive clearly identifies two kings, who are most likely to be identified as Hieron and Gelon (Figure 2.11).[109] As the Neapolis district was being refashioned under royal patronage in the 230s to serve as a zone for mass gatherings of the Syracusans, it was an ideal location to install a monument celebrating dynastic succession.

Hieron may have sought to further strengthen his dynastic ambitions by forging an alliance with the royal house of Epirus through the marriage of Gelon to Nereis, an Epirote princess and daughter of King Pyrrhus II.[110] It was common practice – although not an inviolable rule – for the monarchs of the Hellenistic Mediterranean to seek marriage alliances between the royal houses, particularly among kings and queens.[111] The marriage of Gelon and Nereis in 233/2 forged a connection to the well-established royal house of Epirus.[112] For Hieron, whose own genealogical claims were not particularly illustrious, the advantage gained by linking his family's name to that of the Aiakid clan with its deep ancestry cannot be underestimated. The marriage ensured that children born to the couple could claim descent from the great warrior Achilles, to say nothing of Pyrrhus I. It is in this light that we should view the pair of genealogical monuments dedicated by Nereis and Gelon at Olympia and Delphi to honor the Molossian royal house.[113] Both monuments took the form of long rectangular bases surmounted by statues representing multiple generations of the Aiakid line.[114] Although the Syracusan royal couple do not themselves appear in statuary form, the move to highlight the Aiakid dynasty was clearly a statement that the line would now continue through Nereis and Gelon. The fragmentary base from Olympia has been reconstructed as follows:

[ΝΗΡΙΣ ΚΑ]Ι [ΓΕΛΩ]Ν Τ[ΩΙ ΔΙΙ ΤΩΙ ΟΛΥΜΠΙΩΙ]			
[βασιλέα Ἀλέξανδρον]	βασίλισσαν Ὀλυμ[πιάδα]	[βασιλέα Πύρρον]	[βασιλέα Πτολεμαῖον]
[βασιλέως Πύρρου]	βασιλέως Πύρ[ρου]	[βασιλέως Ἀλεξάνδρου]	[βασιλέως Ἀλεξάνδρου].[115]

Nereis and Gelon [dedicate this monument] to Zeus Olympios			
King Alexander II	Queen Olympias II	King Pyrrhus II	King Ptolemy (of Epirus)
Son of King Pyrrhus I	Daughter of King Pyrrhus I	Son of King Alexander II	Son of King Alexander II

Back in Syracuse, Hieron highlighted his dynastic ambitions on both the miniature and the monumental scale. On the grander scale, we may count his forward-looking epigraphic program in the recently constructed stone theater in Neapolis. As the site of mass gatherings of the Syracusan *dēmos*, the theater offered an ideal venue for Hieron to assert his ideological foundations for dynastic succession. Monumental inscriptions ran along the upper *diazoma* of the theater's *cavea*, with each of the nine *cunei*, or wedge-shaped sections, bearing a dedication to a different figure. At the center was Zeus Olympios, who stood as the embodiment of royal authority and progenitor of regal dynasts.[116] The four western *cunei* were dedicated to members of the Syracusan royal family. The names of Hieron, Philistis, and Nereis can still be read today, each with their royal title. The outermost *cuneus* almost certainly bore Gelon's name, although the inscription is no longer visible. The arrangement of the names makes clear that we are dealing with two royal couples, the current and future king and queen of the Hieronian dynasty. The four eastern *cunei* were dedicated to divine figures, although only the name of Herakles Kraterphron ("Stout-hearted") can be read today. Malcolm Bell has proposed that the three remaining sections were dedicated to Hera, Demeter, and Persephone, who collectively form a divine royal family that could stand as analogous with the Syracusan royal family.[117] The ideological message of orderly succession and divine patronage for the royal house of Hieron conveyed by the theater's epigraphic program is inescapable. Aside from serving as the setting for dramatic performances, Hieron's theater might also have been used for mass gatherings among the Syracusans for royal spectacles designed to reinforce the dynastic messaging of the royal house.[118]

Coinage again played a key role in the promotion of Hieronian ideology, particularly in disseminating the message of dynastic succession following the elevation of Gelon to co-regent and *basileus*. As early as the 230s, the royal mint at Syracuse began issuing a new series of silver coins featuring the

2.11 Fragmentary stone inscription from the Neapolis district of Syracuse. Although damaged, the inscribed stone clearly refers to two kings, presumably Hieron II and his son, Gelon (photo: J. Prag; I.Sicily 003009).

members of the royal household (Figure 2.12). The coins belonging to this new "dynastic" series were related both by a coordinated denominational structure and by a unified iconographic program.[119] The new coinage was clearly part of a calculated program of visual propaganda aimed at establishing Philistis and Gelon as prominent members of the royal house, thereby setting the stage for Gelon's dynastic claim to the throne.

The message of dynastic continuity was plainly articulated in the coin types of these new issues. Hieron appears more mature in his portrait, but still with the idealized features of a man much younger than in actual years, for the king was already in his seventies. The explicitly martial elements found on the reverse types of his bronze portrait coinage are not to be found. Instead, the charging cavalryman was replaced by a Nike driving a quadriga, symbolic of victory in nonmilitary competition.[120] For the first time the king's royal title,

2.12 Silver coins struck by Hieron II, ca. 240/230–215 BCE, bearing portraits of the royal family (top: BM 1987,0649.272; middle: BM 1946,0101.1544; bottom: BM 1841,0726.381; all: © The Trustees of the British Museum).

ΒΑΣΙΛΕΟΣ ΙΕΡΩΝΟΣ, appears on a coin. Hieron wears the cloth diadem in his portrait, an iconographic element he now shares with Gelon, who makes his debut on two silver denominations, each with a distinct reverse type.[121] A Nike driving a biga appears on the larger, eight-litrai denomination, while an eagle grasping a thunderbolt occupies the smaller, four-litrai coins. The eagle bears an uncanny resemblance to the image of the closed-winged eagle on Ptolemaic types, particularly those struck during the reigns of Ptolemy II and Ptolemy III. Setting aside the question of whether the connection is genuine, the image of the eagle grasping a thunderbolt would have certainly carried connotations of Zeus Olympios for a Sicilian viewer, reinforcing the connection between the divine ruler and the future king.[122] Gelon's image bears unmistakable physiognomic similarities to those of his parents – notably in the broad forehead, prominent nose, and meaty chin.

The most important figure of this new regal series was Queen Philistis, judging by the estimated output of her coinage, which far exceeded that of either Hieron's or Gelon's portrait coins.[123] The coinage bearing the portrait of Philistis, like that of Gelon, came in two denominations (16 litrai and 5 litrai) with a Nike driving a quadriga on the reverse of the larger coins and Nike driving a biga on the coins of the smaller denomination. Like her husband and son, Philistis too was depicted wearing a broad cloth diadem, which can be seen emerging from under her veil. The reverse types of both denominations carry the legend ΒΑΣΙΛΙΣΣΑΣ ΦΙΛΙΣΤΙΔΟΣ, "[coinage] of Queen Philistis." Queens played a prominent role in promoting the ideology of dynastic succession within the royal houses of the Successor kingdoms.[124] The decision to mint this dynastic series very well might have been inspired by the Ptolemies, who were fond of minting coins with the portrait of their queens.[125] The portrait coins of Philistis bear striking resemblance to those of Queen Berenike II struck during the reign of Ptolemy III (r. 244/3–222/1), particularly in combining the partially veiled head with a diadem. The similarities extend beyond the costume of each queen to include the addition of the title ΒΑΣΙΛΙΣΣΗΣ.[126]

The massive output of these coins – and particularly the Philistis denominations – had the effect of bringing individuals throughout Hieron's kingdom face to face with the royal family. The hoard evidence suggests that these regal issues circulated throughout the kingdom, but most abundantly in and around Syracuse.[127] This raises the question of the intended audience for these coins and their message of dynastic succession. The seemingly obvious answer, the military, would make sense in light of current views that Hellenistic kings struck silver coinage primarily for paying troops.[128] This interpretation also aligns with the role that the army would play in conferring legitimacy to the next king. Yet the timing of the production of these coins as well as the range of denominations in which they were minted may indicate that the coins were struck as gifts or payments made to members of the civic elite whose support Hieron would need to ensure the successful transfer of power to his son. Whatever the case, it is safe to conclude that the intended audience was Hieron's Sicilian subjects. The fact that none of these coins have turned up beyond the shores of Sicily suggests they did not enjoy wider circulation throughout the Mediterranean.

2.13 Silver portrait coin of Hieronymos, struck ca. 215–214 BCE, depicting the young king wearing a broad cloth diadem (BM 1841,0726.395, © The Trustees of the British Museum).

Despite Hieron's best efforts at securing the line of dynastic succession with Gelon, his son's unforeseen death in 216 left the aged king to find a successor at short notice.[129] The choice of his fifteen-year-old grandson, Hieronymos, was perhaps the king's only remaining option to ensure the continuity of his *dynasteria* and preservation of his kingdom (Figure 2.13). Hieronymos would reign for only 13 months, during which time he reportedly comported himself more like a vicious tyrant than a benevolent king. His murder at the hands of his royal bodyguard in the year 214 was swiftly followed by the gruesome massacre of the surviving members of the royal household at the urging of the Syracusan *dēmos*.[130] It is a somber reminder that no matter how well Hieron's image may come across in surviving historical accounts, such accounts tend to reflect the interests of an imperialistic Roman state and not necessarily those of the communities that had long lived under the king's authority, communities that appear to have had no affection for autocratic rule.

NOTES

[1]   Suda, s.v. βασιλεία (B 147A); Austin (2006, no. 45). For discussion, see Shipley (2000: 65). The definition is generally considered to derive from a source of Early Hellenistic date and, thus, should reflect political thought of the later fourth and third centuries.

[2]   Gehrke (1982); from this point forward, reference will be made to Gehrke (2013), which is an updated English translation of the earlier article.

[3]   Weber (1978: 1111–14).

[4]   Weber (1947: 358–64; 1978: 1114ff.).

[5]   Gruen (1985: 256).

[6]   An idea explored in detail by Chaniotis (2005: esp. 57–77).

[7]   "Victory thus offered a good opportunity to dignify and legitimate one's leadership, through the support of subjects and especially of the army, with the aura of kingship"; Gehrke (1982: 254 = 2013: 77).

[8] See *supra* nn. 72 and 73 in Chapter 1.

[9] Ancient sources routinely describe Hieron as being the "king of Syracuse"; e.g., Polyb. 1.8.3, 1.16.10, 7.8.3; Diod. 24.1.4; Liv. 21.49.3; Plut. *Marc.* 8.6. This, however, should be understood not as reflecting the king's actual political standing, but simply as a convenient label applied by sources external to the Hieronian royal court. Based on these references, Schenck von Stauffenberg (1933: 22–3) argued that Hieron's authority was constitutionally determined by the Syracusans and that the other *poleis* that formed the kingdom were technically allies of the Syracusans, not Hieron. This position has been thoroughly refuted by De Sensi Sestito (1977). Similarly, references to Hieron as "king of Sicily," such as recorded in the Fasti Triumphales for the year 263 (*M'. Valerius M. f. M. n. Maxim. Messalla cos. de Poeneis et rege Siculor. Hierone xvi. K. April*), are most likely etic in origin; Eutropius (3.1) refers to Hieron as *rex Siciliae*.

[10] Gehrke (2013: 78–9) cites numerous examples of kings leading their troops into battle and distinguishing themselves in combat. For Hellenistic kings fighting in battle, Eckstein (2009: 257–8).

[11] Just. *Epit.* 23.4.12.

[12] For *Idyll* 16, see Gow (1952: II.305–24); Hunter (1996: 77–109). On Theokritos and Hellenistic praise poetry, see Gutzwiller (1983: 214–15). González (2010) offers an alternative and compelling interpretation of *Idyll* 16 that foregrounds the civic aspects of Theokritos' text.

[13] Theok. *Idyll* 16.73–81 (trans. A. Verity). Coincidentally, the marriage of Hieron's son, Gelon, to the Molossian princess, Nereis, would bind the Hieronian dynasty to the Aiakids, who claimed ancestry from both Achilles and Telemonian Ajax.

[14] One thinks of the fear-inducing horsehair crest of Achilles helmet donned by Patroklos in *Iliad* 16 (137–8) – κρατὶ δ' ἐπ' ἰφθίμῳ κυνέην εὔτυκτον ἔθηκεν | ἵππουριν· δεινὸν δὲ λόφος καθύπερθεν ἔνευεν – a formula also used for the arming of Paris in *Iliad* 3 (336–7).

[15] For discussion of the spear as potent symbol attached to Hellenistic kingship, see Strootman (2007: 31–53).

[16] Barbantani (2007) explores what she defines as the "spear theme" in Hellenistic court poetry, with particular reference to the Ptolemaic court.

[17] Theok. *Idyll* 16.85–99 (trans. A. Verity); Verity and Hunter (2002).

[18] For a succinct overview of Punic settlement on Sicily, see Spanò Giammellaro et al. (2008), which can be supplemented by De Vincenzo (2019: 537–52).

[19] On kings utilizing the rhetoric of Greeks versus Barbarians for political gain, see Strootman (2005); Eckstein (2009: 253–4). For the reception of "Greek versus Barbarian" discourse by both Greek and non-Greek communities in Magna Graecia, see Dench (2003).

[20] XLI.122–6; and see Higbie (2003: 139–40).

[21] On the date of Hieron's offering, Brinkmann and von Steuben (1995: 244–5) and Lehmler (2005: 201) place it after the battle at Longanus; cf. Higbie (2003: 139–40), who suggests the dedication came after the earthquake that struck Rhodes in 227. Kings dedicating weapons after battle: Pyrrhus (Paus. 1.14.2–3; Plut. *Pyrrh.* 26.5); Demetrios Poliorketes (Plut. *Demetr.* 17.1).

[22] Squillace (2013) discusses the sanctuary of Athena Lindia as a locus for competition among kings, focusing on Alexander and Ptolemy I.

[23] The inventory records the dedication of weapons by at least three other kings: Alexander (XXXVIII.103–9), Pyrrhus (XL.114–21), and Philip [V?] (XLII.127–31). In Pyrrhus' case, the chronicle notes that the weapons offered to the goddess were those belonging to the king himself, which had been used in battle. Berve (1959: 81) offers another potential motivation for Hieron's dedication, namely, to further his connection with Deinomenes, the eponymous founder of the Deinomenid dynasty, from whom Hieron would come to claim ancestry. The Lindian Chronicles (XXVIII.29–35) record the dedication of a gorgon sculpture, executed in acrolithic technique, by this Deinomenes at the sanctuary; for discussion, see Higbie (2003: 111–12).

[24] For Rhodian involvement in the Mediterranean grain trade, see Casson (1954: 168–74) .

[25] Paus. 6.12.2–4, 6.15.6.

[26] For discussion of the martial qualities of Hellenistic equestrian statues, see Siedentopf (1968). Mirone (1919: 58) considered the image of the charging cavalryman on the reverse type of Hieron's bronze coinage to be a representation of the equestrian monument at Olympia mentioned by Pausanias.

[27] For *editio princeps* and discussion of the base's archaeological context at the sanctuary, see Kunze and Eckstein (1958: 205–9); see also Dimartino (2006: 703–4), who provides a recent bibliography. Pausanias (6.12.4) identifies this same Mikion, son of Nikeratos, as the sculptor of two honorific statues of Hieron at Olympia.

[28] Implied by Finley (1968: 112); specifically stated by Portale (2004: 230–7; 2013: 57). The number of honorific statues dedicated to Hieron at Olympia has been a subject of some debate; Eckstein (1958: 205ff.) and Lehlmer (2005: 198) both accept Pausanias' account, while Levi (1970: 153ff.), most notably, has called into question the reliability of Pausanias' account, arguing that the actual number of honorific statues for the king totaled only three. Portale (2004: 230–7) offers a thorough rebuttal of Levi's argument, establishing that there were at least six honorific monuments dedicated to Hieron II at Olympia.

[29] Antigonos Monophthalmos, by comparison, had three statues dedicated in his honor at the sanctuary; Hyde (1903: 103d, 147f, 151b).

[30] *Syll.*³ 427; *IG* XIV.2. The base has a lengthy publication record, starting with Lupi (1734: 90). Dimartino (2017a) provides a comprehensive *lemma* for the inscription. The stone is currently housed in the Museo Archeologico Regionale "Paolo Orsi" in Syracuse; inv. 6489.

[31] Holding the opinion that the dedication celebrated Hieron's victory at Longanus, Berve (1959: 42) and Dimartino (2017a: 244). Manganaro (1965: 315) has argued instead that the monument was erected to celebrate the victory over the Carthaginians in 241, which brought to a close the First Punic War. De Sensi Sestito (1977: 182–3) suggests the dedication followed on the elevation of Gelon to the position of co-regent.

[32] The evidence for the existence and operation of a *koinon* is treated in Chapter 3, pp. 100–103.

[33] For stylistic conventions in the portraiture of Hellenistic kings, see Smith (1988: esp. 12–14 for discussion of coin portraiture). And for a survey of regal coinage from the Early Hellenistic period, see Mørkholm (1991).

[34] Smith (1988: 34–8) provides concise discussion of the diadem's development as a royal symbol associated with Hellenistic, Macedonian-style kingship; see also the recent work of Haake (2012), who explored the connection between the diadem and title of *basileus*. For wreaths worn by Hellenistic rulers, see Smith (1988: 43). Attalos I struck silver tetradrachms bearing a laureate portrait of Philetairos, the founder of the Attalid dynasty who did not take the title of *basileus*; Westermark (1961); Mørkholm (1991: no. 410). Ptolemy III struck a series of bronze coinage in which he is depicted wearing a laurel wreath; Svoronos (1904: nos. 997–1000, pl. 30.4–8); *BMC Ptolemies*, pl. 12.2; Kyrieleis (1975: 27, pl. 17.5). The Spartan king Nabis also wears a laurel wreath wrapped around a diadem on his silver tetradrachms; Grunauer-von Hoerschelmann (1978: 28–9, pl. 6.17).

[35] One suggestion is that Hieron's choice of the laurel wreath aimed at establishing a visual connection with Agathokles, the first Syracusan to declare himself king in the fashion of the Successors, who by some accounts (i.e., Diod. Sic. 20.54.1) wore a laurel wreath, not a diadem, after taking the title of *basileus* because he came to power while serving as a priest of Apollo. If there is any veracity to the story, the wreath might have come to symbolize royal authority for the Syracusans.

[36] Smith (1988: 34–8).

[37] Gehrke (2013: 80) on coinage as a popular medium for communicating victory. Hieron's early regal coinage was no exception, as the image of the laureate king on the coin's obverse and that of the galloping spearman on the reverse served as double reference to militarism and kingship.

38 Smith (1988: 13) states as much for the so-called usurper and break-away dynasts of Asia Minor. Along these lines, the decision to mint coinage by the Spartan kings Areos, Cleomenes, and Nabis was clearly motivated by the model set by the Successor kings; on this, see Walthall (2013).

39 The cavalry motif on Hieron's bronze coinage, Carbè (2004: 268–74).

40 With specific reference to Alexander III and cavalry iconography, see Stewart (1993: 123–57).

41 Most notably, Demetrios Poliorketes (see Mørkholm 1991: 80, no. 174) and Seleucus III (see Mørkholm 1991: 114, no. 341). In both instances, Mørkholm speculates that the horseman might be the king himself. The image of a mounted warrior spearing a fallen soldier was used on the reverse types of several coins struck by the Paeonian king Patraeus; see Mørkholm (1991: 83, nos. 186–7).

42 Such capitulation reminds one of the "Day of Eleusis" and the great embarrassment faced by the Seleucid king Antiochos IV in 168 when forced to accept the decision of the Roman Senate conveyed to him by the Roman envoy, C. Popillius Laenas, as the king stood on the precipice of capturing Alexandria; Polyb. 29.27.1–9. The month-long military spectacle at Daphne in 166, at which some 50,000 troops reportedly paraded through the streets, certainly reads as compensation for a shattered ego as much as it was a conspicuous assertion of the Seleucid king's power; Polyb. 30.25–6; 31.16.1; Ath. 5.194c.

43 Gotter (2013: 208).

44 Haake (2013: 116).

45 On the composition of Hieron's royal army, Berve (1959: 44–5). See also Livy (24.7.1–2), who mentions that some 19,000 infantry and cavalry forces marched under the command of Hieronymos and his generals in 214. Given that the young king had just come to power, it may be reasonably inferred that the majority of these soldiers would have formed part of the standing army during Hieron's lifetime as well.

46 Cordiano (1997) also points to evidence that the king appears to have imposed certain administrative features, such as the dual gymnasiarchy, on the institutional structure of the *gymnasia*. Prag (2007) investigates the adoption and expansion of this Hieronian institution by the Romans after 210, observing that in the system of state-sponsored *gymnasia*, we see another element of Hieron's administrative system co-opted by the Romans in much the same way as they were to maintain the Hieronian tax laws.

47 During the First Punic War, Hieron sent aid to the Romans besieging Akragas in 262, as well as during their assault on Kamarina in 258. During the Hannibalic wars, he provided additional military support including 1,500 light-armed soldiers in 217 (Polyb. 3.75.7) and 1,000 archers and slingers in 216 (Liv. 22.37.7–9).

48 Plut. *Marc.* 8.6. By Diodorus's account (24.14.1), the *spolia* sent to Hieron was considered repayment for the grain he had sent to the Rome during their war against the Insubres.

49 Liv. 24.21.9–10.

50 Millino (2003: 124) suggests these spoils came from the First Illyrian War (230–228). Campagna (2004: 161) makes two important points regarding Hieron's dedication of Gallic armor in the Olympieion at Syracuse. First, he notes that by mounting these weapons to the temple's walls, Hieron was most likely exaggerating his role in Rome's campaigns by, in essence, behaving as a military victor would in dedicating spoils. Second, he brings up the appealing possibility that Hieron might also have framed this dedication in terms of a victory over "barbarian" enemies, sustaining a familiar propagandistic theme from the early stage of his rule.

51 Regarding the role of Hellenistic kings as "protectors," see Strootman (2011: 145–6); Chaniotis (2003: 431ff.).

52 Serrati (2008: 84, n. 22) provides a lengthy list of kings who were identified as *sōtēr*.

53 Chaniotis (2003: 431–3).

54 Initial publication of the altar by Agnello (1949: 208–9).

55 Favoring an interpretation that this represents a private act of worship: Habicht (1970: 259–62); De Sensi Sestito (1977: 188–9); Lehmler (2005: 148–50). Serrati (2008) argues that the altar is but

one piece of evidence that points to the existence of a ruler cult for Hieron and the royal family at Syracuse. Dimartino (2006: 710) has provocatively suggested that the inscription may likely be a modern forgery, basing her conclusions on paleographic grounds.

[56] Akragas: Polyb. 1.19.15; Diod. 23.9.1. Myttistraton: Diod. Sic. 23.9.4. Selinus: Bovio-Marconi (1957: 73ff.). Diodorus (23.9) gives a brief overview of the violence orchestrated by both Roman and Carthaginian forces in the early years of the First Punic War. Reflecting on the toll of the First Punic War, Wilson (2013: 99–100) surmises that the devastation experienced by the cities of central and western Sicily set the region back by nearly two generations with respect to local, civic investments in urban development.

[57] Polyb. 1.62.8.

[58] Lehmler (2005: passim).

[59] Bringmann (1993; 2001).

[60] For excavations in the area, see Orsi (1915; 1925); Gentili (1951; 1954; 1956); and, more recently, Messina (2009).

[61] Recent excavations have revealed the remains of an earlier structure on the site, possibly those of an earlier theater dating back to the fifth century; see Voza (2007).

[62] The richly decorated *skene* of the third-century building has been largely obliterated by later renovations during the Roman period and by even later spoliation. The remains of elaborately carved limestone and stucco caryatid and satyr figures, which adorned the Hieronian *skene*, offer some indication of the structure's original decoration; Rizzo (1923: 97–101); Lehmler (2005: 128–30); Portale (2013).

[63] Marconi (2012: 204–5) provides a comprehensive bibliography related to the theater and its excavation, including important contributions by, among others, Rizzo (1923) and Polacco and Anti (1981). For discussion of the theater as vehicle for Hieronian ideology, see Campagna (2004); Lehmler (2005: 122–35); Veit (2008).

[64] Regarding the excavations, see Voza (1984–5: 675; 1999: 98–105), who notes that the archaic *temenos* also contained two later fifth-century burials, which he speculates might have belonged to Gelon I, the Deinomenid tyrant, and his wife, Damarete. Voza's hypothesis, if correct, would fit with other efforts believed to have been made by Hieron II to integrate himself and his family into the Deinomenid dynasty. But, as both Wilson (1995–6: 67) and Serrati (2008: 89) have observed, the only literary evidence (Diod. 11.38.4; 14.63.3) that speaks of Gelon's final resting place locates his tomb outside the city.

[65] For the promotion of the cult of Zeus Olympios by Hieron II, see Veit (2013: 35) and Serrati (2008).

[66] Wolf (2016: 33–56) offers the most up-to-date architectural study of the Great Altar. For its function and connection to Hieronian political institutions, see Karlsson (1997); Parisi Presicce (2004); Lehmler (2005: 135–45).

[67] Diod. Sic. 16.83.2. Cicero (2.*Verr*.4.119) also mentions the temple, referring to it as extraordinary (*egregium*) in scale. For discussion, see Campagna (2004: 157–61), who endorses Voza's attribution of a monumental stereobate (Voza 1976–7: 551–2), discovered in the vicinity of the city's Roman forum, to the Hieronian Olympieion. The area of the Roman forum has long been identified as the probable location of the city's Hellenistic agora, but this assumption has yet to be verified through archaeological excavation.

[68] Regarding the location of Hieron's palace, see Berve (1959: 65); Cic. *Verr*. 2.4.118. For discussion of other regal amenities at Hieron's palace, see Veit (2013: 32). Disagreements remain over whether Agathokles had a palace on Ortygia; Berve (1959: 70–1).

[69] Livy (24.21) mentions fortified stone granaries on Ortygia in his account of the turmoil that followed the assassination of Hieronymos in 214. Although he refers to the buildings as public granaries (*horrea publica*), most scholars have identified them – on account of their location and fortified nature – as being structures built to house the royal proceeds of the agricultural tithe.

[70] For overview of fortifications, including the Euryalos fortress, during the reign of Hieron II, see Lehmler (2005: 178–84). Lawrence (1946) championed the idea that Archimedes, acting

on behalf of and with support from Hieron, was responsible for major renovations to the Euryalos fortress, including the addition of the *proteichisma* with ditches and catapult emplacements along the western side of the fortress. His position has been challenged by Beste and Mertens (2015: 287–94, esp. 292), who attribute these elements to Agathokles (Phase IV) and suggest that renovations to the fortress completed during the Hieronian period (Phase V) were decidedly less significant. See also Dimartino (2006: 709) for several fragmentary inscriptions that were discovered by Paolo Orsi at the dipylon gates of the fortress and which appear to attest to intervention by a *basileus*. Dimartino dates the inscriptions to the third century on paleographic grounds, suggesting they belong to renovations carried out by Hieron II or his son, Gelon. On the fortifications of Syracuse, more generally, see Livy (24.34.12–14), Polyb. (8.7.2–3), and Berve (1959: 76).

[71] On the water galleries of Syracuse, see Wilson (2000: 12–15; 2013: 94–5) and Collin Bouffier (2009: 72–5).

[72] Hieron's sponsorship of *gymnasia* is discussed in Chapter 3, p. 99–100.

[73] This idea was first explored at length by Wilhelm von Sydow (1984), based on his detailed study of architectural moldings from Syracuse, Megara Hyblaia, and several other sites in eastern Sicily. Campagna (2004: esp. 162–4) has called into question von Sydow's original premise, along with his dating of certain monuments, arguing that his position fails to give full consideration of the potential for civic agency in such construction projects.

[74] The monumentalization of Morgantina's agora is a topic thoroughly explored by Bell (1984–5: 506–10; 1993; 2007a; 2007b), who cites the coherence of the overall architectural plan, including shared construction units and the coordinated alignment of certain buildings, as evidence for a unitary program of construction, rather than organic growth over time. Deussen (1994) goes as far as to suggest the East Granary at Morgantina was a gift from Hieron II to the city.

[75] For Heloros, see Wolf (2016: 57–71).

[76] On the identification of the temple as sacred to Demeter, see Voza (1973: 123, n. 385), who reports the discovery of a clay altar inscribed ΔΑΜΑΤΡΟΣ inside a building, identified as part of the cult complex, immediately behind the temple.

[77] The archaeological materials recovered in the course of the excavation of these buildings support a date in the latter half of the third century for their construction; see, Voza (1968–9: 362) and Martin and Vallet (1980: 296); cf. Campagna (2006: 31), who suggests the stoa building was constructed later, during the second century BCE.

[78] Megara Hyblaia: Wolf (2016: 83–4), who echoes von Sydow's (1984: 282–5, 340–3) initial assertion that the temple should date to the Hieronian period by virtue of its architectural decoration. Tauromenion: Wolf (2016: 13–26). The temple under S. Caterina, a peripteral temple of the Doric order, has been variously dated between the second half of the fourth century and the middle of the third century BCE, largely on stylistic grounds; von Sydow (1984: 280–5, 340–3) suggested a construction date around 260, while Vallet and Villard (1966: 54–61) placed its construction to the late fourth century by comparison to the so-called fourth-century temple at Megara Hyblaia. Recent excavations have produced material evidence that corroborates a mid-third-century date for the temple; Campagna (2011: 18ff.).

[79] For instance, see the review of Wolf (2016) by Campagna (2018).

[80] For instance, see Campagna (2019: 66–9).

[81] See discussion in Chapter 8, pp. 314–15. Campagna (2004: esp. 162–4) has raised doubts about the degree of royal intervention in the refashioning of Morgantina's agora, arguing instead that greater attention should be placed on the civic agency behind the monumental building program.

[82] Polybius (1.16.10–11, 7.8.6) explicitly states that Hieron's benefactions won him a good reputation throughout the Greek world; see also Eckstein (1985: 269).

[83] Polyb. 5.88.5–8; and see Diod. Sic. 26.8.

[84] A sentiment echoed by Polybius's praise of the king (7.8.6): εὐεργετικώτατος δὲ καὶ φιλοδοξότατος γενόμενος εἰς τοὺς Ἕλληνας μεγάλην μὲν αὐτῷ δόξαν, οὐ μικρὰν δὲ

Συρακοσίοις εὔνοιαν παρὰ πᾶσιν ἀπέλιπε (And having shown himself most beneficent to the Greeks, and most anxious to earn their good opinion, he left behind him not merely a great personal reputation but also a universal feeling of goodwill toward the Syracusans).

85 Ath. 5.40–5. The *Syrakosia* has long captured the attention of scholars. Lehlmer (2005: 210–32) offers an extensive discussion of the ship; but see also Di Pasquale (2010); Portale (2013).

86 For an overview of the material evidence related to the interaction of the two kingdoms, see the collected papers in Caccamo Caltabiano (1995), as well as subsequent contribution by De Miro (2009). Regarding artistic exchange, in particular, see Portale (1995); Pisani (2011). For the presence of Syracusans (and Sicilian Greeks) in Alexandria, see La'da (2002: 212, 284–5, 289–91) and Manganaro (1989), who discusses the movement of people between Egypt and Sicily during the Hellenistic period with particular focus on material and numismatic evidence related to commercial exchange. And for discussion of such interactions in the field of numismatics, see Caccamo Caltabiano et al. (1995: 236–45); Lehmler (2005: 84–96); Wolf and Lorber (2011).

87 Arguing that there was, in fact, a formal treaty between Hieron and the Ptolemies, Serrati (2000) speculates that Hieronymos sent a delegation to Alexandria to announce his succession to the throne (Polyb. 7.2.2) and suggests that the young king might have also sought to renew a peace treaty with Ptolemies at that time.

88 Regarding the connection between the Hieronian agricultural tithe and the Ptolemaic system of agricultural taxation, see Carcopino (1914) and Bell (2007a; 2007b).

89 For Hieron's gifts of grain to the Romans, see Diod. 23.8.1, 24.1.4, 25.14; Eutr. 3.1.3; and Liv. 23.21.5. For shipments of grain to Carthage during the Mercenary War (241–237), see Polyb. 1.83.2–4 and Berve (1959: 75). Rome was by far the largest beneficiary of Hieron's grain dispensation. Dalheim (1968: 27) suggests that Hieron's appearance in Rome for the *ludi Romani* in 237, coupled with his gift of grain that same year, was a demonstration of his loyalty to Rome, shortly after the Romans and Carthaginians had again run afoul of one another, this time over control of Sardinia (Polyb. 1.88.8–12). The great ship reportedly sent by Hieron to Ptolemy II (Ath. 5.206e–209c) was said to hold, among other gifts, 60,000 *medimnoi* of grain, an amount roughly equivalent in weight to 2,425 metric tons of wheat grain.

90 Eckstein (1980: 200); Garnsey (1988: 183–5). Today the residents of Syracuse might describe the king with respectful deference as "*furbo*" or "*spertu*."

91 Polyb. 1.83.2–4; Eckstein (1985: 271–3) offers further discussion.

92 Livy (22.37) gives the amounts at 300,000 *modii* of wheat and 200,000 *modii* of barley.

93 Liv. 23.38.13.

94 Haake (2013) offers the most thorough analysis to date regarding Hieron's attempt to establish a *dynasteria* in the mold of the Successor kings.

95 Polyb. 7.8.1.

96 This detail was also given in the *Epitome historiarum* of Zonaras (8.6).

97 Just. *Epit.* 23.4.1–4. On the possible noble origins of Hierokles, see Goldsberry (1973: 161, n. 4).

98 Berve (1959: 7); De Sensi Sestito (1977: 17–18); Rutter (1993: 186).

99 For Damerete, see Liv. 24.22.8, 24.25.11. On Hieron's other daughters and sons, see Haake (2013: 110–11). Hieron may have taken additional steps to strengthen his connection with the Classical dynast. The idea has been advanced by Giuseppe Voza that a group of burials enclosed within a small precinct wall on the Belvedere plateau above Hieron's theater might have been considered the tombs of the Classical tyrant and his wife. The construction of the massive pi-shaped stoa complex around these tombs during the Hieronian period might have been a means of honoring the adopted ancestors; Voza (1984–5: 675); cf. Wilson (1996: 67) and Serrati (2008: 89), who question Voza's interpretation on the grounds that Diodorus (11.38.4, 14.63.3) states that Gelon's tomb was located outside the city.

100 On the need for Hellenistic rulers to highlight their own connection with such *progonoi*, see Smith (1988: 24–6).

[101] Rutter (1993).

[102] Diod. 11.26.

[103] Hesychius, s.v. φιλιστίδειον νόμισμα; Rutter (1993: 187).

[104] Regarding the connection between acts of beneficence (*philanthrōpia*) and Hellenistic kingship, see Samuel (1993: 190–2).

[105] Pearson (1987: 21); cf. Rutter (1993: 176–7), who notes that, contra Pearson, if Ptolemaic titulature was indeed the influence in constructing this passage, this was not based on a text derived from Timaeus, who was deceased by the time Ptolemy III Euergetes came to the throne. Instead, Rutter persuasively suggests that Diodorus' text here drew on general Hellenistic notions of ideal kingship.

[106] For co-regency of Gelon, see Berve (1959: 57); De Sensi Sestito (1977); Haake (2005: 164–5); Zambon (2006: 89). The date is inferred from a passage in Polybius (1.62.8) that purports to give the terms of the treaty that brought to a close hostilities between Rome and Carthage in 241. In the preserved text, only Hieron is mentioned with regard to the kingdom, a fact that most have taken as evidence that Gelon had not yet been made co-regent. Nevertheless, many scholars consider that the promotion of Gelon to king took place not long after 241. At any rate, we know Gelon was co-regent by the time of the earthquake on Rhodes in 227.

[107] Regarding the utility of co-regency for Hellenistic monarchs, see Walbank (1984: 66–7). Among the Ptolemaic kings, the practice began in 284 when Ptolemy II was elevated to the status of co-regent with his father, Ptolemy I.

[108] *Syll.*³ 428; De Sensi Sestito (1977: 129); Dimartino (2006: 705).

[109] For further discussion of this monument, see Gentili (1959–60); Dimartino (2006: 709); and cf. Manganaro (1977), who posits that the two royal figures named in the inscription were Hieronymos and Gelon.

[110] It surely brought the additional advantage of strengthening the king's connections in the Adriatic, which was a key area linking Syracuse with Aegean traders and markets. On Syracusan commercial contacts in the Adriatic at this time, see Millino (2003).

[111] On the topic of royal marriage alliances, see Seibert (1967). The general exception to this rule was the Ptolemies, who tended to marry within the royal household. More recently, Ager (2017).

[112] Polyb. 6.12.3, 7.4.5. There is some confusion over whether Nereis was the daughter of Pyrrhus I or his son, Pyrrhus II. In this respect, Hieron could look to both Agathokles and Pyrrhus for recent precedent. Agathokles married Theoxena, a stepdaughter of Ptolemy I. Agathokles' daughter, Lanassa, was initially married to Pyrrhus I (Plut. *Pyrrh.* 9.1; Diod. Sic. 21.4; Consolo Langher 2000: 304–5) but left him and married Demetrios Poliorketes (Plut. *Pyrrh.* 10.7; Consolo Langher 2000: 365–7).

[113] On the monuments dedicated by Nereis and Gelon at the panhellenic sanctuaries of Olympia and Delphi in honor of the Epirote royal house, see Dimartino (2006: 705–7); Lehmler (2005: 193–6).

[114] The statues that stood on either base do not survive – or, at least, have not been identified – but we might glean some sense of what these monuments could have looked like from the so-called Daochos Monument at Delphi; see Dohrn (1968); Geominy (2007). The dedication, made during the 330s by one Daochos, son of Agias, of Pharsalos, held honorific statues of the dedicant and seven family members from various generations.

[115] This is the reconstruction offered by Bringmann and von Steuben (1995: n. 61 [E]). Although the stone is extremely damaged, the reconstruction of the text benefits from comparison with the similar monument erected at Delphi.

[116] Barbantani (2011) for the assimilation of Hellenistic kings with Zeus in the poetry of Callimachus.

[117] Bell (1993: 270–2).

[118] On the use of the theater for promotion of royal agenda, see Veit (2013: 33). Lars Karlsson (1993; 1997) has also advanced a compelling thesis that the theater and altar served as the

setting for meetings of the Koinon Sikeliotan, a federal union composed of the *poleis* subject to Hieron. If correct, the dynastic messaging of the theater would have also been intended for the consumption of the representatives sent to Syracuse by the affiliated *poleis*. We know of at least one such gathering that very likely took place in the theater following Hieron's death in 215, when the Syracusan Assembly was convened so that king's will could be read aloud and Hieronymos, his grandson, publicly recognized as Hieron's successor and king; Livy 24.4.4–7. Gelon had, of course, died in 216, leaving Hieronymos the next in line of succession.

[119]   For the most thorough discussion of Hieron's so-called regal issues, see Caccamo Caltabiano et al. (1997), where it is argued that that these coins were struck within a narrow window of time between 217 and 215; cf. Arnold-Biucchi (2002), who argues in favor of a longer period of minting, beginning perhaps around the year 240. Further discussion of this coin series can be found in Chapter 7, pp. 259–66.

[120]   Carroccio (2004) associates the image of the Nike with competition in the Olympic games, although it should be noted that there is no direct evidence to corroborate this idea that Hieron entered chariots into the races at Olympia. Yet even if Hieron II never entered chariots at Olympia, Hieron I certainly did, so the image of the victorious quadriga could be another dynastic claim linking Hieron II to the achievements of his homonymic predecessor.

[121]   Both coins bear the legend ΣΥΡΑΚΟΣΙΟΙ ΓΕΛΩΝΟΣ on their reverse types. This enigmatic inscription, with its rare use of the nominative case in the legend, has been variously interpreted, e.g., Hill (1903: 192); Holm (1898: 695, n. 21); Holloway (1962: 17–27); and more recently, Carroccio (2004: 262–3). De Sensi Sestito (1977: 128–9) proposed that the Syracusans struck these coins to celebrate the reinstatement of their right to operate a civic mint upon the announcement of Gelon's co-regency. That we are likely dealing with the product of the royal mint and not a civic issue is suggested by the fact that they are so intimately tied to Hieron's other dynastic issues, with respect to both their iconography (all three family members wear diadems and share physiognomic features) and their metrology. Moreover, the letters BA, which accompany the reverse legend ΓΕΛΩΝΟΣ on both denominations, are most plausibly interpreted as an abbreviation for ΒΑ[ΣΙΛΕΟΣ] ΓΕΛΩΝΟΣ, "[coinage] of king Gelon"; cf. Holloway (1962: 18), who suggests that BA is an abbreviated form of Βασιλικὸν ἀργύριον, following Franke's (1958: 75) observation that the royal title would have been written in full, and not abbreviated.

[122]   The eagle also appears in sculptural form on Hieron's Great Altar in Neapolis and as an *akroterion* on the third-century temple at Megara Hyblaia.

[123]   While estimating total output based on die counts remains a controversial topic (see Buttrey 1993; Buttrey and Buttrey 1997), there is a growing consensus among numismatists that it is nevertheless possible to arrive at the general order of magnitude of an emission based on die estimates; de Callataÿ (1995; 2011).

[124]   Carney (1995). Carney (1992: 171–2) observes that in cases of royal polygamy, one wife would take preeminence over others when her son was elevated to the status of co-regent and heir. While the available evidence does not suggest Hieron took multiple wives, that the promotion of Philistis as queen mother around the time that Gelon is elevated to the status of co-regent and successor of Hieron fits within the understood conventions.

[125]   See discussion in Morkholm (1991).

[126]   This was the first time the queen's title appeared on a Ptolemaic coin, or for that matter on any coin from Sicily. On the similarities between the coinage of Berenike II and Philistis, see Franke (1958); Caccamo Caltabiano et al. (1997: 53–9). This is an issue discussed in further detail in Chapter 7, pp. 263–65.

[127]   Hoards containing coinage of Hieron's silver regal series include Noto (1853) = *IGCH* 2217; Syracuse (1964) = *IGCH* 2218; Vizzini (1931) = *IGCH* 2219; Syracuse (1838) = *IGCH* 2220; Rosolini (1907) = *IGCH* 2221; Morgantina (1966) = *IGCH* 2232; Syracuse (1972) = Storaci and Manenti (2013: 218); Syracuse (1993) = Storaci and Manenti (2013: 218–22).

[128] De Callataÿ (2014).

[129] According to Livy's account (24.4.1–6), Hieron reportedly proposed to dissolve his kingdom and restore freedom to the Syracusans following Gelon's death but was dissuaded from doing so by his daughters and sons-in-law, who wished to wield power by controlling the young Hieronymos. Berve (1959: 84) has rightly questioned the authenticity of this account. Rather, the story of Hieron's deathbed wish to relinquish his power to the *dēmos* rather than let it pass to Hieronymos reads more as a reflection of Roman attitudes that vilified Hieronymos for his decision to seek an alliance with Carthage as well as their readiness to absolve Hieron from the anti-Roman sentiments of his successor.

[130] For the assassination of Hieronymos, Liv. 24.7.2–7; Silius Ital. 14.99–104. Livy (24.25.11, 24.26) reports that the murders of the surviving family members were carried out with popular support from the Syracusan Assembly for the purpose of extinguishing the royal blood line.

THREE

CITIES IN THE KINGDOM

prorogata imperia provinciaeque, M. Claudio Sicilia finibus eis, quibus regnum Hieronis fuisset, Lentulo propraetori provincia vetus ...

These generals were continued in command, and their provinces assigned to them as follows: to Marcus Claudius, so much of Sicily as lay within the limits of the kingdom of Hieron; to Lentulus, the propraetor, the old province in that island ...
—Livy 24.44.4

In 1749, a heavily damaged gray granite block inscribed with small, finely carved letters was discovered at Syracuse in the vicinity of the ancient agora (Figure 3.1).[1] Although measuring only 36 centimeters × 13 centimeters and broken along all four sides of the inscribed surface, this small and fragmentary inscription captured the attention of noted Sicilian antiquarians of the day, including Gabriele Lancillotto Castelli, principe di Torremuzza, who was the first to publish the stone in his *Siciliae et objacentium insularum veterum inscriptionum Siciliae nova collectio* (1769). Castelli published only a partial transcription of the inscribed text, based on an apograph provided to him by fellow antiquarian Cesare Gaetani della Torre. The partial text provided by Gaetani was accompanied by only the briefest of comments from Castelli, who could say little more about the inscription than "*fragmentum inscriptionis, quae duabus columnis erat inscripta.*"[2] Castelli's laconic remark was due, no doubt, to the fact that he himself would not have the opportunity to view the stone, which resided in the private collection of Giuseppe Maria Capodieci, a priest and local historian of Syracuse. In 1813, Capodieci would publish *Antichi monumenti di Siracusa*, in

3.1 Fragmentary inscription of letter from Hieron II to the Syracusans (inscription: Museo Archeologico Regionale Paolo Orsi, inv. 4) (courtesy of the Parco Archeologico e paesaggistico di Siracusa, Eloro, Villa del Tellaro e Akrai; apograph: after Dimartino 2015).

which he provided his own apograph and transcription of the inscribed stone (which remained in his private household museum), along with his interpretation that the text had something to do with a marriage and a public oath taken by the Syracusans.[3] Several decades later, the German epigrapher Johannes Franz would offer his own take on the text and, importantly, observe that its manufacture dated to the reign of Hieron II.[4] It was not until 1900, however, that Adolf Wilhelm would come to identify the inscription as we know it today – as the transcript of a royal letter.[5] Subsequent scholars have offered various opinions regarding the potential content of the document, but all agree that it records part of a letter written by Hieron II to the Syracusans.[6]

The epistolary mode was the common means by which Hellenistic monarchs communicated with cities.[7] That Hieron employed the genre too should come as no surprise, following on the discussion from Chapter 2. The letter itself offers valuable confirmation that Hieron conducted his administrative relationships with the cities of southeastern Sicily in much the same manner as his royal counterparts in the eastern Mediterranean communicated with the cities in their own spheres of influence.[8] Across the Hellenistic world, royal letter-writing came to employ a standard formula that couched interaction in a personal tone with terms like "I" or "we" (king) and "you" (city). On multiple occasions in the surviving portion of his letter, Hieron directly addresses the Syracusans using this personal tone (e.g., A.2: [ὑμὶ]ν φροντίζειν; B.2: διδῶτε). This stereotypical language of royal correspondence served to mask the asymmetry of power between kings and cities, as John Ma has persuasively explored in his study of the Seleucid king Antiochos III.[9] The epistolary mode allowed both king and *polis* to scaffold the vast disparity of power that lie between them in terms of familiarity and reciprocity. On one hand, kings could express their power through euergetic benevolence (rather than by military violence), and, on the other, cities operated from a position of parity by granting honors to the king and by framing their acceptance of the king's bidding in terms that emphasized the community's autonomy in the decision to accede to royal requests.[10]

We see this dynamic at play elsewhere in Hieron's letter. The king emphasizes the goodwill (A.5: *eunoia*; εὔνοια) that the Syracusans have shown him in the past, thereby framing the requests and benefactions offered in the letter within a context of reciprocity and euergetic exchange. Such language further establishes the relationship between the king and the Syracusans within what Ma describes as "a chronology of benefaction and gratitude." In other words, neither Hieron's current act of *euergesia* nor the Syracusans' *eucharistia* (expression of gratitude) is viewed in isolation – outside a history (and implied future) of reciprocity between the two parties.[11] In defining how such discourse served the needs of a king, Ma writes,

> Gifts, the evocation of past gifts, the promise of future gifts, the ruler's proclaimed initiative in thinking up new gifts, his beneficent character, manifested in his decisions: reference to these themes created legitimacy for the king, represented his power, and deproblematized it by shifting the focus of discourse from power to benefaction. This discourse played its role in fostering consent and making power acceptable.[12]

Although the fragmentary state of the Syracusan inscription precludes any substantial restoration of the original text, what survives certainly admits a relationship fused by royal beneficence and civic appreciation, one that is showcased by the very existence of the stone itself. That the Syracusans acquiesced to Hieron's requests on this particular occasion is apparent simply by the fact that the letter, along with the corollary oath, was inscribed on stone and then (presumably) set up in the city's agora. In doing so, the Syracusans endorsed the legitimacy of Hieron's *basileia*.

There is good reason to believe that Hieron's authority was constructed from a network of individual agreements such as this, forged between him and the cities that formed his kingdom.[13] The personal nature of Hieron's rule can be inferred from the details of an episode that played out at Leontinoi in the turmoil that followed the assassination of Hieronymos in the year 214. Seeking to inflame anti-Roman sentiments among the cities formerly under Hieronian control, the Carthaginian envoy and agitator Epikides divulged to the Leontinoi that the Syracusans had made peace with Rome on the condition that all the cities formerly subject to Hieron's control were now to be considered subject to Syracusan rule. According to Livy, the response from the *dēmos* of the Leontinoi was sharp and unequivocal – they had neither given the Syracusans a mandate to conclude a treaty with Rome on their behalf, nor were they bound by the treaties not of their own making.[14] Underpinning this episode is the idea that the Syracusans had overstepped by assuming a preroga-tive that belonged to the king alone. Livy makes this clear in his summary of the arguments laid forth by Epikides, who reportedly told the Leontinoi that the Syracusans were no longer content simply with their own freedom, but sought now to rule as kings and exercise dominion over others (*etiam regnent ac dominentur*). The reaction of the Leontinoi confirms what was inferred from Hieron's letter to the Syracusans – the treaties that bound together Hieron's kingdom were made directly between individual cities and the king.[15] This marked a reshuffling of political hierarchy for many of the smaller *poleis* in the region, which had long been subject to Syracusan domination.

CITIES IN THE KINGDOM

The Hieronian sphere of influence was never particularly large, especially when compared with the vast Successor kingdoms. What Hieron's kingdom lacked in size, however, it made up for in performance. Hieron ruled over a fertile pocket of the Mediterranean whose agricultural assets had achieved near-legendary fame by the Hellenistic period (Figure 3.2).

At its greatest extent, Hieron's control stretched from Halaisa on the island's north coast to Kamarina on the south coast, encompassing most of the *poleis* in the eastern half of Sicily except Mamertine-controlled Messana. This, of course, was a short-lived maximum, lasting no more than a half a decade after his victory at the Longanus river. The arrival of Manius Otacilius Crassus and Manius Valerius Maximus in the year 263 precipitated the swift dissolution of Hieron's spear-won kingdom, particularly following the forceful capture of

3.2 Map showing the hypothetical extent of the kingdom of Hieron II after 263 BCE (after Walthall 2013b; courtesy of Getty Publications, J. Paul Getty Museum).

Adranon and Kentoripe, both Hieronian allies. Faced with the threat of such an overwhelming military force, no fewer than sixty-seven cities reportedly sent envoys offering their voluntarily submission to the Roman generals, either during or shortly after the siege of Kentoripe.[16] These included many of the *poleis* that were at the time allied with the king, with the result that Hieronian control along Sicily's north coast was effectively eliminated only a short time after it had been established there.[17] We see this in the unfinished stretches of fortification walls at Tyndaris that have been attributed to aborted efforts undertaken by Hieron to fortify his outposts along the island's Tyrrhenian coast in the brief span of time between the battle at Longanus and his capitulation to the Romans in 263.[18]

The treaty of 263 recognized Hieron's authority over a diminished area in the southeastern portion of the island. The frontiers of the kingdom were sufficiently well defined in antiquity that the Roman senate could delineate between kingdom and province in their annual consular appointments. For instance, Livy reports that for the year 213, the consular assignments fell "to Marcus Claudius, so much of Sicily as lay within the limits of the kingdom of Hieron (*quibus regnum Hieronis*); and to [P. Cornelius] Lentulus, the *propraetor*, the old province (*provincia vetus*) in that island."[19] These territorial boundaries were also recognized in practice by Roman generals operating in Sicily, as is suggested by the fact that in 214, sensing the prospect for an outbreak of conflict following the assassination of Hieronymos, the consul Appius Claudius reportedly "collected all his forces on the boundary of the province and the kingdom."[20] From what is known about the demarcation of space in this instance, the territorial limits recognized by both Hieron and the Roman senate must have been coterminous with the territorial boundaries of the *poleis* that fell to the king's authority by way of the treaty. Rather than choosing a series of geographical features (rivers, mountain ranges, etc.) to demarcate the limits of the Hieronian kingdom, Rome recognized Hieron's dominion over a number of *poleis* and their territories, the whole of which, when added together, constituted the territory over which Hieron exercised sovereignty. Today, we do not share the same degree of certainty about the territorial limits of Hieron's kingdom, as did Appius Claudius in the year 214. This, of course, has not deterred modern scholars from attempting to delineate the boundaries of the kingdom.[21]

Any reconstruction of the territorial extent of the Hieronian kingdom must start with Diodorus' summary of the treaty of 263. The historian names six *poleis* – Leontinoi, Megara Hyblaia, Neaiton, Heloros, Tauromenion, and Akrai – in addition to Syracuse that were to remain subject to Hieron by the terms of the treaty.[22] Most scholars have readily accepted Diodorus' account with respect to the political status of these seven *poleis* vis-à-vis Hieron. After all, many of these cities had long been in the orbit of Syracusan economic and military power. Yet, while certainly the most descriptive source on the subject, few scholars have considered Diodorus' list to be exhaustive, and, as a result, a wide range of proposals regarding the full extent of Hieron's kingdom have been put forward over the past century.

Jérôme Carcopino and Alexander Schenk von Stauffenberg, for instance, both argued that the king's authority initially extended no farther than to the seven cities mentioned by Diodorus, but that he was later ceded additional territory following the renewal of the peace treaty with Rome in 248 due to his loyalty during the First Punic War.[23] This position has not received much scholarly support, particularly given the silence of our historical sources regarding the conjectural expansion of Hieron's territorial control.[24] Thomas Lenschau proposed that Hieron ruled over a far more expansive kingdom after 263, one that included the cities of Kentoripe and Agyrion.[25] Diodorus makes a brief and unsatisfying reference to the sponsorship of monumental architecture in his hometown of Agyrion, which Lenschau took as evidence for royal patronage by Hieron II and thus evidence for the city's status within the kingdom.[26] But, as later scholars would rightly point out, the identification of Hieron as patron of this particular construction project is far from certain.[27] As will be discussed below, the available evidence favors the exclusion of Kentoripe and Agyrion from the kingdom. While most scholars have readily accepted Diodorus's statement that Tauromenion was among the cities that fell to Hieron's control by the terms of his peace with Rome, Helmut Berve considered the city's presence on Diodorus' list to be a mistake, arguing that the city was not subject to Hieronian control after 263. At the time Berve was writing his book, *König Hieron II*, it was generally believed that Tauromenion had continued to strike civic coinage throughout the third century, behavior he deemed incompatible with the semi-autonomous status of a *polis* that recognized the authority of the king.[28] While not wrong in his belief that the cities that recognized Hieron's political authority also accepted some form of royal oversight, Berve's case for excluding Tauromenion has not been widely accepted by subsequent scholars. This may be due, in large part, to the timely discovery of an inscribed base in the Sanctuary of Zeus at Olympia that once held an honorific statue of Hieron II dedicated by the *dēmos* of Tauromenion. This key piece of material evidence surfaced in 1958, the same year that Berve completed *König Hieron II*. The text of the inscription (discussed in Chapter 2) plainly recognizes Hieron's status as *basileus* and essentially confirms Diodorus' assertion that Tauromenion was among the *poleis* subject to Hieronian authority.[29] Whether the Tauromenitani enjoyed a special status compared with other cities in the kingdom is a matter that we shall return to in the second part of this chapter.[30]

With the advance of scientific excavations in eastern Sicily after the Second World War, archaeological evidence has begun to play an increasingly important role in efforts to define the territorial extent of Hieron's kingdom.[31] In this spirit, I offer my own assessment of the cities subject to Hieron's authority based on the available literary and archaeological evidence. The combined weight of this evidence suggests that following the resolution of Hieron's treaty with Rome in 263, the Hieronian kingdom consisted of at least fifteen *poleis*: Syracuse, Leontinoi, Megara Hyblaia, Neaiton, Heloros, Akrai, Tauromenion, Herbessos, Morgantina, Kamarina, Echetla, Menai, Hybla Magna, Mutyka, and Euboia.[32]

Several of the smaller communities listed here, including those on the order of Echetla, Menai, and Hybla Magna, are not mentioned by Diodorus. Yet they very likely fell within the confines of the Hieronian kingdom by the simple fact that these communities were located between the territory of Syracuse and those of the larger allied *poleis*, like Morgantina or Kamarina.[33] Their omission from Diodorus' account might be readily explained by their modest size or, perhaps, a prior status as politically dependent to Syracuse.[34] We also see some of these smaller cities taking part in a coordinated resistance to Rome in the years following Hieron's death, an effort that appears to have been shared by the *poleis* formerly allied with the king.[35] Among this group are three large cities – Herbessos, Morgantina, and Kamarina – that Diodorus does not mention among those ceded to the king by terms of the treaty, yet there are strong arguments in favor of counting all three *poleis* as being among those subject to Hieron. The inclusion of any one of these *poleis* would substantially enlarge the territory subject to the king. For this reason alone, it is useful to review carefully the evidence in favor of counting each of these cities as part of the kingdom.

Herbessos

Herbessos (mod. Montagna di Marzo), despite its absence from Diodorus' account, has strong claim to being counted among the *poleis* subject to Hieron II.[36] Situated on a high massif along the western flanks of the Heraian mountain range, Herbessos would have been the westernmost city in Hieron's kingdom. The settlement held commanding views of the surrounding territory from its upland vantage point overlooking the fertile Olivo River valley below.

Our ancient historical sources speak little about the city's political status in the late fourth and early third century. Herbessos was not among the cities that reportedly sought alliance with Hieron during his campaigns against the Mamertines in the 260s, but this does not necessarily warrant its exclusion from the kingdom. Given its remote inland location, the city presumably faced little direct threat from the Mamertine incursions that had plagued portions of eastern Sicily for much of the previous two decades. Herbessos possibly came under Hieronian control in the years following the battle at Longanus, as the king sought to extend his control over free *poleis* on the island.[37] Alternatively, the city may have been conceded to Hieron by the Romans as part of their renewed peace treaty of 248, although this is purely speculative.[38] During the First Punic War, the city served as a supply depot for the Romans besieging Akragas, but was captured in a surprise raid by the Carthaginian general Hanno in 262.[39] Malcolm Bell has suggested that Hieron might have allowed the Romans to use the city as a base of operations during their assault on the Carthaginian-held Akragas.[40] Little more is said about the city or its political situation in the decades to follow.

Perhaps the strongest evidence that Herbessos was among the cities subject to Hieronian authority relates, in fact, to events that transpired after the king's death. In his account of the events taking place in Sicily during the year 212, Livy describes a widespread revolt that broke out among the *poleis* that had allied themselves with Carthage against Rome after the fall of Syracuse. In highlighting Marcellus' efforts to suppress these revolts, Livy notes that Herbessos gave shelter to Hippokrates and Epikides, envoys sent by Hannibal with the goal of fomenting anti-Roman sentiments among Hieron's former allies. Livy discusses the reception of these Carthaginian envoys at Herbessos within the context of the revolts breaking out at Syracuse, Leontinoi, Megara Hyblaia and Heloros – all cities that unquestionably belonged to the kingdom.[41] That Herbessos formed part of this constellation of cities in revolt is certainly suggestive of its prior political affiliation with Hieron, as we know to have been the case with the other four *poleis* named by Livy. More significant still is the fact that it was Marcus Claudius Marcellus who was responsible for quashing the revolt in which Herbessos played a part. We will recall that for the consular appointments of 212, Livy notes that the Roman senate had assigned the territory of the former Hieronian kingdom to Marcellus, while the remainder of the island (the *provincia vetus*) was given to P. Cornelius Lentulus and, moreover, that the boundary between these two areas of jurisdiction was well defined in antiquity.[42] It follows then that if Herbessos did lie outside the political boundaries of the kingdom and in the territory of the *provincia vetus*, it would have fallen to Lentulus, not Marcellus, to deal with suppressing the revolt there. The fact that Marcellus reportedly ordered troops to retake Herbessos, coupled with the city's apparent participation in the revolt spurred on by Hippokrates and Epikides, strongly suggests it was among the *poleis* subject to Hieron.

Archaeological excavations along the plateau of Montagna di Marzo have revealed traces of the ancient settlement, which appears to have been permanently occupied for about 500 years between the sixth century and first century (Figure 3.3).[43] By the third century, the urban center was organized according to an orthogonal grid plan with three major avenues running through the

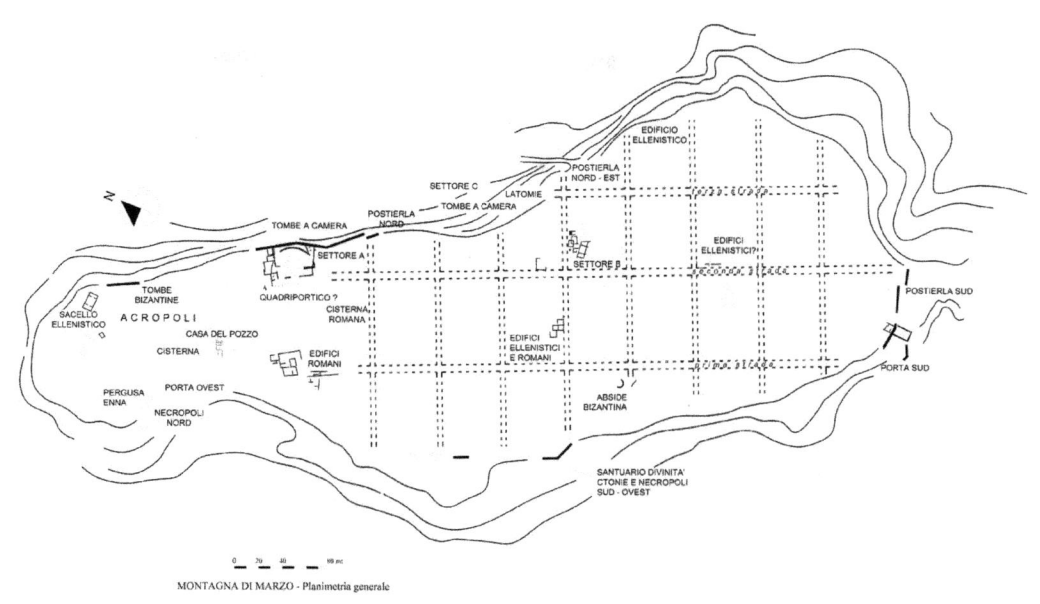

3.3 Plan of Herbessos (after Guzzardi 1999; drawing: G. Filantropi).

city.[44] While much of the ancient settlement remains buried, the limited excavations on the site have brought to light remains of public architecture, residential buildings, and multiple *necropoleis*. Little can be said at present about developments taking place inside the urban center during the Hieronian period.[45] Yet the discovery of a large hoard of bronze coins at the site in the early twentieth century may lend further credibility to our identification of Herbessos as a city politically subject to Hieronian control. The hoard contained a considerable number of bronze coins struck by Hieron II (258 of 319 coins; 81%).[46] Such a large proportion of the king's own currency is to be expected within the political boundaries of the kingdom, where the small-denomination bronzes issued by the royal mint would have enjoyed privileged status as legal tender. In fact, the high percentage of Hieronian coinage represented in the hoard at Herbessos is comparable to that of other bronze hoards found within the territories subject to Hieron. The circulation of Hieronian coinage is a subject to which we will return in Chapters 7 and 8. Taken together, the combined weight of the literary and archaeological evidence tips the scales in favor of counting Herbessos among the cities subject to Hieronian rule.

Morgantina

Morgantina is the second *polis* that has strong claim to inclusion in Hieron's kingdom despite its omission from the account of Diodorus. The ancient

3.4 Plan of Morgantina (drawing: E. Thorkildsen; courtesy of the American Excavations at Morgantina).

settlement was located roughly 15 kilometers due east of Herbessos, in the eastern foothills of the Heraean range. Situated along the broad Serra Orlando plateau, Morgantina overlooked the Plain of Catania and a fertile territory fed by the Dittaino and Gornalunga Rivers (Figure 3.4). The surviving historical record is silent on Morgantina's political situation during the period of Hieron's rise to power in the 270s, but there is good reason to believe that the city had long fallen within the political and economic orbit of Syracuse. The citizens of Morgantina had reportedly welcomed Agathokles in the year

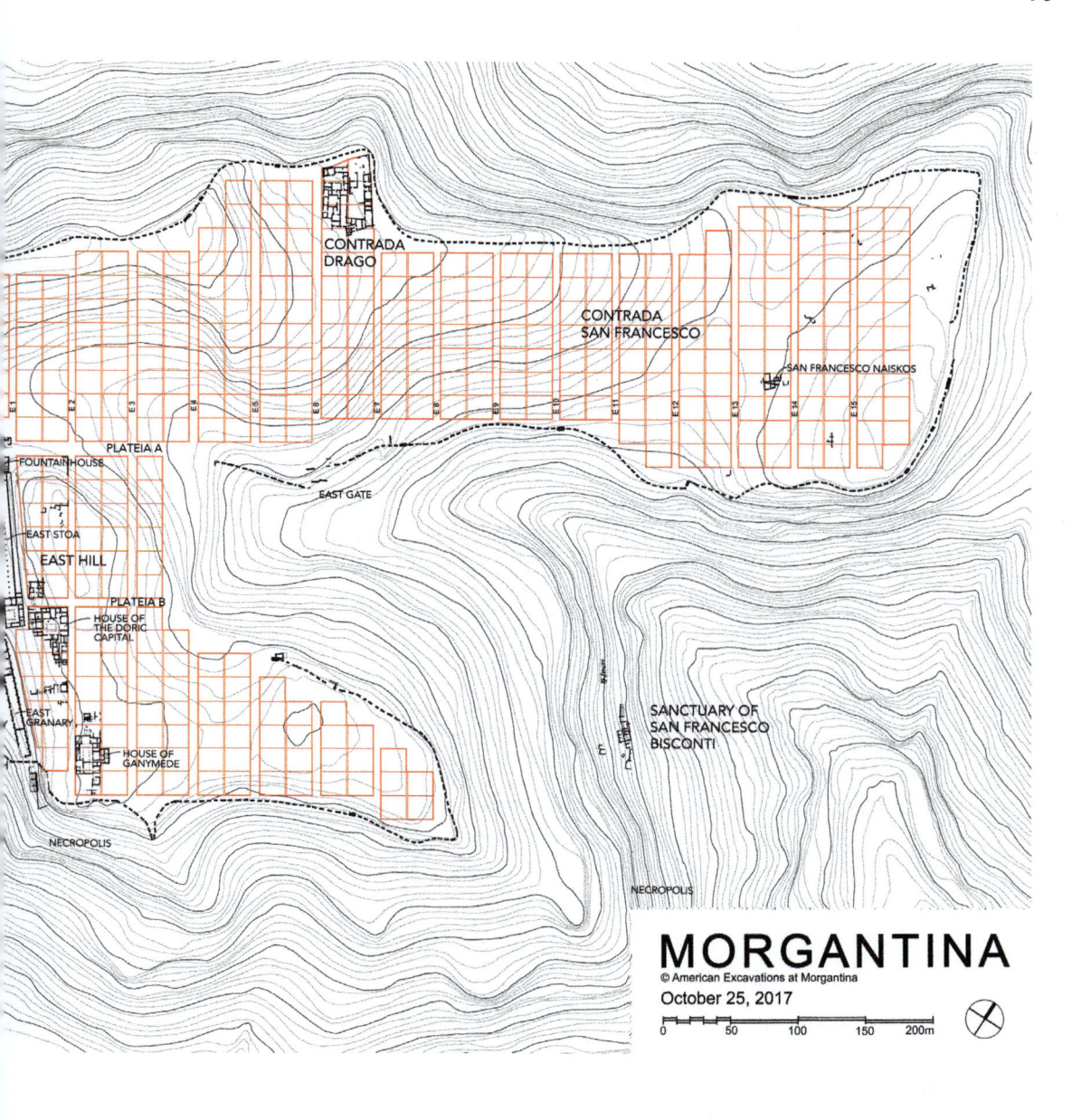

317 and offered the exiled leader military support in his bid to regain control at Syracuse.[47] The city's participation in the coordinated resistance to Rome, following the capture of Syracuse in 213, may offer further indication that – like Herbessos – Morgantina was politically subject to Hieron II.

While historical sources remain largely silent on the question of Morgantina's political fortunes during the early third century, the archaeological record speaks volumes. More than 65 years of archaeological excavations at the site have produced a wealth of material evidence connecting the city to Syracuse and to the Hieronian kingdom.[48] As discussed in the previous chapter, the most prominent expression of this connection was certainly the monumental building program that transformed the city's agora in the second half of the third century. Malcolm Bell has convincingly attributed this architectural transformation to a combination of Hieron II's patronage and the stable political environment fostered within the kingdom.[49] The three large stoa buildings, stone theater, and monumental fountain house reflect not simply a level of investment previously unseen in the city's public architecture, but also a high degree of coordination and planning, which Bell credits to the work of an architect sent from the royal court at Syracuse.[50]

In the following chapters, we will encounter three additional bodies of material evidence that further sustain the idea that Morgantina was politically linked to the Syracusan monarch. Among the public monuments of the new building program, those that reveal the strongest connection with royal oversight are two above-ground granaries constructed in the city's lower agora. These monumental warehouses and their connection to the Hieronian tithe administration will be discussed in Chapter 6. Further evidence that Morgantina was subject to royal oversight are the remains of ceramic measuring vessels of standardized form and capacity. In Chapter 5, I build a case that these handheld instruments were related to broader administrative policies carried out by the royal court in service of facilitating the assessment and collection of agricultural taxes throughout the kingdom. Numismatic evidence, as well, supports the hypothesis that the city was politically and economically attached to the Hieronian kingdom. As will be discussed in greater detail in Chapter 8, the king's bronze coinage makes up more than a quarter of the total number of coins (ca. 3,000 of 12,000) recovered at the site since controlled excavations began in 1955.[51] Such numbers evoke sustained economic and political contact with Syracuse during much of the third century, and are comparable to the concentrations of Hieronian coins found at other sites within the kingdom, including Herbessos and Kamarina.

Kamarina

The case for Kamarina's inclusion among the *poleis* subject to Hieronian authority after 263 is still nascent and, perhaps, the most open to debate.[52] During the late fourth century, the city had passed back and forth between Syracusan and Carthaginian control on several occasions (Figure 3.5). Kamarina would ultimately fall to Syracuse by the terms of Agathokles' peace with Carthage in the year 306/5, which established the boundary of the two powers' respective *epikrateia* at the Halykos river (mod. Platani). Following Agathokles' death, the city appears to have remained under Syracusan control, although historical sources suggest both the city and its territory suffered from military incursions by the Akragantine ruler Phintias, as well as by the Mamertines.[53] Diodorus reports

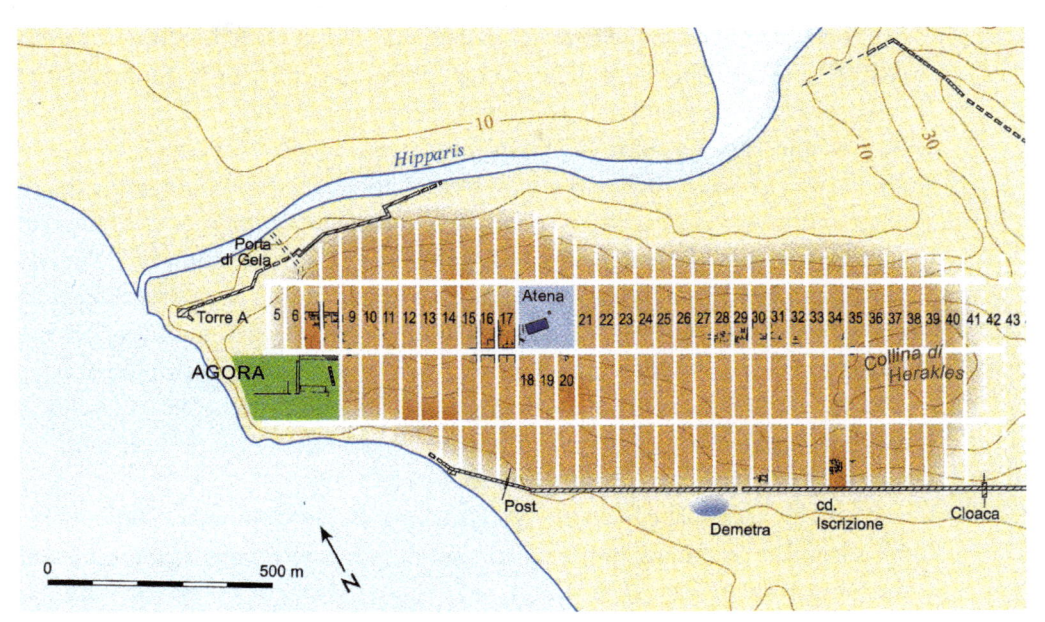

3.5 Plan of Kamarina (after Mertens 2006).

that in the opening years of the First Punic War, a political faction at Kamarina handed over the city to Carthaginian forces led by Hamilcar, an event that precipitated the Roman assault on the city in the year 258.[54] After failing in their initial attempt to capture the city, the Romans succeeded in their second assault, now reportedly aided by siege engines supplied by Hieron.[55] According to Diodorus (23.9), the Romans sold most of the city's inhabitants into slavery – an event that many scholars considered an irreparable blow to the vitality of Kamarina.[56] Reassessment of archaeological evidence from Hellenistic levels within the urban center of Kamarina, however, has upended such long-held beliefs.[57] The material record presents a consistent picture of economic vitality throughout the latter half of the third century. In both the private and public spheres, new construction soon replaced what was damaged in the siege. On the slopes of the hill immediately north of the city's agora, archaeologists have uncovered the remains of large, well-appointed houses dating from the second half of the third century – evidence, indeed, that the city was far from abandoned after 258.[58] New construction in the agora was laid immediately over the remains of buildings thought to have suffered damaged in 258, like the so-called West Stoa, a long, rectangular structure in which archaeologists discovered several hundred amphoras that had been sealed within the building when it was demolished.[59] Commerce also continued without clear signs of interruption, judging from the numismatic material recovered in the city's agora during excavations of the 1980s and 1990s.[60] Of the 708 legible coins found during these excavations, the bronze coins of Hieron II ($n = 265$) accounted for more than one-third of these and nearly 90 percent of all coin finds datable to the third century. Lucchelli and Di Stefano, who published the numismatic finds from the agora excavations, found no evidence of disruption caused by the events of 258. Rather, the large amount of Hieronian coinage found in the agora certainly points to sustained commercial connections with Syracuse throughout the king's reign and is, moreover, closely comparable to the concentrations of Hieronian coinage found in contemporary commercial contexts at Morgantina.[61] Perhaps the strongest indication that Kamarina numbered among the cities subject to Hieronian control are the remains of numerous standardized measuring vessels found in the city's agora, including one that bears a stamp indicating that its capacity was validated by a royal magistrate. Together with the standardized measures from Morgantina, I argue in Chapter 5 that these vessels must be related to the tithe administration of Hieron II.[62]

The archaeological evidence from Kamarina invites us to reconsider conclusions based on surviving historical accounts alone. Hieron reportedly provided the Romans with siege engines in their assult on the city in 258, a detail that has led many to conclude the Kamarina was not under the king's protection . Yet if Diodorus was correct in reporting that the Carthaginians had captured Kamarina by treachery only months before the Roman siege, it may have been the case that Hieron was acting with the intention of regaining control of the city.[63] Even from the limited details provided by the historical record, Kamarina does appear to have been under Syracusan control at the start of the First Punic War. By the time of the Second Punic War, moreover, the city was recognized by Silius Italicus as being allied with Syracuse and Hybla Magna in their resistance to Rome following the death of Hieron.[64] As with the case of Herbessos and Morgantina, such coordination on the part of Kamarina certainly suggests that the city was allied with Hieron during his lifetime.

When Herbessos, Morgantina, and Kamarina are added to the seven *poleis* mentioned by Diodorus, the boundaries of the Hieronian kingdom are greatly expanded to encompass a large swath southeastern Sicily, including much of the fertile *mesogeia*. It is unclear why these three cities were not included in Diodorus' account. Perhaps they were not specifically named in the terms of the initial peace treaty with Rome and were only later ceded to Hieron by the Romans. This second line of reasoning was advanced by Lenschau more than a century ago, when arguing that control of Herbessos was granted to Hieron by the Romans in 248 as repayment for his unwavering support during the First Punic War.[65] While such territorial accretions to the kingdom cannot be ruled out, there is no positive evidence to corroborate this hypothesis or lead us to choose it over another. What is certain is that archaeological evidence from all three sites appears to reflect a sustained period of economic stability throughout much of the middle decades of the third century, during which time there are strong signs of close commercial and administrative contact with Syracuse.

In our effort to ascertain the frontiers of the kingdom, it is equally valuable to identify the *poleis* of eastern Sicily that lie outside Hieron's direct political authority. The kingdom's northern border likely followed the course of the Chrysas river (mod. Dittaino), which springs from headwaters in the Heraian Mountains and flows west to join the Symaithos river (mod. Simeto) about 30 kilometers from the Ionian coast. The Symaithos divided the territory of Leontinoi from that of Katane to the north. While Katane had been an ally of Hieron in the early 260s, the city was among those that sought alliance with Rome in 263.[66] The city appears to have retained a degree of independence afterward as an ally of Rome.[67] Similarly, the territories of Kentoripe and Agyrion, which lie to the northwest of Katane in the foothills of the Nebrodi mountain range, were removed from Hieronian control by the treaty of 263.[68] The Chrysas river likely formed the southern border of both the territories of Kentoripe and Agyrion, effectively separating them from the Hieronian kingdom.[69] These two cities appear to have remained outside Hieronian control after 263.[70] Bordering on the territory of Herbessos was that of Henna, a city that had hosted a Carthaginian garrison until 258, when it was captured by the Romans.[71] Henna remained in Roman hands for the duration of the war, which is not surprising given its strategic position overlooking much of central Sicily. After the First Punic War, Henna was granted the status of a Roman *civitas libera atque immunis*, situating it firmly outside Hieronian control.[72] Bordering Herbessos' territory to the south was the territory of Phintias-Gela (mod. Licata). Given the notable presence of Roman and Carthaginian forces in the area throughout period of the First Punic War, the city and its territory most likely fell outside Hieronian control along with the rest of the Geloan Plain.[73] Thus, the southwestern frontier of the Hieronian kingdom must have followed an uneven path through the foothills of the Heraian range, presumably corresponding to the limits of Morgantina's southern border, and then along the Hyblaeus river (mod. Dirillo), which formed the western limit of Kamarina's territory.[74] Set apart from the main body of the kingdom was Tauromenion, Hieron's outpost north of the Symaithos river.

Considered together, Hieron's control after 263 extended over a territory comprising approximately one-quarter of the island (ca. 6,000 square kilometers). This was indeed minuscule by comparison with the kingdoms of the eastern Mediterranean.[75] But Hieron's pint-sized kingdom certainly punched above its weight thanks to its outsized agricultural capabilities. To Hieron fell among the most fertile portions of the island's *mesogeia*, including a large swath of the Plain of Catania, renowned in antiquity for its bountiful yields of grain.[76] His kingdom encompassed the major ports at Syracuse, Tauromenion, and Kamarina, as well as smaller harbors along the east and south coast. Four major rivers – the Chrysas, Hyblaeus, Gornalunga, and Symaithos – served as navigable arteries connecting the interior to the coast. Tauromenion provided the king with access to the old-growth forests that scaled the slopes of Mt. Etna, a source of precious timber resources.[77] Hieron's task was how to effectively extract resources from his kingdom, a subject that will be the focus of the second part of the book.

DEFINING THE RELATIONSHIP BETWEEN CITIES AND KING

Negotiating Power between King and City

If Hieron's letter to the Syracusans gives us an idea about how the king and the communities subject to his rule interacted, what inferences can we draw about the process in which they initially came under his control? For the Hieronian kingdom, we lack details about where this process ran smoothly and where it met with resistance from local stakeholders, insights occasionally afforded by the epigraphic record of other Hellenistic kingdoms.[78] We have only later historical accounts, like that of Diodorus, which tend to condense what was undoubtedly a complicated process into a few short lines.[79] Nonetheless, there are good reasons to believe that the manner in which cities found themselves politically linked to Hieron was not all that dissimilar from what we know was taking place in the Successor kingdoms. After all, we have already seen that Hieron showed himself to be quite aware of and receptive to the political maneuvers taken by his perceived counterparts in the Aegean. Based on the few surviving literary references that mention communities surrendering to or welcoming Hieron's troops, we could imagine that the process worked along the lines of Elias Bickerman's "surrender and grant" model, based on his study of the Seleucid kingdom.[80] Following Bickerman's paradigm, a city would first surrender to the king, who, through royal proclamation (πρόσταγμα, *prostagma*), would then restore the city's autonomous status, although often with certain limitations like the obligation to pay taxes or garrison the king's soldiers. The result was that the city and king were now both legally bound by treaty, as well as by a relationship of reciprocity.

In recognizing Hieron's sovereignty, the *poleis* of southeastern Sicily forfeited a degree of their local autonomy in return for benefactions and protection from the king. This was an experience shared across the Mediterranean world as the political autonomy of the *polis* was becoming increasingly eclipsed by the political and military authority of Hellenistic monarchs.[81] Yet it bears noting here that the condition of limited civic autonomy was not a novel experience for the cities in southeastern Sicily, many of which had been subject to Syracusan domination for generations.[82] For smaller *poleis* like Akrai and Neaiton, long within Syracuse's sphere of influence, the conclusion of a treaty with Hieron might have constituted little more than a new legal framework for their interaction with a more powerful sovereign, albeit one that effectively removed them from direct Syracusan control.

Perhaps the clearest limitation placed on the autonomy of the cities of southeastern Sicily was their concession to pay the king an annual tithe, a *dekatē*, on agricultural production within their territories.[83] The details of the Hieronian tithe will be explored further in Chapter 4. For the present discussion, it is enough to underscore that the payment of taxes or tribute to an external state constituted a forfeiture of sovereignty for an autonomous *polis*.[84] Moreover, taxation opened the door for the encroachment of royal interests into the civic sphere. The assessment and collection of taxes by royal officials, for instance, brought about new forms of external oversight. A proportional tithe on agricultural production, like that collected from the cities of the Hieronian kingdom, required *poleis* to comply with a range of externally enforced measures, such as the reporting of annual census data to royal officials and the adoption of new units of measurement.

Beyond taxation, the *poleis* subject to Hieronian control likely faced other forms of royal interference. Many scholars have suggested that Hieron restricted the autonomy of *poleis* to issue their own civic coinage; and, indeed, it appears that none of the cities under Hieron's control struck coinage during the 54-year period that he reigned as king.[85] Whether or not this inactivity was the result of direct interference from the royal court is a question to be explored further in Chapter 7. Some scholars have suggested that *poleis* may have also been expected to train and contribute local military forces for the king's army. Hieron does seem to have promoted the construction and operation of *gymnasia* in the cities under his control.[86] In his study of the role played by Sicilian *gymnasia* in the training and maintenance of local military units during the Roman Republican period, Jonathan Prag convincingly argues that the institution – as with so many other aspects of Rome's administration of Sicily – began during the reign of Hieron II.[87] An inscription found at the site of Neaiton, one of the cities undisputedly under Hieronian control during the third century, may support this view. Although partially damaged, the inscription, which was originally carved into the living bedrock above the entrance to what is believed to have been a civic *gymnasion*, can be read:

> Ἐπὶ γυμνασιάρχων
> Ἀριστί[ω]νος τοῦ Ἀγαθ[άρχου]
> Φιλιστίωνος τοῦ Ἐπικράτ[εος]
> νεανίς[κοι Ἱε]ρώνειο[ι].

> When Aristonos, son of Agatharchos, and Philiston, son of Epikrates, were
>   *gymnasiarchs*
> The Hieronian *neaniskoi* [dedicated this].[88]

The inscription clearly belongs to a dedication made by an otherwise unknown group called the Hieronian *neaniskoi*. By the Hellenistic period, the term *neaniskoi* and its cognates (e.g., *neoi*) often carried the connotation of young men involved in military service.[89] If these *neaniskoi* were, in fact, trained for possible conscription into the king's army, Hieron's promotion of civic *gymnasia* would certainly reflect royal intervention beyond mere benefaction.[90]

Despite the evidence for royal infringement on certain aspects of *polis* sovereignty, the cities of Hieron's kingdom continued to exercise a fair degree of civic autonomy. This is to be expected in light of recent scholarship on the Hellenistic *polis* that has profitably replaced the narrative of decline, which had long defined the fate of the *polis* in the age of the Successor kings, with one of dynamism and growth.[91] The vitality of the Hellenistic *polis* is no longer seen as mutually exclusive with political domination by sovereign monarchs.[92] With regard to the cities of southeastern Sicily, we have ample evidence for the continued operation of democratic bodies like the *ekklēsia* (often attested in the Doric form, *halia*) and *boulē*, as well as for the appointment of civic magistrates. Even at Syracuse, Hieron's de facto capital, there is abundant evidence for self-governance.[93] The inscription with which we began the chapter records an oath sworn jointly by the Syracusan *boulē*, civic magistrates (*stratēgoi*), and the Syracusan *dēmos*.[94] Equally impressive is the inscribed text of a decree passed by the council (*boulē*) and assembly (*halia*) of Kamarina in 242, which recognized a request of the Koans to accept their nascent games for Asklepios and grant *asylia* to the god's temple.[95] The surviving text not only attests to the continued activity of these civic organs at Kamarina but further demonstrates the high degree of autonomy that *poleis* within the Hieronian kingdom exercised over civic affairs, even to the point of engaging in diplomatic policy with foreign states.[96] The vitality of civic institutions under Hieronian rule is further manifest at Akrai and Morgantina, where archaeologists have discovered the remains of democratic assembly spaces, like *bouleutēria* and *ekklēsiasteria*.[97] At both cities, in fact, the construction of these deliberative spaces occurred during the Hieronian period.

Negotiating Power between King and koinon*?*

Finally, it bears consideration that beyond his direct communication through letter-writing and royal orders, Hieron may have interacted with the *poleis* of southeastern Sicily through the intermediary structure of a *koinon*, or federal league. The existence of such a federal league operating within the kingdom was first proposed by Giacomo Manganaro, who restored the phrase τό τε κοινὸ[ν τῶν | Σικελιωτᾶν] (*koinon tōn Sikeliōtān*; the *koinon* of the Sikeliotai) to a partially preserved section of Hieron's letter to the Syracusans that opened this chapter.[98] In his initial restoration of the text, Manganaro advanced the idea that the letter contained a direct address from Hieron to the "*koinon* of the Sikeliotai," which he argued was comprised of all the *poleis* subject to the king.

Although Manganaro would come to dismiss his initial interpretation in favor of the more plausible reading, τό τε κοινὸ[ν τᾶς | βουλᾶς καὶ τοῦ δάμου ὅρκιον] (to te koinon tās Boulās kai toū damou horkion, the common oath of the council and the people), arguments in support of the existence of a koinon tōn Sikeliōtān have multiplied over the years.[99]

The Hellenistic period of course saw a proliferation of federal leagues, many of which were initially formed and sustained by kings.[100] These did not always take the form of massive hegemonic federations, such as the League of Corinth convened by Philip II in 338 or the Hellenic League revitalized by Antigonos I and Demetrios Poliorketes in 302.[101] Often, they were smaller, regional federations that kings could leverage to further their own administrative and military objectives.[102] As for the putative koinon of the Sikeliotai, it is true that the inscribed letter from Hieron to the Syracusans does not admit a convincing restoration of the phrase τό κοινὸν τῶν Σικελιωτᾶν. Yet in his error, Manganaro might very well have hit on a vein of underlying historical fact in positing the existence and operation of a koinon formed by the poleis subject to Hieron.

Deprived of direct reference to the koinon in the letter, we can instead look to historical events taking place in the years following Hieron's death and the dissolution of his kingdom, when the cities of southeastern Sicily again found themselves in the midst of the struggle between Rome and Carthage. Ancient authors do not directly attest to the operation of a federal league within the former kingdom but do report several episodes of well-coordinated anti-Roman resistance by many of the poleis formerly subject to Hieron. We have already encountered the coordinated revolt by Syracuse, Leontinoi, Heloros, Megara Hyblaia, and Herbessos that occurred in the years 213 and 212.[103] An even larger group of insurgent poleis is described in the Punica of Silius Italicus, who names Herbessos, Morgantina, Menai, Mutyka, Neaiton, Heloros, and Syracuse as being among the cities to align themselves with Carthage against Rome.[104] These are all, of course, cities once found within the confines of the Hieronian kingdom. One simple explanation for this wholesale realignment of allegiance on the part of these cities is the continued operation of a regional league, the existence of which would have helped to facilitate the type of rapid coordination and troop mobilization described in Livy's account of the events that transpired in southeastern Sicily at this time.

Complementing the historical evidence is a series of gold and silver coins, struck around this very same window of time, that bear the reverse legend ΣΙΚΕΛΙΩΤΑΝ, "(coinage) of the Sikeliotai" (Figure 3.6). Although long recognized as some form of "alliance coinage" by early scholars of Sicilian numismatics, Erik Sjöqvist was the first to decisively connect the coinage to the anti-Roman resistance movement following the assassination of Hieronymos.[105] Both the silver and gold issues of the ΣΙΚΕΛΙΩΤΑΝ coinage bear obvious stylistic and iconographic similarities with the silver coinage struck at Syracuse during the

3.6 Silver two-litra and four-litra coins of the Sikeliotai, ca. 213–211 BCE (top: ANS 1983.38.7, courtesy of the American Numismatic Society; bottom: ANS 1997.9.217, courtesy of the American Numismatic Society).

period of the Fifth Syracusan Democracy (214–212). Yet based on the provenance of known and reported find spots for these coins, there is every reason to believe that the ΣΙΚΕΛΙΩΤΑΝ coinage was struck at Morgantina in the narrow window of time between the investment of Syracuse by Roman forces in 213 and the capture of Morgantina itself in the year 211. The stylistic affinities shared by the dies used for the last coinage struck by an independent Syracuse and those used for the ΣΙΚΕΛΙΩΤΑΝ coinage suggest more than casual inspiration; they indicate that, in all likelihood, the die-cutters for both series were one and the same.[106] This stylistic connection, coupled with the speed with which production of these coins commenced, certainly supports the view that the ΣΙΚΕΛΙΩΤΑΝ coinage emerged not from a nascent resistance movement hastily marshaled by the *poleis* of southeastern Sicily but rather from the remnants of the Hieronian *koinon* making one last, coordinated push for political survival.[107]

While not absolutely decisive, the weight of the historical and material evidence does appear to indicate that some form of federation came into existence during the reign of Hieron II. That the term "ΣΙΚΕΛΙΩΤΑΝ" appears on coins struck by this purported league may justify our use of the label *koinon tōn Sikeliōtān*. It stands to reason that during his lifetime Hieron would have served as the league's *hegemon*, or leader. In fact, we may recall from our discussion in Chapter 2 that an inscribed statue base found in the vicinity of the Syracusan agora identified Hieron with the dual titles of *basileus* and *hegemon*.[108] Could this have been a title reflective of the king's status vis-à-vis a Sikeliote *koinon*? If the league's provisions also called for military commitments and pacts of mutual aid on the part of the member states, the federal structure of a *koinon* might have served as the means of organizing civic military training and enrollment in conjunction with the evidence for the royal sponsorship of civic *gymnasia* discussed above. The rapid coordination of anti-Roman resistance among those *poleis* formerly subject to Hieron certainly points to the existence of such provisions for mutual aid in the event of a military crisis.[109]

Last, judging from the structure and organization of those better-known *koina* found elsewhere in the Hellenistic Mediterranean, the existence of a *koinon* of the Sikeliotai would have provided Hieron with means to efficiently implement and enforce administrative policies throughout his kingdom.[110] The League of the Islanders (*koinon tōn Nēsiōtōn*), formed by Ptolemy II in the early third century, was one such regional league perhaps more akin in scale and function to what we might envision for the *koinon tōn Sikeliōtān*.[111] In surviving decrees passed by the Nesiotic League's representative council (*synedrion*), we see the federation largely involved in deciding administrative matters.[112] Along these lines, Lars Karlsson has argued that Hieron's prodigious expansion of the theater at Syracuse during the 230s, along with the construction of the enormous altar to Zeus, was completed, in part, to serve as a meeting place for the general assembly of the *koinon tōn Sikeliōtān*.[113] The scale of both monuments would be fitting for meetings and sacrifices conducted by a group as large as the representative assembly of the *koinon*.[114]

While the very existence of a *koinon* of the Sikeliotai remains a matter open for further consideration and debate, the surviving historical and material evidence suggests we should not rule out the possibility that a federal league was in operation during the period of Hieronian rule. There is no question that Hieron looked to the Successor kingdoms when articulating his own form of political ideology, so we should not be surprised if he modeled his approach to the organization and administration of his kingdom similarly. It is to this larger question of royal administration – and specifically how Hieron went about mobilizing the vast resources of his kingdom – that we now turn our attention.

NOTES

[1]   *IG* XIV 7. For an excellent historiographic summary of the text and its various interpreters, see Dimartino (2015). The dark-colored granite stone used for the inscription is unlike anything quarried on Sicily; Manganaro (2005: 141) speculates the stone may have come from a quarry in Egypt or Greece.

[2]   Castelli (1769: 280): "a fragment of an inscription, which was inscribed in two columns."

[3]   Capodieci (1813: 178–83).

[4]   *CIG* III (1853), 564, no. 5367.

[5]   Wilhelm (1900). Wilhelm's publication would appear in the same year that the Museo archeologico di Siracusa acquired the inscription from the Capodieci collection, allowing it to be viewed by a far wider audience. Today, the inscription is displayed in the Museo archeologico "Paolo Orsi" in Syracuse.

[6]   Manganaro (1965), for instance, believed that the letter outlined the political privileges that would remain with the Syracusans, if they recognized Gelon as Hieron's legitimate successor and heir to the throne. His rather generous emendations did not receive wide support, particularly with respect to his supposition that among the privileges granted to the Syracusans was the right to mint coinage. Manganaro (2005) offered a revised interpretation, which avoided the issue of the mint entirely. In her recent reanalysis of the inscription, Dimartino (2015) offers a convincing interpretation that the surviving text actually preserves the two separate elements of a single dossier. She suggests that, in addition to the transcript of the royal letter, the second column preserves a portion of an oath taken by the Syracusans. Although the nature of the oath is uncertain, the juxtaposition of the letter and the oath suggests that they were somehow related to one another.

[7]   For royal letters, Welles (1934) remains indispensable, with updated treatment by Bencivenni (2014) and Ceccarelli (2013: 297–330).

[8]   Regarding the fragmentary letter from Kos (*SEG* XII.370) that Herzog and Klaffenbach (1952: no. 3) initially attributed to Hieron II or Gelon, see Rigsby (1996: 121–4), who convincingly argues that the document should be associated instead with one of the Spartocid dynasts of the Bosporan kingdom, citing the work of Robert and Robert (1953: 156–7). The letter's association with Hieron was reiterated by Mattingly (2000: 45), alluding to the fact that the royal letter was inscribed on the same block (opposite side) as a letter from the Geloans at Phintias; but cf. Klaffenbach's observation that the spatial organization of these texts was immaterial; Herzog and Klaffenbach (1952: 30).

[9]   Regarding the standardized syntax and vocabulary of royal correspondence, see Ma (2000: 191–3).

[10]   Ma (2000: 240–1).

[11]   Ma (2000: 186). That the king and the Syracusans had, in fact, shared more than two decades of *euergesia* and *eucharistia* at the point in time when the letter was written is indicated by the use of the term *basileus* in the plural (A.3: *basileōn*), confirmation that the letter postdates 241/240 when Gelon was made Hieron's coregent.

[12]   Ma (2000: 200–1).

[13]   The Ptolemaic monarchs being the principal exception. Both before and after the treaty of 263, Hieron's status as a sovereign monarch was mediated directly with cities.

[14]   Livy, 24.29.7–12; *iubentibus ferociter responsum est neque mandasse sese Syracusanis ut pacem pro se cum Romanis facerent, neque teneri alienis foederibus*; "and they (the Syracusan ambassadors) received a fierce response, 'that they (the Leontinoi) had neither placed themselves at the disposal of the Syracusans to make a peace for them with the Romans, nor were they bound by the treaties of other people.'"

[15]   These treaties between king and *poleis* were presumably renewed when Hieronymos assumed kingship in 215.

[16]   Diod. 23.4; cf. Eutropius (2.19.1), who puts the number at fifty-two cities to seek alliance with Rome. Neither of these two estimates has found much consensus among modern

historians, who generally consider the total number to be inflated. See Zambon (2008: 208, n. 45) for additional discussion and bibliography on the subject.

[17] For instance, Halaisa is specifically mentioned by Diodorus as among the sixty-seven cities to send envoys to the Roman consuls in 263; cf. Diodorus (22.13.2), who previously mentioned Halaisa when its inhabitants surrendered themselves to Hieron, during one of his campaigns in northern Sicily. Other cities specifically mentioned by Diodorus as surrendering to or allying themselves with Hieron, prior to the Roman invasion of 264, include Mylai and Ameselon (22.13.1), Abakainon, Tyndaris, and Tauromenion (22.13.2).

[18] On the fortifications, see Karlsson (1993: 39–40, n. 25), who makes a similar observation about the construction of fortifications at Troina, a settlement located farther inland, on the southern side of the Nebrodi mountain range. At both sites, coinage struck by Hieron II was found among the material used to date the construction of the walls; see Trendall (1960–1: 50) for Tyndaris; and Militello (1961: 328, 350) for Troina.

[19] Livy, 24.44.4. The area of the *provincia vetus* being that fell to Rome following the First Punic War or, in other words, the rest of the island.

[20] Livy, 24.7.9: *ad provinciae regnique fines omnia convertit praesidia*. Similarly, Livy (24.29.2–4) elsewhere describes raids made by the Syracusan general Hippokrates across the provincial border (*Hippocrates enim finitima provinciae Romanae primo furtivis excursionibus vastare coepit*) just north of Leontinoi with the intention of laying waste to the countryside belonging to Rome's allies, possibly that of Katane.

[21] Synopses of the various positions taken over the past century can be found in Karlsson (1993: 41–5); Bell (1999: 257–9); and Zambon (2008: 211–21).

[22] Diod. 23.4.1. Polybius (1.17), who also mentions the treaty of 263, makes no direct reference to the extent of Hieron's territorial control.

[23] Carcopino (1914: 49); Schenck von Stauffenberg (1933: 37), who would argue that the Romans later ceded control over Kentoripe and Agyrion to Hieron in 248.

[24] Berve (1959: 38) and Karlsson (1993: 48) both reject Schenck von Stauffenberg's hypothesis that additional territories were granted to Hieron in 248. De Sensi Sestito (1977: 116–17) advocated in favor of Schenck von Stauffenberg's position, positing herself that the territories of Herbessos, Agyrion, and Kentoripe were given to Hieron by the Romans as an inducement to reaffirm their peace treaty because they feared that the king might throw his support to the side of the Carthaginians. While certainly a possibility, there is nothing that makes this hypothesis particularly plausible.

[25] Lenschau (1913: *RE* 8.2, s.v. "Hieron").

[26] Diod. 16.83.3.

[27] In particular, see Berve (1959: 38), who rightly points out that the specific passage of Diodorus refers to construction accomplished by Timoleon, even though set within a general discussion of Hieron's building program at Syracuse. Berve's position is accepted by both Goldsberry (1973: 126) and Karlsson (1993: 43).

[28] Berve (1959: 36–7). He also enlists the support of ancient *testimonia*, including that of Eutropius (2.19.1), who lists Tauromenion among the fifty-two cities that sent envoys to surrender to the Roman consuls during the siege of Kentoripe in 263, and that of Zonaras (8.9), who states that Hieron lost control over all the cities that had sought alliance with Rome in 264/263. The important question of whether or not the city continued to operate its civic mint will be addressed in Chapter 7.

[29] Kunze and Eckstein (1958: 205–9, *ed. pr.*); subsequently, *SEG* XVII, 196, *SEG* XIX, 332, and Dimartino (2006: 703–4).

[30] On the relationship between Hieron and Tauromenion, see De Sensi Sestito (1977: 113–16). Following another thread, Manganaro (1963: 21–2; 1965: 319) has suggested that Tauromenion gained independence from Hieron sometime after 241, an argument he bases on his dating of a list of civic *strategoi* (*IG* XIV.421) from Tauromenion and on the opinion that Hieron would not have supported or allowed for democratic reforms within the cities subject to his rule. Manganaro's position on this issue seems untenable given

current scholarly thinking about local civic autonomy during the Hellenistic period; see, too, Goldsberry (1973: 176, n. 98), who offers a thoughtful rebuttal to Manganaro's conclusions.

[31] See, especially, Bell (1993: 258–69); Karlsson (1993); Walthall (2011).

[32] Regarding the identification of smaller communities that certainly fell within the confines of the kingdom, see Goldsberry (1973: 126).

[33] See Bell (2007a: 195, n. 35), who lists a number of the smaller *poleis* that must have fallen to Hieronian control.

[34] See Goldsberry (1973: 126), who discusses the examples of Bidis and Talaria, which she suggests may have been villages or towns politically subordinate to a larger *polis* in the third century BCE.

[35] Sil., *Pun.* 14.198ff.; and see the discussion of the *koinon Sikeliōtān* that closes this chapter.

[36] Regarding the identification of Montagna di Marzo as the site of ancient Herbessos, see Moreschini (1992); Manganaro (1999a: 7–33).

[37] Counting Herbessos among the Hieron's subjects are Berve (1959: 37–8) and Bell (2007a: 195).

[38] This is the opinion of Schenck von Stauffenberg (1933: 45) and De Sensi Sestito (1977: 116–17).

[39] Polb. 1.18.5–9. Carthaginian control of the city was presumably short-lived, given that Hanno's forces were soon thereafter routed by the Roman troops encamped around Akragas. Any Carthaginian forces left to garrison Herbessos were likely expelled following the fall of Akragas in 262.

[40] Bell (2011: 198).

[41] Liv. 24.30.2–13, 24.35.1; cf. Manganaro (1999a: 16), following Marino (1988: 19), who argues that Livy's narrative does not offer compelling evidence to warrant the inclusion of Herbessos within Hieron's kingdom. Rather, he suggests the city was part of a *koinon* of *poleis* in southeastern Sicily that formed following the assassination of Hieronymos in 214.

[42] Liv. 25.3.6.

[43] For summary of the various excavation campaigns at Montagna di Marzo, see Mussinano (1966); Gentili (1969); Guzzardi (1999).

[44] Adamesteanu (1962; 1963) considered the grid plan to have been laid out in the fourth century, perhaps during the Timoleonic period.

[45] Guzzardi (1999: 546–7), following Mussinano (1966), considers the remains of a small theater, which has been identified in the northwest quadrant of the site believed to be the area of the agora, to be a product of the second century, based on architectural similarities with contemporary Roman theaters. While not to deny such parallels, these may have been added at a later point in time, as occurred with the theater at Morgantina, which has been definitively dated to the third century on archaeological grounds.

[46] *IGCH* 2242; initially published by Orsi (1930: 105–16). The hoard contained 319 coins, most of which were lost during the Second World War. Of that number, 258 (81%) were bronzes of Hieron II. The remaining contents were a mixture of Syracusan, Carthaginian, Roman, and Mamertine issues. The hoard was buried around the year 213/212, judging from the latest coins it contained. The date would certainly suggest that burial was connected to military violence during the Second Punic War, possibly as a result of events described by Livy. See also Manganaro (1999a: 17–18), who discusses the so-called Barrafranca Hoard (*IGCH* 2241) in the context of monetary circulation in the area of ancient Herbessos. This small bronze hoard, initially published by Orsi (1909: 67), contained 84 coins, of which 74 (88%) were Hieronian Poseidon/Trident bronzes, 5 Syracusan bronzes struck during the time of the 5th Democracy (214–212), and 5 Roman Republican fractions (4 *unciae* and 1 *sextans*), all of which were overstruck on Hieronian Poseidon/Trident flans.

47 Justin, *Epit.* 22.2.1.

48 Sjöqvist (1960a: 131) was the first to suggest that Morgantina may have been part of Hieron's kingdom. This position has been championed in recent decades by Malcolm Bell, who has published extensively on the association between Morgantina and Hieron II; see, e.g., Bell (1993; 2007a; 2007b). Accepting Morgantina's inclusion within the kingdom: Wilson (2013: 90, n. 31); cf. Campagna (2004: 155–7).

49 Bell (1988) provides the most extensive bibliography on the monuments of the agora with references to the preliminary reports of the 1950s and 1960s. For the development of this idea, see Bell (1999; 2007a: 195, n. 35).

50 Syracusan influence at Morgantina during the Early Hellenistic period also took material expression in the artwork that was both imported to and produced locally at the city; see, e.g., Phillips (1960); Bell (1981: 43–4); Bell (2011: 198–206).

51 For coinage, see Holloway (1965: 135–50); Bell (1984–5; 1995); Buttrey et al. (1989, nos. 363–8); and Walthall (2017).

52 See Walthall (2011), where the argument is first advanced that Kamarina and its territory did, in fact, fall to Hieronian control. Accepted by Rempe (2018); Brancato (2020).

53 Regarding the Mamertine incursions, see Diod. 23.1.4. This is further suggested by the discovery of two small coin hoards, composed of bronze coinage struck by Agathokles, Hiketas, and Pyrrhus, which may attest to the presence of mercenaries formerly in the employ of the Syracusan military leaders or, simply, to the circulation of Syracusan coinage in the urban center that was buried in a moment of crisis. For details about the contents and archaeological context of these hoards, see Pelagatti (2001).

54 Diod. 23.9.5.

55 Eckstein (1980: 189–91).

56 Polybius (1.24.12) also mentions the siege but omits any mention of the population being sold into slavery. In her recent study of urbanism in Roman Sicily, Pfuntner (2019: 43ff.) notes the ancient *testimonia* regarding the siege of 258, but rightly highlights the ample archaeological evidence for continued economic and demographic vitality at the settlement.

57 See, in particular, Mattioli (1995: 229–70) and Di Stefano (2001–2; 2006, 157–76), who compare the commercial vitality of Kamarina after 258 with that of Morgantina in the third century.

58 For discussion of these houses, see Pelagatti (1984–5: 686), and Uggeri (2015: 181–4).

59 Interpretation of the "West Stoa" at Kamarina is complicated by the fact that only a small portion of the building has been excavated; see Pelagatti (1984–5: 683–94). In her report, Pelagatti notes that the appellation "stoa" was given to the building due to its form and location in the city's agora, but that the limited excavation to date had yet to reveal much evidence with respect to the internal organization of space or how the building was entered from the public space. She allows for the possibility that the building may have originally served as a civic warehouse. Destruction and abandonment of the building is generally associated with the Roman capture of the city in 258, although this seems to be established largely on historical grounds. A later abandonment date remains a possibility pending the completion of the excavation and complete identification of all amphoras sealed within the building when it was demolished.

60 Lucchelli and Di Stefano (2004) provide a comprehensive catalog of the numismatic finds from the agora excavations between 1983 and 1995.

61 Lucchelli and Di Stefano (2004: 56).

62 Walthall (2011).

63 Diod. 23.9.4.

64 Sil., *Pun.* 14.198ff.

65 Lenschau (1913: 1507). Schenck von Stauffenberg (1933: 46) makes a similar argument for the late absorption of Kentoripe and Agyrion under Hieron's political authority, suggesting the Romans relinquished control over these *poleis* in 248 when renewing their peace treaty with the king. Neither position has found much favor with subsequent scholars.

66   Eutropius (2.19.1) specifically names Katane as one among the fifty-two *poleis* to voluntarily submit to Rome; Hoyos (2015: 37) suggests, rather, that the city was first captured and plundered by the Romans before establishing an alliance.

67   For discussion of Katane and its territory in the third century, see Manganaro (1996) and Brancato (2020). The decision not to relinquish the city to Hieron in 263 could have stemmed from Roman interests in keeping an open port on the island's Ionian coast. Katane would later serve as a Roman base of operations in Sicily during the Second Punic War. Numismatic evidence points to the presence of a Roman mint in operation at Katane during this period; Crawford (1985: 110). The city remained a *civitas decumana*, subject to paying the annual agricultural tithe, during the Republican period.

68   According to Strabo (6.2.4), the territory of Kentoripe was bordered by that of Katane to the east and stretched to the Symaithos river. Hieron reportedly divided the territory formally controlled by the Mamertine-held Ameselon between Kentoripe and Agyrion in 270 (Diod. 22.13.1), an act generally taken as evidence of their loyalty to Hieron at the time.

69   For an overview of settlement in the territory of Kentoripe, see Biondi (2002), who notes a discernible uptick in material collected from intensive survey dating from the latter half of the third century and first half of the second century BCE. The ancient settlement at Assoros (mod. Assoro), which lies southwest of Agyrion, was also separated from Hieronian control by the course of the Chrysas river.

70   See *supra*, n. 24.

71   Diod. 23.9.4–5; Polyb. 1.24.12.

72   Livy 24.37–9. Henna lost its privileged political status after an attempted revolt in 214, from which point it was a designated a *civitas decumana*, responsible for paying an annual tithe to Rome.

73   Diod. 24.1.7. There is no evidence to suggest that either Morgantina or Kamarina took advantage of the depopulation in the *chora* of Gela to expand their control into the neighboring territory.

74   On Dirillo river as the boundary between Gela and Kamarina, see Di Stefano (1987); Daverio Rocchi (2009).

75   Even the Attalid kingdom far eclipsed the Hieronian kingdom in terms of scale; see Hansen (1971: 166–233), who estimates the Attalid state encompassed an area of approximately 66,750 square miles (ca. 172,881 square kilometers), following the Peace of Apamea (189/8), which gave new definition to its political boundaries.

76   On the fertility of the territory of Leontinoi, see Diod. (5.2.4). Pliny (*NH* 18.10) reports implausible yields of 100-to-1 in the *ager Leontinus*, while Cicero (2 *Verr.* 3.112) gives a more credible, but still bountiful, estimate of eight-fold yields, which on a good year might even reach ten-fold.

77   Etna and timber: Diod. 14.42.4. Hieron's *Syrakosia* was reportedly constructed with timbers felled from the slopes of Mt. Etna; Athn., *Deip.* 5.206f.

78   Ma (2000: 2–3) gives the examples of Smyrna and Lampsakos, two cities that initially resisted submission to Antiochos III, but later submitted in response to threats of military violence; Liv. 33.38.1–7.

79   Referring to Hieron's campaign of 269, Diodorus (22.13.4) reports the surrender of Halaisa, Abakainon and Tyndaris (τὴν μὲν Ἅλαισαν παραδόσει προσηγάγετο, ὑπὸ δὲ τῶν Ἀβακαινίνων καὶ Τυνδαριτῶν προθύμως προσδεχθεὶς ἐκυρίευσε τῶν πόλεων τούτων).

80   Bickerman (1938).

81   The continued vitality of cities throughout the Hellenistic period is a subject for which there is a growing body of scholarship; see, especially, Billows (2007); Strootman (2011); Boehm (2018).

82   Strootman (2011: 143) makes a similar point regarding the Greek *poleis* of Asia Minor, which faced limits placed on their local autonomy by Persian satraps (largely expressed in the payment of tribute to the Persian king) long before they became subject to political domination by Alexander III and the Successor kings.

[83] This was not a payment of rent, as argued by Carcopino (1914: 67–70), since Hieron did not claim ownership over all the land within his kingdom.

[84] For excellent discussion, see Kaye (2018). See also Strootman (2011: 145, n. 15), who summarizes that "gift-giving was honourable while being taxed was tantamount to loss of *autonomia*," in regard to Antiochos II's letter to Erythrai (*OGIS* 223), wherein the king acknowledges receipt of the city's gift of gold, and in return confers benefactions upon the city, including exemption from paying tribute.

[85] For discussion, see *infra* Chapter 7, pp. 274–85.

[86] Cordiano (1997); Ferruti (2004). Archaeological and epigraphic evidence attests to the existence of *gymnasia* in at least five cities within the kingdom: Syracuse, Neaiton, Akrai, Heloros, and Tauromenion. For a recent synthesis of the available evidence for eastern Sicily, see Trümper (2018).

[87] Prag (2007).

[88] *IG* XIV.240; ISic 1060 (http://sicily.classics.ox.ac.uk/inscription/ISic1060). The date of the inscription remains a subject of debate, specifically whether it refers to a dedication made during or after Hieron's lifetime. Based on the letter forms, Manganaro (1963: 55–6) considered the inscription a product of the second century. His position has been accepted by some scholars (e.g., Lehmler 2005: 185) and considered too late by others (e.g., Cordiano (1997: 61), who prefer a third-century date. In either case, the reference to the "Hieronian" youths remains a marker of possibly royal sponsorship or intervention in the realm of military training.

[89] On the military role of *neaniskoi/neoi*, see Prag (2007: 90–1), citing earlier work by Forbes (1933) and Roesch (1982).

[90] Cordiano (1997: 95–112) posits that further evidence of royal intervention into civic governance was the institution of the dual gymnasiarchy, attested in the Neaiton inscription, which he argues was an institutional structure applied to all *poleis* by royal order during the Hieronian period. Cordiano's position has been accepted by Prag (2007: 92) but contested by Ferruti (2004: 204–5).

[91] For points of departure, see Wörrle and Zanker (1995); Boehm (2018); Börm and Luraghi (2018). Gruen (1993) captures the sense of decline. Strootman (2011), on the other hand, distills many of the arguments in support of viewing the Hellenistic period as one of continued vitality for the *polis*.

[92] For two recent contributions on the subject, see Grieb (2008) and Carlsson (2010).

[93] Strootman (2011: 146) notes similar evidence for democratic institutions at Alexandria, Pergamon, and Antioch.

[94] Based on the conventional reconstruction of the text at B.7–8: Ὅρκιον Βουλᾶς κα[ὶ στραταγῶν] | καὶ τῶν ἄλλων [πολιτᾶν]; see Dimartino (2006: 707–8).

[95] For text and interpretation of the inscription, see Herzog and Klaffenbach (1952: no. 12); Manganaro (1964: 415–19); Rigsby (1996: 148–50).

[96] Such behavior is not outside the bounds of what could be expected for a city that was politically subordinate to a king. For Hellenistic *poleis* exercising agency in diplomatic affairs and policy-making, even while politically subject to a king, see Ma (2003: 29–30); Strootman (2011: 144).

[97] Regarding the *bouleuterion* at Akrai, see Bernabò Brea et al. (1956: 44–51); for that at Morgantina, see Bell (1988: 327–31). On *bouleuteria* in the Hieronian kingdom generally, see Lehmler (2005: 169–72), who holds a decidedly less optimistic opinion about the true independence of these civic bodies, suggesting they were principally leveraged to ensure continued prosperity for the community through open displays of loyalty to the king.

[98] Manganaro (1965: 317).

[99] For opposition to Manganaro's initial restoration, see Roussel (1970: 141) and Dalheim (1977: 24, n. 24). Manganaro (1979: 19, n. 56) himself would soon after propose an alternate reading, wherein the text refers to common oaths, repeated in Manganaro (2005: 144–7). Karlsson (1993; 1997) offers the most complete presentation of evidence in support of the

existence of a *koinon* of the Sikeliotai during the reign of Hieron II; also see De Sensi Sestito (1977: 116–23), who develops Manganaro's original hypothesis.

[100]   Mackil (2013) remains an essential study on the structure and organization of Late Classical and Hellenistic *koina*.

[101]   For overview, see Smarczyk (2015).

[102]   Boehm (2018: 121–6) discusses several such regional *koina* established and fostered by the Antigonid kings.

[103]   See *supra*, n. 39.

[104]   Sil., *Pun.* 14.258–78.

[105]   Sjöqvist (1960b), who provides a concise summary of previous scholarship concerning the ΣΙΚΕΛΙΩΤΑΝ coinage and its chronology.

[106]   As observed by Sjöqvist (1960b: 57–8).

[107]   Karlsson (1993) notes further that a corporate body referred to by Cicero (2 *Verr.* 2.145ff.) as the *commune Siciliae* might have descended from the *koinon tōn Sikeliōtān*. Bell (2007a: 195–6) discusses the possible role of the *commune Siciliae* with respect to Roman administration of Sicily, including the operation of the tithe, during the first century BCE.

[108]   *Syll.*³ 427; *IG* XIV 2.

[109]   Similar pacts may have existed for the *koinon* of Athena Ilias; Boehm (2018: 122).

[110]   See, e.g., Boehm (2018: 122–3), commenting on the administrative and economic advantages derived by both Antigonos I and the cities that comprised the *koinon* of Athena Ilias.

[111]   Regarding the date of the Nesiotic League's foundation, see Meadows (2013), who convincingly argues in favor of Ptolemaic agency behind its formation; Meadows' position has been accepted by Brumbaugh (2019: 172), but cf. Buraselis (2015), who remains steadfast in his interpretation (1982: 60–75) of the League's Antigonid origins.

[112]   See, especially, the discussion by Constantakopoulou (2017: 31–57), who highlights the agency of the Nesiotic League, taking a bottom-up approach to its organization and interactions with the Ptolemies and Antigonid kings.

[113]   Karlsson (1997: 85–7). The league's council (*synedrion*) was presumably small enough to meet elsewhere, but could have certainly been accommodated by the expanded *cavea* of the theater. By way of comparison, Scholten (2000: 27) estimates the *synedrion* of the Aetolian League to have reached approximately 1,500 members by the late third century BCE, citing Larsen (1968: 198–202).

[114]   One hesitates to speculate on the objectives or frequency of such meetings, particularly for a league whose very existence remains unproven, yet the elevation of Gelon to the status of co-regent would certainly have provided an opportune moment to convene the *koinon*.

PART II

MEASURING A KINGDOM

FOUR

SEEING THE HIERONIAN STATE

The premodern state was, in many crucial respects, partially blind; it knew precious little about its subjects, their wealth, their land holdings and yields, their location, their very identity. It lacked anything like a detailed "map" of its terrain and its people. It lacked, for the most part, a measure, a metric, that would allow it to "translate" what it knew into a common standard necessary for a synoptic view.

—James Scott, *Seeing like a State*

For the state, taxation was an exercise in knowledge. By counting and classifying its subjects it could establish how much surplus it could extract from them, and simultaneously demonstrate its total knowledge and therefore its control.

—Michael Given, *The Archaeology of the Colonized*

Of the many magnificent sights described in the *Deipnosophistai* of Athenaeus of Naucratis, it is no wonder that the great ship of Hieron II, the *Syrakosia*, has long captured the attention and imagination of historians and archaeologists.[1] With its libraries, law court, gymnasium, and pleasure gardens, the vessel was nothing short of a floating city, a marvelous feat of engineering brought to life by the combination of the unmatched genius of Archimedes and the consummate wealth of the Syracusan king (Figure 4.1). And while there are good reasons to dismiss many details about the ship's outlandish scale and sumptuous adornment as simply the products of literary exaggeration, Athenaeus' anecdote may still contain an undercurrent of reality, particularly with regard to the spirit of competitive display that thrived among Hellenistic monarchs. In the contest of royal expenditure, the *Syrakosia* was certainly Hieron's bid to rank among the true heavyweights of the Hellenistic Mediterranean.

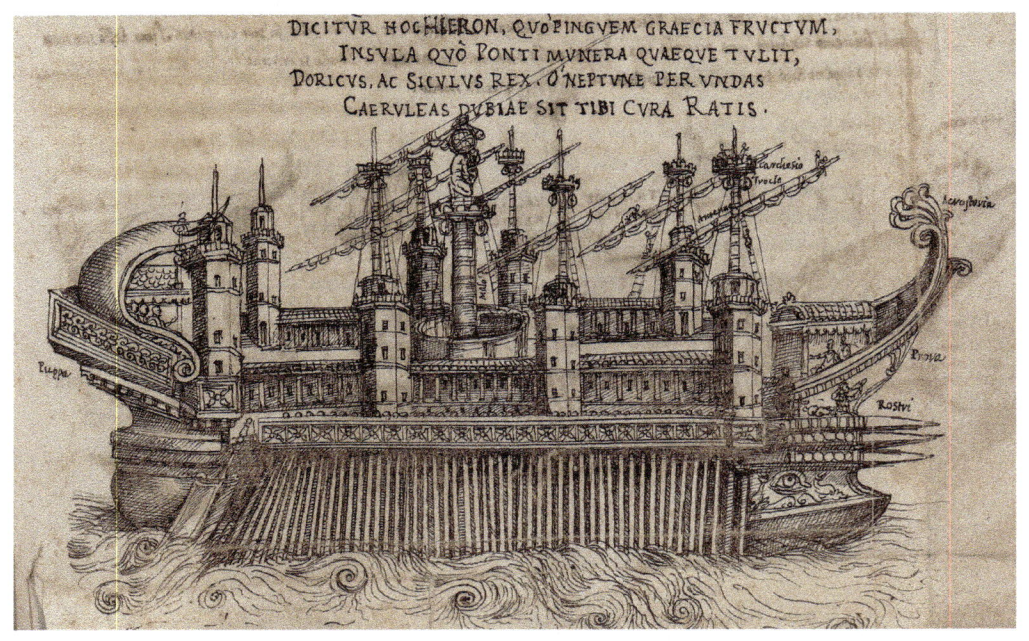

DICITVR HOC HIERON, QVO PINGVEM GRAECIA FRVCTVM,
INSVLA QVÒ PONTI MVNERA QVAEQVE TVLIT,
DORICVS, AC SICVLVS REX, O'NEPTVNE PER VNDAS
CAERVLEAS DVBIAE SIT TIBI CVRÁ RATIS.

4.1 Sketch of the *Syrakosia* by Pirro Ligorio, *Delle antichità*, Vol.12 Libb.XIII–XIIII (courtesy of the Archivio di Stato di Torino).

For as much attention as has been spent substantiating details about the size and decoration of the *Syrakosia*, far too little has been given to considering how the description of the ship makes a bold statement about the agricultural basis of Hieron's wealth.[2] In its very materiality, the *Syrakosia* reflected Hieron's ability to mobilize the vast resources of his kingdom. The ship was built using timbers from the slopes of Mt. Etna, reportedly equivalent to the amount needed to construct sixty triremes. And then there is the description of the ship's cargo, destined for Alexandria, which reads like a précis of the agricultural wealth at Hieron's disposal: "On board were loaded ninety thousand *medimnoi* of grain, ten thousand jars of Sicilian salt-fish, twenty thousand talents of wool, and other cargo amounting to twenty thousand talents." These – as much as the ivory-inlaid doors, marble bathtubs, or tessellated mosaics that we are told were also on board – were the ship's truly stupendous assets. It was a point not lost on Hieron himself, who reportedly had carved into the ship's prow an inscription that announced the *Syrakosia* carried the "gifts of a rich harvest" (*karpon piona dōrophorōn*) that the king wished to share with his allies in the Aegean. As the *Syrakosia* episode makes clear, Hieron's great wealth was measured in part by his access to the vast agricultural resources of eastern Sicily. If it grew, walked, or swam, the king would take his share. How he went about extracting this bounty – from stalk to storeroom – is the subject of this chapter.

After securing his position as king, Hieron turned his attention to harnessing the productive capacity of his new kingdom by means of taxation. While military adventurism and lavish expenditure continue to captivate our imaginations and animate conventional attitudes toward Hellenistic monarchy, there is a growing awareness of the essential role that taxation held for the operation and livelihood of the Successor kingdoms, which Arthur Eckstein has aptly described as "machines for extracting wealth from the population."[3] Kings and their courts expended no small effort in devising ever-more-efficient means of profiting from their kingdoms through a dizzying array of direct and indirect taxes.[4] For his part, Hieron used the agricultural wealth extracted from the *poleis* under his control to enrich himself and maintain his authority through outward expressions of power, whether they were maintaining a standing army, sponsoring building projects in allied cities, or sending aid in the form or grain and cash to international allies.[5]

We know precious little about the full range of taxes collected by the Hieronian state. Much of what can be inferred about the king's fiscal administration ultimately derives from casual comments found in later literary sources or rests on comparison with contemporary practices in the Successor kingdoms. At any rate, Hieron certainly appears to have operated in the spirit of his contemporaries by adopting a mixture of direct and indirect taxes, collected both in cash and in kind.[6]

Among the revenue sources that can confidently be attributed to Hieron's portfolio of wealth extraction is the collection of harbor dues (*ellimenia*; sing. *ellimenion*) from merchant ships exchanging goods at Syracuse and, very likely, other major ports around his kingdom. Following the great earthquake of 227, Hieron granted Rhodian traders carrying goods from Syracusan ports an exemption (*ateleia*) from these harbor duties, which may have been on the order of 5 percent of the total value of goods imported and exported from the kingdom.[7] It follows that if Hieron collected customs fees on goods being imported and exported into the kingdom by sea, similar taxes were collected on goods entering or leaving the kingdom by overland routes as well.[8] The Roman practice of collecting a pasture tax (*scriptura*) on heads of cattle in Sicily may very well have its origins in third-century Hieronian law.[9] Given the enduring importance of herding to the agricultural economy of eastern Sicily, there is every reason to suspect that Hieron derived a portion of his revenue from taxing animal husbandry within the kingdom. This is certainly the impression given by Athenaeus' report that some 20,000 talents of wool were loaded onto the *Syrakosia* bound for Alexandria.[10]

Undoubtedly the most important source of revenue for Hieron was the collection of taxes on agricultural production within the kingdom, a mainstay of imperial resource extraction in the Classical and Hellenistic Mediterranean. By the early fourth century, the Athenians sustained their expanding urban population through the collection of an annual harvest tax from their cleruchies on Imbros, Lemnos, and Skyros.[11] Hellenistic kings regularly collected agricultural taxes in kind, amassing for themselves astonishing stores of grain and other foodstuffs, which they converted into both financial and political capital.[12] Taxes derived from land and agricultural production were considered the principal source of revenue within the royal economy, at least according to the author of the *Oikonomika*, a work of late fourth- or early third-century date, written with reference to the fiscal administration of the Seleucid kingdom.[13] Testimony of the variety of revenue generated by royal taxation on agricultural production can be found in the text of a fragmentary inscription from Aigai in Aolis, a city that passed back and forth between Attalid and Seleucid control throughout the course of the third century.[14] The inscription in question refers to payments made in kind to the royal treasury, specifically listing taxes collected on cereal production, on the harvest from fruit trees, on flocks of sheep and goats, and on the honey produced by beehives. It even specifies that a portion taken from the hunting of wild animals, specifically one leg from each deer and boar killed, was owed to the king. Should such a decree ever be discovered in Syracuse, it would only confirm much of what we already know about the agrarian wealth available to Hieron.

PROLEGOMENON TO THE HIERONIAN TITHE

During the Hieronian regime, Sicily's famed agricultural resources were, for the first time, comprehensively assessed, taxed, and mobilized under a centralized administrative system. Hieron, of course, did not introduce the imperial mode of agricultural taxation to Sicily. This distinction should fall to the Carthaginians and Syracusans, who had for centuries extracted various forms of revenue from the communities under their political and military control. Aside from a few brief notices in the text of Diodorus, we know very little about the nature of assessment and collection that took place in the Sicilian territory subject to Carthaginian control.[15] Fortunately, we are better informed, if only just slightly, regarding methods of resource extraction from the Syracusan-controlled territories in eastern Sicily during the Archaic and Classical periods. Judging from surviving literary sources, large-scale and systematic exploitation of agricultural labor developed early in the city's history, as cultural and wealth inequities grew between an aristocratic landholding faction of the population and the burgeoning lower class, comprising both Greeks and a subjugated population called the *Kyllirioi*, which may have been a group composed of the indigenous "Sikel" inhabitants of southeastern Sicily.[16]

During the ascendency of the Deinomenid tyrants in the first half of the fifth century, Syracuse sought to exploit the resources of an expanding territorial dominion that came to include the city's subcolonies (e.g., Akrai, Heloros) along with several formally autonomous Greek *poleis* (e.g., Leontinoi, Megara Hyblaia).[17] After 450, this territorial control expanded to include a large swath of the island's *mesogeia*, territory that formerly had been in the control of the Sikel leader Douketios.[18] Throughout the fifth century, the revenues collected from this large and agriculturally productive swath of southeastern Sicily brought the Deinomenid tyrants and the city's aristocratic element renowned wealth, which they profitably diverted to military endeavors and grand architectural projects.[19] Following their conquest of the Sikel-held interior, for instance, Diodorus relates that the Syracusans began to collect heavy tribute (*phoros hadros*) from these communities in order to fund their planned military expansion across the island.[20] It is within this context that we can situate the Herodotean account of the Athenian and Spartan embassy to the Syracusan tyrant, Gelon, in the lead-up to Xerxes' invasion of Greece in 480.[21] As the story goes, in return for supreme military command of the Hellenic forces, Gelon offered to provide enough grain and rations to feed the entire Greek army for the duration of the war – an enormous amount by any estimate. Although of dubious historicity, the episode remains a forceful testimonial that Gelon's wealth was predicated on the extraction of agricultural resources from the communities under his rule and, furthermore, that the control of these resources could be effectively translated into political authority and military power.[22] Following the collapse of the Deinomenid dynasty in 465, the Syracusans restored their democratic constitution, initiating what is commonly referred to as the "Second Syracusan Democracy" (465–405). Even under this new dispensation, the Syracusans maintained their hegemonic interests in the region, albeit over a reduced territory.

Surviving literary sources that describe this period of Syracusan ascendency reveal little about the mechanisms put in place to accomplish such large-scale resource extraction. Scholars have long wondered whether it is to the period of the Deinomenid tyrants or the Second Democracy that we should seek the origins of the proverbial Syracusan *dekatē* (lit. one-tenth).[23] Later ancient authors would come to associate the phrase "ἡ Συρακωσίων δεκάτη" (*Syrakōsiōn dekatē*) with great excesses of wealth, but offer few details about the mechanisms behind this mode of extraction, the regularity of its enforcement, or even the date when it was first instituted.[24] The earliest known reference to the Syracusan *dekatē* belongs to a fragment attributed to the third-century Atthidographer Demon, which relates that the proceeds of the *dekatē* were used by the Syracusans for the maintenance of religious sites and festivals, but offers no indication as to the regularity of such payments.[25] Lacking secure testimony regarding these early efforts taken by Syracuse to exploit the agricultural resources of their territorial empire, scholars have been left to speculate whether such extractions involved regular payments, in the form of an annual tithe, or were collected only in extraordinary circumstances as tribute payments (*phoros, aparchē*).[26]

It is generally assumed that some form of agricultural tax was collected by the fourth-century Syracusan tyrant Dionysius I as well as by his son and successor, Dionysius II, although explicit literary or material evidence to the fact is lacking. The author of the pseudo-Aristotelian *Oikonomika*, for instance, describes multiple efforts taken by the elder Dionysius to generate capital revenue from the Syracusan populace in order to fund his military escapades.[27] These efforts, perhaps better described as "schemes" due to their reliance on fraud and deception, reportedly included forcing the Syracusan aristocracy to make compulsory contributions of jewelry and precious goods into a temple-building fund, which Dionysius plundered for his own use.[28] Regardless of where opinions fall on the veracity of any single anecdote attributed to Dionysius in the *Oikonomika*, it is worthwhile to note that his taxes are typically presented as extraordinary incidents, almost uniformly relying on some form of duplicity, and as orchestrated to collect revenue for a particular purpose and not as part of any systematic effort to extract resources on a regular basis.

Equally little is known about the fiscal policies of Hieron's immediate predecessors. Agathokles, of course, required vast amounts of grain and cash to support his campaigns against the Carthaginians, both in Sicily and in North Africa.[29] It is unclear whether the king acquired these resources through a regularized system of taxation or from the ad hoc collection of tribute in the lead-up to each new campaign.[30] Judging from surviving literary accounts, the Agathoklean fiscal regime appears to have hewn closely to the Dionysian model by embracing episodic plunder rather than systematic assessment.[31] Pyrrhus' sojourn in Sicily was all too brief and tumultuous to have allowed the king to institute any form of regularized assessment or collection. The king, however, was certainly swift in demanding tribute from the cities of eastern Sicily. These burdensome demands just as swiftly led to the collapse of support for his presence on the island.[32]

Although our evidence is far from complete, Syracusan efforts geared toward extracting agricultural resources from the territories under their political and military sway during the Classical and Early Hellenistic periods show few signs of having achieved the complexity or sophistication of the royal tax administration that developed under Hieron II. Earlier efforts taken by Syracusan rulers bear the hallmarks of irregularity and reliance on exceptional tactics backed by threats of violence, which are often described by ancient sources as tantamount to piratical raids on the material wealth of the Syracusan aristocracy. This is not to say that regular taxation could not have formed part of the Syracusans' mode of imperial extraction prior to the reign of Hieron II, simply that the surviving literary and material evidence shows no sign that these earlier methods ever rose to the level of administrative oversight characteristic of the Hieronian period.

Hieron's great accomplishment was to introduce an unprecedented degree of structure and organization to the collection and administration of agricultural taxation in Sicily. This meant that while the Hieronian system may have shared a passing resemblance to antecedents employed by the Syracusan rulers of the Classical and Early Hellenistic periods, it did not simply adopt or adapt a preexisting Syracusan practice. Rather, Hieron's tax laws bore a striking resemblance to the expansive fiscal regimes that were developing in the Successor kingdoms.[33] This is not a novel observation; for more than a century, in fact, scholars have taken note of the affinity that the Hieronian tax administration shared with contemporary systems of royal taxation found within the Ptolemaic and Seleucid kingdoms. These royal tax systems share many similarities in their basic structural and operational elements, including their reliance on tax farming and the collection of a proportional harvest tax.

Scholars have long sought to identify the source for Hieron's tax system.[34] Most, by far, have seen elements of Ptolemaic institutions in the Hieronian system, a position championed in the early twentieth century by Michael Rostovtzeff and Jérôme Carcopino. The publication of the Ptolemaic *Revenue Laws* papyri (*P.Rev.*) in 1896 by B. P. Grenfell undoubtedly influenced both historians in making this association.[35] At the time, the details of the newly discovered Ptolemaic law, documented by the *P.Rev.* dossier, followed the contours of what had long been known about the Hieronian tithe from surviving literary sources (discussed below). The assumption then followed that Hieron must have adopted the tax laws of Ptolemy II, an opinion fully embraced by Carcopino, writing that "*c'est donc le roi de Syracuse qui a copié le roi Egyptien.*"[36] While consensus long held in favor of Carcopino's position, a countercurrent developed later in the century with the groundbreaking study of Hieron's kingship by Giovanna De Sensi Sestito, who argued for less direct dependence between the Ptolemaic and Hieronian systems of taxation, going so far as to advance the originality of the Hieronian law. For De Sensi Sestito, the Hieronian laws were a local response to the particular socio-economic and political conditions of his Sicilian kingdom and, thus, could not have been simply a copy of the Ptolemaic laws.[37]

This question of dependence on the Ptolemaic system has several implications, not least for establishing the date of the Hieronian tithe. If Carcopino was correct, Hieron's law would necessarily postdate the incorporation of practices like tax farming in the Ptolemaic code, which is generally believed to have taken places in Egypt by the year 259 at the very latest.[38] There is of course no doubt that Hieron enjoyed a close relationship with the Ptolemaic kings and may have even received financial support from Ptolemy II during his campaigns against the Mamertines in the 260s.[39] It is not out of the question that the fledgling king sought direct input from the Ptolemaic court for the institution and design of his tax laws. If, however, the Hieronian laws were independently conceived, the institution of the tax administration in eastern Sicily could have begun as early as 269, when Hieron's *basileia* was recognized by the Syracusans and other *poleis* in eastern Sicily.[40]

Rather than frame the question in terms of direct or indirect influence, a more profitable approach may be to view both the Ptolemaic and Hieronian tax laws as products of a common tradition, one that had gained ground in the wider Mediterranean region as the first two generations of Successor kings began to grapple with the need to generate reliable revenue from their respective kingdoms through nonmilitary means. Malcolm Bell has argued in favor of decoupling the two institutions, suggesting that the Ptolemaic and Hieronian systems found common inspiration from tax-farming structures that had developed on mainland Greece, such as that codified in the Athenian Grain-Tax Law of 374/373.[41] The argument for decoupling the Ptolemaic and Hieronian laws is further supported by Jean Bingen's reevaluation of the Ptolemaic *P.Rev.* papyrus. Bingen observed that the procedures and regulations outlined in the dossier belonged, in fact, to a collection of various documents that reveal the gradual refashioning of Ptolemaic fiscal policies over time. These were not, he stresses, evidence of a fully developed or unified "code" issued by the central administration.[42] Carcopino, greatly influenced by Grenfell's initial publication and analysis of the *P.Rev.* dossier, considered the papyri evidence of a fine-tuned apparatus at work in Egypt that could naturally serve as the model for the Hieronian system. If, as now seems to be the case, these documents instead attest to a rather different situation in Egypt, where fiscal policies were still undergoing development and adaptation well into the 260s, the notion that Hieron copied a Ptolemaic model is decidedly less appealing. Perhaps then, we are dealing with two systems that developed largely independent of one another, but which nevertheless adopted common administrative elements (e.g., reliance on tax farming, the collection of a proportional tax, etc.) to deal with a shared problem, namely, how to tax a territorial kingdom.

Leaving behind this thorny question of *Quellenforschung*, there remains the profitable discussion of the marked similarities between the Hieronian and Ptolemaic laws. These shared qualities are particularly evident at the operational level, where we see common provisions like the annual auctioning of the right to collect taxes and the reliance on an extensive administrative apparatus (officials, contracts completed in triplicate, etc.). Where the Hieronian administration most resembled its Ptolemaic counterpart was arguably in its reach and scale. The institutional restructuring of the political landscape brought about by the creation of the Hieronian kingdom led to the introduction of a new, centralized state that overlay the fragmented mosaic of *poleis* in southeastern Sicily. The fiscal well-being of this new state required a far greater degree of administrative oversight and royal intervention at the *polis* level than ever before in Sicily.

SOURCES ON THE HIERONIAN TITHE

The mass of documentary material – tax registers, contracts, receipts, and so on – that was once created to serve as the informational basis of Hieron's third-century tax administration no longer survives today. In our attempts to reconstruct the underlying structural and operational elements of the Hieronian tithe, we cannot rely on detailed papyrological dossiers or an extensive epigraphic corpus, as is possible for many Successor kingdoms. Nor do we have recourse to consult Hieron's own agricultural treatise, which may have detailed aspects of the king's agrarian laws alongside more typical agronomic themes.[43] In fact, that any details of Hieron's agrarian laws are known to us today is owed largely to the survival of the *De frumento*, the third book of the second *actio* of Marcus Tullius Cicero's prosecutorial speeches against the infamously rapacious Gaius Verres, who served as provincial governor of Sicily between 73 and 71.[44] Throughout the *De frumento*, Cicero details the myriad abuses perpetrated against Sicilian cultivators by then-governor Verres and his henchmen. It is from this bountiful field of transgressions that scholars have gleaned the essential details of provincial taxation in Sicily during the late Republic.[45] In Cicero's day, and surely in the preceding century, the collection of laws governing the Sicilian tithe and its administration was known as the *lex Hieronica*, named, as Cicero reminds his audience, after the original author of the laws. The Romans, recognizing the efficiency of the Hieronian tithe, had simply adopted the laws established during the reign of Hieron II and applied them to the whole of the island, or, at least, so we are told by Cicero, who states in his second speech against Verres:

> videte nunc maiorum sapientiam, qui cum Siciliam tam opportunum subsidium belli atque pacis ad rem publicam adiunxissent, tanta cura Siculos tueri ac retinere voluerunt ut non modo eorum agris vectigal novum nullum imponerent, sed ne legem quidem venditionis decumarum neve vendundi aut tempus aut locum commutarent, ut certo tempore anni, ut ibidem in Sicilia, denique ut lege Hieronica venderent. voluerunt eos in suis rebus ipsos interesse, eorumque animos non modo lege nova sed ne nomine quidem legis novo commoveri.

> See now the wisdom of our ancestors, who, when they had added Sicily, so valuable an assistant both in war and peace, to the republic, were so careful to defend the Sicilians and to retain them in their allegiance, that they not only imposed no new tax upon their lands, but did not even alter the law of putting up for sale the contracts of the farmers of the tenths, or the time or place of selling them; so that they were to put them up for sale at the regular time of year, at the same place, in Sicily – in short, in every respect as the law of Hieron directed; they permitted them still to manage their own affairs, and were not willing that their minds should be disturbed even by a new name to a law, much less by an actual new law.[46]

Even allowing for artistic license, Cicero's statement makes clear that the Romans, on seizing control of Sicily, made few – if any – substantive modifications to the underlying structural and operational aspects of the Hieronian tithe.[47] Given the centrality of themes involving the exploitation of Sicily's agricultural resources to narratives of Rome's imperial expansion, scholars have long been drawn to Cicero's description of the *lex Hieronica*.[48] Jérôme Carcopino was the first scholar to systematically address the question of identifying which elements of the first-century law, as it was described by Cicero, belonged to the original third-century version.[49] Stripping away the accretions from two centuries of Roman rule is made possible by the fact that Cicero, although describing the law of his day to an audience of contemporaries, framed many of Verres' abuses as stemming from the intentional distortion of laws and norms that had been operative since the time of Hieron II. To follow Cicero's argument, it was Verres himself who modified the original laws to better suit his predatory behavior. Cicero (2. *Verr.* 3.38–9), for example, held that Verres had passed an edict that required cultivators to appear before any court on the island that was chosen by the tax farmer, when a dispute arose over their tithe contract. Not only did this edict run counter to the *lex Hieronica* and the customs set forth by previous Roman governors; Cicero claimed that the modification was expressly intended to allow corrupt tax farmers to exort hapless cultivators. Thus, in presenting anecdotes and testimony regarding the many ways that Verres had violated or manipulated the *lex Hieronica*, Cicero leaves us a remarkably detailed account of how the tithe was administered in Sicily from as far back as the reign of Hieron II.

For more than a century, Carcopino's methods of excavating the *De frumento* have remained the most viable and popular scholarly approach to reconstructing Hieron's third-century system of taxation.[50] This is even as some have rightly cast doubt on the reliability of Cicero's testimony, given that the orator's prosecutorial aims might not have always led him to deliver a wholly objective account, free of embellishment or amplification.[51] While caution is always advisable when working from ancient literary material, it remains the case that many of the structural and operational aspects of the first-century *lex Hieronica* described in the *De frumento* share unmistakable parallels with well-documented elements of royal fiscal administration of Ptolemaic Egypt. Where such overlap exists, it is reasonable to posit that these features belonged to the third-century Hieronian law.

A further avenue of inquiry, one that has shown promise in recent decades, foregrounds the archaeological record as a means of accessing new sources of data on the operation of the tithe in third-century Sicily, rather than working backward from a first-century text.[52] Much of what follows in the subsequent chapters takes this approach, giving priority to the material remains that we can plausibly associate with Hieron's royal administration and the taxation of agricultural goods, in particular. In developing an archaeology of the Hieronian tithe, we can appeal not only to the artifacts involved (e.g., official measuring devices, seals, coinage) but also to the spaces where the procedures or rituals of taxation were performed (e.g., threshing floors, state granaries).

STRUCTURAL FEATURES OF THE HIERONIAN TITHE

Before surveying the operational details of the Hieronian tithe, let us first consider the broader principles that served as scaffolding for its day-to-day operation, what I will refer to as its structural elements. Here, analysis will benefit from the work of economists and political scientists, who have advanced more sweeping theories to explain how rulers and states throughout history went about extracting revenue from the populations subject to their authority. In this respect, Margaret Levi's theory of predatory rule offers a heuristic lens through which to view the decision-making behind the Hieronian system to extract revenue from taxation.[53] Levi's theory holds that rulers will attempt to maximize state revenue, but are constrained in their capacity to do so by several factors, which ultimately determine the nature of the "revenue production policies" adopted and enforced by the state. A powerful, autocratic ruler, for instance, will adopt a different set of policies than a ruler whose authority is constitutionally limited.

In *On Rule and Revenue*, Levi identifies three principal constraints that shape revenue production policies. The first factor constraining a ruler's ability to maximize revenue is his bargaining power relative to that of his constituents, on whose compliance a ruler's authority is legitimated and sustained. Accordingly, a ruler may choose not to adopt policies that would generate the most revenue for the state because doing so would risk alienating constituents and potentially undermine his ability to maintain power. The greater the constituents' bargaining power, the less likely it is for a ruler to adopt revenue-maximizing policies at their expense, since as Levi aptly notes, "*[h]olding* the office of ruler is the *sine qua non* of rule" after all.[54] Rulers are further constrained in their choice of revenue sources by what Levi refers to as "transaction costs," or the costs involved in implementing and enforcing revenue-generating policies, which, in essence, would be debited against the value of the potential revenue. Transaction costs are accrued by the state when efforts are made to assess the value of available revenue sources, monitor compliance among taxpayers, and enforce uniform standards of measurement. Again, a ruler's power relative to that of his constituents will directly influence the transaction costs involved in implementing a given set of revenue-generating policies. A stronger ruler with fewer limits placed on his authority might be able to monitor and enforce compliance more effectively in areas where a weaker ruler could not, thereby generating greater revenue for himself. Alternatively, a ruler whose authority extends over vast or difficult-to-govern areas might be more open to policies that generate less revenue for the state but place more of the financial burden of compliance monitoring onto private actors. The third constraint faced by a ruler is what Levi calls the "discount rate," which she describes as "the extent to which [a ruler] values the future relative to the present. The higher the discount rate, the less concern for the future."[55] This has a direct bearing on the choice of revenue policy, according to Levi's model, which holds that rulers with higher discount rates will aim to maximize revenue without placing much concern on the lasting impacts that these policies may have in the long term, whether for the security of their rule or for the welfare of the state. Rulers threatened by instability during times of war, for instance, might seek to maximize revenue in the short term through burdensome extractions levied on their constituents, while those who enjoy the prospect of long-term security are more likely to adopt less exploitative means of generating revenue, so as to continue on better terms with their constituents.

With Levi's theory of predatory rule in mind, I hope to demonstrate that a similar set of constraints might very well have played a decisive role in the shaping Hieron's fiscal policies, particularly with regard to the three principal structural elements of the tithe system, namely, the proportional rate of taxation, the reliance on tax farmers, and the administrative checks put in place to protect both the taxpayers and tax collectors. Let us consider each of these features in turn.

A Proportional Harvest Tax

One of the first decisions facing the king and his advisors was to determine the method and rate of taxation. Following Levi's thesis, Hieron's choice of revenue extraction should reflect a balance between his "predatory" interest in extracting maximum revenue from his kingdom and the existential need to maintain the loyalty of the *poleis* that recognized his authority as *basileus*. Imposing a tax burden that was deemed excessive by his subjects could lead to instability and risk the reliability of his revenue sources or, worse yet, the collapse of his regime. Hieron had need only reflect on Pyrrhus' recent failure in Sicily as evidence that overly burdensome demands for revenue risked diminishing one's claims to legitimacy and undermined the general support among the *poleis* of eastern Sicily. The king and his advisors needed to strike a balance, such that the constituents of the Hieronian state were obliged to hand over both their economic resources (i.e., agricultural produce) and political resources (i.e., acknowledgment of Hieron's *basileia*) to the king while viewing this transaction as one that garnered them favorable compensation in terms of the protection and benefactions gained. Such considerations may well have been behind the decision to make a proportional tithe the backbone of Hieron's fiscal regime.

The Hieronian tithe was a proportional harvest tax collected in kind on the annual production of cereals, wine, oil, and other agricultural goods (i.e., legumes, pulses, tree fruits) within the kingdom.[56] Cultivators paid a fixed percentage (10%) on their total annual production. This meant that the actual amount paid by the individual cultivator to the state was subject to change from year to year, depending on the total amount that one took in during the harvest. In years of poor harvest, collecting a percentage of total harvest was far less burdensome on cultivators than a land tax, by which a fixed amount was collected – irrespective of the total harvest – based on the amount of land put under cultivation (e.g., X *medimnoi* of grain per unit of land under cultivation).[57] Understood in terms of the decision calculus propounded by Levi, this relatively humane tax rate (particularly when compared with tax rates collected by some of his contemporaries) suggests that Hieron set higher store on compliance than on aggressive assessment strategies.

When compared with taxes collected by other Hellenistic states, which might regularly take upward of one-third of the annual harvest, the Hieronian tithe was not particularly oppressive.[58] During the reign of Ptolemy II, by comparison, tenants who cultivated royal land paid a combination of proportional tax, amounting to one-sixth of the harvest on vineyards and orchards, and a fixed land tax, which had to be paid at a uniform rate in years of surplus or shortfall.[59] Situating this in terms of Levi's model, the comparatively low tax rate collected on agricultural produce in Sicily may reflect a fairly modest level of bargaining power on Hieron's part vis-à-vis the *poleis* that constituted his kingdom. Unlike the Ptolemies, who found themselves in control over a kingdom comprising hundreds of small communities that had long been subject to a powerful central authority, Hieron was ultimately constrained in his profit-seeking behavior by the fact that his kingdom was composed of *poleis* that continued to exercise a relatively high degree of autonomy even after recognizing his *basileia*.

Reliance on Tax Farming

A second essential structural element of the Hieronian tax system was its reliance on tax farmers, or private contractors who purchased the right to collect the tithe on agricultural production owed to the state. Under Hieronian law, tax farmers annually bid on contracts, which granted them the right to collect the tithe on a specific product (e.g., wheat, wine, oil) in a specific territory (e.g., Syracuse, Akrai, Morgantina). They did so with the expectation of making a profit when the total taxes collected from cultivators exceeded the amount paid to win the contract.

Reliance on tax farming as a revenue-generating policy for the state likely found its origins in the second millennium BCE.[60] In the sixth century, tax farming took on a far more important role in the fiscal administration of the Babylonian kingdom, whose rulers faced challenges extracting revenue from their expansive territorial empire. The practice further developed under Achaemenid rule from where it most likely spread to the Greek world by the early fourth century.[61] This is most clearly documented at Athens, where epigraphic evidence attests to the operation of a well-developed tax-farming system designed to ensure a steady supply of grain for the urban populace from the Athenian cleruchies on Imbros, Lemnos, and Skyros.[62] Tax farming found expression on a grand scale during the Hellenistic period, due to its adoption by several of the Successor kings, whose vast territorial empires and constant need for resources provided the ideal conditions for the institution.[63]

To the best of our knowledge, tax farming made its debut in Sicily during the Hieronian period, a fact that will have greater significance in the subsequent discussion of the wider institutional changes brought about by the introduction of a royal tax administration. Here too, Levi's model of predatory rule offers valuable insight into the conditions that may have informed Hieron's decision to farm out the collection of the agricultural tithe – his principal source of royal revenue – to private individuals. Levi specifically addresses the practice of tax farming in the context of the Roman Republic, arguing that the choice to sell off the rights to collect taxes was a solution preferred by rulers who wished to reduce transaction costs tied up both in the collection of taxes and in the monitoring of compliance among the taxpaying populace.[64] While Levi explores the rise and fall of the institution in the context of the changeover from the Republic to Principate, her observations are equally insightful for thinking through the integration of tax farming into the fiscal regimes of Hellenistic kingdoms.[65]

The farming-out of tax collection to private actors played a central role in the fiscal administration of the Hieronian state. As an alternative to centralized bureaucratic collection, the institution brought about many advantages for the king, such as reducing state expenditure associated with the monitoring of compliance.[66] This burden was partially placed on the tax farmers, who held a keen financial interest in ensuring that noncompliance among cultivators was kept at a minimum. This was useful even for a relatively small territorial kingdom like Hieron's in southeastern Sicily, where a small army of royal agents would be needed simply to monitor compliance.[67] Perhaps a more attractive benefit to the king was that the tax-farming structure guaranteed predictable revenue for the state, while shifting financial risk onto the tax farmers, who offered sureties of payment even in the event of a disastrous harvest.[68] Hieron took a small loss in revenue (i.e., the amount collected by the tax farmer over the amount that was bid) for assurance of payment.[69] Political stability, especially following the conclusion of his treaty with Rome in 263, would have afforded Hieron a low discount rate, to borrow Levi's term, such that he would be more willing to incur a small reduction in his profit margin in return for reliable income.

The application of Levi's theory to explain the adoption of tax farming in antiquity has drawn criticism for its focus on the profit-maximizing interests of rulers while overlooking other political or social factors that might motivate them to adopt certain revenue-generating policies. Joseph Manning highlights this in the case of Ptolemaic Egypt, arguing that the decision to introduce tax farming stemmed, in part, from efforts taken by Ptolemy II to encourage the settlement of Greeks in Egypt. In Manning's view, tax farming was not simply an opportunity for Ptolemy II to efficiently maximize short-term revenue; it was also an effective mechanism for solidifying his political base.[70]

The political landscape of eastern Sicily during the Hellenistic period – for centuries home to independent Greek *poleis* – was, of course, quite distinct from that of Ptolemaic Egypt. Still, Manning's conclusions about the political factors at play in the adoption of tax farming may be profitably applied to the Hieronian context. Hieron's challenge was not to attract more Greeks to his kingdom but to maintain the support of the powerful aristocratic families that had long exercised authority within the *poleis* forming his kingdom. As demonstrated by his own marriage to Philistis and by the marriage of his daughters to the sons of elite Syracusan families, Hieron appears to have found it more politically expedient to mollify these potential political rivals than to attempt to eradicate them. In this respect, the decision to farm out tax collection to private agents makes perfect sense. The tax-farming system aligned the interests of the king and local elites by creating shared sources of revenue within a framework that allowed aristocratic families to both profit and project their status.[71]

Here an analogy from early modern Europe may prove illuminating. In his analysis of royal salt taxes (*gabelle*) collected around Nice during the sixteenth century, Matthew Vester found that the dukes of Savoy, who controlled the region, had powerful political motives for choosing to farm out the *gabelle* rather than directly administer their assessment and collection.[72] Vester concluded that while the dukes might have stood to generate greater revenues through direct administration, they chose to farm out the collection in order to conciliate elite political actors in the region, who might otherwise have found cause to challenge their authority if deprived of the opportunity to benefit from the wealth and status that the tax-farming system conferred.[73] Hieron's system could be viewed in a similar light. Elites from all the *poleis* of eastern Sicily could leverage their financial resources to profit from the new tax system by becoming tax farmers. As we will discuss below, the nature of Hieron's tax laws meant that prospective tax farmers were able to bid on the right to collect tithes in the territory of their home *polis*, where they would benefit from local knowledge and contacts, as well as those of all the other *poleis* within the kingdom. By permitting local elites to share in the profit from taxation, Hieron vested these minor political actors (and potential rivals) with a stake in maintaining the well-being of the system and, ultimately, his authority as king. In this way, the royal tax institutions established under Hieron played an essential role in promoting political stability.[74]

Protecting the Actors

Ensuring that both cultivators and tax farmers complied with the laws governing taxation was the underlying rationale for the third structural feature of the Hieronian tithe, legal protections for the main actors. In *On Rule and Revenue*, Levi introduces the concept of "quasi-voluntary compliance" among taxpayers, which she further defines as "*voluntary* because taxpayers choose to pay. It is *quasi*-voluntary because the noncompliant are subject to coercion – if they are caught."[75] Rulers bring about quasi-voluntary compliance through a combination of legal incentives and punishments. According to Levi, quasi-voluntary compliance is best achieved when a ruler can demonstrate that a tax system is not overly exploitative and has a perceived benefit for the constituents. Most importantly, a ruler must demonstrate that the benefits of participation, as well as the sanctions following from nonparticipation, are fairly applied to all constituents.[76] In order to balance these expectations, a ruler needs to discourage freeloading (i.e., the evasion of payment) by instituting clear punishments or disincentives for noncompliant subjects, while at the same time establishing protections for those subjects who voluntarily comply. The Hieronian tithe system would have involved protecting cultivators from predatory tax farmers as well as punishing cultivators who attempted to avoid payment.

Here, Levi's model finds corroboration in Cicero's statement at the outset of the *De frumento*, where the prosecutor argues that, at least in principle, the Hieronian tax administration was initially devised to provide the utmost protections to those who complied and equally severe punishments to those who did not. It is worth quoting the passage here in its entirety:

> tu, homo minimi consili, nullius auctoritatis, iniussu populi ac senatus, tota Sicilia recusante, cum maximo detrimento atque adeo exitio vectigalium totam Hieronicam legem sustulisti? at quam legem corrigit, iudices, atque adeo totam tollit. acutissime ac diligentissime scriptam, quae lex omnibus custodiis subiectum aratorem decumano tradidit, ut neque in segetibus neque in areis neque in horreis neque in amovendo neque in exportando frumento grano uno posset arator sine maxima poena fraudare decumanum. scripta lex ita diligenter est ut eum scripsisse appareat qui alia vectigalia non haberet, ita acute ut Siculum, ita severe ut tyrannum; qua lege Siculis tamen arare expediret; nam ita diligenter constituta sunt iura decumano ut tamen ab invito aratore plus decuma non possit auferri.

> [B]ut you (Verres), a man of no wisdom, of no authority, without the bidding of the people or senate, while all Sicily objected, abrogated the whole law of Hieron, to the greatest injury and even destruction of the revenue. But what law is this, O judges, which he (Verres) amends, or rather totally abrogates? A law framed with the greatest acuteness and the greatest diligence, which gives up the cultivator of the land to the collector of the tenths, guarded by so many securities, that neither in the fields of grain, nor on the threshing floors, nor in the barns, nor while removing his corn privately, nor while carrying it away openly, can the cultivator defraud the collector of one single grain without the severest punishment. The law has been framed with such care, that it is plain that a man framed it who had no other revenues; with such acuteness that it was plain that he was a Sicilian; with such severity, that he was evidently a tyrant: by this law, however, cultivating the land was an advantageous trade for the Sicilian; for the laws for the collectors of the tenths were also drawn up so carefully that it is not possible for more than the tenth to be extorted from the cultivator against his will.[77]

While perhaps overly confident in the structural efficiency of the tithe administration, Cicero nevertheless describes a system that appears to have been designed to incentivize quasi-voluntary compliance from all actors by the equitable application of protections and punishments. Throughout the *De frumento*, Cicero even appears to foreshadow Levi by emphasizing that the successful administration of the *lex Hieronica* had long relied on the willingness (*voluntas*) of both cultivators and tax farmers to comply with the letter of the law. This equilibrium was undermined during the governorship of Verres, whose special edicts had supplanted *voluntas* with threats, violence, and compulsion. The outcome, so Cicero told his audience in Rome, was a steep decline in agricultural productivity across the island, as cultivators chose to abandon their fields rather than fall victim to exploitation and unchecked abuse from tax farmers like Apronius.[78]

As Cicero's testimony makes clear, state officials played a vital role in promoting *voluntas*. Hieron's third-century laws presumably established provisions that called for royal officials to settle disputes between cultivators and tax farmers, like those that eventually drove cultivators off their land during the governorship of Verres.[79] From the king's perspective, ensuring the swift resolution of conflicts that arose over the assessment and payment of the tithe was critical to maintaining operational efficiency and ensuring that royal storerooms brimmed with the proceeds of the harvest. When dissatisfaction among constituents leads to noncompliance, the state risks losing critical revenue.[80] By the same token, intervention by royal administrators played an equally important role in maintaining confidence in the fairness of the tithe administration, thus discouraging corruption on the part of both cultivators and tax farmers.

Here, we could look to the Ptolemaic kingdom to better understand what form these provisions might have taken within the Hieronian sphere. The Ptolemaic *P.Rev.* dossier, for instance, details the procedures taken by royal officials when called on to act as arbiters in the event of a disagreement between cultivator and tax farmer over the amount owed in taxes.[81] In this respect, the tax-farming structure ultimately invited oversight by royal administration, as the intermediary between taxpayers and tax farmers, since both sides relied on the state to protect their rights and enforce contracts. Absent royal intervention, both sides stood to subvert the system to their gain.[82] Cultivators might seek to evade taxes by concealing portions of their harvest or underreporting amounts of seed sown.[83] Tax farmers, if left unchecked, faced little disincentive not to extort payments far beyond their rightful share. Royal oversight served a necessary check against evasion by cultivators as well as against predatory behavior by tax farmers. Allowing unimpeded abuse or fraud by either side threatened to destabilize the agricultural base upon which Hieron depended for revenue.

THE HIERONIAN TITHE IN OPERATION

Having outlined the three principal structural elements of the Hieronian tithe, let us turn our attention to the operation of the tithe itself. From the outset, we should acknowledge two major limitations in our approach, which leave us to begin at a deficit. The first is the loss of the documentary evidence produced in the service of Hieron's tithe administration, once abundant but now lost to time. As we will discuss below, the successful functioning of the Hieronian tax laws relied on the creation of thousands and thousands of documents – census lists, contracts, receipts – on an annual basis. Despite such absolute loss of these primary documents, we may nevertheless reconstruct the key procedural stages in the tithe operation with a relatively high degree of certainty by drawing on both the testimony of Cicero and comparison to the operational details of the Ptolemaic tax administration during the third century.

The second limitation we face, and perhaps one of the greatest injuries that time has inflicted on our understanding of the Hieronian tithe, is the loss of contemporary third-century accounts of the taxpayer's experience in the process. We know that for most this must have been a deeply unwelcome, and even traumatic, experience. As Michael Given notes in *The Archaeology of the Colonized*, the payment of agricultural taxes was typically a cultivator's "most personal and direct contact with the state ... The fruits of your year's work, which will support you and your family through the coming year, lie there in the barn or on the threshing floor. As you watch, helpless to do anything other than protest at any apparent unfairness, your crop is measured, divided, and a significant portion removed."[84] In the following pages, our discussion of the Hieronian tithe's operational aspects may present the process as dispassionate and methodical, but we should not forget the multitude of personal experiences that are now lost to time.[85]

First and foremost, the Hieronian law required the collection and reporting of essential information related to agricultural production from each territory in the kingdom. The foundation of this data was an annual census of all farmers cultivating land within a city's territory. Cicero referred to this census register as the *subscriptio aratorum*, which according to the provisions of the *lex Hieronica* required cultivators to self-report to the appropriate magistrate during an appointed time each year.[86] Given the fact that tithes were sold and collected on the basis of the *polis* unit, it seems most plausible that cultivators reported to a magistrate stationed within each *polis*, although not necessarily to a civic magistrate. Ptolemaic accounts of the third century refer to a similar register of names that was compiled by royal officials.[87]

Already in this first step of the process, the Hieronian state was gathering a significant amount of information about its constituents. At the time that the Hieronian equivalent to the *subscriptio aratorum* was being compiled, cultivators were required to report additional information, including the types of crop being cultivated, the amount of seed sown for each crop, and, quite possibly, the amount of land under cultivation.[88] These last two declarations were certainly features of the *lex Hieronica* during the late Republic, which Cicero refers to as the *professio sationum* (declaration of the amount of seed sown) and *professio iugerum* (declaration of the amount of land cultivated), respectively.[89] Regarding the *professio iugerum*, Cicero held that it was not an original feature of the third-century tax law, but rather a requirement introduced by Verres.[90] Most scholars have followed Carcopino in dismissing Cicero's testimony on the subject, arguing instead that the *professio iugerum* was, in fact, part of the original Hieronian law. Yet there are good reasons to trust Cicero on the matter. Declarations related to the amount of land under cultivation were not strictly necessary for the proper operation of a truly proportional harvest tax, like that collected by Hieron, but were more germane to fixed land taxes like those collected on royal land in Egypt.[91] As will be discussed in further detail below, a prospective tax farmer interested in bidding on wheat production in the territory of Tauromenion, for instance, would need only to consult records related to the amount of seed sown and that collected as tax over the preceding years in order to make an informed decision about the yield of an upcoming harvest. This sentiment is echoed by James Scott, who notes in *Seeing like a State* that measurement of land by surface area was not a particularly useful manner of communicating its productive potential, relating that "[t]he amount of seed sown to a field is in fact a relatively good proxy for average yield, as the sowing is done in anticipation of average growing conditions."[92]

Accepting for the moment that the *professio iugerum* was not strictly necessary to the operation of the Hieronian tithe system, there still remained a significant amount of information gathering to be accomplished at this initial stage. Moreover, it is clear from Cicero's account that the Hieronian law required at least two copies of the *subscriptio aratorum* and *professio sationum* be made for each city, with one copy deposited in the civic archive and one copy sent to Syracuse, where it was held by royal administrators. This duplication of records played an essential role in the operational sequence of the tithe, as it gave both potential tax farmers and royal administrators an intelligible, arithmetic view of the agricultural productivity of the territories that formed the Hieronian kingdom.

Over the years, differing opinions have formed around the identity of the magistrates responsible for gathering the *subscriptio aratorum* and *professio sationum*. The long-held view that the responsibility fell to civic magistrates in each *polis* has recently been challenged by Malcolm Bell, who posits a much greater role for royal officials in the administration of the tithe.[93] Bell argues that during the third century the initial collection of census data fell to the jurisdiction of royal agents stationed in each *polis*, who served as local representatives of the Hieronian court. In support of his argument, Bell points to the figure of the *magistratus Siculus*, an official referred to by Cicero on several occasions in the *Verrines*, who is specifically invoked as an arbitrator of disputes between cultivators and tax farmers. Elsewhere, Bell argues, the *magistratus Siculus* is described as having authority germane to the operation of the tithe administration including, on one occasion, responsibility for collecting the *subscriptio aratorum*.[94] Bell's hypothesis has much to recommend it, especially when one considers that the Ptolemies and Seleucids assigned royal magistrates to jurisdictions over similar tax-related matters.[95]

If such royal magistrates were to be found in cities across the Hieronian kingdom, one might expect to have encountered them headquartered in a space like the so-called Public Office at Morgantina, a large building that faced onto the city's agora (Figure 4.2).[96] Constructed in the middle decades of the third century, the building has been identified as the likely seat of a royal magistrate due to its axial siting with respect to the speaker's platform (*bema*) of the city's *ekklesiasterion* and on account of peculiar architectural features within that may point to its function as a royal bank.[97] A possible counterpart to the Public Office at Morgantina is Building VI A at Megara Hyblaia, which was also built sometime in the third century and shares a similar, though not identical, arrangement of rooms around three sides of a courtyard (Figure 4.3).[98] The building's location, situated between the agora and the city's western gate, would have made it readily accessible to individuals coming and going between the urban center and the surrounding territory. While Henri Tréziny has recently posited that Building VI A might have served a commercial purpose, he nevertheless draws attention to the large rooms along the building's north side, which he suggests could have stored agricultural

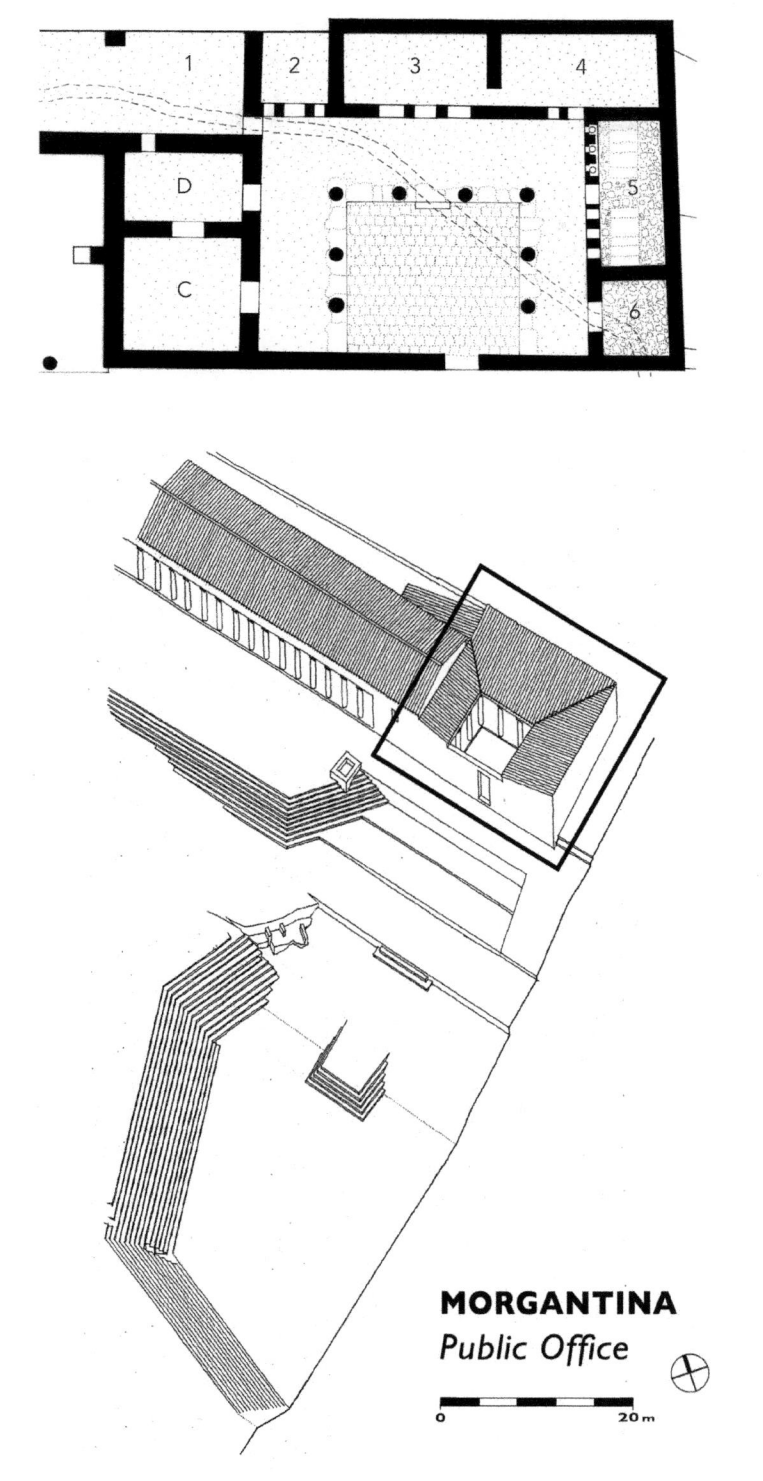

MORGANTINA
Public Office

0   20 m

4.2 The Public Office at Morgantina, third century BCE (after Bell 2007b; drawings: E. Thorkildsen; courtesy of the American Excavations at Morgantina).

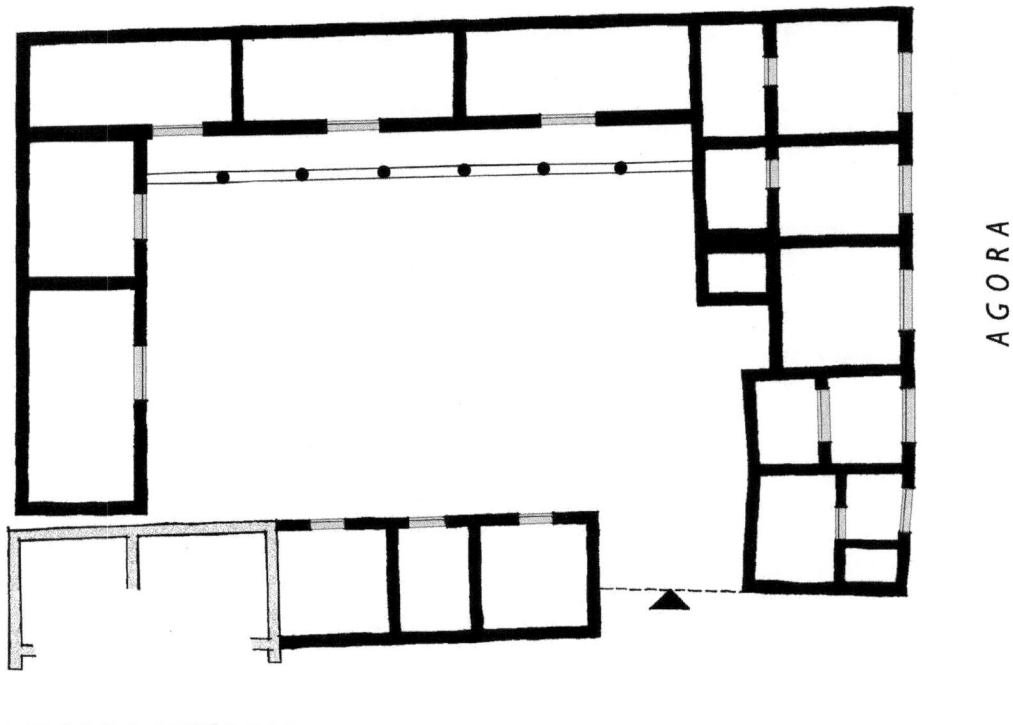

MEGARA HYBLAIA
Le bâtiment VI A

4.3 Building VI A at Megara Hyblaia, third century BCE (after Tréziny 2018).

produce owed to Hieron. This is obviously an intriguing, if unprovable, suggestion, but one that might be further substantiated by the long and narrow form of the northern rooms as well as their heavy ashlar foundations, which loosely resemble the monumental granary buildings at Morgantina, which we will encounter in Chapter 6. During the portion of the year in which the *subscriptio aratorum* was being compiled, we would expect that administrative buildings like the Public Office at Morgantina became bustling sites of interaction between cultivators and royal officials charged with gathering the statistics vital to the operation of the tithe.

Only once this information had been collected and reported could the auctioning of tithe contracts take place. These contracts were sold at auctions that were held at different times throughout the year, but always in Syracuse under the jurisdiction of the king and his administrators.[99] Tithe contracts were auctioned separately by city and by crop.[100] This meant that a prospective tax farmer could bid on the right to collect his tenth of the wheat harvest in the territory of Akrai or of the legume harvest in the territory of Morgantina. In Cicero's day, cities could bid on contracts at auction as a corporate entity, acting in the same way as an individual tax farmer. The orator describes a frustrated attempt by the citizens of Thermai to purchase the right to farm the tithe on wheat in their own territory.[101] This was very likely a feature of the Hieronian law (a concession made by the king to the *poleis* that recognized his authority) and not a privilege introduced by Rome, particularly in light of the preceding discussion of Hieron's need to engender quasi-voluntary compliance among the tithe-paying *poleis*.

Naturally, the timing of an auction was tied to the agricultural calendar and took place only after crops had been sown. Tithe contracts for grains like wheat and barley, for instance, could be auctioned no earlier than the fall after fields were under seed. This was due to the fact that both tax farmers and royal administrators relied on sowing figures (i.e., the farmer's *professio sationum*) to properly estimate the size of the total harvest. Given that tithes were sold for crops with different planting and harvesting seasons, we must imagine that multiple auctions were held each year. It fell to the royal administrators to circulate announcements of upcoming auctions well in advance, so as to give prospective tax farmers time to consider their bid. A record of provisions related to the announcement of upcoming auctions in Ptolemaic Egypt is preserved in the third-century *P.Rev.* dossier, where it is specified that:

> The royal scribes shall notify [the] tax farmers within 10 days of the [opening of the public auction] the number of vineyards or of orchards [in] each nome, the [number] of aruras they contain, [and] the number of vineyards or of orchards belonging to persons on [the tax list] which paid taxes to the temples before the [22nd] year.

> If they fail to give this notice or are shown to have done it incorrectly, they shall be tried and condemned, and shall pay the tax farmers 6,000 drachmas for each offense of which they have been convicted and twice the amount of loss.[102]

We cannot say whether such specific provisions regarding timing and sanctions were also implemented within the Hieronian sphere, but the underlying concern for both transparency and integrity captured within this Ptolemaic text was almost certainly shared by the royal officials responsible for ensuring the efficacy of the Hieronian system.

Civic archives held the annual census of cultivators for each city's territory alongside their planting declarations. Prospective tax farmers could consult them to inform their decisions about whether to bid in an upcoming auction and, if so, what amount. By taking into account planting and harvest data compiled in previous years, an individual could estimate the average harvest for territories or even individual estates.[103] Although individuals with local knowledge and connections might have always enjoyed an advantage when bidding on contracts to collect tithes, the Hieronian system of reporting served to remove certain asymmetries of information that would otherwise privilege local stakeholders at the time of auction.[104] In theory, the greater transparency engendered by the royal tax system would have made it possible for a tax farmer from Syracuse to make an educated bid on the barley tithe from Leontinoi, for instance, even if they were not intimately familiar the territory or its cultivators. This was made possible by the collection and dissemination of information related to agricultural productivity that was required by Hieronian law for the proper operation of the tithe.

Following an auction, the winning bidder(s) for each territory and crop would next conclude a contract with the king that stipulated the conditions of the sale, including the total amount to be turned over the royal granary and the date by which the payment was to be made. During the Republican period, these contracts were concluded between the tax farmers and the governor of the province, who took over the role as the central authority on the island.[105] We can get some idea of what these contracts might have looked like from surviving examples from Egypt like *P. Berlin* 13535, which records the details of three tax farmers who have jointly won the concession to collect the salt tax at Elephantine during the eleventh year of Ptolemy III's reign (236).[106] Of particular note is the oath sworn by the three tax farmers in the names of King Ptolemy and Queen Berenike and the stipulation that payments (cash, in this case) were to be paid in installments at royal banks.

As with any other tax-farming system, the winning bidders would have been required to offer sureties against the failure to make the payment in full.[107] Such a stipulation, of course, would ensure that the king received his revenue regardless of the outcome of the harvest. The financial resources involved in putting forward sureties of payment would have ensured that participation in the tax farm was largely restricted to wealthy elites or to the *poleis* themselves. Still, the fact that tithes were divided by crop and by territory allowed for the possibility of greater participation in the system.[108] In Cicero's day, copies of the contract between tax farmer and governor were made in triplicate, a practice that surely had its roots in the third-century law. This would allow one copy to remain in Syracuse, where it could be held in the royal archive, and one copy to be sent to the appropriate city, where it could be deposited in the local archive for future consultation. The third copy was held by the tax farmer as evidence of his authority to collect a particular tithe.

The next critical step in the process involved the conclusion of agreements between tax farmers and individual cultivators. Cicero referred to this agreement as the *pactio*, in which the amount owed by the cultivator was specified along with, presumably, a fixed location and date for the payment.[109] Similar contracts signed between tax officials and cultivators in third-century Egypt were known as *sungraphai* (sing. *sungraphē*, συγγραφή).[110] Under the Hieronian law, these contracts were made in triplicate and signed by both the tax farmer and the cultivator. The tax farmer and cultivator each retained a copy of the contract, while the third copy was deposited in the appropriate civic archive, where it could be consulted in the event of a dispute between a tax farmer and cultivator.[111]

Precisely when these contracts were concluded under the third-century Hieronian law is a matter of some debate. Most scholars contend that agreements were worked out only after the harvest had been completed and the year's total yield laid out on the threshing floor, in the case of cereals and legumes, where it would be open and visible for all parties to see and assess.[112] Drawing parallels from later Roman practice, a handful of scholars have contended instead that tax farmers and cultivators could conclude contracts prior to the harvest, throughout the late spring or early summer in the case of wheat and barley, while the grain was still maturing on the stalk.[113] Following this view, the contract would be settled at the threshing floor only in the event that an agreement could not be reached prior to harvest.[114] Each option had its advantages. Concluding contracts before the harvest had the potential of increasing the overall speed of the process in transferring agricultural goods from the productive hinterlands to the royal stores at Syracuse. Yet waiting until the year's harvest was completed and visible for all to see ensured that neither the cultivator nor the tax farmer could easily misrepresent the total amounts harvested and owed in payment to the king.

Of course, the two choices are not mutually exclusive. We can envision a scenario in which tax farmer and cultivator were free to conclude their contract prior to harvest, should both sides find the terms acceptable. Alternatively, if the parties could not agree on a fair amount, they might wait until harvest time, when the actual proceeds could be measured under close observation. Protracted disagreement following the harvest may have required the intervention of royal officials, as we know to have been the case in the Ptolemaic kingdom. That careful measurement of grain did, at times, take place on the threshing floor is suggested by the discovery of officially endorsed measuring devices at a farmhouse excavated in the territory of ancient Akrai.[115]

While it is rather easy to discuss this process in uncomplicated, abstract terms, there can be no doubt that the assessment and collection of the tithe was rarely a dispassionate experience for those involved. Michael Given captures a sense of the tumult that awaited all parties at the moment of assessment on the threshing floor: "where tax collector and peasant family stand opposed on either side of the grain heap, taxation is a morass of disagreements, partial payments, negotiations, claims and counter claims."[116] This was certainly the grim experience of the cultivators harassed to the point of abandoning their farms by the abusive tax farmers who thrived during Verres' governorship.[117] We can find a still more engrossing description of the events that took place on the threshing floor in Gustaf Dalman's meticulous account of tax payments in agrarian communities of Palestine during the early twentieth century.[118] As Dalman recounts, the measurement of tithe payments was a highly ritualized event that took place on the threshing floor, where the process could be closely surveilled by the community leader, the tax farmer (or a representative), the cultivator (and often his family), and even Allah, who was invoked to watch over the entire process. Assessments were carried out at noon or at sunset, but not in the morning or afternoon when the sun cast deceptive shadows over the piles of heaped grain. When possible, the measuring was performed by an experienced measurer (*mekaijel, kaijal*). Even still, the measurement was carried out six times, so as to dispel any suspicion among the interested parties (Figure 4.4). The measurer used a wooden measuring vessel, usually with a volume between 12.5 and 15 liters, and would announce aloud the number of each measurement, so that all who witnessed the process could

4.4 Measuring grain on the threshing floor at el-Bīre, Palestine, early twentieth century (after Dalman 1933).

follow along and keep count.[119] When every measure could mean holding back the perils of hunger and starvation for even one more day, it is no wonder that the moment of assessment took on a solemn and protracted tone. Although worlds apart, we should not expect the assessment of taxes in the agrarian communities of Hellenistic Sicily to have been drastically different with respect to the life-or-death stakes and perennial anxieties that accompanied it.

Once the harvest had taken place and taxes been assessed, grain and other goods needed to move from the threshing floor to Hieron's royal granaries. In Cicero's day, tithe grain was conveyed to ports, either on the sea or along a navigable river at a stage in the process he refers to as the *deportatio ad aquam*.[120] Once the grain had reached the port, it was loaded onto transport ships and brought to Rome. Unfortunately, Cicero's statements on the *deportatio ad aquam* are opaque; there is no scholarly consensus on whether the responsibility for transporting the tithe "*ad aquam*" lies with the tax farmers or the cultivators, or even if this provision belonged to the original third-century law.[121] Here, archaeological evidence may offer some insight into how this critical stage in the process was accomplished during the reign of Hieron II. The remains of two monumental granaries found in the agora of Morgantina have been identified as warehouses built to house the tithe owed to Hieron from the surrounding territory. The granaries and their role within the third-century administrative system will be the focus of Chapter 6. If correctly identified as royal warehouses, they bear mention here because of their potential function as regional collection points where tax farmers or cultivators could make payments under the watchful eye of royal agents. Unlike the Romans, who had every interest in moving the proceeds of the agricultural tithe off Sicily as quickly as possible in order to feed their citizen and soldier populations, Hieron might have preferred to distribute his resources by stockpiling grain and other goods in royal warehouses around the kingdom.

The scale and geographic diversity of the territory subject to Hieron meant that grain was harvested at different times throughout the summer season. Even around the territory of Morgantina today, which now belongs to the Comune of Aidone, wheat is harvested over a roughly two-month period across June and July, as fields planted closer to the valley floor ripen well before those at higher elevations on the hills above. Cultivators in the territory of Aidone today adopt different strategies for the harvest, often deciding whether to reap their grain early in the season (mid- to late June) or to wait until later in the season (early to mid-July). Opting to harvest grains later in the summer when more of the crop has ripened on the stalk holds the promise of a larger yield, but also carries the potential risk of losing a significant portion of the crop to a devastating late summer rainstorm or brush fire.[122] Although we cannot fully appreciate an ancient cultivator's decision-making process with respect to timing a harvest, we can be certain that the ruin of late summer rain was likely at the forefront of every cultivator's mind as one gambled against time with each passing day. The crushing tragedy of such a loss is captured by Virgil in his *Georgics*, who writes of the late summer storm:

> Quid tempestates autumni et sidera dicam,
> atque, ubi iam breuiorque dies et mollior aestas,
> quae uigilanda uiris? uel cum ruit imbriferum uer,
> spicea iam campis cum messis inhorruit et cum
> frumenta in uiridi stipula lactentia turgent?
>
> saepe ego, cum flauis messorem induceret aruis
> agricola et fragili iam stringeret hordea culmo,
> omnia uentorum concurrere proelia uidi,
> quae grauidam late segetem ab radicibus imis
> sublimem expulsam eruerent: ita turbine nigro
> ferret hiems culmumque leuem stipulasque uolantis.
> saepe etiam immensum caelo uenit agmen aquarum
> et foedam glomerant tempestatem imbribus atris
> collectae ex alto nubes; ruit arduus aether
> et pluuia ingenti sata laeta boumque labores
> diluit;
>
> Need I describe what men must watch for
> when the weather changes under autumn's stars,
> the days grow shorter, with a gentler heat;
> or when spring downpours soak the bristling cornfields
> as the milky grain is swelling on green stalks?
>
> A farmer and his reaper reach his golden acres
> and begin to strip the barley from its fragile stems.
> Just then, the winds from every quarter join in battle,
> tearing the laden harvest far and wide,
> uprooting it and hurling it on high,
> as if it were light chaff and flying stubble
> scattered by a whirlwind to the darkening air.
> I've often seen it. Often, too, I've seen
> a mighty mass of waters gather in the sky;
> inside the toppling clouds black showers form.
> Heaven falls to earth; the deluge
> drowns the smiling crops and wastes the oxen's labour.[123]

Some degree of inspection or oversight by royal agents was necessary to ensure fair reporting at the payment of the tithe by cultivators.[124] Otherwise, there would be little to prevent either party from acting in a duplicitous manner and later claiming falsely either that a cultivator had underpaid his tithe or that a tax farmer had taken more than the amount stipulated in the *sungraphē*. A guarantee was needed to assure not only that the amount paid was proportionate to the total harvest but also that the produce was of good quality. We know that Ptolemaic administrators required a sample, or *deigma* (generally a container of representative grain, sealed under the supervision of an official), to be sent along with larger shipments of tithe grain headed to the royal granaries at Alexandria in order to reduce the temptation to adulterate the grain by the addition of hay or dirt.[125]

Inspection would most easily take place when the cultivator paid the amount owed as tithe. It could be that a royal official accompanied the tax farmers to the properties of individual cultivators, or that officials armed with a list of the *sungraphai* arranged between cultivators and tax farmers oversaw the individual payments at a regional collection point, like the granaries at Morgantina. We should expect that some form of receipt was issued at the time of payment. Whether this involved the creation of a new document or took the form of an addendum to the cultivator's personal copy of the *sungraphē* is open to speculation. Regardless of the precise form of these documents, every cultivator would have had strong incentive to retain them in a personal archive should questions arise about the status of their payment.[126] If Ptolemaic practice can provide some guidance here, copies of these receipts might also have been held in the archives of the regional collection points operated by royal officials.[127]

For all that remains obscure about the particulars of its day-to-day operation, we can be certain that over time, the tithe accomplished its primary goal, namely, the vast transfer of wealth and resources out of the agriculturally productive *mesogeia* of southeastern Sicily and into the royal granaries at Syracuse. In doing so, the Hieronian tax laws introduced an unprecedented degree of administrative oversight into the politically segmented landscape of the kingdom, binding individuals and communities in ways both profound and mundane. Indeed, cultivators found themselves increasingly drawn into contact with the royal state and its administrators, as the age-old rhythms of the agrarian calendar were now punctuated by the mandatory reporting of planting data and trips to regional collection points, where the fruits of one's labor were handed over to representatives of the king. Such a massive undertaking was matched by an equally impressive institutional framework designed to gather and disseminate data throughout the kingdom. At nearly every step of the operation outlined above, information about the people, places, and produce of Hieron's kingdom was generated, recorded, or transferred. It is to this centrality of data collection for the success of the Hieronian tax laws that we now turn.

"SEEING" THE HIERONIAN STATE

Sometime around the year 240, the famed mathematician Archimedes composed a treatise in which he set out to demonstrate that he could determine the number of grains of sand that fit into the universe and, in doing so, estimate the size of the universe itself. This treatise, commonly referred to as the *Sand Reckoner*, has long captured the attention of mathematicians and scholars.[128] Beyond its ambitious aims, the form of the treatise itself has garnered particular interest, as it was written in an epistolary mode and addressed to Hieron's son, Gelon. The letter begins, "There are some, King Gelon, who think that the number of the sand is infinite in multitude" – a salutation that helps to establish the date of the work, which must have been written after Gelon had been elevated to the position of co-regent. As the opening line names the king as the intended audience for the discussion that followed, Archimedes goes on to conclude his treatise by again directly addressing Gelon in a somewhat conspiratorial tone:

> I suppose that these matters, King Gelon, will seem not well-believable to the many and those who have not shared in learning, but to those who have understood and given thought about the distances and the sizes of the earth, the sun, the moon, and the entire universe they will be believable on account of the proof. Therefore, I think that to you too it is not unfitting to have considered these matters.[129]

The implicit claim here, as Marquis Berrey aptly deduces, was something akin to "Thanks to Archimedes' treatise Gelon is now included in the group of wise humans who understand the deep structure of the natural world."[130] We might rightly wonder whether the young king was indeed an amateur enthusiast of mathematical inquiry, or if Archimedes was simply seeking to solidify his position in the Syracusan royal court by adulating Hieron's would-be successor. In either case, Archimedes casts himself as an indispensable advisor, one uniquely capable of assisting the king when it came to assessing and measuring what the unnamed "some" had deemed otherwise immeasurable.

While couched in terms of cosmic scale, the underlying message of Archimedes' treatise was likely one of contemporary political significance to the Syracusan king, namely, that the seemingly limitless could, in fact, be quantified, enumerated, and, ultimately, known. Gelon and his father probably cared little for estimating the grains of sands that formed the shores of Syracuse, let alone tabulating the number that could fill the entire cosmos. Yet they certainly shared a genuine concern for knowing all they could about other vast sums, like the number of *medimnoi* of wheat sown or the total number of talents of wool shorn each year within their kingdom. Herein lay a very practical application for the outwardly impractical exposition of the *Sand Reckoner*.[131] This was bound to be of interest to Hieron and Gelon, since from their perspective, only that which could be counted could be taxed.

Across the Hellenistic world, many great minds sought patronage in the royal courts of kings. The presence of individuals like Archimedes of Syracuse and Eratosthenes of Cyrene among the inner circle of a king's most trusted friends and advisors reveals the centrality that knowledge acquisition could hold for the livelihood of a kingdom. Within this context, the *Sand Reckoner* belongs to a small, but significant, corpus of scientific treatises that were addressed to Hellenistic kings.[132] While the *Sand Reckoner* does not explicitly deal with matters of practical administration, its principal assertion was one designed to resonate with a ruler whose fiscal interests lie in calculating the potential revenue of the state. In this light, Archimedes' treatise bears some relation to Eratosthenes' *Letter to Ptolemy*, which demonstrated the mathematician's solution to a longstanding geometric problem known as "doubling the cube." In his brief text, Eratosthenes both gives the geometric proof of his solution and offers up an intriguing description of a device that he had created, which would allow for the mechanical replication of his solution to calculating and doubling the volume of a solid. It is Eratosthenes' own appreciation for the practical utility of his device that requires our attention:

> Once this [device] is discovered, we will be able to set in general a given solid bound by parallelograms into a cube, or change the shape from one [solid] into another [solid], and do likewise to even enlarging [a given solid] by preserving its likeness, such as altars and temples. We will also be able to set both wet and dry measures into a cube, I mean a *metretes* or a *medimnos*, and by the side of this [device] to measure the volumes of these receiving vessels. The invention will also be useful for those wishing to enlarge catapults and stone throwing engines.[133]

Why King Ptolemy should have any interest in the mathematician's geometric proofs is explained by Eratosthenes, who frames the utility of his invention with respect to construction projects, administrative tools, and siege engines – all matters of great concern for the king. Of particular note is Eratosthenes' reference to the *metretes* and *medimnos*, two common units used for measuring liquid and dry goods, which made them essential tools for the assessment of agricultural taxes. We will return to Eratosthenes' device in Chapter 5, when our focus shifts to the archaeology of measurement in the Hieronian kingdom.

As we have seen, the fiscal administration of the Hieronian kingdom, viewed through the lens of the agricultural tithe, was predicated on extensive data collection. From the royal capital at Syracuse, the king and his court were confronted with the tremendous task of gathering meaningful information about territories under his control. Herein lay the promise of employing mathematicians like Archimedes and Eratosthenes, whose mathematical treatises offered a potential avenue for removing (if only by degrees) one of the principal obstacles to effective taxation – the ignorance of available resources. We will likely never know if either Archimedes or Eratosthenes directly applied their mathematical genius to the mundane affairs of administration, but their rapport with the Hieronian and Ptolemaic courts was certainly enduring.

While his lot was not to control an expansive and culturally diverse territorial empire like those of the Ptolemaic or Seleucid kings, Hieron's *basileia* nevertheless comprised more than a dozen *poleis* distributed across a geographically varied landscape. From the vantage of the royal court, efficient resource extraction was predicated on possessing reliable information about the taxpaying sector of the polity. In this respect, the Hieronian state was from the outset hindered in its efforts to effectively extract resources due to the fact that, like all premodern states, it suffered from a partial "blindness" (as James Scott might describe it) around the types of information critical to effective taxation (i.e., land ownership, yields, etc.). As a consequence, Hieron needed to render his kingdom legible. One step toward this goal was to establish common standards of measurement. Hieron's ability to extract revenue from his kingdom was closely tied up with his ability to measure its productive capacity.[134] Uniform standards served, in essence, as a common vocabulary with which resources and productivity could be assessed and compared across a politically fragmented landscape. The evidence for metrological standardization in the Hieronian kingdom is discussed in the following chapter.

Together with establishing uniform measurement, it was necessary to gather a wide range of information about potential revenue sources. While warfare was a much more visible aspect of Hellenistic kinship, great effort went into developing the mechanisms for gathering information about a kingdom's constituents, information that provided the essential, if less glorious, foundation of an empire. In antiquity, as today, such data collection was difficult to accomplish and never perfectly executed. One dilemma faced by Hellenistic monarchs was how to maximize data collection without expending excessive resources or intervening too heavily in the day-to-day lives of their tax-paying constituents. In the case of the Hieronian kingdom, the solution was to build this data-gathering into the operational structure of the tithe administration, such that critical information was collected for the Hieronian state at various stages in the process.

By its very nature, the proportional tithe levied on annual harvests, which were subject to interannual variability, required regular assessment and reporting – far more than, say, a direct tax on land use that was paid at the same, fixed rate year after year. The success of Hieron's tax laws rested on what was surely an unprecedented degree of information gathering for the time and place. The agricultural tithe alone required the completion of an annual census of cultivators, as well as the reporting of figures covering, at minimum, the amount of seed sown, the amount of the harvested crop bid by the successful tax farmer, and the amount paid by the cultivators. This is to say nothing of the reporting of customs fees, port duties, or any of the other taxes collected to fill royal coffers. Even the tax-farm auctions themselves served as measuring instruments by which Hieron could get a relatively up-to-date assessment of the revenue that his kingdom was capable of producing in a given year.[135]

It further bears consideration that the collection of census data like the *subscriptio aratorum* and *professio sationum* (or their third-century equivalents) beyond the level of the *polis* appears to have been first introduced in eastern Sicily during the Hieronian period alongside the institution of tax farming. At first glance, this is to be expected as these census figures were essential to the operation of an imperial tax administration that utilized tax farming. Absent their compilation, there could be no accurate assessment of agricultural productivity nor systematic collection of tithes. Yet despite their essential nature, we should not overlook the fact that the introduction of the procedures to collect this data marked a categorical expansion of the king's power at the expense of *polis* autonomy. It also represented a layering of institutional control over the multiple territories that formed the kingdom, binding together the communities of eastern Sicily in ways not formerly experienced under earlier manifestations of the Syracusan territorial state. One novel outcome of this *supra-polis* layer of organization might very well have been the formation of the *koinon tōn Sikeliōtān*, which could have served as an intermediary between the king and the *poleis* subject to his rule.

A concomitant product of the extensive data-gathering operation required by the tithe administration was the creation of large numbers of documents and the maintenance of extensive archives. Jean Andreau estimates that in the mid-first century between 10,000 and 20,000 new documents were created annually, simply to accommodate the normal operation of the *lex Hieronica* during Cicero's day.[136] The Hieronian administration likely produced tax-related documents on this same order of magnitude despite comprising a far smaller share of the island.[137] The creation and maintenance of so many documents required not only a small army of officials and administrators, but also the physical spaces for their storage, such as might have been served by the so-called Public Office at Morgantina. These documents may have been recorded using any number of available media, but given the large numbers produced each year, it would make sense that papyrus was used extensively. The use of papyrus for documents at Hellenistic Morgantina is attested by several clay seals (*cretule, bullae*) that preserve the impression of papyrus on one side and that of a signet ring on the other (Figure 4.5).[138] Those shown here were discovered in the agora at Morgantina. That the same signet ring appears to have been used for both seals suggests these could have belonged to a larger archive, although not necessarily a civic archive or one connected with the tithe administration.[139]

The Hieronian administrative system necessitated a growing reliance on tax-related documents; not only were copies of census data, planting reports, and contracts all stored in civic and royal archives, but cultivators were required to hold on to copies of their contracts with tax farmers, as well as receipts for the payment of taxes. These documents did not render static the information

4.5 Two *cretule* from Morgantina, each bearing the impression of papyrus fibers and the stamp of an identical signet stone (Museo Archeologico Regionale di Aidone, inv 60-1665 and inv. 60-1683; photos: author; courtesy of the American Excavations at Morgantina).

required by the tithe administration; they mobilized it and accelerated its transfer in ways previously unseen in eastern Sicily. The efficacy of the tax-farming system and, ultimately, the fiscal well-being of the Hieronian state relied on the dissemination of formerly privileged knowledge. In the *De frumento*, Cicero demonstrates just how much information a private individual could learn from consulting the tithe-related records held in *polis* archives. He was able to determine not only the number of individual cultivators in a particular territory, but their names along with the types and amounts of seed crops they planted, harvested, and paid in taxes.[140] Moreover, he could calculate the total harvest for a given territory in a specific year, and even track changes in land use and productivity over time. Cicero's access to such information was not exceptional to him, as the tithe system rested on the premise that potential tax farmers could base their prognostications on the same basic information. What was exceptional about this system of infor-mation gathering and dissemination was the capacity it offered the state to view the island's productive capacity in a fashion and to a degree not previously achieved by the political rulers of Sicily.[141]

While the motivation to collect information ultimately lay with the royal prerogative to extract revenue, the outcomes were shared by far more than just the king and his court. This flow of information, from fields to civic and royal archives, moving around in all manner of documents, bound together the cities and citizens of southeastern Sicily in an unprecedented fashion. Whether they knew it or not, cultivators now played a role (indispensable, in fact) in assisting the king and his agents to tax more effectively their agricultural produce by self-reporting census data. Local elites too were co-opted into the system by performing key administrative roles in the oversight and administration of the tithe, whether as civic magistracies or tax farmers. Indeed, the system functioned best when civic magistrates, royal officials, and private individuals acted in concert.

To return to the passage by James Scott that introduced this chapter, I want to underscore that while the Hieronian state was certainly "blind" in many respects, the tax administration served as a corrective to its impaired vision by bringing into focus a diverse agrarian landscape. From Syracuse, Hieron and his advisors could take in the productive landscape of southeastern Sicily with greater breadth and clarity than had ever before been possible. Hieron's view of the territories under his control may not have been detailed with respect to geographical features or topographic boundaries, but it was clear-sighted in terms of what mattered most to the monarch – the names, places, and amounts of whom and what could be taxed. These, collectively, offered the king a commanding perspective over his kingdom.

NOTES

[1] Ath. 5.206d–209e, who quotes Moschion's description of the ship (*FGrH* 575 F1). For a recent reappraisal of the *Syakosia* narrative, see Barbera (2019).

[2] Lehmler (2005: 210–32).

[3] Eckstein (2009: 255).

[4] For a recent survey of royal taxation in the Hellenistic East, see Kaye (2018). Monson (2015) explores the central role of taxation in the fiscal regimes of the Seleucid, Antigonid, and Ptolemaic kingdoms. With regard to direct taxes, both the Ptolemies and Seleucids collected various forms of poll tax (*syntaxis*), including a salt tax, collected in cash on a per capita basis; Monson (2015: 180, 191). It is in the realm of indirect taxation that Hellenistic kings truly excelled, generating revenue both in cash and in kind from the collection of taxes on everything from commercial transactions in the agora to the hunting of wild game. For an overview of the variety of revenue sources exploited by the Seleucid kings, see Aperghis (2004: 137–79).

[5] Examples of the reallocation of tax-derived revenues from the royal coffers back to cities can be found in Bringmann (1993; 2001).

[6] Leaving aside the description of the *Syrakosia* found in the *Deipnosophistai* of Athenaeus, the Polybian account of Hieron's benefactions to Rhodes following the earthquake of

227 underscores the vast quantities of grain and other agricultural resources available to the king.

7   The exemption granted to Rhodian merchants is listed among the gifts given by Hieron and Gelon to Rhodes following the earthquake; Polyb. 5.88.5–8; Diod. 26.8. Berve (1959: 47) took this as evidence that Hieron collected customs duties at ports throughout his kingdom, not only at Syracuse. Cicero (2.*Verr*.2.185) refers to the collection of a 5 percent harbor tax (*portorium*) during the Republican period, which may have been the amount originally collected under Hieronian law. See Goldsberry (1973: 321–7) regarding the administration of the *portorium* in Sicily under Roman rule. For the collection of port fees and customs duties by the Seleucid kings, see Aperghis (2004: 157–60); and, on the broad applicability of the term *ellimenion* for many types of duties and fees paid at port, see Carrara (2014).

8   We know that other Hellenistic kings collected taxes in the form of tolls and customs duties charged for goods carried along overland routes; see Aperghis (2004: 160–2); *IGBulg* V, 5557 (3).

9   Cicero's (2.*Verr*. 3.167) reference to the *scriptura* collected in Sicily makes clear that – at least during the late Republic – the collection of this tax was farmed out to private collectors (*publicani*). That the collection of pasture taxes in Sicily predated Roman fiscal administration, see Rostovzeff (1902: 410); the fourth-century Syracusan tyrant, Dionysius I, also reportedly raised revenues by taxing heads of cattle, *Oik.* 2.1349b. Pasture taxes (*ennomion*) were a common source of revenue for Hellenistic kings; for collection in the Ptolemaic kingdom, see *C.Ord.Ptol.*21 (= Austin [2006: no. 260]), which preserves a portion of an ordinance extending the tax on livestock to the Ptolemaic territory of Coele-Syria.

10   Ath. 5.209b. Depending on the weight standard and size of the talent, this figure would be equivalent in weight to anywhere between ca. 262 metric tons ("reduced" Sicilian talent of 13.08 kilograms) and ca. 524 metric tons (Sicilian talent of 26.16 kilograms, itself roughly equal to an Attic talent); for the mass of a Sicilian talent, see Parise (1979: 303–4). The figure of 20,000 talents is almost certainly exaggerated to fit the exaggerated scale of the ship; but, here, the accuracy of the reported figure is less important than the scale of the figure, which was clearly intended as an expression of Hieron's access to vast agricultural resources.

11   This system of taxation has been largely reconstructed on the grounds of the so-called Athenian Grain-Tax Law of 374/3 BC, the text of which was discovered in the Athenian agora in 1986; see Stroud (1998) for *ed. pr.* and commentary; cf. Harris (1999) with additional insights on the text; and see Sorg (2015) for discussion of the law's historical context. By Stroud's estimate, annual revenues amounted to 31,000 *medimnoi* of wheat and barley, which he estimates was roughly sufficient to feed the population of Athens for one month. While not an enormous amount we should not dismiss the importance of having surplus grain on hand and available for purchase during the late winter and spring months, before the harvest, when household stores were likely to be at their lowest. Moreno (2003) provides evidence that irregular collection of a harvest tax from Athenian cleruchies on Euboea was already taking place by the last quarter of the fifth century.

12   According to Briant (1994), kings sold grain garnered from taxes and rents to raise cash; cf. Bringmann (2001), who offers an alternative interpretation of how Hellenistic monarchs leveraged their material resources for greater political capital.

13   For text and recent discussion, see Aperghis (2004: 117–35), who suggests the content reflects the administration during the reign of Antiochos I. Manning (2010: 123) notes similarities between the sources of revenue generated by Ptolemaic taxation and those outlined by the author of the *Oikonomika*. On the connection between the second book of the *Oikonomika* and the organization of the Hellenistic royal economy more generally, see Descat (2003).

14   For text and commentary, see Malay (1983), who suggests on paleographic grounds that the inscription may date to the reign of Antiochos I (281–261).

15   Diodorus (13.59.3, 13.114.1) twice mentions the payment of tribute (*phoros*) to the Carthaginians by Sicilian cities that fell within their eparchy during the late fifth century.

Along these lines, Polybius (1.71) mentions, in the context of the Mercenary War (240–238), that the Carthaginians had relied on some form of tribute collected from their Libyan territory to fund public and military expenditure. A surviving fragment of Appian (*Sic.*, Frag. 2) mentions that, after their victory in 241, the Romans collected some form of tribute (again, using the term *phoros*) from the portion of Sicily formerly under Carthaginian control. Serrati (2000: 124–5) has used this to argue that the Romans retained the Carthaginian system of taxation in western Sicily. That this included some form of proportional tax on agricultural production collected in kind remains an issue of dispute; see Prag (2013: 61), who concludes that any form of Roman taxation in western Sicily prior to 210 was likely collected in cash and that in-kind payments in the newly formed Roman *provincia* were introduced only after the expansion of the *lex Hieronica* across the whole of the island.

[16] Regarding the subjugation and exploitation of the *Kyllirioi*, see Frolov and Gaudey (1995); Morakis (2015: 43–4); cf. De Angelis (2016: 163–4).

[17] Di Vita (1956); Luraghi (1994: 273–373).

[18] Diod. 12.29.

[19] Morris (2009: 161–2); FGrH 327 F14.

[20] Diod. 12.29–30.1. Along these lines, see Thuc. 6.20.4, where the payment of an *aparchē* ("first-fruits") by an undefined group of *barbaroi* to the Syracusans is mentioned. This is generally taken as reference to the collection of tribute from Sikel communities in southeastern Sicily; Ampolo (1984: 31–2).

[21] Hdt. 7.156–62.

[22] De Angelis (2006: 35–8).

[23] On the origins of the Syracusan *dekatē*, see Ampolo (1984); see also Manganaro (1999a: esp. 115–16); Carcopino (1914: 51–6).

[24] From Strabo (6.2.4) we get the most explicit connection of the phrase with wealth: Συρακούσσας δὲ ἐπὶ τοσοῦτον ἐκπεσεῖν πλοῦτον ὥστε καὶ αὐτοὺς ἐν παροιμίᾳ διαδοθῆναι, λεγόντων πρὸς τοὺς ἄγαν πολυτελεῖς ὡς οὐκ ἂν ἐξικνοῖτο αὐτοῖς ἡ Συρακουσσίων δεκάτη. See also Steph. Byzan. s.v. Συράκουσαι.

[25] FGrH 327 F14: τὴν Συρακουσίων δεκάτην· Δήμων Συρακουσίους εὐδαιμονήσαντάς φησι ψηφίσασθαι τὴν δεκάτην τῶν ὑπαρχόντων ἀποδίδοσθαι εἰς ἐπισκευὴν ναῶν τε καὶ ἀναθημάτων καὶ θεωριῶν· πολλοῦ δὲ χρήματος συναχθέντος εἰς παροιμίαν ἐλθεῖν. Based on the reference to voting in this passage, Ampolo (1984: 32) argues the introduction of the *dekatē* should be dated to the period of the Second Democracy, and not to the period of the Deinomenid tyranny; he allows for the possibility that this passage could also refer to the brief period of the Third Democracy (337–317), which fell between the tyranny of Dionysius II and the reign of Agathokles. While Ampolo must be correct in his assertion that the Demon passage refers to a period of democratic rule at Syracuse, the passage per se does not indicate that the *dekatē* originated as a result of that vote, only that the Syracusans voted at some point in time to utilize the proceeds of the tithe to pay for religious festivals.

[26] Ampolo (1984: 33–4) advocates in favor of the irregular collection of tribute by the Syracusans in the fifth century; cf. De Angelis (2016: 300, n. 422), who suggests otherwise, citing Boehringer (1929: 76).

[27] Ps.-Arist. *Oik.* 1349a.15–1350a.7. In addition, see Arist. *Pol.* 5.1313b, where Dionysius is said, rather implausibly, to have collected taxes equaling the total wealth of his subjects over the course of five years. Underlying the details of all of these stories is the shared theme of a tyrant's rapacity. For discussion of what is known about the fiscal policies of Dionysius I, see De Angelis (2016: 307–8, 316).

[28] For this particular episode, Ps.-Arist. *Oik.* 1349a. Perhaps most plausible of the sundry episodes recounted in the *Oikonomika* is that which involved the levying of taxes on heads of cattle and sheep; McInerney (2010: 179–80). Still better evidence of regularized tax assessment in this period may be found in Diodorus' account (14.106.3–4) of Dionysius' campaigns in South Italy, where the tyrant is said to have transferred the inhabitants of

Kaulonia to Syracuse and, following their resettlement, offered them Syracusan citizenship and exemption from taxation (*ateleia*) for five years.

[29] Grain, at least, seems to have been in short supply for Agathokles. For instance, Diodorus mentions a grain shortage at Syracuse (20.29, 20.32) and the arrival of grain convoys (20.5), suggesting the city or king was forced to purchase grain from abroad. According to Polybius (9.23.2), in 306, Agathokles reportedly received a payment of 200,000 *medimnoi* of grain and 150 talents of silver from the Carthaginians in exchange for relinquishing control over Selinus, Segesta, and other cities in the Carthaginian *epikrateia*.

[30] Certainly the most in-depth discussion of the evidence for fiscal policy during the reign of Agathokles is that of Consolo Langher (2000: 271–5), and even this does not rise above speculation on account of the dearth of evidence.

[31] Diodorus (20.4.5–8) describes the preparations for the invasion of North Africa in 310 as involving the confiscation of property from aristocratic families hostile to Agathokles as well as the seizure of temple offerings and women's jewelry.

[32] Santagati (2016: 70).

[33] For a detailed treatment of Seleucid administration, see Aperghis (2004) as well as contributions in Chankowski and Duyrat (2004); and for formative spatial structuring of the kingdom more broadly, see Kosmin (2014). The fiscal and administrative structures of the Ptolemaic kingdom have received a great deal of attention since Préaux's seminal work, *L'économie royale des Lagides* (1939); most notably, Manning (2003; 2010, esp. 73–201); von Reden (2007) with a focus on monetization and banking; and Monson (2012).

[34] Carcopino (1914: 45–56) explores the antecedents of agricultural taxation in Sicily and possible local models, before arriving at the Ptolemaic laws.

[35] Grenfell (1896); Rostovzeff (1902: 350–6); Carcopino (1914: 57–66).

[36] Carcopino (1914: 66): "it is thus the Syracusan king who copied the Egyptian king." The Ptolemaic influence on the Hieronian laws is echoed by Préaux (1939: 458) and Scramuzza (1937: 3.238). While not denying an affinity between the Hieronian and Ptolemaic tax laws, Berve (1959: 69) observed that the Hieronian system bore similarities to Seleucid practices.

[37] De Sensi Sestito (1977: 158) notes several key differences in the Hieronian and Ptolemaic systems, including that as far as we know the Hieronian tax was applied equally to all land under cultivation, rather unlike the Ptolemaic laws, which differentiated between various types of land (e.g., royal land, land belonging to temples, land cultivated by cleruchs, etc.).

[38] The Revenue Law Papyrus (*P.Rev.*) itself is conventionally dated to the years 259–258, suggesting that elements of the fiscal administration like tax farming had been introduced some time prior.

[39] Wolf and Lorber (2011).

[40] Preferring an even earlier date, Malcolm Bell has argued that the introduction of the Hieronian laws may have occurred by the 270s, while Hieron was still *stratēgos autokrator*. Bell (2011: 197), citing Hieron's contributions of grain to Roman forces at Rhegium in 270 and Akragas in 263 as evidence that the taxation of agricultural produce may have begun even prior to his rise to kingship. While this is not out of the question, the establishment of a centralized fiscal regime geared toward the regularized extraction of agricultural resources from subject communities more closely fits within the period of Hieron's kingship.

[41] See Bell (2011: 196–7), emphasizing differences in the underlying political landscape of the two kingdoms, which do not support the long-held belief that the Hieronian tax came about through Ptolemaic influence. On the influence of the Athenian tax-farming system on the Ptolemaic system, see Bingen (2007: 165–8).

[42] Bingen (2007: esp. 157–62), who notes that the initial publication of the (multiple) papyri by Grenfell (1896) under the sobriquet "the Revenue Laws papyrus" helped to initially establish the notion that they formed a single, internally cohesive document. This mischaracterization, in turn, was used to support the interpretation that the *P.Rev.* contained portions of a "code" promulgated by a royal authority that sought to control even the

most minute aspect of the economy, a position most fully developed by Préaux (1939). Building on Bingen's work, Manning (2010: 154) has described the contents of the *P.Rev.* papyri as "an ad hoc practical solution for economic administration that established the rules for Greek fiscal institution, tax farming, and the contractual obligations and expectations of both tax farmers and tax payers."

43 The work was known to later Roman authors, including Varro (*Rust.* 1.8.1), Columella (*Rust.* 1.1.8), and Pliny (*HN* 18.5), all who make mention of the king's treatise but do not offer any details as to its content. Hieron was not the only Hellenistic monarch known to have authored a treatise on agriculture, but was joined in this distinction by Attalos III and Herod Archelaus, according to Pliny. For the suggestion that Hieron's treatise was more than an agronomic text, see Bell (2011: 193), who posits the work may also have laid out elements of the royal tax laws.

44 Unless otherwise stated, all references to the *De frumento* are made to the text and translation by Yonge (1903).

45 Pritchard (1970; 1971).

46 Cic. 2.*Verr*.3.14. Trans., Yonge (1903) with modifications.

47 Pinzone (1999). And see Dubouloz (2021) for a recent analysis of Cicero's rhetorical framing of the *lex Hieronica* in his prosecution of Verres, particularly as regards asserting a sense of continuity and stability within Roman legal structures.

48 The classic example being Cicero's reference (2.*Verr*.2.5) to a statement purportedly made by Cato the Elder to the effect that Sicily was a storehouse for the republic and wet nurse for the Roman people: *Itaque ille M. Cato Sapiens cellam penariam rei publicae nostrae, nutricem plebis Romanae Siciliam nominabat.* This passage is set within a section of the speech where Cicero explicitly connects Roman military success with the resources taken from (or, in his words, "supplied by") the island.

49 Carcopino (1914).

50 For instance, see Pritchard (1970); De Sensi Sestito (1977: 138–59).

51 In particular, see Steel (2007), who addresses Cicero's rhetorical style in the *De frumento*. Regarding Cicero's use of numbers in the *De frumento* as a rhetorical strategy, see Pittia (2007); Cioffi (2011).

52 Bell (2007a; 2007b).

53 Levi (1988). While Levi's work has long been a subject of discussion and debate among economic historians and political scientists (e.g., Kiser 1994), her theory of predatory rule has only recently begun to receive more attention among ancient historians who study the economies of the Mediterranean region. I first encountered these ideas in an article by Monson (2007), who offers a compelling model for how Levi's theories can be profitably applied to the study of the fiscal regimes of Hellenistic kingdoms. See subsequent work by Manning (2010); Monson (2015); and Tan (2017).

54 Levi (1988: 13), italics my own.

55 Levi (1988: 13).

56 In addition to grain, Cicero (2.*Verr*.3.18) mentions the tithe collected on wine, olive oil, and *fruges minutae*, which has been understood as a reference to both tree fruits and legumes, as, for instance, by Carcopino (1914: 3).

57 For a concise overview of a fixed land tax (*ekphorion*, or, sometimes, *epigraphē*) collected on land subject to royal administration within the Ptolemaic kingdoms, see Monson (2015: 182–4), who notes that while the Ptolemaic *ekphorion* is sometimes translated as "harvest tax," it was not proportional or based on the amount of the actual harvest, but rather was a fixed rate paid on the amount of land under cultivation. Significantly, Monson observes that even the most common rate set by Ptolemaic administrators could routinely amount to payments on the order of 60 percent of an individual's total harvest.

58 For tax rates that far exceeded the Hieronian *dekatē*, Bresson (2016: 103–4) cites the figure of 50 percent paid by Egyptians as harvest tax on cereal cultivation under the Ptolemies. Along similar lines, Monson (2015: 189) points to evidence that the Seleucid kings, like the

Ptolemies, collected a fixed land tax (*ekphorion*) from tenants cultivating royal land and suggests that these rates might translate to roughly 30–60 percent of a cultivator's total harvest. Rates were not consistent even within a kingdom, as some cities and regions could enjoy privileged treatment or, alternatively, bear excessive burdens. An example of the latter situation would be the region of Judea and Samaria in the Seleucid kingdom, which paid agricultural taxes on the order of 30 percent of grain production and 50 percent of the yields from orchards; Monson (2015: 190). Kaye (2018: 5) observes that even the term *dekatē*, which per se indicates a 10 percent rate, was at times used for taxes on arable land that amounted to well over one-tenth of production.

[59]   The one-sixth tax on vineyards and orchards (*apomoira*) was collected by temples from tenants of temple lands during the reign of Ptolemy I. In the twenty-second year of the reign of Ptolemy II (264) the *apomoira* on vineyards and orchards was extended to private landowners, who could choose to pay in either cash or kind, as lease in the case of vineyards; for the *apomoira* tax, see Clarysse and Vandorpe (1995; 1998); Muhs (2005: 7–9).

[60]   Jursa and García (2015: 121).

[61]   Jursa and García (2015: 137–8).

[62]   As documented in the Athenian Grain-Tax Law of 374/3; see Stroud (1998); Osborne and Rhodes (2003: 118–27, no. 26); *SEG* XLVII.96.

[63]   Tax farmers played an important role within the fiscal administration of the Ptolemaic state, a fact that has been much discussed and debated; see, e.g., Bingen (2007); Monson (2007); Manning (2010: 152–7). Beginning in the reign of Ptolemy II, the state appears to have relied on royal officials (*logeutai*) to carry out the actual collection of taxes, while still farming out contracts to private individuals (*telōnai*), who stood to the profit when the actual tax revenues exceeded the amount paid for the contract; see Préaux (1939: 450ff.). Judging from the surviving documentary sources, the Seleucid kings appear to have placed very little reliance on tax farming, except in the collection of taxes and tribute from Judaea and Samaria; see Aperghis (2004: 168–9, 283–5).

[64]   Levi (1988: 71–94); and see Kiser and Kane (2007), who take up this question. Tan (2017) offers a thoughtful and up-to-date discussion of tax farming during the Roman Republic.

[65]   See Monson (2007), for discussion of Levi's theory in light of the transition from Ptolemaic to Roman rule in Egypt.

[66]   Tan (2017: 41) enumerates several reasons that rulers historically adopted tax farming rather than have the state collect its own taxes.

[67]   In discussing the economic rationale behind the adoption of tax farming by rulers in early modern Europe, Kiser (1994: 290–1) frames the decision as being one based, in part, on a choice between the amount of revenue lost due to different types of potential corruption – there was the corruption engendered, on one hand, by the coercive and overly burdensome collection practices of tax farmers and, on the other, by underreporting and lower assessments by royal agents susceptible to bribes. In some respects, the Ptolemaic system avoided this problem by its novel formulation of removing tax farmers from the actual collection of agricultural taxes and instead placing that responsibility in the hands of royal officials; see Bingen (2007: 166–7).

[68]   Predictability of revenue has been used to explain the adoption of tax-farming systems in later periods, such as in the farming-out of customs in seventeenth-century England; here, see Ashton (1956). Manning (2010: 157) and von Reden (2007: 107) emphasize the role of tax farming in reducing risk on the part of the Ptolemies.

[69]   The Hieronian laws might have actually been open to wider participation, given that rights were auctioned off for different crops, which might not have required such a financial outlay. Still, tax farming within the kingdom must have largely remained the preserve of the wealthy, who were capable of offering sureties of payment. Cicero's assertion that Verres allowed his own poor clients to win tax-farming contracts, despite the fact that they lacked the finances to offer surety of payment, was in itself an indictment against the governor for inverting customary norms that restricted the practice to elite investment.

[70] Manning (2010: 155–6).

[71] On the role that tax farming has played in attempts by rulers to incorporate powerful local elites within the state, see Goldstone and Haldon (2009: 16); Tan (2017: 47–8).

[72] Vester (2004). Weber (1978: 965–6) also observed that the specific form and operation of a tax-farming system in a particular state would depend on the relative power held by the ruler and the tax farmer. This he situated in terms of the competing interests of the two parties, which he saw as a tension between the tax farmer's interest in extracting as much as possible from the tax-paying subjects and the ruler's interest in maintaining the support of his constituents by checking the predatory behavior of tax farmers.

[73] Vester (2004: 777–8). The operation of local elites as tax farmers in Ptolemaic-controlled territories outside Egypt is documented for Judea (Joseph., *AJ* 12.4.4–5) and, possibly, in Lycia: Gygax (2001: 175).

[74] On the role that tax institutions played in creating political stability in early modern Europe, see Vester (2004: 750); Brooks (1974). Kiser (1994: 300) highlights the potential risks, noting two examples from early modern Europe when individual tax-farming syndicates gained control over a majority of the state revenue and were able to exercise undue power over a ruling monarch. The provision in the Hieronian tax law that stipulated that tithes were sold separately by territory and by crop may have been conceived with the intention of limiting any single individual or group, apart from the king, from gaining control over a large percentage of the kingdom's resources.

[75] Levi (1988: 32), italics in original.

[76] Levi (1988: 53).

[77] Cic. 2.*Verr*.3.19–20. Trans., Yonge (1903) with modifications.

[78] Cic. 2.*Verr*.3.14; 3.36–37. And for discussion, see Pritchard (1970: 357).

[79] Cic., 2.*Verr*.3.34; 3.117. Bell (2007a: 189–95) discusses the *magistratus Siculus* and possible third-century antecedents.

[80] Levi (1988: 53–4).

[81] *P.Rev*. Col. 28.; Austin (2006: 520, no. 296).

[82] For instance, Kiser (1994: 290–1); Given (2004).

[83] In Egypt, cultivators were required to declare under royal oath the total amount of their annual taxable produce; *P.Rev*. (cols. 27–8).

[84] Given (2004: 26).

[85] In this respect, Cicero's *De frumento* remains a valuable (if occasionally melodramatic) account of the hardships suffered by individual cultivators, like Xeno of Menai, Polemarchus of Morgantina, and Nymphodorus of Aitna, at the hands of Verres and his malicious henchmen. For these and other examples, Cic. 2.*Verr*.3.53–7.

[86] Cic. 2.*Verr*.3.120. As Carcopino (1914: 6) notes, the amount of territory under cultivation was likely to fluctuate from year to year due to alternation in land actively cultivated and land left fallow; "*Dans un pays de culture extensive comme la Sicile, l'alternance très variable de la jachère et de la culture sur un meme sol s'imposait comme une précaution indispensable*."

[87] For treatment of the Ptolemaic census, the work of Clarysse and Thompson (2006: esp. 10–35 for overview) is essential for the combination of its scope and detail. Rostovtzeff (1902: 352–3) suggests the term ἀπογραφὴ ὀνόματος for the Ptolemaic census of cultivators.

[88] Carcopino (1914: 7) saw an essential connection between the *subscriptio aratorum* and the reporting of the crops cultivated and the extent of land under cultivation.

[89] Cic. 2.*Verr*.3.112.

[90] Cic. 2.*Verr*.3.38–9.

[91] Carcopino (1914: 6–12); accepting Carcopino's position, Schenck von Stauffenberg (1933: 65–6); Berve (1959: 68); Pritchard (1970: 256). But cf. Schwahn (RE s.v. "tributum" cols. 16–17) and, more recently, Bell (2007b: 191, n. 23), who both consider Cicero's statement to be accurate on the late introduction of the *professio iugerum*.

[92] Scott (1998: 26). For the measurement of land in pre-modern societies by scale of labor or amount of seed sown, see Kula (1986: 29–39).

[93] Bell (2007a: 189–94); Rostovtzeff (1910: 235). This runs counter to the widely held opinion that the *magistratus Siculus* was a civic magistrate, whose title varied from *polis* to *polis*; Carcopino (1914: 6–12, 68–9), followed by Berve (1959: 53–4) and De Sensi Sestito (1977: 147).

[94] Bell (2007a: 190), with reference to Cic. 2.*Verr*.3.120.

[95] Bell (2007a: 194) speculates that the title of the *magistratus Siculus* during the third century could have been something along the lines of *oikonomos*, by way of comparison with the financial officials operating within the Ptolemaic administration. For the panorama of opinions expressed regarding the role of the *oikonomos* within the royal administration of the Seleucid kingdom, see Aperghis (2004: 208, n. 41); Ma (2000: 135–6); Capdetrey (2007: 360–1).

[96] Bell (2007b: 124–30); he notes that recent excavations inside the so-called Public Office produced evidence that places its construction in the second half of the third century.

[97] Bell (2004: 140; 2007b: 124–30). Royal banks in Egypt: von Reden (2007: 253–79).

[98] Treziny (2018: 240–4).

[99] On the auction at Syracuse, see Cic. 2.*Verr*.3.14, 3.149. By way of parallel, auctions for contracts to collect taxes in Ptolemaic-controlled Lycia were held in Alexandria; see *P.Tebt*. 8. During the Republic, the Roman governor of Sicily was responsible for supervising the sale of the tithes; Cic. 2.*Verr*.3.83 and 3.117; Pritchard (1970: 354–5).

[100] As evidenced by references in the *De frumento* to civic documents recording the sale of the tithe belonging to a specific territory; e.g., Leontinoi (2.*Verr*.3.117), where in the text of his speech, Cicero indicates that he or a colleague read aloud the accounts from the auction specific to the tithes collected from the territory of Leontinoi during the governorship of G. Norbanus: *cedo mihi C. Norbani decumas venditas. C. NORBANI DECVMAE VENDITAE AGRI LEONTINOI.* At various places in the *De frumento*, Cicero refers to separate contracts to collect wheat (2.*Verr*.3.148–9) and barley (2.*Verr*.3.78), as well as the individual tithes for olive oil, wine, and other minor crops, like legumes and tree fruits (2.*Verr*.3.18).

[101] Cic. 2.*Verr*.3.99.

[102] *P.Rev.* Col. 33; trans. taken from Austin (2006: 522, no. 296). For a recent treatment of public auctions in Ptolemaic Egypt with focus on their role as fiscal institution, see Hogan (2019: 107–22).

[103] That census information was held for multiple years in civic archives is attested by Cicero's own experience in gathering data for his prosecution of Verres; 2.*Verr*.3.117, 3.120–1. See also Andreau (2007: 83).

[104] Kiser (1994: 287) underscores this by stressing that tax collectors who possessed local and specific knowledge regarding the types of taxes they were collecting (e.g., merchants who doubled as tax collectors of indirect taxes) stood a better chance of profit off their position.

[105] Cic. 2.*Verr*. 3.117.

[106] For translation and commentary, see Porten (2011: 363–5, C32).

[107] In Egypt, tax farmers who won bids to collect the *apomoira* tax (1/6th of production from orchards) were required to provide sureties totaling 1/20th above the closing bid within 30 days of the auction; *P.Rev.* Col. 34; Austin (2006: 522, no. 296).

[108] From the king's perspective, dividing up the tithe contracts into smaller units also may have served the purpose of discouraging any individual or group from gaining control over a too great a quantity of a single resource.

[109] On possible deadlines set by Hieronian law for the delivery of grain, see Goldsberry (1973: 136); Carcopino (1914: 22–3). Cicero (2.*Verr*.3.36) mentions that tithe grain was to be delivered by the first of August (*ante Kalendas Sextilis*) to prearranged transshipment points on the water.

[110] See *P.Rev.* Col. 42, where it is specified that these contracts between tax farmers and cultivators were to be drawn up in duplicate.

[111] Cicero (2.*Verr*.3.102) states that he obtained the *sationes* and *pactiones* from the civic registers (*ex litteris publicis*) of Hybla and Menai. And for the tax farmer's copy, see Cic. 2.*Verr*.3.112.

See also Carcopino (1914: 12–13); Scramuzza (1937: 237–8), regarding the necessity of having multiple copies of the *pactio*.

[112] This idea appears to have originated with Carcopino (1914: 18–19), who cites the requirement during the governorship of Verres; Cic. 2.*Verr.* 3.36–7. He is followed in this view by, among others, Berve (1959: 68) and Pritchard (1970: 358).

[113] Schwahn (RE s.v. "tributum" cols. 20–1); Scramuzza (1937: 237). This practice is documented in the *Lex Manciana*, a law of the early second century CE, which stipulated terms regarding tenancy on imperial estates in North Africa.

[114] Frank (1928: 795); Goldsberry (1973: 136–7).

[115] Discussed *infra* Chapter 5, pp. 184–5; and see Pelagatti (1970) for publication of the farmhouse.

[116] Given (2004: 31).

[117] Cic., 2.*Verr.*3.36–7.

[118] Dalman (1933). I initially learned of Dalman's study in Given (2004).

[119] Dalman (1933: 149–51).

[120] Soraci (2011: 50–2) offers a detailed discussion of the evidence for the *deportatio ad aquam* in the Late Republic, but does not weigh in on whether or not this procedural aspect of the first-century *lex Hieronica* had its roots in the third-century law.

[121] For discussion, see Pritchard (1970: 358–9), who ultimately concludes that the third-century law did, in fact, include a provision equivalent to the *deportatio ad aquam* and that the responsibility fell to the tax farmer, from the Hieronian period throughout the Republic.

[122] Personal communication with Sig. Bruno Cristiano and Sig. Filippo Campanella, both residents of Aidone. Similarly, Scalisi (2007: 69) notes that the within the modern province of Enna, cereal harvests around cities and towns in the central part of the province (e.g., Aidone, Raddusa, Valguarnera) generally begin several weeks earlier than the harvest in the northern part of the province.

[123] Verg. G. 311–26; translation by John Richmond. Many thanks to Richard Thomas for bringing this passage to my attention.

[124] In Ptolemaic Egypt, the presumed solution to this problem was to pass on the responsibility of assessment to local officials, who were more intimately aware of local land tenure and conditions of climate and harvest; see Manning (2007: 456). For an example from a significantly later period, see Vester (2004: 774, n. 70).

[125] E.g., *P.Hib.* 98, a transit receipt from the year 251, which specifies a *deigma* of barley accompany the larger shipment of grain. For additional discussion, see Thompson (1983: 65–7).

[126] As noted by Given (2004: 96–7).

[127] See, for instance, Zola Packman's study of receipts from the Diospolis Magna granary, which were issued at the time of payment, signed by the taxpayer and countersigned by a granary official, and stored in the granary's archive; Packman (1968).

[128] For the date of the *Sand Reckoner*, see Knorr (1978: 234–8), who characterizes the treatise as a "popularizing effort" that set forth no "serious mathematical result." As Knorr notes, this might very well have been due to the professed audience of the work. For more detailed discussion of the treatise and Archimedes' method, see Netz (2003; 2009).

[129] Archim. *Sand Reckoner* 258.5–12 (Heiberg). Translation after Berrey (2017: 134).

[130] Berrey (2017: 135).

[131] Again, see Knorr (1978: 238), who deemed the treatise to have "no serious scientific objective."

[132] For discussion of four such treatises, see Berrey (2017).

[133] Eutocius *In Libros Archimedis de Sphaera et Cylindro* II 90.13–27 (Heiberg); translation after Berrey (2017: 166).

[134] The importance of standardizing units of measurement and the relationship between measurement costs and a ruler's choice of revenue system are topics explored by Levi (1988: 29).

[135] Kiser (1994: 292) notes that rulers might effectively use auctions to measure assets, particularly when variations in value were frequent and unpredictable.

136 Andreau (2007: 82–4). Cicero (2.*Verr*.3.112) himself noted the need for extensive documentation in the operation of the tithe. On the variety of written texts referred to in the *Verrine Orations*, see Butler (2002: 35–60).

137 Regarding the production and storage of documents related to the Hieronian tax laws, see Bell (2007a: 128–9).

138 See Bell (2007a: 129–30) for the question of whether or not papyrus grew in Sicily during the Hellenistic period, as it does today, or was a species introduced by Arab settlers in the ninth century. The discovery of several inkwells from third-century-BCE contexts at Morgantina may also point to the habit of writing on papyri; for discussion see Sjöqvist (1959); Stone (2014: 99–100).

139 An archive of papyri documents that were once held in Temple C at Selinus has been discussed on the basis of a large number of surviving cretule found in the immediate vicinity of the temple, where they appear to have been burned during the capture of the city in 250; see Salinas (1883; 1889) and Zoppi (1996).

140 That even this amount of detail only scratched the surface of what was possible to know is suggested by the level of documentation that survives from the Ptolemaic Egypt; see, for instance, Clarysse and Thompson (2006), who present copious evidence related to the collection of census data and the salt tax, and, similarly, Monson (2012), regarding land survey and assessment.

141 This, of course, is not to suggest that data collection was flawless in either its execution or outcome, as we should fully expect there to have been resistance at the local level and blind spots stemming from imperfect implementation of novel or unpopular administrative practices. On this point, see Manning and Scheidel (2010), who in reviewing the work of Clarysse and Thompson (2006) draw attention to the limitations of royal surveillance revealed by the papyrological evidence. Yet even accounting for such limitations and blind spots, the amount of centralized data collected by the Hieronian state was surely vast and arguably unprecedented for its time in the context of Sicily.

FIVE

STANDARDS AND THE STATE

Almost every town in Sicily, and even various articles, had a different weight and measure, til his Sicilian Majesty, by a Decree dated the 31st December, 1809, ordered, that from the 1st of January, 1811, there should be an uniformity of Weights and Measures, throughout the island, upon the following metrological system.
—John Galt, *Voyages and Travels* (1812)

They [uniform measures] also enhanced administrative control over matters of taxation and economic development. At the same time, an impressive display of state power was required to enact the new system in the first place.
—Theodore Porter, *Trust in Numbers* (1995)

On the morning of January 8, 1790, President George Washington delivered his first Annual Message to a joint session of the United States Congress at Federal Hall in New York City. In what would become a model for all future State of the Union addresses, the president laid out what he saw as the principal administrative challenges and legislative priorities facing the new country. Washington's concerns for the defense and well-being of the young nation were paramount, so it cannot be overlooked that in such a short speech – numbering only seven handwritten pages – the president would proclaim that "[u]niformity in the currency, weights, and measures of the United States is an object of great importance," and would go on to urge the Congress to swiftly attend to creating a common set of standards for the country.[1] Washington's call for the creation of a common currency and uniform system of measurement may serve as a useful, if unorthodox, introduction to the discussion of metrological standardization in the Hieronian kingdom more than two millennia earlier.

While not to push the analogy beyond its useful limits, there is certainly common ground to be found in the shared concern for establishing a shared standard for weights and measures. After all, both president and king found themselves as the preeminent political leader of their respective states, each newly fashioned from a number of smaller polities and each host to a motley array of metrological units.[2] Indeed, one of the foundational acts performed by new rulers throughout history has been to validate or establish standards of weight and measure within the territory subject to their authority. In circumstances involving the political unification of previously independent communities, common standards furnished an expedient means of integration under a single, central authority.

On his accession to kingship, Hieron found himself exercising authority over a patchwork of communities ranging from large *poleis* to smaller satellite towns and agrarian villages. Each of the formerly autonomous polities that now recognized his *basileia* had itself previously controlled the selection of its own civic standards according to norms determined by local authorities and dominant commercial networks. Consolidating authority over this mosaic of communities required the imposition of kingdom-wide metrological standards for currency, weights, and measures that comported with the royal purse. To be certain, Hieron's principal concern lay not with strengthening the unity of his fledgling state, as seems to have been on President Washington's mind. Rather, it was a decidedly less noble ambition: the need to facilitate taxation and generate revenue, which motivated him to seek metrological consolidation.[3]

As we established in the previous chapter, the administration of the Hieronian tithe rested on the efficient collection and dissemination of large amounts of data. Because the king relied on the revenue generated from this tax on agricultural production, it was in his interest to remove the obstacles to data collection that made his kingdom less intelligible and thus less taxable. A multiplicity of civic standards was one such obstacle. Without a common set of standards – a shared language of measurement by which royal officials, tax farmers, and cultivators could communicate – the collection of royal taxes within the Hieronian kingdom would have been costly and inefficient.

STANDARDS AND THE STATE

For as long as states have extracted resources, rulers have sought to establish and enforce metrological standards.[4] Together with the power to mint coinage, the authority to establish the standards for "legitimate" weights and measures has historically been the prerogative of the state, which Hector Vera aptly describes as possessing a "monopoly on the legitimate means of measure."[5]

In many ancient states, the relationship between sovereign rulers and units of measurement found personal expression.[6] We see this relationship between ruler and metrological standards manifest already by the third millennium in a number of stone weights that date to the reign of the Sumerian king Shulgi (c. 2094–c. 2046). One such weight, carved from black diorite (Figure 5.1), bears a well-preserved inscription that reads:

> For the god Nanna, his lord,
> Shulgi, mighty man, king of Ur, king of the four lands
> Confirm[ed] (this stone weight to be) one half mina.[7]

Here, the unit value of the physical weight is validated by Shulgi, whose authority over such matters is implicitly communicated by attaching his name and titles (king of Ur, king of the four lands) to the stone itself. While lacking such boastful grandiloquence, fifth-century Athenian weights were occasionally inscribed with the word ΔΕΜΟΣ or ΔΕΜΟΣΙΟΝ to serve the very same purpose, since in democratic Athens, the *dēmos* became guarantor of officially sanctioned units of weight and measure (Figure 5.2).[8] In each of these cases, it

5.1 Stone weight inscribed with name of the Sumerian king Shulgi, ca. 2094–2046 BCE (Musée du Louvre, inv. AO 22187; image: © 2005 RMN-Grand Palais, musée du Louvre/ Franck Raux).

is understood that the legitimacy of a notional set of standards, along with the validity of the physical devices created to represent it, rests on endorsement by the state's prevailing sovereign authority.

In much the same way, Hellenistic monarchs exercised their authority to designate and enforce state-sanctioned standards for measurement.[9] This took a variety of forms, some more overt than others. The large number of inscribed weights from the Seleucid kingdom often bear evidence of their validation by the addition of royal titulature or symbols, such as found on a lead mina weight produced during the reign of Antiochos IV Epiphanes (r. 175–164) and now held in the Bibliothèque nationale de France (Figure 5.3).[10] As Paul Kosmin's recent study of the Seleucid dating system so persuasively argues, even the measurement of time was subject to royal intervention.[11] Certainly, the most recognizable expression of this prerogative to control the legitimate means of measurement came with the production of coinage – an arena in which Hellenistic kings truly excelled.[12] Yet, apart from the rich corpus of coinage struck by kings in this period, the material culture associated with royal efforts to promote and enforce metrological standards has not elicited sufficient

5.2 Official terracotta dry measure from Athens, ca. 450-425 BCE (Agora inv. AP 1103; Ephorate of Antiquities of Athens City, Ancient Agora, ASCSA: Agora Excavations; © Hellenic Ministry of Culture and Sports/Hellenic Organization of Cultural Resources Development [HOCRED]).

5.3 Lead mina weight produced during the reign of the Seleucid king Antiochos IV Epiphanes, r. 175–164 BCE (left: after Rostovzeff 1941; right: after Babelon and Blanchet 1895).

attention, even as scholars increasingly recognize such efforts as vital to royal administration.

That this essential element of kingdom-building has long fallen outside the mainstream discussions of Hellenistic kingship is understandable for several reasons. The otherwise considerable documentary record left behind by the major Successor kingdoms reveals very little by way of explicit testimony about the administrative deliberations behind standardization, let alone a public appeal of the kind issued by George Washington.[13] Moreover, with the exception of coinage, the material evidence associated with measurement has rarely escaped the orbit of its affiliated subdisciplines (e.g., historical metrology) to serve broader investigations of ancient economy and administration.[14] Few if any scholars have expressed honest vexation that the utilitarian tools of administration have not garnered the same degree of attention as the spectacular monuments erected by kings to communicate their wealth and military might. Astonished, indeed, would we be to discover a bronze equestrian statue of a Hellenistic king, wielding a measuring rod instead of a spear, or a votive dedication that boasted of his victory over the armies of incommensurate measures that once occupied one's kingdom.[15] So, even as greater attention is paid to advancing our understanding of the fiscal regimes and administration of Hellenistic kingdoms, our appreciation of this vital aspect of ancient statecraft has remained relatively static. In an effort to advance this conversation and provide avenues for future research, let us examine the evidence for the standardization of volumetric measurement within the Hieronian state. In this, we are aided by the survival of a relatively large body of material evidence that only recently has gained the attention of archaeologists working in parts of Sicily that formerly comprised the kingdom of Hieron II. Here, I refer to the remains of ceramic measuring vessels, which in their form, capacity, and decoration show adherence to a coherent metrological standard.

SETTING STANDARDS IN HIERONIAN SICILY

Based on the discussion in Chapter 4, there can be no doubt that a shared standard of volumetric measurement was essential at every step of the tithe operation, from the initial reporting of planting statistics to the final reckoning of payments due to the crown. Without common units of measurement, Hieron could provide no equitable grounds for collecting reliable information about his kingdom's productivity or synthesizing the vast amount of information required for the successful operation of the tithe. Only with a unified system of measurement could the amount of grain sown and harvested in the territory of Akrai, for example, or the quantity of olive oil produced in the territory of Syracuse be accurately assessed, reducing the potential for under-reporting or misreporting of amounts due to errors in conversion.[16] The king and his administrators could not afford reporting in disparate units. Disputes over incommensurate measurements at any stage in the collection process threatened administrative gridlock and public disaffection, both potentially disruptive to the operations that brought agricultural produce from farmland across eastern Sicily to the royal storerooms at Syracuse. The absence of a common standard for measuring volume would be stifling, as producers, tax collectors, and royal authorities would be forced to make sense of a variety of local units of measure, not to mention variations in the actual vessels themselves.[17] A single, kingdom-wide volumetric standard would increase the efficiency of assessment by reducing the need to make conversions between local civic standards and royal tax standards.

Fixed volumetric units would have also benefited the individuals who came to Syracuse to bid on the right to collect the tithes. Without access to accurate data on annual harvests, potential tax farmers would be less inclined to bid at auction, since any inconsistency in amounts reported and actual amounts harvested increased the risk of lost revenue. Common standards for measuring volume allowed for greater transparency on the part of both taxpayer and tax collector. Thinking back to Levi's concept of quasi-voluntary compliance, fostering such transparency was of paramount concern since the perception of unfair or unequal assessment could undermine public willingness to comply with taxation. Thomas Figueira recognized wide compliance as one of the intangible benefits of metrological consolidation within the Athenian *arkē* during the fifth century. Transparency, he contends,

> fostered by even a partial convergence of metrological standards would not only promote facility of administration, an obvious concern of the

Athenians, but would also enhance allied ability to judge for themselves whether Athens had assessed their own city's tribute fairly and commensurably with the assessments of others. Reciprocal policing of assessments by different allied governments helped to create equitable treatment as well as the perception that all the allies bore a proportionate burden.[18]

In this way, unified measurement served as a shared vocabulary with which royal officials could translate harvest data to assess productivity across the kingdom; it was an intelligible grammar with which tax farmers could estimate yields from far-flung territories and a common language with which cultivators could defend themselves against potential abuses of tax farmers.

In the following sections, we turn our attention to a distinctive class of ceramic vessel that first appears in the archaeological record during the reign of Hieron II. Consideration of the formal characteristics exhibited by the majority of known specimens leads to the conclusion that these vessels are capacity measures used for liquid and dry goods. Having established that these vessels belonged to a coherent system of measurement, I go on to argue that the physical measures are themselves evidence of Hieronian efforts to promote metrological standards, basing my conclusions on both the overall uniformity they exhibit and their contemporaneous debut in the archaeological record at disparate sites across eastern Sicily. This conclusion is corroborated by the survival of several measuring vessels that were stamped by a royal official who confirmed their volumetric accuracy. Taken together, these artifacts reveal much about the Hieronian administration's efforts to promote the use of common volumetric standards throughout the kingdom, observations that might in turn be profitably applied to the study of efforts made by other Hellenistic monarchs to bring about metrological standardization within their respective kingdoms.

A STANDARD EMERGES

A farmer entering the agora at Morgantina around the year 250, intending to pay their share of agricultural taxes and perhaps purchase some goods at market, would have encountered a novel type of measuring device in the hands of those officials stationed at the massive new granary buildings that overlooked the entrance to the city. After handing over the king's share of the harvest, the farmer, now venturing to purchase additional provisions, would have found merchants wielding nearly identical vessels as they hawked their goods from the market stalls scattered around the public square. Knowingly or not, the farmer was witness to the outcome of a royal initiative that had originated in Syracuse and was intended to facilitate the assessment and collection of the agricultural taxes that the farmer and other cultivators now owed each year to the king. Although our farmer had encountered measuring devices in the hands of merchants for as long as could be recalled, the older vessels had always varied in their form and appearance to a far greater degree than those which now pervaded the city in both public and private contexts. In fact, the farmer now kept several measuring vessels of this new type in their small farmstead down in the *chora*, where grain was threshed in the late summer after the harvest. These were essential tools, indeed, as individuals now arrived each summer to fix the amount of produce owed in taxes to the king. These individuals purportedly carried measures of identical capacity to those in the possession of the farmer, but one could never be too careful when it came to something as important as parting with one's hard-earned harvest.

While the emergence of this measuring technology would have been immediately apparent to our third-century denizen of Morgantina, it has only recently come into focus for archaeologists working in Sicily, for whom ancient volumetric measures are not an especially well-known class of artifact.[19] The new devices used for measuring out dry goods were cylindrical in shape with straight, almost vertical, sides that were often marked on the exterior with incised horizontal bands. These dry measures came in a variety of sizes, ranging from small, handheld devices that might contain enough grain to feed an individual for a day or two to much larger vessels that were good for bulk transactions. New standardized liquid measures also appeared at this time. These took the form of small single-handled pitchers with bulbous bodies and narrow necks to prevent spillage.

It was not that these vessels took a radically different form compared with the capacity measures that our farmer had previously encountered in the hands of merchants and traders who sold goods in the agora at Morgantina. What the farmer might have found remarkable, however, was the consistency of appearance that the new measures exhibited. This was particularly evident in their simple decoration, which tended to be limited to a series of horizontal bands incised around the exterior of the vessels. On the smaller dry measures, these bands might decorate the entirety of the vessel, while the larger ones, particularly those with tripod-like feet, tended to have bands only around the uppermost portion of the body. Even the liquid measures had these distinctive bands incised around the neck of the vessel. Here, it is worth noting that the number of incised bands appears to have no direct correlation to a vessel's volume (i.e., 12 grooves $\neq$ 12 units). Moreover, the bands did not serve as some form of graduation, like the lines found on a modern measuring cup. Rather, the banding likely served as a simple visual signifier of the vessel's function, one that allowed for easy identification as a measuring device.[20] The addition of a light-yellow slip applied to the exterior surface of these vessels before the firing process served to further elide any discernible inconsistency in their appearance, heightening the sense of uniformity among this new class of capacity measure. So consistent, in fact, was the visual appearance of these new measures that a merchant traveling from Syracuse might have carried with them a set of measures nearly identical to those used by a merchant in the agora at Kamarina or a cultivator in the territory of Akrai.[21]

To date, the remains of over 100 individual measures belonging to this new volumetric system have been identified at five different locations in eastern Sicily: Syracuse, Megara Hyblaia, Kamarina, Morgantina, and Contrada Aguglia, a site that lies in the territory of ancient Akrai. Judging from the archaeological record, this new class of measuring vessel first arrived at urban centers and rural sites around southeastern Sicily in the second quarter of the third century. As will be discussed in further detail below, the geographic distribution of these measures not only corresponds to what is known from surviving historical sources about the territorial extent of the Hieronian kingdom, but may even be used as the basis for extending the boundaries far beyond what has come down to us in the histories of Diodorus Siculus and Polybius.

Dry Measures

Among the quantity of identifiable measures that survive today in museums and archaeological storerooms, the majority appear to have been of the variety used for measuring out dry goods like cereals, legumes, and dried tree fruits. These can be categorized into three types, which are primarily distinguished from one another by size and form.[22] With few exceptions, I have chosen to represent the capacity of these and the other measures discussed below with integers that most closely approximate the actual or estimated volume of these vessels. This is not to ignore the appreciable variation in volume, which might today be considered unacceptable for a calibrated measuring instrument. Rather, this is done to highlight the proportional relationship shared by the different vessel types and sizes with respect to their capacity. It is not the precision of any individual measure vis-à-vis a theoretical norm expected for an ancient capacity unit that serves as a criterion for a vessel's association with the standard describe here, but rather the broader set of shared stylistic characteristics and proportional relationships exhibited by the class of artifacts on the whole.

Type 1: These are the smallest dry measures in terms of volume and are the most well represented in the archaeological record by number of identifiable fragments. They are characterized by their simple, cylindrical form and incised banding, which tends to extend over the entirety of the vessel's exterior (Figure 5.4). The walls of some well-preserved specimens curve slightly inward around the middle, an attribute that may have helped one to grip the vessel when scooping or filling it with dry goods. Type 1 vessels tend to range in diameter between 10 and 16 centimeters, depending on their capacity. At

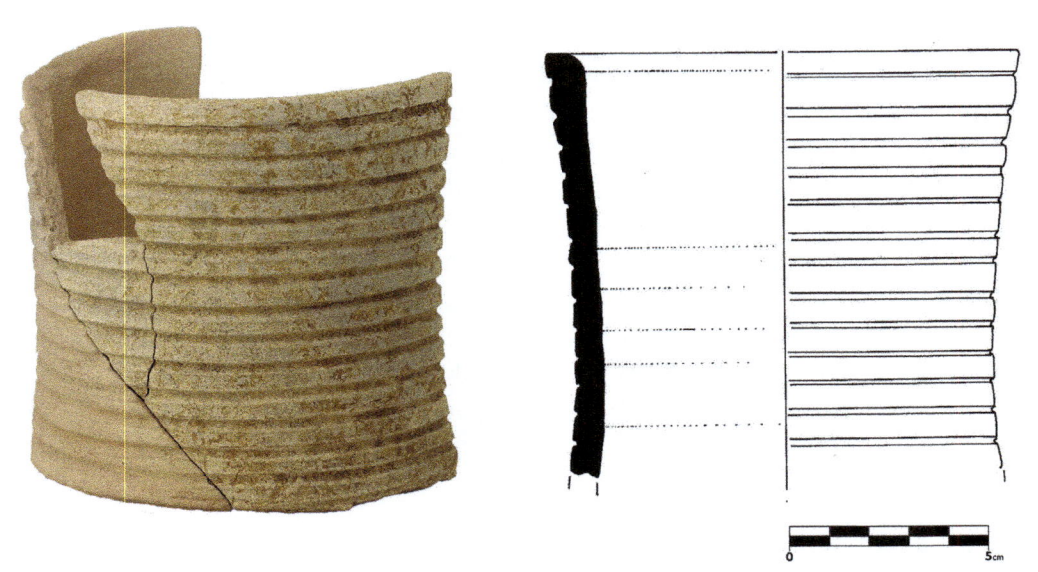

5.4 Type 1 dry measure from Morgantina, third century BCE (Museo Archeologico Regionale di Aidone, inv. 84-193; photo: A. Maggio; drawing: F. Pisciotta; courtesy of the American Excavations at Morgantina).

5.5 Type 2 dry measure from Morgantina, third century BCE (Museo Archeologico Regionale di Aidone, inv. 62-1447; photo: C. Williams; drawing: F. Pisciotta; courtesy of the American Excavations at Morgantina).

Morgantina, Type 1 vessels of two different sizes have been securely identified. The smaller vessels held ~1 liter, while the larger size had a capacity of ~2 liters.

Type 2: These vessels are slightly larger than the Type 1 measures with respect to both their size and capacity. Type 2 measures have straight, inward-sloping walls, flat bases, and a single vertical strap handle, which gives the vessel the appearance of an oversized mug (Figure 5.5).[23] Type 2 measures tend to have little or none of the incised banding found on other types. That they belonged to the same system of standardized measurement as the other vessels described here is established by the archaeological contexts in which these vessels are found, as well as by their capacities, which exhibit a volumetric relationship with the other standardized types. Type 2 measures may have been

5.6 Type 3 dry measure from Morgantina, third century BCE (Museo Archeologico Regionale di Aidone, inv. 62-1448; photo: A. Maggio; drawing: F. Pisciotta; courtesy of the American Excavations at Morgantina).

manufactured in multiple sizes like their Type 1 counterparts. Of the known specimens from Morgantina, at least two individual vessels have estimated volumes on the order of ~3.2 liters.[24] There are also a number of Type 2 measures of a smaller capacity that, for the most part, survive in only fragmentary states. One nearly complete vessel of this smaller scale, however, has been recovered in recent excavations at the site; this has a volume of ~2 liters.[25] At the moment, it is unclear whether these larger and smaller vessels were intended to hold two discrete volumetric units or just one, in which case we should interpret the surviving specimens as having been manufactured in such a way that their capacities strayed by degrees from their intended value, resulting in vessels that were slightly larger or slightly smaller than the ideal unit. Here, we shall treat the vessels as representative of two distinct units.[26]

Type 3: These are the largest class of standardized dry measure belonging to the new system. They are cylindrical in form with straight vertical walls and are decorated with the characteristic exterior banding found on Type 1 vessels, although never for the entire elevation of the body (Figure 5.6). Rather, these bands are typically confined to the upper portion of the body, extending down from the vessel's lip to cover upward of one-quarter of the exterior surface. Many, although certainly not all, Type 3 vessels have a vertical strap handle, which may have facilitated emptying the vessel when filled or provided a sturdy means of carrying the vessel when empty. The largest vessels of the Type 3 variety were occasionally manufactured with three small, tripod-like feet. The dimensions of these larger measures vary according to capacity, with rim diameters tending to fall between 30 and 40 centimeters. Type 3 vessels appear to have been manufactured in at least two standard sizes with capacities corresponding to roughly ~16 liters and ~32 liters.

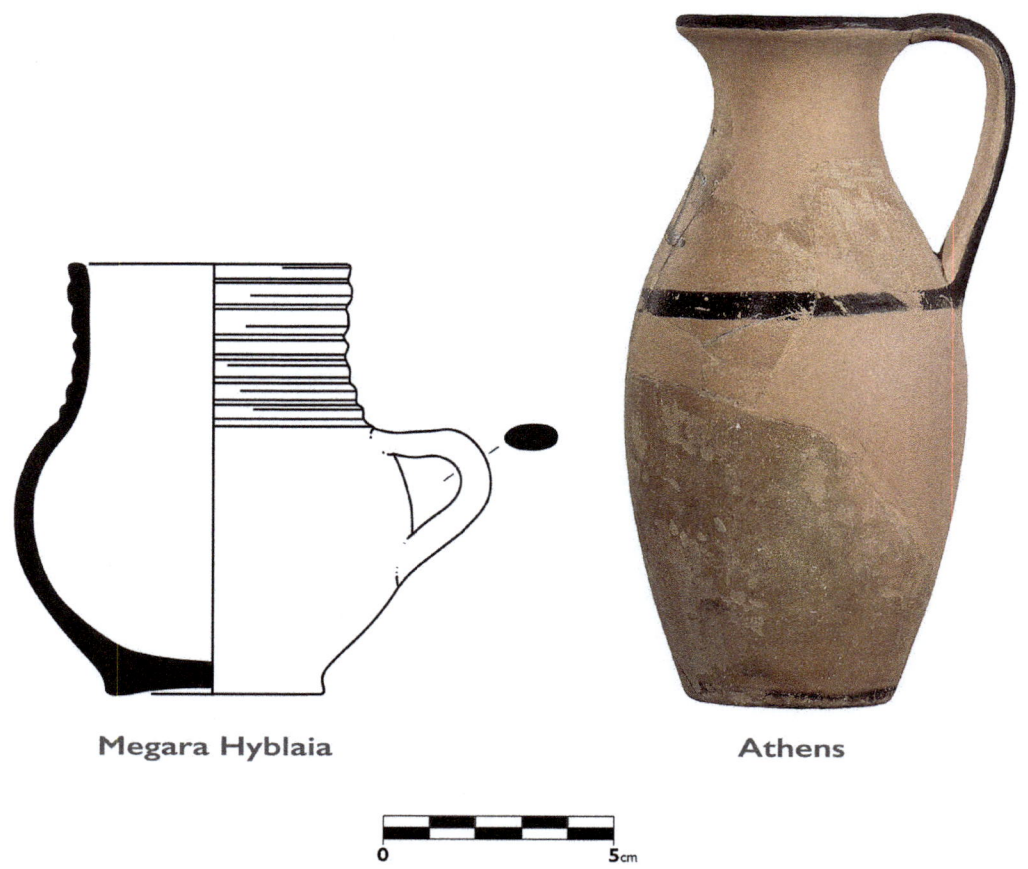

Megara Hyblaia   **Athens**

5.7 Left: Line drawing of liquid measure from Megara Hyblaia, third century BCE (after Tréziny 2018); right: official liquid measure from Athens, fifth century BCE (Agora inv. P 13429; Ephorate of Antiquities of Athens City, Ancient Agora, ASCSA: Agora Excavations; © Hellenic Ministry of Culture and Sports/Hellenic Organization of Cultural Resources Development [HOCRED]).

Liquid Measures

We possess far fewer examples of standardized liquid measures belonging to this new system. Of this number, only those from Megara Hyblaia have been published.[27] The surviving specimens all appear to share a rather uniform body type, resembling that of an *olpe* with a bulbous body, single handle, and high, narrow neck to prevent spills (Figure 5.7). In its basic form, this shape is similar to the standardized liquid measures found at Athens and Olympia.[28] As noted above, these vessels share the same horizontal banding found on the dry measures, decoration that may have served to distinguish them as part of the new system of standardized measurement.[29] This banding seems to have been restricted to the neck of the vessel. Like the dry measures, these liquid measures were manufactured in a range of sizes, although only one liquid measure of this system has survived in sufficiently good condition to accurately determine its capacity. The vessel in question, which was found at Megara Hyblaia, held ~0.3 liter.[30] Henri Trénziny, who published this and the other standardized measures from Megara Hyblaia, has noted the existence of fragments belonging to several larger liquid measures, which he speculates may have had a capacity closer to ~1 liter.

From the preceding discussion, we may note that consistency of both form and appearance served to distinguish this new class of standardized capacity measures. Next, we will consider the date and distribution of surviving specimens of this system. Looking ahead, I will argue that the swift adoption of this new, highly standardized technology was prompted by royal initiative from the Hieronian court.

Date and Distribution

Judging from the archaeological record, this new class of standardized measuring vessel found its way into daily use across southeastern Sicily within a very narrow window of time. The best evidence for establishing the chronology of the new system comes from Morgantina, where the remains of over seventy-five individual measures have come to light during the American-led excavations taking place at the site since 1955. Collectively, the evidence from Morgantina tells a story of the swift adoption and diffusion within both private and public sectors of the ancient city during the second and third quarters of the third century. The markedly increased presence of these vessels in archaeological contexts dating to this relatively narrow period of time stands in stark contrast to the near total absence of identifiable volumetric measures from contexts of preceding or successive centuries.

These third-century contexts may themselves be further distinguished by association with two important events in the city's history, events that left behind a clear impression in the archaeological record. The first was the realization of a monumental building program that radically transformed the city's agora around the middle of the third century (ca. 260/250).[31] The second event took place in the year 211 when, during the course of the Second Punic War, the city was besieged and eventually captured by Roman forces under the command of the praetor M. Cornelius Cethegus.[32] Archaeologists have identified sealed stratigraphic deposits produced by both events and, within those deposits, recovered the remains of standardized measures of the types outlined above.

The earliest archaeological contexts at Morgantina in which dry measures of this new standard turn up are those associated with the destruction of the northern wing of the Central Shops, a suite of six rooms located in the city's lower agora (Figure 5.8). During the 260s, these rooms were intentionally razed nearly to their foundations and then covered over with a thick leveling

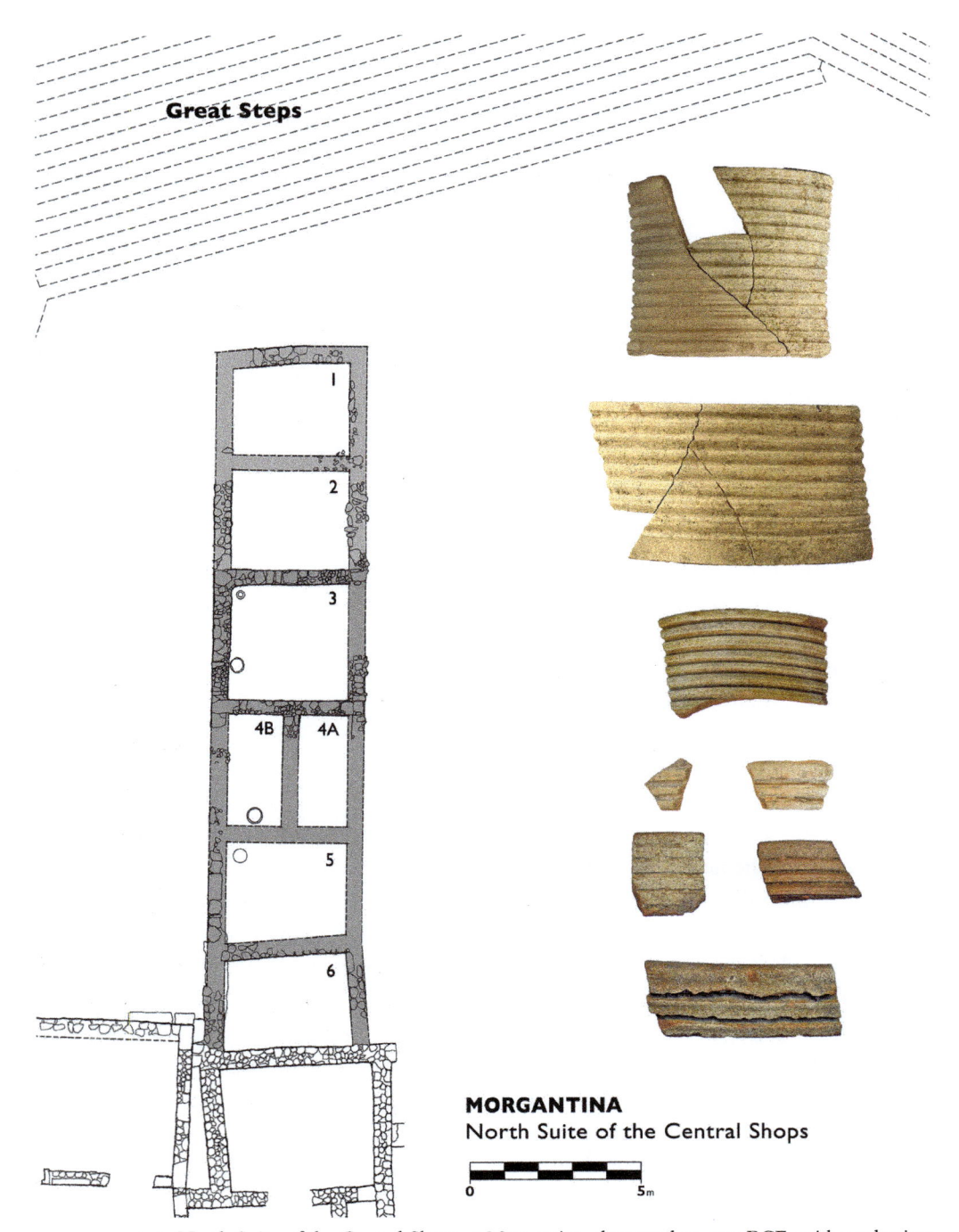

5.8 North Suite of the Central Shops at Morgantina, destroyed ca. 250 BCE, with a selection of standardized measuring vessel fragments found within the shop rooms shown at the right (drawing: E. Thorkildsen; photos: author; courtesy of the American Excavations at Morgantina)

fill that raised the surface of the surrounding area by more than 30 centimeters.[33] This was done to accommodate the construction of the Great Steps, a monumental flight of stairs that connected the upper and lower agora and likely served as the meeting place of the city's *ekklesia*. Archaeologists recovered fragments belonging to at least fifteen individual measures of Type 1 and Type 3 varieties from the stratified contexts inside the shop rooms, as well as from within the layer of intentional fill above, establishing beyond a doubt that measures of this new standard were in use by the year 260.

The second major event, the Roman siege of 211, left traces in the archaeological record resulting from the actual violence that befell the city (at times distinguished by layers of ash and debris), as well from the "clean-up" efforts that took place in the aftermath of the siege. The archaeological contexts associated with the post-siege recovery are characterized by activities like infilling of domestic cisterns with ceramic debris and rubble.[34] Excavators found fragments belonging to dozens of individual liquid and dry measures in these archaeological deposits, which help to establish a *terminus ante quem* of ca. 211 for the manufacture and use of both the liquid measure and all three types of dry measure belonging to this new system.

Among the buildings that suffered irreparable damage during the siege were the North and South Demeter Sanctuaries. Inside the South Demeter Sanctuary, excavators discovered a Type 2 measure and a Type 3 measure lying together, smashed on the floor of the sanctuary's storeroom.[35] The two measures share a 1:10 volumetric relationship (~3.2 liters to ~32 liters), suggesting that they were used in conjunction with one another. From among the destruction debris inside the North Demeter Sanctuary, archaeologists recovered a nearly complete Type 2 measure with an approximate capacity of ~3.2 liters, as well as several large fragments belonging to a Type 3 measure with a capacity of ~16 liters.[36] Standardized measures were also found inside many of the houses that suffered damage or were abandoned around the time of the siege, including among the well-appointed Hellenistic residences that clustered on the hills nearest the agora.[37] More were recovered in large numbers within the sub-elite neighborhoods farther from the city center. From one such residential complex east of the agora, in a district known today as Contrada Drago, portions of several dry measures were found inside what appears to have been a domestic storeroom.[38]

The picture that emerges from Morgantina offers clear indication that both liquid and dry measures of this new system came into use by the second quarter of the third century and remained a common feature in the city for the next several decades, down to the time of the Roman siege. As noted above, the remains of standardized measures belonging to this system have yet to turn up in deposits predating the second quarter of the third century. Moreover, there is no compelling evidence that these vessel types continued to be manufactured or used much beyond 211. The number of identifiable measures found in contexts dated to the second and first centuries can be counted on a single hand. Moreover, these are so fragmentary that they are most convincingly interpreted as the by-products of residual circulation within construction fills and refuse deposits, rather than as instruments found in context of primary use. Thus, the broader perspective afforded by the archaeological remains at Morgantina certainly supports the claim that the adoption and floruit of this system of standardized volumetric measure was very much a third-century phenomenon.

We find corroborating evidence at several other sites in southeastern Sicily. Excavations in the agora of Kamarina produced fragments belonging to roughly two dozen measuring vessels of the new system. Among this number, upward of half were recovered in and around the so-called West Stoa, a long, rectangular building (ca. 6.5 meters × 60.5 meters) that delimited the western edge of the city's Classical and Early Hellenistic agora (Figure 5.9).[39] The discovery of a cache of several hundred Greco-Italic amphoras within the building has led to its identification as a public warehouse.[40] Within the West Stoa, archaeologists also recovered ceramic fragments belonging to several standardized measures of both liquid and dry types.[41] In her initial publication of the building, Paola Pelagatti suggested that the abandonment of

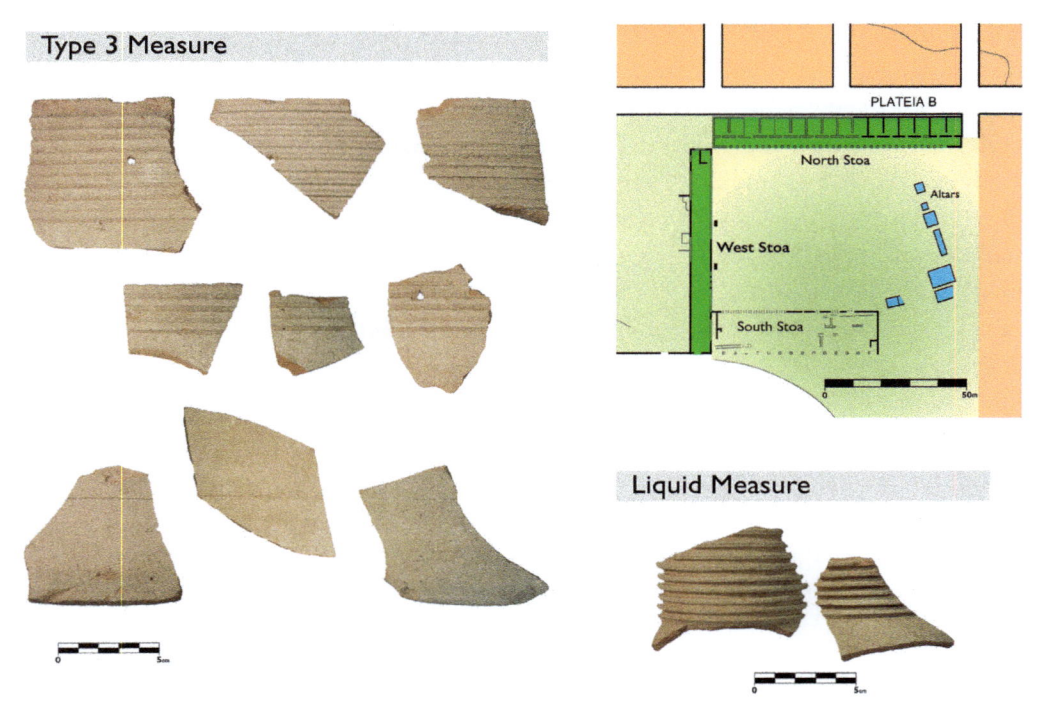

5.9 Remains of two standardized measuring vessels recovered from the Hellenistic agora at Kamarina, third century BCE (photos: author; courtesy of the Polo Regionale di Ragusa per i siti culturali e per i Parchi archeologici di Kamarina e Cava d'Ispica).

the West Stoa might have been the result of the Roman siege of 258.[42] If correct, the measures found sealed by the abandonment layers of the West Stoa would confirm that adoption of the volumetric standard at Kamarina occurred around the same time as at Morgantina. Yet whatever damage was caused by the Roman siege of 258, it did not permanently disrupt the livelihood of Kamarina. In fact, subsequent excavations in the area immediately surrounding the West Stoa have brought to light ample evidence that the ancient agora remained a locus of commercial activity throughout the third century. In particular, the excavations conducted by Giovanni Di Stefano in the space between the West Stoa and North Stoa brought to light fragments belonging to various liquid and dry measures along with a large number of bronze coins of the Hieronian mint.[43] It is within this third-century milieu that the standardized measures from Kamarina belong, a situation that finds close analogy with the contemporary use of the measures at Morgantina.

Fragments of many vessels belonging to this new standard have been unearthed throughout the decades at Syracuse, especially around the Neapolis district of the city, which not incidentally was first systematically developed during the reign of Hieron II (Figure 5.10). These, however, have largely come to light in the course of rescue excavations conducted in advance of new construction around the modern city and thus lack secure archaeological context. Nevertheless, the fact that these vessels so clearly resemble their counterparts from Kamarina and Morgantina leaves little doubt as to their association with this new system. From the neighboring city of Megara Hyblaia, archaeologists have identified fragments of fourteen individual liquid and dry measures from occupation contexts of Hellenistic date.[44] Among this number was one well-preserved liquid measure of this new standard, which had been buried in a sealed well deposit of secure third-century date. Rounding out this number are the measures discovered at the farmstead at Contrada Aguglia in the territory of Akrai.[45] The archaeologists responsible for excavating the farmstead reported fragments belonging to at least two distinct Type 3 measures, which had been thrown down a well inside the property. One of the two was sufficiently well preserved to estimate a volume of ~32 liters.[46]

When we step back to consider the geographic distribution of these standardized measures, they are clearly clustered in the southeastern portion of the island (Figure 5.11). To date, no standardized measures belonging to the new system described above have come to light at sites in western Sicily, either in published excavation reports or within museum collections.[47]

To fully grasp the magnitude of the third-century proliferation of standardized measures in southeastern Sicily, we must take account of the comparable dearth of identifiable measures from the preceding centuries. The number of published measures of pre-Hieronian date from Sicily can be counted on one

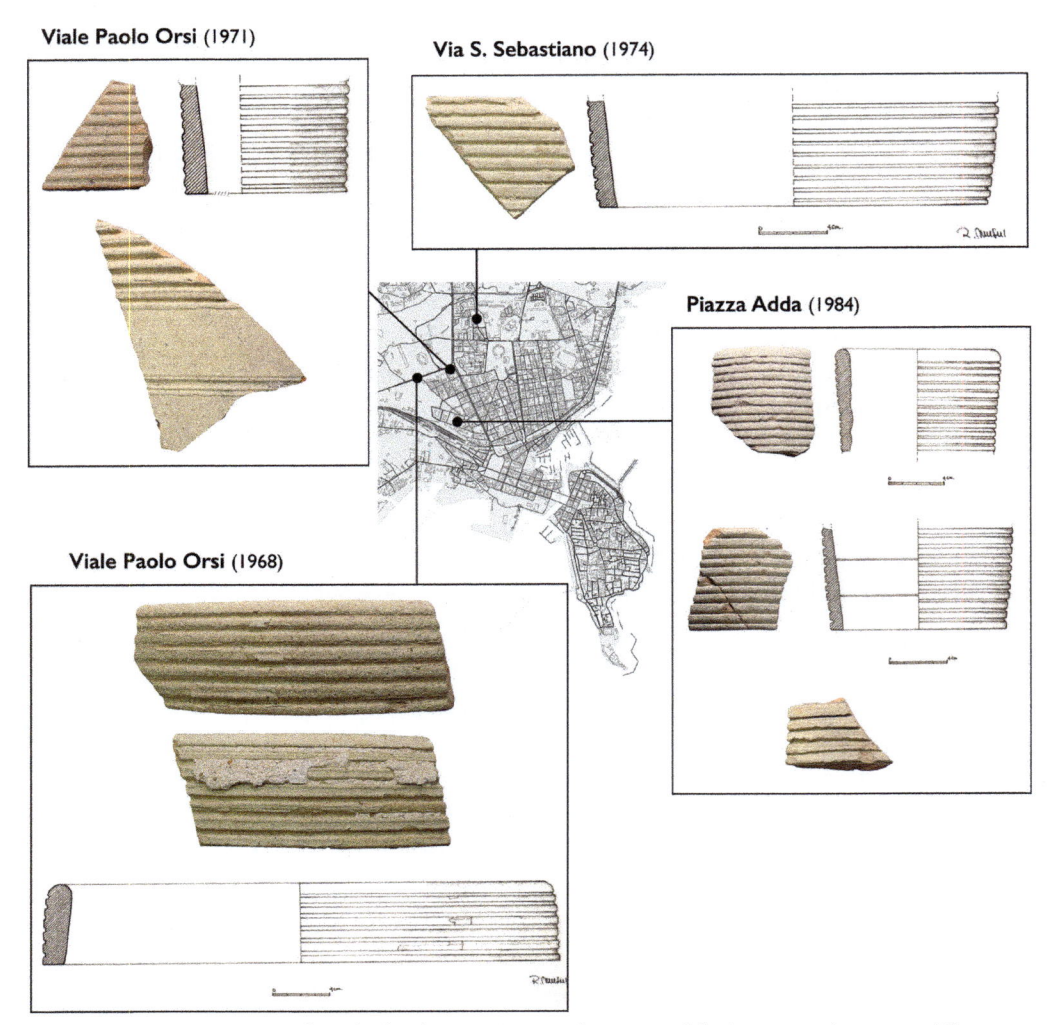

5.10 Remains of standardized measuring vessels recovered during excavations around Syracuse, third century BCE (photos: author; drawings: R. Musumeci; courtesy of the Parco Archeologico e paesaggistico di Siracusa, Eloro, Villa del Tellaro e Akrai).

hand.[48] The four known specimens share no stylistic affinities, aside from their general cylindrical form and the telltale presence of horizontal bands, incised around the vessels' exteriors. The vessels come from three sites – Naxos, Leontinoi, and Kamarina – and all have been dated on archaeological grounds to the fourth or early third century. Three of the four vessels appear to have been produced in Sicily, while the fourth – that discovered at Naxos – may be an Attic import. Notably, the vessels of Sicilian manufacture appear to share some relationship with contemporary Attic units of measure. The excavator of the Kamarina measure, for instance, associates its capacity with the Attic *trihemikotylon* (~0.41 liter), while the better-preserved of the two measures from Leontinoi (vol. ~0.65 liter) approximates the volume of an Attic

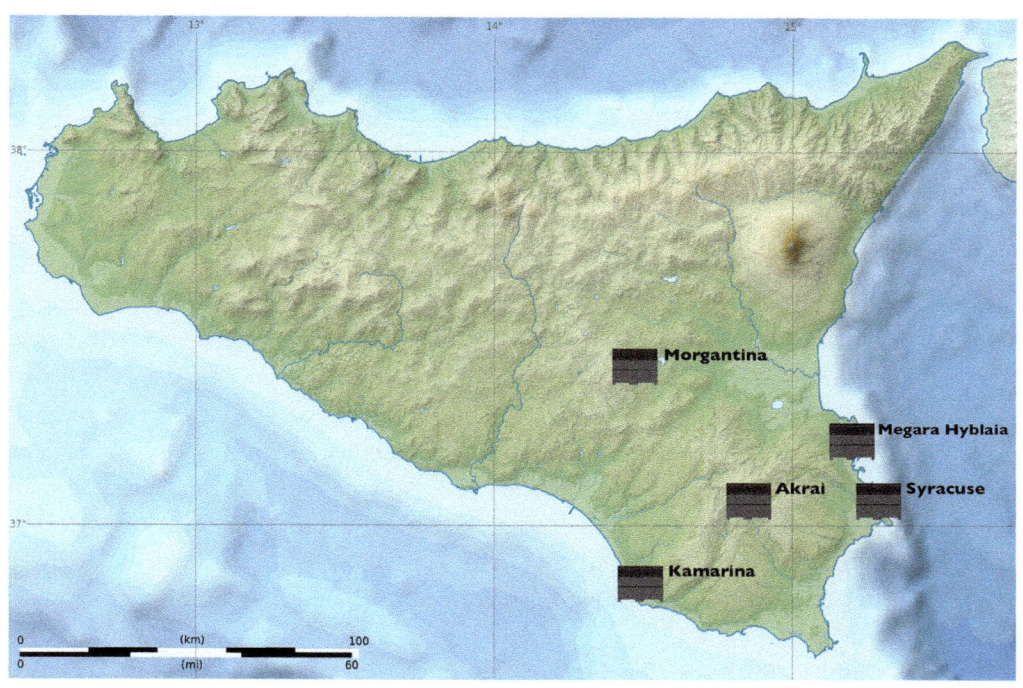

5.11 Locations where standardized measuring vessels of the Hieronian type have been discovered (base map © Sémhur/Wikimedia Commons/CC-BY-SA-Figure 3.0).

dikotylon.[49] Maria Costanza Lentini has suggested that the imported vessel found at Naxos may have served as a three-*choinix* measure, noting its similarity to many of the dry measures found in the Athenian agora.[50] While this is an admittedly small sample size, the pre-Hieronian measures appear to reflect more than a passing familiarity with Attic units of measure. Athens was certainly an importer of Sicilian grain during the fourth century and had long enjoyed close political and economic ties with many Sicilian cities, not least Kamarina and Leontinoi.[51] Given the importance of agricultural exports for all three of these cities, the frequency with which Attic units of measurement turn up is to be expected for the time and place.

The meager quantity of pre-Hieronian measures documented from excavations in Sicily may be attributed in part to their simple, unadorned form, a factor that can contribute to greater discard rates of vessel fragments deemed "undiagnostic" by archaeologists. Alternatively, it could be the case that these older measures were more commonly manufactured from materials that tend not to survive in the archaeological record, like wood and bronze. Yet, even allowing for both possibilities to be true, the most convincing explanation for the paucity of reported measures of pre-Hieronian date must be that their manufacture never remotely approached the scale of production that was evidently achieved for the new, third-century system.

Metrology

Thus far, we have seen evidence for the emergence of standardized measuring vessels at multiple sites around eastern Sicily during the middle decades of the third century. These vessels appear to have been manufactured according to a common and well-defined volumetric standard. It remains for us to attempt to identify the metrological system to which they belonged.

From the outset, it is important to acknowledge that ancient metrological instruments rarely achieved the degree of precision that we have come to expect from our modern measuring devices.[52] Nearly all ancient metrological devices (i.e., measures, weights, scales, etc.) exhibit some degree of variance from the theoretical standard to which they were manufactured to conform. Such inconsistency has been well documented with respect to ancient weights.[53] The same holds true for volumetric measures. In their study of such measures from the Athenian agora, Mabel Lang and Dorothy Crosby found that the capacity of any given vessel – even those authenticated by Athenian magistrates as accurate – might diverge from the expected norm by as much as 10 percent.[54]

As noted above, the Sicilian dry measures for which we can calculate capacity tend to cluster around a few discrete volumetric units. Among the Type 1 vessels, the well-preserved specimens held either ca. 0.97 liter (~1 liter vessels) or about twice that capacity at ca. 1.84 liters (~2 liter vessels), which may be reasonably identified as two distinct units – one the double of the other. Of the vessel fragments cataloged from sites in eastern Sicily, the majority belonged to Type 1 measures with dimensions analogous to those of the smaller, single-unit vessels described above. These ~1 liter measures, as I refer to them here, represent the smallest identifiable unit of the new system, although we cannot rule out the possibility that vessels which held even smaller units might be hiding out among the Type 1 fragments. At the other end of the spectrum, the largest ceramic vessels of the new system held ~32 liters. Example of these large Type 3 measures with capacity of ~32 liters have been identified at multiple sites, including Morgantina, Kamarina, Syracuse, and Akrai (Contrada Aguglia). The frequency with which these vessels appear suggests that they must represent another unit of the system. In between the largest (~32 liters) and smallest (~1 liter) units are Type 3 measures that held ~16 liters and Type 2 measures that seem to have volumes that cluster around ~3.2 liters and ~2.4 liters.

If we treat the ~32 liter measure as the full unit, assigning it a value of 1, the remaining measures fall into tolerably regular fractional subdivisions, including 1/2 (~16 liters), 1/10 (~3.2 liters), 1/12 (~2.4 liters), 1/16 (~2 liters), and 1/32 (~1 liters).[55] Our third-century volumetric standard emerges from the objects themselves (Figure 5.12). If a unit larger than ~32 liters was regularly employed

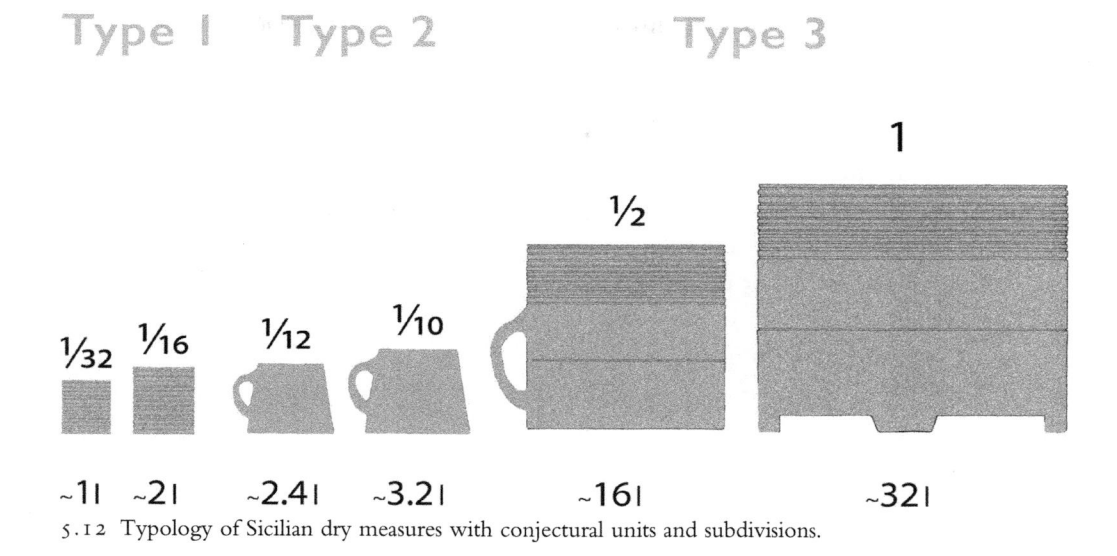

5.12 Typology of Sicilian dry measures with conjectural units and subdivisions.

in Sicily during the third century, there is at present no surviving material evidence of its existence. Perhaps it was simply impractical to use a ceramic vessel of larger capacity; indeed, the ~32 liter vessels themselves are quite cumbersome even when empty. For larger units, standardized containers made of perishable materials, like cane baskets or cloth sacks, may have been employed.[56]

While the physical measures themselves reveal a fidelity to a common volumetric standard, it remains an open question as to precisely which ancient standard these vessels were intended to represent and whether any of the physical measures can be associated with known, ancient units. The problem of attributing these third-century measures to a known standard of measurement rests, in part, with the wide gulf that lies between, on the one hand, the volumetric calculations derived from surviving documentary sources and, on the other, those derived from the material remains of the measures themselves. Take the ~32 liter vessels, for instance. These Type 3 measures certainly appear in sufficient numbers to justify their identification as representative of a shared ancient unit of measuring dry goods. But to what ancient unit did these ~32 liter vessels conform? One possibility is the *medimnos* (μέδιμνος), a volumetric measurement used for dry goods, typically cereals and foodstuffs, that was found throughout much of the Greek world. As we might expect, the capacity of a *medimnos* varied from region to region and even from city to city, depending on the predominant standards at play. The most well-attested variant of the *medimnos* conforms to the Attic standard, which is generally considered to have had a capacity of approximately 52.5 liters.[57] The Attic *medimnos*, then, was much larger than the unit represented by the Type 3 vessels of ~32 liters.

Are we then dealing with a regional variant of the *medimnos*? On face, this is a difficult question to answer as anything approximating a "Sicilian" or "Syracusan" volumetric standard, akin to the Attic standard, remains ill-defined in a modern sense. The physical measures themselves may shed light on the matter, but they do not give up their secrets easily. Polybius, in fact, refers to a "Sicilian" *medimnos* (Σικελικὸς μέδιμνος, *Sikelikos medimnos*) on at least three separate occasions in his *Histories*.[58] Elsewhere he refers to an "Attic" *medimnos* (Ἀττικὸς μέδιμνος, *Attikos medimnos*), giving the impression that the Sicilian and Attic varieties were recognizably distinct units of measurement, although he does not give specific details about the capacity of either unit.[59] Things get rather thorny when we consider that long-held metrological calculations of the Sicilian *medimnos* tend to place its capacity between 52.24 liters and 52.39 liters, making it nearly indistinguishable from the Attic measure of the same name.[60] These calculations, however, draw largely on the work of Epiphanius of Salamis, who composed his treatise *On Weights and Measures* in the late fourth century CE, roughly 500 years after Polybius' death. Thus, while it is quite possible that in the intervening centuries the Sicilian *medimnos* came to be essentially conflated with its Attic counterpart, it would appear that the two units were recognizably distinct at the time Polybius composed his *Histories*.

Could the "Sicilian" *medimnos* of the Polybian narrative be the ~32 liter unit attested by the material evidence emerging from various sites within the Hieronian kingdom? While not explicitly corroborating this hypothesis, Polybius (6.39.13) describes the monthly grain rations provided to Roman infantry soldiers during the Second Punic War as "about two-thirds of an Attic *medimnos*" (σιτομετροῦνται δ' οἱ μὲν πεζοὶ πυρῶν Ἀττικοῦ μεδίμνου δύο μέρη μάλιστά πως). This would amount to roughly 34.95 liters of grain, a figure relatively close to the ~32 liters of the Type 3 Sicilian measures. Additionally, we know from epigraphic sources that in Sicily around this time grains and other dry goods were measured by the *medimnos*, *hemimedimnos* (1/2 *medimnos*), and *hemihekteus* (1/12 *medimnos*).[61] We see this same fractional relationship $(1:\frac{1}{2}:\frac{1}{12})$ among the physical measures themselves (~32 liters:~16 liters:~2.4 liters), when the ~32 liter vessel is treated as a full unit analogous with a *medimnos* in this scenario. Perhaps taxation in the Hieronian kingdom relied on a much smaller *medimnos* than most of the rest of the Greek world at the time, one that was roughly two-thirds the size of the Attic *medimnos*.

Given Hieron's close political and economic ties with both Ptolemaic Egypt and Rome, it seems worth noting that the ~32 liter unit may have shared some affinity to standard units of each state's respective volumetric system. Calculated at 8.62 liters, the Roman *modius* was about one-fourth the size of the ~32 liter unit.[62] The 40-*choinix artaba* measure, a unit attested in tax documents from Ptolemaic and Roman Egypt, was even closer to our Sicilian unit, if estimates of its volume (ca. 32 liters) are correct.[63] At present, it is only possible to draw attention to the proximity between these various units. Further work aimed at identifying points of intersection between these three volumetric systems may yield important insights about the nature and origin of the Sicilian measures. For the moment, it is sufficient to underscore the fact that this third-century Sicilian system appears to have provided no clear point of interoperability with Attic units of volume. As we will see in Chapter 7, this shift away from the Attic volumetric standard mirrors changes made by Hieron with respect to his minting operations, where we have evidence of a clear break from the Attic standard and shift to issuing coinage based on the Sicilian litra unit.

Diffusion of the Standard

The range of archaeological contexts in which these standardized vessels have been found reveals that the new measures were thoroughly diffused across contemporary society. That fragments of these vessels turn up in greatest concentration in and around the agorai of Morgantina and Kamarina is not unexpected, given the importance of these spaces for both commercial activity and administrative oversight. The notable assemblage of standardized measures found within the Central Shops at Morgantina and around the area of the West Stoa at Kamarina certainly reinforces their identification as instruments involved in routine commercial exchange. Standardized measures show up in domestic contexts of all types at Morgantina, from the well-appointed, aristocratic residences that occupied the hills near the agora to the modest dwellings of Contrada Drago and Contrada Agnese farther from the city center. Within the house, measures could have served for the provisioning of foodstuffs or in the sale of goods produced by the household. This latter function may apply to a house recently excavated in the Contrada Agnese quarter of Morgantina, where excavators found a nearly complete Type 2 measure within a small shop room that fronted onto one of the main avenues of the city.[64] The occupants of the house appear to have specialized in milling grain into flour, which they may have sold from the small shop attached to their house.[65]

The standardized measures found in the farmstead at Contrada Aguglia in the territory of ancient Akrai demonstrate that the use of these vessels was not restricted to urban centers. As will be argued in the following section, the measures from Contrada Aguglia have a strong claim to identification as instruments used for the assessment and collection of agricultural taxes. At Morgantina, standard measures have even been discovered in spaces identified as sanctuaries dedicated to Demeter and Persephone.[66] It is tempting to imagine these vessels being used to measure out dedications made to the goddesses, or perhaps to assess rents paid in kind by tenants on agricultural lands owned by the sanctuary.[67]

From their ubiquitous presence in households, commercial spaces, and even sacred contexts, we are left with an impression that standardized measures were thoroughly integrated into the rhythms of daily life for the residents of these communities. The fact that the same vessel types with roughly uniform volumes turn up around the same point in time at different sites across southeastern Sicily is compelling evidence that we are witness to the enforcement and adoption of a coherent system of volumetric measurement. As I argue below, the genesis of this standardization was undoubtedly to be found in the court of Hieron II.

STANDARDIZATION AS ROYAL INITIATIVE

Let us now take up my contention that the widespread and contemporaneous adoption of a common volumetric standard – unprecedented in Sicily up until that point in time – was the outcome of an exceptional political mandate and a literal materialization of Hieronian administrative policy. From the outset, we should admit that state-backed enforcement of a single volumetric standard is, of course, not the only conceivable explanation for the appearance of uniform measures in southeastern Sicily at this time. Alternatively, one could adopt a "commerce-driven" explanation by viewing metrological unification as the response to economic forces. Along those lines, one might argue that standardization came about as individual *poleis* independently aligned their local civic standards with a more widely recognized standard. This would certainly have held the advantage of facilitating commercial exchange and trade by reducing transaction costs involved in converting units between two or more standards. Such an economic rationale is considered by most to be the motive behind the gradual adoption of Attic standards for coinage, weights, and measures during the fifth century by *poleis* that fell outside the Athenian *arkē*.[68]

The prevalence of uniform measures certainly held economic advantages for the residents of the region, who stood to benefit from greater transparency even in the most routine of commercial operations. Yet this gradualist model seems incompatible with the sudden and widespread emergence of the new system documented above. A commerce-driven explanation is easier to accept when accounting for the behavior of an individual *polis*, but less satisfactory when trying to account for the rapid appearance of a single standard at numerous *poleis*, as occurred around southeastern Sicily. When broad adoption of a common metrological standard did occur in the ancient world, it was generally slow and piecemeal, and often required intervention by a more powerful political actor.[69] This remains the most compelling interpretation of the "Athenian Coinage Decree," which prescribed the use of Attic coins, weights, and measures by Athens' tributary allies.[70] The Athenian law provides one of the most clear-cut examples of top-down, state-sanctioned enforcement of metrological standards in the ancient world. Moreover, it offers valuable insight into how metrological consolidation was achieved across an extensive geographic area comprising diverse polities. Punishment and penalties for noncompliance were involved. We see this, for example, in a portion of the decree's text that required members of the Athenian Council of the Five Hundred to swear an oath to the effect that, "If anyone strikes silver coinage in the cities and does not use Athenian coins or measures or weights but (instead uses) foreign (i.e. non-Athenian) coins and measures and weights, I shall punish and penalize him according to the earlier decree that Klearchos proposed."[71] Moreover, copies of the text were likely distributed to all affected by the new law, as portions of the Coinage Decree have been discovered in at least six locations around the Aegean, each in territories known to have been subject to Athenian control during the fifth century. While the potential commercial value of common units was sufficient grounds to motivate the adoption of Attic standards by some trading partners, the Athenians clearly found it more efficient to enforce the use of their units of measure among their tributary allies, rather than wait for voluntary adoption.

While the territorial extent of the Hieronian kingdom came nowhere close to the vast empire controlled by the Athenians during the fifth and fourth centuries, the Sicilian *mesogeia* did not necessarily lend itself to an organic process of integration as presupposed by economic explanations for metrological consolidation. A historical case study from a later period in Sicilian history may help us to understand why. For most of the medieval and early modern periods there was no common standard for measuring grain in Sicily, despite the many efforts made by the island's rulers to promote and enforce standardization.[72] Take, for instance, the *salma*, a unit of capacity used across the island for measuring out cereals and other dry goods, much like the *medimnos* of antiquity. While the term "*salma*" enjoyed island-wide currency as a unit of measure, it conformed to no single standard. A merchant ship moving between Syracuse and Agrigento would find that the *salma* used by cities in the eastern half of the island was nearly 20 percent larger than that found in cities west of the river Salso.[73] In the fifteenth century, not only did each of the island's three administrative regions use different *salma* measures, but the capacity of a *salma* measure varied from city to city even within a single region. This was the case in the Val di Mazara, where several different cities within the region, including Agrigento, Palermo, Polizzi, and Castellamare, each used its own incommensurate *salma* measure.[74] Such fragmentation created problems for merchants and rulers alike, all of whom had a financial interest in bringing about greater uniformity among the island's measures.[75]

Between the twelfth and eighteenth centuries, numerous kings and rulers attempted to unify the island's measures for grain and other dry goods, yet none succeeded in bringing about lasting change.[76] The efforts of Charles I of Anjou to standardize weights and measures throughout the Kingdom of Sicily during the thirteenth century met with resistance.[77] The island's Aragonese rulers did not enjoy much greater success, and despite the promulgation of royal edicts by Frederick III in 1296, Alfonso V in 1434, and Ferdinand II in 1509, lasting unification of measurement across any significant portion of the island, let alone the entirety of Sicily, was not fully achieved until centuries later.[78] Stephan Epstein has underscored the intractability of the situation, noting that "[d]uring the late Middle Ages, neither of the forces that ordinarily increase market integration and act to standardize measurements – trade and a central political authority – was sufficiently strong to achieve anything like a complete unification of the Sicilian market."[79] Throughout the centuries, royal officials found themselves in a drawn-out struggle with local aristocracies that fought to preserve their feudal prerogative to determine local units of weight and measure.[80]

As late as 1809, standardization of measures across the island remained an elusive goal.[81] In that year, the ruling Bourbon monarch, Ferdinand III, sent officials to Sicily to carry out a town-by-town survey of existing metrological standards as the first step in the process of introducing metric units as the island-wide standard. The great variety of measures encountered by Ferdinand's technicians was detailed in a report, the *Codice metrico–siculo*, totaling nearly 600 pages (Figure 5.13). The epigraph that introduced this chapter was written by the Scottish author John Galt, who had traveled through Sicily not long after Ferdinand's royal order took effect. Galt's brief statement – and its oblique praise for the efficacy of royal fiat – belies the difficulties that lie ahead. Today, one can still encounter marble conversion plaques affixed to the exteriors of churches and civic buildings across Sicily. These plaques, placed outside local centers of social and political authority like churches and town halls, give standard rates of conversion between what are regularly described as the "ancient" (*antiche*) pre-metric units of volume, weight, and distance and their modern metric equivalents. What Ferdinand initiated in 1809 was hardly the last step in a process that had begun so many centuries before; this is evident on the conversion table that still hangs outside the church of San Francesco d'Assisi in the municipality of Petralia Sottana (Figure 5.14). The date inscribed on the lower right-hand corner of the plaque, 28 April 1862, is an unambiguous reminder that even 50 years after Ferdinand's decree ordering the adoption of the metric system, the "ancient" measures remained firmly embedded in daily life.[82]

Comparison with medieval and early modern Sicily is illustrative, not least for what it reveals about the barriers to bringing about metrological unification regardless of the implicit benefits to trade and commercial exchange that followed from the use of a common system of measurement. Standardization was never a straightforward or organic operation. Even within a geographically limited area like Sicily, a great diversity of measuring technologies might flourish due to the strength of local communities and their powerholders. The coeval appearance of standard measures at multiple cities in the highly

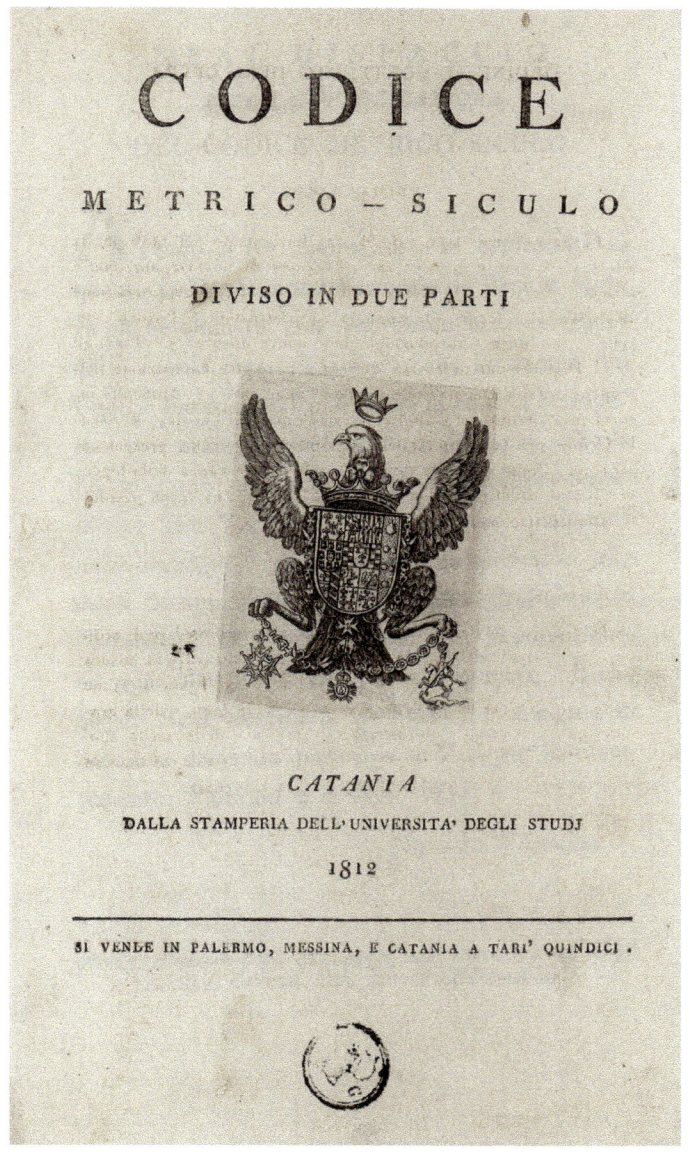

5.13 Title page of *Codice metrico siculo*, 1812 (courtesy of Ghent University Library; BIB.JUR.001454).

segmented political landscape of Hellenistic Sicily thus seems possible only as a consequence of aggressive royal intervention.[83]

FINGERPRINTS OF THE ROYAL HAND: STATE-ENDORSED MEASURES

Any remaining doubts about the vital role played by the Hieronian state in bringing about the new volumetric standard are dispelled by the discovery of

5.14 Standards plaque affixed to the façade of the church of San Francesco d'Assisi, Petralia Sottana (photo: K. Bowes).

measuring vessels that bear a tangible mark of royal oversight. To date, the remains of three such measures have been found at three distinct locations in southeastern Sicily. One was discovered in the agora at Kamarina by archaeologists working in the vicinity of the West Stoa. A second was found at Morgantina in a residential quarter of the ancient city just west of the agora. The third was recovered in a Hellenistic farmhouse at Contrada Aguglia in the territory of ancient Akrai.[84] Although fragmentary, all three can be readily distinguished on morphological grounds as Type 3 dry measures of the ~32 liter variety. Each was stamped before firing on the outer surface of one foot with a short, two-word inscription contained within a narrow, elliptical frame (Figure 5.15). The inscription reads, ΑΚΡΙΒΑΙΟΝΤΟΣ ΑΡΤΕΜΙΔΩΡΟΥ (ἀκριβάζοντος Ἀρτεμιδώρου, *akribazontos Artemidōrou*), which translates along the lines of "when Artemidoros was serving as magistrate, he verified the accuracy [of this measuring device]" (Figure 5.16).[85] Nothing more is known about this Artemidoros, but the force of the participle ἀκριβάζοντος, "he verified the accuracy [of this measuring device]," implies the existence of a prescribed volumetric standard against which the capacity of the stamped vessel was compared and then confirmed. Given that the three stamped vessels can all be positively identified as Type 3 dry measures of the new typology, the implied standard must be one and the same as that outlined earlier in this chapter.

Close inspection of the surviving fragments of these measures has revealed that an identical device was used to stamp all three vessels. That we are, in fact, dealing with the very same device is confirmed by the distinctive smudging of the letters tau and epsilon in Ἀρτεμιδώρου, visible on all three inscriptions (Figure 5.17). Coupled with the uniformity shown in the placement of the stamp on the three vessels — at a point on or just above one of the feet — we might reasonably conclude

Morgantina

Kamarina

Akrai (Contrada Aguglia)

5.15 Fragments of three Type 3 measures, each stamped with the same die, which reads ΑΚΡΙΒΑΙΟΝΤΟΣ ΑΡΤΕΜΙΔΩΡΟΥ (after Walthall 2011).

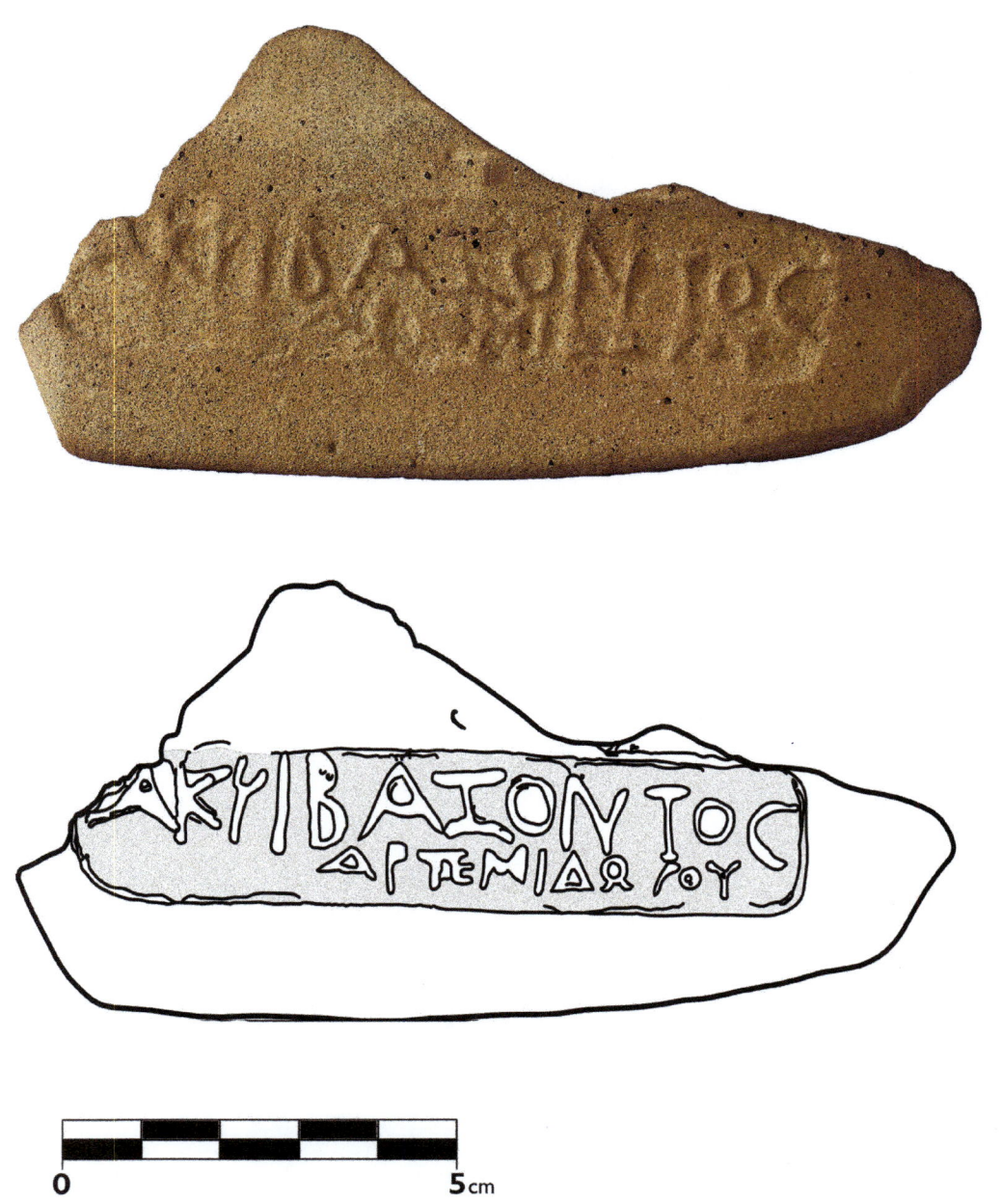

5.16 Detail of the stamped measure from Morgantina (inv. 58-916; photo: A. Maggio; drawing: G. Guadagnino; courtesy of the American Excavations at Morgantina).

that all three of the stamped vessels were manufactured at a single location, according to a prescribed volumetric standard against which their capacity was tested and confirmed, and then subsequently distributed to sites around south-eastern Sicily. Under the circumstances, we would expect this to have taken place at Syracuse, an inference supported by the fact that all three appear to have been manufactured from a medium-red clay typical of the area around Syracuse.[86]

Morgantina

Kamarina

0   5cm

5.17 Detail of the stamped inscriptions found on the measures from Morgantina and Kamarina; the smudging of the letters tau and epsilon in the name Ἀρτεμιδώρου is highlighted (photos: author; courtesy of the American Excavations at Morgantina and the Polo Regionale di Ragusa per i siti culturali e per i Parchi archeologici di Kamarina e Cava d'Ispica).

The broad distribution of the stamped measures indicates that the individual responsible for verifying the accuracy of the measures (a certain Artemidoros) either held rather far-reaching authority or himself operated as a functionary under such an authority. If only one stamped measure existed or if all three extant vessels had been recovered from the territory of a single *polis*, there would be no reason to question Artemidoros' credentials as a civic magistrate, akin to the *metronomos* in Athens. A parallel could be drawn to contemporary dry measures stamped with the names of civic magistrates attested from *poleis* in the Black Sea region.[87] Yet the stamped measures from Sicily confirm that the jurisdiction of Artemidoros was geographically expansive, extending from Kamarina on the southern coast up to Akrai in the Hyblaean range and beyond to Morgantina at the western edge of the Plain of Catania. The authority that lay behind Artemidoros' remit to certify the accuracy of measures found in the territories of three distinct *poleis* must have been far greater than that of a civic magistrate. During the third century, the only conceivable source for such sweeping authority in southeastern Sicily was of course the royal administration of Hieron II. It follows that Artemidoros likely served as a royal magistrate operating within the Hieronian kingdom. Such an official, charged with overseeing the accuracy of weights and measure, would have played an indispensable role in the administration of the agricultural tithe. The near-universal association between sovereign authority and the power to establish legitimate units of measure allows us to safely dismiss the possibility that Artemidoros was a private individual somehow involved in marketing accurate capacity measures. It may very well have been the case that Artemidoros was simply responsible for overseeing the manufacture of these state-sanctioned vessels, after which point they were passed along to another official with broader remit over the assessment and collection of royal taxes, akin to a *dioiketes* in the Ptolemaic state. [88] Even so, this would in no way invalidate our identification of the ἀκριβάζοντος-stamped vessels as markers of royal authority, nor would it diminish the underlying argument that their broad geographic distribution reflects the reach of the Hieronian state in matters of measurement and, by extension, taxation.

It is worth reminding ourselves that the small sample size of surviving ἀκριβάζοντος vessels should not hinder our interpretation of either their function or their role within the royal administration. That three such objects have been identified is, in fact, rather remarkable, and speaks in favor of the existence of far larger numbers in circulation during the third century. By way of comparison, analogous devices from Egypt are, to date, practically non-existent in contexts of Hellenistic and Roman date, despite the fact that documentary papyri attest to the widespread diffusion of physical measures of both officially sanctioned and private varieties.[89] Equally astonishing is the relatively far-flung distribution of the stamped vessels in Sicily, given what it reveals about the nature and scope of Hieron's royal administration. As alluded to in Chapter 3, the discovery of the ἀκριβάζοντος measures at Kamarina and Morgantina all but confirms their political subordination to Hieron and, moreover, compels us to reassess the size of the Hieronian kingdom by redrawing the political boundaries to include the territories of both *poleis*.

Function of the ἀκριβάζοντος Measures

The geographic distribution of the ἀκριβάζοντος measures invites reflection on the mechanics of royal administration within the Hieronian kingdom, particularly with respect to the introduction and enforcement of uniform, state-sanctioned standards. If the unruly metrological landscape of medieval Sicily is any model, there is good reason to believe that the process by which the independent *poleis* of Hellenistic Sicily were brought to share the royal standards of measurement was itself a complex and challenging operation. While many details of this process are lost to us, the stamped measures hold clues to its inner workings. One can imagine several ways in which the ἀκριβάζοντος measures functioned within the Hieronian kingdom.

The ἀκριβάζοντος Measures as *sekōmata*

We know little about how new standards were initially introduced across the Hieronian kingdom or, for that matter, across any Hellenistic kingdom.

Within the Sicilian context, the initial step might have involved the transmission of a message from the king to each *polis*, perhaps via the representatives of the *koinon tōn Sikeliōtān*, outlining the requisite adoption of a kingdom-wide standard for volumetric measurement that would be utilized in the administration of the annual agricultural tithe. A royal mandate would necessarily be accompanied by technical information about the new standard. As our detour through medieval Sicily made clear, Hieron could not have simply declared that taxes were now to be reported, assessed, and collected by the *medimnos* unit if every *polis* used its own, distinct civic *medimnos*. The king might have designated the *medimnos* used in Syracuse as the standard by which all taxes were to be assessed and paid, but, even so, such a proclamation would have necessarily required accompanying specifications about the capacity or dimensions of the Syracusan *medimnos*.

One possibility is that this information was communicated as a set of linear measurements according to which all new measuring devices used in the assessment of taxes needed to conform. Along these lines, Mabel Lang has suggested that "laws introducing or enforcing measures of capacity must have included specifications of interior dimensions," citing the text of a fifth-century inscription found on the island of Thasos that appears to give the interior dimensions of four volumetric measures.[90] In this light, it is worth revisiting Eratosthenes' *Letter to King Ptolemy* and, in particular, the mathematician's description of the practical purposes to which his mathematical proof for the doubling of the cube might be realized. Among them was the ability to verify the capacity of volumetric measures accurately. In his letter, Eratosthenes writes,

> δυνησόμεθα δὲ καὶ τὰ τῶν ὑγρῶν μέτρα καὶ ξηρῶν (λέγω δέ, οἷον μετρητὴν ἢ μέδιμνον), εἰς κύβον καθίστασθαι καὶ διὰ τῆς τούτου πλευρᾶς ἀναμετρεῖν τὰ τούτων δεκτικὰ ἀγγεῖα, πόσον χωρεῖ.

> We can also reduce into a cube both liquid and dry measures (I mean, such as a *metretes* or a *medimnos*), and we can then measure how much the vessels of these liquid or dry materials hold, using the edge of the cube.

Eratosthenes knew that his method for reducing a volumetric unit, like a *medimnos*, into linear measurement would hold great appeal for Ptolemy II, who, like Hieron, relied on the use of uniform measures to efficiently assess and collect agricultural taxes from his kingdom. Translating the capacity of "royal" units of measure into a mathematical proof not only allowed for physical measures to be tested for their accuracy, as Eratosthenes notes, but also presumably would have allowed for widespread replication of precise instruments used in the service of taxing the agricultural wealth of the Ptolemaic kingdom.

Yet while the transmission of linear measurements or a mathematical proof may have offered an appealing solution for swiftly disseminating new royal standards, we lack corroborating evidence that such a method was ever utilized by Hieron, let alone by the Ptolemaic court. We do, however, possess a relative abundance of archaeological, epigraphic, and papyrological evidence from the Hellenistic world that attests to the dissemination of physical devices for the purpose of ensuring the faithful transmission of metrological standards. One well-known case appears in an Athenian decree of the year 222/221 (*IG* II² 1013), which records the decision of the Assembly to adopt new civic standards for units of weight and volumetric measures. The text of the surviving decree specifies a number of actions to be taken by civic officials in their effort to promote and enforce the use of the new standards. Central among these efforts was the creation of *sekōmata* (sing. *sekōma*), or physical models of the metrological units. These *sekōmata* for weights and measures were held in the care of public officials and displayed in public spaces around various points in the city; one set was placed in the Skias (Tholos), which lie at the edge of the agora, one set deposited in a public building in the market at the Piraeus, and one set sent to Eleusis. In these locations, the *sekōmata* could be accessed should questions arise about the accuracy of a private measure used in routine market exchange.[91]

Sekōmata may have played an important role within the Hieronian kingdom, considering the vital need for accurate measurement in the administration of the agricultural tithe. Given the degree to which the cities of the kingdom were geographically isolated, there would have been a clear advantage to disseminating official measuring devices when first communicating the specifications of the new royal standards. Once distributed among the *poleis* subject to royal oversight, such devices might then have been adopted for manufacturing new measures or testing the capacity of private devices used in the assessment or collection of royal taxes. If the Hieronian method of ensuring the accuracy of capacity measures used in the administration of the tithe was to distribute physical models, the ἀκριβάζοντος measures might very well have served as *sekōmata*.

Ptolemaic measures used in the administration of royal taxation were often made of bronze, so far as papyrological sources relate.[92] These were deposited in every administrative district (*nome*), where they could be referred to by officials when problems arose.[93] It seems reasonable to posit that a similar procedure was followed within the Hieronian kingdom as well, although no evidence for the use of bronze measuring vessels survives today. The use of bronze *sekōmata* had certain advantages over terracotta, like durability and precision, yet terracotta offered its own benefits, being inexpensive, quick to manufacture, and relatively lightweight.[94] The Athenians produced *sekōmata* in both terracotta and bronze, so we should not rule out the possibility that both materials were also used for *sekōmata* in Hieronian Sicily; those fashioned out of bronze simply no longer survive, or have yet to be identified, in the archaeological record.

The ἀκριβάζοντος Measures as Tools of Assessment

Of course, the ἀκριβάζοντος measures could also have been used for the actual assessment of tithe payments or other transactions taking place along the operational sequence of the tithe administration. Ptolemaic Egypt provides ample evidence for the deployment of state-sanctioned instruments used in the service of administering agricultural taxes. At times this appears to have involved the on-site testing and endorsement of a local measuring device by a royal official.[95] Elsewhere, we encounter royal magistrates employing what appear to be officially sanctioned vessels for the assessment and collection of taxes. We possess numerous references to the use of a "receiving measure" (μέτρον δοχικόν, *metron dochikon*) by Ptolemaic officials in the documentation of grain shipments destined for the royal granaries at Alexandria.[96]

Within the Hieronian context, one could envision the need for state-sanctioned measures at collection points where cultivators paid the portion of the harvest owed as tithe. At Morgantina, this may have occurred at one of the two massive granaries that dominated the city's lower agora. But more localized venues required the same equipment too, as we can clearly infer from the stamped measure found inside the farmhouse at Contrada Aguglia. Chapter 4 explained how, after a farm gathered its harvest, the assessment of the Hieronian tithe could take place directly at its threshing floor. This seems the most credible scenario to explain the presence of the ἀκριβάζοντος measure in such a remote location as Contrada Aguglia.

The ἀκριβάζοντος Measures as Expressions of Royal Authority

Certainly, one of the chief reasons behind disseminating *sekōmata* throughout the kingdom was that it worked to minimize the likelihood of cheating on the part of both cultivators and tax farmers.[97] The profusion of measures with authenticated capacities meant that there was little room for cultivators to evade payment, while at the same time limiting potential abuse by tax farmers looking to take more than their fair share. Thinking back to Hieron's need to foster quasi-voluntary compliance among his constituents, the widespread distribution of state-sanctioned measures would have played an important role in increasing transparency and trust between cultivators, tax farmers, and royal officials. An ancillary, though not inconsequential, outcome of having these vessels distributed around the kingdom was that they served to subtly reinforce the presence of royal power in the lives of his subjects, since the expectation of accuracy rested on the authority of the king and his officials.

The mechanisms by which such transparency and trust were maintained remain obscure, but an effective state policy would have included not only creative ways to incentivize compliance, but also a formidable and versatile apparatus to enforce it. The dangers of lax enforcement are evident in a royal edict issued by Ptolemy VIII in the year 118, following a long civil war in

Egypt, during which time corruption – even among royal officials – had run rampant. In his letter, the king responds to complaints made by farmers that royal magistrates, including granary officials and scribes, were using measures larger than the state-sanctioned devices deposited in each administrative territory (*nome*). The steps taken to correct the situation are outlined in the edict:

> And since it sometimes happens that the *sitologoi* and *antigrapheis* use larger measures than the correct bronze measures appointed in each *nome* . . . in estimating dues to the State, and in consequence the cultivators are made to pay (more than the proper number of *choinikes*), they [the King and Queen] have decreed that the *strategoi* and the overseers of the revenues and the royal scribes (*basilikogrammateis*) shall test the measures in the most thorough manner possible . . . and the measures must not exceed the bronze (i.e. official) measure by more than the two . . . allowed for errors. Those who disobey this decree are to be punished by death.[98]

Faced with distrust among his tax-paying subjects, Ptolemy responded by dispatching royal magistrates throughout the kingdom to test the accuracy of the measures held in each *nome*, which were used for the collection of agricultural taxes. The imposition of the death penalty for transgressors underscores the gravity of the situation, for the loss of public trust in the apparatus of state presented an existential threat to the royal court. We do not know if Hieron and his administrators faced similar problems of corruption, but he would have undoubtedly recognized the importance of emphasizing the trustworthiness of his administration and very likely adopted similarly harsh penalties for transgressions involving royal instruments of measurement and extraction. As in Ptolemaic Egypt and probably every other Hellenistic kingdom, offenses committed using disreputable weights and measures were tantamount to offenses against the king's own authority.

SIZING UP A KINGDOM

Historical evidence leaves no doubt that the widespread unification of volumetric measurement on the scale observed in eastern Sicily during the third century was rarely achieved in the premodern world. When metrological unification was achieved, a powerful central political authority almost always propelled it. In the case of third-century Sicily, our historical and archaeological evidence has led us to the conclusion that the standardization of volumetric measures was a product of royal mandate and, moreover, was symptomatic of greater institutional changes brought about by the development of infrastructure required for the administration of the Hieronian tax laws. The commercial and economic implications of this metrological consolidation, a topic addressed in Chapter 8, must be understood as by-products or consequences of standardization, not as the motivation.

Hieron's prerogative to define valid units of measurement and mint coinage – and then to enforce the use of those standards throughout his kingdom – was more than a symbolic manifestation of his sovereignty. The physical measures were a tangible expression of his royal authority, much like the coinage bearing his name and portrait. If we follow James Scott in concluding that "[e]very act of measurement was an act marked by the play of power relations," we can view the enforcement of a kingdom-wide set of standards as a clear incursion of royal authority into the sphere of civic autonomy, since the regulation and enforcement of legitimate measurement had long remained within the jurisdiction of the individual *polis*.[99]

Hieron's authority percolated down not just to the larger urban centers of the kingdom, but even to the level of the individual taxable estate, like the farmhouse at Contrada Aguglia, which lies more than 11 kilometers from the urban center of ancient Akrai. That a state-validated measuring vessel ended up at this relatively small and otherwise unremarkable farmstead speaks to the scope of oversight and surveillance throughout the territory under the king's administrative control. Hieron's capacity to reach deep into the pockets of his subjects would not be seen again in Sicily until the nineteenth century, when Ferdinand III dispatched technicians to survey the terra incognita of the island's fractured metrological landscape.

Yet for all that the material evidence speaks to the impressive reach of the Hieronian state, it is worth briefly reflecting on what it reveals about the limits of royal authority in these matters. To take just one example, we lack any indication that Hieron took steps to similarly enforce a single, uniform weight standard. To date, no state-sanctioned trade weights endorsed by the king, like those produced by the Seleucid monarchs, have been found in third-century Sicilian contexts. Moreover, a recent survey of trade weights from third- and second-century contexts at Morgantina revealed that devices calibrated to diverse weight systems were used concurrently during the period of Hieronian rule.[100] This is not to say that the king took no interest in promoting or enforcing a single, royal standard for weight measurement; but if such a standard existed, it is not immediately discernible in the material record. Was this due to pushback from the *poleis* of the kingdom, a concession made by the king to maintain the quasi-voluntary compliance of his constituents? Or is it simply a reflection of imperfect representation in the archaeological record? One suspects this may be related in some fashion to the relative insignificance of weight-based measurement compared with that of volume-based measurement in the operation of the Hieronian tax laws, but evidence from one site alone does not allow us to draw definite conclusions in this matter. Further analysis of a larger dataset, representing weights found at sites across southeastern Sicily, may shed much-needed light on the question. And if our brief venture into the measured world of Hieronian Sicily demonstrates anything, it is that there is much to be discovered when greater attention is paid to the archaeology of metrological consolidation. Doing so will only expand our awareness of these long-overlooked instruments of royal power and enrich our appreciation for how they served the fiscal, administrative, and ideological goals of the Hellenistic kingdom.

NOTES

1   Twohig (1993: 543–9). Not long thereafter, Thomas Jefferson, then secretary of state, came to submit his "Plan for Establishing Uniformity in the Coinage, Weights, and Measures of the United States" to the US House of Representatives on July 13, 1790. In his report, Jefferson highlighted the great diversity exhibited by units of weight and measure commonly used in the States at the time. It would be several more years before a joint Congress would pass legislation to adopt a common standard of measurement.

2   Despite the fact that English units of measure were utilized by all the American colonies, there appears to have been no cohesive or uniform standard among them. The great heterogeneity that could be found in the ostensibly standard units is outlined in Thomas Jefferson's 1790 "Plan for Establishing Uniformity in the Coinage, Weights, and Measures of the United States." Jefferson's report incorporates the findings of two metrological surveys commissioned by the English House of Commons in 1757 and 1758 that found all manner of variation in standard measures employed in England at the time, units on which the colonies had based their own standards.

3   Along these lines, ensuring the Roman state had ample revenue was certainly the governing motive behind a well-known passage from the *History* of Cassius Dio (52.30.9), in which Gaius Maecenas reportedly advised Octavian that effective fiscal administration of an empire required that "[n]one of the cities should be allowed to have its own separate coinage or system of weights and measures; they should all be required to use ours." While we may comfortably dismiss the historicity of the statement itself, the content of the message was certainly appropriate to any would-be ruler; Millar (1964); Kuhlmann (2010).

4   For general treatment of this subject, the work of economic historian Witold Kula (1986) remains essential. Herodotus (2.109), for instance, attributes the origins of land measurement in Pharaonic Egypt with taxation. The so-called Palermo Stone, part of the Royal Annals of the Old Kingdom of Ancient Egypt, dates to the 5th Dynasty and records the height of the Nile at the peak of its annual flooding, an essential factor for assessing tax burdens on agricultural land; Wilkinson (2000).

5   Vera (2011: 121–35). For the historical association between sovereignty and control of legitimate measurement, Kula (1986: 18–23).

6   Berriman (1953: 4). Connection to divine authority is found in the Sumerian myth of "Inanna's Descent to the Nether World," in which the goddess Inanna is described as bearing a measuring rod and measuring line; see Kramer (1950).

7   The inscription suggests the weight was once deposited in the temple of the moon god, Nanna, at Ur. It now resides in the Louvre (inv. AO 22187); translation by Frayne (1997: 153–4, no. 50), who also publishes three additional inscribed weights (nos. 51–3), each confirmed by Shulgi using the same formula. For similar formula used on a verified weight of the Babylonian king, Nebuchadnezzar II (r. ca. 605–562), now in the British Museum (AN150338001), see Berriman (1953: 57–8; 1955: 193–201).

8   Broneer (1938: 222–4).

9   Manning (2010: 134).

[10] The weight, now in the Bibliothèque nationale de France (inv. Bronze 2245), was donated in 1862 by Honoré Théodoric d'Albert, duc de Luynes. For publication, see Babelon and Blanchet (1895: 679–80, no. 2245); and, more recently, Gatier (2014: 141–7).

[11] Kosmin (2018).

[12] For recent overview, see De Callataÿ (2012). And see comments by Meadows (2014: 174) regarding Alexander III's adoption of the Attic weight standard for his coinage.

[13] In a certain sense, this is seen in the so-called Amnesty Decree (= *P. Tebt.* 5; Austin 2006: 594, no. 290) issued by Ptolemy VIII, Cleopatra II, and Cleopatra III in the wake of a tumultuous period of dynastic infighting, as the edict specifically acknowledges the abuses of royal administrators who took advantage of the military and political chaos by employing larger measures than those officially sanctioned when collecting taxes.

[14] The excavation of what has been identified as a Seleucid administrative center at Tel Kedesh offers a much-needed look into royal oversight at the provincial level; see Herbert and Berlin (2003). Among the artifacts found within the sprawling administrative complex were over a dozen massive storage vessels that once held wheat (*Triticum aestivum*), several dozen amphoras, and more than 2,000 clay *bullae*.

[15] To see that such a message does not always lie outside the realm of artistic expression, we can look to the *Allegoria ed effetti del buono e del cattivo governo* (*Allegory of Good and Bad Government*), a series of frescoes completed by the fourteenth-century Sienese painter Ambrogio Lorenzetti. These decorate the walls of Siena's Palazzo Pubblico, where they served as a vivid precept to the city's civic leaders. On the panel representing the Allegory of Good Government, the large, seated figure of Justice holds out a set of balance scales from which an angel distributes measuring devices to two kneeling figures.

[16] One needs only to consult Zupko's *Italian Weights and Measures from the Middle Ages to the Nineteenth Century* (1981) to grasp the very real possibility for metrological chaos within even as small a geographical area as eastern Sicily.

[17] Ashworth (2004: 1314).

[18] Figueira (1998: 299).

[19] Lack of familiarity among archaeologists with this class of artifact has naturally led to its underrepresentation in archaeological reports and publications, particularly in the case of measures from Sicily. Pelagatti (1970: 490–3) was among the first Sicilian archaeologists to publish the volumetric measures from her excavations and, more importantly, recognize their value for interpreting the broader fiscal operations of the Hieronian kingdom.

[20] Such banding, either painted or incised, also appears on capacity measures from numerous sites in mainland Greece. As I conjecture for the banding on the Sicilian devices, the number of bands on the mainland examples appears to bear no direct relationship to a vessel's capacity; Lang and Crosby (1964: 51–63) note the presence of similar banding decoration on both dry and liquid measures from the Athenian agora.

[21] For reference to one such vessel, see Walthall (2013c: 55; and inv. M-16).

[22] At present, the most extensive catalog of these Sicilian measures can be found in Walthall (2013c), which includes information about the remains of just over 100 individual vessels that can be attributed to this third-century system of volumetric measurement.

[23] Occasionally, the base of a Type 2 vessel is raised on a shallow ring foot, which is visible only when viewed from the underside. Whether it was the intended purpose, this can give the impression that a vessel has a slightly larger capacity.

[24] Both are listed in Walthall (2013c: cat. M-2, M-12), where they are erroneously identified as having volumes of ~2.75 liters because, well, Walthall (2013c) was clearly pretty bad at math.

[25] Morgantina Excavations Inv. 18-161, which was found in the recent excavations of the House of the Two Mills; Walthall (2021).

[26] This is certainly an issue that will eventually find greater clarity as more specimens of these Type 2 measures are discovered in archaeological excavations or identified in museum storerooms, adding to the sample size from which we can calculate volumes more precisely.

[27] Unpublished fragments attributable to standardized liquid measures have recently been identified by the author in the museum storerooms at Syracuse, Kamarina, and Morgantina.

[28] Lang and Crosby (1964: 56–64).

[29] Given that they were manufactured along similar lines, it can be difficult to distinguish between fragments belonging to the neck of a liquid measure and those of a Type 1 dry measure. The size of the diameter may be the best means of making an informed decision as to whether a fragment belongs to one or the other. Although overlap exists, the necks of the liquid measured have smaller diameters (~5–12 centimeters), on average, than those of the Type 1 dry measures (~10–16 centimeters).

[30] Tréziny (2018: 244–7).

[31] For scholarship related to the building program at Morgantina, see *supra* Chapter 3, p. 94.

[32] The Roman siege of Morgantina is mentioned by Livy (26.21.14–17), who notes elsewhere (24.36.8–10) that the inhabitants of the city had previously expelled a Roman garrison in 213 BCE. On the timeline and historical narrative of the siege, see Erim (1958); Bell (2000); Walthall (2017: 102, n. 2); and Buttrey (1965; 1979), who presents an overview of the archaeological evidence for violent destruction associated with this event.

[33] The ceramic and numismatic material contained within the stratigraphic layers associated with intentional destruction of the shops and leveling fill is consistent with a date in the first half of the third century.

[34] See Stone (2014: 27–47) for summary of the deposits associated with cleanup efforts following the siege of 211.

[35] For discussion of the building's excavation, see Stillwell (1963: 169–70); referring to a recently excavated portion of the South Sanctuary, then known as the Priest's House, Stillwell writes, "The accumulation of evidence regarding the destruction of the Demeter sanctuaries in Morgantina in the sack of 211 B.C. has grown so impressive that there can be little doubt that the destruction of this house – as well as that of the sanctuary which it served – must have occurred in 211, and no later."

[36] Walthall (2013c: cat. M-12, M-14).

[37] From the residential quarter located on the West Hill, excavators found the remains of several measures, including two Type 3 vessels with capacities of ~32 liters (Walthall 2013c: cat. M-3, M-13), one of which had been tossed down a courtyard cistern.

[38] For discussion of the remains associated with the Contrada Drago complex, see Allen (1974: 362–6). Within the storeroom, excavators found fragments belonging to at least two distinct Type 1 vessels and a Type 3 vessel with capacity of ~16 liters.

[39] For initial publication, see Pelagatti (1984–5: 683–94), with subsequent discussion by Di Stefano (2001: 693–700).

[40] A recent estimate puts the number at roughly 800 vessels; cited by Uggeri (2015: 140) and discussed by Mattioli (1995: 267–8); cf. Pelagatti (1984–5: 688), who indicates the total to be at least 300 amphoras. Due to their orientation, lying horizontally on their sides in the sand and sometimes stacked three deep, the vessels appear to have been empty at the time of their burial and were probably located in an underground storeroom below the ground floor of the building.

[41] A preliminary catalog of the vessels from Kamarina is published by Walthall (2013c).

[42] Pelagatti (1984–5).

[43] Lucchelli and Di Stefano (2004) publish the coins excavated in the agora between 1983 and 1995.

[44] Tréziny (2018: 244–7).

[45] Pelagatti (1970).

[46] See Walthall (2013c: 164).

[47] The nearest in terms of geographic location and date is the measuring vessel found at Monte di San Fratello (anc. Apollonia), which bears strong formal similarities to the dry measures of Hieronian date under consideration here. On account of its archaeological context, the measure from Monte di San Fratello is likely a product of the second or first century BCE;

for the vessel and archaeological context, see Bonanno and Perrotta (2008: 28–9, 43–4). This vessel was found in what appears to be a house occupied between the late fourth century and late first century BCE. The dimensions of the vessel, as published by Bonanno and Perrotta, correspond to a device with a capacity of ~27.2 liters. This could have passed for half of an Attic *medimnos* of ~52.5 liters, although it would have been slightly too large. A more attractive possibility, given Monte di San Fratello's location along the Tyrrhenian coast, would be a Roman *trimodius*, a unit of ~26.2 liters (based on a *modius* unit of 8.73 liters). The *trimodius* measure is mentioned by Plautus in the *Menaechmi* (l. 15), attesting to its use from at least the third century.

48 Fragments of only four pre-Hieronian measures are published. One was recovered at a kiln site, located on the outskirts of Kamarina: Pisani (2008: 126, no. 299, fig. 24; Inv. 2854. height 8.2 centimeters, diameter 9.3 centimeters, est. vol. 0.41 liter). This vessel is currently on display at the Museo Archeologico Ibleo in Ragusa. Fragments belonging to two different vessels found inside a well at the site of Caracausi, in the territory of Leontinoi: Grasso and Musumeci (1989: 145, nos. 647–8; pl. 16). A fourth measure was discovered during excavations of a votive deposit, located west of the urban center at Naxos: Lentini (2002: 237, fig. 18; inv. 2572). The vessel had a preserved height of 13.5 centimeters and a base diameter of 16.5 centimeters.

49 For comparable estimate of *dikotylon*, see Lang and Crosby (1964: 47–8).

50 Lentini (2002: 237) cites affinities with measures from the Athenian agora, specifically DM 29–36 in Lang and Crosby's catalog.

51 Sicilian grain is thought to have reached Athens in great quantities during the fourth century BCE; see, for instance, Dem. 32.4 (*Against Zenothemis*) and 56.9 (*Against Dionysodorus*); *IG* II² 283, honoring a Salaminian grain-trader with connections to Sicily; *IG* II² 408, honoring two traders from Herakleia, who sold Sicilian grain at reduced prices in Athens; Garnsey (1988: 151–4). Regarding alliances, that with Leontinoi is better attested in both historical and epigraphic sources; see, *IG* I² 52; Meritt (1946b); Wick (1976); Enos (1992). On the contours of an Athenian alliance with Kamarina, see Thuc. 6.75.3, as well as discussion by Bosworth (1992).

52 Riggsby (2019).

53 With respect to the accuracy of ancient weights, Hitzl (1996: 105–20), who studied the weights from the sanctuary at Olympia, argued that variance of up to 20 percent from the theoretical norm would have been considered acceptable in antiquity. In their analysis of over two dozen basalt weights from Pompeii, Damerow et al. (2002: 96–7) note a similarly high degree of variation among these ostensibly standardized objects. The inaccuracy of Bronze Age weights has also been a topic of conversation among specialists; see, e.g., Hafford (2012) and Ialongo et al. (2018).

54 Lang and Crosby (1964: 47–8).

55 A broadly similar range of fractional relationships has been observed for dry measures used in Ptolemaic Egypt, where the standard *artaba* unit was divided in various fashion; see Shelton (1977); Fowler (1983); and Bagnall (2011: 186–7), where a 1/10 fractional unit of the *artaba* (a *metron*) is discussed.

56 On the use of sacks of standardized volume for the conveyance of grain in Egypt, see Mayerson (1998: 189–94). *Cannizzi*, or large containers made of tightly woven reeds, were used by Sicilian famers to store grains well into the twentieth century; for discussion and image, see Scalisi (2007: 81–2).

57 According to Hultsch (1882: 104–7), who estimated the ideal volume to be 52.53 liters. Additionally, see Lang and Crosby (1964: 41–8); dry-measure units based on a *kotyle* of ~0.27 liter, a *choinix* of 1.087 liters, and a *medimnos* of ~52.2 liters.

58 For references to the Sicilian *medimnos*: Pol. 2.15.1, 9.11a.3–4, and 34.8.7 (= Ath. 8.330c).

59 Pol. 6.39.13.

60 Lombardo (1982: 885) calculates 52.39 liters; Viedebantt (*RE* 15.1, s.v. "Μέδιμνος") calculates 52.24 liters, based on a passage in the treatise *On Weights and Measures* by Epiphanius of

Salamis (sec. 21), which appears to indicate that by the late fourth century CE, the Sicilian *medimnos* was reckoned as equivalent to 4.5 *modii xystos*, a unit that Duncan-Jones (1976b: 55) estimates to have a held somewhere between 11.63 and 11.85 liters.

61 See, e.g., Entella Tablet A1 (= Nenci no. 5), lines 19–23; Ampolo (2001: 93–6); and the so-called Financial Inscriptions from Tauromenion (= *IG* XIV 423–30); Aranjo-Ruez and Oliveri (1965: no. I, lines 25–34, and no. III, lines 21–8).

62 Like all volumetric measures, the capacity of the Roman *modius* changed over time. Throughout much of the Republican and Imperial periods, the ideal volume of the *modius* seems to have been relatively constant with most estimates of its capacity clustering around 8.62–8.74 liters; for a detailed discussion, see Duncan-Jones (1976a; 1976b), who refers to this *modius* (giving a more precise figure of 8.6185 liters) alternatively as a *modius Italicus* or "basic" *modius*.

63 The 40-*choinix* Ptolemaic and Roman *artaba* measure, commonly referenced in tax documents from Egypt, comes much closer in volume, itself believed to have held approximately 32 liters; Duncan-Jones (1976b: 50).

64 Schirmer et al. (2021: 10–11).

65 Tharler et al. (2020: 15–18); Walthall (2021).

66 For the North Demeter Sanctuary, see Sjöqvist (1958a: 158–60; 1958b: 7–12) and Stone (2014: 41–3). For the South Demeter Sanctuary, see Stone (2014: 43–4).

67 Along these lines, the Herakleia Tablets (*IG* XIV 645) attest to the payment of rents in kind on the leasing of land sacred to Athena and Dionysus; for discussion, see Uguzzoni and Ghinatti (1968). If, as Bell (2008: 155–9) has posited, the urban lots occupied by the sanctuaries at Morgantina represent allotments made to Demeter and Persephone in a fashion analogous to the allotment of land made to citizens, then the goddess may have also received allotments of agricultural land in the city's *chora*, which could be leased for cultivation. By way of comparison, the Accounts of the Eleusinian Epistatai (329/328; *IG* II² 1672, ll. 252ff.) record the rents paid in kind for short-term leases on land sacred to Demeter. Also of note is the Athenian *aparchai* decree of the fifth century (*IG* I³ 78a), which records payments of tribute in the form of grain to the sanctuary of Demeter; Fornara (1983: 160–3, no. 140); Evans (2010: 127–8).

68 For overview, see Kroll (2009: 205), who notes with respect to Athenian coinage that "during the second half of the fifth century, Athenian silver was assuming a role as the most sought-after trade specie of the Eastern Mediterranean world." The adoption of Attic standards for measurement is also attested in the archaeological record, such as by a lead trade weight in the Ashmolean Museum that, although manufactured on the Attic mina standard, bears the *parasema* of both Cyzicus (tuna fish) and Athens (owl). Meyer and Moreno (2004) persuasively argue that this weight attests to steps taken by the Cyzicaeans to align their civic standards with those of the more commercially dominant Attic standard. They go on to note (213) that it should be viewed as a materialization of a "complex and long process of metrological standardization that occurred naturally as the Aegean world adapted to Athenian commercial hegemony."

69 Bresson (1993: 162–4) suggests that the Rhodians enforced the use of their civic coinage within a zone that encompassed the neighboring islands.

70 The bibliography for the Coinage Decree is extensive, yet there remain ongoing disputes surrounding many aspects of the law, from its date to the very essence of its underlying intention, whether an expression of imperial grandstanding by Athens (Mattingly 1996; Hatzopoulos 2014) or a practical policy driven by administrative interests (Figueira 1998). See also the observations by Kallet (2001: 205–25), who perceptively notes that in prescribing the metrological norms within their *arkē*, the Athenians were simply behaving as any *polis* with regard to establishing the units of measure considered legitimate within their political borders.

71 Text, omitting lacunae, taken from Meiggs and Lewis (1969: no. 45, sec. 12) and Fornara (1983, no. 97).

72 For overview, see Epstein (1992: 120–2).

73 Backman (1995: xix). As with the ancient *medimnos*, such variation has naturally led to a
    difference of opinion by scholars attempting to estimate the capacity of the *salma*; see
    Gyllenbock (2018: 1724) for differing estimates on the *salma*.

74 While the variation in the size of the *salma* used at Agrigento and that used at Palermo may
    be partially explained by the distance between the cities or the relative size of these two
    cities, it is far more remarkable that the smaller towns of Polizzi and Castellamare used
    measures different from neighboring Palermo, the largest political and commercial center in
    the region; see Epstein (1992: 121, n. 114). It was this multiplicity of measures that
    prompted the fifteenth-century merchant Giovanni da Uzzano to remark, "*Cicilia ae piu
    salme*" (Sicily has many *salme*); Epstein (1992: 120).

75 A treaty of 1156 negotiated between William I and Genovese merchants makes provision
    for the royal curia at Messina to supply a standard measure (*cisto*) to the merchants; Mathews
    (1992: 76–7).

76 Among the earliest attempts on record for this period is the *Liber Augustalis*, or Constitutions
    of Melfi, a new legal code imposed by Frederick II in 1231 for the Kingdom of Sicily.
    Frederick's constitution set forth regulations related to various economic, legal, and insti-
    tutional practices within the kingdom, including the mandated use of common weights and
    measures for commercial transactions. Despite the harsh punishments set forth for those
    who transgressed the laws, Zecchino (2017) has found that Sicily remained home to a
    multiplicity of metrological instruments.

77 Runciman (1958: 128).

78 In 1434, King Alfonso issued an edict "on the standardization of measurements," which
    prescribed the *salma* of Catania to be the common measure of grain used throughout the Val
    di Demone and Val di Noto.
    The edict appears to have had little success; see Epstein (1992: 121); Cordova (1890: 42).

79 Epstein (1992: 121).

80 Kula (1986)

81 Epstein (1992: 122).

82 Porter (1995: 26) notes the process of metrification was similarly drawn out in France,
    taking upward of 40 years to enact the new system of measurement.

83 This is not to completely dismiss the role that merchants might have played in furthering
    standardization within the Hieronian context. Indeed, commercial use of state-sanctioned
    metrological instruments would have almost certainly accelerated adoption and led to even
    greater ubiquity.

84 Pelagatti (1970: 491–3) first published the vessel from Contrada Aguglia. For the fragments
    from Kamarina and Morgantina, see Walthall (2011).

85 For further discussion of the inscription, see Walthall (2011).

86 This is supported by visual comparison with ceramics locally produced at Morgantina. The
    fabric of the stamped measuring vessel found at Morgantina, for instance, has a perceptibly
    darker reddish hue (MSC 2.5YR 6/6) than the local clay, quarried near the site, which generally
    fires pale reddish brown (MSC 5YR 6/3–4) to lighter yellowish brown (MSC 5YR 7/4).

87 Molev (2003: 846, pl. 4) publishes a stamped dry measure of third-century date from Kyrta.
    Similarly, Treister and Vinogradov (1993: 531–2) publish a stamped dry measure from
    Tyras, also of third-century date; Kleyman (1989: 19–25). Manganaro (2001: 149–56)
    publishes a grain measure of much later date (probably early sixth century CE), inscribed
    with the name of the individual who certified its validity (Εἰταλικὸς τῆς δεσποτίας τοῦ
    κόμητος Οὐαδίλα, | ἀπὸ κελεύσεως τοῦ ἄρχοντος, ἔγραψα κα(τ)εζα|γιασμένον ζέστιν ἀπὸ
    ὀνόματος Ἑορτασίου | δίκαιον ὀνκίων ἴκοσι τε(σ)άρων στρατιοτικῶ|ν), arguing on pros-
    opographic grounds that the measure originated in Sicily.

88 Various scholars have posited the operation of such royal officials within the Hieronian
    kingdom; Carcopino (1914: 6–12); Berve (1959: 53–4, 58); Bell (2007a: 194).

89 Of possible exception are the three bronze vessels discovered by Flinders Petrie at Tell
    Dafana in 1887, two of which are now held in the British Museum (1887,0101.776,

BM 1888,0208.146) and while the third ended up at the Boston Musem of Fine Arts (87.496a–b). None of the vessels, which are heavily corroded, bear any visible sign of having been authenticated by a state official. As far as I am aware, these are among only a handful of objects that have been identified as measuring devices of Ptolemaic date found in Egypt. All are small and have capacities no greater than 1 liter. The attribution of Ptolemaic date stems from Petrie's notation that they were discovered in the excavation of a Ptolemaic-era waste heap.

[90]   Lang (1952: 18–31) argues the inscribed stone was intended to be placed in a public space, such as the agora of Thasos, where individuals could consult it; cf. De Ste. Croix (2004: 340–6), who argues against Lang's position, stressing the paucity of evidence to corroborate it.

[91]   In many cities, *sekōmata* took the form of stone tables with cavities carved out to correspond to fixed volumetric units, the names of which were sometimes inscribed on the stone itself. Remains of these so-called *mensae ponderariae* have been found across the Mediterranean region and tend to date from the Hellenistic and Roman periods; Cioffi (2017).

[92]   For instance, *P.Hib.* I.98, a receipt from the year 252, which records the shipment of 4,800 *artabas* of barley to the royal granaries in Alexandria. The receipt certifies that the grain was "justly measured" using a bronze measuring vessel and leveling rod, which had been brought from Alexandria.

[93]   As suggested by *P.Tebt.* 5. It is worth noting that for the use of standard measures in Ptolemaic Egypt, we are solely reliant on references found in the papyrological record.

[94]   See Broneer (1938: 224) on problems arising from manufacturing volumetric measures in terracotta.

[95]   *P.Rev.* cols. 25 and 40.

[96]   Although these particular receipts date to the 150s and 140s, the use of the μέτρον δοχικόν dates back to at least the middle decades of the third century BCE, as evidenced by *P.Hib.* 1.74 ll.2. At least one receipt (*P.Lille* I.21) mentions that the volume of the μέτρον δοχικόν was tested (συμβλέπτειν) against that of a bronze measure (πρὸς τὸ χαλχοῦν) and with the aid of a leveling rod (σκυτάλη δικαία).

[97]   Bell (2007a: 190–3). The importance of trustworthy measures is emphasized time and again in the Athenian decree *IG* II² 1013, discussed above.

[98]   *P.Tebt.* 5; translation from Austin (2006: 594, no. 290).

[99]   Scott (1998: 27).

[100]   Walthall (2023).

SIX

MONUMENTAL GRANARIES

Murgantiam primum prodito ab ipsis praesidio Romano recipit, ubi frumenti magna vis commeatusque omnis generis convecti erant Romanis.

He (Himilco) first regained control of Morgantina – the Roman garrison having been betrayed by the inhabitants of the city themselves – where the Romans had stored a great quantity of grain and supplies of all kind.

—Liv. 24.36.10

Imagine entering the agora of Morgantina around the year 240 (Figure 6.1). You climb the steep path leading to the city gate on the south side of the fortifications. Once inside, you are immediately confronted by an imposing sight – a massive stone façade on your right, stretching north for 90 meters, circumscribing the eastern edge of the public space. While long and rectangular like the monumental stoa buildings that frame the city's upper agora, this structure does not present an inviting, permeable colonnade. Rather, the heavy walls, reinforced by imposing stone buttresses, convey a sense of restriction and control – a message further accentuated by the armed guards stationed at the building's main entrance. Looking left, you see a similar monument, shorter by half but constructed with the same massive, buttressed walls. This monument stands in parallel arrangement on a high outcrop of limestone some 45 meters away. Together, they flank the approach into the marketplace, forming a corridor into the agora that you have no choice but to take (Figure 6.2).

These two buildings were almost certainly monumental granaries, large warehouses built to store a portion of Morgantina's agricultural wealth, cultivated in

6.1 Veduta of the lower agora at Morgantina, ca. 240 BCE, looking south (illustration: J. Blid).

the territory below. Arguments for this identification emerged shortly after their discovery and rested largely on observations about their open floor plan and architectural form. For literary corroboration, archaeologists pointed to Livy, who in his account of the Sicilian conflict during the Second Punic War explicitly mentions that Morgantina harbored large stores of grain.[1] The passage in question, which forms the epigraph for this chapter, refers to the capture of the city in the year 214 by the Carthaginian commander Himilco. Having only recently abandoned an attempt to confront the Roman general Marcellus on his march to Syracuse, Himilco now sought to undermine the Roman military effort by sparking uprisings among the cities of southeastern Sicily. At Morgantina, he found both a populace willing to expel the Roman soldiers garrisoning their city and great stores of grain. As we shall see, archaeological evidence confirms that the two granaries were standing while the events described by Livy unfolded; indeed, they seem to be the only buildings of any period at Morgantina that could have accommodated the *frumenti magna vis* to which the historian refers.

In this chapter, we will explore the two monumental granaries at Morgantina from the ground up. We begin with a discussion of their architectural form and date, before turning to consider the place of these warehouses within administrative structure of the Hieronian kingdom. Following on the observations drawn in Chapter 4, I argue that the granaries at Morgantina served an essential role in the operation of the Hieronian tithe. Like the standardized measures of Chapter 5, Morgantina's granaries provide important material witness – albeit on

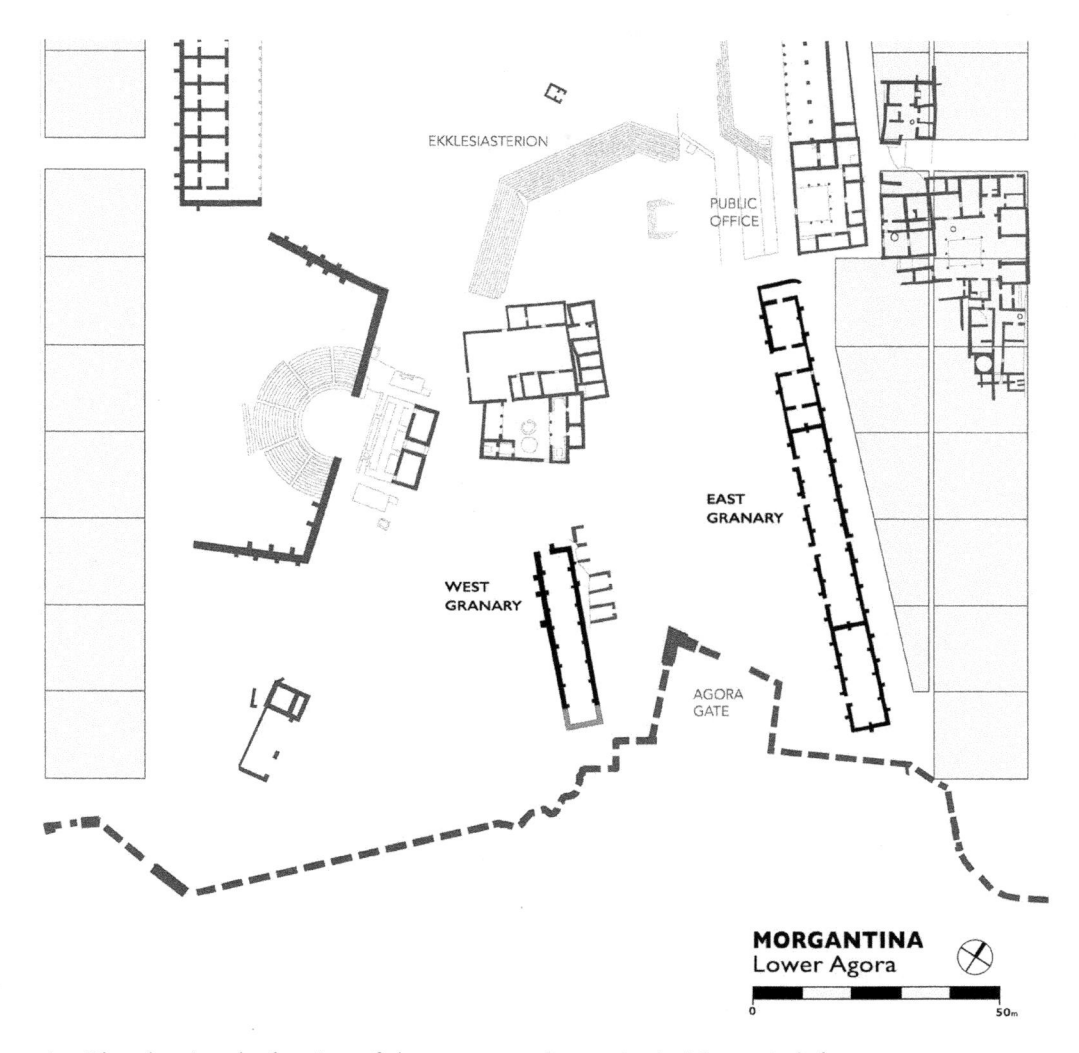

6.2 Plan showing the location of the monumental granaries in Morgantina's lower agora (drawing: E. Thorkildsen; courtesy of the American Excavations at Morgantina).

a far more monumental scale – to the operation and reach of the Hieronian state. Finally, I discuss the ideological function of these buildings and their role in projecting Hieron's authority to the western end of his kingdom. In this light, I consider other evidence for the close relationship between granary buildings and the ideology of kingship in the Hellenistic world.

THE GRANARIES AT MORGANTINA: IDENTIFICATION, CONSTRUCTION, AND FORM

Even a cursory glance at these two buildings framing the lower agora of Morgantina reveals a number of shared architectural features that speak to their common purpose. Most striking is their shape: narrow rectangles

6.3 Plaster coating on the exterior of the West Granary at Morgantina (courtesy of the American Excavations at Morgantina).

enclosing long, open rooms. Both monuments were constructed with thick masonry walls set on deep foundations. Unusually, the ancient builders had applied several thick coats of plaster to the exterior walls of both buildings – not over time, but in quick succession during the building's later phases of construction. Notably, these exterior preparations had been carried down below the visible surface of the ancient wall face to the very foundations (Figure 6.3). Meant to function as a shield against moisture, the plaster was applied even before the foundation trenches had been filled. Massive stone blocks, some weighing well over two tons apiece, were used in the lower masonry courses of both buildings. Exterior buttresses punctuated the otherwise plain and unadorned façades. Pairs of buttresses also ran along the interiors of both buildings. Current interpretations hold that these interior buttresses carried heavy timber beams over which rested an elevated wooden floor. This would have the effect of creating a long, covered hall suitable for large-scale storage.

The architectural form and construction techniques readily identify both buildings in the lower agora as large warehouses.[2] If the repeating pairs of interior buttresses did indeed carry an elevated wooden floor, as is the current *communis opinio* among archaeologists working at the site, this design feature almost certainly was intended for grain and other agricultural produce that benefited from ventilated storage on raised floors.[3] Several authors of ancient

Greek and Roman technical treatises and agronomic texts advise storing cereals in raised granaries as a means of reducing the destructive effects brought on by moisture and excessive heat.[4] This was one among two favored techniques employed for large-scale, long-term grain storage in the ancient Mediterranean, the other being storage in subterranean silos.[5] Raised granaries certainly appear to have been preferred when grain needed to be stockpiled for upward of a year, yet remain accessible for finite consumption or incremental distribution.[6] Purpose-built, raised granaries have a long history stretching back into the Bronze Age and find material expression in the archaeological record across the world up to the present day.[7]

The East Granary

Portions of the so-called East Granary were first revealed during the 1959 season of the Princeton-led excavations at the site under the direction of Erik Sjöqvist. Work continued over the course of the next two field seasons; by 1961, archaeologists had exposed all of the building's standing architecture (Figure 6.4).[8] Between 1989 and 1992, and again between 2011 and 2013, small-scale excavations were undertaken in and around the building to address unresolved questions about its chronological development.[9]

The East Granary measures 92.85 meters × 7.80 meters along its exterior (Figure 6.5), making its length roughly twelve times the width. The building comprises only six rooms (Rooms A–F) of unequal lengths, but all sharing a uniform interior width (6.30 meters). Rooms A and B together constitute roughly two-thirds of the building's total length. The fact that Room B, at 40 meters, is almost exactly twice the length (and thus twice the surface area) of Room A, at 20.25 meters, suggests an intentional proportional relationship of 2:1. A suite of four smaller rooms (Rooms C–F) occupies the remaining third of the granary at the northern end.

The walls of the building were unusually thick (avg. width 76 centimeters) compared with those of many other buildings at the site (avg. width ~45 centimeters). They follow a standard "double-faced" construction technique common to both private and public architecture of Hellenistic date at Morgantina: large blocks of local limestone form the exterior faces enclosing a fill of smaller chunks of limestone rubble.[10] The lowest courses of the building were formed of large, sometimes exceedingly large, ashlars (Figure 6.6). These were set on broad stone foundations (avg. width 1 meter) that extended beyond the vertical plane of the wall on both the interior and exterior of the building, providing deeply rooted stability to an already substantial structure.

The alternating pairs of interior and exterior stone buttresses are undoubtedly the most distinctive feature of the building's design. The massive exterior

6.4 Excavations of the East Granary in 1960, looking south (courtesy of the American Excavations at Morgantina).

buttresses measure 70 centimeters wide and project roughly 70 centimeters from the surface of the wall. With few exceptions, these external buttresses were symmetrically positioned along the building's longitudinal walls and spaced at regular intervals of 4.45 meters.[11] Pairs of interior buttresses were also built into the walls of Rooms A and B. These are of slightly smaller dimensions than the exterior buttresses, measuring 50 centimeters wide and projecting out 50 centimeters toward the center of the room. They too are spaced at regular intervals of 4.65 meters. There are no internal buttresses in Rooms C, D, and E. Room F, however, does have a single pair of internal buttresses, located approximately halfway along the eastern and western walls of the room. In their dimensions and construction, these resemble the internal buttresses found in Rooms A and B. As was suggested above, the parallel

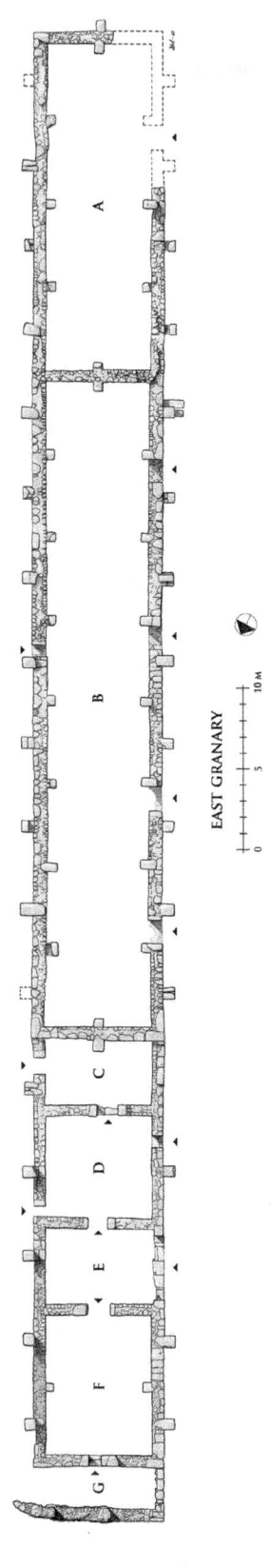

6.5 State plan of the East Granary; scale 1:400 (drawing: J. Blid; courtesy of the American Excavations at Morgantina).

6.6 Detail of ashlar construction of the East Granary, showing the separation of the northern and southern suites of rooms (courtesy of the American Excavations at Morgantina).

arrangement and regular spacing of the interior buttresses recommends the hypothesis that they carried heavy timber beams used to support an elevated wooden floor.[12] Such an arrangement would serve to distinguish Rooms A and B (and possibly Room F as well) as spaces dedicated to storage, whereas the layout of Rooms C, D, and E suggests these spaces served a different function, one likely associated with the broader administrative activities necessitated by the large-scale stockpiling of grain and other agricultural goods (e.g., record-keeping and oversight, garrisoning of troops for protection, etc.).

Archaeological evidence suggests the building rose in two major phases, the first of which involved the construction of Rooms A and B, followed in quick succession by the addition of the northern suite of rooms (Rooms C–F). Their seamless bonded masonry construction clearly indicates that the two largest rooms were built as part of a single construction phase. These rooms, moreover, share a single foundation, one that is clearly distinct from the foundation underlying the rooms to the north. The addition of the northern suite as a subsequent construction unit was confirmed in 1960, when archaeologists excavated a small trench against the exterior face of the building's western façade at the point where Rooms B and C meet. There, they found clear indication of the temporal construction sequence: the western wall of Room C did not bond with that of Room B, but simply abutted it. Further, they observed that the foundations of Room C (and presumably those of the other rooms belonging to the northern suite) were bedded some 40 centimeters higher than those of Room B. The more substantial foundations underlying Rooms A and B support the supposition that these were the principal loci of grain storage within the building. Although constructed in two distinct phases, it is nevertheless clear that all six rooms were planned together from the very start.

Construction of the East Granary was preceded by two major engineering projects required to prepare the area for a building of its orientation, scale, and function. First, a substantial portion of the bedrock along the western slope of the East Hill was excavated away. Archaeologists working on the excavations of 1959 and 1960 found the hillside had been cut back in roughly uniform fashion along the entire axis of the building. This achieved the desired orientation of the building (on which more below), and it allowed space for proper ventilation and drainage along its eastern side. Notably, the cutting back of the hillside encroached on space that had been reserved for private residences along the slope of the East Hill that faced the agora. Although archaeologists have yet to find evidence that the construction of the granary required the uprooting of preexisting private construction on the lots of *insula* E1/2S, there is no question that the building crews, literally and figuratively, carved away the space of private urban land allotments as they excavated away the hillside.[13] The second preparatory task involved the construction of a broad platform that would become the beaten-earth floor of the granary. This surface was leveled using a mixture of clay-rich soils and the unconsolidated limestone bedrock that had been quarried from the hillside. Once it was completed, the builders appear to have built a massive bonfire across the entire platform, which had the effect of "baking" the soil down to a depth of 3–5 centimeters. Archaeologists encountered traces of this burnt soil layer, identifiable by its bright red color and dense compaction, at similar levels in both the southeast corner of Room A and the northeast corner of Room F, suggesting that the entire platform was constructed in a single phase.[14] That this burning did not take place after the building had been finished is made clear by the fact that the builder's trench dug for the placement of the walls cut through the burnt surface. Burning the surface of the soil platform may have been a measure to prevent moisture or insects from entering the building from the soils below.[15]

Function

Material evidence recovered from within the building does not unequivocally confirm its identity as a granary. This is primarily because grains and other foodstuffs, unless carbonized, typically do not survive in the archaeological record in Sicily.[16] Nevertheless, the building's distinctive architectural footprint most plausibly identifies it as a granary. With their open floor plans, heavy

6.7 Reconstruction of the East Granary; section, looking south (drawing: J. Blid).

masonry construction, and provisions for an elevated floor, Rooms A and B were certainly designed for the purpose. The wide external buttresses would have played an essential role both by reinforcing the walls against the lateral forces of heaped grain, whether stored loose or in sacks, and by supporting the wide, overhanging eaves necessary for keeping rainwater away from the building and its precious contents (Figure 6.7).

Taking a closer look at the northern suite of rooms, we can tentatively designate discrete functions to these spaces based on the standing architecture alone (Figure 6.8).[17] That these rooms served as the locus of administrative activity associated with the movement of grain or other agricultural goods in and out of the building seems appropriate, judging from their relatively small size and organization. This is consistent with what is known of the activities that took place in the royal granaries of Ptolemaic Egypt, where archiving and administrative oversight took place on the premises of the warehouse.[18] Room E, for instance, with its monumental doorway (width 3.95 meters) along the

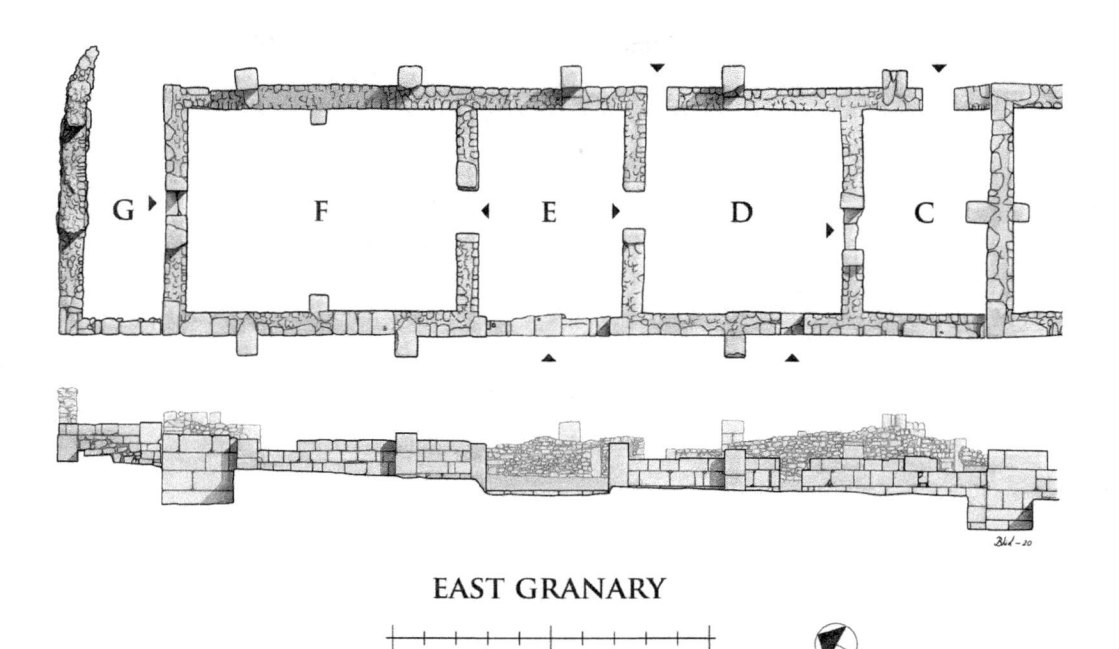

EAST GRANARY

0   5   10 M

6.8 East Granary, plan of the northern suite of rooms (C–F) with preserved wall elevations below (drawing: J. Blid).

building's western façade, would have offered a suitable entrance for carts or wagons. Adjoining it to the north, Room F was the only room of the suite equipped with a pair of interior buttresses like those found in Rooms A and B. By analogy, Room F may have served as an intermediate site of grain storage, used perhaps when security was needed in loading or offloading large shipments of grain. Within Rooms C and D, we might expect to find the officials tasked with the overseeing the operation of the granary and, with them, the necessary documents and records. Room D, which could be entered either from a doorway that opened onto the public space or from the adjacent offloading Room E, controlled access to Room C, which was the smallest room of the building and could not be directly accessed from the agora. Room C, however, could be accessed from a doorway in its eastern wall, which led to a narrow, alley-like space that ran between the granary building and the excavated slope. One possible interpretation for this configuration is that it provided a secure means of accessing the stores held in Room B, which was also equipped with a single doorway along its eastern side, without having to exit the building from the western side, facing the open agora.

Dating
Diagnostic artifacts recovered from stratified deposits excavated inside the East Granary help establish an unambiguous timeline for the building's

construction, use, and eventual abandonment. The granary surely rose in the second or third quarter of the third century BCE, at a time when Morgantina was subject to the political control of Hieron II.[19] This is confirmed even by the small amount of ceramic and numismatic evidence that excavators collected from the soil fills laid down at the time of the building's construction. The most important diagnostic find in this respect is a small bronze coin of a type struck at Syracuse between 276 and 269, during the years that Hieron held power as *stratēgos autokrator*. Archaeologists recovered this coin from within the building's construction fill, establishing a *terminus post quem* of 269 for the granary.[20] Notably, the coin shows little sign of wear, suggesting that it was not in circulation long before finding its way into the ground.[21]

The East Granary ceased to function as a warehouse around the year 211, when Morgantina fell to Roman troops. As I argue in greater detail below, Rome's priorities regarding the agricultural tithe differed from those of Hieron; no longer was there any need to stockpile large stores of grain or other agricultural goods at interior sites like Morgantina. In the years that followed the siege, the granary likely fell victim to spoliation and gradually lapsed into disuse, as is evident from the accumulation of sediments in and around the building. In the third quarter of the second century, the massive warehouse once again came to life – this time not as a granary but as a sprawling ceramics workshop specializing in the production of fine wares, lamps, and architectural elements like roof tiles and bricks.[22] While the large-scale storage of agricultural goods had doubtless ceased long before, the installation of pottery kilns marked a definitive end to the building's use as a granary.

The West Granary

Like its counterpart, the West Granary was excavated over the course of several field seasons, spanning nearly six decades (see Figure 6.2). Portions of the building were first exposed in 1956 during the second season of the Princeton-led excavations at the site. At the time – three years *prior* to the discovery of the East Granary – the building was not recognized as a monumental warehouse and was largely ignored for much of the next three decades. Excavations resumed only in 1980 when archaeologists dug a long trench across the building's transverse axis that located both interior and exterior buttresses, architectural features that pointed to its function as a raised-floor granary. Work continued in the newly dubbed West Granary during the 1981 and 1982 seasons.[23] In 2011, archaeologists returned to the West Granary with the goal of refining details of its chronology, which had remained a subject of some debate.[24]

Only the footprint of the West Granary survives today. The building, a victim of aggressive spoliation over time, has been largely reduced to its

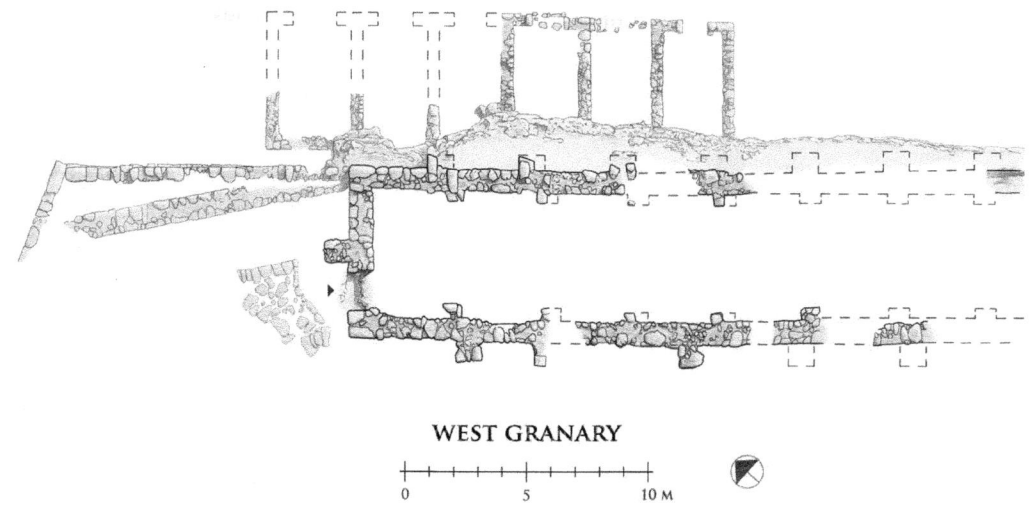

WEST GRANARY

0   5   10 M

6.9 State plan of the West Granary; scale 1:200 (drawing: J. Blid; courtesy of the American Excavations at Morgantina).

foundations. In only a few places do the stones of the lowest courses remain in situ. Yet despite its poor state of preservation, sufficient portions of the foundations remain to allow for an accurate reconstruction of its overall plan and superstructure (Figure 6.9). At its maximum, the building measures 7.50 meters across and is preserved to a length of 32.90 meters. Its full length is unknown, as its southernmost portion was destroyed by the construction of a seventeenth-century palazzo, the ruins of which still stand today at the edge of the agora. Considering the building's orientation and its immediate topographic situation, the full length may have been originally closer to 40 meters. This would bring the exterior dimensions of the West Granary (~40 meters × 7.50 meters) very close to those of Room B of the East Granary (40 meters × 7.80 meters), and would suggest, moreover, that the two buildings were planned using an analogous construction module.

Judging from the surviving remains, builders employed the same heavy masonry walls, doubly reinforced by interior and exterior buttresses, as found on the East Granary. The interior buttresses measured 50 centimeters × 50 centimeters and formed opposing pairs spaced uniformly along the longitudinal walls at intervals of 3.80 meters. The building's exterior buttresses have dimensions similar to those of the East Granary, but these do not appear to be spaced at regular intervals or in a paired configuration.[25] It appears that the building's only entrance was a wide doorway (1.70 meters) in the short north wall set between the central buttress and northwest corner of the building. The placement of a single doorway at one of the building's short ends differs from the arrangement found in the East Granary, which had at least six doorways in the long western wall. Locating the door in the north wall was a prudent choice from the standpoint of access, as one could not reach the building from the south or the east due to its position atop the high limestone outcropping. This short north side of the granary was the first point one would reach when approaching the building from the lower agora. Leading to the entrance from the north was a ramp formed of large limestone paving stones.

The building stood on a natural outcropping of limestone bedrock that rises several meters above the ground level of the lower agora to the east. This was, topographically speaking, quite different from the location chosen for the East Granary, which sat at the base of the East Hill. Nevertheless, the two buildings were clearly constructed to share a nearly parallel alignment, the effect of which was to create a broad corridor through which individuals moving in and out of the city would pass.

Function

The pairs of interior buttresses are a sign that the building was also equipped with an elevated wooden floor of identical construction to that found in the East Granary. Excavations inside the building revealed no evidence of cross walls dividing the space, indicating that the granary was likely a single, open hall.

Dating

Today, we know that the West Granary followed a chronological trajectory nearly identical to that of the East Granary. Materials recovered from stratigraphic deposits within the building confirm that its construction began during the period of Hieronian rule and, furthermore, that it had ceased to function as a warehouse by the start of the second century. This was not always the case. Excavations inside the building during the 1980s had produced numismatic evidence that supported an interpretation that the West Granary was a forerunner of the East Granary by upward of 40 years.[26] Sustaining this long-held interpretation were stylistic observations about the building's layout and design, which were considered less developed than the "perfected plan" of its counterpart to the east.[27] The discovery of new diagnostic evidence during the 2011 excavations inside the West Granary has led to the critical reassessment of the long-held view regarding the date of the building's construction. From within the plaster-rich leveling fill deposited inside the granary at the time of the its construction, excavators recovered a well-preserved bronze coin struck at the South Italian city of Rhegium between the years 260 and 215.[28] The presence of this coin within the subfloor packing situates the construction of the West Granary firmly within the period of Hieron's rule.

Like the East Granary, the West Granary also ceased to function as a warehouse shortly after Morgantina was captured in 211. No signs have emerged that the building was damaged in a conflagration or destroyed in the violence of the siege. Presumably, what precious comestibles remained within were consumed or carried off, along with useful building materials such as timber beams. At several points around the interior of the building, excavators encountered concentrations of collapsed roof tiles lying on the beaten-earth floor. Sealed below the layer of fallen tiles were several coins, the latest of which were struck between the years 214 and 212 by a Roman mint operating on Sicily during the Second Punic War.[29] As the latest datable objects recovered from below the tile fall layer, the coins clearly demonstrate that the building was in a state of disrepair within only a matter of years after the Roman siege. By the middle of the second century, the building had been largely reduced to its foundations. It was not repurposed as the East Granary had been. Rather, its demolition was prescribed by the construction of a large *temenos* wall that enclosed a sanctuary complex located between the granary and the theater.[30]

The Granaries in the Urban Landscape

Once completed, the East and West Granaries redefined the surrounding landscape of Morgantina's lower agora. Topographically speaking, one cannot imagine a more prominent location in the city than that which was given over to these buildings. Framing the principal entrance to the agora, these monuments created a broad corridor through which individuals entering and exiting the city would pass. Measuring over 92 meters in length and standing as much as 9 meters in height, the East Granary was undoubtedly the dominant architectural feature of the lower agora (Figure 6.10). Its massive, buttressed walls provided an imposing backdrop for all activities taking place in its vicinity. Rising from its foundations on what was already a prominent

6.10 Reconstruction of the East Granary, showing west elevation along the northern suite of rooms (drawing: J. Blid).

limestone outcropping, the West Granary, although less than half the length of its counterpart, would have offered an equally arresting visual statement, towering over the lower agora and blocking views beyond.

That these buildings were the product of careful and deliberate planning is evident not only in their parallel arrangement and analogous proportions but also in the great lengths taken by the architects and construction crews to secure the desired siting for them. Viewed in context of the larger urban setting, the granaries were plainly planned along with the rest of the monumental building program that transformed Morgantina's agora over the course of the third century. And, as is arguably the case with so many other buildings of Morgantina's monumental agora, the ultimate source for the construction and the design of the granaries was probably Syracuse.[31]

Estimating the Capacity of Morgantina's Granaries

Before moving on to consider the East and West Granaries within their wider social and historical context, we might be tempted to speculate regarding the capacity of these warehouses. As fixed units of volume that were constructed for the purpose of preserving grain and other produce, the granaries at Morgantina offer a tantalizing glimpse into agricultural production in the surrounding region. One might reasonably suppose that since the maximum surface area of the two buildings is relatively well known, it is only a matter of inferring the height at which foodstuffs were piled in order to calculate their capacity. Of course, the simplicity of this solution belies the magnitude of complexity that awaits all who venture down this path.

Arriving at accurate estimates for the capacity of ancient raised granaries has long remained an intractable problem for modern scholars. This is largely due to the fact that only the stone foundations of these buildings tend to survive, and so calculations must inevitably rely on guesswork around many unknown details of storage (e.g., the original height of the walls, depth of the heaped grain, etc.). The issue has generated much deliberation and discussion among scholars working with the remains of Roman granaries (horrea), particularly those found in military forts or associated with large rural villas.[32] In recent years, the question of estimating granary capacity has received considerable attention from Javier Salido Domínguez, whose study of Roman granaries on the Iberian Peninsula has ultimately led him to recommend that scholars abandon their quest to quantify storage and instead focus on the qualitative characteristics of raised granaries that may be compared and contrasted with one another.[33] Such "quantitative skepticism," as Salido Domínguez describes his outlook, is necessitated by the many unanswerable questions that, at present, preclude the accurate calculation of a granary's capacity.[34]

Salido Domínguez's recommendations are well taken, and it should be acknowledged from the very outset that the calculations given in the following section are, at very best, impressionistic and intended only to offer a general sense of the building's scale in terms of their volume. Estimating the combined capacity of Morgantina's granaries begins with attempting to answer three deceptively simple questions: What was stored in the buildings? How was it stored? How high was it stored?

When it comes to the question of what was stored in these buildings, there is every likelihood that the monumental warehouses accommodated a variety of agricultural goods grown and produced in the territory of Morgantina. In fact, archaeobotanical remains collected from third-century contexts at the site, contemporary with the use of the granaries, confirm that a wide spectrum of crops were being cultivated and consumed in the area, crops such as barley (*Hordeum vulgare*), bread wheat (*Triticum aestivum*), emmer wheat (*Triticum dicoccum*), lentil (*Lens culinaris*), bitter vetch (*Vicia ervilia*), fava bean (*Vicia faba*), grape (*Vitis vinifera*), olive (*Olea europaea*), and fig (*Ficus carica*).[35] It would not be unreasonable to expect that any number of these crops were to be found in the granaries in one form or another, especially if the buildings were indeed used to warehouse the agricultural tithe owed to Hieron. Yet since we cannot hope to even identify the full range and quantity of each product stored in the granaries, let us opt for the simple (if unlikely) scenario that the granaries held only cereal grains like wheat and barley. The rolling foothills of Morgantina's territory that lie in the direction of the Ionian coast were well suited to cereal production, and it is perhaps no coincidence that the city's first coinage bore the image of a ripe ear of grain as the emblem of its reverse type (Figure 6.11).

Having chosen cereal grains as the hypothetical contents of our granaries, we next need to determine the method of storage. Since the 1970s, scholars

6.11 Silver litra coin of Morgantina, ca. 450 BCE (ANS 1944.100.10021; courtesy of the American Numismatic Society).

specializing in the study of Roman *horrea* have tended to endorse one of two principal methods in their reconstructions – grain stored in sacks or piled loose on the floor.[36] Each method had its own set of advantages and disadvantages, and either was a potentially viable option for the storage of grain inside the Morgantina granaries. Today, scholarly consensus has largely coalesced in favor of the second method – grain heaped directly onto the granary floor. This is informed by inferences drawn from the archaeological remains of ancient granary buildings as well as insights gleaned from documentary evidence that describes the character and operation of granaries in early modern Europe. The primary benefit of storing grain in piles is that it facilitates the maintenance and ventilation needed to control for moisture and humidity, which could trigger germination or allow for the growth of destructive bacteria and fungi. Grains heaped on the raised floor of a granary benefited from the circulation of air and could be regularly shoveled or turned to promote the drying process. This was essential for the long-term storage of cereal grains.

It is now generally held that sacks were a viable option only for the short-term storage of grain despite the many advantages they offered with regard to storage and handling. Sacks could be stacked to a greater height than loose grain, which has a natural tendency to flow when piled on the floor.[37] There were also administrative advantages to using sacks of standardized sizes, which would facilitate the assessment of tax grain moving in and out of state granaries. Philip Mayerson has presented a persuasive case for the use of standardized sacks for the storage and transport of tax grain in Ptolemaic Egypt.[38] Given the widespread adoption of standardized terracotta measures in Hieronian Sicily during this period, it seems altogether plausible that sacks of standardized capacity were used for large units of measurement. Yet for all their logistical promise, sacks are not conducive to the long-term storage of grain, as they do not allow for the ventilation required to prevent the accumulation of moisture in bulk grain.[39] We should thus conclude that the grain stored inside the two granaries at Morgantina was heaped directly on the raised surfaces of the buildings. If sacks played a role, it was likely only for short-term storage or in the process of administrative recordkeeping. To offer one purely speculative scenario, we might imagine that loose grain was heaped on the elevated floor in Rooms A and B, where there was ample space for the maintenance required to keep it cool and dry. When it came time for transport or distribution, the dried grain would have been moved in smaller quantities to Room F, where it was transferred into sacks and stacked awaiting shipment.

Finally, let us consider the height at which the loose grain was heaped as this will give us a key dimension with which to determine capacity. Here too, we must venture down the path of conjecture as no ancient data survive to guide us on the subject. Estimates in the range of 150–300 centimeters have been regularly proposed for the average height of heaped grain in Roman *horrea*.

Several recent voices, however, have raised doubts about these projections, characterizing them as impractical and opting instead for average heights in the range of 30–90 centimeters.[40] In arriving at these much-reduced height estimates, scholars such as Stéphane Martin and Lars Blöck have turned to agronomic treatises of the early modern period, which provide a great amount of detail about the storage of grains in conditions that were not altogether dissimilar from those likely found in ancient Roman *horrea*. Lars Blöck, for instance, cites the *Ökonomische Encyclopedie* (1773–86) of Johann Georg Krünitz, who provides detailed instructions for the construction of raised granaries and for the proper storage of grain therein. The author specifies that dried grain should be heaped no higher than 90 centimeters and that freshly harvested grain piled in heaps of no greater depth than 60 centimeters in order to prevent fermentation and rot.[41] For the present discussion, we will select three arbitrary numbers (30, 60, and 100 centimeters) for the average height and use these to estimate the amount of wheat that could be held by the granaries at Morgantina (Chart 6.1). Again, these numbers are intended only to offer plausible values for the minimum and maximum capacity of the granaries.

	East Granary (369 m²) L. 69.55 m[*] W. 5.3 m[**]	**West Granary (176 m²)** L. 40.0 m[†] W. 4.4 m[††]	
	Total Surface Area: 545 m²		
	@ 30 cm	@ 60 cm	@ 100 cm
m³	163.5 m³	327 m³	545 m³
Liters	163,500 L	327,000 L	545,000 L
Kg (0.79g/L)	129,165 kg	258,330 kg	430,550 kg
Medimnoi (@ 52.25 L)	3,129	6,258	10,430
Type-3 Measure (@ 32 L)	5,109	10,219	17,031

[*] *Rooms A, B, and F.*

[**] *Subtracting 1.0 m from the interior width of 6.3 m.*

[†] *Projected length, based on surviving length of 32.9 m.*

[††] *Subtracting 1.0 m from the interior width of 5.4 m.*

CHART 6.1

Putting it all together, we arrive at capacity estimates for the granaries that fall in the range of 129 to 430 metric tons of wheat grain. This would translate into roughly 163,500–545,000 liters or about 3,100–10,400 *medimnoi*, if we use the figure of 52.25 liter per *medimnos*.[42] To put this into perspective, Livy (22.37) reports that Hieron's grain fleet landed at Ostia with some 300,000 *modii* of wheat and 200,000 *modii* of barley following the battle at Cannae. Allowing for the fact that these numbers are likely to have been embellishments on reality, this would amount to over 83,000 *medimnoi* of grain, or more than eight times our maximum capacity for Morgantina's granaries. Since Morgantina's territory likely accounted for only a small portion of the total area under Hieron's political control, these numbers certainly register as plausible.[43] But, again, this is all mere speculation. Given the cursory route taken in arriving at these numbers, it seems prudent that we avoid using them to further extrapolate demographic figures for the city or speculate about the carrying capacity of the surrounding territory. Those are calculations better left for future work on the Morgantina granaries, which should pay greater attention to details like the structural capabilities of the buildings' masonry walls and elevated wooden floors.

MONUMENTAL GRANARIES IN THE HELLENISTIC MEDITERRANEAN

Less than a decade after Sjöqvist's initial discovery and identification of the East Granary, Geoffrey Rickman drew attention to a comparable kind of storehouse architecture that was already prolifically evident at Roman military forts.[44] These were often constructed with a wooden or stone-slab floor suspended above a stone platform. Rectangular in form and built in a heavy masonry construction style designed to support the weight of amassed grain, these platforms generally supported rows of low, thick interior walls that in turn carried the elevated floor. Narrow vertical slits perforating the lower walls allowed for subfloor ventilation. Well-documented examples of this type of granary, like those excavated at Reniblas and Castillejo in Spain and at Corbridge in Britain, also resembled the Morgantina buildings in their array of external buttresses, which served to fortify the already substantial stone foundations (Figure 6.12).

While their architectural affinity with Roman military granaries may put to rest questions about the function of the Morgantina buildings as monumental granaries, it inevitably raises further questions about the source of inspiration for their design. Although utilizing similar design principles, the Morgantina granaries predate even the earliest known Roman military granaries by upward of a century or more.[45] The obvious, yet evasive, answer lies buried under Syracuse, where Hieron had constructed monumental stone granaries within

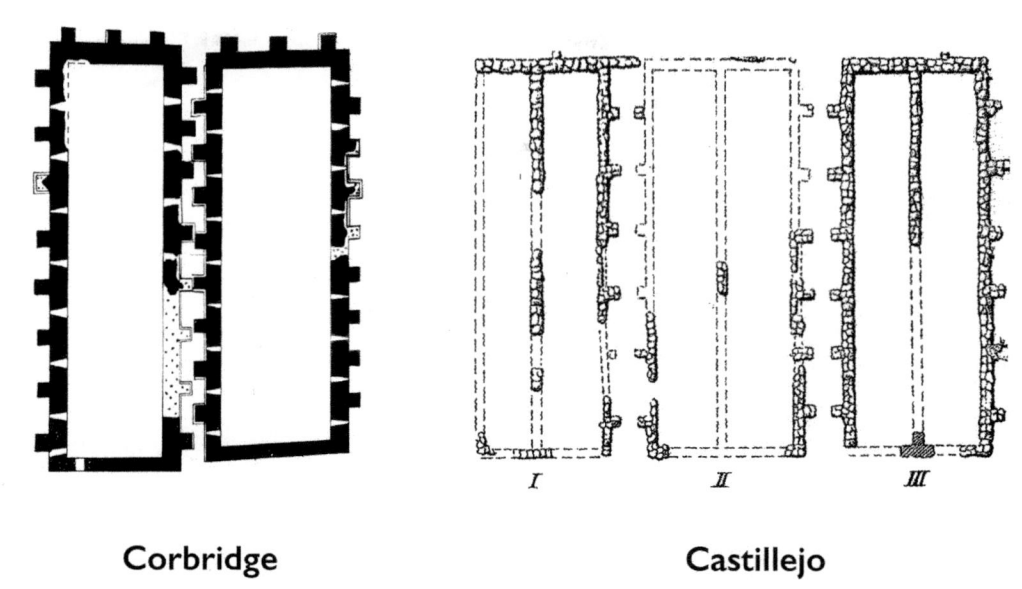

Corbridge   Castillejo

6.12 Plans of Roman military granaries from forts at Corbridge (England, third century CE; after Birley 1954) and Castillejo (Spain, second or first century BCE; after Schulten 1927).

the walls of his fortified palace complex on the island of Ortygia.[46] During his lifetime, these royal granaries surely held the prodigious quantities of grain and other agricultural products collected in taxes from his kingdom. They were the storehouses from which he supplied vast amounts of grain to allies and merchants throughout the Mediterranean. Unfortunately, no trace of these monuments has been recovered archaeologically.

To contextualize the granaries of Morgantina within their contemporary Hellenistic setting, we must look outside Sicily and to the eastern Mediterranean, where, as luck would have it, several monumental granaries of similar form and date have been unearthed. Notable among these are the so-called arsenal buildings excavated during the 1927 season of the German archaeological mission at Pergamon. The five long, rectangular buildings were situated at the highest point of the city's acropolis in the area identified as the Attalid's palace complex, where they overlooked the city and its territory (Figure 6.13).[47] In their 1937 publication of these monuments in the *Altertümer von Pergamon*, von Szalay and Boehringer rightly adduced the function of the buildings as warehouses on the basis of their architectural form in much the same manner as Sjöqvist would do roughly two decades later at Morgantina. They even went on to note the stylistic similarities shared by the Pergamene warehouses and those granary buildings excavated at Roman forts in Spain, Germany, and England, highlighting common design elements like the elongated proportions and the arrangement of longitudinal walls in the foundations to support an elevated wooden floor.[48] Yet, while the German

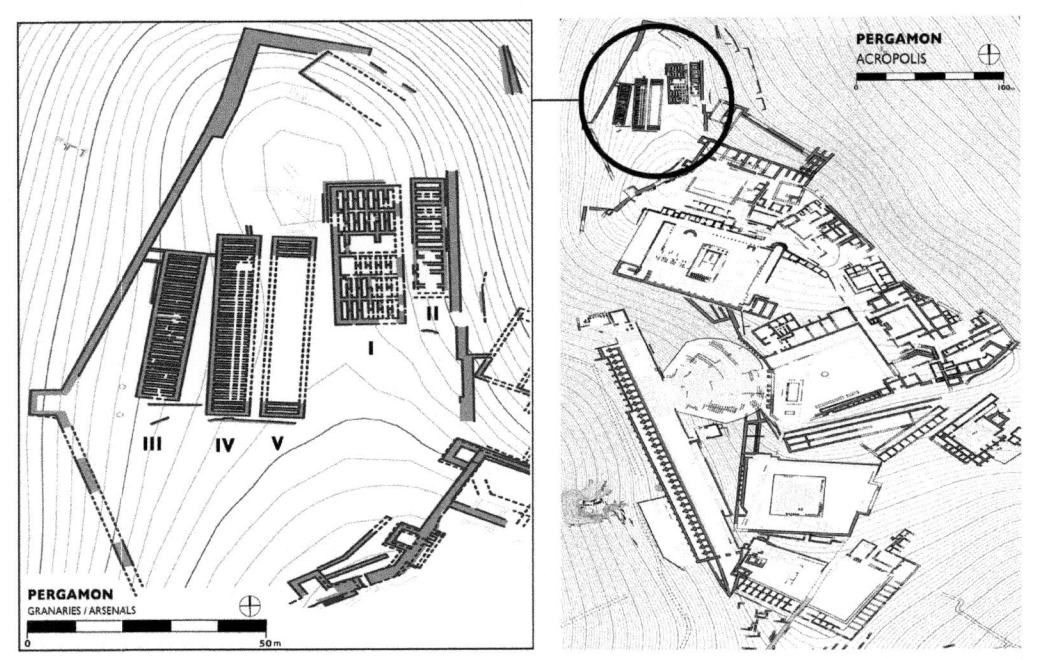

6.13 Plan of the acropolis of Pergamon, showing location of the monumental granaries and arsenal buildings (base map: © DAI 2020; courtesy of the Pergamon Excavation of the DAI).

scholars would posit that one among the five buildings (Arsenal I) might have been constructed for the purpose of grain storage, they would ultimately characterize the Pergamene warehouses as arsenals built principally to hold the armaments (i.e., stone ballista balls, iron arrowheads, etc.) found in great quantities around the immediate vicinity of this walled section of the acropolis, although not necessarily within the buildings themselves. While the "arsenal" label has long followed these buildings, there is every reason to believe that their principal function was the long-term storage of grains and other agricultural produce, not that of military implements alone.[49]

What survives of the Pergamene warehouses today are the massive stone platforms upon which originally rested elevated wooden superstructures (Figure 6.14). These platforms sat on deep foundations formed by rows of low interior walls that were spaced at regular intervals, similar to those seen in later Roman military granaries. Narrow ventilation slits located along the lower masonry courses and within the stretches of interior walls are unmistakable design features of granary architecture. Raised and ventilated floors would have been ideal for the storage of grain, but presented no obvious benefit for stone or metal munitions. Their elongated proportions resemble those of the Morgantina granaries. Compare, for instance, Arsenal III (39.22 meters × 7.95 meters) and the West Granary (~40 meters × 7.5 meters), which were constructed with a length-to-width ratio of about 5:1. That the East Granary

6.14 Excavation of the Pergamene granaries (after von Szalay and Boehringer 1937; courtesy of the Staatliche Museen zu Berlin – Antikensammlung, photo archive PM 6499).

at Morgantina had a far more exaggerated length-to-width ratio (12:1) than any of the Pergamene buildings may have been a consequence of available space in their immediate topographic settings. Atop the fortified acropolis at Pergamon, where builders had to contend with the combined limits imposed by the course of the circuit wall and the steep topography under foot, constructing a building of a corresponding length to that of the East Granary would prove prohibitively difficult. The solution arrived at by the architects and builders of the Pergamene granaries seems to have been simply to construct multiple buildings of fixed dimensions that, collectively, could hold the desired volume of produce. This is perhaps most clearly seen in the construction of Arsenals IV and V, which are contemporary buildings of identical dimensions (47.65 meters × 8.07 meters) and parallel orientation. The construction of these dual warehouses in a single campaign is consistent with the interpretation that architects were tasked with building granaries of specified total capacity on a site with limited space.[50]

While not a precise match to the granaries at Morgantina, the Pergamene arsenals nevertheless share important attributes of design, like their elevated floors and elongated rectangular form, that should lead us to believe they served a similar purpose – namely, to store foodstuffs. They were also of contemporary date, according to the chronology proposed by von Szalay and Boehringer, who placed the earliest of these buildings (Arsenals I and II) in the first half of the third century BCE. Specifically, they suggest that Arsenals I and II were constructed during the reign of Philetairos (r. 282–263), patriarch of the Attalid dynasty, at a time when the city was undergoing major expansion. They considered the remaining three buildings also to have been products of the third century, constructed as the city continued to flourish under Eumenes I (r. 263–241) and his adoptive son Attalos I (r. 241–197).[51]

Outside Pergamon and beyond the confines of the Attalid kingdom, another raised granary of similar form and design has been discovered at Mount Karasis in central Turkey. This remarkably well-preserved building belonged to a fortified palace or administrative complex built in the third century, most likely during the reign of the Seleucid king Antiochos III (r. 222–187). Located on an isolated mountain in the southern reaches of the Taurus Mountains, the site itself was only rediscovered by archaeologists in the 1990s.[52] Like those found at Morgantina and Pergamon, the granary building at Mount Karasis is an elongated rectangle (~60 meters × ~12 meters) constructed of heavy masonry walls that were built to support an elevated wooden floor on a series of interior stone piers (Figure 6.15).[53] Its location, along the uppermost ridgeline within the fort, mirrors that of the Pergamene buildings. The choice to situate these buildings at topographically remote points within their respective settlements surely reflects a concern with safeguarding the valuable contents within. No one, of course, wanted vital food supplies to fall into enemy hands, particularly during times of war or protracted siege. And while keeping provisions out of reach was surely of paramount concern, there was clearly attention paid to increasing the visibility of these buildings by placing them at prominent, conspicuous locations.

Collectively, the number of archaeologically attested granary buildings of Early Hellenistic date remains rather small, but as the relatively recent discovery of the granary atop Mount Karasis should remind us, many more Hellenistic granaries surely await identification, whether through excavation or intensive survey. Along these lines, Radt has posited the existence of a monumental granary of similar size and dimensions to those discussed here among the remains of a fortified residence at the site of Teke Kale in southwestern Turkey.[54] Another large granary building of comparable form has been credibly identified inside the citadel at Jebel Khalid in northern Syria.[55] Here, archaeologists have excavated the remains of a fortified settlement that began its life as a Seleucid garrison and administrative center of the late third century. Although the building in question has been subject only to intensive survey, not stratigraphic excavation, its architectural form, clearly visible from aerial photographs, supports its identification as a monumental granary of analogous form to those of Pergamon and Mount Karasis.

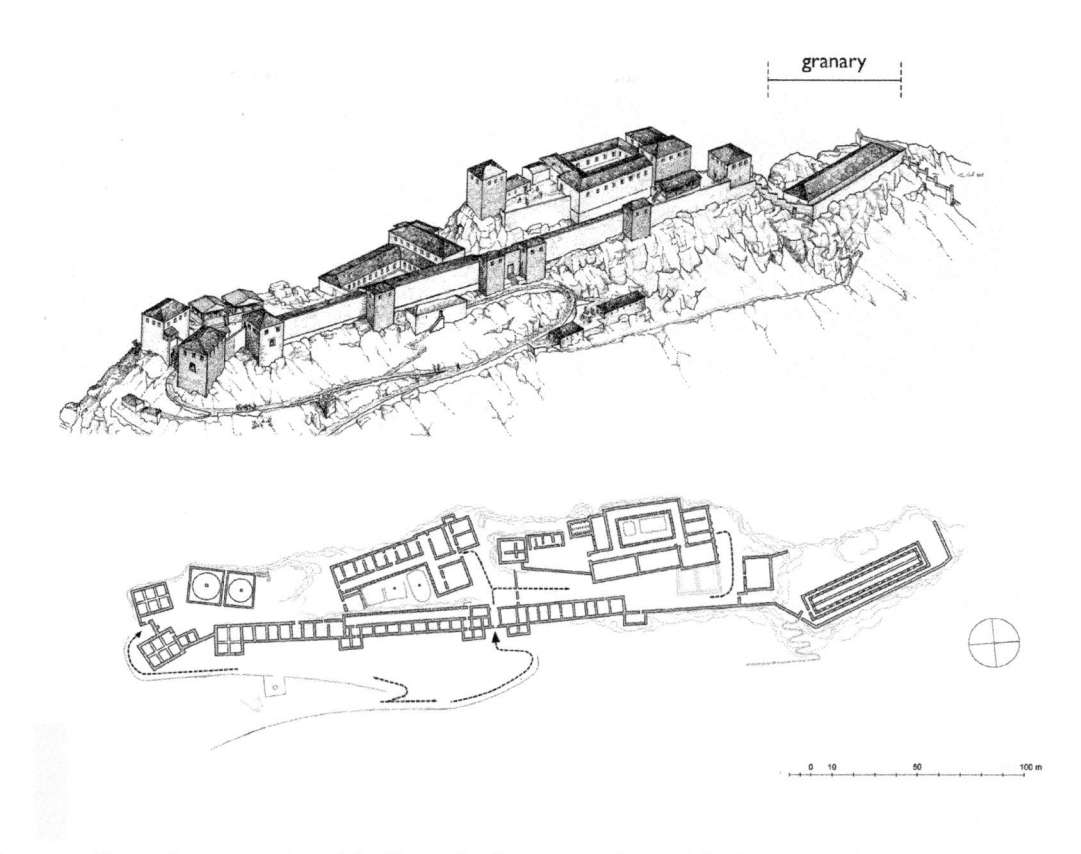

6.15 Plan and reconstruction of the Upper Castle at Mount Karasis (after Radt 2016; drawing: T. Radt).

Still, much can be said with respect to the current assemblage of Early Hellenistic granaries. Individually, each of these buildings exhibits some small degree of variation from the others with respect to layout and design, even among those found at the same site. These minor architectural differences might be attributed to any number of regional, or even local, factors, such as the availability of timber. Minor differences aside, one is struck by the overwhelming similarity shared by all of these monuments. Most significant in this respect, these buildings exhibit a consistency of form and design that points to a shared approach to constructing purpose-built monumental granaries, one that preceded the better-known examples found at Roman military forts.[56]

While it cannot be said to have served as a direct source of inspiration for any of the buildings considered here, the *Poliorcetica* of the third-century tactician Philo of Byzantium also provides contemporary reference to this type of monumental granary.[57] Philo's treatise on siege craft offers a lengthy description of techniques for building at least two types of above-ground granary (σιτοβολών, *sitobolōn*), one constructed primarily of stone and the other of timber.[58] The text of the treatise is regrettably quite fragmentary around the discussion of granaries, and hardly anything survives of Philo's recommendations for constructing timber granaries. Yet the surviving portions offer several recommendations for effective granary construction that mirror the surviving remains at Morgantina, Pergamon, and Mount Karasis. For instance, Philo emphasizes the importance of keeping grain dry and cool to prevent destruction by moisture and rot, and so recommends storing it in buildings with elevated (ὑπερῷος, *hyperōos*) floors.[59] He also describes how to construct a building with a relatively fixed and narrow width but an unspecified length. The modular quality of Philo's proposed building would allow communities to construct granaries according to their specific needs and limitations, such as population size or the availability of space within the city's walls.[60] This fixed ratio could, in theory, be repeated ad infinitum such that the volume of a granary was augmented by increasing its length but not its width. We can see evidence of such modularity employed in the design and construction of the granaries at both Morgantina and Pergamon. Although it remains our best surviving source on the matter of granary construction during the Early Hellenistic period, Philo's *Poliorcetica* was unlikely to have been the only technical treatise in circulation around the middle decades of the third century that offered its reader a detailed description of granary construction.[61] The similarities exhibited by the eight granary buildings from the three sites discussed above would certainly be best explained in terms of the circulation of such technical treatises.

MONUMENTS OF ROYAL PERSUASION?

Beyond similarities of form and function, the granaries discussed above share a further connection in that they all were built at sites closely associated with the projection of political and military authority held by Hellenistic monarchs. The granaries of Pergamon stood within the segment of the city's acropolis belonging to the palace complex of the Attalid kings. Those of Mount Karasis and Jebel Khalid belonged to fortified outposts built by Seleucid kings. While the granaries in the agora of Morgantina might, at first glance, appear to stand out from the group, there is good reason to view their role in projecting the royal power of Hieron II. The construction of two monumental granaries within a single generation certainly marked a significant departure from earlier practices at Morgantina, where archaeologists have discovered no evidence for public or communal storage from an earlier date. It is surely no coincidence that these granaries appear as Hieron was consolidating his political power over much of southeastern Sicily, and that the buildings rose as part of the monumental redevelopment of Morgantina's agora, a project that, as discussed above, has been credibly associated with Hieron's royal benefaction.

Their location within the city certainly appears to reflect the pragmatic considerations involved in conveying large amounts of grain and other agricultural goods up into the urban center from the *chora* below. Situating the granaries next to the agora gate reduced the need to move bulky cargo through the city's streets. Yet their siting, seemingly so practical from the standpoint of security and management, should not distract from the ultimately impractical task of hauling grain and other agricultural products up from the countryside to fill these massive warehouses. Even at minimum capacity estimates, the sheer volume of grain that could be stored in these buildings would have required no small investment of time and energy to transfer it from the surrounding countryside into the city, a trip that would easily involve an elevation change of several hundred meters. What conditioned this behavior was almost certainly the obligation to pay the agricultural taxes imposed by the king. Indeed, that such prominent locations in the city's political and commercial center were given over to these buildings is consistent with the interpretation that their purpose was as much a symbolic expression of royal power as it was a functional tool of administration.

Granaries and Royal Administration

Within the context of the Hieronian kingdom, state granaries likely played an essential role in the administration of the agricultural tithe.[62] Hieron, of course, possessed monumental granaries on Ortygia, but these were surely the last stop for grain and other produce that moved through the system of royal taxation outlined in Chapter 4. Effective taxation of the relatively expansive territory controlled by Hieron after 263 would surely have been aided by a dispersed network of royal granaries, situated at strategic points around the kingdom. Beyond simply serving as distributed sites for grain storage, regional granaries provided the additional benefit of extending administrative oversight and gathering the vital information that accompanied it.

We can again look to the Ptolemaic kingdom to better understand how the granaries at Morgantina might have fit within the administrative infrastructure of Hellenistic Sicily.[63] The Ptolemies maintained a network of royal granaries throughout Egypt; these served as nodes of local and regional collection for various harvest taxes, and were used as transshipment points for moving agricultural goods from the interior to the capital at Alexandria.[64] The documentary record reveals vivid details about ecosystem of the "typical" royal granary within the Ptolemaic kingdom. Royal officials (*sitologoi*) were charged with keeping track of grain stores in these granaries, accounting for both income and expenditures, as well as issuing receipts to taxpayers. Surviving tax receipts reveal that cultivators typically made payments in installments rather than in a single bulk outlay, which would have involved making multiple visits to one of these administrative centers throughout the year.[65] At these granaries, one could observe the routine encounters between royal tax officials and cultivators, as the latter approached leading donkeys laden with sacks of threshed and dried grain, only to depart thereafter clutching a receipt of payment, written in ink on a piece of papyrus or the outer wall of a broken pot. It is also from documentary papyri that we know tax grain warehoused at these regional granaries could be distributed locally as state payments (e.g., as salaries for officials, as loans of seed grain) or, when needed, transferred to other state granaries. Typically, it seems, grain was held until it was needed in Alexandria, at which point it was moved by ship down the Nile to the royal granaries in the capital city.

Thinking along similar lines, the granaries at Morgantina could have served as sites for the collection of taxes on cultivation in the surrounding territory. Given their size and arrangement, the northern suite of rooms (Rooms C–F) in the East Granary may well be identified as the administrative headquarters of officials (*sitologoi?*) charged with receiving the tax payments owed by cultivators working in the territory of Morgantina. Within those rooms, we can suppose that the great majority of tax receipts could be stored and consulted by cultivators, tax farmers, and royal officials.[66] In this scenario, the East Granary served as much a role in information-gathering as it did warehousing the king's grain. The valuable contents contained within the walls of the granary thus took two forms: the obvious stores of agricultural produce and the all-important records of deposits, payments, and withdraws. As sites where individual cultivators came face-to-face with royal officials in order to play out the annual ritual of paying the harvest tax, the granaries would have further served to project the king's power outside the royal capital. This was very likely the closest that most individuals who dwelt in and around Morgantina – or, for that matter, any of the *poleis* subject to Hieron's authority – would have come to experiencing the power of the Hieronian state.[67]

One shortcoming of this hypothesis is, of course, the lack of archaeologically attested granaries at other urban centers within the Hieronian kingdom.[68] It is admittedly tenuous to envision a network of regional granaries across southeastern Sicily when only those at Morgantina are known. Whether comparable granaries were constructed elsewhere inside the political boundaries of the Hieronian kingdom remains an open question – but a question that, even now, has not been adequately tested on the ground. That one cannot, at present, point to the physical remains of similar monuments at other cities within the kingdom is unsurprising given the limited scale of excavations carried out in most other major urban centers around eastern Sicily, particularly when compared with Morgantina. At Akrai, for instance, large portions of the Hellenistic agora remain unexcavated, while only the basic outline of the

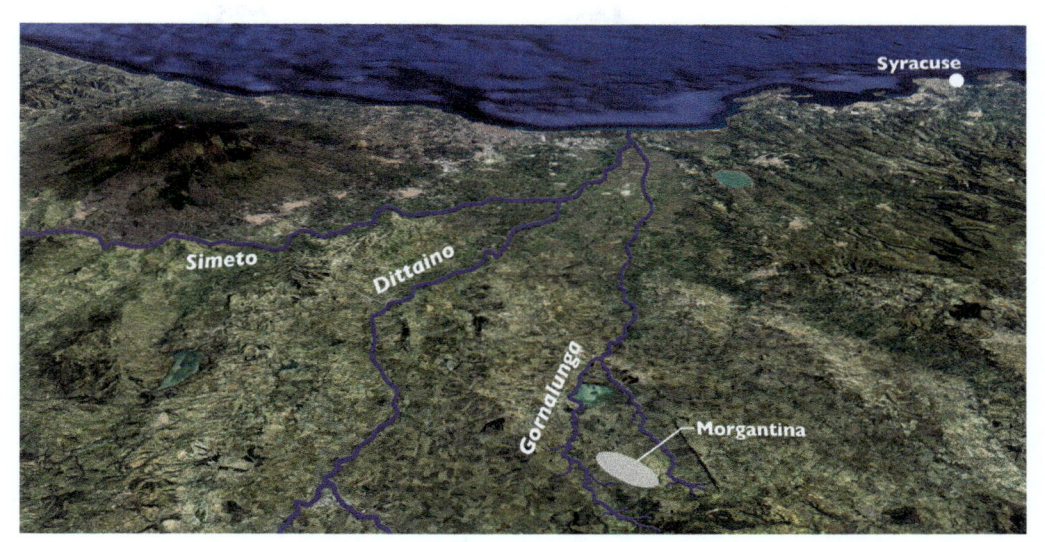

6.16 Map showing the course of the Gornalunga, Dittaino, and Simeto rivers (map data: Google © 2022 Landsat/Copernicus Data: SIO, NOAA, US Navy, NGA, GEBCO).

third-century agora at Tauromenion has been defined.[69] The paucity of comparable warehouses elsewhere in the kingdom does not preclude the identification of the Morgantina granaries as monuments of royal character. There were the central granaries within the king's palace complex on Ortygia, which we might imagine as oversized versions of those built at Morgantina.[70]

One practical aspect of the tithe administration that would certainly necessitate the existence of state granaries at points like Morgantina was the logistics of transport involved in moving masses of grain from inland agricultural zones to the royal granaries at Syracuse.[71] Overland transport, even within the relatively small kingdom, would have been a far more costly and labor-intensive operation than moving grain downriver by boat. Morgantina itself lies between two branches of the Gornalunga river (Figure 6.16).[72] That the Gornalunga served as a well-traveled route of transshipment is suggested by the results of an intensive survey conducted in the territory around Morgantina in the 1990s, which identified several large sites located close to the ancient river course.[73] Yet even as the Gornalunga provided vital access to the coast, it may have only been navigable in the winter and spring when the water level was at its annual maximum.[74] Since the cereal harvest took place during the summer months when the water levels were at their lowest, the massive warehouses at interior sites like Morgantina may have served the essential function of storing the proceeds of the tithe until they could be moved downriver by transport vessel in the winter or spring.

In addition to reducing transport costs, the king may have accrued additional benefits by keeping tax grain in reserve at storage facilities closer to areas of cultivation and away from the capital at Syracuse. There was certainly the potential for financial gain in doing so. While the bulk of his profits surely derived from supplying the international market, Hieron may also have held back grain to sell within Sicily, including to the very *poleis* from which he collected taxes in the first place.[75] The time of year when inland sites were most accessible by river was also when domestic grain stores were likely approaching their lowest levels and market prices, consequently, were nearing their peak. Keeping back large stores of grain that could be released on the market in the spring when prices were at their highest may very well have been an important financial consideration for Hieron, who would have largely relied on the market to convert his agricultural wealth into silver reserves.

For an example of this dynamic at work, we can look to a letter written by the Antigonid king Antigonos I to the Teans regarding their recent *synoikism* with Lebedos (*Syll.*[3] 334). Both communities, it seems, had petitioned the king for the privilege to establish a fund to import grain with the goal of stockpiling it in the event of shortage.[76] Although he made an exception in their case, Antigonos explained that he did not usually permit cities the right to import grain (*ta sitēgēsia*) nor to stockpile it, claiming that cities did not need to spend money importing grain when it could be supplied from tribute-bearing land in the area. As Aperghis notes in his discussion of the letter, the king's objection – while couched in the language of philanthropy and concern for the well-being of Teans and Lebedoi – surely stemmed from the desire to protect his own profit margins. Maintaining his profits from grain sales to the communities under his control was likely on his mind, for once the Teans and Lebedoi could purchase grain on the open market, Antigonos would lose two captive customers for his own surplus grain.[77] Elsewhere in the Hellenistic world we can find instances where royal interests were at odds with civic autonomy over matters of food supply, and we would expect Hieron to have advanced his own interests much as Antigonos I did when it came to making the most of his stockpile of grain and agricultural goods.[78]

Now, a quite reasonable objection could be leveled here, namely, that the case for identifying the granaries at Morgantina as monuments of Hieronian royal administration is largely based on circumstantial evidence and, further, that an equally persuasive case could be put forth in which the granaries are identified as civic monuments constructed as provision against food shortage or as monumental statements of the community's own agricultural wealth. Such an argument is not without merit, particularly when set within the growing discourse concerned with the continued vitality of the *polis* in the Hellenistic period.[79] However, several factors count against it.

As civic monuments, the granaries would have presumably held grain in anticipation of food shortage caused by a widespread crop failure or a lengthy siege. Communal strategies for alleviating the burden of food shocks are well attested in the Hellenistic period. Often, this appears to have involved the intervention of wealthy citizens, who in an act of euergetic largesse purchased large amounts of grain or other foodstuffs at their own expense only to resell it to the community for prices below what they had paid.[80] Rather than rely on the fortuitous intervention by an individual, some Hellenistic *poleis* approached the perennial menace of food shortage by establishing a permanent fund (*sitōnikon*) that could be used to purchase grain in times of food crisis precipitated by local crop failure or drastic increases in the market price of grain.[81] Although we might expect that such a monetary fund was matched by provisions to store imported grain, this does not always seem to have been the case. Rather, the grain imported with public funds appears to have been promptly sold or distributed to the community and was rarely stockpiled for disbursement at a later date. Judging from the surviving epigraphic accounts that detail the creation and operation of *sitōnikon* funds, purchases made with public funds tended to occur only when there was a communal need, whether imminent or perceived.

Moreover, as Migeotte has observed, grain purchases were generally small in scale and intended as no more than stopgap measures to help the community through a few lean months until harvest.[82] In no attested circumstance do we know of a *polis* purchasing grain from *sitōnikon* funds with the express intention of stockpiling it throughout the year. Long-term storage of grain and other produce is never prioritized in these documents, nor is the construction of physical granaries ever mentioned. Rather, the legal and administrative mechanisms governing many of the known *sitōnikon* funds only took effect after cheap grain was needed by a community, suggesting that in most cases the grain purchased with the fund was distributed as quickly as possible, thus obviating the need for the long-term stockpiling of grain. Even when a regular system of purchasing was put in place, such as recorded in the so-called Samian Grain Decree (*Syll.*[3] 976), the amount of grain purchased seems to have been relatively small and would not have required buildings of the scale found at Morgantina.[83] We may conclude, then, that storage on the scale of the East and West Granaries is simply not commensurate with such ad hoc civic strategies, even among *poleis* far more populous than Morgantina.

Alternately, one might consider the construction of the granaries as a precaution taken by the city in the event of a lengthy siege. If so, the sheer size of the structures may have communicated a sense of security to the community. It was certainly the case that the Morgantinoi had seen their fair share of military violence in the decades preceding the construction of the granaries. Were they acting on advice of the kind Philo issues in the *Poliorcetica*, which urges communities to stockpile enough stores for a year-long siege? The timing and context surrounding their construction, however, suggest otherwise, since during the middle decades of the third century Morgantina was enjoying the peace and protection brought about by the treaty signed in

263 between Hieron and Rome. Allowing for the possible discovery of dispositive evidence to support one interpretation or another, we are left to weigh the available facts. The date, siting, and size of these buildings support the interpretation that they were more likely constructed to hold the agricultural tithe owed to the king than to serve as bulwarks against famine or siege.

It is ultimately the abandonment of the granaries in the years following the Second Punic War that offers the surest confirmation of their vital role in the administration of the Hieronian tithe. As noted above, the archaeological record reveals that both the East and West Granaries did not maintain their original function into the second century, but appear to have swiftly fallen out of use in the years following the Roman siege of 211. Their abandonment did not follow from irreparable damage by fire. Rather, it appears they had simply ceased to serve the purpose for which they were built. How could this be if the Romans, as we know, retained the *lex Hieronica* and, moreover, endeavored to revitalize agricultural production on the island almost immediately after the Carthaginians ceded control of the island in 210? The answer must surely lie in the divergent needs of Hieron and Rome with respect to the annual proceeds of the tithe. Once in control of the island, Rome had no need for grain to remain on Sicily, let alone to stockpile it at inland sites like Morgantina. Their interest was to ensure that grain reached the coast as soon as possible, where it could be loaded onto transport ships and supplied to meet the bottomless needs of Rome's urban and soldier populations. From the perspective of the Roman state, the island's agricultural surplus was to be promptly mobilized. Maintaining stores of grain on Sicily, particularly at inland sites like Morgantina, played no part in the administration of the *lex Hieronica* by the Roman state. By the first century, the *lex Hieronica* certainly required cultivators to bring their tithe grain *ad aquam*, a provision that reflected Rome's interest in moving grain swiftly to the coast and, moreover, obviated the need for massive warehouses at inland sites like Morgantina.[84]

Granaries and the Projection of Royal Power

Beyond their function as administrative outposts, monumental granaries certainly appear to have played an essential role in advancing the military interests of Hellenistic monarchs. We see this most visibly in the coexistence of garrisons and granaries at sites of strategic value for kings. Philip V, for instance, maintained fortified granaries at Chalcis, a site located far from his capital at Pella but of great strategic value as one of three garrisoned "fetters" that allowed him to exert his military control over central Greece.[85] Similarly, the granary buildings at Mount Karasis and Jebel Khalid belonged to what have been identified as fortified Seleucid outposts (*phrouria*), small settlements of a military character that served to extend the immediacy of royal power throughout the kingdom.[86] The role that granary buildings played amid the broader actions taken by Hellenistic rulers to project "hard power" through the garrisoning or mobilization of troops was only one side of the coin. We should not discount the flip side, which might be framed in terms of extending a king's "soft power." In widening our perspective, we might consider how these buildings, through their very function and monumentality, served to communicate the virtues of sovereign authority in the Hellenistic world.

We have long recognized that monumental architecture played an instrumental role in shaping and affirming ideologies of political power, particularly as it inscribed and reinforced the sovereign authority of the state.[87] Academic discussions among archaeologists and anthropologists have typically focused on manifestations of this relationship in the context of early civilizations of the Bronze Age Near East and pre-Columbian New World. Yet Bruce Trigger's assertion that "monumental architecture makes power visible and hence becomes power rather than merely a symbol of it" also finds its mark in the monumentality of the Hellenistic world, which took on its consummate expression in the foundation and planning of entire cities – a degree of hyper-monumentality befitting the awesome power of the Successor kings.[88] Granary buildings seem almost to typify how Trigger and others have come to regard the political ideology borne out in the relationship between the state and monumental architecture.[89] With a monumental granary like those found at Pergamon, Mount Karasis, and Morgantina, we are dealing not only with the ability of the state (in our case, the king) to mobilize energy, labor, and resources to construct something beyond the scope of the nonstate actor. There was the attendant expectation that it would be filled *repeatedly* with agricultural surplus appropriated from the territories subordinate to the political authority of the state. These were not static forms of monumentality, but it was through their periodic replenishment at the hands of taxpaying subjects that monumental granaries served to actively reinforce the political ideology of the state.[90]

For Hellenistic rulers, the capacity of monumental granary buildings to promote the ideology of legitimate rule rested on reaffirming the ability of the king to exercise control over vast supplies of food in a world where the threat of food shortage was an ever-present danger for even the most well-off *polis*.[91] The epigraphic record of the Hellenistic period is rife with situations in which wealthy individuals were honored for mobilizing their private wealth and resources for the benefit of a community in distress, whether to ameliorate an imminent food shortage or to mitigate financial hardship. Hellenistic monarchs regularly found themselves in this position of *euergetes*, whose ability to marshal great surpluses of agricultural goods conferred prestige and legitimacy to their *basileia*. It also gave them the power of the life and death over a community in a very literal sense.[92] When amounts and figures are given in the historical record, it is not surprising to find gifts of grain or other agricultural goods made by kings reckoned in colossal sums, commensurate with their vast wealth, which far surpassed that of any private individual or *polis*.[93] When Demetrios Poliorcetes attempted to capture Rhodes in 306/5, for instance, no less than 12,000 metric tons of grain were reportedly dispatched by Ptolemy I, Cassander, and Lysimachos to help the island's residents withstand the siege.[94] Even this tremendous outlay pales in comparison to the nearly 30,000 metric tons of grain purportedly sent by Ptolemy III to Rhodes following the earthquake of 227.[95]

In addition to their precious contents, the impressive scale of these buildings likely would have served to further reinforce a message of royal power and prosperity. While not to deny the pragmatic considerations governing their capacity, there can be no question that the size of these Hellenistic granaries was also clearly intended to make an impression upon the viewer.[96] Their immense scale communicated plentitude, whether or not they were actually full.[97] It is easy to see how monumental granaries translated a king's euergetic persona in architectural form. In the right context, they were physical reminders of a king's privileged ability to forestall famine and economic crisis, behavior that might earn him the honorific title of *euergetes* or *sōtēr* from an indebted community. Yet, just as these warehouses stood as material witness to a king's outsized wealth and his capacity for equally outsized euergetism, these heavily fortified structures, impervious and inaccessible to the ordinary person, stood as stark reminders of a king's power to take the agricultural surplus of his kingdom and use it as he saw fit. We saw this fundamental imbalance of power that divided kings and the communities under their control laid bare in Antigonos I's letter to the Teans, a communiqué that presupposed a considerable degree of royal control over the community's food supply.

Coupled with their imposing scale, the siting of these buildings underscores the fact that their function was as much to communicate a message of royal power as it was to safeguard the foodstuffs therein. Those that survive today share conspicuous locations in the landscape, as construed with respect both to their visibility and to their inaccessibility.[98] The remote or unobtainable quality of the buildings and their contents was most clearly expressed in their topographic siting at hard-to-reach points within a settlement. The prominent topographic settings in which we find the granaries on the citadel at Pergamon and in the upper fortress on Mount Karasis plainly demonstrate that these buildings were meant to be seen by many, but accessed by few (Figure 6.17). This spatial separation of the buildings was reinforced by locating them within palace complexes or other areas where there was an understood demarcation of royal authority within which access by the ordinary citizen was limited and heavily surveilled. The granary building at Mount Karasis, for instance, rose on the rocky cliffs of the palace's so-called Upper Castle area, where it was accessible only to those who had passed through two layers of heavy fortification.[99] The situation of the Pergamene granaries was no different. Along similar lines, we know that Hieron's granaries at Syracuse were physically removed

6.17 Remains of the monumental granary at Mt. Karasis. view from the south, overlooking surrounding territory (photo: T. Radt).

from the city by their placement within the king's fortified palace complex on Ortygia. These too were likely conspicuous features in the landscape, if we follow Caroline Lehlmer's attractive suggestion that they were oriented in such a fashion as to make them highly visible to all those arriving to Syracuse by sea.[100]

Let us return to view the Morgantina granaries against this same discussion of monumentality, visibility, and accessibility. Their siting in the city would have set them out as prominent monuments on the horizon, visible to those approaching the urban center from the south and imposing in their magnitude to all who passed through the agora gate. This certainly made them more accessible than the granaries located atop the Pergamene acropolis or within the fortifications of the Upper Castle at Mount Karasis. Yet their place within the agora should not lead us to discount the overwhelming message of restriction and control communicated by their formidable construction and heavily buttressed walls. These were certainly not freely accessible spaces for the average citizen of Morgantina, who might only expect to receive admittance into these massive warehouses or to interact with their officials when taking part in the closely surveilled routines surrounding taxation. As I speculated above, the East Granary likely served as a site where cultivators from the territory of Morgantina would have handed over payments of their agricultural tithe to royal officials, who represented the king's interests and authority on the ground. Through the performative and recursive nature of the bureaucratic rituals taking place at these administrative buildings, the granaries served to reify the narrative of legitimacy on which the king laid claim to his authority to rule and, with it, his prerogative to extract resources from the land under his control. Even as this remains a speculative scenario in the case of the Morgantina granaries, we possess ample documentary evidence from the Ptolemaic kingdom that confirms the identification of royal granaries as sites where such status-affirming rituals took place. By their very nature, the granaries were sites that reinforced the political imbalance between Hieron and the city, where grain and equally precious information flowed in one direction – that is, out of the hands of the cultivators and into those of the king.

It was, arguably, for the local audience – the residents of Morgantina – that these buildings carried their most potent message about the reach of Hieron's authority. This is most clearly revealed in the orientation of the granaries themselves, which followed neither the axial plan established by the city's orthogonal grid nor the arrangement of the colonnaded stoas that framed the edges of the upper agora. Rather, the granaries appear to have been roughly aligned with the broad flight of steps that served as the city's *ekklesiaterion*. For citizens gathered in assembly, the two massive warehouses acted much like a frame that focused one's gaze out into the *chora* and to the fertile territory below (see above, Figure 6.1). They were, above all, material embodiments of Hieron's royal prerogative to take his share of Morgantina's agricultural resources, and a not-so-subtle reminder to the assembled citizens of the limits placed on their autonomy by royal power.

NOTES

[1]   Liv. 24.36.10.

[2]   From the initial publication following its discovery, Sjöqvist (1960a: 131) identified the East Granary as a monumental warehouse and further suggested the building was intended to hold the agricultural tithe owed to Hieron II by the residents of Morgantina. In his discussion of the building's architectural design, Sjöqvist drew on the comparison with the open floor plan and wide aisles of the Naval Arsenal of Philo at the Piraeus in Athens, the physical remains of which have not been identified but are described at length by an inscription detailing its construction (*IG* II^2 1688); Lorenzen (1964) and Winter (2006: 149ff.). The physical remains of a large (~44.40 meters × 17.62 meters) arsenal building of Hellenistic date have been identified on the Kolonos Agoraios hill in Athens; for description and identification, see Pounder (1983).

[3]   For reconstruction, see Bell (1988: 323) with further discussion *infra*. Since the 1970s, archaeologists and historians have paid greater attention to raised-floor granaries, particularly those structures found at Roman military forts along provincial limes. The groundbreaking work by Rickman (1971) remains essential. In recent years, investigations have turned to addressing methodological questions, such as whether a building's original capacity can be estimated from surviving archaeological remains and if this data can be used for the quantification of agricultural production in a particular locale or region. For one such recent survey, see the collected papers in Martin (2019) with extensive and up-to-date bibliography.

4   Philo, *Polior.* B10–24 [87.2–51]; Columella, *Rust.* 1.6.10; Varro, *Rust.* 1.57; Plin. *HN* 18.73, where a variety of methods are discussed with regard to specific crops. Storing grain in elevated lofts is also recommended by the author of the *Geoponica* (2.27.1–2).

5   The use of grain silos, or pits, also has a long history, stretching well back into the Bronze Age; Privitera (2014) with bibliography and discussion of Mycenaean examples. Here, I distinguish from conservation of grains and foodstuffs in large storage vessels (e.g., *pithoi*, *dolia*), which in sufficient numbers could constitute a strategy, albeit not one typically used for long-term storage beyond the household level. Features interpreted as subterranean grain pits or silos have been identified in the archaeological record at various sites in Sicily, including at Megara Hyblaia, where five large silos have been discovered in connection with both private and public space of the eighth and seventh centuries BCE; see De Angelis (2002) for discussion and reference to other known subterranean grain silos on the island.

6   Such was not the case with subterranean silos, which functioned only so long as they remained hermetically sealed. Philo (*Polior.* B6–9 [86.39–87.1]) recommends steps for construction and proper storage of grain in sunken pits. For further discussion of subterranean storage in Europe into the nineteenth century, see Sigaut (1988: 10–12).

7   The structures identified as elevated granaries of the Indus Valley civilizations excavated at Harappa and Mohenjo-daro, among other locations, share this same functional design element – that is, storing grain on elevated surfaces to allow for ventilation – with raised granaries of the later Hellenistic and Roman periods; see Vats (1974) for those of Harappa. Currid (1985) publishes above-ground granaries of the "beehive" variety from Bronze Age sites in Palestine, which, while typologically distinct from the rectangular variety, were provided with stone supports to create an elevated surface.

8   Initial reporting of these excavations was made by Sjöqvist (1960a: 129–31) and Stillwell (1961: 277–8), then co-directors of the Princeton-led American Excavations at Morgantina.

9   The results of the campaigns completed under the supervision of Paul Deussen during the 1989–92 seasons remain unpublished. For a preliminary report on the excavations of 2011–13, see Walthall (2015).

10   Tsakirgis (1984: 318–19). Mège (2014: 166–7) notes the use of similar construction techniques for third-century domestic architecture at Megara Hyblaia.

11   The large doorway leading into Room E disrupts the regular spacing of the exterior buttresses along the western façade of the building.

12   The availability of substantial timber resources at Morgantina is not in question, as evidenced by the use of wooden columns and entablature for the contemporary North Stoa and East Stoa buildings; see Bell (1993: 332). Furthermore, the presence of forests in the vicinity of the ancient settlement is borne out by palynological data collected in the environs of Morgantina, as well as by the large numbers of fallow deer bones recovered from third-century contexts inside the city. Pollen cores taken from the nearby Lago di Pergusa suggest a landscape that was still rich in deciduous cover, although decidedly less so in the centuries following the establishment of permanent Greek settlements on the island; for data and discussion, see Sadori and Narcisi (2001); Sadori et al. (2013). Bones of red deer from third-century contexts at Morgantina are reported by Bell (1988: 329). Hieron reportedly exploited the rich timber resources of his kingdom, particularly when it came to his ship-building enterprises. The classic example is the famed *Syrakosia* described in the *Deipnosophistai* of Athenaeus (5.206d–209e); with technical discussion in Turfa and Steinmayer (1999).

13   Bell (2022) observes that a similar expansion of public architecture into private space occurred with the construction of the East Stoa, which also required trimming back the hillside to the north of the granary into land that had been allotted for private use.

14   This is clearly visible in the southeast corner of Room A, where excavations in 2013 revealed evidence for the point at which the builder's trench cut through the burnt layer on both the east and south sides of the room; for further discussion and photograph of the builder's trench, see Walthall (2015: 87–8).

15   As far as I know, there is no immediate parallel for this practice in an ancient Mediterranean context. Several ancient authors recommend using materials like vinegar, urine, or *amurca*

(olive oil lees) to repel vermin and pests; Columella, *Rust.* 1.6.12–13, Philo, *Polior.* B10.1–3. An alternative approach to pest-proofing is prescribed in the *Opus agricultura* of the fifth-century author Palladius, who recommends builders create an impervious floor fashioned from crushed-tile mortar and brick pavers. As Wilson (2015: 200) notes, Palladius was describing not an elevated granary, but one seeming closer in form to the type excavated at the site of Gerace in southeastern Sicily, which was built with a floor of cut stone pavers set into a mortar bedding.

[16] Regarding this issue of preservation, see Halstead (1997: 103–4). The archaeological methods of the mid-twentieth century did not regularly incorporate the systematic collection and sampling of soils for archeobotanical remains. As a result, the East Granary was excavated to a point where, today, there is little or no chance of finding undisturbed stratigraphic layers within the building or in its immediate vicinity that might preserve archeobotanical remains from the time when the building functioned as a granary. Despite this, there is little reason to believe that even if such layers were preserved they would have produced very much in terms of carbonized material, given that at no point does the building seem to have suffered from destruction by conflagration.

[17] The artifacts recovered from within these rooms during the initial excavation of 1959–61 reveal little about the use of the space in the third century, given that the building was repurposed in the second century as a pottery workshop.

[18] See *infra* nn. 64 and 65.

[19] The association of the building with the period of Hieronian rule is an idea that was originally advanced by Sjöqvist (1960a: 130) in his preliminary report on the 1959 excavation campaign at the site. Sjöqvist's initial judgment was correct, despite the fact that he could only draw inferences based on the discovery of large number of bronze coins of Hieron II in contexts associated with the building's primary use phase. At the time, he could not point directly to material from contexts created *at the time* of the building's construction to support his conclusion, as we can today. This was due in part to the fact that, at the time of his publication, the single coin recovered from a context associated with the building's construction was considered by scholars to be a product of the Agathoklean mint at Syracuse and not, as we now know to be the case, that of Hieron II. Additional details of this coin given *infra*, n. 21.

[20] This conclusion is further sustained by the ceramic material recovered from within the fill of a builder's trench excavated at the southeast corner of Room A in 2013, discussed, briefly, in Walthall (2015: 87–8).

[21] Inv. 59-1832. AE. 19mm, 6.19g, 12h. *Obv.* Head of Persephone l./*Rev.* Bull butting l.; above, club, ΘE; below, IE. Date: ca. 276–269. Ref: *MS* II, no. 324. For discussion of where this coin fits into the chronology of Hieron's minting operations, see *infra* Chapter 7, pp. 249–50.

[22] The renovations have been discussed in detail by Cuomo di Caprio (1992), who focuses on the kilns, as well as by Stone (2014), who publishes the ceramics manufactured by the pottery.

[23] Bell (1988: 321–4) published a preliminary report of the 1980–2 excavations, where the building is first identified as a monumental granary of similar design to that of the East Granary.

[24] For summary of this work, see Walthall (2015: 83–7).

[25] Surviving only at the level of their foundations, the external buttresses on the West Granary share nearly identical dimensions (ca. 1.0 meter × 1.0 meter) to those of the East Granary, leading to the conclusion that they were of comparable proportions in elevation as well.

[26] See Bell (1988: 323, n. 36) and Deussen (1994: 232) citing, in particular, a bronze coin of Agathoklean date (inv. 80-281; *MS* II, no. 321; ca. 310–290) found within the packing of the building's beaten-earth floor. While the coin was rightly recognized only as evidence of a *terminus post quem* for the granary's construction date, stylistic arguments were mustered to support the conclusion that the West Granary must have been conceived and constructed prior to the East Granary.

[27] Deussen (1994: 232).

[28] Inv. 11-35. AE; ∅ 21mm, 6.86g, 10h. *Obv.* Head of Apollo l./*Rev.* Tripod, РΗΓΙ-Ν Ν. Date: ca. 260–215. Ref.: *MS* II, no. 50; and, for date, Rutter and Burnett (2001: no. 2543). For photo and excavation context, see Walthall (2015: 84–6).

[29] Inv. 82-272. AE; ∅ 20mm, 5.34g, 2h. *Obv.* Head of Mercury r./*Rev.* Prow r. Date: ca. 214–211. Ref.: *MS* II, no. 504; *RRC* 42/5.

[30] For the location and plan of the *temenos* and sanctuary complex, see Bell (1988: 315). A short stretch of wall, possibly belonging to the post-211 sanctuary, was found overlying the western wall of the granary during the 2011 excavations; Walthall (2015: 84).

[31] Deussen (1994: 232–3) alludes to the possibility of a Syracusan prototype, namely, the royal granaries on Ortygia mentioned by Livy (24.21.11–12). Syracuse has been considered the inspiration for other architecture at Morgantina during this period, most notably the West Baths; see Lucore (2009; 2015).

[32] See, e.g., work by Manning (1975); Gentry (1976); and, more recently, Schubert (2016).

[33] For earlier work, see Salido Domínguez (2008; 2009; 2017).

[34] Salido Domínguez (2019: 31–2) lists a host of factors he considers essential, but largely unknowable, for accurately calculating capacity.

[35] For brief summary, see Walthall (2015: 89–90; 2021: 63–4). Unfortunately, none of these remains were recovered from within stratigraphic contexts associated with the use of the two granaries themselves, as these were largely excavated away in the 1960s when environmental sampling was not de rigueur.

[36] For overview of the various positions taken by scholars over the past several decades, see Martin (2019: 36–40).

[37] Citing statistics from the Food and Agriculture Organization of the United Nations (FAO), Boetto et al. (2016: 218) note that grain-filled sacks can be stacked to a height of approximately 6 meters when a pyramidal arrangement is employed.

[38] Mayerson (1998).

[39] This is a limitation discussed by Virlouvet (2015: 680) and in Boetto et al. (2016: 213–14).

[40] Martin (2019: 34–5); Blöck (2019: 13).

[41] Blöck (2019: 14). Martin (2019: 40–6) suggests depths of 20–40 centimeters were more plausible still, basing her judgment on a combination of archaeological data derived from storage contexts ranging in date from the Roman imperial to early modern periods as well as from agronomic and historical texts from the eighteenth and nineteenth centuries.

[42] For capacity of the *medimnos*, see *supra* Chapter 5, pp. 177–8.

[43] In Chapter 3 (*infra* p. 97), I propose that the area under Hieron's political control after the year 263 totaled roughly 6,000 square kilometers, or about one-quarter the area of Sicily (~25,711 square kilometers). Thompson (1999: 495–6) suggests the size of Morgantina's territory in the third century at the time when the granaries were in use may have reached 300 square kilometers.

[44] Rickman (1971) was the first to draw an explicit parallel between the Morgantina buildings and the raised-floor granaries found at Roman military camps. For a survey of Roman military granaries, see Rickman (1971). And for recent work focused on Roman granaries from Spain, see Salido Domínguez (2009); North Africa, Papi and Martorella (2007); Dacia, Petculescu (1987); and Roman Gaul, Martin (2019). The principal difference between the Morgantina granaries and their Roman counterparts lies in the method used to elevate the wooden floor. While the examples from Morgantina appear to have relied on heavy wooden beams to span the gap between interior buttresses, the Roman granaries instead were almost consistently built with rows of low interior walls that held the elevated platform.

[45] The earliest extant Roman examples, those excavated at Valdevorrón and Castillejo in Spain, are generally considered to date to the period of Scipio's campaigns in 134/133; Salido Domínguez (2009: 681); Schulten (1927: 207ff.).

[46] Livy (24.21.11) refers to these buildings in his narrative of the events following the assassination of Hieronymos. He refers to these buildings as public granaries (*horrea publica*), but this is surely an anachronism reflective of their continued use as warehouses following

the collapse of the Hieronian dynasty. Their location on Orytgia, site of Hieron's royal palace, is all but confirmation that these buildings originally served royal ends.

47 Initial publication of the buildings by Wiegand (1928) was followed shortly by the comprehensive publication of von Szalay and Boehringer (1937) in the *Altertümer von Pergamon*.

48 Von Szalay and Boehringer (1937: 25–8).

49 Even at the time of their initial publication, von Szalay and Boehringer (1937: 27) suggested this was a possible function for "Arsenal I," which they maintained was the only building of the five on the acropolis with a sufficient width (12.95 meters) for grain storage. Alone, this is an indefensible metric, given that the majority of granary buildings in Roman forts of Republican and Imperial date tended to have widths measuring between 8 and 10 meters. For instance, the granaries of the fort at Castillejo measured ~8 meters (Schulten 1927: 207ff.) and that from the fort at Thamusida measured 10.43 meters (Papi and Martorella 2007: 91).

50 It is noteworthy, yet surely coincidental, that the combined length of Arsenals IV and V (~95.30 meters) is approximate to that of the East Granary (92.85 meters).

51 For discussion of chronology, see von Szalay and Boehringer (1937: 55–6). See also Radt (1999: 76–7).

52 For initial identification of the site, long known to residents in the area, see Sayar (1995). Between 2003 and 2006, a series of archaeological investigations (incorporating both an architectural survey and an excavation) were conducted at the site on Mount Karasis. The preliminary results of this work have been published by Hoffmann and Sayar (2007) with subsequent analysis by Radt (2011; 2016).

53 Backmann (2011).

54 Radt (2011: 58–9).

55 For the Jebel Khalid complex, see the considerable publications by Clarke (1994; 2001; 2002) and members of the Australian team responsible for its excavation, e.g., Clarke et al. (2016). I follow Radt (2011: 57) in his identification of the building in question as a granary of comparable form to those found at Mount Karasis and Pergamon.

56 This emphasis on the long and narrow rectangular shape will be a characteristic shared with later Roman military granaries, as well as with many large private granaries built to store the agricultural wealth amassed by villa owners. For excellent discussion, see Wilson (2015: 191–202), who publishes the remains of a large granary building belonging to a villa of Imperial date at the site of Gerace in central Sicily.

57 Philo, *Polior.* B10–24 [87.2–57]. For text and commentary, see Garlan (1974) and Whitehead (2016: 84–7, 232–7).

58 Here, aboveground granaries are distinguished from subterranean pits (*siros*) used for storing grain, the latter of which Philo discusses in a preceding section (B6–9 [86.39–87.1]) on provisioning for a siege.

59 Philo, *Polior.* B10.1–4 [87.2–5]. In his commentary on the text here, Whitehead (2016: 232–3) calls attention to the similarities shared by Philo's description of elevated granaries and those on Pergamene acropolis.

60 The use of fixed units has been recognized in the layout and design of the Morgantina granaries, as well as those from Pergamene acropolis. That a common module was used when laying out the buildings is suggested by the consistency of dimensions used within the individual buildings (e.g., size of exterior buttresses, spacing of interior buttress) as well as between the two buildings, such as the consistency in their width. Deussen (1994: 232) suggests a unit of measure equal to 19.4 centimeters was used in designing the layout of the East Granary.

61 We know, for instance, that granaries played a role in texts on siege craft; e.g., Polyaenus, *Strat.* 5.1.3, recounts a story about the Akragantine tyrant Phalaris, who reportedly bribed the individuals responsible for guarding the granaries of his besieged enemy and in doing so convinced them to intentionally damage the building's roof, such that the grain stored inside was eventually destroyed by water and rot. The story is also found in the *Strategemata* of Frontinus (3.4.6).

62 State-controlled granaries were an indispensable element of any imperial system that extracted resources through the in-kind taxation of agricultural goods. With reference to

centralized state control of agricultural resources in the context of early civilizations of Mesopotamia, see Childe (1950: 12); and Middle Kingdom Egypt, see Ezzamel (2002: esp. 69).

63 While the particulars of taxation varied from region to region even within the Ptolemaic kingdom and, thus, cannot be claimed as definitive evidence for the existence of any particular practice in Sicily, the basic operational functions of royal granaries within the Ptolemaic context can nonetheless provide valuable clues as to how the Hieronian system would have benefited from a similar framework; regarding the regional diversity of Ptolemaic administrative practices, see Manning (2010: 143).

64 A brief overview of the administration of royal granaries under the Ptolemies can be found in Muhs (2016: 233–4), who notes that the Ptolemaic system of documenting and transporting grain likely resembled the systems put in place during periods of Saite and Persian rule. For more detailed treatments of the Ptolemaic granary system viewed through the documentary record, see Packman (1968), who publishes a collection of tax receipts from the royal granary at Diopolis Magna. Although dating to the second and first centuries BCE, the corpus of tax documents from Diopolis Magna offers valuable insight into aspects of the day-to-day administration of a royal granary; see too Mayerson (1998); Youtie (1950).

65 This was observed by Packman (1968: 54–9), who notes (54), "In short, it seems fairly certain that installment paying was the regular, rather than the exceptional, practice for the payers of royal grain taxes, and it is probably safe to assume that single payments, even by taxpayers to whom no other published receipts were issued in the same year, are ordinarily only installments towards the total amount of one year's tax."

66 Bell (2011: 197) goes further to suggest that this suite of rooms might also have held other relevant documents, related to the tithe, including the planting census and copies of the contracts concluded between cultivators and tax farmers.

67 Given (2004: 93ff.) makes this point, generally, with respect to resource-extraction by the state. With specific reference to spheres of interaction between taxpayer and the state in Hellenistic Egypt, see Manning (2003: 141–52).

68 Costanzo (1996) surveys the evidence for granaries of Hellenistic date on Sicily. Of those buildings with extant archaeological remains (i.e., not Hieron's royal granaries on Ortygia), only to those at Morgantina can be securely attributed a date prior to the first century BCE. Prestianni Giallombardo (2004) takes up the issue of granary construction within the Hieronian kingdom. She too notes the lack of physical remains, but considers the construction of monumental warehouses, like the addition of fortification walls around allied *poleis*, to be a logical expression of Hieronian authority. The remains of four buildings excavated in the agora of Kamarina have recently been identified as granaries by Di Stefano (2001–2: 693–e4), who compares their long, rectangular form to the granary buildings at Morgantina. Based on their orientation and stratigraphic relationships with other monuments in the agora, these buildings are believed to postdate the fall of the city to Roman troops in 258, although evidence to establish a more precise chronology has yet to be presented. While their narrow, rectangular form and elongated dimensions (~5.2 mters × ~75 meters) certainly fit within the granary typology, further investigation of the buildings is likely required before this identification can be confirmed.

69 For Akrai, Wilson (2012: 251) provides a brief summary of the archaeologically attested monuments in the city's agora. A new series of excavations within the urban center at Akrai led by Roksana Chowaniec and a team from the University of Warsaw have improved our understanding of the ancient city; see, generally, Chowaniec (2015; 2017; 2018). Regarding the location and potential layout of the Hellenistic agora (possibly agorai) at Tauromenion, see Campagna (2011; 2019), as well as Campagna and La Torre (2009).

70 An opinion expressed by Wilson (2013: 91–2, n. 33).

71 Assuming that the cost of transporting grain from regional granaries to the capital fell to the king, as was the situation under the Ptolemies; Muhs (2016: 233–4).

72 This may also have been true of the ancient Chrysas river (mod. Dittaino), a larger river than the Gornalunga, which is located about 12 kilometers north of Morgantina. For discussion

of Morgantina's setting within the surrounding landscape, see Thompson (1999: 22–7) and Leighton (2012: 189–94) with passing reference to the rivers. A preliminary survey of the Gornalunga's ancient flood terraces by Judson (1963) suggests that around the middle of the third century BCE, the river could have reached depths of 8–10 meters and upward of 100 meters in width where it passed by the ancient settlement.

73 Thompson (1999).

74 The number of navigable rivers in Sicily was much larger in antiquity and the medieval period than today, as even the Simeto (anc. Symaithos) is reduced to little more than a creek during the hot summer months; Wilson (1990: 6). Writing at the turn of the twentieth century, Sladen (1907) writes for his entry on "Rivers" that "Sicily has no navigable rivers. The Simethus (sc.) near Catania is the best apology for one. Hardly any but it and the Anapo has even a row-boat on it," before concluding, "It is of no use enumerating the rivers, for in Sicily they imply only three things – irrigation, floods, and malaria, unless we count them as roads" (the last being a practice of the Messinese). While worlds apart from Sicily, Chiverrell and Archibald (2009) come to a similar conclusion regarding the seasonal navigability of the ancient river near the settlement at Vetren (anc. Pistiros?) in central Bulgaria.

75 While documentary evidence for grain sales by kings is fugitive, the practice is generally considered to have been a major source of revenue and means of converting agricultural wealth into precious metal reserves; e.g., Bringmann (1993: 20); Briant (1994); Reger (2003: 349); and Boehm (2018: 101–3) with reference to *Syll.*³ 334. Casson (1984: 76–7) suggests that increasing market share was a clear motivation behind many of the gifts of grain made by Hellenistic kings to cities, such as Athens, Delos, and Rhodes. He cites, for instance, the grain given by the Numidian king Massinissa to Delos in 179 BCE, arguing that Massinissa's gift represented a "first move" in an effort to curry favor with the merchants who were once supplied with Sicilian grain by Hieron II. Thonemann (2013: 26–7) offers a compelling interpretation of the large gifts of grain given by Eumenes II to Rhodes and Miletos in the 160s, suggesting that the king was having difficulty selling the grain on the market.

76 For discussion, see Gabrielsen (2011: 238–45), who views this episode as an example of the agency that cities could still retained in their relationship with kings.

77 Aperghis (2004: 185).

78 One example from the Ptolemaic sphere is *Syll.*³ 502, a decree of Samothrace dating to the reign of Ptolemy III, which acknowledges that the king or his governor allowed the city to export grain free of taxation; Austin (2006: 467–8, no. 269); Bagnall (1976: 159–68).

79 Campagna (2019: 66–69) and Battistoni (2011: 180) argue, for instance, that major transformations taking place in the political and architectural landscape at Tauromenion during the late third century may be best interpreted as expressions of civic identity aimed at countering the political reach of Hieron II.

80 Such acts of euergetism are recorded with greater frequency in the epigraphic record, often in the context of an honorific decree, from the fourth century onward; see, e.g., Mussa (2017) with focus on fourth-century Athens.

81 For general review of epigraphic attestations of *sitōnikon* funds at various locations in the Mediterranean, see Fantasia (1989; 1998; 1999) and Migeotte (1991). Garnsey (1988) remains an accessible treatment of famine and food shortage in the ancient Mediterranean.

82 Migeotte (2009: 168–9), who further observes that even those *poleis* that are known to have established relatively large *sitōnika* do not appear to have utilized these funds on an annual basis. For amounts of grain supplied by Hellenistic *sitōnika*, see Migeotte (1991).

83 Gargola (1992: 17) finds that, except in rare instances, the total amount of grain purchased and distributed by Hellenistic *sitōnika* funds was small. For instance, he calculates that the total amount of grain purchased with the annual funds available from the Samian *sitōnikon* was around 1,000 *medimnoi* of wheat.

84 Cic. 2.*Verr*.3.36.

85 Destruction mentioned by Liv. 31.23.5–7; Polyb. 18.10–11. An inscription discovered in 1932 at the site of Chalkis confirms the existence of the granaries; Hatzopoulos (1996: no. 13); Welles (1938: 251–5). It records a *diagramma* from Philip V to the officials (referred

to as *oikonomoi* in the text) responsible for maintaining the garrison's stores of grain, wine, and wood. More importantly, it reveals the great interest that the king held for managing the details of grain storage at his garrisons to the point where the *oikonomoi* were instructed to inspect stores of grain after each rain in the summer months and every 10 days during the winter (ll. 21–4) so as to ensure that water had not infiltrated the building. The discovery of a portion of a nearly identical inscription found in the vicinity of ancient Kynos in 1985 has led Hatzopoulos (2001: 30–1) to suggest that copies of this royal *diagramma* were set up at the other cities fortified by Philip's garrisons.

[86] For the role that these and other such settlements played in terms of surveillance and control of landscapes, see discussion by Kosmin (2014: 202–3).

[87] Childe (1950); Moore (1996); Osborne (2014). See also the collected papers in Bretschneider et al. (2007), which focus on the relationship between architecture and manifestations of political power in the context of the Bronze Age Near East and Aegean.

[88] Trigger (1990: 122). For city foundations and the ideology of royal authority within the Seleucid kingdom, see Kosmin (2014: 208–21).

[89] Trigger (2003: 564); Pollock (1999: 181), with reference to monumental architecture of ancient Mesopotamia, discusses the notion that the generally involuntary participation of the ruled in the construction of monumental architecture was often cast in terms of contributing to a "common good," particularly in situations involving the construction of religious monuments that were intended to ensure the continued survival of the ruler or state, which, in turn, would offer protection to those subjects.

[90] An idea more thoroughly discussed by Given (2004: 36–7) in the context of estate granaries in medieval England.

[91] The link between food storage and political authority has long been recognized as a dominant driver in state organization of ancient and early modern periods. Within the realm of the ancient Mediterranean, an especially well-developed body of scholarship has developed in this respect with regard to Aegean Bronze Age palatial societies, e.g., Halstead (1995; 1997); Christakis (2004; 2011).

[92] For a modern analog, see Given (2004: 30) with reference to the paternalistic ideology that developed around the person of the Ottoman sultan, who as the "father of the peasants" both exercised power to extract critical resources from peasant communities through the mode of taxation and later provided the very same life-sustaining produce back to those communities in times of famine or food shortage.

[93] Bringmann (2001) and Casson (1954) provides numerous examples.

[94] Diod. 20.96.1.

[95] Polyb. 5.89.

[96] Regarding private granaries built on the properties of Late Roman villas, Wilson (2015: 200) and Brown (2013: 14) make similar observations. Brady (1996: 143–59) notes that barns and storehouses on estates in medieval England were typically the largest structures on the estate and often much larger in scale than what was needed in terms of routine storage, an example of overbuilding that reflected on the wealth of the landowner.

[97] Hendon (2000) explores the social implications of shared-but-unequal knowledge among community members with respect to the storage of commodities like foodstuffs.

[98] Moore (1996: 116–18) highlights the active role that the siting and visibility of monumental buildings in the Andes played for broadcasting control over territories subject the Inca authority.

[99] This may have been a function of the military character of the settlement at Karasis, which may have been conceived with the prospect of having to weather a protracted siege.

[100] Lehlmer (2005: 177).

SEVEN

THE HIERONIAN MINT

What currency clearly reflects is the presence of the state – made visible in the form of the king's face and the king's name, but also implicitly in the validity (or not) of the coin in the marketplace after it had been issued by the state and used by the state for the payments that enabled the operations outlined above (war, consumption, gifts).
—John Ma, *Hellenistic Empires*, 346

This chapter focuses on the coinage struck by Hieron II and explores evidence for what might be described as the king's policies toward minting. Like the standardization of volumetric measures and construction of monumental granaries, the issuance of coinage offers important material insight into the consolidation and reach of Hieron's royal authority. As an instrument of dual economic and political value, coinage held a privileged position in the toolkit of the Hellenistic monarch. Beyond their essential role in facilitating state payments and generating revenue for the royal treasury, coins operated as a premier medium for disseminating information and extending state control over territorial kingdoms formed by collections of semi-autonomous polities.[1] It is no wonder that coinage was a tool favored by Hellenistic kings, who showed themselves consummate virtuosi of large-scale minting operations. Due to this multifarious quality, coinage – as John Ma crisply summarizes in the passage above – can help us to reveal the unseen contours of the Hellenistic state.

Understanding the output of Hieron's mint promises to elucidate how the king used coinage to bolster his political authority over the *poleis* of southeastern Sicily. On one level, the chosen iconographic motifs, disseminated as obverse and reverse types, speak to the construction of his royal image. In his minting activity, Hieron demonstrated a readiness to embrace current fashions manifest on the coinages produced by Hellenistic monarchs of the eastern Mediterranean while still retaining features characteristic of Sicilian, or more specifically Syracusan, practices. On another level, coinage sheds light on what might be identified as the king's monetary reforms and interventionist policies intended to shape the fiscal structures of the Hieronian kingdom and, ultimately, to consolidate power through the accumulation of wealth and resources. In this chapter, we will review evidence for a number of such interventions – namely, the manipulation of monetary standards and the suppression of civic minting – and reflect on what they reveal about the fashioning of the royal economy under Hieron II.

A BRIEF SKETCH OF HIERONIAN COINAGE

This section offers an introductory overview of the coinage struck by Hieron II, beginning with his time as *stratēgos autokrator* of the Syracusans. This is a sketch in that it intends only to familiarize the reader with the relative sequence and variety of coins minted in the name of Hieron. While the chronological arrangement presented here draws on the most recent archaeological evidence and numismatic scholarship, further revisions to this schema will undoubtedly be required as numismatists continue to produce new studies of individual issues and archaeologists publish excavated coins from secure stratigraphic deposits. A systematic study of the Hieronian mint remains a major desideratum for all whose work intersects with third-century Sicily.[2]

The coins produced during the reign of Hieron II have been objects of admiration and study from as far back as the Renaissance, when many of the great European numismatic collections started to be formed. We know that at least one Hieronian coin was counted among the personal collection of the sixteenth-century bishop and noted antiquarian Laevinus Torrentius.[3] By the late eighteenth century, images of Hieron's coinage began to appear in print, such as in Castelli di Torremuzza's 1796 *Siciliae et objacentium insularum veterum inscriptionum nova collectio*, where the illustrated coin is erroneously labeled "*Hieronis I Syracusorum Tyrannis*" (Figure 7.1).[4] Over a decade later, Castelli would illustrate a far greater number of Hieron's coins in his 1781 study, *Siciliae populorum et urbium regum quoque et tyrannorum veteres nummi Saracenorum epocham antecedentes*. Here too, the coins struck in the name of Hieron II are attributed to his Deinomenid namesake, as are the coins struck in the name of Hieron's son, Gelon.[5] Around the same time, Hieron's coinage had even become the occasional subject of discussion among early scholars of numismatics.[6] It was not until the late nineteenth century and the pioneering work of Barclay Head

7.1   Illustration of a Hieronian coin from Castelli di Torremuzza's *Siciliae et objacentium insularum veterum inscriptionum nova collectio* (after Castelli 1769).

that a concerted effort was made to understand the relative sequence of these coins.[7] Head's *History of the Coinage of Syracuse* (1874), a work that drew on the significant holdings of the British Museum, was the first comprehensive treatment of Hieron II's coinage, and remains a valuable starting point for any survey of it. He was followed in the early twentieth century by several scholars whose contributions clarified details of the Head's chronological arrangement or simply augmented the growing catalog of known specimens.[8]

Well into the second half of the twentieth century, numismatic scholarship concerned with Hieron's coinage dealt primarily with coins held in private and public collections, although this work was occasionally aided by the discovery and publication of an important coin hoard, such as that from Polizzi Generosa.[9] Major change came in the 1950s and 1960s with the publication of numismatic material from archaeological excavations at major urban centers like Morgantina and Gela.[10] Excavated coins recovered from sealed stratigraphic deposits gave further definition to debates over both the absolute and relative chronology of Hieron's coinage. This was particularly true with respect to the king's bronze denominations, which were predominant among the numismatic finds from archaeological sites around eastern Sicily. In this respect, the appearance of *Morgantina Studies, vol. 2: The Coins* (Buttrey et al. 1989) was a major milestone in the publication of coin finds from controlled archaeological excavations. In recent decades, the study of Hieronian coinage has been championed by Maria Caccamo Caltabiano and her colleagues from the Università di Messina, who have carried out a several systematic studies of Hieron's bronze, silver, and gold coinage.[11] Collectively, members of the so-called Messina School have advocated for sweeping chronological revision to Hieron's minting output, applying a range of detailed metrological arguments to advance a series of dates substantially later than those set forth by prior scholars. Such bold assertions have received mixed reception by numismatists and archaeologists alike.[12] Yet we cannot discount the great value of their work, which collectively stands as the most significant contribution to the study of Hieronian numismatics since Head's *History of the Coinage of Syracuse*.

For our present purposes, establishing an absolute chronology for the coinage struck by Hieron II is far less consequential than understanding its relative chronology. Fortunately, the relative sequence of output by the mint at Syracuse has been established on stylistic and archaeological grounds by more than a century's worth of scholarship. I have chosen to divide Hieron's coinage into three broad periods of minting, each defined by a significant stage in his political career.[13] This is not to suggest that a single event, political or otherwise, can or should be attributed to the inception of each period of minting activity outlined below. Rather, it is simply that proximate historical factors recommend attribution to one period over another (i.e., Hieron's years as *stratēgos autokrator* or as *basileus*). We have already encountered several of Hieron's coin types in Chapters 1 and 2, when our focus was directed on the question of how iconographic choices reinforced his claims toward legitimate kingship. Here, we will address the question of how minting intersected with the major political events during his reign and ask to what degree changes in minting habits reflect significant political and historical events.

Period I (ca. 276–269)

The first coins minted by Hieron II were struck while he held power as *stratēgos autokrator* of the Syracusans (ca. 276–269). During this period, the Syracusan mint issued gold, silver, and bronze coinage in the name of Hieron. If one dominant attribute could be ascribed to the coinage of Period I, it would be continuity. As discussed in Chapter 1, the style and iconography of Hieron's earliest coinage reflects an interest in maintaining a level of homogeny with the coinage of his predecessors: Pyrrhus, Hiketas, and especially Agathokles. Continuity was also maintained with respect to the denominations and weight standards chosen for his silver and gold coins. We saw this, for instance, with Hieron's gold hemistaters that were struck on the Attic-Euboic weight standard with obverse and reverse types nearly identical to those of Hiketas and Agathokles.[14] So striking a resemblance, in fact, that it is only by the addition of his name in the genitive, ΙΕΡΩΝΟΣ, on the reverse type that Hieron can be identified as the authority responsible for issuing these coins.[15]

In continuing to produce gold, silver, and bronze denominations with readily identifiable types and on universally recognized weight standards, Hieron was almost certainly striking coinage to pay troops employed in his military campaigns against the Mamertines, many of whom may have been formerly in the employ of the men whose coinage he was emulating.

7.2 Gold hemistater of Hieron II, ca. 276–269 BCE (ANS 1997.9.102; courtesy of the American Numismatic Society).

Gold

1. AU. Head of Persephone l./Nike driving biga r.; below, ΣΥΡΑΚΟΣΙΩΝ (avg. 4.30 grams).[16]
2. AU. Head of Persephone l./Nike driving biga r. (or l.); below, ΙΕΡΩΝΟΣ[17] (avg. 4.30 grams) (Figure 7.2).

These gold issues were struck on the Attic-Euboic standard.[18] The coins are stylistically reminiscent of gold hemistaters struck by Hiketas, as well as bronze denominations of the preceding Syracusan Fourth Democracy.[19] Surviving specimens struck with the legend ΣΥΡΑΚΟΣΙΩΝ are extremely rare and have been attributed variously to Pyrrhus and Hieron II.[20] If their attribution to Hieron is correct, their meager numbers may point to a restricted period of minting lasting no more than two years between 276 and 274. As suggested in Chapter 1, the switch to striking hemistaters with the legend ΙΕΡΩΝΟΣ most likely occurred after the battle at Kyamosoros in 274.[21]

Silver

1. AR. Head of Athena l./Pegasos r. (or l.); below, ΙΕΡΩΝΟΣ[22] (avg. 5.66 grams) (Figure 7.3).

Hieron struck only a single silver denomination during this period, its weight nearly identical to the silver octobols struck by Pyrrhus during his campaigns in Sicily.[23] The obverse and reverse types were remarkably similar to those of the silver staters struck by Agathokles.[24] They can be distinguished from these by the addition of Hieron's name on the reverse type as well as by their lighter average weight.

7.3 Silver octobol of Hieron II, ca. 276–269 BCE (BM G1874,0715.116; © The Trustees of the British Museum).

Bronze

1. AE. Head of Persephone l./Pegasos flying r.; below, IEΡΩΝΟΣ[25] (avg. 11.34 grams).
2. AE. Head of Persephone l.; at l., ΣΥΡΑΚΟΣΙΩΝ/Bull butting l.; above, club; below, in exergue, IE[26] (avg. 5.66 grams).
3. AE. Head of Artemis (or Arethusa) l./Pegasos flying l.; below, IEΡΩΝΟΣ[27] (avg. 2.83 grams).

Hieron's bronze coinage of Period I (Figure 7.4) also shows reliance on earlier types, especially the Persephone/Bull IE series, which quoted directly from Agathoklean types.[28] So close, in fact, are these coins in appearance to the earlier series that for a time they were considered Agathoklean themselves. Most early scholars ascribed these Persephone/Bull IE coins to Hieron II, interpreting the letters IE as an abbreviated form of IEΡΩΝΟΣ. This attribution fell out of favor for a time after specimens of these coins were recovered in the Capo Soprano excavations at Gela in the 1950s.[29] Taking their presence at the site as indication that these coins were in circulation prior to 282, when the city was reportedly destroyed by Phintias, scholarly consensus swung to favor an Agathoklean date.[30] Today, however, *communis opinio* has now swung back in favor of attributing these small bronze coins to the period of Hieron's tenure as *stratēgos autokrator*, following a close review of the archaeological contexts from which these coins have been recovered.[31]

Among the bronzes struck by Hieron during his time as *stratēgos autokrator*, those of the Persephone/Bull IE series were issued in prolific quantities, judging from the number of extant specimens.[32] The Persephone/Pegasos

7.4 Bronze coinage struck during Period I, ca. 276–269 BCE; top: Head of Persephone l./Pegasos flying r. (BM EH,p219.15.Hiell; © The Trustees of the British Museum); middle: Head of Persephone l./Bull butting l., club above, IE in exergue (BM RPK,p259X.53.Syr; © The Trustees of the British Museum); bottom: Head of Artemis l./Pegasos flying l. (BM 1841, B.345; © The Trustees of the British Museum).

and Artemis/Pegasos types are attested in much smaller numbers.[33] Their relationship can be evinced on the grounds that all three types share a metrological standard with the Persephone/Pegasos coins representing a full unit and the Persephone/Bull IE and Artemis/Pegasos types representing one-half and one-quarter units, respectively.[34] On the basis of their abundance in hoards reported from northeastern Sicily and southern Italy, Mariangela Puglisi has argued that these small bronze denominations were used principally as payment for soldiers campaigning with Hieron against the Mamertines.[35]

Period II (ca. 269–241/230)

The starting point for the second major period of mint activity was the beginning of Hieron's kingship, which followed shortly after the Battle of Longanus in 269.[36] Among the most prominent innovations introduced by the royal mint were the types chosen for the first coinage issued after Hieron declared himself king. While still *stratēgos autokrator*, Hieron had consciously embraced coin types and styles that conveyed a clear message of continuity with the military potentates who had preceded him. After taking the title of *basileus*, Hieron adopted new types that served to distinguish his coinage from that of his predecessors. This period is defined, in particular, by two significant modifications in his minting habits: first, the introduction of portrait coinage, and second, the switch to monometallic output with the sole production of bronze coinage.

Undoubtedly the most conspicuous change to occur in Period II was the appearance of the king's idealized portrait on the obverse types of new, large-denomination bronze coins. We first encountered Hieron's portrait coinage in Chapter 2 when discussing the nature of his rule vis-à-vis the political ideology of Hellenistic kingship.[37] Hieron struck portrait coins in two successive types; in the first he wears a laurel wreath; in the second, a cloth diadem. In the fashion of contemporary royal portraiture, the king never appears to age much past his forties even as new coins presumably continued to be issued well into the final years of Hieron's life.

The choice to issue portrait coins shortly after becoming king may seem rather unsurprising, as the production of portrait coinage was becoming almost a sine qua non for Hellenistic kings of his day.[38] By the time Hieron took the title of *basileus* in the early 260s, a standard visual language for the portraiture of Hellenistic rulers had already begun to emerge on coinage.[39] He had only to draw on preexisting iconographic conventions used to communicate a message consonant with legitimacy (e.g., youthful appearance, royal headgear, etc.) when selecting his own coin types.[40] Yet it is difficult to overstate the significance of this move within its contemporary Sicilian context, as this was the first time that a political leader in Sicily had struck coins bearing his own image. For Hieron, this bold break with the visual language of earlier Sicilian leaders announced the start of a new political order organized around the person of the king. In a sense, it brought the residents of eastern Sicily face-to-face with their ruler; furthermore, this forced familiarity intensified through frequent encounters, for the coins were ubiquitous.[41] The widespread diffusion of Hieron's royal portrait within the sphere of daily commercial exchange – a fact well attested by individual coin finds in the archaeological record – was further aided by the choice of bronze, the metal favored for everyday transactions, as the principal medium for this novel coinage.[42]

Bronze

While the relative sequence of the bronze series issued during Period II has been established with a high degree of certainty, the absolute dates for the production of many types remain a subject of some debate. Several, including the Poseidon/Trident and diademed Hieron/Horseman types, appear to have been struck over the course of several decades. For this reason, grouping the coins loosely by weight and series highlights the range of coinage produced in this period. It is important to note that some coin types that first appear in Period II continued to be struck into the decades encompassed by Period III.

Large-Denomination Bronzes

Large-denomination bronzes struck during this period are shown in Figure 7.5.

Portrait Series
1. AE. Portrait of Hieron l., wearing laurel crown/Horseman charging r.; below, ΙΕΡΩΝΟΣ (avg. 17.36 grams).[43] Date: ca. 269–263.
2. AE. Portrait of Hieron l., wearing diadem/Nike driving a biga r.; below, ΙΕΡΩΝΟΣ (avg. 35.45 grams). Date: ca. 263–215.
3. AE. Portrait of Hieron l., wearing diadem/Horseman charging r.; below, ΙΕΡΩΝΟΣ (avg. 17.27 grams). Date: ca. 263–215.

Both the laureate and diadem Hieron/Horseman coins were struck on large flans of similar dimensions and were of comparable weight, clustering around 17.1 grams. With an average weight of ~35.45 grams, the Hieron/Biga issue was clearly intended to serve as a double unit to the Hieron/Horseman denomination.[44] Based on their shared iconography of the obverse types, these larger units clearly belong to the phase of minting in which the diadem Hieron/Horseman coins were issued. They were struck on a far more limited scale than the diadem Hieron/Horseman coins, judging from the comparative numbers of surviving specimens and their resulting die types.[45]

It is generally agreed that the laureate Hieron/Horseman series preceded the diademed Hieron/Horseman series in order of production. This arrangement

7.5 Large-denomination bronze coinage struck during Period II, ca. 269–241/230 BCE; top: Portrait of Hieron II, wearing laurel wreath / Horseman charging r. (BM RPK,p256C.7.Hie; © The Trustees of the British Museum); middle: Portrait of Hieron II, wearing diadem/Nike driving a biga r. (BM 1946,0101.1553; © The Trustees of the British Museum); bottom: Portrait of Hieron II, wearing diadem/Horseman charging r. (BM 1918,0204.87; © The Trustees of the British Museum).

rests largely on stylistic grounds, as Hieron appears visibly younger in the laureate series than in the diadem series. Welcome confirmation of this sequence is provided by the archaeological record in that the laureate portrait coins often turn up in contexts where Syracusan coins of the early third century (including those of Period I) are present and specimens of the diadem portraits are absent, indicating that they entered circulation first.[46] The two series share the image of the charging horseman as their reverse type, signaling continuity, but they share no dies, further suggesting there was no overlap in their production. It is likely, then, that the diadem series commenced not long after the laureate types ceased to be struck.[47]

Scholarly opinion is far more divided when it comes to determining the absolute date range for the production of these two series; we may characterize the opposing opinions as favoring "high" and "low" chronologies. Proponents of a high chronology have long held that production of the portrait series began shortly after Hieron came to power as *stratēgos autokrator* and continued throughout his reign with the diadem portrait coins replacing those of the laureate type around 269, when he took the title of *basileus*.[48] In recent decades, advocates for a low chronology have strenuously argued that the majority of Hieron's coinage, including the diadem Hieron/Horseman coins, were not introduced until the final decades of the third century, some only within the final years of the king's death.[49] According to this view, the diadem portrait coins were not struck until the 220s at the earliest and may not have even been minted until the years 218–215.[50] That these two groups could arrive at such radically different dates for the Hieron/Horseman coinage is, in part, a reflection of the different means by which they approached the question; proponents of the high chronology have consistently viewed the issue through the lens of coins found in archaeological contexts, while advocates of the low chronology have largely applied numismatic methods (e.g., die study, metrological and stylistic comparison) in structuring their chronological arguments.[51]

In discussing Hieron's portrait coinage here and in Chapter 2, I have adopted a slightly modified version of the high chronology, which has the portrait series beginning only after Hieron declared himself king, but well before the 220s as favored by proponents of the low chronology. This best reflects the available archaeological evidence – which unequivocally substantiates the conclusion that both laureate and diadem varieties of the Hieron/Horseman type were in circulation by 250. It also most closely aligns with the model set by other Hellenistic monarchs, who took the momentous step of issuing portrait coinage only after their ascent to kingship was complete. Portrait coinage was symptomatic of their royal status. Had Hieron struck coins with his portrait while still *stratēgos autokrator*, his actions would be truly exceptional.

Imitation Ptolemaic "diobols"

4. AE. Head of Zeus r./Eagle standing on thunderbolt l.; at right, Galatian shield; ΒΑΣΙΛΕΩΣ ΠΤΟΛΕΜΟΥ (avg. 17.15 grams).[52] Date: ca. 265/4. Wolf-Lorber's "West Greek" style.

The early portrait coinage of Hieron must now be understood in relation to a series of large bronze denominations that by outward appearance claim to be struck by a mint operating under the authority of Ptolemy II (Figure 7.6). Iconographically, their types closely resemble those used by the Ptolemaic mint for a number of their large-denomination bronze coinages, which is why these coins are traditionally referred to as diobols. The presence of these coins in eastern Sicily has long been taken as evidence for commercial contacts between Alexandria and Syracuse during the Hieronian period. A recent reappraisal of these coins, however, now suggests that they may reflect an even stronger link between Hieron and Ptolemy II than previously recognized. On the basis of detailed stylistic, metrological, and distribution analysis, Wolf and Lorber have persuasively argued that a large number of these coins with "Alexandrian" style and fabric are in fact evidence of the operation of a Ptolemaic mint on Sicily during the 260s.[53]

According to their hypothesis, Ptolemy II may have sent soldiers and bullion to help support Hieron's war against the Mamertines. Wolf and Lorber identify two distinct phases of minting for these Zeus/Eagle coins found around Sicily, based on differences in style and minting techniques. In the earliest phase, minting was carried out by Ptolemaic officials. At some point (they propose 265/4) Ptolemy withdrew his support and Hieron continued to strike a nearly identical series of coins in Ptolemy's name, doing so perhaps because he continued to employ mercenaries accustomed to receiving payment in Ptolemaic currency.[54] While no historical sources report Ptolemaic support for Hieron in this period, the Ptolemaic kings were known to have actively supported Pyrrhus and Agathokles with cash and soldiers to aid in their military endeavors.[55] It was also around this same time that Ptolemy II was sending aid to Sparta and Athens in order to prop up their war against king Antigonos II Gonatas. In similar fashion, Ptolemy II might have backed Hieron in his campaigns against the Mamertines, seeing it as a way of extending his influence in the western Mediterranean. The notable presence of these Zeus/Eagle denominations on Sicily certainly speaks in favor of this hypothesis, particularly given the fact that coins with matching die types and weights are found exclusively in Sicily and (in much smaller numbers) southern Italy.

Whatever the motives were for continuing to strike coins in Ptolemy's name, these denominations appear to have been recognized as a valid currency within Hieron's kingdom, judging from their presence alongside coinage that bore the king's own name in both hoards and commercial contexts.[56] Both Hieron's portrait coins and the Ptolemaic Zeus/Eagle coins minted on Sicily

7.6 Ptolemaic Zeus/Eagle imitation diobols; top: "West Greek" style (ANS 1944.100.76066; courtesy of the American Numismatic Society); bottom, "Alexandrian" style (ANS 1944.100.76056; courtesy of the American Numismatic Society).

were struck on flans of remarkably similar dimension and with a nearly identical mean weight of ~17.1 grams.[57] Following a reassessment of these large-denomination coins, Wolf has recently argued that this correspondence in their mean weight was not coincidence, but rather a sign of close coordination between the Ptolemaic and Hieronian states.[58] He notes that the ~17.1 gram unit finds no clear precedent in Syracusan coinage or traditional Sicilian weight standards, but is remarkably close to one-quarter the Ptolemaic bronze drachm unit of ~68.5 grams that was struck following the coinage reforms carried out by Ptolemy II in the 260s.[59]

Further peculiar is the fact that the ~17.1 gram unit was never a denomination struck by Ptolemy II, either before or after the coinage reforms. The imitation Ptolemaic Zeus/Eagle coins struck on Sicily are often erroneously referred to as diobols on account of their large size and nearly identical iconography to Ptolemaic diobols minted prior to the coinage reform of the 260s. Their ~17.1 gram unit weight, however, falls between the ~15.43 gram unit of actual pre-reform Ptolemaic diobols and the ~22.8 gram unit on which the post-reform Ptolemaic diobols were struck. In fact, the Ptolemies would almost never strike a bronze coin equivalent to one-quarter of a bronze drachm, preferring *obol*-fractions (1/6) instead.[60] The ~17.1 gram unit then appears to be an innovation of early Hieronian date, one that rests on the post-reform Ptolemaic bronze drachm (~68.5 grams) but does not otherwise find ready correspondence with Ptolemaic units. It would seem then that the introduction of this new, heavy bronze coinage on Sicily was the result of a coordinated policy by Hieron and Ptolemy II.

Small-Denomination Bronzes

Small-denomination bronzes struck during this period are shown in Figure 7.7.

Poseidon/Trident Series
1. AE. Head of Poseidon l./Ornamental trident, flanked by two dolphins; IEP-ΩΝΟΣ (avg. 8.50 grams). Date: ca. 269–241. "Large-flan" series.
2. AE. Head of Poseidon l./Ornamental trident, flanked by two dolphins; IEPΩ-ΝΟΣ (avg. 6.24 grams). Date: ca. 241–215. "Small-flan" series.

Like the Hieron/Horseman coinage, the Poseidon/Trident coinage was also issued in two series, the earlier of the two struck on heavier flans of larger dimension ("large-flan" series) than those of the later, lighter series ("small-flan" series).[61] And much like the debates swirling around the chronology of the Hieron/Horseman coinage, there is a wide divergence in scholarly opinion about the absolute dates of both Poseidon/Trident series. Again, archaeological evidence supports the high chronology, which locates the large-flan Poseidon/Trident series early in Hieron's reign (ca. 269–241) and the small-flan series in the decades following 241.[62] It bears noting that a sizable number of these Poseidon/Trident denominations were halved in antiquity by cutting along the vertical axis of the reverse type. This was done to coins of both the large-flan and small-flan series, specimens of which have been found at sites around the island with the greatest concentrations reported from *poleis* in eastern Sicily that were subject to Hieron II. The purpose behind this large-scale fractioning of Hieron's coinage will be explored in greater detail below.

Other Small Bronzes
3. AE. Head of Persephone l./Bull butting l. or r.; above, club; below, in exergue, IE (avg. 4.1 grams). Date: ca. 269–215.

7.7 Small-denomination bronze coinage struck during Period II, ca. 269–241/230 BCE; top: Head of Poseidon l./Trident, "large-flan" series (BM TC,p85.3.Hiell; © The Trustees of the British Museum); middle, upper: Head of Poseidon l./Trident, "small-flan" series (ANS 1944.100.57167; courtesy of the American Numismatic Society); middle, lower: Head of Persephone l./Bull butting l., club above, IE in exergue (BM 1946.0101.1562; © The Trustees of the British Museum); bottom: Head of Apollo l./Horse running r. (BM 1926.0205.8; © The Trustees of the British Museum).

4. AE. Head of Apollo l./Horse rearing r.; below ΙΕΡΩΝΟΣ (avg. 4.2 grams). Date: ca. 269–215.

The Persephone/Bull IE types assigned to Period II closely resemble those minted in Period I with the exception that they do not bear the legend ΣΥΡΑΚΟΣΙΩΝ on their obverse type and the bull on the reverse can appear facing right.[63] These were also typically struck on slightly smaller flans with a lower average weight (~4.1 grams) than their Period I counterparts (~5.66 grams), making them, on average, roughly half the weight of the large-flan Poseidon/Trident coins. The same can be said of the Apollo/Horse bronzes, which are broadly dated to this period on account of what appears to be a shared unit weight with the lighter Persephone/Bull IE coins as well as a number of control marks shared with the Poseidon/Trident small-flan series. In all likelihood, the Apollo/Horse bronzes were issued subsequent to the lighter Persephone/Bull IE coins; this conjecture is also reinforced by the number of control marks shared with coins of the Poseidon/Trident small-flan series, which continued to be struck until the end of Hieron's reign. Neither of these small denominations appears to have been struck in particularly large quantities, certainly nowhere near the scale of production reached for both Poseidon/Trident series. To this point, we will return when addressing the question of Hieronian monetary policy.

Period III (ca. 240/230–215)

Period III is distinguished principally by the renewed production of silver coinage by the royal mint at Syracuse. This was a period of bimetallic output, as several of the bronze types that were first issued in Period II continued to be struck down to the death of Hieron in 215. Silver output was represented in large part by the so-called dynastic series, which featured portraits of the royal family – Hieron, Philistis, and Gelon – on obverse types of no fewer than five denominations. The ideological messaging behind these silver issues was clearly directed at paving the way for the peaceful succession of Gelon to the throne. Historically, these efforts aimed at promoting the continuity of his dynasty appear to have taken on a greater urgency for Hieron in the 230s and 220s. It was in these decades when we first encounter deliberate steps to highlight Gelon's status as co-regent and king, culminating with the completion of the monumental building program that transformed the Neapolis district of Syracuse.

Silver
Silver coinage struck during this period is shown in Figure 7.8.

1. AR. Portrait of Hieron l., wearing diadem/Nike driving a quadriga r.; above, ΒΑΣΙΛΕΟΣ; below, in exergue, ΙΕΡΩΝΟΣ (avg. 27.70–28.20 grams).[64]

7.8 Silver coinage struck during Period III, ca. 240/230–215 BCE. From top: Portrait of Hieron II, wearing diadem/Nike driving quadriga r. (BM 1987,0649.272; © The Trustees of the British Museum); Portrait of Philistis, wearing diadem/Nike driving quadriga r. (BM 1946,0101.1544; © The Trustees of the British Museum); Portrait of Gelon, wearing diadem/ Nike driving biga r. (BM 1841,0726.381; © The Trustees of the British Museum); Portrait of Philistis, wearing diadem/Nike driving biga r. (ANS 1944.100.57111; courtesy of the American Numismatic Society); Portrait of Gelon, wearing diadem/Eagle standing on thunderbolt r. (BM 1947,0406.121; © The Trustees of the British Museum); Head of Apollo l./Wingless Nike advancing, holding scroll and palm branch (BM 1841,0726.327; © The Trustees of the British Museum); Tripod/Mark of value XIIΓ (BM 1963,0311.2; © The Trustees of the British Museum); Head of Artemis r./Owl facing (BM 1841,B.303; © The Trustees of the British Museum); Head of Athena l./Mark of value (three dots) XIII (BM 1847,0208.1; © The Trustees of the British Museum); Head of Herakles r./Mark of value XII (BM 1928,0120.49; © The Trustees of the British Museum).

2. AR. Portrait of Philistis l., veiled and wearing diadem/Nike driving a quadriga r.; above, ΒΑΣΙΛΙΣΣΑΣ; below, in exergue, ΦΙΛΙΣΤΙΔΟΣ.

    (avg. 13.20–13.60 grams).

3. AR. Portrait of Gelon l., wearing diadem/Nike driving a biga r. (or l.); above, ΣΥΡΑΚΟΣΙΟΙ; below, in exergue, ΓΕΛΩΝΟΣ.[65]

    (avg. 6.60–6.76 grams).

4. AR. Portrait of Philistis l., veiled and wearing diadem/Nike driving a biga r. (or l.); above, ΒΑΣΙΛΙΣΣΑΣ; below, in exergue, ΦΙΛΙΣΤΙΔΟΣ.[66]

    (avg. 4.45 grams).

5. AR. Portrait of Gelon l., wearing diadem/Eagle standing on thunderbolt r.; at left, ΣΥΡΑΚΟΣΙΟΙ; at right, ΓΕΛΩΝΟΣ.[67]

    (avg. 3.20–3.35 grams).

6. AR. Head of Apollo l./ΣΥΡΑΚΟΣΙΟΙ; Wingless Nike advancing to front, holding a scroll in r. hand and, in l., a palm branch (avg. 2.10–2.20 grams).

7. AR. Tripod, ΣΥΡΑΚΟ – ΣΙΟΙ/Mark of value ΧΙΙΠ [68] (avg. 1.56 grams).

8. AR. Head of Artemis r./ΣΥΡΑΚΟΣΙΟΙ; Owl facing (avg. 0.95–1.10 grams).

9. AR. Head of Athena wearing Corinthian helmet/Mark of value (three dots) ΧΙΙΙ; ΣΥΡΑΚΟΣΙΟΙ (avg. 0.70–0.75 grams).

10. AR. Bust of Herakles wearing diadem r.; at l., club/Mark of value ΧΙΙ; ΣΥΡΑΚΟΣΙΟΙ (avg. 0.45–0.50 grams).

Beyond the royal portraits on the obverse types of the five largest denominations, we can see aspects of the ideology of the ruling house expressed on the reverse types as well as in some of the less-explicitly royal iconography of the smaller denominations struck during this period. The lack of explicit military themes is fitting with our discussion in Chapter 2, considering what we saw as a "refashioning" of Hieron's *basileia* in the years following the conclusion of his treaty with Rome in 263. Even though he could not stake legitimacy on persistent military success, Hieron had recourse to agonistic victories of a different type. Particularly striking in this respect is the recurrence of chariot iconography on four of the five portrait coins. The figure of Nike appears driving a quadriga on the reverse type of the two largest denominations and a biga on the two smaller portrait coins.

The iconography of chariot racing had long held symbolic expression of the power and prestige commanded by Syracusan political and military leaders. The image of a charioteer adorning the reverse type of a large Syracusan silver coin may bring to mind the tetradrachms of the Deinomenid tyrants (ca. 485–465) or the mammoth decadrachms issued under the Dionysii (ca. 405–344), but we cannot know for certain if an ancient viewer with one of Hieron's silver coins in hand would have made the same connection. Agathokles too had minted tetradrachms with a galloping quadriga.[69] Still closer in date and iconography to the Hieronian types are the gold decadrachms of Hiketas, where it is Nike – and not a mortal charioteer – who guides the horses with reigns and *kentron* in hand.[70]

If the chariots of Hieron's coins referred to a specific event (i.e., a victory at one of the Panhellenic games), we are unaware of the details. Comparison could be made to the gold staters struck by Philip II of Macedon to celebrate his victory in the *synoris* (two-horse chariot race) during the Olympic games of 348, but the reverse types of the Macedonian coinage clearly depict a mortal charioteer, much like those depicted on Syracusan tetradrachms of the fifth and fourth centuries. Rather, the chariots of Hieron's dynastic series – driven by the divine personification of victory – may simply have communicated an all-embracing message of wealth, status, and success in competition.

Further in line with the ideology of dynastic succession, the image of an eagle grasping a thunderbolt that appears on the reverse types of the smallest portrait coins of the series (those depicting Gelon) may be plausibly associated with an expression of divine legitimization by Zeus. Stylistically, associations have been drawn between the eagle on the reverse of Gelon's portrait coin and the coinage of Ptolemy II and Ptolemy III.[71] While not to discount the Ptolemaic types as possible source of inspiration for the Syracusan die-cutters, it must be remembered that the iconography of Zeus pairing the eagle and thunderbolt had Syracusan precedents going back to the time of Timoleon and the Third Syracusan Democracy (ca. 344–316).[72] Within the context of the Hieronian regal portrait series, the eagle and thunderbolt might be reasonably viewed as symbolic of divine approbation of Hieron's plans for dynastic succession.[73]

Among many of the smaller denominations of Hieron's silver coinage, we face greater ambiguity with respect to the messaging of the royal house. Nike again makes an appearance on the reverse type of the largest fraction (no. 6 above), where the goddess is shown swiftly approaching on foot with a scroll (proclaiming victory?) held in her outstretched right hand. This message of victory is repeated in the obverse type of the tripod (no. 8 above). The image of the owl (reverse type, no. 7 above) and Athena (obverse type, no. 9 above), together with the eagle from Gelon's portrait coin (reverse type, no. 5 above), might collectively reference the story of the Hieron's first campaign, during which an eagle alighted on his shield and owl on his spear, an omen that was held to presage his future kingship.[74] Herakles, who appears on the obverse of the smallest denomination (no. 10 above), was also among the deities whose names were inscribed on the *cunae* of the theater at Syracuse, a monument that we have seen held a central function in promoting Hieron's program of succession. Apollo and Artemis ranked among the tutelary deities of the Syracusans, who were worshipped in the city since the Archaic period. Here we find no clear connection to royal ideology and may simply be dealing with a nod to those who were likely the intended audience of these coins – the

7.9 Gold decadrachm of Ptolemy III, ca. 246–222 BCE, with portrait of Berenike II (BM 1923,1108.1; © The Trustees of the British Museum).

Syracusans themselves. This, of course, might also account for the unusual legend ΣΥΡΑΚΟΣΙΟΙ in the nominative, a feature we will return to later in this chapter.

Returning to the question of chronology, the date of Hieron's "dynastic series" coinage has been the topic of much discussion in recent decades. As with so much of his bronze coinage, the higher chronological time frame adopted by most earlier scholars has been disputed by Caccamo Caltabiano and Carroccio, who have marshaled an array of metrological and stylistic arguments in support of their hypothesis that these silver portrait coins were struck only within the narrow window ca. 217–214.[75]

One of the central pillars supporting their argument in favor of this low chronology is the perceived stylistic dependence of Philistis' portrait types on those of the Ptolemaic queen, Berenike II, whose portrait appears on gold and silver denominations struck during the reign of Ptolemy III (r. 244–222).[76] The similarities are indeed quite remarkable. Both queens wear a broad cloth diadem under a light veil pulled over their heads and both are identified as ΒΑΣΙΛΙΣΣΑ on the reverse type (Figure 7.9).[77] Caccamo Caltabiano has argued that the coinage bearing the portrait of Philistis must have taken that of Berenike II as its model, which she dates controversially to the months shortly after the death of Ptolemy III. While the iconographic correspondence between these coins is undeniable, there are serious problems with Caccamo Caltabiano's line of reasoning on the issue.

The first is Caccamo Caltabiano's assertion that the coinage depicting Berenike II in this fashion was struck only between 222 and 221, corresponding to the brief window of time between the death of Ptolemy III and that of Berenike herself. This suggestion has not been accepted by other scholars, who have preferred to maintain the broader date range, between 244 and 222, for the production of the Berenike portrait coins.[78] This is significant, for even if we are to accept the premise that the numismatic portrait of Philistis was modeled after that of Berenike II, the window of opportunity for influence was much wider than Caccamo Caltabiano is willing to admit. We could thus accept Caccamo Caltabiano's hypothesis that the Ptolemaic series influenced the Hieronian die-cutters, and still reasonably expect production of the Philistis types – and by extension the entire dynastic series – to begin in the 230s.

Second, Caccamo Caltabiano gives no serious consideration to the possibility that it was the Hieronian coins that actually came first, originating without taking the Berenike type as a direct model. It is indeed a tendency among scholars to consider the primary direction of cultural influence in this period to flow from Alexandria to Syracuse, yet this runs the risk of overlooking the innovative capacity of the Hieronian court and its ability to influence wider cultural trends.[79] We might be better served still by setting aside questions of influence in either direction and simply note that when considering the iconography of the Philistis types, there is no shortage of possible sources of "local" Sicilian influence. For instance, the image of Philistis with veil drawn over her head resembles common numismatic representations of Demeter, a goddess with stronger roots in Sicily than Egypt. Furthermore, Syracusan die-cutters had a local precedent to draw on when representing a female member of the royal house in the bronzes struck by Pyrrhus at Syracuse with the portrait of his mother, Phthia, as the obverse type (Figure 7.10).[80] On these coins, the Aiakid queen mother is depicted wearing a veil and oak-leaf wreath, flanked by her name in the genitive, ΦΘΙΑΣ. The resemblance, while

7.10 Bronze coin of Pyrrhus, ca. 278–276 BCE, with portrait of Phthia (ANS 1944.100.57085; courtesy of the American Numismatic Society).

admittedly not as striking as that of Philistis and Berenike, is nonetheless close enough to warrant consideration as a possible inspiration for Hieron's issues. Given the recent marriage alliance forged between Hieron and the Aiakid line through Gelon's marriage to Nereis, the visual reference to Phthia – queen mother to Pyrrhus, as Philisitis was to Gelon – may have been an intentional move on the part of the die-cutters.

To return to the question of the date of the dynastic series, production beginning around 230 makes far greater sense from a historical perspective than in the narrow three-year period (ca. 217–214) advocated by Caccamo Caltiabiano. Proponents of this low chronology suggest the production of these coins was somehow animated by a heightened need to pay soldiers during the initial years of the Second Punic War, but fail to address the specific utility that a truly massive output of silver would have held for the Hieronian kingdom at a time when Sicily had not yet become a war zone. A more plausible explanation for the reintroduction of silver coinage is as part of the efforts taken by the king to ensure the peaceful transition of power to his son, Gelon. We might reasonably consider their role as gifts or rewards for courtiers, local elites, and royal officials whose support would be indispensable for realizing Hieron's dynastic ambitions. Recall that winning the support of powerful factions of the Syracusan aristocracy was vital to Hieron's initial claims to kingship in the 260s. In this light, we should view the coins as part and parcel of Hieron's broader efforts to reinforce an ideology of divinely sanctioned regal succession that was so clearly expressed in the monumental building program taking place at Syracuse in the 230s and 220s. That these coins and their dynastic message were intended for consumption by a local audience is underscored by the distribution of their known findspots, which shows a distinct concentration in and around Syracuse at sites within the political boundaries of the Hieronian kingdom.[81]

Bronze

1. AE. Portrait of Hieron l., wearing diadem/Nike driving a biga r.; below, ΙΕΡΩΝΟΣ (avg. 35.45 grams). Date: ca. 263–215.
2. AE. Portrait of Hieron l., wearing diadem/Horseman charging r.; below, ΙΕΡΩΝΟΣ (avg. 17.1 grams). Date: ca. 263–215.
3. AE. Head of Poseidon l./Ornamental trident, flanked by two dolphins; ΙΕΡΩΝΟΣ (avg. 6.24 grams). Date: ca. 241–215.
4. AE. Head of Apollo l./Horse rearing r.; below ΙΕΡΩΝΟΣ (avg. 4.2 grams). Date: ca. 269–215.

Hieron continued to produce bronze coinage during Period III. According to my arrangement no new bronze types were introduced at the time that the silver dynastic issues were minted. Rather, we see a continuation of several bronze types first struck in Period II. Given the uncertainty that remains around the chronology of Hieron's bronze coinage, I list here the four types that are generally considered to be among the latest struck by the king. It bears repeating that all four types listed here were almost certainly in circulation prior to ca. 230, the approximate date that I have assigned for the beginning of Period III. In all likelihood, the Hieron/Horseman and Poseidon/Trident series continued to be struck at intervals into the final years of Hieron's reign.

WAS THERE A HIERONIAN "MONETARY POLICY"?

Having assessed the output of the Syracusan mint throughout Hieron's long reign as both *stratēgos* and king, let us now turn to address the role that coinage and minting played in the consolidation of the king's power. Specifically, we will consider evidence for what might be casually described as "monetary policy" pursued by the king. I apply the term "monetary policy" loosely to define actions or decisions made by the king or his court that affected the circulation of currency in his kingdom. This is not to imply that Hieron pursued monetary policy in a modern economic sense, being those actions taken by a central authority to manipulate money supply as a means of improving the overall health of a state economy. So far as we can tell, ancient states and their rulers rarely, if ever, acted in this fashion with respect to minting practice.[82] Nevertheless, there was clearly an awareness by the Early Hellenistic period that coinage – as an economic instrument uniquely commanded by the state – could be employed to achieve various purposes for the benefit of the state, and, as such, the operation of a royal mint could be a matter of sophisticated decision-making.[83]

With respect to monetary decision-making and "policy" pursued by the Hieronian court, we must rely principally on the archaeological record, basing our conclusions on the material evidence available to us in the form of hoards and coins recovered in the course of excavations. From the material record, we can see at least three ways in which Hieronian policy came to shape the economic and monetary landscape of eastern Sicily throughout the greater part of the third century.

A Switch to Monometallic Minting

Whereas Hieron had minted a tri-denominational coinage during the time he held power as *stratēgos autokrator* of the Syracusans, the inauguration of his kingship brought about a major currency reform that ushered in a period of monometallism and the exclusive production of bronze coinage by the royal mint. This momentous shift occurred at the outset of Period II, simultaneous with the introduction of Hieron's laureate portrait coinage. Depending on when we date the beginning and end of the Period II coinage, the Hieronian mint appears to have exclusively minted bronze coinage for upward of five decades. This first – and arguably most significant – intervention by Hieron would come to transform the monetary landscape of eastern Sicily for over a generation.

Let us first consider the possible motivation behind this policy shift and then briefly address its consequences. Several motives have been inferred to explain the transition to striking only bronze coinage. One explanation holds that the decision was necessitated by the terms of the 263 treaty with Rome, which required that Hieron make annual payments on an indemnity totaling 100 talents of silver.[84] Advocates of this thesis argue that such payments would have essentially depleted the royal coffers, leaving Hieron financially unable to support a tri-metallic monetary system.[85] While this is not inconceivable, it is nevertheless improbable that such a modest indemnity – especially when paid in installments over several decades – could have resulted in the crippling economic hardships this scenario implies.

If the 263 treaty between Hieron and the Roman did, in fact, have a hand in the currency reform, it is probably because it helped to eliminate Hieron's ability to conduct large-scale military campaigns. After 263, Hieron no longer needed to retain a sizable mercenary force or, consequently, to strike the high-value silver and gold denominations customarily used to pay it.[86] Bronze coinage, however, was occasionally struck in large quantities by Hellenistic kings for military expenditure related to the settlement or garrisoning of soldiers.[87] By forestalling Hieron's military ambitions, the treaty – not the indemnity itself – likely obviated the need to produce the high-value denominations required to maintain a large mercenary force. This alone, however, does not fully explain what seems to have been the discontinuance of gold and silver coinage in the early years of Hieron's kingship.

Surely a contributing factor, if not the principal motivation, behind this switch to an all-bronze currency was the fact that Hieron had no access to natural deposits of either silver or gold, and so was left to rely on trade for augmenting his stores of the precious metals.[88] By striking a heavy bronze coinage for state payments, Hieron could avoid depleting his precious metal reserves. In this respect, the Hieronian policy found common ground with contemporary Ptolemaic efforts to restrict the removal of silver from Egypt, efforts that included striking silver coinage on a lighter standard than the common Attic drachm and minting a heavy bronze coinage for internal circulation within the political boundaries of the kingdom.[89] In fact, both the Ptolemaic and Hieronian currency reforms seem to have come into being around the same time in the middle years of the 260s.

Although we lack documentary evidence that might speak in detail to the impact of Hieron's coinage reform on the communities under his control, the archaeological record offers some tantalizing information. One unmistakable consequence of the shift to monometallic output was a massive increase in the amount of bronze coinage that entered circulation in the areas subject to Hieronian control. This was especially true of the Hieron/Horseman and Poseidon/Trident series, which must have left the royal mint at a rate rivaling the productivity of even the largest Hellenistic mint. A cursory glance over surviving specimens reveals that the number of obverse and reverse dies used in the production of each of these common issues reached well into the hundreds, figures that could easily translate into millions of coins entering circulation.[90]

That there was indeed a veritable flood of bronze coinage leaving the royal mint at Syracuse and reaching urban centers around eastern Sicily is substantiated in the archaeological record. At Kamarina, for instance, Lucchelli and Di Stefano report 264 bronzes of Hieron II discovered during the excavations of the city's agora between 1983 and 1995.[91] This accounts for roughly 37 percent of the 708 legible coins recovered during excavations in the agora, a corpus of material that ranged in date from the fifth century BCE to the twentieth century of the common era. The number of Hieronian bronzes is quite substantial on its own and represents the largest body of coins found at Kamarina attributed to a single ruler or state. The real significance of this number is best understood when considered in context of the Syracusan coinage from the agora excavations struck during the years encompassing Agathokles' rise to power in 316 and Hieron's death in 215.[92] Hieron's coinage accounts for over 85 percent of the coin finds (264 of 310), outnumbering the coinage of his autocratic predecessors by a ratio of more than 15 to 1 (Figure 7.11). Even accounting for coin loss through attrition among the older coinage, the overall numbers surely reflect a considerable influx of bronze coinage entering circulation during Hieron's reign. Stepping back again to view the totality of numismatic material from the agora at Kamarina, the impression of an upsurge in monetization during this period is borne out further when we consider that the number of Hieronian coins recovered in the excavations (again, $n = 264$) is only slightly lower than the total number of coins found in the agora struck in the four centuries between 215 and the end of the second century CE ($n = 287$).[93]

The numerical dominance enjoyed by Hieron's coinage at Kamarina compares favorably with the numismatic data from Morgantina, where well over 10,000 coins have been recovered in excavations across the ancient urban center. Of the 9,898 coins published by the authors of *Morgantina Studies, vol. 2: The Coins*, just over 25 percent ($n = 2,647$) are attributable to Hieron II.[94] As at Kamarina, the chronological range of the coins published in the *Morgantina Studies* series spans nearly 25 centuries. That one in every four coins recovered at the site was struck by the Hieronian mint points to the enormous

MORGANTINA | Syracusan Coins by Issuing Authority

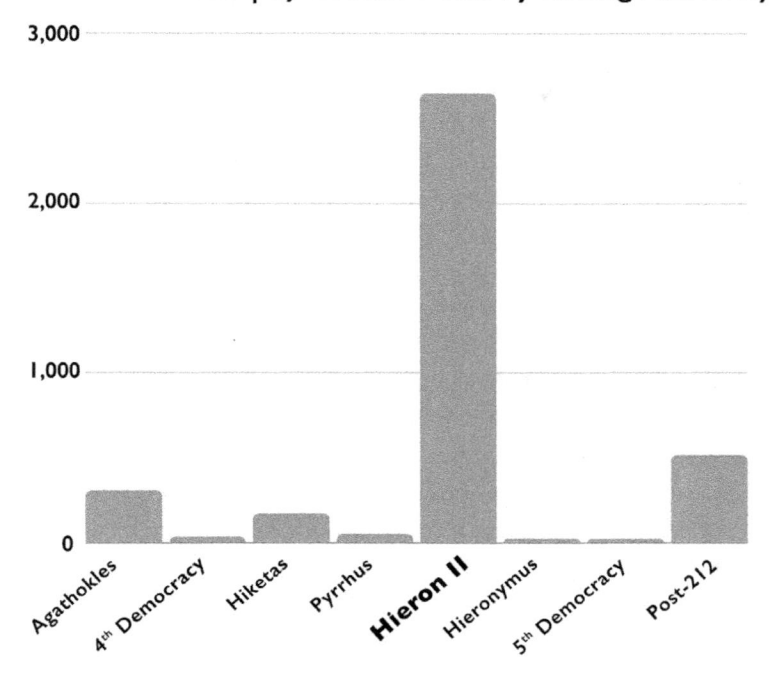

KAMARINA | Syracusan Coins by Issuing Authority

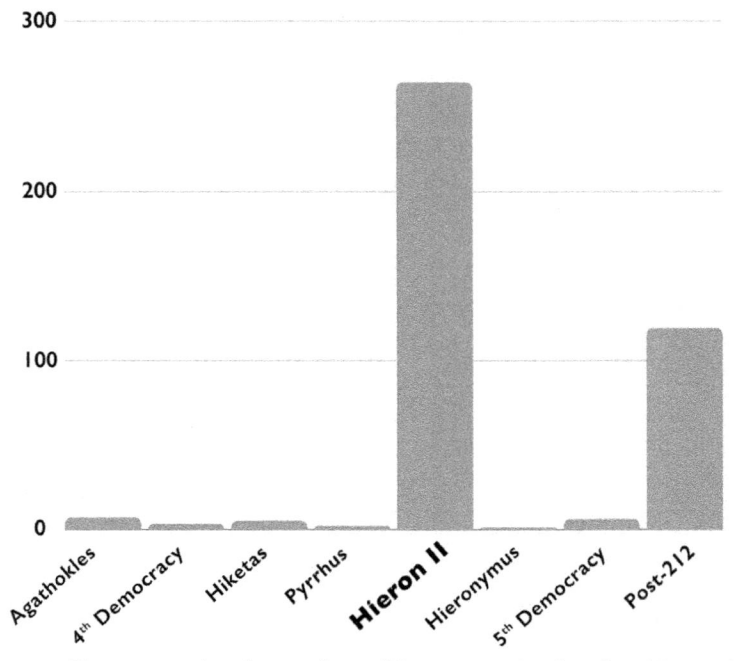

7.11 Chart comparing the number of Syracusan coins found at Morgantina and Kamarina arranged by minting authority.

quantity that once circulated in the city. Within commercial contexts, the bronze coinage of Hieron was ubiquitous by the middle of the third century.[95] Again, the overall numbers from Morgantina show a substantial uptick in the amount of bronze coinage that reached the city compared with previous generations. A survey of total coin finds from Morgantina reveals a nearly 400 percent increase over the amount of Syracusan coinage that had reached the city in the previous 40-year period spanning the reigns of Agathokles, Hiketas, and Pyrrhus (see Figure 7.11). The numbers suggest there was an equally sharp drop in the amount of Syracusan coinage reaching Morgantina in the late third and second century, following Hieron's death.

While excavation coins from other sites within the kingdom are not as well published as those from Kamarina and Morgantina, the hoard evidence from the region is fairly robust and confirms the numerical dominance of Hieron's coinage.[96] There is little reason to doubt that a similar wave of bronze reached most of the communities within the political boundaries of the Hieronian kingdom at the same moment. Understandably, Hieron's bronze coinage does not appear to have circulated to the same degree outside the political boundaries of the kingdom. While I do not wish to make too much of comparisons with sites that followed their own distinct political trajectories over the course of the third century, it is nevertheless worth highlighting that the numbers of Hieronian coins reported from well-excavated sites in the western part of the island, like Selinus and Iatas, are far smaller than those from eastern Sicily.[97]

In the following chapter, we will revisit these bronze denominations, paying attention to their presence within commercial contexts at the urban centers of Morgantina and Kamarina and, in the process, arrive at a better understanding of how Hieron's bronze currency became a common medium of exchange in southeastern Sicily. For the present discussion, the massive output of bronze coinage by the Hieronian mint might be profitably viewed in light of Sitta von Reden's important observations about the role that coinage played in the process of state formation and the consolidation of political authority in the Ptolemaic kingdom, as she writes:

> Coinage and monetization are closely linked to state building, state power, and the representation of it to the citizens or subjects. . .In the State's control over the fiscal organs and its symbolic identification with a standardized medium of exchange lies a significant potential to integrate a country. Monetization can be seen as a strategy of political integration and state formation.[98]

While von Reden was principally concerned with the efforts of early Ptolemaic kings to introduce coinage and promote its use throughout the largely non-monetized Egyptian *chora*, her commentary on the use of coinage to foster political and economic integration is nevertheless applicable to the

Hieronian kingdom. This is especially true for the early decades of Hieron's rule, when the king's bronze coinage reached an unprecedented level of ubiquity in the commercial landscapes of southeastern Sicily.

Striking a "Light" Silver Coinage

A second major policy move that we can ascribe to Hieron involved the weight standards of the silver dynastic coinage issued by the king in Period III. As we recall, in the first period of minting activity, Hieron struck gold and silver denominations on what was the most widely adopted Mediterranean standard of the day, the Attic-Euboic standard. At the time, Hieron needed to pay troops who fought in his campaigns against the Mamertines, and it was common practice to pay mercenaries in coinage struck on the Attic-Euboic standard.

As was just discussed above, the early decades of Hieron's kingship saw a profound shift from tri-metallic production to one of monometalism. When he did eventually resume minting silver coinage with the release of the dynastic series, Hieron appears to have abandoned the Attic-Euboic standard, choosing to issue coins instead on the local Sicilian litra standard.[99] The silver litra standard developed on Sicily around the middle of the fifth century, possibly as a means of facilitating trade between Greek *poleis* and indigenous communities, who had long used a larger, bronze unit known as the litra.[100] By the late fifth century, the silver litra unit had come to normalize around 0.87gram of silver, which, beyond its local bronze equivalences, shared points of approximate interconvertibility with both Attic drachms (~4.3 grams for a ratio of 1:5) and Corinthian staters (~8.6 gram for a ratio of 1:10), making it an effective tool of exchange. Yet Hieron's adoption of the litra standard for his own silver denominations did not immediately ensure he would have units easily convertible with denominations struck on other weight standards. For instance, the Philistis/Quadriga denomination, typically identified as a 16-litra unit, was struck with a median weight of ~13.5 grams. This falls short of the ideal weight of an Attic tetradrachm (~17.1 grams) by nearly 25 percent.

Scholars have long debated the motivation behind this shift from the Attic drachm to the litra standard, since while the silver litra could present itself as interoperable with the Attic-Euboic standard, the inefficiencies of conversion and exchange are readily apparent. Nevertheless, scholarly opinion has largely returned to the assumption that Hieron adopted a new weight standard as means of facilitating international trade. George Francis Hill, the first to recognize that Hieron's dynastic issues were not minted on the Attic-Euboic standard, argued that it was the king's intention to bring his coinage closer in line with Ptolemaic weight standards. In support of his thesis, Hill noted that the nominal weight of the Gelon/Eagle 4-litra denomination (~3.20–3.35 grams) was roughly equivalent to the Ptolemaic silver drachm (~3.6 grams).[101] Along these lines, the average weight of the Philistis/Quadriga 16-litra denomination (~13.5 grams) approximated that of the contemporary Ptolemaic tetradrachm (~14.25 grams), falling short by roughly three-quarters of a gram.[102] Some years later, Giesecke argued that Hieron had sought to align his monetary standards with that of the Roman denarius system, which at the time was still erroneously thought to have begun in 269.[103] De Sensi Sestito would come to reject these earlier claims, positing instead that Hieron did not base his silver dynastic series on any existing standard, but rather created a coinage that could circulate in different monetary zones, including those dominated by Roman and Ptolemaic standards.[104] This interest in identifying the "international" aspects of Hieron's silver coinage has found its greatest expression in the recent work of Benedetto Carroccio, who perceives points of compatibility between Hieron's silver denominations and contemporary coinages struck on no fewer than five different monetary standards.[105]

The hypothesis that Hieron aligned his monetary standards with those of more powerful trading partners is very appealing, as it holds potentially far-reaching implications for our understanding of economic integration in the region.[106] Yet while metrological studies favor this idea of monetary coordination on the part of Hieron, the archaeological record appears to tell a different story altogether. If achieving such interoperability was the desired outcome of Hieron's currency reforms, would we not expect to find evidence that Hieronian silver circulated widely within the Mediterranean, or at least within favorable monetary zones? Quite the opposite appears to be the case, as no specimens of Hieron's dynastic series have ever been found beyond the shores of Sicily or even in parts of the island that fell outside the political boundaries of the kingdom (Figure 7.12). And while Carroccio, as Hill before him, rightly demonstrates the numerous points of metrological convergence with Ptolemaic units, the archaeological record suggests the amount of Ptolemaic silver in circulation on Sicily during the third century was meager to the point of irrelevance.[107]

How then do we account for the perceived coordination of monetary standards alongside the near-total absence of foreign coinage circulating within the Hieronian kingdom? Why did Hieron's internationalized currency not enjoy any appreciable circulation outside Sicily? The answer may lie in the *approximate* interoperability of Hieronian units with those more widely exchanged currencies. Hieron, of course, ruled over a kingdom lacking in natural deposits of silver and gold, and so relied on international trade and taxation at home to boost his stores of these precious metals. He may have sought to prevent the outflow of silver resources through trade by issuing coinage that was slightly lighter than the more widely circulating Attic-Euboic standard. Here, as with his bronze coinage reforms of the 260s, Hieron may

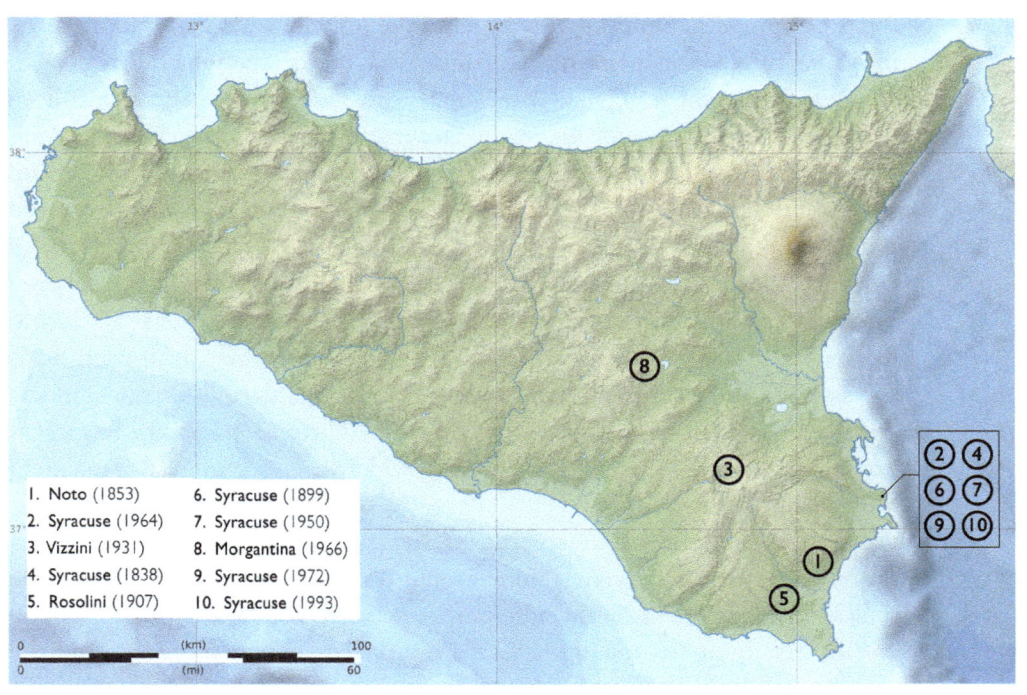

7.12 Map showing the locations of known hoards containing silver coins struck by Hieron II (base map © Sémhur/Wikimedia Commons/CC-BY-SA-3.0).

again have found inspiration in the monetary policies of the Ptolemies, who had struck lightweight silver coins since the reign of Ptolemy I.[108] By enforcing the use of his own royal coinage for commercial transactions taking place within the kingdom, Hieron would have been able to, in essence, "trap" silver by taking advantage of favorable exchange rates forced on foreigners seeking to do business in eastern Sicily. We might envision conversion taking place between an Attic tetradrachm (~17.1 grams) or Ptolemaic tetradrachm (~14.25 grams) and the nearest Hieronian counterpart, the Philistis/Quadriga 16-litra denomination (~13.5 grams). Better still were potential profit margins for the king if he enforced the exchange of foreign silver denominations for their state-sanctioned equivalent in his own bronze coinage.

We are aware that the Ptolemies enforced such a policy, requiring merchants to exchange their foreign coinage and bullion for lighter Ptolemaic coins of an "equivalent" value.[109] Evidence for this practice may survive in a letter written in the year 258 by a certain Demetrios, who is typically identified as an official of the royal mint in Alexandria during the reign of Ptolemy II. In his letter, Demetrios appears to write to a superior, reporting that an untimely administrative pronouncement has led to disruptions in the routine practice by which "the foreigners who come here [Alexandria] by sea and the merchants and middlemen and others bring both their local money of unalloyed metal and the gold pentadrachms, to be made into new money for them in accordance with the decree which orders us to receive and remint."[110] Demetrios goes on to state that the merchants have expressed their frustration due to the fact that they could not exchange their foreign coinage at either the mint or royal banks, and were thus stymied from purchasing agricultural goods in the countryside, where (as Demetrios need not elaborate) only the king's coinage was accepted. That some form of currency conversion or exchange was indeed enforced by the early Ptolemaic kings is borne out in the archaeological record by what appears to be the general dearth of foreign coins in Egypt by the early third century.[111] Outside the Ptolemaic kingdom, merchants found little use for their underweight silver coins – let alone for the overvalued bronze – with the result that Ptolemaic silver did not tend to circulate widely as a commercial instrument around the Mediterranean.[112]

No smoking gun like Demetrios' letter survives to confirm whether a similar policy was enforced at the entrepôts of the Hieronian kingdom. Still, the combination of a lightweight silver coinage, which shows no signs of having circulated beyond the political boundaries of the kingdom, and the near-complete absence of foreign silver coinage found within the kingdom both urge the conclusion that Hieron took these measures to limit the amount of silver lost through trade.[113]

Royal Interference to Civic Minting

In stark contrast to the tremendous output registered by the royal mint at Syracuse, the archaeological record points to an abeyance of civic minting by the *poleis* of the kingdom throughout the five decades of the king's reign and up to the death of Hieronymos in 214, which brought about the dissolution of the Hieronian kingdom. It would appear that not one of the roughly fifteen *poleis* within the Hieronian kingdom issued coinage while subject to the king's political authority. How can we explain this situation? Was this inactivity the result of royal interference aimed at suppressing the operation of civic mints, or was it simply the consequence of *poleis* voluntarily interrupting their local mint operations due to the widespread availability of the king's own coinage? Identifying the cause or motive for the inactivity of these civic mints throughout much of the third century may shed additional light on the nature and extent of Hieron's authority over the *poleis* that constituted his kingdom.

The question of royal intervention within the realm of civic minting is one that has received much attention by scholars concerned with the phenomenon in the context of the wider Hellenistic world. Since Berve first made the argument in his *König Hieron II*, scholars have largely accepted the premise that the *poleis* subject to Hieron's rule did not mint coinage. Early opinions were focused on the presumption that Hieron restricted civic mints for political reasons. This perspective aligned with the prevailing belief that during the Classical and Hellenistic periods, no *polis* minted civic coinage in its own name while subject to the political authority of another state.[114] Accordingly, the fact that *poleis* of eastern Sicily did not mint coinage was considered clear evidence of their political subjugation to Hieron. In the past three decades, however, opinions have shifted away from this political etiology, as recent scholarship has emphasized other, mainly economic, factors driving the closure of civic mints by cities subject to an external authority like a king. Let's first take up the argument that civic mints were closed by royal intervention.

For scholars such as Berve and De Sensi Sestito, who grappled with this question of civic minting within the Hieronian kingdom, two cities – Syracuse and Tauromenion – stood out from the rest for what was perceived at the time as evidence for the persistence of their civic mints even under subjection to royal authority. For De Sensi Sestito, Syracuse and Tauromenion were considered exceptions that proved the general rule about a royal prohibition on civic minting; that is, their privileged status reflected the two cities' relative size and influence for which Hieron was willing to make concessions in return for their acknowledgment of his political authority.[115] Berve, on the other hand, considered the prolonged operation of the civic mint at Tauromenion a valid reason to exclude the *polis* from his list of cities under Hieron's control.[116] Regardless of their respective merits, both positions can now be shown to rest on shaky ground, particularly in the case of Tauromenion, which almost certainly ceased civic minting activity for the duration of Hieron's reign.

With an array of bronze and silver issues traditionally dated around the middle decades of the third century (ca. 275–210), Tauromenion was long considered to be the exception to the rule that allied cities did not mint coinage during Hieron's lifetime. Today, this viewpoint has been convincingly challenged by Anna Carbè, whose reappraisal of Tauromenion's third-century coinage demonstrates that the *polis* did, in fact, cease to strike coinage around the time that Hieron became king. Moreover, Carbè's work suggests that in the years leading up to Hieron's declaration of kingship, the *polis* may have even coordinated its coin types and denominations with those issued by Hieron while he was still *stratēgos autokrator* of the Syracusans.[117] Given the far-reaching implications of her conclusions to the present discussion, Carbè's argument merits a closer look.

After surveying the coinage conventionally dated ca. 275–210, Carbè identifies two distinct periods of output, which she distinguishes on metrological and stylistic grounds.[118] In the earlier period of minting, Tauromenion struck both bronze and silver denominations that in many resembled the coinage issued by Hieron while he held power as *stratēgos autokrator*. This correspondence is perhaps most clearly seen in the city's silver coinage, which bore the

7.13 Silver octobol of Tauromenion, ca. 276–269 BCE (BM 1841,0726.365; © The Trustees of the British Museum). Compare with Figure 7.3.

head of Athena wearing a Corinthian helmet on its obverse type, and a flying Pegasos on its reverse (Figure 7.13). In terms of both iconography and metrology, these coins remind one of the Athena/Pegasos octobols struck in Hieron's name. This period of minting was followed by a long interval of inactivity, which Carbè suggests lasted more than half a century. In support of her hypothesis, she rightly observes that the coins belonging to the later period of civic minting at Tauromenion exhibit far greater stylistic and metrological affinities with coinage struck at other Sicilian *poleis* in the years after the Second Punic War. From these observations, Carbè concludes that Tauromenion's mint ceased its operation for the greater part of the third century, arguing that the city did not strike civic coinage between the time that Hieron became king and his death in 215.

Carbè's conclusions appear to be fully corroborated by the archaeological record at Morgantina, where excavations have revealed well over 100 coins of the types she assigns on stylistic and metrological grounds to the post-215 period of mint activity at Tauromenion. Significantly, only one single coin of this number has been recovered from a context considered to predate the Roman siege of Morgantina in 211.[119] Given the great abundance of coins recovered from commercial and domestic spaces that were active up to and at the time of the Roman siege, the conspicuous absence of these coins from pre-211 contexts strongly suggests that they had only just entered circulation shortly before the time of the siege, thus adding further confirmation to the validity of Carbè's thesis about the interruption of Tauromenion's mint.

The situation at Syracuse is not as clear cut. Being the de facto capital of the kingdom, Syracuse naturally served as the base for Hieron's royal minting operations, as it had for both Agathokles and Pyrrhus before him. It was also the largest and most powerful of the Sicilian *poleis* to recognize Hieron's claim on autocratic legitimacy. Mollifying the aristocratic factions that had long held power in the city may have required special concessions on the part of Hieron. For this reason, scholars have long assumed that the city may have retained some control over its civic mint in return for acknowledging Hieron's *basileia*. The Syracusans had enjoyed visibility on the coinage struck by Agathokles and Pyrrhus in the form of the city's ethnic ΣΥΡΑΚΟΣΙΩΝ, "[coinage] of the Syracusans," appearing as a legend on many coins and may have even continued to have a hand in issuing civic coinage.[120] So too during the years that Hieron held power as *stratēgos autokrator* was the city's ethnic minted on the obverse types of the Persephone/Bull IE series. Reference to the Syracusans, however, vanished shortly after Hieron took the title of king and began to issue his first series of portrait coins. For the next half a century, the coin types issued by the royal mint at Syracuse exhibited a consistency in their promotion of the king's personal rule and, consequently, his sole authority to strike coinage. The latter message is evident in the replacement of the city's ethnic by the legend ΙΕΡΩΝΟΣ, "[coinage] of Hieron."[121] Coinage bearing the ethnic legend ΣΥΡΑΚΟΣΙΩΝ would not reemerge again until the time of the Fifth Syracusan Democracy (213–212), following the assassination of Hieronymos.[122]

Judging from the bronze coinage alone, it would appear that Hieron made no such concessions in allowing the Syracusans continued operation of their mint. It is with the silver coinage of Period III, however, where interpretative difficulties arise. While the largest and most prolifically struck types, those of the so-called dynastic series, are fully imbued with the iconography and language of autocratic rule, a number of the smaller silver denominations of this period were struck with the legend ΣΥΡΑΚΟΣΙΟΙ. Some scholars have adduced this as evidence for the continuation of civic minting by the Syracusans, and while the impulse to identify these coins as the products of an independent civic mint is understandable, closer inspection reveals several details that collectively suggest these coins were wholly contrived and produced under direct royal control.[123] Leaving aside the atypical nominative form of the ethnic legend, a detail that has yet to receive convincing explanation, these coins were intrinsically bound to Hieron's dynastic series with respect to both their metrology and their iconographic program.[124] This is most clearly observed in the 4-litra and 8-litra denominations, which juxtapose the legend ΣΥΡΑΚΟΣΙΟΙ alongside that of ΒΑ ΓΕΛΩΝΟΣ on the coins' reverse types, possibly an abbreviated form of ΒΑ[ΣΙΛΕΟΣ] ΓΕΛΩΝΟΣ, "[coinage] of king Gelon," or Β[ασιλικὸν] Α[ργύριον] ΓΕΛΩΝΟΣ, "[coinage struck from] the royal silver of Gelon." Arguments that these coins should be considered evidence for the special status of the Syracusans, which granted them privileges to operate a civic mint, are unconvincing, particularly given that Gelon, Hieron's son and co-regent, is depicted wearing a royal diadem on the obverse types, much in the same fashion as his father and mother on their respective portrait coins. The message here is overwhelmingly one of promoting the legitimacy of Gelon's ascension to power, not celebrating Syracusan autonomy.

A number of smaller silver denominations, believed to have been struck at the same time as the portrait coins of Hieron, Philistis, and Gelon, also bear the legend ΣΥΡΑΚΟΣΙΟΙ without any overt iconographic reference to the royal family. These, of all coins struck in this period, have the best claim to representing a degree of independence on the part of the Syracusans to operate their civic mint. They are, nevertheless, closely bound to the larger, portrait series by their apparent denominational structure, making it far more likely that they were struck by the royal mint. The reference to the civic body of the ΣΥΡΑΚΟΣΙΟΙ, by my reading, may reflect some concession or attempt made by the king to reinforce Syracusan support behind the idea of Gelon's succession to the throne as legitimate heir.

If this reading of the evidence is correct, we are left with what appears to have been the total suspension of civic minting during the reign of Hieron II, and – even more significantly – with credible evidence from Tauromenion of a civic mint shuttering its activity at the start of Hieron's reign. The manifest silence of these civic mints for the greater part of the third century speaks volumes in support of the long-held idea that there was indeed a degree of royal interference aimed at restricting the operation of civic mints. The fact that none of the *poleis* subject to Hieron appear to have minted coinage with their own ethnic legends for the duration of his reign certainly corroborates this point of view.

The inactivity of civic mints during this period is even more remarkable when viewed in light of the florescence of civic coinages struck in the period that followed the dissolution of the Hieronian kingdom. In the last decade of the third and first half of the second century, many of the cities formerly subject to Hieronian control issued small bronze coinage in their own name. Leontinoi, Syracuse, and Tauromenion all reactivated civic mints and struck coinage bearing their ethnic legend.[125] More remarkable still is the fact that around this same moment in time, three *poleis* formerly allied with Hieron – Akrai, Hybla Magna, and Menai – issued a civic coinage for the first time in their history (Figure 7.14).[126]

We might be tempted, then, to view the uptick in civic minting that followed Hieron's death as predicated on these communities' collective desire to visually express their renewed civic autonomy following a period of political suppression. Yet as clear-cut as the evidence for royal intervention may appear, it is constructive to consider alternative explanations for the lack of civic minting during this period. In fact, aside from the shuttering of the mint at Tauromenion and the royal appropriation of the Syracusan mint, it is difficult to speak of active

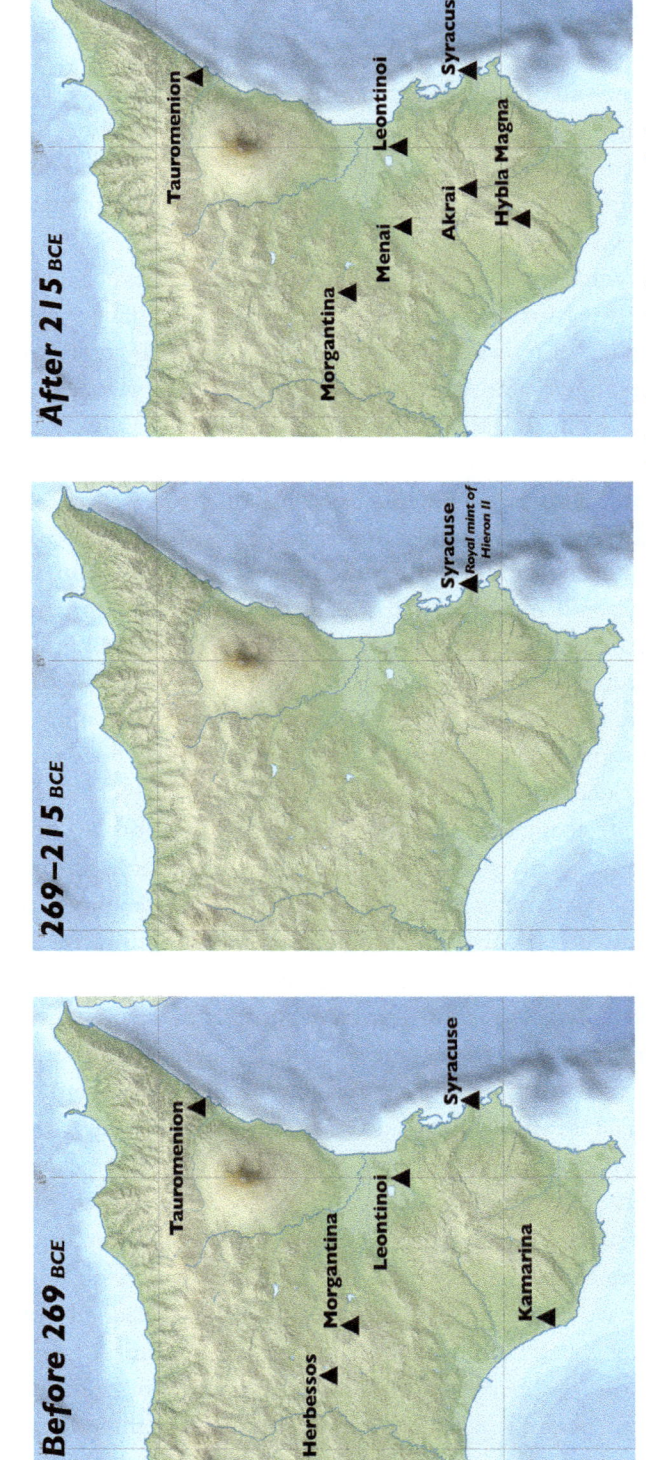

7.14 Map of eastern Sicily showing cities subject to Hieron II that operated a civic mint before, during, and after the period of Hieronian rule (base map © Sémhur/Wikimedia Commons/CC-BY-SA-3.0).

suppression or intervention by the Hieronian state when most other *poleis* within the kingdom either had never minted civic coinage (e.g., Akrai, Hybla Magna) or had not operated an active mint for more than a generation prior to Hieron's rise to power (e.g., Leontinoi, Morgantina). Moreover, the belief that Hellenistic kings perforce suppressed the minting activity of the *poleis* under their control has been steadily eroded in recent decades, most forcefully by Thomas Martin, whose *Sovereignty and Coinage in Classical Greece* delivered a powerful blow to the long-established belief that Macedonian kings actively suppressed civic mints during the Classical period.[127]

In reviewing the evidence for the closure of Thessalian mints during the fourth century, Martin found that Macedonian royal policy played no direct role in the cessation of civic minting; instead, he argued, "[a] combination of practical factors made it easy for Macedonian royal coinage eventually to supplant local coinage to such an extent that further local production would have been superfluous even for purposes of convenience in exchange." Among the "practical factors" Martin considered to be influential was the likelihood that Macedonian coinage abundantly circulated as a well-known and trusted medium of exchange throughout the region. Absent the need to produce new coinage, Thessalian cities could simply rely on Macedonian tetradrachms for their civic expenditure. In the wake of *Sovereignty and Coinage*, scholars have begun to adopt a more flexible outlook that recognizes a spectrum of attitudes and actions taken by Hellenistic monarchs toward civic mints.[128] A growing consensus supports Martin's thesis that an economic – not political – rationale drove most decisions about whether or not to produce coinage.

In light of changing scholarly views on the relationship between political autonomy and a city's ability to operate a mint, should we instead view the inactivity of civic mints inside Hieron's kingdom as economically motivated? Hieron himself certainly put a spectacular quantity of bronze (and later silver) coinage into circulation – so much, in fact, that the cities of southeastern Sicily may credibly have found the market sufficiently saturated with Hieronian bronze to the point where there was little economic motivation to produce their own coinage.[129] Following this line of reasoning, the uptick in production of small bronze coinage by civic mints following the dissolution of Hieron's kingdom might have simply been a response to economic pressures resulting from the steep drop in output by the Syracusan mint and not, as previously suggested, an expression of renewed civic autonomy.

Given the available data, how can we best explain the inactivity of the civic mints? Are we witness to the outcome of a heavy-handed policy emanating from Hieron's royal court at Syracuse, or a constellation of individual, *polis*-level responses to a perceived abundance of coinage in circulation? Arriving at a definitive answer regarding royal interference seems out of the question, short of discovering a new royal letter forbidding the operation of civic mints.

In the absence of other documentary sources, we are best served by turning to the coins themselves, especially when the numismatic evidence can be viewed in its archaeological context.

As we will come to see, there are reasons to question whether the economic explanation holds true in the case of southeastern Sicily. This position hinges on the supposition that the existing currency was in sufficiently high circulation that a *polis* like Tauromenion would have found little or no incentive to strike its own coinage. Yet there are two clear signs that even as Hieronian bronze became the common medium for commercial exchange throughout the kingdom, communities still found themselves facing a shortage of low-denomination coinage. That these *poleis* did not respond to local shortages by minting their own civic coinage does recommend the conclusion that they were prohibited from doing so by command of royal decree.

One sign of a persistent shortage of small change is the continued circulation of older coinage struck by previous Syracusan regimes, as well as by external mints, at centers like Kamarina and Morgantina, albeit in very limited quantities. Valued at best for their intrinsic weight in bronze, these older and non-Syracusan coins likely remained in circulation to serve the need for low-denomination currency in these communities.[130] A second, more telling sign that communities both faced a scarcity of small change and were prohibited from striking new coins to address this problem is the large number of intentionally halved Poseidon/Trident denominations that have turned up in excavations around southeastern Sicily. The practice of cutting these bronze coins along their central axis to create two roughly equal halves occurred with great frequency throughout the third century, judging from the hundreds (if not thousands) of surviving specimens recovered from sites around eastern Sicily (Figure 7.15).[131]

To some, the mass cutting of coinage at first glance may appear a means of demonetizing the currency by physically altering its appearance. Yet the mass demonetization of coinage in the ancient world was rarely accomplished through the physical mutilation of specie, judging from the available material

7.15 Halved Poseidon/Trident coins of Hieron II (courtesy of the American Excavations at Morgantina).

evidence. The wholesale demonetization of coinage at this period would have more likely been accomplished by the recall of currency to the central mint, where the coins could be melted down and re-minted, or simply re-tariffed with a countermark.[132] A closer look at the halved Poseidon/Trident coins themselves reveals several important details that belie such a motive.[133] For instance, the manner in which the fractioning occurred suggests that considerable care went into the process. With few exceptions, the flans were divided into two roughly equal pieces by carefully cutting along the axis formed by the trident shaft on the coin's reverse type. Such regularity could only be achieved by systematic effort to produce consistent units, whereas cutting coins simply to destroy or demonetize them would have produced a far greater degree of variation in the orientation of the cut and, naturally, in the sizes of the cut pieces themselves.[134]

The impressive scale at which the fractioning occurred lends further credibility to the argument that this was not done to demonetize the coins. At Morgantina alone, halved specimens account for roughly 26 percent of the total number of Poseidon/Trident coins from the site.[135] Comparably high percentages are reported among the coins recovered in the agora at Kamarina.[136] Such large quantities suggest that these were not the products of occasional discovery and seizure by regulatory officials, as was the charge of the *agoranomoi* patrolling the markets in Athens when they encountered a fraudulent coin. Finally, evidence that these halved coins continued to circulate in commercial contexts alongside uncut Hieronian money establishes beyond a doubt that these fractions continued to serve a monetary function.[137] Around the agora at Morgantina, halved Poseidon/Trident coins have been found alongside full specimens in ancient shops.[138] The occasional inclusion of these halved coins in hoards further speaks to their enduring monetary value.[139]

If these coins clearly continued to serve a monetary function, why were they cut? Both the rationale for and the time frame of the fractioning of the Poseidon/Trident coinage have long been a subject of debate.[140] For many decades, the halving of Poseidon/Trident bronzes was considered a phenomenon of the Second Punic War, datable to a narrow window of time between 214 and 211. Holloway, who first advanced this chronological argument, observed that during the war's Sicilian campaigns, Roman commanders had used Hieron's Poseidon/Trident bronze denominations as an emergency payment for their soldiers fighting in Sicily by overstriking Roman types onto the Hieronian coins.[141] According to Holloway's thesis, once the Roman weight system dropped to the point of the sextantal level and there were no longer Syracusan bronzes light enough to overstrike, some adroit quaestor turned to cutting Poseidon/Tridents in half as a means of meeting the need for small change paid out to the Roman soldiers.[142] In the past several decades, however, Holloway's captivating thesis has been thoroughly undermined by a spate of fresh archaeological discoveries, which demonstrate beyond a doubt that the phenomenon of halving was more attenuated, beginning sometime in the first half of the third century with the large-flan Poseidon/Trident series.[143]

Holloway's thesis was correct in at least one respect, namely, in identifying the practice of halving as a mechanism for increasing the supply of small bronze coinage in circulation. The most plausible explanation for this phenomenon is to view it as a response to an

7.16 Halved Short Cross silver penny, minted 1180 CE in York, England (BM 1985,0415.86; © The Trustees of the British Museum).

unmet demand for small change during the reign of Hieron II. While worlds apart, the cutting of silver pennies to form fractional denominations (half pennies, farthings) appears to have been rather common practice in medieval England and may offer a reasonable point of comparison to the practice in Hieronian Sicily.[144] Like the Poseidon/Trident issues, these small medieval coins were carefully cut along the axis of the double cross of the reverse type (Figure 7.16). Reflecting on the scale at which the fractioning of these coins occurred, David Metcalf noted that "cutting a penny in half was not an occasional expedient ... it was provision made on a large scale; a million chisel cuts neatly done."[145] While the scale of medieval fractioning may have gone far beyond that of the Hieronian period, the spirit of Metcalf's statement rings true for the halving of the Poseidon/Trident issues in the third century, down to the uniformity of cuts along the trident shaft. Since halving of English pennies took place at different times over several centuries, scholars have observed that fractioning occurred with greater frequency when small change was in short supply and, conversely, became less common when smaller denominations were abundantly struck by the central mint.[146] It would not be surprising if a similar set of conditions led to the fractioning of the small Hieronian denominations.

The fractioning of Poseidon/Trident coins, then, seems to have been a response to demand for more small denomination coins.[147] What drove this need for small change? Deflationary pressure could be to blame, if the purchasing power of Hieron's bronze coins increased to the point where they were impractical as instruments of routine commercial transactions. An alternative, and perhaps more likely, explanation is that production of small bronzes by the royal mint at Syracuse lagged behind the steady demand for smaller denominations.[148] Looking at the overall number of coin finds from this period, it would certainly appear that the smallest bronze units (i.e., the Apollo/Horse and Persephone/Bull IE series of Phases II and III) were struck in nowhere near the same quantities as the larger Poseidon/Trident or Hieron/Horseman issues.

Confirmation that small change was indeed scarce may be evinced by the number of Apollo/Horse issues (avg. 4.2 grams) found at Morgantina compared with that of the large-flan Poseidon/Trident issues (avg. 8.11 grams): a remarkably imbalanced ratio of 59 examples of the *less* valuable coin against 411 examples of the higher denomination.[149] This variance confirms what is otherwise the logical inference regarding money supply within the Hieronian kingdom – that the scarcity of small denominations was felt more strongly as distance from Syracuse increased. That no halved Poseidon/Trident coins have yet to be reported from excavations at Syracuse itself may further support this conclusion.[150]

It should not surprise us that the royal mint did not step in to meet demand by increasing production of smaller and smaller denominations needed for commercial exchange taking place in the cities of the kingdom. Ensuring that there is an ample amount of currency in circulation to facilitate commercial exchange may be a pillar of modern monetary policy, but it does not seem to have been a primary concern of the ancient state. Moreover, there was likely little financial incentive for Hieron to issue low-denomination coins, as small coins did not generate nearly the same level of seigniorage for the state as it accrued by striking larger denominations.[151] Rather than issue additional low-denomination coins like the Apollo/Horse types, Hieron may have simply allowed the halving of Poseidon/Tridents to take place, assuming, of course, that the royal court itself did not have a hand in regulating or coordinating the fractioning. The consistency of the cuts and regularity of the fractioning does indeed suggest a degree of oversight and attention to the process that went beyond random individuals simply picking up a hammer and chisel to clip coins when the need presented itself. Could oversight of the process have rested in the hands of royal officials or even with the royal mint itself? Further analysis of the half coins themselves with attention paid to the technical nature of the cuts may shed light on who was ultimately responsible for the practice.

Taking a step back, we have seen evidence that low-denomination coins were likely in short supply around the Hieronian kingdom and that the fractioning of the Poseidon/Trident coins is best explained as a response to this scarcity of small change. The fact that Morgantina, Tauromenion, Kamarina, or any other *polis* within the kingdom did not themselves issue coins to meet the demand for low-denomination coinage points decidedly to a royal policy forbidding local minting. The relative speed at which former subjects of Hieron resumed minting activity following the dissolution of the kingdom – to strike primarily low-denomination bronze coinage, no less –

demonstrates all the more clearly that the inactivity by these mints during the middle of the third century was a by-product of royal interference.

ADDING IT UP

While much important work remains to be done in advancing our understanding of Hieron's minting policies and, in particular, the role that coinage played in the administration of his Sicilian kingdom, the preceding discussion has laid out several areas in which we see the Hieronian state engaging in what might broadly be deemed monetary policy. In many respects, Hieronian policy resembled efforts taken by contemporary Ptolemaic kings to shape the monetary landscape of their own kingdom. Large quantities of bronze coinage were minted for internal circulation, as silver denominations were struck on a light standard that discouraged circulation outside the political boundaries of the kingdom. For both Hieron and the Ptolemies, the circumstances of unequal resource distribution undoubtedly shaped their minting practices. Sicily, like Egypt, lacked natural reserves of silver. Whether or not Hieron's actions were directly influenced by Ptolemaic policy is a matter that will remain the subject of debate. There is certainly ample evidence that the two kingdoms enjoyed a close relationship, especially when it came to trade and diplomatic contacts between the royal courts at Syracuse and Alexandria. Moreover, the recent work by Wolf and Lorber has persuasively established that this relationship extended into the realm of minting and, very likely, served as a catalyst for the bronze coinage reform implemented by Hieron in the 260s.

One area of monetary policy where Hieron likely found little guidance from the Ptolemies' experience was in his dealings with the *poleis* of southeastern Sicily that had traditionally exercised autonomy over the operation of their civic mints. In this respect, I have argued that the inactivity of civic mints in eastern Sicily during Hieron's reign may be related to intervention on the part of the Hieronian court. The shuttering of Tauromenion's mint in the 260s supports this conclusion, as do the many hundreds and thousands of halved Poseidon/Tridents coins found at sites all around eastern Sicily – a response, I suggest, to shortages in small change that would have been redressed by the production of local, civic coinages, if only it had been allowed for the *poleis* subject to Hieron's authority to operate their mints.

This intercession by the Hieronian state to block local, civic minting was surely motivated by practical, administrative interests on the part of the king and not – as long held by some scholars – by ideological views concerning the relationship between minting and *polis* autonomy. Such an interpretation accords well with our understanding of the Hieronian state's role in gathering harvest data and promoting the unification of volumetric standards throughout the kingdom as a means of facilitating the extraction of resources through taxation. As Sitta von Reden has persuasively demonstrated in the case of Ptolemaic Egypt, the combination of a widely available state coinage and policies designed to exclude foreign coinages from internal circulation facilitated administrative oversight by royal officials, lowered transaction costs related to taxation, and allowed the state to extract even more resources than would be possible if solely reliant on taxation in kind.[152]

While we lack the rich documentary record available to scholars of Hellenistic Egypt, the material evidence available to us from Hellenistic Sicily certainly sustains the notion that Hieron II, like his Ptolemaic counterparts, actively used coinage as an instrument to further strengthen his rule.

NOTES

[1]   Ma (2013: 346). See Gabrielsen (2013: 348) and von Reden (2007: 296–302) for similar sentiments.
[2]   This is not to discount the significant contributions made thus far to this end, including most notably that of Caccamo Caltabiano et al. (1997) and Carroccio (2000; 2004).
[3]   De Callataÿ (2013: 138).
[4]   Castelli (1769: pl. 1, no. 14).
[5]   Castelli (1781: pls. 97–100), who correctly attributes several of Hieron's II bronze denominations (pl. 104).
[6]   Notably, Eckhel (1792: I.249–67), who considered the portrait coins depicting Hieron II wearing a diadem to be posthumously struck by Hieronymos; see Caccamo Caltabiano et al. (1997: 25) for an excerpt from the relevant passage of Eckhel's *Doctrina numorum veterum*.
[7]   Head (1874a: 60–9); printed also as Head (1874b). Head's *History of the Coinage of Syracuse* was the among the first numismatic works to recognize the value of ancient coins as historical documents. It was followed shortly by the *British Museum Catalog: Sicily* (1876), which he edited with R. S. Poole and P. Gardner. The chronology set forth in Head (1874a and 1874b) for the Hieronian mint was retained in *BMC: Sicily*.
[8]   Most notably, Giesecke (1920; 1923); Gabrici (1927); and Franke (1958), all of whom adopted – with minor alterations – the chronological framework laid out in *History of the Coinage of Syracuse*.
[9]   Cutroni Tusa (1960–1: 78–90).
[10] For the excavations on Capo Soprano at Gela, see the pair of seminal articles by Adamesteanu and Orlandini (1956; 1960). While the monograph-length publication of the coin finds from Morgantina would not appear until 1989, as Buttrey et al., *Morgantina Studies, vol. 2: The Coins* (1989), the annual preliminary reports published by co-directors Sjöqvist (1958a; 1960a; 1962) and Stillwell (1961; 1963) made frequent mention of numismatic material recovered in the course of excavations. These were augmented by the work of Holloway (1960; 1965) and Buttrey (1965; 1973), each of whom produced several numismatic contributions with specific reference to the Morgantina excavations.
[11] Caccamo Caltabiano et al. (1995; 1997); Carroccio (1994; 2000; 2018).
[12] Arnold-Biucchi (2002); Mattingly (2000); Walthall (2017).
[13] A tripartite periodization for Hieron's coinage is presented by Buttrey et al. (1989: 104–6). I follow their organization with various emendations to both the absolute and relative chronology of the coins.
[14] *Supra* p. 27, Figure 1.2.
[15] Regarding the addition of Hieron's name to his coinage while still *stratēgos autokrator*, see discussion *supra* Chapter 1, n. 58, with response to Caccamo Caltabiano's objection that

Hieron could not have struck coins in his name prior to assuming kingship. Hieron was, in fact, simply following a precedent set by Agathokles; see Ierardi (1995–6); Armagrande (2000: 224–9); and De Lisle (2017).

[16] Unless stated otherwise, average (mean) weights are taken from Caccamo Caltabiano et al. (1995).

[17] Coins in this series were struck with multiple variations in the type; Carroccio (1993) argues the types were used at different points in Hieron's reign, one at the start of Hieron's career and two in the final years of his life.

[18] Caccamo Caltabiano et al. (1995: 200–1).

[19] For the Persephone/Biga coins of the Fourth Syracusan Democracy, see Holloway (1962: 5–17); and on the gold hemistaters of Hiketas, see Buttrey (1973).

[20] For their association with Hieron II, see Carroccio (1993) and Manganaro (1981–2). Head (1874b: 56–8) considered these to date from the time of Pyrrhus' campaigns on Sicily.

[21] In addition to the stylistic and metrological similarities these coins share with those of Hieron's predecessors, attribution of the Persephone/Biga hemistaters to the period of Hieron's tenure as *stratēgos autokrator* is supported by the presence of four specimens in the Carlentini hoard (*IGCH* 2206), which has a burial date of ca. 260, based on Jenkins and Lewis' (1963) study of the Carthaginian coins found within the hoard. This is not to completely dismiss Carroccio's thesis (*supra* n. 17) that the Persephone/Biga types were revived by Hieron nearly 50 years later and struck alongside the silver issues of the "Regal Series" (below, Period III).

[22] Ref. *MS* II, no. 358; *SNG ANS*, no. 868. For the placement of these coins early in the sequence of Hieron's mint output, see Franke (1958: 62–3); Caccamo Caltabiano et al. (1995: 204–7).

[23] De Callataÿ (2000).

[24] See, e.g., *SNG ANS*, nos. 554–7.

[25] Ref. *MS* II, no. 359; Gàbrici (1927), nos. 497–9; *SNG Cop.*, no. 857; *SNG ANS*, no. 1016.

[26] Ref. *MS* II, no. 324.

[27] Ref. *MS* II, no. 362; *SNG ANS*, no. 1018.

[28] De Lisle (2017: 12–13).

[29] Among the early works to attribute these coins to Hieron II: Holm (1906: 213); Giesecke (1923: 118); and Franke (1958: 59–61). Head (1874b: 68–9) also assigned these coins to Hieron, noting that they shared control marks with several of Hieron's other bronze issues. Head further noted the invariable presence of the letters IE on this series, which he took for a contraction of IEPΩNOΣ.

[30] For the Gela excavations, see Adamesteanu and Orlandini (1956; 1960). For the attribution of these coins to Agathokles, see Holloway (1979: 90–1). The Agathoklean date is repeated by the authors of *Morgantina Studies, vol. 2: The Coins* (Buttrey et al. 1989: nos. 324–5).

[31] On the Hieronian date for these coins, see De Sensi Sestito (1971: 526–8); Caccamo Caltabiano et al. (1995: 201–4); Bell (1995: 291–2); Mattingly (2000: 42–3); and, more recently, Frey-Kupper (2013: 156–9).

[32] On the size of this series, see Caccamo Caltabiano et al. (1995: 203, n. 38).

[33] Puglisi (2009: 330, nos. 337–8).

[34] Regarding the metrological relationship between these three types, see Carroccio (2004: 165), who classifies them as a litra (1), hemilitra (½), and tetras (¼), respectively.

[35] Puglisi (2004: 313–14; 2011: 193–4) focuses principally on the distribution of the Persephone/Bull IE coinage along with two bronze series struck early in Period II – the laureate Hieron/Horseman and large-flan Poseidon/Trident coinages – underscoring her argument by comparing the relative concentration of these coins in the northeastern portion of the island with that of later Hieronian bronzes, which enjoyed wider circulation around the island.

[36] For the date of the battle, see *supra* Chapter 1, pp. 28–31.

[37] *Supra* Chapter 2, pp. 50–1.

[38] On Hellenistic royal portrait coinage, generally, see Mørkholm (1991); Smith (1988: 9–14 and passim); and Kroll (2007).

[39] Thonemann (2015: 148–54).

[40] Hieron's portrait coins can be compared with those minted by Antiochos I (ca. 280–261; Houghton and Lorber, nos. 327–8), Ptolemy I (ca. 294–282; = Svoronos, nos. 365–6), or Ptolemy II (ca. 282 = Svoronos, nos. 548, 558–9). Aside from the uncharacteristic use of the laurel wreath, the significance of which was discussed in Chapter 2 (*supra* pp. 50), one notable peculiarity of Hieron's coinage is the king's left-facing portrait, a marked divergence from the standard right-facing portraiture issued by nearly all of his contemporaries. Thonemann (2015: 162) suggests the choice of the left-facing portrait reflected a long-held preference for left-facing portraits on Syracusan coinage.

[41] Rowan (2014: 78); von Reden (2001: 65). Also see Wynne-Jones and Fleisher (2012: 26) with consideration of coinage as symbolic of power in the context of medieval East Africa.

[42] On the use of bronze coinage for routine commercial transactions, see Marcellesi (2010); Crawford (1970) remains an important commentary on the subject.

[43] Mean weights for the Phase II large-denomination bronze coins taken from Wolf (2022: 130).

[44] Given the uncertainty involved in assigning ancient denominations to these bronze coins, I refrain from labeling them. Discussion of possible denominations can be found in Carroccio (2000: 161–6). And see Wolf (2022), who makes a compelling case that the Hieron/Horseman denominations were litra units and the Hieron/Biga coins were dilitra.

[45] Carroccio (2000: 263).

[46] The Polizzi Generosa hoard (*IGCH* 2229), discovered in 1957, is perhaps the most important published coin hoard for establishing a relative chronology of the Hieron/Horseman series. The contents of the hoard were initially published by Cutroni Tusa (1958–9: 312; 1960–1: 78–90), who dated its burial to the second quarter of the third century (ca. 250), associating its deposition with the general atmosphere of military conflict in western Sicily during the First Punic War. Among the contents of the hoard were at least forty-two Hieronian bronzes, including coins of the laureate Hieron/Horseman series and large-flan Poseidon/Trident series. Conspicuously absent were specimens of either the diadem Hieron/Horseman series and small-flan Poseidon/Trident series. Carroccio (2000), however, has called into question the value of the hoard for establishing the relative chronology of the two series, noting that a portion of its contents was removed in the time between its discovery and publication by Cutroni Tusa. Carroccio's valid skepticism about the Polizzi Generosa hoard is, however, somewhat diminished by the evidence from Morgantina, which supports both the precedence of the laureate series relative to the diadem portrait and a date for their introduction in the decade of the 260s; e.g., see Bell (1995); Walthall et al. (2018: 7–8); Walthall (2020a: 125–8). See also Carbé (2003) with additional evidence from Francavilla di Sicilia in the province of Messina.

[47] I have been able to find at least one pair of control marks – the ligature "AR" on the reverse type, matched with a cloth fillet on the obverse type – which was used for both laureate and diadem series dies. Examples illustrated in Buttrey et al. (1989: nos. 363c and 366a). The stylistic similarities exhibited by the portraits of both types (as well as that of the horseman on the reverse) may indicate that coins struck from these dies were issued around the point of transition between the two portrait types.

[48] This is the basic framework adopted by Buttrey et al. (1989: nos. 363, 365, 366) and echoed subsequently by Bell (1988: 327–31; 1995).

[49] One can find this viewpoint most fully elaborated in the work of Caccamo Caltabiano et al. (1995; 1997) and Carroccio (1993; 2000).

[50] This is the opinion expressed by Carroccio (2000: 264–5). Similarly, Mattingly (2000) suggests the diadem portrait coins were introduced in 227, the year in which the Romans first sent a governor to the western part of Sicily.

51 Compare, for instance, Bell (1995) and Carroccio (2000), representing the high and low camps, respectively.

52 Wolf (2022).

53 Wolf and Lorber (2011); cf. Jones (2020), who argues instead that these coins were struck by Hieron.

54 Wolf and Lorber (2011: 33–4) take Rome's entrance into the war between Hieron and the Mamertines as Ptolemy's cue to stop subsidies to Hieron. This is based on the notion that Ptolemy II and Rome had concluded a treaty of *amicitia* in 273, which Ptolemy did not wish to violate once Hieron became an enemy of Rome. Ancient sources for the treaty: Eutr. 2.15; Liv. *Per.* 14; Zonar. 8.6.11. For excellent analysis, see Westall (2011).

55 For Ptolemaic support of Pyrrhus, see Plut. (*Pyrrh.* 5.1); Hammond (1988); Adams (2008). The establishment of a Ptolemaic camp at Koronai in Attica occurred around this time, along with Ptolemaic subsidies sent to Sparta and Athens to fund the Chremonidean War (267–261). Vanderpool et al. (1962) publish the remains of the camp at Koronai.

56 Example of this comingling is a hoard of thirty bronze coins found at the bottom of a cistern at Morgantina in 1970, see Buttrey et al. (1989: cat. no. 61); Allen (1974: 362–6). Additional hoards with mixed Hieronian and Ptolemaic bronzes include *IGCH* 2029 (Campana, Calabria), *IGCH* 2242 (Montagna di Marzo, Sicily), and *IGCH* 2249 (Avola, Sicily). A minuscule number of silver coins of Ptolemy I and Ptolemy II have also turned up in Sicilian hoards, including *IGCH* 2232 (1 tetradrachm of Ptolemy II) and *IGCH* 2234 (1 tetradrachm of Ptolemy I and 1 tetradrachm of Ptolemy II).

57 Wolf and Lorber (2011: 47).

58 Wolf (2022: 115–17).

59 See Wolf (2013; 2017) where he identifies the ideal drachm unit of Ptolemy II's post-reform bronze as 68.5 grams and not the traditional figure of 72 grams.

60 One exception being the bronze ¼ drachm denomination struck during the reign of Ptolemy III by the Ptolemaic mint that operated on Cyprus; ex. Svoronos 1006. I thank Dan Wolf for this reference.

61 Poseidon/Trident coins of the large-flans series typically measure between 20–23 millimeters in diameter and have an average weight of 8.50 grams, while those of the small-flan variety were typically struck on flans measuring 18–20 millimeters in diameter and weighing 6.15 grams on average. Because these coins were presumably struck *al marco* and not *al pezzo*, that is to say with attention paid to the number of coins struck per batch and not to the weight of individual coins, there are examples of light large-flan coins with measurements approximating those typical of the small-flan series and vice versa. In such cases, the series of the coin can be distinguished by the manner in which the legend appears on the reverse type: on large-flan coins, the legend appears as ΙΕΡ-ΩΝΟΣ with the division in the name made by the vertical shaft of the trident, whereas the legend of the small-flan series appears as ΙΕΡΩ-ΝΟΣ, with the first four letters of the king's name written to the left of the trident's shaft.

62 For a recent summary of scholarship regarding the chronology of the large-flan Poseidon/ Trident series, see Frey-Kupper and Barrandon (2003: 518–19, esp. n. 23), who themselves support the higher chronology. A notable exception to the current consensus dating is Carroccio (2000: 264–5), who has argued on metrological grounds that the introduction of the large-flan series occurred only after 241 or 230.

63 It bears noting that Buttrey et al. (1989: 144–5) considered these smaller Persephone/Bull IE coins to be imitations of the larger, Syracusan variety on account of what they felt were stylistic traits that more closely resembled coinage issued by Tauromenion and Siculo-Punic mints than that of Syracuse. They suggest these were minted somewhere in the interior of the island in response to localize shortages of the larger Persephone/Bull IE coins. While the obverse and reverse types of these smaller coins are certainly rendered with less detail than their larger counterparts, the perceived differences in style might be attributed to any number of factors, such as differences in flan size or differences in the speed at which the

coins were produced, both of which might account for variation in appearance. In favor of their identification with the Hieronian mint, see Caccamo Caltabiano et al. (1995: 219ff.) and Mattingly (2000: 46).

[64] Averages are taken from those provided in Caccamo Calabiano et al. (1997).

[65] As with the preceding Philistis/Biga denomination, Caccamo Caltabiano et al. (1997: 189–200) identify two main reverse types used for the Gelon/Biga denomination, again with the principal distinction being whether the horses are depicted at full gallop (their nos. 239–70) or walking abreast (their nos. 271–84).

[66] Caccamo Caltabiano et al. (1997: 182–8) distinguish several distinct types used for these smaller Philistis/Biga denominations, most notably one group with the reverse type depicting the horses of the Nike-driven biga at full gallop (their nos. 220–7) and one group where the horses are standing or walking abreast (their nos. 228–38).

[67] Gelon's death in late 216 or early 215 marks the obvious *terminus post quem non* for the production of these portrait coins; cf. Caccamo Caltabiano et al. (1997: 49–53), who posit that Gelon's portrait types continued to be minted posthumously, and even beyond Hieron's own death, down to 214, based on shared control marks with the portrait coinage struck by Hieronymos.

[68] A handful of extant specimens belonging to this issue, as well as those of the following two issues listed here (nos. 9 and 10), reportedly have reverse types with the genitive ethnic ΣΥΡΑΚΟΣΙΩΝ. Given their rarity, Caccamo Caltabiano et al. (1997: 103) suggest these may represent errors made by die carvers that left the mint before the mistake was recognized and the dies could be reworked to read the standard ΣΥΡΑΚΟΣΙΟΙ form.

[69] Ierardi (1995–6: 39–49).

[70] Buttrey (1973: 6–12).

[71] E.g., Holloway (1962: 24).

[72] Buttrey et al. (1989: nos. 307 [Third Democracy], 341–2 [Hiketas]).

[73] An eagle stood as the acroterion on the temple at Megara Hyblaia, which has been dated to the period of Hieronian rule; see Vallet and Villard (1966: 26–7), who originally date the temple to the late fourth century; and see Wolf (2016: 83–4) with discussion of Hieronian date for the building.

[74] Just. *Epit.* 23.4.9–10; as noted by Holloway (1962: 25).

[75] The most complete presentation of the arguments can be found in Caccamo Caltabiano et al. (1997).

[76] Caccamo Caltabiano et al. (1997: 53–9).

[77] The earliest appearance of the title Βασίλισσα belongs to a series of silver didrachms struck by Queen Amastris (r. ca. 300–285) of Paphlagnoia; Mørkholm (1991: 96, nos. 279–80); *SNG BM*, no. 1297.

[78] Lorber (2018); Arnold-Biucchi (2002).

[79] Phillips (1960), for instance, posits that refined techniques for constructing tessellated mosaics first developed in the Hieronian court before ultimately spreading to larger cultural centers like Alexandria and Rome.

[80] Head (1874a: 66) was the first to note this similarity.

[81] More on this point *infra* pp. 272–4.

[82] The issue of "monetary policy" of the Seleucid kings is treated variously in Houghton (2004) and Bresson (2005); and see Manning (2008: 91–2) on what he describes as the economic policies of the early Ptolemaic kings. For a broad survey of scholarship on the topic of monetary policy in both Greek and Roman contexts, see von Reden (2002: 152–60).

[83] See recent discussion by Thonemann (2015: 111–15), who offers a balanced view of the decision-making that lie behind royal minting policy.

[84] See *supra* Chapter 1, n. 96 for details of the indemnity.

[85] Caccamo Caltabiano et al. (1995: 209–10).

[86] For the association of silver coinage (particularly tetradrachms) with the payment of mercenaries, especially following long campaigns, see de Callataÿ (2014: 65–72).

[87] For a summary of the various positions, see de Callataÿ (2014: 72–3). Psoma (2009) offers a detailed defense of the use of bronze to pay soldiers' *sitarchia*.

[88] Von Reden (2001: 70) comments on how the lack of local silver resources in Egypt shaped Ptolemaic minting policy.

[89] The literature regarding Ptolemaic monetary policy is vast; for recent work, see von Reden (2007), who associates the lighter silver standard of the Ptolemies with a desire to retain precious metal resources within Egypt.

[90] For example, Carroccio (2018) identified 306 obverse dies, 506 reverse dies, and 695 die pairs from a sample of approximately 2,200 small-flan Poseidon/Trident coins. In terms of the overall numbers of surviving specimens currently held in museums and collections, 2,200 represents only the tip of the iceberg, and we should expect that any future work by Carroccio or others in this vein will yield still larger die counts. While the efficacy of statistical methods that attempt to extrapolate the output of an ancient mint from the numbers of surviving dies remains a subject of debate, there appears to be a growing consensus among numismatists that die numbers can serve as a reasonable index of the magnitude of mint output, if not necessarily reliable for quantifying precise numbers. Estimates involving the "average" productivity of individual dies tend to focus on silver coinage. On the vexed issue of quantifying coin production, see de Callataÿ (2011), who offers a summary of scholarship and, ultimately, takes an optimistic stance on the issue.

[91] Lucchelli and Di Stefano (2004: 79–86).

[92] Lucchelli and Di Stefano (2004: 78–9) report ten coins of Agathokles, five coins of Hiketas, and two coins of Pyrrhus.

[93] Lucchelli and Di Stefano (2004: 41).

[94] See Buttrey et al. (1989: 133–4) for published totals from excavations 1955–82. The number of Hieronian coins found in excavations since 1982 brings the site-wide total closer to 3,000 coins.

[95] The pervasiveness of Hieron's coinage within the commercial sphere is a topic discussed in greater detail in Chapter 8; see *infra* pp. 320–4, where the archaeological evidence from Morgantina (esp. northern suite of Central Shops) supports the conclusion that Hieronian bronzes came to monopolize the commercial landscape by the 250s at the latest.

[96] See, e.g., *IGCH* 2242 (Montaga di Marzo 1929), *IGCH* 2227 (Pachino 1923), *IGCH* 2216 (Burgio 1902), *IGCH* 2241 (Barrafranca 1907–8), as well as a hoard found at Megara Hyblaia in 1967; Manganaro (2012: 32).

[97] From Selinunte, only 20 of the 1,054 coins published by Cutroni Tusa (1957; 1958–9; 1968) are Hieronian. Similarly, Frey-Kupper (2013: 408–11) counts only 76 Hieronian coins among the 1,425 coins she published from excavations at Iatas.

[98] Von Reden (2001: 65–6).

[99] Early scholars, including Hill (1903), identify the base unit of Hieron's dynastic series as the silver litra, equivalent to approximately 0.87 gram of silver. Recent reevaluation of the dynastic series by Caccamo Caltabiano et al. (1997: 123–30) has led to the suggestion that these denominations were instead based on a reduced silver litra of ~0.28 gram. The latter suggestion has not found widespread acceptance among scholars, although further study of the smaller, fractional silver denominations struck around this time may shed new light on the subject. For the purposes of this discussion, I will proceed with the understanding that the base unit of Hieron's Period III silver coinage was a litra of roughly 0.87 gram.

[100] On the introduction of the silver litra, see Parise (1979); Clain-Stefanelli (1987); and Manganaro (1999b).

[101] Hill (1903: 188).

[102] For the weight of the Ptolemaic silver tetradrachm in the third century BCE, see Wolf (2017: 541).

[103] Giesecke (1923: 120–6); cf. Hill (1903: 188–9), who had already rejected this idea. For the possible points of interaction between Hieron's chosen monetary standards and Rome's minting policy, see Caccamo Caltabiano et al. (1997: 121–33).

[104] De Sensi Sestito (1977: 163–4).

[105] Carroccio (2004: 139–45) notes points of metrological correspondence with the Attic-Euboic standard, Corcyran standard, reduced Aeginetan standard, Corinthian standard, Ptolemaic standard, and even the Roman quadrigatus series; reiterated in Carroccio (2013: 62–3, n. 11).

[106] Mixed hoards containing Hieronian and Roman coins are certainly represented in the archaeological record (e.g., *IGCH* 2231, *IGCH* 2241, *IGCH* 2242), but it is important to note that the introduction of the denarius system, even by the most generous estimate, did not occur until *after* Hieron's death in 215; see Walthall (2017: 110–11, n. 25) for discussion and bibliography. Thus, evidence for the joint circulation of Hieronian and Roman silver coinage, documented by mixed hoards buried around the time of Marcellus's siege of Syracuse (213–212), confirms only that such intermingling occurred *after* the collapse of the Hieronian dynasty. If anything, it points to agency on the part of the Romans to coordinate their own monetary standards with those coinages already widely circulating on Sicily.

[107] Previously noted by Arnold-Biucchi (2002), who points out that only two published hoards from Sicily contain Ptolemaic silver alongside Hieronian issues; these are *IGCH* 2232 (the Enna Hoard) and *IGCH* 2233 (the Syracuse 1904 Hoard), which contain a combined total of three Ptolemaic coins. The long-held view that Ptolemaic bronze coinage freely circulated within the kingdom on account of beneficial trade relations between the two kingdoms, as advanced by Manganaro (1989), has been undermined by the work of Wolf and Lorber (2011).

[108] For recent work on the early Ptolemaic coinage reforms, see Lorber (2012a; 2012b: 211–16; 2018); Wolf (2017).

[109] Von Reden (2007: 46–8).

[110] *P. Cair. Zen.* I 59021. For translation and discussion, see Bagnall and Derow (2004: 163–4, no. 102); Le Rider (1986: 49–51); Richter (1992: 177–86); and recent contribution by Panagopoulou (2016).

[111] Again, von Reden (2007: 43–8), who documents the gradual withdrawal of foreign silver coins (typically those of heavier Attic-weight denominations) from circulation in Egypt, as viewed from the evidence of hoards. In many respects, this parallels the situation on the ground in the Hieronian kingdom, where we find limited evidence for the circulation of foreign coins.

[112] Outside Egypt, the circulation of Ptolemaic coins was largely restricted to those areas under Ptolemaic control; Bagnall (1976); cf. Konuk (2004), who notes the increasing number of Ptolemaic bronze and silver coins being reported and published from areas once part of Caria and Cilicia, portions of modern Turkey that for several generations were fiercely contested by the Ptolemies and Seleucids. The coinage of Ptolemy II does turn up with some frequency at sites around Attica; it is typically associated with the king's financial and military support of Athens, Sparta, and their allies during the Chremonidean War; see, e.g., Lagos (1996).

[113] The small quantities of foreign silver coinage that do turn up in hoards around eastern Sicily reveal more about limits to the enforcement of royal policies regarding coinage than undermine the hypothesis that Hieron did enforce some form of exchange between foreign currency and his own monetary units.

[114] The concept is sometimes referred to as the "*lex Seyrig*," a term coined with reference to the work of the French archaeologist Henri Seyrig, whose study of the mint of Aradus proved most influential in advancing the idea that Greek *poleis* lost the right to mint coinage when they came under the control of a Hellenistic monarch; Seyrig (1951: 206–20). The notion that the right to strike civic coinage was lost with the diminished autonomy that followed a

city's subjugation to a king can be found explicitly articulated by Tarn (1913: 197) in his study of Antigonos Gonatas.

[115] De Sensi Sestito (1977: 130); followed by Bell (1993).

[116] Berve (1959: 37).

[117] The continued operation of Tauromenion's mint throughout the reign of Hieron was often considered something of an exception that proved the rule of his royal intervention in the operation of civic mint; see De Sensi Sestito (1977: 130); Bell (2007a: 195, n. 35). Berve (1959: 37), on the other hand, counted this among the reasons for excluding Tauromenion from among the member states of Hieron's kingdom.

[118] Carbè (1995).

[119] The overall absence of these coins was confirmed by cross-referencing their types against the "Catalogue of Stratigraphically Related Coins" listed in Buttrey et al. (1989: 156–99). Furthering Carbè's observations that the production of the Apollo/Butting Bull series at Tauromenion should be dated *after* 215 is the fact that only one example of the ninety-two recorded specimens of this series (Buttrey et al. 1989: nos. 411–12) found at Morgantina was recovered from a context considered to predate the Roman siege of Morgantina in 211; for this coin, see Buttrey et al. (1989: 167, Deposit 33). This would suggest that these coins had only just entered circulation shortly before the time of the siege. Furthermore, as Buttrey et al. note, a published specimen of the Apollo/Butting Bull coinage in the Hunterian Collection (Macdonald 1899: I, 256, no. 18) that was overstruck on a Poseidon/Trident of Hieron II offers strong indication that these coins must not have entered circulation until after Hieron's death, since one would not expect to see an overstrike over the king's legal currency.

[120] For instance, the Herakles/Athena Alkidemos bronze series (*SNG ANS*, nos. 845–6) struck at Syracuse during Pyrrhus' time in Sicily bore iconography associated with the royal Epirote line alongside the legend ΣΥΡΑΚΟΣΙΩΝ.

[121] This had begun even earlier with the gold and silver denominations struck during Hieron's tenure as *stratēgos autokrator* (Period I).

[122] For coin types associated with the period of the Fifth Syracusan Democracy, see Puglisi (2009: 332–3).

[123] See, in particular, De Sensi Sestito (1977: 128–9) and Holloway (1962: 17–27).

[124] Regarding the metrological relationships between the silver denominations, see Carroccio (2013).

[125] For these issues, see Puglisi (2009: 281–2, 332–5, 338–9).

[126] Puglisi (2009: 238–9, 267, 285–6); And for a recent assessment of the coinage of Akrai, see Więcek (2018).

[127] Martin (1985).

[128] Taking up the example of third-century Athens under Antigonos Gonatas, see Oliver (2001); and see Meadows (2001), citing multiple examples.

[129] Price (1991: 76–9) proposes a similar phenomenon occurred during the lifetime of Alexander III, whose precious metal coinage became so ubiquitous that many local mints around the Aegean region ceased to produce civic issues in silver and gold. Only following Alexander's death did civic mints resume their production of silver coins (notably in the form of posthumous Alexanders types), which Price interprets as a response to a need for more coinage.

[130] Stannard (2018: 138–40) discusses evidence for the continued use of similarly "residual" coins as a partial remedy to what he sees as severe shortages of small-denomination bronze coinage in the area of central Italy during the second century BCE.

[131] For site finds from Morgantina, see Buttrey et al. (1989: nos. 367–8); Walthall (2017: 111–14). And from Kamarina, see Lucchelli and Di Stefano (2004: 82–6).

[132] Kroll (2011) reconstructs evidence for one such mass recall of Athenian silver coinage around the middle of the fourth century.

[133] More often, the practice of mutilating coins was one applied in circumstances of destroying false or counterfeit specimens, as documented in Classical Athens, where, by mandate of

Nikophon's Law on Silver Coinage (375/4), market attendants (*agoranomoi*) were instructed to confiscate and physically mutilate any false or counterfeit coins found circulating in the city's market places; Stroud (1974), and see Martin (1991) with illustrated examples of mutilated coins.

[134]   Of the ca. 527 known specimens from Morgantina, nearly all were cut along the vertical shaft of the trident on the reverse type. Autopsy of the coins from Morgantina suggests fewer than 1 percent were cut from the obverse side, or without care to follow the line of the trident shaft.

[135]   This is roughly 51 percent of the large-flan series coins from the site, and approximately 14 percent of the small-flan series. See Bell (1988) for arguments related to the proportion of halved large-flan to small-flan coins.

[136]   Lucchelli and Di Stefano (2004: 82–6) list 70 examples (29 of the large-flan type and 41 of the small-flan type) recovered during excavations in the agora at Kamarina.

[137]   That the coins continued to circulate for long periods after fragmentation is evident from the wear patterns along the cut edge of many of the coins. Fractioning produced sharp edges along the axis of the trident that, over time, would be dulled by circulation. Different degrees of wear can be readily observed on the cut edges of halved coins, indicating that they continued to circulate long after fractioning; see, e.g., Walthall (2017: 112, fig. 8).

[138]   For halved coins in commercial contexts at Morgantina, see Bell (1993); Walthall (2017: 111–20); and Chapter 8, with additional discussion.

[139]   Walthall (2020a: 123–5).

[140]   The most thorough discussion of this phenomenon, to date, is laid out in a pair of articles by Holloway (1960) and Bell (1988). These scholars agree that the halved coins continued to circulate as valid currency, but they offer differing explanations for the motivation behind the fractioning of these coins; for a more recent treatment, see Walthall (2017).

[141]   Roman overstrikes on Hieronian bronze are a well-documented phenomenon: see Hersch (1953: 41–3); Crawford (1974: 107–14).

[142]   Holloway's low dating has been echoed in the scholarship of Carroccio (2000; 2004).

[143]   Bell (1988) was the first to present archaeological evidence in support of a pre-250 date for the halving of these coins, drawing attention to specimens found within primary contexts in the agora at Morgantina. Now, see Walthall (2017: 111–15) and, more importantly, Gandolfo (1997: 323, nos. 67–8), who publishes examples from Montagna dei Cavalli (ancient Hippana) discovered in contexts predating 258. For the identification of Montagna dei Cavalli as ancient Hippana, see Vassallo (1988–9: 313). According to Polybius (1.24.10–11), the city was besieged and captured by the Romans in 258; see also Diodorus (23.9.5). Vassallo (1997: 304) discusses the sealed destruction contexts from which the halved coins were recovered, attributing the destruction to the events described by Diodorus. Caminneci and Di Carlo (2017) publish a halved large-flan Poseidon/Trident recovered in their recent excavations at Monte Adranone (Sambuca di Sicilia). The coin was found among grave goods in one rock-cut tomb in the city's South Gate Necropolis. Archaeologists working at Monte Adranone discovered extensive evidence of violent destruction sometime in the first half of the third century BCE. This has been associated with the capture of the site by Roman forces during the First Punic War, as mentioned by Diodorus (23.4.2); see additionally Fiorentini (1995) and Di Noto (1992).

[144]   For general introduction and discussion of the practice, see Metcalf (1998) and Rampling (2011).

[145]   Metcalf (1998: 79).

[146]   See discussion by Rampling (2011).

[147]   Bell (1988: 340–2) first proposes the possibility that the halved coins filled a need for smaller change; cf. Mattingly (2000: 45–6), who agrees with Bell that the Poseidon/Trident coins were halved to meet demand for smaller denominations, but prefers an initial date for the halving of large-flan Poseidon/Trident coins between 242 and 227. That the practice of fractioning was largely restricted to the Poseidon/Trident issues and not the larger Hieron/

Horseman coins makes sense from a pragmatic perspective, as the portrait coins were twice the value of the Poseidon/Trident coins. Halving the Hieron/Horseman coins would only create denominations equal to that of the Poseidon/Trident, which were certainly not in short supply. We might also entertain the idea that there was a proscription against defacing the king's portrait, although there survives no indication of such a mandate.

[148] The availability of smaller denominations increases opportunities for commercial transaction in both number (more instances of one-on-one exchange) and type (potential buyers can purchase goods in smaller amounts from sellers, rather than waiting to purchase a larger amount with a larger coin), and as a result leads to a greater frequency of commercial transaction by opening up exchange to smaller transactions. For the presence of halved bronze coins in the Athenian agora, see Kroll (1993: 92–3), who takes the position that halving was an unofficial means (due to small percentage of total coin finds, less than 2%) of meeting a demand for half-unit fractions.

[149] Buttrey et al. (1989: nos. 360 and 367).

[150] This may simply be due to the lack of comprehensive publication of numismatic finds from excavations, rather than a true reflection of their general absence from the city. For a summary of numismatic finds from published excavations at Syracuse, see Puglisi (2009: 131–2). Gentili (1954) reports the discovery of roughly thirty Poseidon/Trident coins (all intact), recovered from small votive deposits made in the vicinity of the Great Altar at Syracuse.

[151] With respect to minting, seigniorage is the difference between the face value of a coin and the cost required to produce and place it in circulation. Concerning the low return from minting small denominations, see Bransbourg (2011: 101–2); Stahl (2000: 174–5). With respect to medieval mints, Sargent and Velde (2002: 50–3) note that "[p]er unit of value, the production process made small coins more expensive to produce than larger one, since the same effort was required to strike a coin of any size, and not much less to prepare smaller blanks than larger blanks." For a modern analogy, the US Mint reported that in 2020 the unit cost of producing and distributing a penny and nickel was 1.7¢ and 7.4¢, respectively, while that of quarter and dime was 8.6¢ and 3.3¢, respectively. The US federal government currently loses money with every penny placed into circulation, while the seigniorage it ostensibly gains from every quarter-dollar placed into circulation is 16.4¢.

[152] Von Reden (2007: 301).

EIGHT

INSTITUTIONS AND MARKETS IN HIERONIAN SICILY

Throughout history, institutions have been devised by human beings to create order and reduce uncertainty in exchange. Together with the standard constraints of economics they define the choice set and therefore determine transaction and production costs and hence the profitability and feasibility of engaging in economic activity.... Institutions provide the incentive structure of an economy ...

—Douglass North (1991: 97)

In the quarter century that transpired between Agathokles' death in 289 and the conclusion of Hieron's treaty with the Romans in 263, political conflict and near-constant warfare brought about untold devastation to many communities of eastern Sicily. The damage was not contained to urban centers alone. Violence spilled out into the peripheral territories and rural communities, disrupting the rhythms of agrarian life and robbing the countryside of its agricultural potential. Productive landscapes once celebrated for their fecundity and storied abundance were stifled underfoot by marching armies.

Although ancient authors tend to highlight the destruction suffered by urban centers, the violence inflicted on the countryside by military conflict does not go wholly unaccounted for in surviving accounts of the period. Diodorus, for instance, charged both the armies of Hiketas and Phintias with plundering rural estates and laying waste to the farmland that lay between Syracuse and Gela in the Hyblaean hills.[1] The territory of Syracuse itself suffered multiple invasions. In 279/8, a Carthaginian army had occupied the city's *chora* for several months, laying waste to agricultural land and nearly capturing the city before being turned back by Pyrrhus and his soldiers.[2] And, again, in 264/3 Roman soldiers under the command of Appius Claudius reportedly devastated the *chora* of the Syracusans and their allies.[3] For all the attention paid to the Mamertine assaults on the urban settlements of Gela and Kamarina, much of the lasting devastation they wrought was directed toward laying waste to farmland and pillaging in the territories of these two cities rather than direct attempts on the urban centers themselves.[4]

Unsurprisingly, this quarter-century of nearly perennial violence inflicted on the landscape of eastern Sicily has left an indelible mark in the archaeological record. One of the most compelling illustrations of an agrarian landscape in decline has emerged from the Gela Survey, a multiyear intensive survey led by Johannes Bergemann that investigated a roughly 200-square-kilometer area in the western hinterland of Gela's *chora*.[5] There, archaeologists registered a rise in the number of sites in the territory over the late Classical period, reaching a maximum density of 171 sites in the late fourth and early third century.[6] This was followed by a swift and precipitous decline in identifiable sites, down to just thirty-six, a consequence Bergemann himself attributes to the sustained violence of the early third century, beginning with the incursions made on the city and its territory by the Mamertines and the subsequent relocation of Gela's population by Phintias in 282.[7]

Complementing this picture of disruptions to wider settlement patterns presented by the Gela Survey, archaeologists have identified several rural sites in eastern Sicily that exhibit signs of abandonment or destruction in this period. The remains of a small agrarian village at Scornavacche, located in the *chora* of Kamarina on a small bluff above the Dirillo river, vividly attest to the tumultuous situation in the countryside. Here, archaeologists discovered evidence that the settlement was abandoned as a result of what they describe as a sudden and violent event early in the third century.[8] A similar fate may have befallen the ancient settlement that lies beneath the modern town of Francavilla di Sicilia. The archaeological evidence recovered at several points around the settlement – plausibly identified by its excavators as Kallipolis, a small village in the hinterland of Tauromenion – is indicative of abandonment in the first half of the third century.[9] The settlement at Francavilla lay in a portion of the island heavily contested by Hieron and the Mamertines. Its abandonment may very well have been a consequence of the ongoing conflict in the 270s and 260s as both sides fought to exert control over the area. Smaller settlements, like those at Gagliano Castelferrato in the foothills of the Nebrodi and Contrada Casalrosato near Valverde, southeast of Etna, offer further evidence for the disruptions in the countryside brought about by years of warfare.[10] We can be certain that for every instance of abandonment or destruction attested by ancient literary sources or in the archaeological record, there were myriad others that suffered as soldiers on the march disrupted the cadence of life in the countryside, forcing fields to lie fallow and crops to be left unharvested.

Among the most vivid accounts of the damage inflicted on the productive landscapes of eastern Sicily is to be found in the 16th *Idyll* of Theokritos. As we recall from Chapter 2, the poet calls on Hieron to drive the Carthaginian army out of Sicily, thereby restoring peace and prosperity to the island. Theokritos transports us to an agrarian world uprooted by a generation of conflict, one in which the cycles of the agricultural calendar have been ruptured by warfare, yet in lines 88–97, he conjures the hopeful vision of the future:

> May the cities which enemy hands have cruelly razed
> Be once again peopled by their former inhabitants.
> May rich harvests repay their toil, and may sheep in their
> Countless thousands fatten in pastures, bleating across
> The plain; and may herds of cattle as they wander back
> To their folds quicken the evening traveler's steps.
> May fallow land be ploughed again, ready for seed-time,
> At the season when the cicada, keeping watch over shepherds
> In the noonday sun, sings loudly high up in the tree branches.
> May their armor be covered with spiders' fine-spun webs, and
> Even the name of the battle-cry be forgotten.[11]

With this invocation, the poet captures both the toll that incessant violence had wrought on eastern Sicily and the latent potential of island's fertile landscapes, which have suffered under prolonged devastation. Fields now lie fallow and crops go unharvested; the low bleating of sheep no longer carries across the plain, their tremulous cries replaced by those of soldiers. This was the situation in 275 when he composed his idyll for Hieron. Theokritos, of course, did not remain in Sicily long enough to see an end to military conflict, nor to witness the revitalization that he had predicted would follow an end to war. Peace would return to eastern Sicily, and recovery was swift to follow.

The conclusion of Hieron's treaty with Rome in 263 marked the beginning of a nearly half-century-long period of sustained peace and prosperity for the *poleis* of southeastern Sicily. In establishing the political boundaries of the Hieronian kingdom, the treaty provided a largely inviolate barrier against the military violence that would continue to devastate much of western Sicily throughout the long decades of the First Punic War. For the communities under Hieron's political protection, this long-desired peace meant a return to the countryside free from threat of violence, and with it a return to agricultural productivity.

The lasting peace that followed on the conclusion of Hieron's treaty with Rome has long been recognized as an essential ingredient behind the cultural and economic renaissance that took place in eastern Sicily during the decades of Hieronian rule. Roger Wilson lays out the stark difference between the situation of the cities of Hieron's kingdom and those of the central and western portions of the island, which remained a battleground for another quarter century:

> By contrast with the comparative stability and wealth of eastern Sicily, there is little in the way of major public building which can be dated with certainly to the third century in central or western Sicily, or any hint that this part of the island shared the same prosperity as that enjoyed in Hieron's kingdom. That is not surprising. It is difficult to assess the precise impact that fighting had on the physical fabric and the economy of this western part of the province in the course of two bloody Punic wars, but the hints that we have from the sources, to which can be added an increasing body of archaeological evidence, suggest it was not inconsiderable.[12]

That prosperity followed from peace is itself not an especially novel thesis. This very concept even found clear material expression in contemporary works of art by Sicilian craftsmen.[13] One thinks of the ornate gilt-silver pyxis on which the goddess Eirene (Peace) is depicted holding the baby Ploutos (Wealth) and a cornucopia brimming over with proceeds of the harvest (Figure 8.1).[14] The vessel, which was found at Morgantina but likely manufactured in Syracuse during the height of Hieronian rule, bears contemporary witness – in its literal materiality as well as in its allegorical decoration – to the promise of abundance and wealth that was born of and nurtured by peace. What has yet to receive full consideration, however, are the ways in which the genesis of the Hieronian kingdom, particularly from the standpoint of its political demarcation following the treaty of 263, helped create the conditions for peace and prosperity in the region.

As the de facto capital of Hieron's kingdom, Syracuse would regain its status as one of the premier artistic and intellectual centers of the Mediterranean. The city itself was transformed by the completion of new building projects, much of which was fueled by royal investment. Syracuse was not alone in undergoing a radical transformation to its urban fabric. Most, if not all, of the cities in the kingdom saw a spate of new building and investment in urban infrastructure, some of which we might trace back to royal benefaction and some of which was surely due to the benefaction of local elites, who saw their wealth rebound with that of the countryside.

Peace – although a necessary precondition – was alone not a sufficient catalyst in bringing about the great economic prosperity enjoyed by the *poleis* of the Hieronian kingdom. Eirene, it seems, had some help in the matter and from a rather mundane, and often maligned, source no less: taxation. Here, I suggest that the expansion and amplification of royal authority over eastern Sicily played an important, and even indispensable, role in revitalizing the region's agricultural economy. In particular, it was the administrative systems put in place to facilitate the extraction of agricultural taxes from the

8.1 Gilt silver pyxis lid with seated woman (Eirene?) holding a cornucopia and child (Ploutos?). Buried at Morgantina in 211 BCE (Museo Archeologico Regionale di Aidone, inv. 1982.11.11; courtesy of the American Excavations at Morgantina).

communities subject to Hieronian authority that created the conditions for greater economic integration throughout the region and, ultimately, expanded opportunities to profit from agricultural production.

While Hieron's rule ushered in much-welcomed security for many communities of eastern Sicily, it also introduced novel limitations to civic autonomy, none of these arguably more consequential than the regular collection of an agricultural tithe. Hieron's tax law, along with its attendant administrative machinery, constituted a powerful institution, the likes of which had never before been seen in Sicily. By design, this system of royal taxation served to entangle individuals and cities with the king and his royal agents through the routine collection of planting and harvest data from around the kingdom, through the enforcement and use of state-sanctioned coinage and measuring devices and through the tax-farming system that encouraged participation at a local level from profit-seeking elites. The natural, if unintended, outcome of these new administrative structures was the overall expansion of economic activity, as trade networks between agriculturally productive inland centers and coastal markets intensified and as commercial exchange was facilitated by the promotion of a common currency and shared metrological standards.

INSTITUTIONS AND MARKETS IN HIERONIAN SICILY

Throughout the remainder of the chapter, I highlight some of the ways in which manifestations of royal authority over the cities of southeastern Sicily may have fostered agricultural production, trade, and exchange within the kingdom. To do so, I borrow heavily from the field of new institutional economics (NIE) and, in particular, the scholarship of Douglass North, whose work on transaction costs and the role played by institutions in shaping economic activity has been immensely influential for the study of the ancient economy.[15] One of the basic tenets of the NIE school of thought – and which holds greatest relevance to the present discussion – modifies the neoclassical model of the rational economic actor by demonstrating that economic behavior is (and was) shaped by cultural, societal, and legal structures. North elucidates how institutions, or what he has referred to as the "rules of the game in society," come to define economic activity:

> Institutions are the humanly devised constraints that structure political, economic and social interaction. They consist of both informal constraints (sanctions, taboos, customs, traditions, and codes of conduct), and formal rules (constitutions, laws, property rights). Throughout history, institutions have been devised by human beings to create order and reduce uncertainty in exchange. Together with the standard constraints of economics they define the choice set and therefore determine transaction and production costs and hence the profitability and feasibility of engaging in economic activity.... Institutions provide the incentive structure of an economy; as that structure evolves, it shapes the direction of economic change towards growth, stagnation, or decline.[16]

The emphasis on the role of institutions in shaping economic behavior has found many advocates wishing to better understand the structure and performance of ancient Mediterranean economies.[17] NIE has become so influential, in fact, that it has recently been described as the "default paradigm" in scholarship dealing with economies of ancient Greece and Rome.[18] Any survey of recent scholarship on the ancient economy of the past 15 years will largely confirm this assertion.[19] The application of an NIE framework has been most consistently employed in the study of the ancient Roman economy, for which we benefit from a comparative wealth of documentary evidence. There

is, however, a growing body of scholarship in which the economic performance of Hellenistic kingdoms as well as that of earlier Greek states is viewed
through the lens of new institutionalism.[20]

For North, institutions play a fundamental role in shaping economic behavior – and, by extension, the performance of an economy at large – inasmuch as
they governed transaction costs underlying the process of exchange. Broadly
conceived, transaction costs can be considered barriers that prevent individuals
from full engagement with market exchange and other economic activities.[21]
Often these are abbreviated as barriers resulting from incomplete or asymmet-
rical access to the types of information desired by individuals involved in
exchange. North himself explains, "The costliness of information is the key
to the costs of transacting, which consist of the costs of measuring the valuable
attributes of what is being exchanged and the cost of protecting rights and
policing and enforcing agreements. These measurement and enforcement costs
are the sources of social, political, and economic institutions."[22]

At the level of the individual actor, we tend to think of the ancient
marketplace as being rife with incomplete and asymmetric access to various
types of information. An individual interested in buying a quantity of wine, for
instance, might face a number of uncertainties simply related to gaining
requisite information regarding the valuable attributes – both qualitative and
quantitative – of the product in question, which would ultimately inform
whether or not the transaction takes place. Here, institutions can help. Social
convention may dictate that the seller should allow the prospective buyer to
sample the wine beforehand, so as to remove any doubts about its quality. This
would have the effect of creating a degree of transparency between seller and
buyer, but we are not yet out of the woods because still ahead lie questions
about the size of the seller's measuring vessel (it may look a little small), the
fineness of the buyer's silver coin (it may look a little dull), and the likelihood
that either party will be punished if they violate the contract of the sale (what is
to prevent one party from deceiving the other?). The state can play a role in
lowering some of these transaction costs by, among other things, establishing
and enforcing the use of standardized measures and a single state-sanctioned
coinage, as well as by empowering market officials to monitor activity and
justly sanction violations of prescribed laws governing marketplace exchange.

When transaction costs are low, more business can be done; but, as the costs
of exchange increase, we expect a corresponding decline in economic activity.
This is true at the individual scale, as well as for the economy as a whole. When
viewed from a more global perspective, transaction costs mount up to the
point where they shape the contours of regional production and trade.
Regarding the impact that asymmetry of information will have on the performance of markets, Peter Bang writes that "imperfections, irregularities and
asymmetries in trading conditions enhance friction and hence transaction costs,

the costs of conducting business. When these are high, it will often be either be very difficult, even outright impossible, or at least prohibitively expensive to synchronize developments in markets more closely."[23] Various strategies were developed by ancient merchants and states alike to reduce these asymmetries.[24]

A key concern in many applications of NIE principles for the study of the ancient economy is the state's role in shaping the institutions that in turn determined the costs of doing business. North himself addressed this question with respect to premodern states with a single ruler.[25] While not all elements of North's approach ring true for the ancient Mediterranean, his definition of a state as "an organization with a comparative advantage in violence, extending over a geographic area" certainly describes the forms of autocratic rule manifested by both Hellenistic monarchs and Roman emperors.[26] Thanks to their comparative advantage in violence, states have a hand in establishing and enforcing the formal rules of the game, trading protection or the threat of potential violence in return for revenue from its constituents.[27] Ancient and premodern states are often described as "predatory," a classification North considers to be true of states that come into existence as "the agency of a group or class; its function, to extract income from the rest of the constituents in the interest of that group or class. The predatory state would specify a set of property rights that maximized the revenue of the group in power, regardless of its impact on the wealth of the society as a whole."[28] For a profit-maximizing ruler like a Hellenistic monarch, setting the "rules of the game" to benefit themselves was de rigueur. But this certainly did not preclude the potential for economic benefits to be shared more broadly, since as North notes, "Almost any set of rules is better than none," even when those rules are exploitative.[29]

Here then, we see that the very formation of a state (even a predatory state) can bring about conditions that – in effect, although not necessarily by design – foster exchange and economic activity.[30] Remarking on the conditions created by the political unification of the Mediterranean under Roman rule during the early Empire, Elio Lo Cascio contended:

> The creation of more peaceful and safer conditions ... the diffusion of a "technology of measurement" and of common metrological systems, and above all the creation of a unitary monetary area and of common legal rules are all quite remarkable contributing factors in the reduction of transaction costs, in so far as they reduced uncertainty and determined the availability of more information to the transacting parties.[31]

In highlighting the economic transformation that followed from the lowering of transaction costs across the Roman empire, Lo Cascio just as well might have been describing outcomes that followed the consolidation of Hieronian rule in southeastern Sicily, which, as we have seen, brought about a comparable trifecta of lasting peace, the creation of a single monetary zone, and the widespread dissemination of common metrological systems.

While designed with the ruler's financial interests in mind, Hieron's tax administration was ultimately a stimulus for economic exchange in that it lowered transaction costs associated with routine commercial exchange and facilitated market integration among the tithe-paying *poleis* of eastern Sicily. The state's desire to more efficiently extract resources through taxation led to the adoption of an administrative infrastructure designed to swiftly move goods and information throughout the Hieronian kingdom. While from the vantage point of the state, administrative decision-making was devised to facilitate the extraction of resources from the agriculturally productive areas of the kingdom, the resulting institutional structure had the added effect of linking grain-producing communities in the interior to the island's largest urban market at Syracuse and, ultimately, to international markets around the Mediterranean that were served by merchants and traders intending to bring back cheap grain from Sicily.

Although it is admittedly speculative, I think we can see this play out in two ways. First, the state's role in promoting (or enforcing) the use of a common coinage and common metrological standards among the cities of eastern Sicily would have lowered transaction costs for constituents involved in routine commercial exchange, especially those costs stemming from incomplete access to information. In other words, it became easier – if only marginally so – for individuals to exchange goods and coins within the political boundaries of the Hieronian kingdom. Second, Hieron's efforts to sell tithe grain and other agricultural resources on the market created incentives for constituents to engage in market exchange by selling their agricultural surplus.

Shared Standards and Lowered Costs

The picture that emerged from the discussion of Chapter 5 was one in which volumetric measures of the Hieronian system were thoroughly integrated across the region, turning up in large numbers in commercial and domestic contexts. Standardization came with attendant economic benefits, as the use of common units of measure lowered transaction costs involved in routine commercial interactions by reducing asymmetries of information between buyer and seller.[32] Cultivators who traveled to an urban center to purchase or sell goods at market might be more inclined to do so if they recognized the units of measure used by a merchant. Uniformity of measuring instruments does not eliminate all asymmetries of information; it does not, for instance, solve for uncertainties about the quality of goods being sold. Common standards, however, do certainly create a more level playing field between buyers and sellers, one that would have undoubtedly lowered the cost of commercial transactions to occur across the Hieronian kingdom with greater ease than had previously been enjoyed in the absence of the Hieronian state.

In the previous chapter, we encountered ample evidence to suggest that a vast quantity of bronze coinage was placed in circulation by the royal mint at Syracuse between 269 and 215. This was registered at sites like Kamarina and Morgantina, where coin finds from commercial areas show a considerable uptick of Hieronian coinage. Alongside efforts to promote a common set of volumetric standards, the widespread availability of bronze coinage struck by the royal mint at Syracuse – whether motivated by policy or preference – would have also fostered greater economic integration among the communities of eastern Sicily, as Hieron's bronze coinage became a common medium of exchange.

The value of a unified monetary zone with respect to trade and exchange has again been effectively summarized by Elio Lo Cascio, who, writing of Roman monetary policy during the Principate, adjudges that

> The creation of a single monetary area may have contributed most to the reduction in transactions costs: a centrally produced coinage circulated almost everywhere, and locally issued coins (chiefly small bronze denominations) were linked to the mainstream coinage by a common system of fixed rates of exchange. Moreover, it was a serious offense, indeed a crime, to refuse to accept current coins which carried the *vultus* of the emperor and were not counterfeit. Again, the enforcement of the legal value of the coins can be viewed as instrumental in reducing transaction costs. High levels of coin output and circulation from Augustus to the third century seem to have been instrumental in facilitating safe and smooth exchanges of goods at local, regional, and interregional level.[33]

The same features of the monetary landscape that helped to lower transaction costs during the early Empire (i.e., high levels of production, widespread circulation, the king's portrait used as marker of state-sanctioned value) were also to be found in the highly monetized landscape of eastern Sicily during the reign of Hieron II.

Incentives for Engagement

Beyond establishing the conditions for the formation of a metrological *koine* within the political sphere of the Hieronian kingdom, the wealth-maximizing interests of the king may have helped to bring about conditions that were further conducive to economic growth by incentivizing cultivators to engage in the sale of their agricultural surplus. Here, again, it bears reiterating that we proceed into the realm of the speculative. At the outset, it is possible that Hieron's efforts to profit from the sale of his tithe grain generated greater international demand for Sicilian grain and raised Syracuse's profile as a major

Mediterranean port for purchase of grain during the third century BCE.[34] The increased demand for Sicilian grain was met when Sicilian communities on the island's interior sold agricultural surplus to agents operating between the interior and coast. This piggybacking of trade on top of the existing tithe infrastructure led to increased wealth for a portion of the population.

Engagement with the market would have looked different for different segments of society. Broadly defined, we might divide these into three groups: the king; wealthy, large-scale landowners; and small-scale cultivators, whether tenant farmers or landowners in their own right. At the top, Hieron stood to profit immensely from offloading the proceeds of the annual tithe on the commercial market.[35] As highlighted in Chapter 6, grain sales constituted a principal avenue by which Hellenistic kings converted their agricultural wealth, generated from in-kind taxation, into all-important cash reserves.

All things considered, it was not difficult to generate demand for grain, which constituted the chief source of nutritional calories for most of the Mediterranean's population. Coupled with an unevenness of productivity across the Mediterranean, one had a recipe for constant demand on a region-wide scale. As Keith Hopkins put it, "sharp inter-annual fluctuations of rainfall created local gluts and local shortages and stimulated unpredictable flows of surplus staples to unpredictable markets."[36] Such regional instability meant that on a Mediterranean-wide scale, the demand for grain was constant and inelastic. Localized supply shortages due to crop failure or poor harvests further served to drive the development of markets and trans-Mediterranean trade networks, which by the third century were relatively well developed.[37]

From the perspective of a supplier on the international market, Hieron certainly enjoyed a privileged position. For starters, he ruled over one of the most consistently fertile pockets of the Mediterranean.[38] Moreover, he was guaranteed to reap the annual proceeds of the tithe. Even in years of poor harvests, unexpected downturns in productivity would be offset by the payments made from tax farmers, who were contractually obligated to meet the full amount of their bids. The king's storerooms would have been further augmented from the rents paid by tenants who cultivated the large tracts of land in the territory of Leontinoi over which Hieron claimed direct ownership. The *ager Leontinus*, which lay in the fertile Plain of Catania, was renowned in antiquity for its crop yields.[39] Unlike the tithe, which was fixed at 10 percent of the annual harvest, the rents paid by cultivators of royal lands could have been much higher.[40]

Hieron may have had recourse to additional mechanisms by which he could extract cheap grain and other agricultural goods from his kingdom. We know that under Roman administration of the *lex Hieronica*, the state could require the compulsory sale of grain, equivalent in scale to a second tithe and sometimes even more beyond that. When this occurred, cultivators were paid, in cash, a fixed price per unit of grain that was taken by the state beyond the amount owed in the initial tithe. On several occasions during the second and first centuries BCE, upward of one-third of the total harvest was collected from Sicilian farmers in the form of these additional, compulsory sales to the state. The earliest reference to this practice of collecting a second tithe is found in Livy, where it is stated that the Romans requisitioned two-tenths of the island's grain harvest in the year 190 to supply to their troops fighting against Antiochos III in Aetolia.[41] Livy mentions a double tithe collected again in 171 during the lead-up to the Third Macedonian War.[42] The requisitioning of grain above that paid as tithe may have been a far more regular event than the handful of instances mentioned by Livy, and may even have begun in the third century during the reign of Hieron. Whether or not the requisitioning of a second tithe had its origins in the Hieronian law depends on how closely we believe the Romans held to the third-century precursor to the *lex Hieronica*. Still, that such levies and purchases of additional grain occurred with the frequency they are recorded suggests that at least an additional 10–20 percent of the island's total annual harvest could be mobilized as vendible surplus.

Flush with grain, Hieron faced the challenge of converting the agricultural produce into precious metal resources. Hieron's task was to attract merchants, who supplied foreign markets with grain or other agricultural produce purchased from the king. While Hieron routinely deployed his fleet to transport gifts of grain around the Mediterranean, the bulk of his actual sales most likely took place at Syracuse, where tithe grain could be sold to merchants, who would themselves take over the costs and risks involved in transporting it to foreign markets. Sicily, of course, had long been a chief source of grain for merchants supplying foreign markets.[43] Hieron took additional steps to enhance Syracuse's attractiveness as an essential port of call for merchant ships plying the Mediterranean.

In Chapter 2, we identified several instances in which Hieron reportedly made substantial gifts of grain to major Mediterranean commercial and military powers.[44] While such gifts blossomed into recognition of status and praise, much beloved of monarchs, Hellenistic kingdoms were not run on reputation alone. There were undoubtedly practical reasons for such acts of magnanimity, such as to advertise both the quality and availability of Hieron's grain supply to prospective customers.[45] Such efforts, moreover, helped to establish the reputation of Syracuse as a reliable source of grain, which in turn may have attracted merchants in search of predictable markets to procure grain and other agricultural goods. Although it was unlikely to have played into the king's considerations, we should not underestimate the impact that such gift-giving had on shaping consumer preferences for Sicilian grain. It was certainly the case that by the Roman period, tastes for certain agricultural products, often associated with particular geographic locations or regions, drove the acquisition and trade of specific goods.[46]

In 227, Hieron took a more direct approach to attract merchants to eastern Sicily by granting Rhodian merchant ships freedom from paying customs duties at the ports within his kingdom.[47] This move followed an earthquake of the same year that inflicted great damage on the city of Rhodes. Again, what at first glance appears as an altruistic act by Hieron was, from another perspective, a sensible investment in the long-term enrichment of the royal fisc. The importance of the Rhodian grain fleet for mobilizing the surplus produce accumulated through in-kind taxation by Hellenistic kings – Hieron among them – was certainly the cause for the extraordinary scale of royal benefactions that followed the earthquake. By removing the customs duties collected from Rhodian merchant ships trading at commercial harbors within his kingdom, Hieron made the ports in eastern Sicily a more attractive destination. Rhodian merchants were not alone in frequenting the Hieronian kingdom in search of grain. Epigraphic evidence also attests to the presence of Chian traders and Athenian grain-buyers turning up at Syracuse around the middle of the third century in search of cheap grain.[48]

By encouraging merchants to purchase grain at Syracuse, Hieron's actions strengthened the city's ties to Mediterranean-wide markets. Once in Sicily, merchants may have been required to exchange their foreign coinage for the king's own coinage, a transaction that would have benefited Hieron. While we do not possess any documentary evidence as forthright as the letter written by Demetrios, the Ptolemaic mint official, attesting to this type of mandatory exchange within the Hieronian context, the trivial amount of foreign coinage found in contemporary archaeological contexts in eastern Sicily does suggest Hieron enforced a policy of currency conversion. Merchants may have conducted the entirety of their business at Syracuse or could have dealt with agents operating between inland centers of production and coastal markets – a scenario that might account for the large quantities of Hieron's coinage reaching cities like Morgantina at this time. In addition to supplying foreign markets, Hieron may have also profited by selling off his grain to local ones. Hellenistic kings presumably relied on internal demand from large urban centers within their respective kingdoms to offload their agricultural surpluses. This was the ostensible reasoning behind Antigonos' hesitation behind allowing the Teans and Lebedians to gain autonomy over the importation of grain and the maintenance of their civic grain supplies.[49] By the middle of the third century, Syracuse ranked among the largest cities in the Mediterranean and was certainly the island's largest urban center with a population that may very well have consumed more grain than its hinterland could supply.[50]

Hieron was not alone in profiting from the tithe administration. The mechanisms that allowed the king to effectively tax the agricultural productivity of eastern Sicily also created opportunities for his constituents to engage in market exchange of surplus grain and other agricultural products. This of course did not mean that many would have profited or even actively taken part in the grain trade. For most, especially the small-scale cultivators and tenant farmers, there may have simply been greater incentive to exchange surplus grain for cash and not necessarily for profit-oriented motives. If Hieron required payment of some forms of taxation in cash or landowners expected rents in cash, cultivators may have needed to sell off a portion of their surplus produce in order to obtain the coinage required to pay the state or landlord.[51] For a smaller group, the economic conditions created during Hieron's reign may have spurred profit-driven intensification of agrarian activity and greater investment in agriculture. In almost every respect, the wealthy, large land-owners were better served by the growing number of opportunities to provide grain for the large urban markets of Syracuse and abroad.[52]

Aside from the king, it was the tax farmers who were best equipped to benefit from the administrative structures put in place to extract grain from eastern Sicily. As discussed in Chapter 4, the tax-farming system on which the tithe adminis-tration relied was itself dependent on the profit-seeking behavior of private individuals. Those capable of purchasing the rights to collect tithes did so with the expectation that total production would be higher than the amount initially bid and would hence yield a profit. In practice, tax farmers in Hieronian Sicily operated as de facto merchants, who profited by selling the grain or other agricultural products they collected over and above the amount owed to the state. In all likelihood, these were individuals already engaged in the grain trade, who com-manded resources sufficient both to provide surety for their bids at auction and to transport large amounts of grain from grain-producing areas of the interior to the coast.[53] Here, Hieron's efforts to attract foreign merchants to Syracuse benefited tax farmers and surely incentivized their efforts to bring additional grain to market by purchasing (or unjustly demanding) surplus produce from cultivators.

In addition to tax farmers, wealthy cultivators in possession of large tracts of agricultural land may have also benefited from the growth of market integra-tion between Syracuse and agriculturally productive inland zones brought about by the Hieronian tithe. This was certainly a situation where economies of scale may have encouraged the expansion of landholding, as well as increased specialization in agricultural production of market-bound goods. As more land came into the hands of fewer individuals, there was greater need for land tenancy, which itself led to increased amounts of surplus produce collected in rents and made available for sale.[54] This was further to the benefit of the wealthy since, under the Hieronian law, payment of the tithe fell to individual cultivators, not landowners.[55] This created advantages for owners of large estates, who could collect rents on arable land worked by tenant farmers and pay no tithe on their tenant's harvest.

Those least likely to benefit from the increased opportunity to offload surplus grain on the market were the small-scale cultivators and tenant farmers.

As mentioned above, necessity rather than profit may have motivated most small-scale cultivators to sell surplus produce should they, for instance, be required to pay taxes or rents in cash.[56] The need to purchase goods and materials that could not be manufactured within the household also would have led some cultivators to sell surplus produce at market. Those small-scale cultivators who did direct surplus goods to the market surely faced systemic disadvantages compared with the situation enjoyed by larger landowners. Small-scale cultivators were less likely to withstand the pressure to sell early after the harvest, when grain was most abundant and market prices were at their lowest.[57] They were also more likely to find themselves in a situation in which they were forced to sell or part with non-disposable surplus (e.g., for rents, repayment of loans, etc.), putting themselves in the position of having to buy back grain as the year progressed.[58] Wealthy, large-scale cultivators, conversely, were better equipped to withhold agricultural produce until market prices were more favorable and could even capitalize on their position by buying up grain locally from small landowners at low prices and then supplying it either to merchants operating between the interior and the coast or to coastal markets directly.[59]

Even with these structural disadvantages, small-scale farmers would have likely faced increased incentives (or at least lowered barriers) to mobilize surplus grain as a result of the consolidation of Hieron's political authority in eastern Sicily. This requires us not to embrace the idea of a proto-capitalist, profit-maximizing peasant, but rather to view the sale of surpluses on the market as a form of risk-buffering – akin to storage or communal distribution. It is still a commonly held view that the risk-averse peasant preferred to stockpile surplus produce or participate in communal storage strategies in the event of food shortage, rather than engage in the market.[60] This approach interprets the relationship between small-scale farmers and the market in terms of aversion. Yet if we reframe discussion to focus on access to markets, we might consider how limited access to markets may have resulted in reliance on the subsistence strategies traditionally ascribed to peasant communities (e.g., stockpiling). But if conditions were such that participation in market exchange could serve as a viable risk-buffering strategy, there may have been greater incentive to sell disposable surplus and convert perishable goods into durable coinage. Access was a key component for making participation in market exchange a viable strategy for small-scale cultivators. As ethnographic work in West Africa has shown, when barriers to market exchange were sufficiently low – and even encouraged through state-backed policies such as monetization and farm-gate purchases – small-scale farmers were more likely to participate in market exchange.[61] In the absence of accessible and reliable trade networks, the costs involved in bringing surplus grain to the market could be prohibitively expensive for smaller cultivators.

Within this framework, we can posit several ways in which the tithe administration may have lowered the transaction costs involved in market exchange, effectively removing some barriers that had formerly made it inconvenient for small farmers to sell surplus grain. For starters, the increased availability of standardized measuring devices and a common coinage throughout the kingdom helped to level the playing field when it came to potential asymmetries of information between merchants and cultivators. Moreover, the tithe system's reliance on tax farming increased interaction between cultivators and individuals engaged in supplying grain to larger markets on the coast, who were themselves incentivized to purchase additional grain that could be conveyed to the coast by the same network as the tithe grain. Last, the tithe administration required cultivators to report harvest data in person and even to make tithe payments at granaries in urban centers, like those at Morgantina. This had the effect of bringing more people into urban centers on a routine basis than otherwise might have been the case, making it more likely that they might engage in market exchange.

MARKET INTEGRATION IN HIERONIAN SICILY

I have so far argued that the structure and operation of the Hieronian state helped to create conditions by which interior communities were brought into increased economic contact with Syracuse and, by extension, Mediterranean-wide trade networks. Such market integration was accomplished by, among other things, the advent of long-term peace and stability within the kingdom, the unification of coinage and measures under a single standard, increased monetization, and the administrative structures that facilitated the collection of an annual agricultural tithe. The outcome of greater market integration was growth in economic activity and, for a segment of the population, increased wealth derived from investments in agricultural production and the sale of surpluses.

The piggybacking of trade and intensification of agricultural production as a result of increased taxation by the state has most often been discussed with regard to the Roman imperial *annona*.[62] It is perhaps for this reason that applications of this model with regard to Sicily tend to overlook the developments taking place within the Hieronian kingdom, focusing rather on the situation under Roman rule. Yet it is undoubtedly significant that two recent inquiries concerning the impact of Roman provincial administration on Sicilian communities highlight evidence for economic growth in connection to the *lex Hieronica*. In discussing the economic outcome of Rome's expansion of Hieron's tax system to incorporate the whole of the island after 210, Roger Wilson notes that

> Any remaining surplus Sicilians could sell on the open market. One might have thought that the new taxation burden (in addition to

> municipal taxation) might have crippled the Sicilian communities, and 30 years ago that indeed was the orthodox view of Sicily during the Republic.... Yet, as we shall see, the Sicilian cities enjoyed a building boom in the second and early first centuries.... Perhaps the economic stimulus was provided by the chance to sell their surplus overseas to generate extra cash, resulting in more land coming under cultivation than ever before. So far from being oppressed by excessive taxation, the Sicilian communities rose to the fresh challenge by shifting their economic gear and broadening their horizons.[63]

Wilson attributes the prosperity enjoyed by the island's elite (evidenced by, among other things, a spate of new building projects) to the opportunities created by the tithe system to sell off agricultural surpluses to supply markets abroad.

Phillip Perkins arrived at a similar conclusion when addressing the economic impacts of Roman taxation on the territory of ancient Iatas (modern Monte Iato), located in western Sicily.[64] Drawing on data collected by the Monreale Survey, an intensive pedestrian survey conducted in the Upper Belice Valley of northwestern Sicily, Perkins argued that the Roman administration of agricultural taxes (i.e., the *lex Hieronica*) led to greater market integration between interior communities, like Monte Iato and Monte Maranfusa, and larger markets on the coast. The commercial entanglements that followed from Rome's increased administrative control affected both urban and rural settlements. What this looked like on the ground was a manifest increase in the number of imported goods registered both by the survey and from excavations at the urban center of Iatas. The character of the imports changed over the centuries, but always tended to reflect the broad contours of Rome's administrative supply chain that brought food from productive centers around the Mediterranean to the capital city. During the first two centuries of Roman rule on Sicily, the archaeological evidence from the Monreale Survey reflected the increased importance of the Tyrrhenian shipping lanes that connected Sicily to Rome, as evidenced by the high proportion of Greco-Italic amphoras that once held Campanian wines. The interior's growing connectivity with markets and administrative centers on the coast was also reflected by an influx of bronze coinage struck at Panormus, which served as the region's principal port for shipping tithe grain to Rome. According to Perkins,

> The survey evidence indicates that as W Sicily developed as part of the province, subject to taxation in kind, it became involved in a complex of economic exchanges linking the province to Italy and Rome. This economic nexus drew together the Sicilian elites and the Roman authorities, officials and traders. It also became a driving force in the activities of Sicilian elites responsible for assessing the tax and for organising the territory to be sufficiently productive to meet the tax demands.

> Subaltern classes in Sicily also participated: they produced the corn for the tithe and consumed a portion of the *annona*-linked Campanian wine. Thus this part of the province was drawn into a Tyrrhenian world under Roman hegemony where political power manifested in taxation generated an economic bond that formed a structural part of local society.[65]

Both Wilson's and Perkins' conclusions are particularly relevant for our present discussion since the Roman institution of agricultural taxation that they consider so determinative on the economic landscape of western Sicily is, of course, the *lex Hieronica*. It is now up to us to consider whether the archaeological evidence shows that the Hieronian tax system produced similar conditions on the ground for those communities subject to royal authority during the third century.

Testing the Model: Morgantina

As one of the most extensively investigated archaeological sites on Sicily, Morgantina may serve as a practical case study to better understand the economic integration experienced by the cities within the kingdom of Hieron II. As we will see, the evidence from Morgantina demonstrates that signs of economic integration very much like those observed by Perkins in the area around Iatas had come to take shape in eastern Sicily over the course of the third century. Here too, we find that integration was sustained by the administrative institutions established in the service of facilitating the state's collection of agricultural taxes. Significantly, the material record from Morgantina reflects a further restructuring of dominant trade networks in the second century, once the city had been brought under Rome's provincial administration, a situation that further mirrors patterns of trade noted by Perkins in his study of the Monreale Survey data.

The Urban Settlement

The third century was a time of economic prosperity for Morgantina, which benefited from an extensive and agriculturally productive territory. Peace and an abundance of agricultural land may have attracted newcomers to the city, which witnessed a spike in population around the end of first quarter of the third century.[66] Estimates have placed Morgantina's urban population between 6,000 and 10,000 persons at this time, a substantial increase over that of the previous centuries.[67] This rapid population growth was inscribed on the landscape by the construction of new residential quarters in what previously had been unoccupied portions of the Serra Orlando ridge.[68] Recent excavations in the area of Contrada Agnese, one of these residential quarters located at the western limits of the ancient city, confirm this picture of rapid development around the middle decades of the third century.[69]

The civic wealth enjoyed by the residents of Morgantina is perhaps nowhere better viewed than in the initiation of the building program that radically transformed the appearance of city's agora during the course of the third century. As discussed in Chapters 3 and 6, many elements of this program, including the monumental East and West Granaries, were almost certainly the products of royal patronage (or royal intervention, depending on how one looked at it). Yet even allowing for major investment from the royal court at Syracuse, there are clear signs that Hieron did not hold a monopoly on euergetic benefactions when it came to the transformation of Morgantina's agora. Most notably, a large inscription carved into the stone seats of the theater's *cavea* records a dedication made by a certain Arkhelas, son of Eukleidas.[70] The inscription, still partially visible along the vertical face of the tenth row of seats in the *cavea*, reads,

ΑΡΧΕΛΑΣ ΕΥΚΛΕΙΔΑ ΔΙΟΝΥΣΩΙ

Arkhelas, son of Eukleides, [dedicated this] to Dionysos

While the precise details of Arkhelas' patronage remain open to speculation (Did he pay for the construction of the entire theater? Just a portion of the seating? For something else completely?), the prominent location and scale of the inscription certainly speaks to a major investment in the city's civic architecture by a member of the (presumably) local elite. In the same vein, a limestone sculpture of a draped female figure discovered in the agora during the 1956 excavation season may represent another member of the local elite honored on account their euergetic expenditure on the behalf of the city (Figure 8.2).[71] Malcolm Bell has convincingly demonstrated that the statue originally stood on a stone base situated along the southern wall of the East Stoa.[72] It is tempting to identify the sculpture as an honorific statue erected on behalf of the sponsor of the East Stoa's construction.[73] Bell has posited that the sculpture may represent the Syracusan queen Philistis or possibly the goddess Tyche, but we should not dismiss the possibility that the statue represents a less-regal benefactor from among the prominent families of Morgantina.[74]

Amid the wider backdrop of urban development, there are also unmistakable signs of increased private wealth documented in the construction and elaboration of large peristyle houses, many of which have been excavated on the East and West Hills that flanked the city's agora.[75] Embellished with elaborate mosaic pavements, richly decorated banqueting rooms, and large peristyle courtyards, this new style of residence was undoubtedly designed to be an expression of the owner's wealth and status within the community.[76] Less monumental signs of the prosperity enjoyed by wealthy Morgantinoi include luxury items found inside private houses, such as gold and silver jewelry, drinking vessels, and other objects made from precious metals and exhibiting a high degree of craftsmanship.[77] That even those occupying the middle ranks of society saw greater wealth during this period is evidenced by the recent excavations of the House of the Two Mills, a modestly appointed dwelling of third-century date that was located near the western edge of the ancient urban center. The house, while large enough to fully occupy one of the city's urban allotments, did not boast mosaic floors or peristyle courts; the owners instead apportioned a large extent of the house to light industry and commerce. Yet over the course of the house's occupation (ca. 260–200), there are clear signs of increasing wealth and investment by the owners, who introduce new milling technologies into their production spaces as well as elements of luxury or comfort, such as the addition of

8.2 Limestone sculpture of female figure from the agora at Morgantina, third century BCE (Museo Archeologico Regionale di Aidone, inv. 56-1749; courtesy of the American Excavations at Morgantina).

a small room off the courtyard that appears to have served as a private bathing space.[78]

Economic prosperity, of course, was not shared by all members of the community equally and there are signs that growth was not without consequences. That several of the large peristyle houses flanking the city's agora came to expand into neighboring lots and occupy the space of two allotments of the urban grid plan is just one sign that increased prosperity likely led to greater social stratification in the community. The growing class divide is evident when the large peristyle houses of the East and West Hills are compared with the more humble residences found as one moved farther away from the city center. The so-called House of Eupolemos is an example of one of these smaller residences, which did not undergo expansion in the third century.[79] But even this house only marks a midway point between urban elite and poor, who may have lived at close quarters in residential complexes like that excavated in Contrada Drago, located to the northeast of the agora, or in the small houses excavated along the slopes of Collina Papa.[80] This, of course, does not even take into account those at the bottom of the socioeconomic spectrum, about whom the archaeological record reveals little.

The Territory

At the same time as these developments were taking place inside the urban center at Morgantina, there were major changes occurring in the surrounding hinterland. We have a reasonably good understanding of the broad patterns of rural activity in the territory around Morgantina thanks to the results of an intensive landscape survey carried out during the late 1990s. The Morgantina Survey, conducted under the direction of Steven Thompson, revealed evidence for human occupation in the countryside around Morgantina spanning more than 7,000 years from the Neolithic period to the present day.[81] While the classification of rural sites by surface scatters into several broad chronological periods makes it impossible to establish the proximate cause behind the transformations in rural activity observed by Thompson and his team, the overall settlement patterns during the Hellenistic period are consistent with the evidence for an increase in population and private wealth in the urban center.

The survey identified fifty-six sites classified as Late Classical–Early Hellenistic (LC-EH, ca. 400–200) within the area of the survey universe (ca. 150 square kilometers).[82] While this represents only a slight increase in the absolute number of sites registered from the preceding Late Archaic–Early Classical (LA-EC, ca. 600–400) period, Thompson noted several "fundamental differences" in rural activity between the LA-EC and the LC-EH periods.[83] Notable among these are data that Thompson interprets as evidence of growth in the number of permanent rural residences during the LC-EH period. On a regional level, twenty-four new sites came to be occupied in the LC-EH period, many of which showed high on-site artifact densities, a metric used to identify permanent settlements. Thompson observed that there was movement away from portions of the territory that lie north of the urban center, with an increased number of sites appearing in the area southeast of the Serra Orlando ridge, concentrated around the Belmontino and Aquabianca river valleys, two branches of the Gornalunga river. The LC-EH sites were also less diffusely scattered in the landscape compared with those of the previous period, which may indicate that rural habitation went through a process of nucleation so as to reserve more land for cultivation. Thompson interpreted these trends in the data as being indicative of a qualitative shift in the nature of rural activity toward an intensification of agricultural production and a greater degree of permanent residence in the countryside.[84] This intensification, of course, occurred around the time when the Hieronian tax administration was in full swing, and it is tempting to see a causal link between the tithe and this change in rural activity.

Thompson tentatively identified the majority of LC-EH sites recorded by the survey as farms or sites of agricultural production, based on factors including the composition and the density of on-site artifact scatters.[85] None of the sites identified by the Morgantina Survey have yet to be investigated through excavations. Thompson suggests that the numerous small sites (<0.5 hectare) with medium and high artifact densities may be identified as family farms, comparing them with the findings from the Metaponto Survey, which found that family farmsteads typically covered an area around 0.2–0.25 hectare.[86] Medium-sized sites (0.5–0.88 hectare), Thompson suggests, were probably larger farming establishments, the majority of which (*n* = 19) were located between 2 and 5 kilometers from the urban center. The five largest sites were all located at distances greater than 4.5 kilometers from the city and were found in close proximity to branches of the Gornalunga river. Four of these sites revealed evidence for continued occupation well into the first century.[87] On account of their size, location, and duration of occupation, Thompson posited that these sites might have been points of transshipment, where agriculture produce was collected and processed prior to shipment via river down to the coast. At one of these sites (R88/S1), archaeologists documented a stone fragment they identify as belonging to the lower block of an olive oil or wine press, perhaps an indication of the agricultural processing that took place in the area.[88]

The picture that emerges from the Morgantina Survey is one of a bustling *chora* in the third century when permanent occupation in the territory around the city would reach its highest recorded level. To put this into perspective, Joannes Bergemann and the team responsible for the Gela Survey found that occupation in the countryside of Gela reached its nadir in the third century with the number of recorded sites dropping from the highest recorded number of 171 in the late fourth and beginning of the third century to only 36 sites by the middle of the third century. Bergemann reasonably attributes the precipitous drop in rural occupation to decades of instability and violence that began with the Mamertine assault on the city in 282 and would continue throughout much of the rest of the century, encompassing both the First and Second Punic Wars.[89]

In the territory of Morgantina, Thompson found that the total number of sites occupied between the Late Hellenistic and early Roman Empire (LH-RM, ca. 200 BCE–50 CE) dropped 40–72 percent from the high of the preceding LC-EH period. Of those sites that remained, nearly all showed signs of occupation in the preceding LC-EH period and most were found to cluster along branches of the Gornalunga river. Thompson considered the decline in rural occupation to reflect a similarly steep drop witnessed in Morgantina's urban population in the decades and centuries following the siege of 211. He suggests that the nature of these rural sites continued to be defined by agricultural production in service of the tithe, citing the continued occupation of several of the large LC-EH sites into the LH-RM period as well as the fact that most LH-RM sites were found in proximity to the river.

Taking a step back, we can plausibly view both the changing patterns in rural activity and increased wealth of the urban center as a response to the structural changes instituted by the Hieronian tax laws. There is no evidence to suggest that the population of Morgantina adopted alternatives to agricultural production that would account for the increased wealth that is clearly manifest in the material record at the urban center in the third century. Rather, as Wilson posited for the enrichment of the island's elite during the first two centuries of Roman rule, the prosperity experienced by the citizens of Morgantina in the third century was likely connected to the intensification of agricultural production and the exploitation of newfound opportunities to sell off surplus goods generated by the introduction of the Hieronian tithe.

Aware of the potential to profit from marketing grain through the opportunities created by the tithe, large landowners may have responded by expanding and intensifying production. The shift in larger rural sites toward the river valleys southeast of the city, observed by the Morgantina Survey, might reflect efforts to reduce transportation costs as well as to invest in the infrastructure necessary for processing and shipping grain and other agricultural products to the coast. Wealthier landowners may have found additional opportunities to profit by playing the role of merchant, purchasing surplus grain from smaller cultivators or collecting it as rents from tenants, grain that could be sold for higher prices on the coast, or even locally, as private stockpiles diminished throughout the year. Additionally, local elites might have further profited from the system by winning tax-farm contracts to collect the tithes owed by cultivators in the territory. Such newfound opportunities were likely to have been the source of increased wealth for a certain segment of the population, wealth that in turn was invested in both private and public sectors of the city. In time, social stratification within the polis became more pronounced, manifesting in the construction of large peristyle houses and sponsorship of public buildings like the theater.

Coinage and Trade

Beyond the material signs of increased wealth at the urban center and changes to patterns of land used in the surrounding territory, we find additional evidence that the tithe system shaped the contours of economic activity at Morgantina among the substantial body of numismatic material recovered at the site. As durable instruments of economic exchange, coins may help to shed light on the manner in which the tithe administration encouraged commercial exchange between agriculturally productive centers in the interior and market centers at major port cities along the coast.

To accomplish this, let us consider the coin finds recovered from two commercial complexes located in the agora at Morgantina (Figure 8.3). The earlier of the two, the so-called Central and South Shops, was in operation for the greater part of the third century, while the latter complex, a Roman

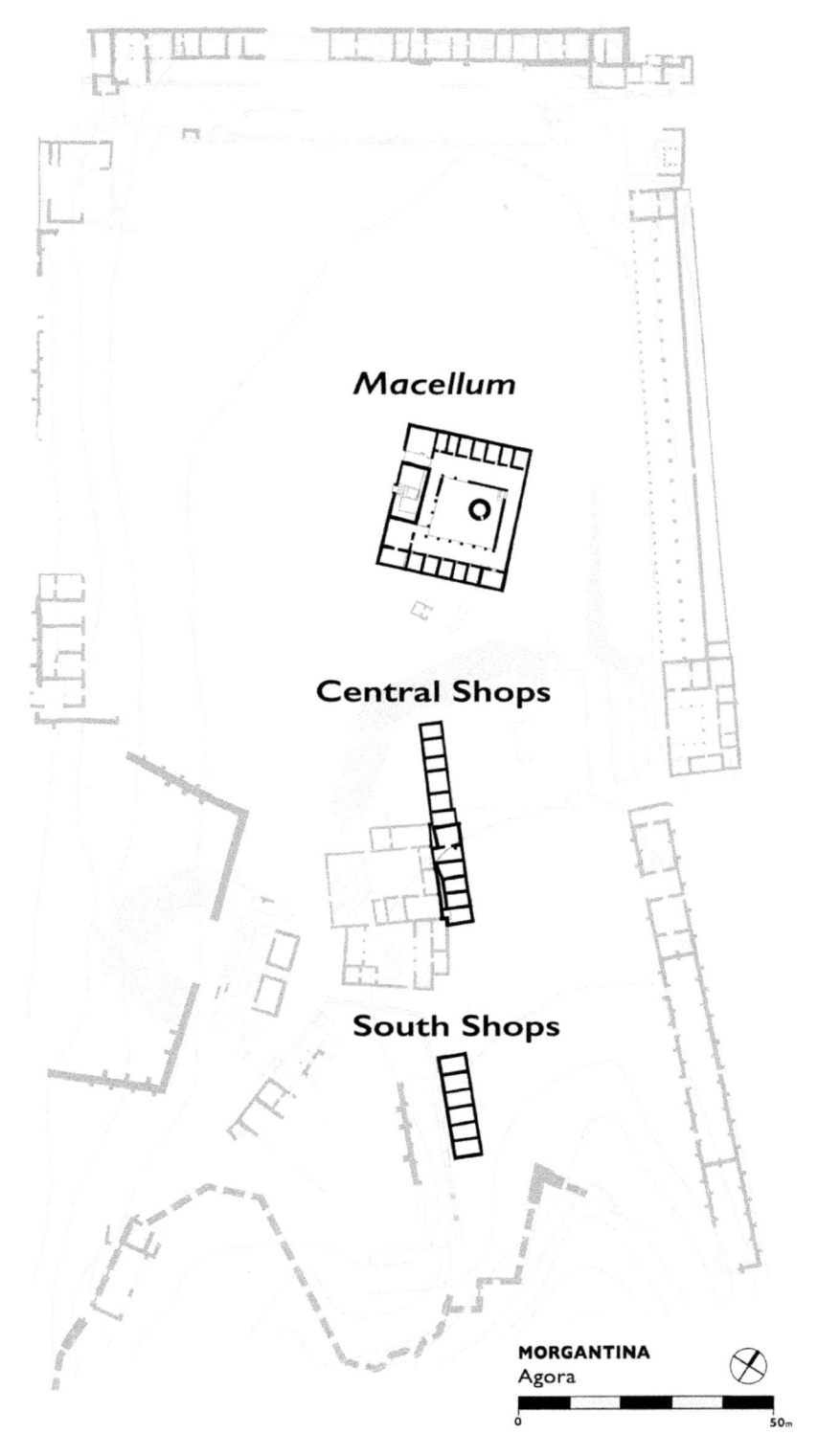

8.3 Plan of the agora at Morgantina with the location of the *macellum* and Central and South Shops indicated (after Bell 1988).

macellum, was in use during the second and first centuries. For our purposes, let us posit that the numismatic material recovered from inside these commercial spaces can serve as a reliable index of overall coin circulation at Morgantina between the third and first centuries, as well as offer some indication as to the direction and intensity of trade taking place between Morgantina and other urban centers around the region. The Central and South Shops and Roman *macellum* represent rare instances of stratified coin deposits recovered from commercial contexts on the island. For this reason, they grant us a view into the use of coinage in a commercial setting that is neither well documented nor regularly scrutinized in the numismatic scholarship for Sicily.[90]

Coins in the Hellenistic Marketplace: The Central and South Shops (ca. 275–211)

The Central and South Shops is the name given to three distinct commercial suites, each made up of six small shop rooms. Aside from their location in the city's agora, the commercial nature of these spaces can be inferred from the artifacts found within the individual rooms, such as trade weights, transport amphoras, and standardized volumetric measures of the types discussed in Chapter 5.[91] Excavations also brought to light hundreds of coins from stratified archaeological deposits within the shops, evidence of sustained commercial activity over a roughly 60-year period that coincides closely with the regnal years of Hieron II.

The northernmost suite of rooms was built first, sometime around the year 275. The shops remained in use for about 25 years, until they were razed to make way for the construction of the Great Steps, a monumental flight of stairs that linked the city's upper and lower agora.[92] The central and southern suites of shop rooms were built around this time, presumably as replacements for the recently demolished northern suite of shops. Both central and southern suites remained in use for roughly 40 years. They were abandoned or destroyed around the last decade of the third century, likely in connection with the Roman siege of the city in 211.[93] We can be relatively certain that commercial activity ceased within these spaces in 211 or not long thereafter, given that no artifacts of second-century date were found sealed below the layer of fallen roof tiles inside any of these rooms.

A total of 476 coins were recovered from contexts related to the use of these eighteen shop rooms. Of this number, 472 (99%) were bronze. The remaining four were silver coins of types struck by Roman and Punic mints during the Sicilian phase of the Second Punic War. These four coins could only have arrived at Morgantina in 213 at the very earliest, and thus are not representative of the coinage in circulation during the reign of Hieron II.[94] The preponderance of small-denomination bronze coinage within these spaces suggests that the commercial transactions were highly monetized.[95]

Of the 462 legible coins recovered from the shops, just over 75 percent (n = 348) were issued by the Hieronian mint (Figure 8.4).[96] This number is made up almost exclusively of Hieron's three largest bronze series, the Persephone/Bull IE series (n = 53), the Hieron/Horseman series (n = 37), and the Poseidon/Trident series (n = 239). The next largest group of coins (10%, n = 46) from the shops belongs to the pre-Hieronian mint at Syracuse and is comprised chiefly of types struck between the period of the Third Syracusan Democracy (330–317) and the years that Hiketas held power as *stratēgos autokrator* (287–278). Almost completely absent from the shop contexts are coins from nearby Sicilian mints. Those present – from the mints of Tauromenion, Akragas, and Tyndaris – comprise less than 3 percent (n = 12) of the total. The remaining number (12%, n = 56) is made up of South Italian, Punic, and Roman coins, the latter of which only first entered circulation in the years after Hieron's death.

Apart from the handful of Campanian and Punic coins dated to the middle decades of the third century, Hieron's Syracusan mint is the only active minting authority represented in these commercial contexts for the greater part of the third century. The proportion of Hieronian coins recovered from deposits within individual shop rooms further supports this conclusion. Inside

Central and South Shops | Distribution of coin finds by mint

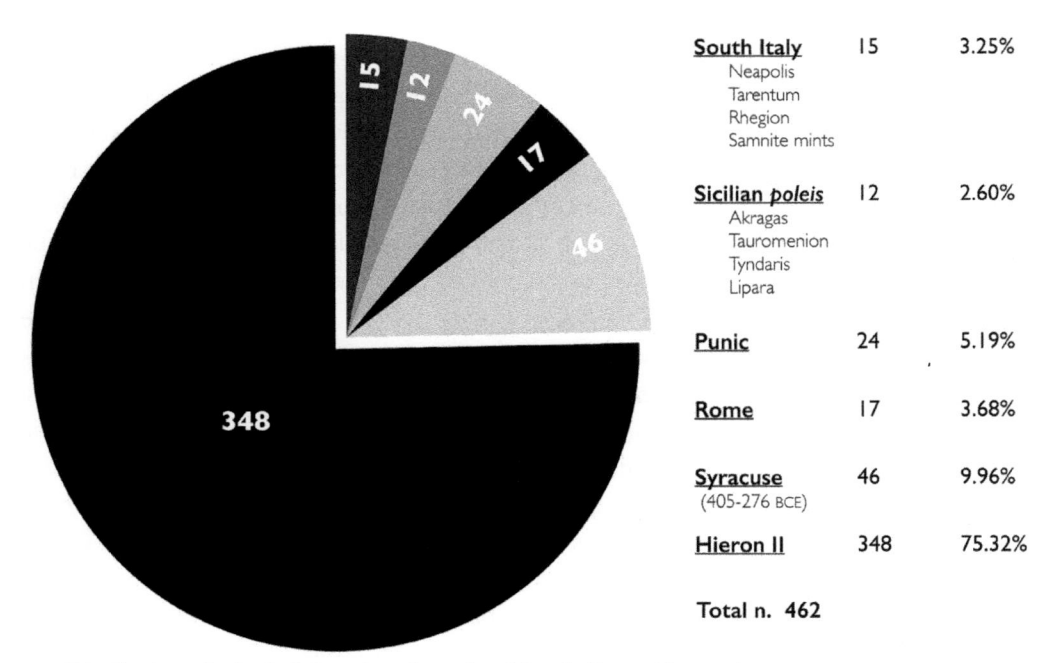

South Italy	15	3.25%
Neapolis		
Tarentum		
Rhegion		
Samnite mints		
Sicilian *poleis*	12	2.60%
Akragas		
Tauromenion		
Tyndaris		
Lipara		
Punic	24	5.19%
Rome	17	3.68%
Syracuse	46	9.96%
(405-276 BCE)		
Hieron II	348	75.32%
Total n. 462		

8.4 Distribution of coin finds by mint, Central and South Shops, Morgantina.

Rooms 3 and 4 of the northern suite, for instance, excavators exposed five successive beaten-earth floor surfaces spanning the roughly 25-year period of occupation and use. Treating each floor as a discrete period in the use of the room, we find that Hieronian bronze represents the better part of the coinage in circulation throughout the lifetime of the shop (Figure 8.5).[97] A similar pattern emerges from a closer look at the coins found inside Room 5 of the central suite. Here, it is worth noting that the five non-Hieronian coins found above the latest floor and below the tile fall layer inside Room 5 were all struck between 214 and 211, after the dissolution of the Hieronian kingdom.

After taking a closer look at the coin finds from the Central and South Shops, one is left with the clear impression that Hieronian coinage was the dominant monetary instrument of commercial exchange at Morgantina for the greater part of the third century. This observation is further sustained by the overall number of coins recovered at the archaeological site. As discussed in Chapter 7, the aggregate numismatic data from the site show a sharp increase in the amount of bronze coinage that reached the city during the decades of Hieron's reign. This widespread availability of a common bronze coinage would have certainly facilitated routine commercial exchange by lowering the transaction costs that arise when multiple currencies are involved and conversion is required to complete purchase or sale.

Can we attribute this influx of bronze coinage at an inland site like Morgantina to increased opportunities for piggybacking trade brought about by the administration of the Hieronian tithe system? Perkins answered in the affirmative regarding the economic opportunities created by the tithe system once it was applied to western Sicily by the Romans. Of particular note are Perkins' observations about the flow of coinage to inland sites like Iatas once the *lex Hieronica* had become the law of the land. Regarding the coin finds recorded from excavations at Monte Iato, Perkins suggested that the preponderance of bronze coinage of Panormus (44% of the total number of coin finds) – which would have served as the region's largest port, supplying grain ships hauling tithe grain destined for Rome – along with those of Rome itself (16%) may have been related to the purchase of grain.[98] While it may be impossible to determine whether the vast number of Hieronian bronzes recovered at Morgantina document the purchase of agricultural surpluses made by merchants or royal officials, the coin finds from Morgantina certainly speak to an intensification of economic exchange with Syracuse during the third century.

A couple of processual questions arise from this interpretation. First, how can we be sure that Hieron's bronze coinage flowed into the interior of the island as a consequence of improved market integration brought about by the tithe system and not, for instance, on account of a more traditional catalyst for coin circulation, such as the payment of troops? And, second, to what degree can coinage reliably reflect the movement of goods (in this case surplus produce) along trade networks, especially given that Hieron seems to have

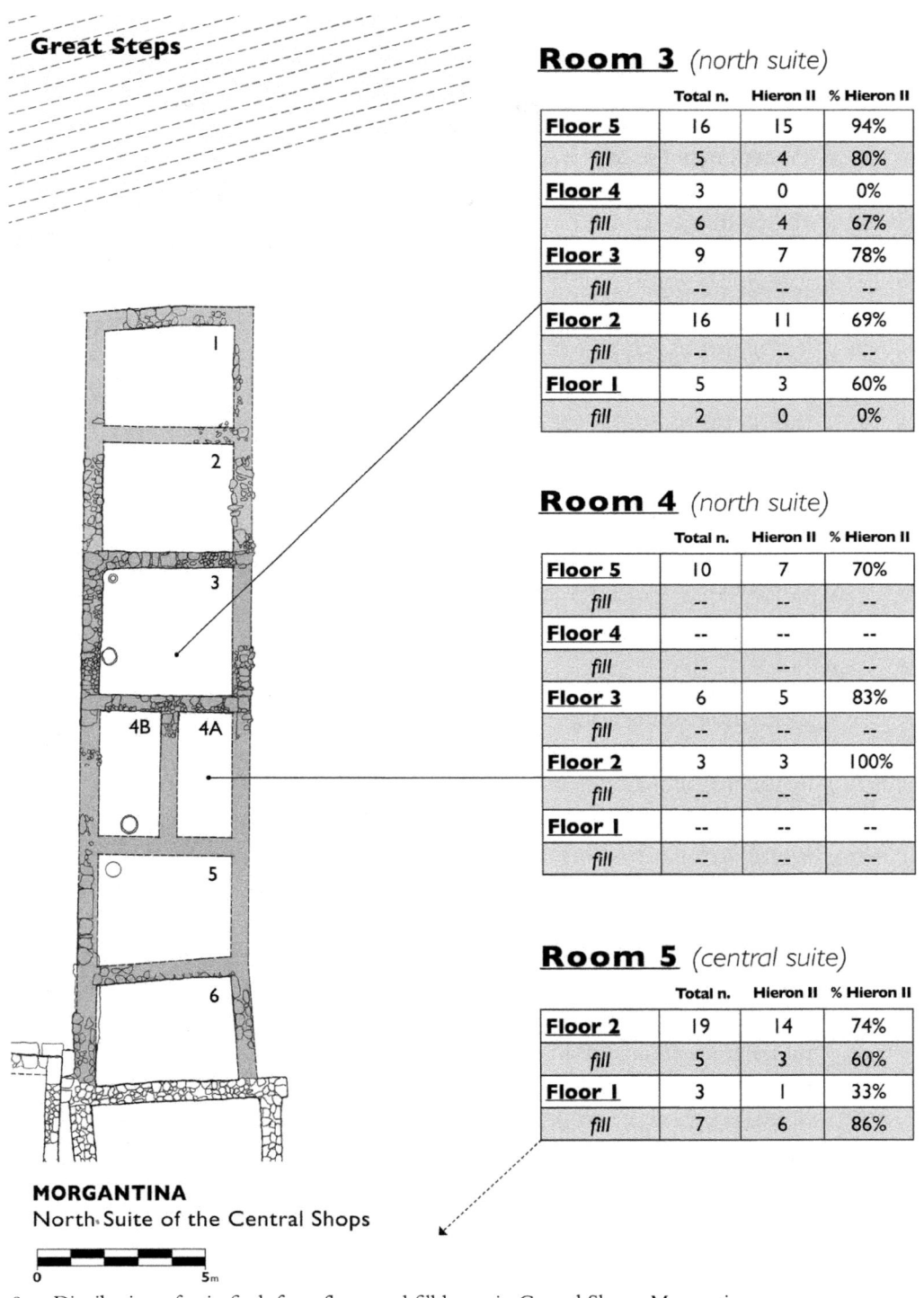

Room 3 *(north suite)*

	Total n.	Hieron II	% Hieron II
Floor 5	16	15	94%
fill	5	4	80%
Floor 4	3	0	0%
fill	6	4	67%
Floor 3	9	7	78%
fill	--	--	--
Floor 2	16	11	69%
fill	--	--	--
Floor 1	5	3	60%
fill	2	0	0%

Room 4 *(north suite)*

	Total n.	Hieron II	% Hieron II
Floor 5	10	7	70%
fill	--	--	--
Floor 4	--	--	--
fill	--	--	--
Floor 3	6	5	83%
fill	--	--	--
Floor 2	3	3	100%
fill	--	--	--
Floor 1	--	--	--
fill	--	--	--

Room 5 *(central suite)*

	Total n.	Hieron II	% Hieron II
Floor 2	19	14	74%
fill	5	3	60%
Floor 1	3	1	33%
fill	7	6	86%

MORGANTINA
North Suite of the Central Shops

0   5m

8.5 Distribution of coin finds from floors and fill layers in Central Shops, Morgantina.

adopted several monetary policies aimed at bolstering the ubiquity of his own coinage among the cities of the kingdom? Both issues are difficult to resolve, looking only at the data from the Central and South Shops. Clarity is gained with respect to both questions, however, when the numismatic data from the Roman period *macellum* are brought into the discussion.

Coins in the Roman Marketplace: The *macellum* (ca. 175–30)

The second commercial complex under consideration was an enclosed market built in the upper agora around the middle of the second century (Figure 8.6). On account of its architectural form, the complex has been identified as a Roman *macellum*.[99] The market remained in use for over a century, until its abandonment sometime in the 30s.[100] The two rows of shop rooms along the north and south sides of the complex were loci of commercial activity, judging from the concentration of coins and other artifacts related to exchange recovered therein.

Archaeologists recovered a total of 432 coins from secure stratigraphic contexts within the *macellum*, 407 of which are legible.[101] This number approaches that from the Central and South Shops ($n = 476$) and should offer a representative sample of the coinage in circulation at Morgantina in the second and first centuries. Again, bronze coinage appears to have been the prevalent medium of exchange, making up roughly 99 percent of the total number of coins found within the shop rooms. As was also the case with the Central and South Shops, silver coins ($n = 5$, all Roman denarii) made up only a tiny fraction of the total.

When the coins from the *macellum* are categorized by their mint of origin, we can immediately observe several important differences between the coins found in the *macellum* and those from the Central and South Shops (Figure 8.7). One is immediately struck by the amount of non-Syracusan coinage in circulation compared with the numbers represented in the Central and South Shops. A far larger number of Sicilian mints – including Aitna, Katane, Kentoripe, Messana, and even Morgantina itself – are represented by substantial numbers of coins. It would appear that Syracusan bronze no longer represented the dominant medium of exchange at Morgantina, as it had while the Central and South Shops were in existence.

By far the most prevalent coin types recovered from the shop rooms in the *macellum* were small bronze denominations minted at Katane. These account for over one-quarter of all the coin finds from the *macellum* shops rooms (27%, $n = 111$). The vast majority of these Katanaian issues are of the type Obv. Head of Apollo l./Rev. Isis standing r. (Figure 8.8), which were struck in great numbers during the first quarter of the second century.[102] Indeed, the archaeological evidence from Morgantina suggests that these bronzes arrived at the city in prodigious numbers in the second century.[103] More than 1,000 specimens of the Apollo/Isis series have been recovered in excavations at the site to date, making

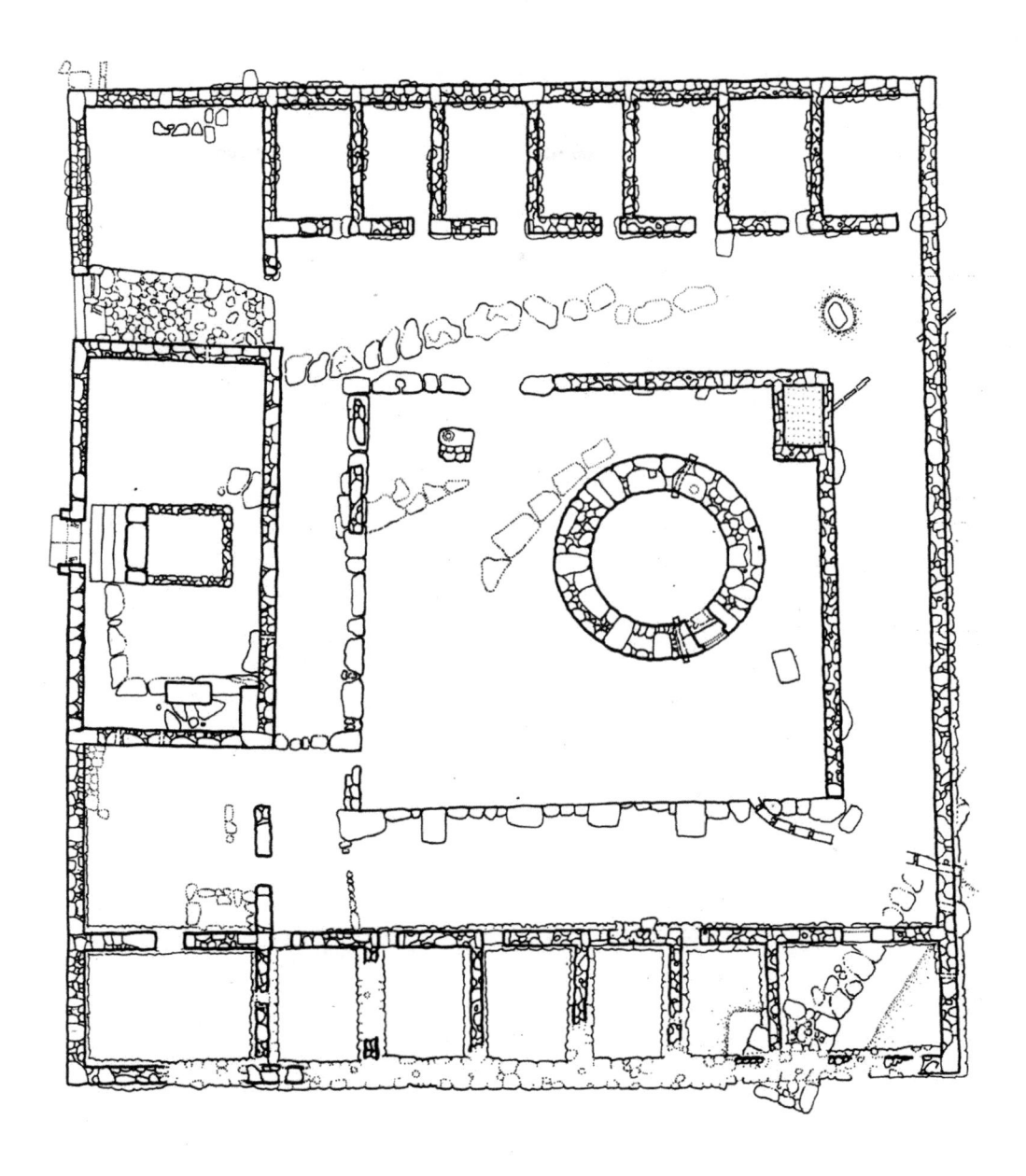

MORGANTINA

Macellum

0　　　　5m

8.6 The *macellum* at Morgantina, ca. 175–35 BCE (courtesy of the American Excavations at Morgantina).

Macellum | Distribution of coin finds by mint

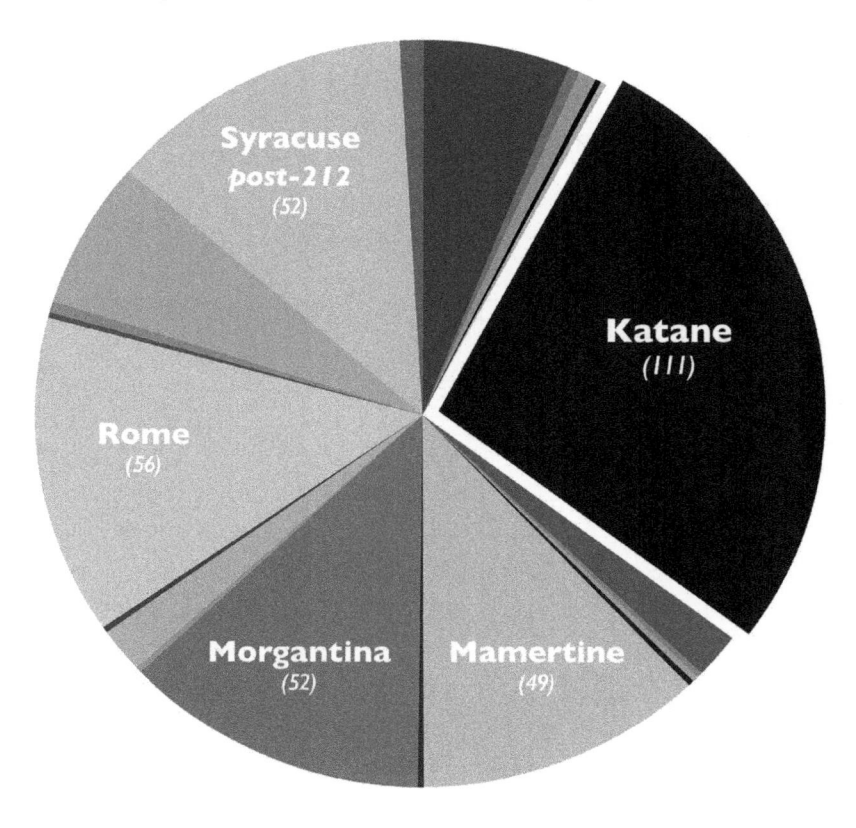

Aetna	25	6.14%	Kentoripe	8	1.97%
Akragas	2	0.49%	Panormus	I	0.25%
Alaesa	3	0.74%	Punic	2	0.49%
Aluntion	I	0.25%	Rhodes	I	0.25%
Gela	I	0.25%	Rome	56	13.76%
Mamertine	49	12.04%	South Italy	10	2.46%
Menaenum	I	0.25%	Syracuse (pre-212 BCE)	27	6.63%
Morgantina (HISPANORUM)	52	12.78%	Syracuse (post-212 BCE)	52	12.78%
Kale Akte	I	0.25%	Tauromenion	4	0.98%
Katane	III	27.27%			

Total n. 407

8.7 Distribution of coin finds by mint, *macellum*, Morgantina.

8.8 Bronze coin of Katane, second century BCE (BM EH,p163.6.Cat; © The Trustees of the British Museum).

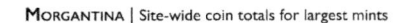

MORGANTINA | Site-wide coin totals for largest mints

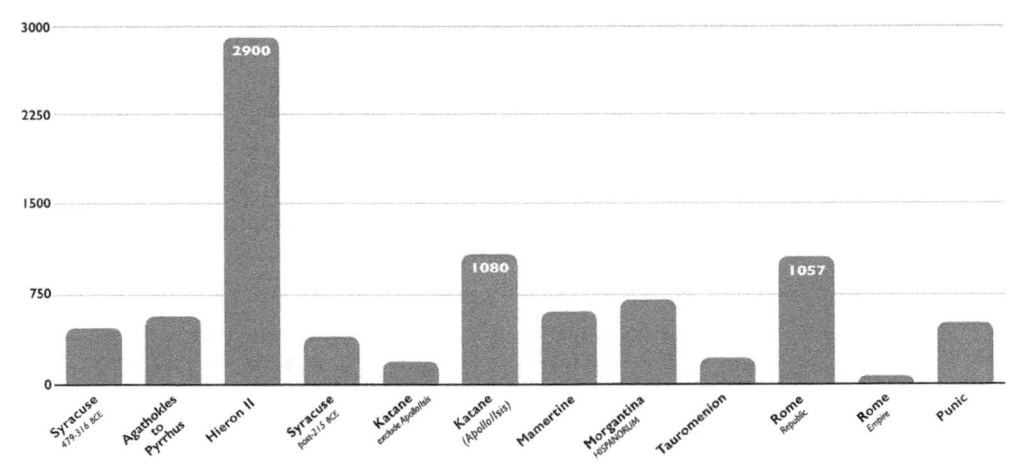

8.9 Totals of site-wide coin finds from the American Excavations at Morgantina.

them the second largest body of coinage found at Morgantina, behind only the total number of Hieronian coins recovered from the site (Figure 8.9).[104]

Based on the preceding discussion, we would expect the dramatic increase in Katanaian bronze reaching Morgantina in the second century would reflect a shift in the destination that tithe grain (and the attendant surpluses) moved – away from Syracuse toward Katane. And, in fact, this very scenario plays out in our historical sources. Once Syracuse had fallen to Marcellus and the Carthaginians were expelled from the island, it was Rome's top priority to redirect grain exports north.[105] Peninsular Italy had suffered terribly during the

Hannibalic campaigns and Sicily offered an immediate source of grain, necessary to keep Rome's urban population content and its armies marching. Livy reports that in the months immediately following the end of hostilities in Sicily, the consul M. Valerius Laevinus encouraged Sicilian farmers to return to cultivating their fields in an effort to restore cereal productivity to prewar levels. In 211, Laevinus reportedly sent word to Rome that he and his troops had

> compelled the Sicilians to lay down their arms at last and turn their attention to tilling the soil, so that the island might not only produce food enough for the inhabitants, but might relieve the grain market of the city of Rome and of Italy, as it had done on many occasions.[106]

By the following year, the newly harvested tithe grain was being sent to Roman troops stationed at Tarentum. Livy specifically names Katane as the port used by Laevinus to send the grain north, noting that

> [Laevinus] made a tour of the island in order to inspect the land and note which parts were cultivated and which were uncultivated, and to commend or rebuke the owners accordingly. Owing to his care and attention there was so large a yield of grain that he was able to send some to Rome, and also accumulate a store at Katane to furnish supplies for the army which was to pass the summer at Tarentum.[107]

With Katane now operating as major port for the export of tithe grain to Rome, large profits stood to be made through the ancillary trade in grain and other agricultural goods being moved by merchants to supply Rome. The Katanaians may have capitalized on their city's newfound status, striking large quantities of small-denomination bronze coinage to serve as instruments of exchange. The movement of merchants within the network would also explain the infiltration of the Katanaian coinage into the island's interior. Katane remained a principal port through which Sicilian grain reached Roman markets throughout much of the second and first century, judging from surviving archaeological and epigraphic evidence.[108] This connection between the two cities is further confirmed by Shelley Stone's analysis of the Hellenistic and Roman ceramics from Morgantina. Stone has found that during the second century both the imported and locally produced varieties of Campana C at Morgantina exhibit a much stronger connection to wares manufactured in the environs of Katane than to those manufactured around Syracuse.[109]

The available evidence surely suggests that Katanaian bronzes most likely reached Morgantina on account of a similar set of mechanisms that had previously brought great quantities of Hieronian coinage into the interior. We can see that the networks that tightly linked the interior and coast during the Hieronian period did not cease with the dissolution of the kingdom or the fall of Syracuse in 213; they were simply redirected to a more convenient port. Bronze coinage continued to flow into the interior of the island, only now bearing the legend of Katane. The influx of Katanaian bronze into Morgantina in the early second century, in fact, confirms the hypothesis that the substantial amounts of Hieronian coinage circulating in the island's interior during the third century was due in large part to the movement of agricultural surpluses from the interior to the coast. Thus, we find that with the dissolution of the Hieronian kingdom, the Syracusan market weakened its hold on Morgantina, and in its place there was an increased presence of bronzes from Katane, which served as an important Sicilian port for grain ships headed north to Rome.

Here, we are reminded of Perkins' inference regarding the prevalence of bronzes from Panormus found at Monte Iato. As a principal administrative center and commercial port on the north coast of the island during the Republican period, Panormus would have played a similar role with respect to the tithe administration for Monte Iato as Syracuse, initially, and Katane, later on, would have for Morgantina. Comparison with the coin finds from Kamarina is again illuminating. We recall that the overall numismatic data reported from Morgantina and Kamarina show that both cities witnessed an influx of bronze coinage struck by Hieron II, with the result that Hieronian bronzes represented the lion's share of coinage in circulation at the two cities throughout the greater part of the third century.[110] I have suggested that this homogeny was due, in part, to Hieronian policy regarding civic minting and, in part, to increased trade stimulated by the tithe system. That was certainly the case while Hieron was alive. But when comparing the representation of civic mints among the coins struck after 215 that were found at Kamarina with those found at Morgantina, we see notable deviation where previously there had been a high degree of conformity. While the coins recovered from the *macellum* at Morgantina reveal the growing presence of coinage from coastal cities in the northeast part of the island (Katane and Messana in particular), Syracusan bronzes of the late third and second century continue to make up the largest percentage of coinage arriving at Kamarina in the century following the dissolution of the Hieronian kingdom (Figure 8.10). This variance in numismatic data among the post-215 material from Morgantina and Kamarina most likely reflects a divergence in the direction of trade for these two cities after the dissolution of Hieron's kingdom. With Rome's embrace of the *lex Hieronica*, both cities continued to pay taxes in kind as they had done while subject to Hieron II, only now the final destination for tithe grain was no longer Syracuse. The Romans were interested in swiftly moving grain and other agricultural produce off the island so that it could be supplied to their citizens and soldiers. Under Rome's administration of the *lex Hieronica*, tithes were brought to the nearest major port, where they could be readily loaded onto transport ships bound for points overseas.[111] This adaptation to the third-

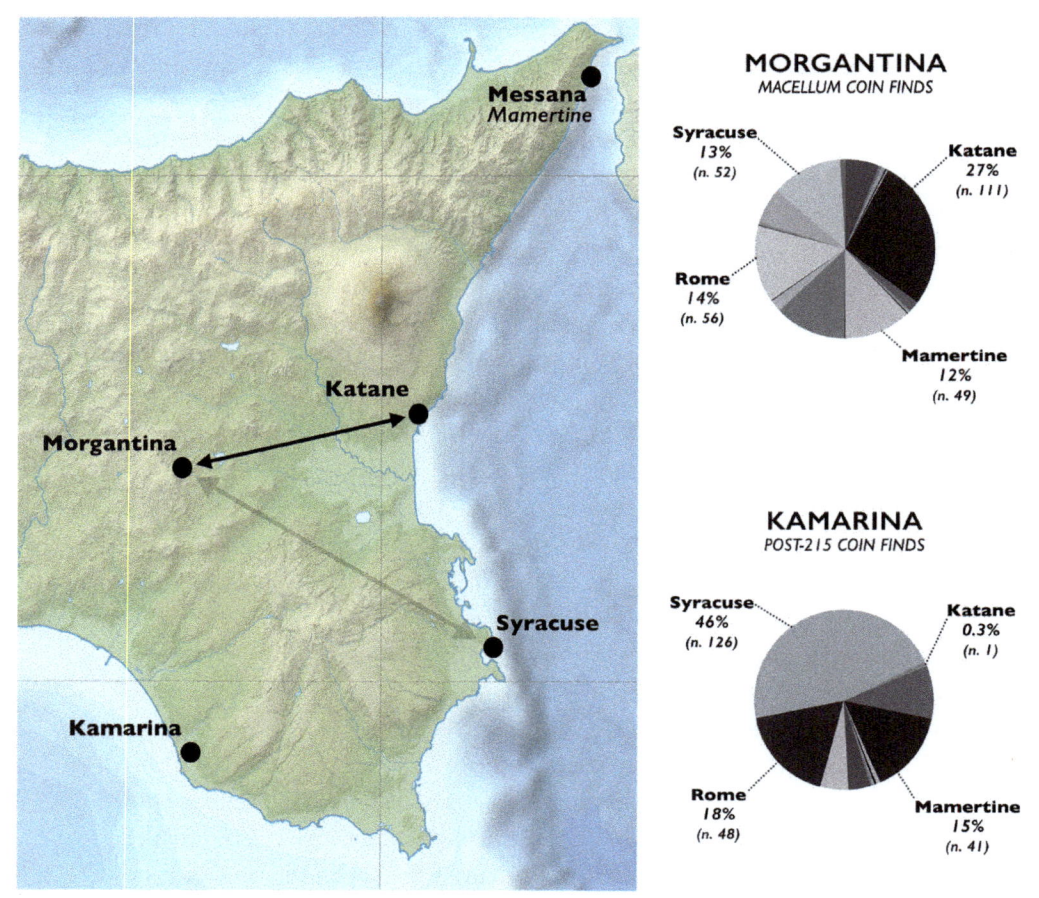

MORGANTINA
MACELLUM COIN FINDS

Syracuse
13%
(n. 52)

Katane
27%
(n. 111)

Rome
14%
(n. 56)

Mamertine
12%
(n. 49)

KAMARINA
POST-215 COIN FINDS

Syracuse
46%
(n. 126)

Katane
0.3%
(n. 1)

Rome
18%
(n. 48)

Mamertine
15%
(n. 41)

8.10 Map showing possible divergence of trade patterns in southeastern Sicily between the third and second centuries BCE, as evidenced by coin finds from Morgantina and Kamarina (base map © Sémhur/Wikimedia Commons/CC-BY-SA-3.0).

century Hieronian system would then account for the different mints represented in the post-215 numismatic material found at Kamarina and Morgantina. Syracuse remained the dominant administrative and commercial port for the portion of southeastern Sicily that included Kamarina. The same was not the case at Morgantina, which in the second century found itself in greater commercial contact with Katane.

As our brief survey of the coin finds from the Central and South Shops and the Roman *macellum* at Morgantina suggests, there is still much to discover with respect to the economic changes brought about by the imposition of the Hieronian tithe. In addition to revealing the existence of trade networks otherwise unattested in our historical sources, the coin finds from the *macellum* serve to highlight the fact that Morgantina did not suffer the severe economic isolation that we generally attribute to communities on the interior of the island during the Roman period.[112] In fact, as the numismatic evidence suggests, Morgantina experienced continued economic vitality into the second and first centuries, as trade networks with urban markets on the coast did not cease to exist, but were simply redefined, shifting from Syracuse to Katane and other cities on the island's north coast.

INSTITUTIONS AND INTEGRATION

I have argued that the formation of the Hieronian kingdom and subsequent constitution of an administrative architecture tied to the collection of agricultural taxes created the conditions for an unprecedented degree of economic integration across eastern Sicily during the third century. Taking a page from NIE, we have encountered four elements that had the potential to transform the economic landscape of the region. First, the creation and enforcement of an annual tithe entailed the regular transfer of surplus grain from areas of high supply to areas of high demand. Second, Hieron's efforts to sell his own tithe grain encouraged mercantile presence in Sicily, especially at Syracuse. Third, the tithe infrastructure created or strengthened commercial links between cities on the interior and those on the coast. Fourth, the royal policy of standardization facilitated interstate exchange by reducing transaction costs related to asymmetry of information.

This is in no way to suggest that Hieron aimed to foster market integration or had any awareness of economic performance within his kingdom beyond a general appreciation that increased agricultural productivity led to greater profits from the tithe. From the perspective of the royal administration, the intended goal was surely to facilitate the efficient assessment and collection of agricultural taxes and no more. The coincidental developments in market integration and economic exchange witnessed by the communities in southeastern Sicily were just that – coincidental.

The overwhelming attention given in this chapter to the material evidence from Morgantina stems from the settlement's rather unique modern history as the site of ongoing archaeological excavation and research for over 65 years, work that has produced an exceptional record of daily life in an ancient city subject to Hieron II. Morgantina, however, was certainly far from unique when it came to the ways in which its citizenry experienced Hieronian rule. Although archaeological investigations at most other cities within the Hieronian kingdom have not reached the scale as those at Morgantina, we can nevertheless find clear expression of increased prosperity in the cities of southeastern Sicily at this time, confirming that Morgantina was in no way an outlier. As archaeological investigations continue to improve our understanding of daily life in the other cities subject to the Hieronian tax laws and their attendant institutions, there is every reason to believe that our picture of economic integration during this period will grow ever more comprehensive.

NOTES

[1]   Diod. 22.2.2.
[2]   Diod. 22.8.
[3]   Polyb. 1.12.4.
[4]   Zambon (2008: 36–7).
[5]   Bergemann (2010; 2011).
[6]   Bergemann (2011: 87–9).
[7]   Bergemann (2010: 159–60; 2011: 89–91).
[8]   Di Stefano (1987: 159–61) posits that the destruction and abandonment might have been caused during the Mamertine assaults on Gela and Kamarina, or by any one of the number of conflicts took place in this area between Syracusan, Akragantine, and Carthaginian troops.
[9]   For a summary of excavations in the area, see Spigo and Rizzo (1993–4: 1039–50) and Spigo (2003). The site is best known for the remains of a sanctuary where terracotta votive plaques of Locrian type were produced in the fifth century BCE. Carbè (2003), who published the numismatic material from the excavations, notes that the latest coins are those struck by Hieron in the 270s and 260s; these include two specimens of the Persephone/Bull IE series, one laureate Hieron/Horseman coin, and one Poseidon/Trident of the large-flan series.
[10]   For Gagliano Castelferrato: Patané (1997); De Angelis (2007: 165). For Contrada Casalrosato: Privitera (1988–9).
[11]   Theok. 16.88–97; trans., Verity and Hunter (2002).
[12]   Wilson (2013: 99).
[13]   Bell (2011).
[14]   The pyxis belongs to a fifteen-piece set of gilt-silver objects that was clandestinely looted from the archaeological site of Morgantina, and later purchased by the Metropolitan Museum of Art in New York. It, together with the rest of the set, was repatriated to the Italian state in 2010. For detailed discussion of the objects, see Guzzo (2002). Bell (2000) takes up the circumstances of its burial (in antiquity) and its illicit discovery and export from Italy in the 1970s.
[15]   In particular, North (1990; 1991).
[16]   North (1991: 97); and see North (1993: 5) for his analogy of institutions as the "rules of the game."
[17]   Among others, Kehoe (2007: 29–52; 2015); Manning (2010); Temin (2013); Ober (2015a and 2015b); Terpstra (2019).
[18]   Terpstra (2019: 13).
[19]   See, e.g., surveys by Bang (2009) and Manning (2018: 27–32) .
[20]   Among others, Manning (2003; 2010); Lyttkens (2013); and Ober (2015a: esp. 101–21).
[21]   North (1992) considered transaction costs to be shaped by four broad variables: (1) the cost of measurement, (2) the size of the market, (3) the cost of enforcing contracts, and (4) ideological attitudes.
[22]   North (1990: 27).
[23]   Bang (2006: 58).
[24]   Regarding the role of commercial partnerships, see Terpstra (2013). Ober (2015b) explores the role of the state.
[25]   North (1979).
[26]   North (1979: 250).
[27]   North (1990: 3–36) distinguishes between what he sees as "formal" institutions, or those backed by the laws of the state, and "informal" institutions or rules, which he describes as "codes of conduct, norms of behavior, and conventions" that derive from a social or community context
[28]   North (1979: 251).
[29]   North (1979: 253).

[30] North (1979: passim) considers the existence of the state to be a basic precondition of economic growth.

[31] Lo Cascio (2006: 221–2).

[32] Akerlof (1970); Curtis (1998: 547–9); Geertz (1978: 28–32). Vera (2008: 139–40), provides a useful summary. See also Iwahashi (2004: 96–8).

[33] Lo Cascio (2007: 627).

[34] For the role of Syracuse as a major port for the grain trade during the third century, see *infra* n. 48.

[35] See Lo Cascio (2006: 224–5) for discussion of how the Roman emperor as the imperial state could both "define the rules of the game" and at the same time be a player in that game.

[36] Hopkins (1980: 103).

[37] Regarding the impact of inter-annual fluctuations in production on the grain market, see Erdkamp (2005: 144–7); Halstead and Jones (1989: 54); and, for the interconnected Mediterranean, generally, Horden and Purcell (2000: esp. 175–230). With reference to trade in commodities due to uneven distribution of resources, see Garnsey and Saller (1987: 50).

[38] For summary of ancient and modern perspectives on the agricultural potential of Sicily, see Walthall (2020b: 318–22).

[39] Cic. 2.*Verr*.3.112. Moreno (2007: 26).

[40] See discussion in Chapter 4, p. 125.

[41] Liv. 37.2.11. For further discussion, see Pritchard (1971: 226).

[42] Liv. 42.31.8.

[43] For exports of grain to Rome prior to Punic Wars, see Gallo (1992). For shipments to Greece, see Fantasia (1993) and Nenci (1993) with particular focus on Akragas. Thucydides (3.86) suggests that one reason the Athenians sent ships to Sicily in 427 BCE was to prevent shipments of Sicilian grain to the Peloponnese. Demosthenes (56.9) mentions a large shipment of Sicilian grain which, upon its arrival at the Piraeus, drove down the price of wheat throughout the city. Westlake (1960) believed that regular import of Sicilian grain was essential to the well-being of Athens; cf. Rathbone (1983: 50), who calls into question the island's reputation as a longtime supplier of grain to mainland Greece.

[44] Hieron reportedly sent large quantities of grain to the Romans on several occasions: Diod. 23.8.1 (262, siege of Akragas); Diod. 24.1.4 (250, siege of Lilybaeum); Diod. 25.14 (220s, during Celtic War). Reference to other grain shipments sent by Hieron include Polyb. 1.83.2–4 (241–238?, grain to Carthage during Truceless War); Athen. 5.206e–209c (240s?, grain, salted fish, wool, etc. sent to Ptolemy III); Polyb. 5.88.7. (227, grain to Rhodes following the earthquake).

[45] Garnsey (1988: 82–4) notes similar profit-driven motives behind private acts of euergetism involving grain supplies during the Hellenistic period.

[46] Pliny (*HN* 18.12), for instance, distinguished at least a dozen different regional varieties of wheat, ranking them by qualities such as whiteness and weight. Among the wheats grown outside Italy, he considers Sicilian wheat to rank second in quality only to that grown in Boeotia, which he judges to be the first among non-Italian wheat varieties.

[47] For further discussion, see *supra* Chapter 5, p. 175. Diodorus (26.8) adds the detail that it was Rhodian *grain* ships that were exempt from Hieron's customs duties. On the detrimental effect that customs duties could have on market integration, see Bang (2006: 69–70).

[48] For Sicilian grain reaching Athens during the reign of Hieron II, see Oliver (2007: 247–9), who cites two Athenian honorary decrees from the middle decades of the third century that attest to the presence of Athenian *sitonai* in Sicily. One decree (*IG* II² 584+679; *SEG* XXXIX.128; *SEG* XLV.108), dating to the year 247/6, specifically mentions Athenian *sitonai* stopping in Syracuse.

[49] For further discussion, see *supra* Chapter 6, p. 230.

50   Demographic studies focusing on ancient Sicily are relatively few and far between; see, e.g., Beloch (1874); Muggia (1997); and De Angelis (2000), who rightly counts demography as a fruitful avenue of future research. With respect to Syracuse, Beloch (1886: 281) estimates that by the year 300 the population reached 300,000. Based on his estimates of the amount of productive land available in the territory of Syracuse, De Angelis (2000: 124) suggests the resources grown on land controlled by the Syracusans could have supported anywhere between ca. 110,000 and ca. 145,000 people. With respect to the provisioning of grain for a Hellenistic capital, see Thompson (1983: 74–5), who highlights efforts by taken by the Ptolemaic kings to purchase additional grain from production zones for transport to Alexandria, where the demand was much greater.

51   This is the principal mechanism behind Hopkins's "Tax and Trade" model; Hopkins (1980). See also Garnsey and Whittaker (1998: 317–20). Von Reden (2007) argues that monetization of the Egyptian countryside was accomplished in part by the collection of a cash tax, which required small farmers to sell surplus produce in exchange for bronze coinage.

52   Erdkamp (2005: 323–6).

53   In his study of European merchants of the sixteenth century, Jeannin (1972) found tax farmers were often prominent merchants, who possessed ample knowledge about the markets and products they were responsible for collecting.

54   Erdkamp (2005: 328–9) discusses the evidence for this phenomenon in the context of the Roman world. Direct evidence for the agglomeration of land into fewer hands is difficult to come by for the period in question, yet data collected from an intensive landscape survey in the territory of Morgantina may reflect this trend of consolidation; see Thompson (1999), and discussion of the Morgantina Survey, *supra* pp. 316–8.

55   Cic. 2.*Verr*.3.53–5; Carcopino (1914: 206–7); Berve (1959: 66–7).

56   Edrkamp (2005: passim) presents a wealth of literary and documentary evidence in support of the position that ancient farmers in the Mediterranean – even those of modest means – sold surplus grain on the market.

57   De Ligt (1993: 137ff.).

58   Erdkamp (2005: 152). McArdle (1978: 110ff.) documents a similar phenomenon in medieval Tuscany, while Saul (1986; 1987) details this practice among the small-scale farms in the grain-producing districts of western Burkina Faso during the second half of the twentieth century.

59   Discussed at length by Erdkamp (2005: 147–64). The ability of larger and wealthier landowners to weather a year or more of poor harvests would even offer additional opportunity to profit, as bad harvests drove up prices; noted by Cicero (2.*Verr*.3.227).

60   For the view of the risk-averse small farmer, see Gallant (1991: 98–9), building on the work of, among others, Chayanov (1986).

61   Saul (1986; 1987). With regard to the Roman world, Erdkamp (2005: 103–4) develops this idea that greater market integration helped to reduce the severity of localized food shortages; and see Morley (1996: 75).

62   Kingsley (2001: 56–7) supports a piggyback model for Judaean wine brought to major urban centers by merchants transporting taxes in kind for the *annona*, describing the situation as "a commercial superstructure overlying the foundation of a state fiscal framework." Similarly, Decker (2001: 77–82) cites evidence for market integration among communities in Northern Syria in the late Roman and early Byzantine periods, based on surplus production of oil and wine purchased by merchants operating in the hinterland of Antioch and Apamea. In his sweeping survey of the paleobotanical data from Gordion, Marston (2017) highlights both the shift to intensive cultivation of bread wheat during the Roman period and the concomitant harm to the landscape brought about by unsustainable agricultural practices.

63   Wilson (2013: 488).

64   Perkins (2007).

65   Perkins (2007: 45).

[66] For further discussion, see Walthall and Souza (2021).

[67] Stone (2014: 12–13).

[68] Bell (2008); Allen (1974: 362–6).

[69] Lucore (2013); Trümper (2017); Souza et al. (2019); Tharler et al. (2020); Schirmer et al. (2021); Walthall (2021).

[70] Sjöqvist (1962: 138); Dubois (1989: 228, no. 191).

[71] Inv. 56-1479; Stillwell and Sjöqvist (1957: 159). Bell (1993: 332, n. 30) dates the sculpture to the second half of the third century BCE, noting the stylistic affinities of the drapery with that of contemporary Syracusan sculpture and terracotta figurines. The statue's head, arms, and feet – all now missing – were likely carved from marble and inserted into the limestone body. Given the lack of marble quarries on Sicily, sculptures rendered in the acrolithic style, or in this case pseudo-acrolithic style (i.e., marble and limestone), are relatively common; see Marconi (2007).

[72] Bell (1993: 332) notes that the low limestone plinth on which the figure stands and the masonry stone base in the East Stoa share nearly identical dimensions.

[73] See Campagna (2019: 66–9) for civic sponsorship of public building at Taormenion during the Hieronian period. And see Prag (2015: 181–6) for discussion of *euergetism* by local elites in Late Hellenistic and Rome period Sicily; Dimartino (2019), similarly, from the perspective of epigraphic evidence; Henzel (2019) on Sicilian honorific sculptures of Hellenistic and Roman date, with focus on evidence from Solunto.

[74] In support of a royal patron of the East Stoa, Bell (1993: 332) cites the examples of Apollonis, wife of Attalos I, who donated funds for the construction of stoa buildings in the sanctuary of Demeter at Pergamon, and Lamis, a mistress of Demetrios Poliorketes, who sponsored the construction of a stoa at Sikyon. For more examples of female patronage (both royal and nonroyal) of civic buildings in the Hellenistic period, see Ridgway (1987: 407–8) and van Bremen (1996). More recently, Bell (2022) has made a compelling argument that the figure should be identified as the goddess Tyche.

[75] For the Hellenistic houses at Morgantina, see Tsakirgis (1984; 1995: 131–8).

[76] Regarding the mosaic pavements generally, see Tsakirgis (1989); and for discussion of the famous Ganymede mosaic, see Phillips (1960).

[77] For an overview of jewelry recovered from third-century contexts at Morgantina, see Manenti (2015).

[78] Walthall (2021).

[79] See Bell (2000; 2010) for the House of Eupolemos.

[80] Allen (1974: 362–6) offers a preliminary report on the building excavated in Contrada Drago. For a brief description of the Collina Papa excavations, see Walthall (2017: 103–5).

[81] Thompson (1999; 2002).

[82] For description of the survey universe, see Thompson (1999: 55–8).

[83] Thompson (1999: 329) recorded fifty-two sites for this period, compared with the fifity-six from the LC-EH period.

[84] Thompson (1999: 412–13), who further notes that the number of sites that could be reasonably classified as sites of permanent settlement (as opposed to seasonally occupied sites, which might show lower-density scatters) rose from eight in the LA-EC period to eighteen in the LC-EH period.

[85] Thompson (1999: 426–8) is quick to point out that – absent excavation – determining the function of a site by its size or artifact-scatter density is, at best, an exercise in speculation. He notes that, among other factors, post-depositional processes like plowing and mass wasting (i.e., the gradual movement of soils across a landscape) can lead to the dispersal and relocation of artifacts.

[86] D'Annibale (1983).

[87] Thompson (1999: 430 = sites R04/S4, R88/S1, MC17/S1, MC52/S1).

[88] Thompson (1999: 431). For the post-211 population decline in the urban settlement, see Stone (2014: 12–17).

[89]   Bergemann (2010: 159–60).

[90]   Bell (1995) presents an overview of the coin finds from the north suite of the Central Shops, focusing more on questions of chronology than issues of commerce and exchange. Current numismatic scholarship regarding questions of monetary circulation in Hellenistic Sicily tends to privilege discussion of its military function, often viewing circulation through the lens of troop movements; e.g., Puglisi (2004; 2005; 2009).

[91]   For a recent discussion of commercial activity in the agora of Morgantina, see Bell (2019).

[92]   Bell (1988: 326–30; 1995).

[93]   Excavators found thick strata of ash and tiles in all the rooms of the central suite, suggesting that they were destroyed in a conflagration, while several rooms in the southern suite appear to have been temporarily used as a makeshift abattoir following the siege of 211. For the excavation of the central suite and numismatic deposits associated with the final phase of use, see Stillwell and Sjöqvist (1957: 156–7); Buttrey et al. (1989: 162–4, deposit nos. 27–8); Walthall (2017). For the southern suite of rooms, see Bell (1988: 324–6) and Buttrey et al. (1989: 187–8, deposit nos. 56–7).

[94]   For types and discussion of date, see Walthall (2017).

[95]   Crawford (1970: 42–3).

[96]   This number includes eight specimens of the imitation Ptolemaic "West Greek" Zeus/ Eagle series found within the shops, which alone represent approximately 1.5 percent of the total coin finds from the shops. If these are excluded, the overall percentage of Hieronian coinage drops to just below 74 percent.

[97]   While we should recognize that any individual coin may have found its way into the space for any number of reasons, such as carried within the matrix of soil added to serve as a leveling fill (per observations of Ellis 2017), the overall concentration of coins, measured both spatially and temporally, lends to the impression that the majority were used for commercial transactions taking place within either the shop or its immediate surroundings.

[98]   Perkins (2007: 44) adduces that the purchases may have been related to the payments made for the collection of the second tithe, for which cultivators were paid a fixed price in cash.

[99]   For discussion of the excavation and identification of the *macellum* at Morgantina, see Stillwell and Sjöqvist (1957: 154–5); Nabers (1967: 126–42); De Ruyt (1983: 109–14). Based on a recent reappraisal of the archaeological evidence recovered from the building during its excavation in the 1950s, Sharp (2015) has posited that the building was constructed around the year 175. This runs counter to the longstanding opinion that the *macellum* was constructed in the 130s, an interpretation that rested largely on the basis of a single coin – a denarius of Sextus Pompeius Fostlus (inv. 55-2097; *MS* II 592, *RRC* 235/1a) struck in the year 137 – said to have been found in the fill of a builder's trench. In his review of the excavation notebooks and stratigraphic drawings from 1955 and 1956, Sharp has convincingly argued that this coin originally formed part of a small hoard of denarii, which had been concealed below the beaten-earth floor inside one of the shop rooms. It was not – as long believed – recovered from the fill of a builder's trench and, thus, does not provide a clear *terminus post quem* of 137 for the construction of the building.

[100]   For the date of the abandonment of the *macellum*, see Stone (1983: 17).

[101]   The majority of these coins (*n* = 351 of 425) came from the seven shop rooms that formed the north side of the market. This is likely due to the fact that the southern portion of the building and its associated ancient strata suffered from heavy erosional activity in the millennia that followed the abandonment of the market and thus preserved relatively little intact stratigraphy. I am grateful to Hal Sharp for providing me with a manuscript draft of his revised archaeological study of the *macellum*, including his detailed inventory of coin finds from the excavations of the building.

[102]   Buttrey et al. (1989: nos. 140–2). In her study of the coinage from Katane, Casabona (1999) concludes that the earliest of the Apollo/Isis issues was struck between 216/15 and 205; cf. Mattingly (2000: 47), who in a review of Casabona's work suggests the introduction of this series should be pushed down into the first three decades of the second century.

[103] We can be fairly certain that these coins were not in circulation at Morgantina in the years prior to the Roman siege, since none have been recovered from secure contexts at the site predating 211; see discussion in Buttrey et al. (1989: 140–1).

[104] Some 1,057 specimens are reported in Buttrey et al. (1989), which dealt with the coins found in excavations at the site between 1955 and 1981. By my rough calculation, an additional two dozen or so of the Apollo/Isis types have turned up in excavations at the site between 1982 and 2019.

[105] Livy (29.1) reports that in 205, Scipio found that Syracuse still had not fully recovered from the violence and turmoil of Marcellus's siege.

[106] Liv. 26.40.15–16; *coegissetque Siculos positis tandem armis ad agrum colendum animos convertere, ut esset non incolarum modo alimentis frugifera insula, sed urbis Romae atque Italiae, id quod multis saepe tempestatibus fecerat, annonam leveret*; trans., Roberts (1905).

[107] Liv. 27.8.18–19; *provinciam peragrabat, ut viseret agros cultaque ab incultis notaret et perinde dominos laudaret castigaretque. ita tantum ea cura frumenti provenit ut et Romam mitteret et Catinam conveheret unde exercitui qui ad Tarentum aestiv*; trans., Roberts (1905) with emendations.

[108] For instance, *CIL* XIV 364, an inscription discovered at Ostia that identifies a certain C. Granius Maturus as patronus of a shipping guild, which had operations based in both Ostia and Katane; as reconstructed by Manganaro (1988: 9). For a recent review of evidence related to the city's harbor from the ancient to modern period, with particular emphasis on geological and topographic analysis, see Castagnino Berlinghieri and Monaco (2008).

[109] Stone (2014: 151–4), who further suggests that one of the potters responsible for operating the large kiln installed in the former granary building at Morgantina may have moved to the city from Katane or, at least, have been trained by a workshop from that area.

[110] Lucchelli and Di Stefano (2004: 56–7) themselves remark on the pronounced similarity (a "parallelism," to use their term) in the types and percentages of coins circulating at Kamarina and Morgantina during the third century.

[111] See *supra* Chapter 4, p. 155, n. 120 for the *deportatio ad aquam*.

[112] See the excellent discussion by Pfuntner (2019) rebutting narratives of "urban decline." Regarding the refashioning of narratives about Morgantina under Roman rule, see the new work by Trümper (2017; 2019).

CONCLUSION

LOOKING BACK

In the chapters that form the first part of the book, I asked the reader to view the monarchy of Hieron II as one fundamentally akin, in both principle and practice, to the forms of autocratic rule familiar to us from the Successor kingdoms of the eastern Mediterranean. The surviving evidence – both literary and material – offers clear witness to the flexible approach taken by Hieron and his court in service of legitimating his political authority over the cities of southeastern Sicily. Moreover, it reveals that the modes of communication and display emanating from the royal capital at Syracuse were fashioned in a manner receptive to contemporary trends taking place in the courts of the Successor kings. We see this, for instance, in Hieron's early efforts to wrap his claims of legitimate political authority in the cloak of military power, grounded in demonstrable success on the battlefield. It cannot be mere coincidence, as I argued in Chapter 2, that Hieron sought acclamation as *basileus* on the heels of his victory over the Mamertines at the Longanus River in 269. The outward displays of the king's militaristic persona inevitably followed in the form of coin types, monumental statuary, dedications of weapons at Panhellenic sanctuaries, and court-sponsored biographies.

At the same time, Hieron's approach to legitimizing his status as an autocratic ruler was clearly responsive to developments occurring closer to home. This is best seen in the rehabilitation that occurred following the conclusion of his peace treaty with Rome in 263 when, stripped of his ability to freely campaign against the Mamertines, the king sought to justify his exceptional political status by casting himself as *euergetēs* and *sōtēr* for those cities under his control. And, indeed, this was no empty promise as the archaeological record attests to a period of great prosperity enjoyed by those cities that flourished under Hieron's protection, all while much of western Sicily suffered in the ongoing war between Rome and Carthage. In many respects, Hieron's relationship with Rome – once seen as antithetical to his classification as a Hellenistic king – was a harbinger of things to come as Roman political and military interests eventually found their way into the eastern Mediterranean.

Building off this foundation, the greater project of this book sought to bring attention to the materiality of royal administration, particularly with respect to the taxation of agricultural resources. Here, my work was informed by that of Margaret Levi, whose theory of predatory rule provided a helpful framework for understanding the structure and operation of Hieron's tax laws. As an institution that existed to maintain the king's power and legitimacy, the Hieronian tax laws ushered in a degree of intervention and oversight over the *poleis* of southeastern Sicily far greater than had previously been exercised by the dominant political powers on the island. Prior to the consolidation of Hieronian rule, taxation had largely been a highly localized privilege of the *polis*. In its very existence, the royal tax administration necessitated sustained communication and interaction at the supra-*polis* level where it had not previously existed. Even within the expansive territorial zones that fell to Syracusan potentates like Agathokles and the Deinomenid tyrants, the available evidence suggests that administrative oversight was loose, intermittent, and reactive. The Hieronian administration, on the other hand, was unitary, constant, and programmatic.

The task of making the productive landscapes more legible to royal authorities and, thus, more effectively taxed was aided by the introduction of specific material tools of the state, namely, terracotta measuring vessels, monumental stone granaries, and bronze coins. Each class of artifact offers a distinct view onto the nature and scale of Hieron's administrative reach. All were part and parcel of the greater institutional transformations brought about by the development of the Hieronian tax laws and of the bureaucratic infrastructure required for their implementation and performance.

In Chapter 5, I argued that the contemporaneous adoption of standardized volumetric measures at sites across southeastern Sicily was a direct consequence of royal mandate. This conclusion was predicated on observations made both at the macroscale with the widespread appearance of these new measuring tools in the archaeological record around the middle decades of the third century and at the microscale with the reading of the stamped ἀκριβάζοντος measures as devices authenticated by a royal official. What I have endeavored to show is that measuring devices need not be relegated to metrological inquiry but rather should be treated as vital documents of the political, commercial, and administrative systems to which they belonged. Alone, a single measure tells us little; when considered in large number, they can reveal the application of abstract systems ordering the tangible world. In our case, the vessels themselves bring new clarity to the territorial contours of the Hieronian kingdom and offer fresh perspective on the scope of Hieron's royal authority. I have every confidence that this corpus of material will continue to grow, further expanding our understanding of ancient standards, trade, and administration both within the Hieronian kingdom and throughout the Hellenistic Mediterranean.

The monumental granaries discussed in Chapter 6 emerged as much more than straightforward warehouses. These buildings were as much sites of administrative oversight as they were visible expressions of royal power, where cultivators from the surrounding territory would have handed over payments of their agricultural tithe to royal officials, who represented the king's interests and authority on the ground. Through the performative and recursive nature of the bureaucratic rituals taking place at these administrative buildings, the granaries served to reify the narrative of legitimacy upon which Hieron laid claim to the authority to rule and, with it, his prerogative to extract resources from the land under his control. The same can be reasonably argued for the monumental granaries constructed at Syracuse, Pergamon, and Mount Karasis, all of which surely communicated similar messages about the nature of royal power, be it Hieronian, Attalid, or Seleucid. In all cases, monumental granaries were physical reminders of a king's outsized wealth and their capacity to forestall famine and economic crisis. Yet these heavily fortified structures, inaccessible to the ordinary citizen, stood as equally stark reminders of a king's power to take the agricultural surplus of his kingdom and use it as he saw fit.

Shifting focus from the monumental to the handheld, Chapter 7 dealt with the coinage struck by Hieron II and considered how the king may have pursued certain monetary policies aimed at bolstering his wealth and political authority over the *poleis* of southeastern Sicily. One such policy was the shift to the monometallic production of bronze coinage and the corresponding intensification of output by the royal mint at Syracuse, with the result that Hieronian bronze became the ubiquitous currency of southeastern Sicily for the much of the third century. When the royal mint resumed production of silver coinage around the decade of the 230s, denominations were issued in units based on the Sicilian litra standard, resulting in coins that were lighter than those struck on the more widely circulating Attic-Euboic standard. Such a policy may have allowed Hieron to effectively reduce the outflow of silver from his kingdom, especially if merchants seeking to do business in southeastern Sicily were required to exchange heavier foreign coins for their lighter

Sicilian counterparts. Last, I considered the question of whether the Hieronian court actively took steps to suppress the operation of civic mints within the areas subject to royal authority. The enforcement of such a policy is reflected by the fact that not one of the roughly fifteen *poleis* within the Hieronian kingdom issued coinage while subject to the king's political authority. The available evidence supports the interpretation that this abeyance of coin production at civic mints was the product of royal interference and not the consequence of *poleis* voluntarily interrupting local operations.

Finally, in Chapter 8, I considered how the consolidation of royal authority affected the agricultural and economic landscapes of southeastern Sicily, paying particular attention to the ways in which the tithe administration may have fostered trade and economic prosperity for the cities of the kingdom. I argued that Hieron's tax laws brought interior communities into increased economic contact with Syracuse and, by extension, Mediterranean-wide trade networks. Several factors enabled this market integration, including the advent of long-term peace and stability within the territories subject to Hieron; the kingdom-wide unification of coinage and volumetric measures under a single, royal standard; and the implementation of an administrative infrastructure designed to move agricultural produce from the interior to the coast. The argument that such dynamic market integration occurred during this period is borne out by the mint distribution of coins recovered from two commercial complexes at Morgantina. I argued that these coins shed light on the way that the tithe administration encouraged commercial exchange between agriculturally productive centers in the interior and market centers at major port cities along the coast, revealing ephemeral networks of trade and exchange that have gone otherwise unattested in our surviving documentary sources.

LOOKING FORWARD

In bringing the archaeology of Hieron's royal administration to the forefront of this discussion, my aim has been to chart productive approaches for future investigations into the internal mechanics of the Hellenistic kingdom. As archaeologists continue to pursue new excavations and publish the results of earlier campaigns, we can only expect our view of this administrative landscape to come into greater focus. I fully expect that such work will lead to new discoveries that may stand to advance some of the ideas set forth here while proving others incorrect. In either case, our understanding of Hellenistic Sicily and, in particular, the Hieronian kingdom will only continue to improve.

For the time being, the archaeology of the tithe administration in Republican Sicily stands as an open field of investigation, one that promises to reward continued research, particularly when informed by the abundance of scholarship that has explored the Roman afterlife of Hieron's tax laws from legal, literary, and historical perspectives. While Cicero was firm in his claim that the Romans changed little when applying the Hieronian tax laws to the whole of the island, we have had occasion in the preceding chapters to address points of apparent discontinuity in the administration of the agricultural tithe following the Sicily's absorption into the Roman empire.

For instance, we saw that the granary buildings at Morgantina ceased to function as monumental warehouses in the years following the collapse of the Hieronian kingdom. Why were these administrative centers, so essential to the operation of the agricultural tithe during Hieron's lifetime, swiftly abandoned once the Romans took control of Sicily? As I argued in Chapter 6, these buildings were rendered obsolete once the island and its agricultural resources fell to Rome with its insatiable demand for grain. There was no longer any need to systematically stockpile tithe grain or other agricultural produce in Sicily, especially around the island's interior, where it did little good for the citizens of Rome. Rather, tithe grain was brought immediately to ports where it could be loaded onto ships and sent off to feed Roman citizens and soldiers.[1]

Indeed, the archaeological record reflects the growing importance of the cities along the north and east coast of the island during the Republican and Early Imperial periods. Many coastal cities flourished during the second and first centuries BCE, likely due, one suspects, to their newfound role as transshipment points for agricultural goods leaving the island for points north.[2] The construction of long, granary-like structures at the coastal sites of Kamarina and Aci Castello, north of Catania, appear to reflect the administrative changes introduced by the Romans.[3] A study of these changing networks of collection and distribution – alongside a more detailed examination of these and other storage facilities at or near coastal sites – is paramount to understanding how the Romans extracted resources from their first province. Such patterns might also be profitably placed in dialogue with the (re)appearance of monumental granary buildings around the island's interior over the course of the third and fourth centuries CE, at sites like Geraci and Piazza Armerina.[4] These sizable warehouses did not appear in urban centers, but were connected to large villas, whose owners likely collected both rents and taxes in kind from tenants working portions of these massive estates. Can the renewed construction of large granary buildings at interior sites be associated with what is known about the administration of taxes during the period of the Late Empire, or are these structures to be associated with the growing power of elites outside Rome?

Important research remains to be done to investigate the apparent disappearance of standardized measures belonging to the types that we see first materialize at sites around eastern Sicily during the third century. I argued that the widespread appearance of these standardized vessels likely represented efforts made by the Hieronian court to promote the unification of volumetric

C.1 Mosaic representations of standard dry measures from the Piazzale delle Corporazioni, Ostia, second century CE (after Becati 1961).

measurement throughout the kingdom, a vital step toward improving the efficacy of the state's efforts to extract taxes. Yet the Roman conquest of the island and the application of the *lex Hieronica* to the whole of Sicily did not result in a multiplication of measuring vessels like those encountered in Chapter 5. Most surprising of all, these standardized vessels even cease to show up in the archaeological record at those sites in southeastern Sicily where they had been so prevalent during the reign of Hieron II. It may be that the materiality of these vessels changed from the third to the second century, such that terracotta was no longer employed as the prevailing medium for volumetric measures. Most of the extant examples of measuring vessels from the Roman world are, in fact, made from materials like wood and bronze, which rarely survive in the archaeological record.

Yet, at least in form, volumetric dry measures of Roman manufacture, known from other parts of the empire, held quite close to the shapes one might have encountered in markets across the Hieronian kingdom or, for that matter, in the Classical agorai of Athens and Corinth. We can see this continuity of form – cylindrical or truncated cones with tripod feet and external banding – most readily in graphic representations of volumetric measures found decorating mosaic floors, funerary reliefs, and coin types of Imperial date (Figure C.1).[5] In its iconography, the typical Roman *modius* measure appears a descendant of Greek types, perhaps even those first encountered in Sicily by Roman traders. This, of course, is merely speculative, but renewed attention by archaeologists working in storerooms and excavating Roman-era sites around Sicily may help to locate the successors of the Hieronian measures. Here, it is worth noting that a brief survey of roughly fifty weights found in the excavations at Morgantina suggests that Roman weight standards gradually replaced earlier standards (i.e., Sicilian litra units; Attic drachma and mina units) over the course of the second century BCE.[6] This transition can be traced both in terms of the outward appearance of the physical trade weights as well as with regard to the base units on which the weights were initially formed and calibrated. If similar changes were made – in form and capacity – to volumetric measures under increased pressure from Roman administrators and merchants, the remains of these otherwise unremarkable vessels may be waiting for identification and study. These, in turn, may shed light on the tools with which Roman administrators made legible the first of their overseas possessions.

Further analysis of the bronze coinages struck by Sicilian *poleis* in the first two centuries of Roman rule promises to bring additional clarity to the continued impact that agricultural taxation had on the island's markets. As noted in Chapter 7, there was an appreciable spike in output by civic mints in the decades after the collapse of the Hieronian kingdom, likely as a response to the dwindling stock of small bronze denominations in circulation caused by the suspension of minting at Syracuse. We have already seen from our narrow case study of coin finds from the excavations in the agora at Morgantina how the chronological distribution of low-denomination coins might shed light on changing networks of trade. As Phil Perkins persuasively argued in the case of the hinterland around Iatas in western Sicily, these trade networks were often shaped by the demands of the prevailing tax regime. If the scope of analysis were widened to accommodate a larger selection of cities, one potential outcome would be the recognition of previously undetected commercial ties that resulted from Rome's growing administrative control of the island. It may, for instance, lead to greater clarity around the enigmatic *deportatio ad aquam*, a vital (but poorly understood) procedural step in the Roman's operation of the *lex Hieronica*.[7]

For these civic issues struck under Roman rule, there is the added layer of analysis that might be applied to the iconographic choices made for the reverse types. Even a cursory glance at the coins issued in the century to follow the formation of the Roman province reveals a preference for agricultural themes, which served to reinforce the connection between a community and the agrarian sources of its wealth. One particularly conspicuous example from this period is the series of bronze coins struck by the *polis* of Kentoripe in the decades around the year 200 (Figure C.2). These coins depict a bust of the goddess Demeter on the obverse, and a plow on the reverse. While the agricultural goddess featured regularly on Sicilian coin types going back centuries, the plow was a relatively new addition to the iconographic reper-toire. It was a symbol adopted by several other Sicilian cities around this time, appearing as a monogram on the coinages of both Leontinoi and Panormus, as well as in larger format on a series struck at the hilltop city of Henna, which depicts a pair of serpents drawing the plow. Returning to the coins of

c.2 Bronze coin of Kentoripe with a plow as reverse type, second century BCE (ANS 1944.100.8401; courtesy of the American Numismatic Society).

Kentoripe, one suspects the selection of the plow was meant to highlight – even advertise – the productivity of its territory. This self-promotion exhibited by Kentoripe and other Sicilian communities with respect to themes of agricultural capacity may have played a role in shaping Roman perceptions of the island and its potential as a grain basket for Rome.

CODA

In writing this book I have sought to bring greater depth and dimension to our appreciation of the Hieronian kingdom and its place within the wider Hellenistic Mediterranean. My approach was to focus on the inner workings of the royal administration and economy, particularly those that are available to us in the archaeological record. Thus, in my telling of the story, monumental granaries, grain measures, and bronze coins took center stage. Collectively, they revealed new aspects of consolidation and control by the Hieronian state, the nature and scale of which had not been registered in the political or productive landscapes of Sicily prior to the third century.

Although much of the preceding discussion centered on the person of Hieron and on the Hieronian state, the point was to reconstruct some of what living under that state looked like for the people who remain unnamed and unknown. By prioritizing archaeology, we have the opportunity to cast a brighter light on the material realities experienced by the inhabitants of the cities and territories of southeastern Sicily at the time, who – measure by measure, year after year – handed over a portion of their harvests to the king. Their personal experiences of royal power, whether through interaction with measure-wielding tax collectors or in the rituals of assessment and reporting, may have gone largely unchronicled by ancient historians but are not completely lost to us. By studying the material instruments of administration, the very tools that bound citizens and cultivators to the Hieronian state, we can better grasp those aspects of daily life otherwise unavailable in the documentary record. Fortunately for us, Sicily holds countless stories of this kind, waiting to be told by future generations of archaeologists and historians.

NOTES

1   Soraci (2011).
2   For an archaeological overview of urban centers on Sicily during the Republican and Imperial periods, see Wilson (1990); Pfuntner (2019); and, with specific reference to the area south of Palermo, Perkins (2007).
3   Mattioli (1995). To this, we might add the so-called Basilica at Tindari, which was constructed along the central *decumanus* leading into the city. The date – along with the function – of this building remains subject to debate.
4   For fullest discussion, see Wilson (2015: 191–202); Wilson and Ramsay (2017: 286–92).
5   Berg (2020) offers a recent summary of the available visual evidence for the Roman *modius*.
6   See Walthall (2023).
7   For an in-depth discussion of the *deportatio ad aquam*, see Soraci (2011: 84–96).

BIBLIOGRAPHY

Adamesteanu, D. 1962. "L'ellenizzazione della Sicilia ed il momento Ducezio." *Kokalos* 8: 167–98.

Adamesteanu, D. 1963. "Note di topografi a siceliota, parte I." *Kokalos* 9: 19–48.

Adamesteanu, D., and P. Orlandini. 1956. *Gela: Scavi e scoperte 1951–1956, fascicolo I*. Vol. 10. Rome: Accademia nazionale dei Lincei.

Adamesteanu, D., and P. Orlandini. 1960. *Gela: scavi e scoperte 1951–1956, fascicolo II*. Vol. 14. Rome: Accademia nazionale dei Lincei.

Adams, G. W. 2008. "The Unbalanced Relationship between Ptolemy II and Pyrrhus of Epirus." In *Ptolemy II Philadelphus and His World*, edited by P. McKechnie and P. Guillaume, 91–102. Leiden: Brill.

Ager, S. 2017. "Symbol and Ceremony: Royal Weddings in the Hellenistic Age." In *The Hellenistic Court: Monarchic Power and Elite Society from Alexander to Cleopatra*, edited by A. Erskine, L. Llewellyn-Jones, and S. Wallace, 165–88. Swansea: Classical Press of Wales.

Agnello, S. L. 1949. "Siracusa: Scoperte nel giardino Spagna." *Notizie degli scavi di antichità* 3: 190–212.

Akerlof, G. A. 1970. "The Market for 'Lemons': Quality Uncertainty and the Market Mechanism." *The Quarterly Journal of Economics* 84: 488–500.

Allen, H. L. 1974. "Excavations at Morgantina (Serra Orlando), 1970–1972: Preliminary Report XI." *American Journal of Archaeology* 78: 361–83.

Ameling, W. 2011. "The Rise of Carthage to 264 BC." In *A Companion to the Punic Wars*, edited by B. D. Hoyos, 39–57. Malden, MA: Blackwell.

Ampolo, C. 1984. "Tributi e decime dei Siracusani." *Opus* 3: 31–6.

Ampolo, C. 2001. *Da un'antica città di Sicilia: I decreti di Entella e Nakone*. Pisa: Scuola Normale Superiore.

Andreau, J. 2007. "Registers, Account-Books, and Written Documents in the *De frumento*." In *Sicilia Nutrix Plebis Romanae: Rhetoric, Law, and Taxation in Cicero's Verrines*, edited by J. R. W. Prag, 81–92. Bulletin of the Institute of Classical Studies Supplement 97. London: Institute of Classical Studies, University of London.

Antonaccio, C. M. 1999. "Κυπάρα, a Sikel Nymph?" *Zeitschrift für Papyrologie und Epigraphik* 126: 177–85.

Aperghis, G. G. 2004. *The Seleukid Royal Economy: The Finances and Financial Administration of the Seleukid Empire*. Cambridge: Cambridge University Press.

Aranjo-Ruez, V., and A. Oliveri. 1965. *Inscriptiones graecae Siciliae et infimae Italiae ad ius pertinentes*. Rome: L'Erma di Bretschneider.

Archibald, Z. H. 2007. "Contacts between the Ptolemaic Kingdom and the Black Sea in the Early Hellenistic Age." In *The Black Sea in Antiquity: Regional and Interregional Economic Exchanges*, edited by V. Gabrielsen and J. Lund, 253–71. Aarhus: Aarhus University Press.

Armagrande, V. 2000. "Agatocle, Kore: Il problema dell'assimilazione del *Basileus* con une dea." In *XII Internationaler Numismatischer Kongress, Berlin 1997*, edited by B. Kluge and B. Weisser, 224–9. Berlin: Staatliche Museen zu Berlin.

Arnold-Biucchi, C. 2002. Review of *Siracusa ellenistica. Le monete "regali" di Ierone II, della sua famiglia e dei Siracusani. Pelorias 2. Collana del Dipartimento di Scienze dell'Antichità dell'Università di Messina*, edited by M. Caccamo Caltabiano, B. Carroccio, and E. Oteri. https://bmcr.brynmawr.edu/2002/2002.08.05/.

Ashton, R. 1956. "Revenue Farming under the Early Stuarts." *The Economic History Review*, new series 8: 310–22.

Ashworth, W. J. 2004. "Metrology and the State: Science, Revenue, and Commerce." *Science* 306: 1314–17.

Austin, M. M. 1986. "Hellenistic Kings, War, and the Economy." *Classical Quarterly* 36: 450–66.

Austin, M. M. 2006. *The Hellenistic World from Alexander to the Roman Conquest: A Selection of Ancient Sources in Translation*. 2nd augmented edition. Cambridge: Cambridge University Press.

Babelon, E., and Blanchet, J.-A. 1895. *Catalogue des bronzes antiques de la Bibliothèque nationale*. Paris: E. Leroux.

Backman, C. R. 1995. *The Decline and Fall of Medieval Sicily: Politics, Religion, and Economy in the Reign of Frederick III, 1296–1337*. Cambridge: Cambridge University Press.

Backmann, M. 2011. "Dachwerk über steinernem 'Fruchtkasten': Der Speicherbau des Karasis." In *Holztragwerke der Antike. Internationale Konferenz 30. März –1. April 2007 in München*, edited by A. von Kienlin, 171–181. BYZAS 11. Istanbul: Ege Yayinlari/German Institute of Archaeology.

Bagnall, R. S. 1976. *The Administration of the Ptolemaic Possessions outside Egypt*. Leiden: Brill.

Bagnall, R. S. 2011. "Practical Help: Chronology, Geography, Measures, Currency, Names, Prosopography, and Technical Vocabulary." In *The Oxford Handbook of Papyrology*, edited by R. S. Bagnall, 179–96. New York: Oxford University Press.

Bagnall, R. S., and P. Derow, eds. and trans. 2004. *The Hellenistic Period: Historical Sources in Translation*. Malden, MA: Blackwell.

Bang, P. F. 2006. "Imperial Bazaar: Towards a Comparative Understanding of Markets in the Roman Empire." In *Ancient Economies, Modern Methodologies: Archaeology, Comparative History, Models and Institutions*, edited by P. F. Bang, M. Ikeguchi, and H. G. Ziche, 51–88. Bari: Edipuglia.

Bang, P. F. 2007. "Trade and Empire: In Search of Organizing Concepts for the Roman Economy." *Past & Present* 195: 3–54.

Bang, P. F. 2009. "The Ancient Economy and New Institutional Economics." *The Journal of Roman Studies* 99: 194–206.

Barbantani, S. 2007. "The Glory of the Spear: A Powerful Symbol in Hellenistic Poetry and Art. The Case of Neoptolemus 'of Tlos' (and Other Ptolemaic Epigrams)." *Studi Classici e Orientali* 53: 67–138.

Barbantani, S. 2011. "Callimachus on Kings and Kingship." In *Brill's Companion to Callimachus*, edited by B. Acosta-Hughes, L. Lehnus, and S. A. Stephens, 178–200. Leiden: Brill.

Barbera, D. 2019. "La nave della città: La *Syrakosia* come allegoria della Siracusa ieroniana." In *Cityscapes of Hellenistic Sicily*, edited by M. Trümper, G. Adornato, and T. Lappi, 159–79. Rome: Edizioni Quasar.

Baron, C. A. 2013. *Timaeus of Tauromenium and Hellenistic Historiography*. Cambridge: Cambridge University Press.

Battistoni, F. 2011. "Time(s) for Tauromenion: The Pilaster with the List of the *Stratagoi* (IG XIV 421) – The Antikythera Mechanism." *Zeitschrift für Papyrologie und Epigraphik* 179: 171–88.

Bell, M. 1981. *Morgantina Studies, vol. 1: The Terracottas.*. Princeton, NJ: Princeton University Press.

Bell, M. 1984–5. "Recenti scavi nell'agora di Morgantina." *Kokalos* 30–1: 501–20.

Bell, M. 1988. "Excavations at Morgantina 1980–1985, Preliminary Report XII." *American Journal of Archaeology* 92: 313–42.

Bell, M. 1993. "Observations on Western Greek Stoas." *Studies in the History of Art* 43: 326–41.

Bell, M. 1995. "Monete ieroniche in nuovi contesti di scavo a Morgantina." In *La Sicilia tra l'Egitto e Roma. La monetazione siracusana dell'età di Ierone II. Atti del seminario di studi, Messina 2–4 dicembre 1993*, edited by

M. Caccamo Caltabiano, 289–93. Messina: Accademia Peloritana dei Pericolanti.

Bell, M. 1999. "Centro e periferia nel regno siracusano di Ierone II." In *La colonisation grecque en Méditerranée occidentale. Actes de la rencontre scientifique en hommage à Georges Vallet (Rome – Naples, 15–18 novembre 1995)*, 257–77. Naples: Centre Jean Bérard.

Bell, M. 2000. "La provenienza ritrovata: Cercando il contesto di antichità trafugate." In *Antichità senza provenienza II: Atti del colloquio internazionale, 17–18 ottobre, 1997*, edited by P. Pelagatti and P. G. Guzzo, 31–41. Bollettino d'Arte Supplement 101–102. Rome: Istituto poligrafico e zecca dello stato.

Bell, M. 2004. "Una banca pubblica sull'agora di Morgantina?" In *Nuove prospettive della ricerca sulla Sicilia del III sec. a.C. Archeologia, numismatica, storia. Atti dell'incontro di studio (Messina 4–5 luglio 2002)*, edited by M. Caccamo Caltabiano, L. Campagna, and A. Pinzone, 135–45. Messina: Dipartimento di Scienze dell'Antichità dell'Università degli Studi di Messina.

Bell, M. 2007a. "An Archaeologist's Perspective on the *Lex Hieronica*." In *La Sicile de Cicéron: Lectures des Verrines*, edited by J. Dubouloz and S. Pittia, 187–203. Besançon: Presses universitaires de Franche-Comté, DL.

Bell, M. 2007b. "Apronius in the Agora: Sicilian Civil Architecture and the *Lex hieronica*." In *Sicilia Nutrix Plebis Romanae: Rhetoric, Law, and Taxation in Cicero's Verrines*, edited by J. R. W. Prag, 117–34. Bulletin of the Institute of Classical Studies Supplement 97. London: Institute of Classical Studies, University of London.

Bell, M. 2008. "*Hiera oikopeda*." In *Demetra: La divinita, i santuari, il culto, la leggenda. Atti del I Congresso internazionale Enna 2004*, edited by C. A. Di Stefano, 155–9. Pisa: Fabrizio Serra.

Bell, M. 2010. "Il tesoro di argenteria e la casa di Eupolemos a Morgantina." In *Sacri agli dei, Argenti della casa di Eupolemos a Morgantina. Il rientro*, edited by E. Caruso, 23–5. Palermo: Regione Sicilia.

Bell, M. 2011. "Agrarian Policy, Bucolic Poetry, and Figurative Art in Early Hellenistic Sicily." In *Krise und Wandel: Süditalien im 4. und 3. Jahrhundert v. Chr.: internationaler Kongress anlässlich des 65. Geburtstages von Dieter Mertens, Rom 26. bis 28. Juni 2006*, edited by R. Neudecker, 193–211. Wiesbaden: Reichert Verlag.

Bell, M. 2019. "Commercio e innovazione nell'agora di Morgantina, ca. 250 a.C." *Cronache di archeologia* 38: 243–67.

Bell, M. 2022. *Morgantina Studies, vol. 7: The Political Agora*. Wiesbaden: Reichert Verlag.

Bellomo, M. 2013. "Polybius and the Outbreak of the First Punic War: A Constitutional Issue." *Studi Classici e Orientali* 59: 71–90.

Beloch, K. J. 1874. "Sulla popolazione dell'antica Sicilia." *Rivista di Filologia e d'Istruzione classica* 2: 545–62.

Beloch, K. J. 1886. *Die Bevölkerung der griechisch-römischen Welt*. Leipzig: Duncker & Humblot.

Bencivenni, A. 2014. "The King's Words: Hellenistic Royal Letters in Inscriptions." In *State Correspondence in the Ancient World: From New Kingdom Egypt to the Roman Empire*, edited by K. Radner, 141–71. Oxford: Oxford University Press.

Berg, R. 2020. "Iconography of the Modius Measure in Ostia: The Visualizing of Economic and Cultural Exchange." In *Trade and Commerce in the Harbour Town of Ostia*, edited by A. Landskron and C. Tempesta, 75–104. Graz: Uni-Press Graz Verlag.

Bergemann, J., ed. 2010. *Der Gela-Survey: 3000 Jahre Siedlungsgeschichte in Sizilien*. Munich: Biering & Brinkmann.

Bergemann, J. 2011. "Il Gela-Survey: 3000 anni di insediamenti e storia nella Sicilia centro-meridionale." *Sicilia Antiqua* 8: 63–100.

Bernabò Brea, L., G. Pugliese Carratelli, and C. Laviosa. 1956. *Akrai*. Vol. 1. Catania: Società di Storia Patria per la Sicilia Orientale.

Berrey, M. 2017. *Hellenistic Science at Court*. Berlin: De Gruyter.

Berriman, A. E. 1953. *Historical Metrology: A New Analysis of the Archaeological and the Historical Evidence Relating to Weights and Measures*. London: Dent.

Berriman, A. E. 1955. "A New Approach to the Study of Ancient Metrology." *Revue d'assyriologie et d'archéologie orientale* 49: 193–201.

Berve, H. 1959. *König Hieron II*. Munich: Verlag der Bayerischen Akademie der Wissenschaften.

Berve, H. 1967. *Die Tyrannis bei den Griechen*. Munich: C. H. Beck.

Beste, H.-J., and D. Mertens. 2015. *Die Mauern von Syrakus: Das Kastell Euryalos und die Befestigung der Epipolai*. Sonderschriften (Deutsches Archäologisches Institut. Römische Abteilung) 18. Weisbaden: Reichert Verlag.

Bickermann, E. J. 1938. *Institutions des Séleucides*. Paris: P. Geuthner.

Billows, R. A. 1990. *Antigonos the One-Eyed and the Creation of the Hellenistic State*. Berkeley: University of California Press.

Billows, R. A. 2007. "Cities." In *A Companion to the Hellenistic World*, edited by A. Erskine, 196–215. Malden, MA: Blackwell.

Bingen, J. 1952. *Papyrus Revenue Laws*. Göttingen: Huber.

Bingen, J. 1978. *Le papyrus revenue laws: Tradition grecque et adaptation hellenistique*. Opladen: Westdeutscher Verlag.

Bingen, J. 2007. *Hellenistic Egypt: Monarchy, Society, Economy, Culture*. Hellenistic Culture and Society 49. Berkeley: University of California Press.

Biondi, G. 2002. "Per una carta archeologica del territorio di Centuripe." In *Scavi e ricerche a Centuripe*, edited by G. Rizza, 41–81. Catania: Consiglio nazionale delle ricerche.

Birley, E. 1954. *Corbridge Roman Station Official Guidebook*. London: Her Majesty's Stationery Office (HMSO).

Blöck, L. 2019. "A Model for Calculating the Capacities of *horrea* and Agricultural Areas of Gallo-Roman Villas in the Province of *Germania Superior*." In *Rural Granaries in Northern Gaul (6th century BCE–4th century CE): From Archaeology to Economic History*, edited by S. Martin, 13–22. Radboud Studies in Humanities, Volume 8. Leiden: Brill.

Boehm, R. 2018. *City and Empire in the Age of the Successors: Urbanization and Social Response in the Making of the Hellenistic Kingdoms*. Los Angeles: University of California Press.

Boehringer, E. 1929. *Die Münzen von Syrakus*. Berlin: De Gruyter.

Boehringer, E. 1993. "Die Münzprägung von Syrakus unter Dionysios: Geschichte und Stand der numismatischen Forschung." In *La monetazione dell'età dionigiana. Atti dell'VIII Convegno del Centro internazionale di studi numismatici, Napoli 29 maggio–1 giugno 1983*, 65–89. Rome: Istituto italiano di numismatica.

Boetto, G., E. Bukowiecki, N. Monteix, and C. Rousse. 2016. "Les grandi horrea d'Ostie." In *Entrepôts et trafics annonaires en Méditerranée: Antiquité-temps modernes*, edited by B. Marin and C. Virlouvet, 177–226. Rome: École française de Rome.

Bonacasa, N. 1995. "Sicilia ed Egitto in età ellenistica: Appunti sulla documentazione archeologica." In *La Sicilia tra l'Egitto e Roma: La monetazione siracusana dell'età di Ierone II. Atti del seminario di studi, Messina 2–4 dicembre 1993*, edited by M. Caccamo Caltabiano, 59–78. Messina: Accademia Peloritana dei Pericolanti.

Bonacasa, N. 2004. "Riflessioni e proposte sulla ricerca archeologica nella Sicilia del III sec. a.C." In *Nuove prospettive della ricerca sulla Sicilia del III sec. a.C. Archeologia, numismatica, storia. Atti dell'incontro di studio (Messina 4–5 luglio 2002)*, edited by M. Caccamo Caltabiano, L. Campagna, and A. Pinzone, 35–48. Messina: Dipartimento di Scienze dell'Antichità dell'Università degli Studi di Messina.

Bonanno, C., and G. Perrotta. 2008. *Apollonia: Indagini archeologiche sul monte di San Fratello, Messina, 2003–2005*. Rome: L'Erma di Bretschneider.

Booms, D., and P. Higgs. 2016. *Sicily: Culture and Conquest*. London: British Museum Press.

Borba Florenzano, M. B. 1991. "Political Propaganda in Agathocles Coins." In *Actes du XIe congrès international de numismatique organisé à l'occasion du 150e anniversaire de la Société royale de numismatique de Belgique, Bruxelles, 8–13 septembre 1991*, edited by T. Hackens, G. Moucharte, and C. Courtois, 71–7. Louvain-la-Neuve: Séminaire de numismatique Marcel Hoc.

Borba Florenzano, M. B. 1992. "The Coinage of Pyrrhus in Sicily: Evidence of a Political

Project." In *The Age of Pyrrhus: Papers Delivered at the International Conference, Brown University, 8–10 April 1988*, edited by T. Hackens, N. D. Holloway, R. R. Holloway, and G. Moucharte, 207–23. Archeologia Transatlantica 11. Providence, RI: Center for Old World Archaeology and Art.

Börm, H., and N. Luraghi, eds. 2018. *The Polis in the Hellenistic World*. Stuttgart: Franz Steiner Verlag.

Bosworth, B. 1992. "Athens' First Intervention in Sicily: Thucydides and the Sicilian Tradition." *The Classical Quarterly* 42: 46–55.

Bovio-Marconi, I. 1957. "Inconsistenza di una Selinunte romana." *Kokalos* 3: 70–8.

Braccesi, L., and G. Millino. 2000. *La Sicilia greca*. Rome: Carocci.

Brady, N. D. K. 1996. "The Sacred Barn: Barn-Building in Southern England, 1100–1550: A Study of Grain Storage Technology and Its Cultural Context." PhD diss., Cornell University.

Brancato, R. 2020. "Paesaggio rurale ed economia in età ellenistica nel territorio di Catania (Sicilia orientale)." *Thiasos* 9: 45–75.

Bransbourg, G. 2011. "'*Fides et Pecunia Numerata*' Chartalism and Metallism in the Roman World Part 1: The Republic." *American Journal of Numismatics (1989–)* 23: 87–152.

Braund, D. C. 1984. *Rome and the Friendly King: The Character of the Client Kingship*. London: CroomHelm.

Breglia Pulci Doria, L. 1985. "Per la storia di Atene alla fine del II sec. a.C. Il decreto sui pesi e misure: *IG* II² 1013." *Mélanges de l'école française de Rome* 97: 411–30.

Bresson, A. 1993. "La circulation monétaire rhodienne jusqu'en 166." *Dialogues d'histoire ancienne* 19: 119–69.

Bresson, A. 2005. "Coinage and Money Supply in the Hellenistic Age." In *Making, Moving and Managing: The New World of Ancient Economies, 323–31 BC*, edited by Z. H. Archibald, J. K. Davies, and V. Gabrielsen, 44–72. Oxford: Oxbow.

Bresson, A. 2009. "Electrum Coins, Currency Exchange and Transaction Costs in Archaic and Classical Greece." *Revue belge de numismatique et de sigillographie* 155: 71–80.

Bresson, A. 2011. "Grain from Cyrene." In *The Economies of Hellenistic Societies, Third to First Centuries BC*, edited by Z. H. Archibald, J. K. Davies, and V. Gabrielsen, 66–95. Oxford: Oxford University Press.

Bresson, A. 2016. *The Making of the Ancient Greek Economy: Institutions, Markets, and Growth in the City-States*. Princeton, NJ: Princeton University Press.

Bretschneider, J., J. Driessen, and K. van Lerberghe. 2007. *Power and Architecture: Monumental Public Architecture in the Bronze Age Near East and Aegean*. Orientalia Lovaniensia Analecta 156. Leuven: Peeters.

Briant, P. 1994. "Prélèvements tributaires et échanges en Asie Mineure achéménide et hellénistique." In *Economie antique: Les échanges dans l'Antiquité: Le rôle de l'État*, edited by J. Andreau, P. Briant, and R. Descat, 69–81. Saint-Bertrand-de-Comminges: Musée archéologique départemental.

Bringmann, K. 1993. "The King as Benefactor: Some Remarks on Ideal Kingship in the Age of Hellenism." In *Images and Ideologies: Self-Definition in the Hellenistic World*, edited by A. Bulloch, 7–24. Berkeley: University of California Press.

Bringmann, K. 2001. "Grain, Timber and Money: Hellenistic Kings, Finance, Buildings and Foundations in Greek Cities." In *Hellenistic Economies*, edited by Z. H. Archibald, J. K. Davies, V. Gabrielsen, and G. J. Oliver, 205–14. London: Routledge.

Bringmann, K., and von Steuben, H. 1995. *Schenkungen hellenistischer Herrscher an Griechische Städte und Heiligtümer*. Berlin: Akademie Verlag.

Broneer, O. 1938. "Excavations on the North Slope of the Acropolis, 1937." *Hesperia: The Journal of the American School of Classical Studies at Athens* 7: 161–263.

Brooks, C. 1974. "Public Finance and Political Stability: The Administration of the Land Tax, 1688–1720." *Historical Journal* 17: 281–300.

Brown, F. E., and R. T. Scott, eds. 1993. *Eius virtutis studiosi: Classical and Postclassical Studies in Memory of Frank Edward Brown (1908–1988)*. Washington, DC: National Gallery of Art.

Brown, P. 2013. *Through the Eye of a Needle: Wealth, the Fall of Rome, and the Making of Christianity in the West, 350–550 AD*. Princeton, NJ: Princeton University Press.

Brumbaugh, M. E. 2019. *The New Politics of Olympos: Kingship in Kallimachos' Hymns*. New York: Oxford University Press.

Bugh, G. R., ed. 2006. *Cambridge Companion to the Hellenistic World*. Cambridge: Cambridge University Press.

Buraselis, K. 1982. *Das hellenistische Makedonien und die Ägäis: Forschungen zur Politik des Kassandros und der drei ersten Antigoniden (Antigonos Monopthalmos, Demetrios Poliorketes und Antigonos Gonatas) im Ägäischen Meer und in Westkleinasien*. Munich: C. H. Beck.

Buraselis, K. 2015. "Federalism and the Sea: The *Koina* of the Aegean Islands." In *Federalism in Greek Antiquity*, edited by H. Beck and P. Funke, 358–76. Cambridge: Cambridge University Press.

Burton, P. J. 2003. "'Clientela' or 'amicitia'? : Modeling Roman International Behavior in the Middle Republic (264–146 B.C.)." *Klio: Beiträge zur Alten Geschichte* 85: 333–69.

Butler, S. 2002. *The Hand of Cicero*. London: Routledge.

Buttrey, S. E., and T. V. Buttrey. 1997. "Calculating Ancient Coin Production, Again." *American Journal of Numismatics* 9: 113–35.

Buttrey, T. V. 1965. "The Morgantina Excavations and the Date of the Roman *Denarius*." In *Atti del Congresso internazionale di numismatica, Roma, 11–16 settembre 1961*, 261–7. Rome: Istituto italiano di numismatica.

Buttrey, T. V. 1973. "The Morgantina Gold Hoard and the Coinage of Hicetas." *The Numismatic Chronicle* 13: 1–17.

Buttrey, T. V. 1979. "Morgantina and the *Denarius*." *Numismatica e antichità classiche* 8: 149–57.

Buttrey, T. V. 1993. "Calculating Ancient Coin Production: Facts and Fantasies." *The Numismatic Chronicle* 153: 335–51.

Buttrey, T. V., K. T. Erim, T. D. Groves, and R. R. Holloway. 1989. *Morgantina Studies, vol. 2: The Coins*. Princeton, NJ: Princeton University Press.

Caccamo Caltabiano, M., ed. 1995. *La Sicilia tra l'Egitto e Roma: La monetazione siracusana dell'età di Ierone II. Atti del seminario di studi, Messina 2–4 dicembre 1993*. Messina: Accademia Peloritana dei Pericolanti.

Caccamo Caltabiano, M., L. Campagna, and A. Pinzone, eds. 2004. *Nuove prospettive della ricerca sulla Sicilia del III sec. a. C. Archeologia, numismatica, storia. Atti dell'incontro di studio, Messina, 4–5 luglio 2002*. Messina: Dipartimento di Scienze dell'Antichità dell'Università degli studi di Messina.

Caccamo Caltabiano, M., B. Carroccio, and E. Oteri. 1995. "Il sistema monetale ieroniano. Cronologia e problemi." In *La Sicilia tra l'Egitto e Roma: La monetazione siracusana dell'età di Ierone II. Atti del seminario di studi, Messina 2–4 dicembre 1993*, edited by M. Caccamo Caltabiano, 195–280. Messina: Accademia Peloritana dei Pericolanti.

Caccamo Caltabiano, M., B. Carroccio, and E. Oteri. 1997. *Siracusa ellenistica: Le monete "regali" di Ierone II, della sua famiglia e dei Siracusani*. Messina: Dipartimento di Scienze dell'Antichità dell'Università di Messina.

Caminneci, V., and N. Di Carlo. 2017. "Monte Adranone (Sambuca di Sicilia). Scavo nella necropoli di età ellenistica." *Fasti On Line Documents & Research* 394: 1–18. www.fastionline.org/excavation/micro_view.php?item_key=fst_cd&fst_cd=AIAC_4494.

Campagna, L. 2004. "Architettura e ideologia della basileia a Siracusa nell'età di Ierone II." In *Nuove prospettive della ricerca sulla Sicilia del III sec. a.C. Archaeologia, numismatica, storica. Atti dell'incontro di studio, Messina, 4–5 luglio 2002*, edited by M. Caccamo Caltabiano, L. Campagna, and A. Pinzone, 151–89. Messina: Dipartimento di Scienze dell'Antichità dell'Università degli Studi di Messina.

Campagna, L. 2006. "L'architettura di età ellenistica in Sicilia: Per una rilettura del quadro generale." In *Sicilia ellenistica, consuetudo italica: Alle origini dell'architettura ellenistica d'Occidente*.

Atti delle giornate di studio (Spoleto 2004), edited by M. Osanna and M. Torelli, 15–34. Rome: Edizioni dell'Ateneo.

Campagna, L. 2007. "Architettura pubblica ed evergetismo nella Sicilia di età repubblicana." In *La Sicilia romana tra repubblica e alto impero. Atti del convegno di studi (Caltanisetta, 20–21 maggio 2006)*, edited by C. Miccichè, S. Modeo, and L. Santagati, 110–34. Caltanissetta: Siciliantica.

Campagna, L. 2009. "Urbanistica dei centri siciliani d'altura in età ellenistica: Il caso di Tauromenion." In *Eis Akra: Insediamenti d'altura in Sicilia dalla preistoria al III secolo a.C. atti del V Convegno di studi*, edited by M. Congiu, C. Miccichè, and S. Modeo, 205–26. Caltanissetta: Salvatore Sciascia Editore.

Campagna, L. 2011. "Tauromenion: Nuove ricerche sull'urbanistica e sull'architettura della città ellenistica." *Forma Urbis* 16: 15–21.

Campagna, L. 2018. Rezension von *Hellenistische Heiligtümer in Sizilien. Studien zur Sakralarchitektur innerhalb und außerhalb des Reiches König Hierons II* by Markus Wolf. *Sehepunkte* 18, www.sehepunkte.de/2018/02/30525.html.

Campagna, L. 2019. "The Making of the Hellenistic City in Sicily: Some Reflections from the Case Study of Tauromenion." In *Cityscapes of Hellenistic Sicily*, edited by M. Trümper, G. Adornato, and T. Lappi, 55–73. Rome: Edizioni Quasar.

Campagna, L., and la Torre, G. F. 2008. "Ricerche sui monumenti e sulla topografia di Tauromenion: Una stoà ellenistica nell'area della Naumachia." *Sicilia Antiqua* 5: 115–46.

Capdetrey, L. 2007. *Le pouvoir séleucide: Territoire, administration, finances d'un royaume hellénistique (312–129 avant J.C.)*. Rennes: Presses universitaires de Rennes.

Capodieci, G. M. 1813. *Antichi monumenti di Siracusa*. Syracuse: Presso le stampe di D. Francesco M. Pulejo.

Carbè, A. 1995. "Nota sulla monetazione di Tauromenion nel III secolo a.C." In *La Sicilia tra l'Egitto e Roma: La monetazione siracusana dell'età di Ierone II. Atti del seminario di studi, Messina 2–4 dicembre 1993*, edited by M. Caccamo Caltabiano, 303–18. Messina: Accademia Peloritana dei Pericolanti.

Carbè, A. 2003. "Ritrovamenti monetari a Francavilla di Sicilia (ME)." In *Archeologia del Mediterraneo: Studi in onore di Ernesto de Miro*, edited by G. Fiorentini, M. Caltabiano, and A. Calderone, 181–201. Rome: L'Erma di Bretschneider.

Carbè, A. 2004. "Il 'cavaliere' di Ierone II: Aspetti iconografici." In *Nuove prospettive della ricerca sulla Sicilia del III sec. a.C. Archaeologia, numismatica, storica. Atti dell'incontro di studio, Messina, 4–5 luglio 2002*, edited by M. Caccamo Caltabiano, L. Campagna, and A. Pinzone, 267–75. Messina: Dipartimento di Scienze dell'Antiquità dell'Università degli studi di Messina.

Carcopino, J. 1914. *La loi de Hiéron et les romains*. Paris: Fontemoing.

Carlsson, S. 2010. *Hellenistic Democracies: Freedom, Independence and Political Procedure in Some East Greek City-States*. Historia Einzelschriften 206. Stuttgart: Franz Steiner Verlag.

Carney, E. 1992. "The Politics of Polygamy: Olympias, Alexander and the Murder of Philip." *Historia: Zeitschrift für Alte Geschichte* 41: 169–89.

Carney, E. 1995. "Women and *Basileia*: Legitimacy and Female Political Action in Macedonia." *The Classical Journal* 90: 367–91.

Carrara, A. 2014. "Tax and Trade in Ancient Greece: About the *Ellimenion* and the Harbour Duties." *Revue des études anciennes* 116: 441–64.

Carroccio, B. 1993. "La monetazione aurea di Ierone II ed il problema dell'organizzazione della zecca siracusana negli anni del suo regno." In *Actes du XIe congrès international de numismatique organisé à l'occasion du 150e anniversaire de la Société royale de numismatique de Belgique, Bruxelles, 8–13 septembre 1991*, edited by T. Hackens, G. Moucharte, and C. Courtois, 65–70. Louvain-la-Neuve: Séminaire de numismatique Marcel Hoc.

Carroccio, B. 1994. *La monetazione aurea e argentea di Ierone II*. Torino: Circolo numismatico torinese.

Carroccio, B. 2000. "Sulla cronologia e metro-logia delle monetazioni bronzi con ritratto di Ierone II di Siracusa." In *XII Internationaler Numismatischer Kongress, Berlin 1997*, edited by B. Kluge and B. Weisser, 261–6. Berlin: Staatliche Museen zu Berlin.

Carroccio, B. 2004. *Dal basileus Agatocle a Roma: Le monetazioni siciliane d'età ellenistica: Cronologia, iconografia, metrologia*. Messina: Dipartimento di Scienze dell'Antichità dell'Università degli Studi di Messina.

Carroccio, B. 2013. "Le monete di Archimede." In *Archimede: Arte e scienza dell'invenzione*, edited by G. Di Pasquale and C. Parisi Presicce, 60–3. Florence: Giunti.

Carroccio, B. 2018. "Influence of Striking Praxis and Chemical Corrosion in Weight Variations of a Big Sample of Syracusan Bronze Coins." In *IMEKO International Conference on Metrology for Archaeology and Cultural Heritage*, 181–4. Red Hook, NY: Curran Associates.

Caruso, E. 2006. "Le fortificazioni di Lilibeo: Un monumentale esempio della poliorcetica punica in Sicilia." In *Guerra e pace in Sicilia e nel Mediterraneo antico (VIII–III sec. a.C.): Arte, prassi e teoria della pace e della guerra*, edited by M. A. Vaggioli and C. Michelini, 283–306. Pisa: Scuola Normale Superiore.

Casabona, M. 1999. "Le monete di Catana ellenistica fra Roma e le influenze orientali." *Rivista italiana di numismatica e scienze affini* 99: 13–46.

Casson, L. 1954. "The Grain Trade of the Hellenistic World." *Transactions of the American Philological Association* 85: 168–87.

Casson, L. 1984. *Ancient Trade and Society*. Detroit, MI: Wayne State University Press.

Castagnino Berlinghieri, E. F., and C. Monaco. 2008. *Il sistema portuale di Catania antica: Studi interdisciplinari di geo-archeologia marittima*. Archeologia Marittima Mediterranea Papers 3. Rome: Fabrizio Serra.

Castelli, G. L. 1769. *Siciliae et objacentium insularum veterum inscriptionum nova collectio, prolegomenis et notis illustrata*. Palermo: G. M. Betivenga.

Castelli, G. L. 1781. *Siciliae populorum et urbium regum quoque et tyrannorum veteres nummi Saracenorum epocham antecedentes*. Palermo: Typis regiis.

Castrizio, D. 1995. "La destinazione dei pegasi agatoclei." *La Sicilia tra l'Egitto e Roma: La monetazione siracusana dell'età di Ierone II. Atti del seminario di studi, Messina 2–4 dicembre 1993*, edited by M. Caccamo Caltabiano, 295–302. Messina: Accademia Peloritana dei Pericolanti.

Castrizio, D. 2011. "Considerazioni sul pagamento del *sitos* ai mercenari nella Sicilia tra Dionisio I e Timoleonte." *Polifemo* 11: 209–32.

Ceccarelli, P. 2013. *Ancient Greek Letter Writing: A Cultural History (600 BC– 150 BC)*. Oxford: Oxford University Press.

Chaniotis, A. 2003. "The Divinity of Hellenistic Rulers." In *A Companion to the Hellenistic World*, edited by A. Erskine, 431–45. Malden, MA: Wiley-Blackwell.

Chaniotis, A. 2005. *War in the Hellenistic World: A Social and Cultural History*. Malden, MA: Wiley-Blackwell.

Chankowski, V., and Duyrat, F., eds. 2004. *Le roi et l'économie: Autonomies locales et structures royales dans l'économie de l'empire séleucide*. Topoi. Orient-Occident. Supplément 6. Lyon: Maison de l'orient méditerranéen.

Chayanov, A. V. 1986. *The Theory of Peasant Economy*. Madison: University of Wisconsin Press.

Childe, V. G. 1950. "The Urban Revolution." *The Town Planning Review* 21: 3–17.

Chiverrell, R., and Z. H. Archibald. 2009. "Flooding and River Evolution: Implications for Human Occupation and Activity at Vetren, Central Bulgaria." *Géomorphologie: Relief, Processus, Environnement* 4: 287–302.

Chowaniec, R., ed. 2015. *Unveiling the Past of an Ancient Town: Akrai/Acrae in South-Eastern Sicily*. Warsaw: University of Warsaw.

Chowaniec, R. 2017. *The Coming of Rome: Cultural Landscape of South-Eastern Sicily*. Warsaw: University of Warsaw.

Chowaniec, R., ed. 2018. *On the Borders of Syracuse: Multidisciplinary Studies on the Ancient Town of Akrai/Acrae, Sicily*. Warsaw: University of Warsaw.

Christakis, K. S. 2004. "Palatial Economy and Storage in Late Bronze Age Knossos." *British School at Athens Studies* 12: 299–309.

Christakis, K. S. 2011. "Redistribution in Aegean Palatial Societies: Redistribution and Political Economies in Bronze Age Crete." *American Journal of Archaeology* 115: 197–205.

Cioffi, C. 2017. "Tavole di misura (*mensae ponderariae e sekomata*): Un approccio metrologico all'archeologia." In *Étalons monétaires et mesures pondérales entre la Grèce et l'Italie*, edited by C. Doyen, 265–286. Louvain-la-Neuve: Association Professeur Marcel Hoc.

Cioffi, R. L. 2011. "Fuzzy Math: The Place of Numerical Evidence in Cicero *In Verrem* 3.116." *Mnemosyne* 64: 645–52.

Clain-Stefanelli, E. E. 1987. "On Some Fractional Silver Coinages of Sicily and Magna Graecia during the Fifth Century BC." *Revue belge de numismatique* 133: 39–66.

Clarke, G. W. 1994. "Jebel Khalid on the Euphrates: The Acropolis Building." *Mediterranean Archaeology* 7: 69–75.

Clarke, G. W. 2001. "A Seleucid Governor's Palace: Jebel Khalid on the Euphrates." In *The Royal Palace Institution in the First Millennium BC*, edited by I. Nielsen, 215–47. Athens: Danish Institute of Athens.

Clarke, G. W. 2002. "Jebel Khalid on the Euphrates: The Acropolis Building." In *Jebel Khalid on the Euphrates*. Vol. 1: *Report on Excavations 1986–1996*, edited by G. W. Clarke, P. J. Connor, L. Crewe, B. Frohlich, H. Jackson, J. Littleton, C. E. V. Nixon, M. O'Hea, and D. Steele, 25–48. Mediterranean Archaeology Supplement 5. Sydney: Meditarch.

Clarke, G. W., P. J. Connor, L. Crewe, B. Frohlich, H. Jackson, J. Littleton, C. E. V. Nixon, M. O'Hea, and D. Steele, eds. 2002. *Jebel Khalid on the Euphrates*. Vol. 1: *Report on Excavations 1986–1996*. Mediterranean Archaeology Supplement 5. Sydney: Meditarch.

Clarke, G. W., H. Jackson, C. E. V. Nixon, J. Tidmarsh, K. Wesselingh, and L. Cougle-Jose. 2016. *Jebel Khalid on the Euphrates*. Vol. 5: *Report on Excavations 2000–2010*.

Mediterranean Archaeology Supplement 10. Sydney: Meditarch.

Clarysse, W., and D. J. Thompson. 2006. *Counting the People in Hellenistic Egypt, vol. 2: Historical Studies*. Cambridge: Cambridge University Press.

Clarysse, W., and K. Vandorpe. 1995. *Zenon, un homme d'affaires grec à l'ombre des pyramides*. Leuven: Presses Universitaires de Louvain.

Clarysse, W., and K. Vandorpe. 1998. "The Ptolemaic *Apomoira*." In *Le culte du souverain dans l'Egypte ptolémaïque au IIIe siècle avant notre ère*, edited by H. Melaerts, 5–42. Leuven: Peeters.

Coarelli, F. 1980. "La cultura figurativa in Sicilia nei secoli IV–III a.C." In *La Sicilia antica*. Vol. 2, no. 1: *La Sicilia greca dal VI secolo alle guerre puniche*, edited by E. Gabba and G. Vallet, 157–82. Naples: Storia di Napoli e della Sicilia.

Collin Bouffier, S. 2009. "L'eau en Sicile grecque: Nouvelles perspectives de recherches." *Pallas* 79: 65–79.

Consolo Langher, S. N. 2000. *Agatocle: Da capoparte a monarca fondatore di un regno tra Cartagine e i Diadochi*. Messina: Dipartimento di Scienze dell'Antichità dell'Università degli Studi di Messina.

Constantakopoulou, C. 2017. *Aegean Interactions: Delos and Its Networks in the Third Century*. Oxford: Oxford University Press.

Cordiano, G. 1997. *La ginnasiarchia nelle "poleis" dell'Occidente mediterranea antico*. Pisa: ETS.

Cordova, V. 1890. *Le origini della città di Aidone e il suo statuo*. Rome: Forzani.

Costanzo, M. A. 1996. "Granai di età ellenistica in Sicilia." In *Atti delle giornate di studio sugli insediamenti rurali nella Sicilia antica (Caltagirone 29/30 Giugno 1992)*, 67–70. Catania: Edizioni Greco.

Cougle-Jose, L., et al. 2002. *Jebel Khalid on the Euphrates*. Sydney: MEDITARCH Publications; Sydney University Press.

Crawford, M. H. 1970. "Money and Exchange in the Roman World." *The Journal of Roman Studies* 60: 40–8.

Crawford, M. H. 1974. *Roman Republican Coinage*. London: Cambridge University Press.

Crawford, M. H. 1985. *Coinage and Money under the Roman Republic: Italy and the Mediterranean Economy*. London: Methuen.

Crawford, M. H. 2007. "The Mamertini, Alfius and Festus." *Collection de l'Institut des sciences et techniques de l'antiquité* 1030: 273–80.

Cuomo di Caprio, N. 1992. *Morgantina Studies, vol. 3: Fornaci e officine da vasaio tardo-ellenistiche*. Princeton, NJ: Princeton University Press.

Curcio, A. 1979. "Resti di fattorie antiche nella vallata del Tellaro." *Sicilia archeologica* 12: 79–90.

Currid, J. D. 1985. "The Beehive Granaries of Ancient Palestine." *Zeitschrift des Deutschen Palästina-Vereins* 101: 97–110.

Curtis, B. 1998. "From the Moral Thermometer to Money: Metrological Reform in Pre-Confederation Canada." *Social Studies of Science* 28: 547–70.

Cutroni Tusa, A. 1957. "Vita dei medaglieri [Selinunte 1956]." *Annali dell'Istituto italiano di numismatica* 4: 201–3.

Cutroni Tusa, A. 1958–9. "Vita dei medaglieri [Selinunte 1957–1958]." *Annali dell'Istituto italiano di numismatica* 5–6: 306–16.

Cutroni Tusa, A. 1960–1. "Ripostigli monetali del Museo di Palermo." *Annali dell'Istituto italiano di numismatica* 7–8: 73–90.

Cutroni Tusa, A. 1968. "Vita dei medaglieri [Selinunte 1964–1967]." *Annali dell'Istituto italiano di numismatica* 15: 190–218.

Dalheim, W. 1968. *Struktur und Entwicklung der römischen Völkerrechts im dritten und zweiten Jahrhunderts v. Chr.* Vestigia 8. Munich: C. H. Beck.

Dalheim, W. 1977. *Gewalt und Herrschaft: Das provinziale Herrschaftssystem der römischen Republik*. Berlin: De Gruyter.

Dalman, G. 1933. *Arbeit und Sitte in Palästina*. Vol. 3: *Von der Ernte zum Mehl: Ernten, Dreschen, Worfeln, Sieben, Verwahren, Mahlen*. Gütersloh: C. Bertelsmann.

Damerow, P., J. Renn, S. Rieger, and P. Wenig 2002. "Mechanical Knowledge and Pompeian Balances." In *Homo Faber: Studies on Nature, Technology, and Science at the Time of Pompeii*, edited by J. Renn and G. Castagnetti, 93–108. Rome: L'Erma di Bretschneider.

D'Annibale, C. 1983. "Field Survey of the *Chora* of Metaponto." In *Archaeological Survey in the Mediterranean Area*, edited by D. Keller, 191–3. BAR International Series 155. Oxford: BAR Publishing.

Daverio Rocchi, G. 2009. "Confini e frontiere della *polis*: Spazio di vita e categorie geografica." *Geographia Antiqua* 18: 47–62.

De Angelis, F. 2000. "Estimating the Agricultural Base of Greek Sicily." *Papers of the British School at Rome* 68: 111–148.

De Angelis, F. 2002. "Trade and Agriculture at Megara Hyblaia." *Oxford Journal of Archaeology* 21: 299–310.

De Angelis, F. 2006. "Going against the Grain in Sicilian Greek Economics." *Greece and Rome* 53: 29–47.

De Angelis, F. 2007. "Archaeology in Sicily 2001–2005." *Archaeological Reports* 53: 123–91.

De Angelis, F. 2016. *Archaic and Classical Greek Sicily: A Social and Economic History*. New York: Oxford University Press.

De Callataÿ, F. 1995. "Calculating Ancient Coin Production: Seeking a Balance." *The Numismatic Chronicle* 155: 289–311.

De Callataÿ, F. 2000. "Un 'octobole' de Pyrrhus surfrappé sur un statère de type corinthien: Réflexions sur les masses monnayées par Pyrrhus en or et en argent." *Annali dell'Istituto italiano di numismatica* 47: 189–213.

De Callataÿ, F. 2011. "Quantifying Monetary Production in Greco-Roman Times: A General Frame." In *Quantifying Monetary Supplies in Greco-Roman Times*, edited by F. De Callataÿ, 7–29. Bari: Edipuglia.

De Callataÿ, F. 2012. "Royal Hellenistic Coinages: From Alexander to Mithradates." In *The Oxford Handbook of Greek and Roman Coinage*, edited by D. M. Metcalf, 175–90. Oxford: Oxford University Press.

De Callataÿ, F. 2013. "The Numismatic Interests of Laevinus Torrentius (1525–1595), One of the Foremost Humanists of His Time." In *Translatio nummorum: Römische Kaiser in der Renaissance. Akten des internationalen Symposiums Berlin 16.–18. Novembre 2011*, edited by U. Peter and B. Weisser, 125–40. Ruhpolding: Rutzen-Verlag.

De Callataÿ, F. 2014. "For Whom Were Royal Hellenistic Coins Struck? The Choice of Metals and Denominations." In *Bildwert: Nominalspezifische Kommunicationsstrategien in der Münzprägung hellenistischer Herrscher. Kolloquium vom 17.–18. Juni 2010 in Münster*, edited by A. Lichtenberger, K. Martin, H.-H. Nieswandt, and D. Salzmann, 59–77. Bonn: Habelt-Verlag.

De Ligt, L. 1993. *Fairs and Markets in the Roman Empire: Economic and Social Aspects of Periodic Trade in a Pre-Industrial Society*. Dutch Monographs on Ancient History and Archaeology 11. Amsterdam: J. C. Gieben.

De Lisle, C. 2017. "The Coinage of Agathokles of Syracuse: Sicilian and Hellenistic Influences." *Numismatic Chronicle* 177: 9–28.

De Miro, E. 2009. "La Sicilia e l'Egitto nel periodo ellenistico-romano: Sintesi e nuovi dati." *Mare Internum: Archeologia e Culture Del Mediterraneo* 1: 85–98.

De Ruyt, C. 1983. *Macellum: Marché alimentaire des Romains*. Louvain: Institut supérieur d'archéologie et d'histoire de l'art.

De Sanctis, G. 1916. *Storia dei romani*. Vol. 3, pt. 1: *L'età delle guerre puniche*. Milan: Fratelli Bocca.

De Sanctis, G. 1967. *Storia dei Romani*, Vol. 3, pt. 1, 2nd ed. Florence: La Nuova Italia.

De Sensi Sestito, G. 1971. "La politica di Gerone II dal 275 al 269 a.C." In *Umanità e storia: Scritti in onore di Adelchi Attisani*, edited by R. Franchini, 497–536. Messina: Giannini.

De Sensi Sestito, G. 1977. *Gerone II: Un monarca ellenistico in Sicilia*. Palermo: Edizioni Sophia.

De Sensi Sestito, G. 1980. "La Sicilia dal 289 al 210 a.C." In *La Sicilia antica*. Vol. 2, no. 1: *La Sicilia greca dal VI secolo alle guerre puniche*, edited by E. Gabba and G. Vallet, 343–70. Naples: Storia di Napoli e della Sicilia.

De Sensi Sestito, G. 1995. "Rapporti tra la Sicilia, Roma e l'Egitto." In *La Sicilia tra l'Egitto e Roma: La monetazione siracusana dell'età di Ierone II. Atti del seminario di studi, Messina 2–4 dicembre 1993*, edited by M. Caccamo Caltabiano, 17–57. Messina: Accademia Peloritana dei Pericolanti.

De Ste. Croix, G. E. M. 2004. *Athenian Democratic Origins and Other Essays*. Edited by D. Harvey and R. Parker with the assistance of P. Thonemann. Oxford: Oxford University Press.

De Vincenzo, S. 2013. *Tra Cartagine e Roma: I centri urbani dell'eparchia punica di Sicilia tra VI e I sec. a.C.* Berlin: De Gruyter.

De Vincenzo, S. 2019. "Sicily." In *The Oxford Handbook of the Phoenician and Punic Mediterranean*, edited by B. R. Doak and C. López-Ruiz, 537–52. New York: Oxford University Press.

Decker, M. 2001. "Food for an Empire: Wine and Oil Production in North Syria." In *Economy and Exchange in the East Mediterranean during Late Antiquity*, edited by S. Kingsley and M. Decker, 69–96. Oxford: Oxford University Press.

Denaro, M. 1995. "La distribuzione delle anfore ellenistico-romane in Sicilia (III sec. a.C.–III sec. d.C.)." *Kokalos* 41: 183–203.

Dench, E. 1995. *From Barbarians to New Men: Greek, Roman, and Modern Perceptions of Peoples of the Central Apennines*. Oxford: Clarendon Press.

Dench, E. 2003. "Beyond Greeks and Barbarians: Italy and Sicily in the Hellenistic Age." In *A Companion to the Hellenistic World*, edited by A. Erskine, 294–310. Malden, MA: Wiley-Blackwell.

Descat, R. 2003. "Qu'est-ce que l'économie royale?" *Pallas* 62: 149–68.

Deussen, P. W. 1994. "The Granaries of Morgantina and the *Lex Hieronica*." In *Le ravitaillement en blé de Rome et des centres urbains des débuts de la République jusquau Haut Empire. Actes du Colloque international Naples, 14–16 février 1991*, 231–5. Naples: Centre Jean Bérard.

Di Noto, A. 1992. "Monte Adranone." In *Bibliografia topografica della colonizzazione greca in Italia e nelle isole tirreniche*, edited by G. Nenci, G. Vallet, and G. Panessa, 10: 257–65. Pisa: Scuola Normale Superiore; Rome: École française de Rome.

Di Pasquale, G. 2010. "The 'Syrakousia' Ship and the Mechanical Knowledge between Syracuse and Alexandria." In *The Genius of Archimedes: 23 Centuries of Influence on*

Mathematics, Science and Engineering, edited by S. A. Paipetis and M. Ceccarelli, 289–301. Dordrecht: Springer Netherlands.

Di Stefano, G. 1987. "Il territorio di Camarina in età arcaica." *Kokalos* 33: 129–207.

Di Stefano, G. 2001. "La *chora* di Camarina." In *Problemi della chora colonial dall'Occidente al Mar Nero. Atti del XL Convegno di studi sulla Magna Grecia*, 689–705. Taranto: Istituto per la storia e l'archeologia della Magna Grecia.

Di Stefano, G. 2001–2. "L'attività di ricerca della Soprintendenza a Camarina e nella provincia de Ragusa fra il 1996 e il 2000." *Kokalos* 47–8: 687–728.

Di Stefano, G. 2006. "Aspetti urbanistici e topografici per la storia di Camarina." In *Camarina: 2600 anni dopo la fondazione. Nuovi studi sulla città e sul territorio*, edited by P. Pelagatti, G. Di Stefano, and L. De Lachenal, 157–76. Rome: Istituto poligrafico e zecca dello stato.

Di Vita, A. 1956. "La penetrazione siracusana nella Sicilia sud-orientale alla luce delle più recenti scoperte archeologiche." In *Kokalos* 2: 177–205.

Di Vita, A. 1999. "Siracusa, Camarina, Selinunte: quale frontiera?" In *Confini e frontiere nella Grecia d'Occidente. Atti del XXVII convegno di studi sulla Magna Grecia*, 361–79. Taranto: Istituto per la storia e l'archeologia della Magna Grecia.

Dimartino, A. 2006. "Per una revisione dei documenti epigrafici siracusani pertinenti al regno di Ierone II." In *Guerra e pace in Sicilia e nel Mediterraneo antico (VIII–III sec. a.C.). Arte, prassi e teoria della pace e della guerra*, edited by M. A. Vaggioli and C. Michelini, 703–17. Pisa: Scuola Normale Superiore.

Dimartino, A. 2015. "L'epistola di Ierone II e l'*orkion boulas* (IG XIV, 7): Un nuovo dossier epigrafico?" *Epigraphica* 77: 39–65.

Dimartino, A. 2017a. "Dedica dei Siracusani a tutti gli dèi." *Axon: Iscrizioni storiche greche* 1: 241–6.

Dimartino, A. 2017b. "Iscrizioni del teatro di Siracusa." *Axon: Iscrizioni storiche greche* 1: 267–76.

Dimartino, A. 2017c. "Iscrizioni del teatro di Taormina." *Axon: Iscrizioni storiche greche* 1: 301–8.

Dimartino, A. 2019. "Epigrafia greca e pratiche onorarie in Sicilia durante l'età ellenistica e romana." In *Cityscapes of Hellenistic Sicily*, edited by M. Trümper, G. Adornato, and T. Lappi, 197–218. Rome: Edizioni Quasar.

Dohrn, T. 1968. "Die Marmor-Standbilder des Daochos-Weihgeschenks in Delphi." *Antike Plastik* 8: 35–62.

Doyen, C. 2016. "Réformes métrologiques grecques à la fin du IIe s.: Pour une réévaluation de l'influence romaine." In *Étalons monétaires et mesures pondérales entre la Grèce et l'Italie*, edited by C. Doyen, 187–208. Louvain-la-Neuve: Association de numismatique Professeur Marcel Hoc.

Dubois, L. 1989. *Inscriptions grecques dialectales de Sicile: Contribution à l'étude du vocabulaire grec colonial*. Rome: École Française de Rome.

Dubouloz, J. 2021. "Accommodating Former Legal Systems and Roman Law: Cicero's Rhetorical and Legal Viewpoint in the Verrine Orations." In *Legal Engagement: The Reception of Roman Law and Tribunals by Jews and Other Inhabitants of the Empire*, edited by K. Berthelot, N. Dohrmann, and C. Nemo-Pekelman, pp. 47–68. Publications de l'École française de Rome, 579.

Dunbabin, T. J. 1948. *The Western Greeks: The History of Sicily and South Italy from the Foundation of the Greek Colonies to 480 B.C.* Oxford: Clarendon Press.

Duncan-Jones, R. P. 1976a. "The *Choenix*, the *Artaba* and the *Modius*." *Zeitschrift für Papyrologie und Epigraphik* 21: 43–52.

Duncan-Jones, R. P. 1976b. "The Size of the *Modius Castrensis*." *Zeitschrift für Papyrologie und Epigraphik* 21: 53–62.

Eckhel, J. H. 1792. *Doctrina numorum veterum*. Vienna: Sumptibus J. Camesina.

Eckstein, A. M. 1980. "*Unicum subsidium populi Romani*. Hiero II and Rome, 263 B.C.–215 B.C." *Chiron* 10: 183–203.

Eckstein, A. M. 1985. "Polybius, Syracuse and the Policy of Accommodation." *Greek, Roman, and Byzantine Studies* 26: 265–82.

Eckstein, A. M. 1987. *Senate and General: Individual Decision-Making and Roman Foreign*

Relations, 264–194 B.C. Berkeley: University of California Press.

Eckstein, A. M. 2009. "Hellenistic Monarchy in Theory and Practice." In *A Companion to Greek and Roman Political Thought*, edited by R. K. Balot, 247–65. Malden, MA: Wiley-Blackwell.

Eckstein, F. 1958. "Inschriften." In *Bericht über die Ausgrabungen in Olympia*. Vol. 6: *Winter 1953/1954 und 1954/1955*, edited by E. Kunze, 205–25. Berlin: De Gruyter.

Ellis, S. 2017. "Reevaluating Pompeii's Coin-Finds: Monetary Transactions and Urban Waste in the Retail Economy of an Ancient City." In *The Economy of Pompeii*, edited by M. Flohr and A. Wilson, 293–338. Oxford: Oxford University Press.

Enos, R. L. 1992. "Why Gorgias of Leontini Traveled to Athens: A Study of Recent Epigraphical Evidence." *Rhetoric Review* 11: 1–15.

Epstein, S. R. 1992. *An Island for Itself: Economic Development and Social Change in Late Medieval Sicily*. Cambridge: Cambridge University Press.

Erdkamp, P. 2005. *The Grain Market in the Roman Empire: A Social, Political and Economic Study*. Cambridge: Cambridge University Press.

Erim, K. T. 1958. "Morgantina." *American Journal of Archaeology* 62: 79–90.

Erskine, A., ed. 2003. *A Companion to the Hellenistic World*. Malden, MA: Wiley-Blackwell.

Evans, N. 2010. *Civic Rites: Democracy and Religion in Ancient Athens*. Berkeley: University of California Press.

Ezzamel, M. 2002. "Accounting and Redistribution: The Palace and Mortuary Cult in the Middle Kingdom, Ancient Egypt." *Accounting Historians Journal* 29: 61–103.

Fantasia, U. 1989. "Finanze cittadine, liberalità private e *sitos demosios*: Considerazioni su alcuni documenti epigrafici." In *Serta Historica Antiqua II*, 47–84. Pubblicazioni dell'Istituto di Storia Antica e Scienze Ausiliarie dell'Università degli Studi di Genova 16. Rome: G. Bretschneider.

Fantasia, U. 1993. "Grano siciliano in Grecia nel V e IV secolo." *Annali della Scuola Normale Superiore di Pisa* series III, 23: 9–31.

Fantasia, U. 1998. "Distribuzioni di grano e archivi della *polis*: Il caso di Samo." In *La mémoire perdue: Recherches sur l'administration romaine, Actes de la Table Ronde (Rome, 19–20 mai 1995)*, edited by C. Moatti, 205–28. Rome: École Française de Rome.

Fantasia, U. 1999. "I SITOPHULAKES e i SITONIA di Tauromenio." In *Sicilia Epigraphica I. Atti del convegno di studi (Erice, 15–18 ottobre 1998)*, edited by M. I. Gulletta, 251–79. Pisa: Scuola Normale Superiore.

Ferruti, F. 2004. "L'attività di Ierone II a favore dei ginnasi." In *Nuove prospettive della ricerca sulla Sicilia del III sec. a.C. Archeologia, numismatica, storia. Atti dell'incontro di studio (Messina 4–5 luglio 2002)*, edited by M. Caccamo Caltabiano, L. Campagna, and A. Pinzone, 191–212. Messina: Dipartimento di Scienze dell'Antichità dell'Università degli Studi di Messina.

Figueira, T. J. 1998. *The Power of Money: Coinage and Politics in the Athenian Empire*. Philadelphia: University of Pennsylvania Press.

Figueira, T. J. 2003. "Economic Integration and Monetary Consolidation in the Athenian *arkhe*." In *Moneta mercanti banchieri: I precedenti greci e romani dell'euro: Atti del convegno internazionale, Cividale del Friuli, 26–28 settembre 2002*, edited by G. Urso, 71–92. Pisa: ETS.

Finley, M. I. 1968. *A History of Sicily*. Vol. 1: *Ancient Sicily to the Arab Conquest*. London: Chatto & Windus.

Fiorentini, G. 1988. "Attività della Soprintendenza Beni culturali e ambientali per la Sicilia centro-meridionale (Agrigento, Caltanissetta, Enna): (1984–1988)." *Kokalos* 34–5: 491–502.

Fiorentini, G. 1995. *Monte Adranone*. Rome: Istituto poligrafico e zecca dello stato.

Forbes, C. A. 1933. *Neoi: A Contribution to the Study of Greek Associations*. Middletown, CT: American Philological Association.

Fornara, C. W. 1983. *Archaic Times to the End of the Peloponnesian War*. Translated Documents of Greece and Rome 1. Cambridge: Cambridge University Press.

Fowler, D. H. 1983. "A Note on Fractions of an Artab." *Zeitschrift für Papyrologie und Epigraphik* 52: 273–4.

Frank, T. 1928. "Rome after the Conquest of Sicily." In *Cambridge Ancient History*. Vol. 8.2: *The Hellenistic Monarchies and the Rise of Rome*, edited by F. W. Walbank, A. E. Astin, M. W. Frederiksen, and R. M. Ogilvie, 793–821. Cambridge: Cambridge University Press.

Franke, P. R. 1958. "Historisch-numismatische Probleme der Zeit Hierons II von Syrakus." *Jahrbuch für Numismatik und Geldgeschichte* 9: 57–85.

Frayne, D. 1997. *Ur III Period (2112–2004 BC)*. Toronto: University of Toronto Press.

Frey-Kupper, S. 2013. *Die antiken Fundmünzen vom Monte Iato 1971–1990: Ein Beitrag zur Geldgeschichte Westsiziliens*. Lausanne: Éditions du Zèbre.

Frey-Kupper, S., and J. N. Barrandon. 2003. "Analisi metallurgiche di monete antiche in bronzo circolanti nella Sicilia occidentale." In *Quarte giornate internazaionali di studi sull'area elima (Erice, 1–4 dicembre 2000)*, edited by A. Corretti, 507–36. Pisa: Scuola Normale Superiore.

Frolov, E. D., and J. Gaudey. 1995. "*Gamoroi* et *Killyrioi*: Analyse de la structure sociale dans la Syracuse archaïque." In *Esclavage et dépendance dans l'historiographie soviétique récente*, edited by M.-M. Mactoux and E. Geny, 73–92. Paris: Les Belles Lettres.

Gabrici, E. 1927. *La Monetazione del bronzo nella Sicilia antica*. Palermo: Boccone del povero.

Gabrielsen, V. 2011. "Profitable Partnerships: Kings, Cities, and Trade." In *The Economies of Hellenistic Societies, Third to First Centuries BC*, edited by Z. H. Archibald, J. K. Davies, and V. Gabrielsen, 216–50. Oxford: Oxford University Press.

Gabrielsen, V. 2013. "Finance and Taxes." In *A Companion to Ancient Greek Government*, edited by H. Beck, 332–48. Malden, MA: Wiley-Blackwell.

Gallant, T. W. 1991. *Risk and Survival in Ancient Greece: Reconstructing the Rural Domestic Economy*. Stanford, CA: Stanford University Press.

Gallo, L. 1992. "La Sicilia occidentale e l'approvvigionamento cerealicolo di Roma." *Annali della Scuola Normale Superiore di Pisa* series III, 22: 365–98.

Gandolfo, L. 1997. "Ricerche a Montagna dei Cavalli: Rinvenimenti monetari." In *Archeologia e territorio*, edited by C. A. Di Stefano, 315–31. Palermo: G. B. Palumbo.

Gargola, D. 1992. "Grain Distributions and the Revenue of the Temple of Hera on Samos." *Phoenix* 46: 12–28.

Garlan, Y. 1974. *Recherches de poliorcétique grecque*. Athens: École française d'Athènes.

Garnsey, P. 1988. *Famine and Food Supply in the Graeco-Roman World: Responses to Risk and Crisis*. New York: Cambridge University Press.

Garnsey, P., and R. Saller. 1987. *The Roman Empire: Economy, Society and Culture*. London: Duckworth.

Garnsey, P., and C. R. Whittaker. 1998. "Trade, Industry and the Urban Economy." In *Cambridge Ancient History*. Vol. 13: *The Late Empire, A.D. 337–425*, edited by A. Cameron and P. Garnsey, 312–37. Cambridge: Cambridge University Press.

Garoufalias, P. 1979. *Pyrrhus, King of Epirus*. London: Stacey International.

Garraffo, S. 1993. "La monetazione dell'età dionigiana. Contromarche e riconiazioni." In *La monetazione dell'età dionigiana: Atti dell'VIII convegno del centro internazionale di studi numismatici, Napoli 29 maggio–1 giugno 1983*, edited by A. Stazio, S. Ceccoli, and M. Taliercio Mensitieri, 191–242. Rome: Istituto italiano di numismatica.

Gatier, P.-L. 2014. "Poids et vie civique du Proche-Orient hellénistique et romain." In *La mesure et ses usages dans l'Antiquité: La documentation archéologique*, edited by C. Saliou, 125–62. Besançon: Presses Universitaires Franche Comté.

Geertz, C. 1978. "The Bazaar Economy: Information and Search in Peasant Marketing." *American Economic Review* 68: 28–32.

Gehrke, H.-J. 1982. "Der siegreiche König Überlegungen zur Hellenistischen Monarchie." *Archiv für Kulturgeschichte* 64: 247–78.

Gehrke, H.-J. 2013. "The Victorious King: Reflections on the Hellenistic Monarchy." In *The Splendors and Miseries of Ruling Alone: Encounters with Monarchy from Archaic Greece to the Hellenistic Mediterranean*, edited by N. Luraghi, 73–98. Studies in Ancient Monarchies 1. Stuttgart: Franz Steiner Verlag.

Gelzer, M. 1933. "Römische Politik bei Fabius Pictor." *Hermes* 68: 129–66.

Gentili, G. V. 1951. "Siracusa: Scoperte nelle due nuove arterie stradali, la Via di Circonvallazione, ora Viale Paolo Orsi, e la Via Archeologica, ora Viale Francesco Saverio Cavallari." *Notizie degli scavi di antichità* 5: 261–360.

Gentili, G. V. 1954. "Siracusa: Ara di Ierone. Campagna di scavo 1950–1951." *Notizie degli scavi di antichità* 8: 333–85.

Gentili, G. V. 1956. "Siracusa: Contributo alla topografia dell'antica citta." *Notizie degli scavi di antichità* 10: 99–116.

Gentili, G. V. 1959–60. "I busti fittili di Demetra e Kore da Siracusa." *Archivio storico siracusano* 5–6: 5–20.

Gentili, G. V. 1969. "Piazza Armerina (Enna). Le anonime città di Montagna di Marzo e di Monte Navone. Testimonianza archeologiche." *Notizie degli scavi di antichità* 7–8: 14–102.

Gentry, A. P. 1976. *Roman Military Stone-Built Granaries in Britain*. British Archaeological Reports 32. Oxford: British Archaeological Reports.

Geominy, W. 2007. "The Daochos Monument at Delphi: The Style and Setting of a Family Portrait in Historic Dress." In *Early Hellenistic Portraiture: Image, Style, Context*, edited by P. Schultz and R. von den Hoff, 84–98. New York: Cambridge University Press.

Giesecke, W. 1920. *Das münzwesen Hierons II von Syrakus*. Berlin: Berliner Münzblätter.

Giesecke, W. 1923. *Sicilia numismatica: Die Grundlagen des griechischen Münzwesens auf Sizilien*. Leipzig: K. W. Hiersemann.

Giesecke, W. 1935. "Eine unbekannte Silbermünze Hierone II von Syrakus." *Deutsche Münzblätter* 55: 361–4.

Given, M. 2004. *The Archaeology of the Colonized*. London: Routledge.

Goldsberry, M. A. S. 1973. "Sicily and Its Cities in Hellenistic and Roman Times." PhD diss., University of North Carolina at Chapel Hill.

Goldstone, J. A., and J. Haldon. 2009. "States, Empires and Exploitation: Problems and Perspectives." In *The Dynamics of Ancient Empires: State Power from Assyria to Byzantium*, edited by I. Morris and W. Scheidel, 3–29. Oxford: Oxford University Press.

González, J. M. 2010. "Theokritos' *Idyll* 16: The Χάριτες and Civic Poetry." *Harvard Studies in Classical Philology* 105: 65–116.

Gotter, U. 2013. "The Castrated King, or: The Everyday Monstrosity of Late Hellenistic Kingship." In *The Splendors and Miseries of Ruling Alone: Encounters with Monarchy from Archaic Greece to the Hellenistic Mediterranean*, edited by N. Luraghi, 207–30. Studies in Ancient Monarchies 1. Stuttgart: Franz Steiner.

Gow, A. S. F. 1952. *Theocritus*. 2nd ed. Cambridge: Cambridge University Press.

Grainger, J. D. 2017. *Great Power Diplomacy in the Hellenistic World*. London: Routledge.

Grasso, L., and A. Musumeci. 1989. *Caracausi: Un insediamento rupestre nel territorio di Lentini*. Catania: Università di Catania, Istituto di archeologia.

Green, P. 1990. *Alexander to Actium: The Historical Evolution of the Hellenistic Age*. Berkeley: University of California Press.

Grenfell, B. P. 1896. *Revenue Laws of Ptolemy Philadelphus*. Oxford: Clarendon Press.

Grib, V. 2008. *Hellenistische Demokratie: Politische Organisation und Struktur in freien griechischen Poleis nach Alexander dem Großen*. Historia Einzelschriften 199. Stuttgart: Franz Steiner Verlag.

Gruen, E. S. 1985. "The Coronation of the Diadochoi." In *The Craft of the Ancient Historian: Essays in Honor of Chester G. Starr*, edited by J. W. Eadie and J. Ober, 253–71. Lanham, MD: University Press of America.

Gruen, E. S. 1993. "The *Polis* in the Hellenistic World." In *Nomodeiktes: Greek Studies in Honor of Martin Ostwald*, edited by R. Rosen and J. Farrell, 339–54. Ann Arbor: University of Michigan Press.

Grunauer-von Hoerschelmann, S. 1978. *Die Münzprägung der Lakedaimonier*. Berlin: De Gruyter.

Gutzwiller, K. 1983. "Charites or Hieron: Theocritus' '*Idyll*' 16." *Rheinisches Museum für Philologie* 126: 212–38.

Guzzardi, L. 1999. "Montagna di Marzo: Nuovi dati sulla storia e sulla topografia del sito." *Kokalos* 45: 535–51.

Guzzo, P. G. 2002. "A Group of Hellenistic Silver Objects in the Metropolitan Museum." *Metropolitan Museum Journal* 38: 45–94.

Gygax, M. D. 2001. *Untersuchungen zu den lykischen Gemeinwesen in klassischer und hellenistischer Zeit*. Bonn: Habelt Verlag.

Gygax, M. D. 2016. *Benefaction and Rewards in the Ancient Greek City: The Origins of Euergetism*. Cambridge: Cambridge University Press.

Gyllenbok, J. 2018. *Encyclopaedia of Historical Metrology, Weights, and Measures*. Vol. 3. Cham: Birkhäuser.

Haake, M. 2005. "Agathokles und Hieron II. Zwei 'basileis' in hellenistischer Zeit und die Frage ihrer Nachfolge." In *Διάδοχος τῆς βασιλείας: La figura del sucesor en la realeza helenística*, edited by V. Alonso Troncoso, 153–75. Madrid: Universidad Complutense, Servicio de Publicaciones.

Haake, M. 2012. "Diadem und basileus: Überlegungen zu einer Insignie und einem Titel in hellenistischer Zeit." In *Das Diadem der hellenistischen Herrscher: Übernahme, Transformation oder Neuschöpfung eines Herrschaftszeichens?*, edited by A. Lichtenberger, K. Martin, H.-H. Nieswandt, and D. Salzmann, 293–313. Bonn: Habelt-Verlag.

Haake, M. 2013. "Agathocles and Hiero II: Two Sole Rulers in the Hellenistic Age and the Question of Succession." In *The Splendors and Miseries of Ruling Alone: Encounters with*

Monarchy from Archaic Greece to the Hellenistic Mediterranean, edited by N. Luraghi, 99–127. Studies in Ancient Monarchies 1. Stuttgart: Franz Steiner.

Habich, G. 1917. "Falscher Aureus des Königs Hieron II. von Sicilien." *Frankfurter Münzzeitung* 17: 247–9.

Habicht, C. 1970. *Gottmenschentum und griechische Städte*. Munich: Beck.

Habicht, C. 1997. *Athens from Alexander to Antony*. Cambridge, MA: Harvard University Press.

Hafford, W. 2012. "Weighing in Mesopotamia: The Balance Pan Weights from Ur." *Akkadica* 133: 21–65.

Halstead, P. 1995. "From Sharing to Hoarding: The Neolithic Foundations of Aegean Bronze Age Society." In *Politeia: Society and State in the Aegean Bronze Age. Proceedings of the 5th International Aegean Conference, University of Heidelberg, Archäologisches Institut, 10–13 April 1994*, edited by R. Laffineur and W.-D. Niemeie, 11–21. Brussels: Université de Liège; Austin: University of Texas at Austin.

Halstead, P. 1997. "Storage Strategies and States on Prehistoric Crete: A Reply to Strasser." *Journal of Mediterranean Archaeology* 10: 103–7.

Halstead, P., and G. Jones. 1989. "Agrarian Ecology in the Greek Islands: Time Stress, Scale and Risk." *Journal of Hellenic Studies* 109: 41–55.

Hammond, N. G. L. 1988. "Which Ptolemy Gave Troops and Stood as Protector of Pyrrhus' Kingdom?" *Historia: Zeitschrift für Alte Geschichte* 37: 405–13.

Hansen, E. V. 1971. *The Attalids of Pergamon*. 2nd ed. Ithaca, NY: Cornell University Press.

Harris, E. M. 1999. "Notes on the New Grain-Tax Law." *Zeitschrift für Papyrologie und Epigraphik* 128: 269–72.

Hatzopoulos, M. B. 1996. *Macedonian Institutions under the Kings*. MELETHMATA 22. Athens: Research Centre for Greek and Roman Antiquity.

Hatzopoulos, M. B. 2001. "Macedonian Palaces: Where King and City Meet." In *The Royal Palace Institution in the First Millennium BC: Regional Development and Cultural Interchange* between East and West, Monographs of the Danish Institute at Athens, edited by I. Nielsen, 189–99. Aarhus: Aarhus University Press

Hatzopoulos, M. B. 2014. "The Athenian Standards Decree: The Aphytis Fragments." Τεκμήρια 12: 235–69.

Head, B. V. 1874a. History of the Coinage of Syracuse. London: Russell.

Head, B. V. 1874b. "On the Chronological Sequence of the Coins of Syracuse." The Numismatic Chronicle 14: 1–80.

Head, B. V. 1876. Catalogue of the Greek Coins, Sicily: In the British Museum. London: Longmans.

Hendon, J. A. 2000. "Having and Holding: Storage, Memory, Knowledge, and Social Relations." American Anthropologist 102: 42–53.

Henzel, R. J. 2019. "Ehrenstatuen im hellenistichen Sizilien." In Cityscapes of Hellenistic Sicily, edited by M. Trümper, G. Adornato, and T. Lappi, 179–95. Rome: Edizioni Quasar.

Herbert, S., and A. Berlin. 2003. "A New Administrative Center for Persian and Hellenistic Galilee: Preliminary Report of the University of Michigan/University of Minnesota Excavations at Kedesh." Bulletin of the American Schools of Oriental Research 329: 13.

Hersch, C. A. 1953. "Overstrikes as Evidence for the History of Roman Republican Coinage." The Numismatic Chronicle and Journal of the Royal Numismatic Society 13: 33–68.

Herzog, R., and G. Klaffenbach. 1952. Asylieurkunden aus Kos. Berlin: Akademie-Verlag.

Hicks, J. 1969. A Theory of Economic History. Oxford: Clarendon Press.

Higbie, C. 2003. The Lindian Chronicle and the Greek Creation of Their Past. Oxford: Oxford University Press.

Higgs, P. 2016. "The Rise of Tyrants." In Sicily: Culture and Conquest, edited by D. Booms and P. Higgs, 72–131. Ithaca, NY: Cornell University Press with the British Museum Press.

Hildebrandt, B., and C. Veit, eds. 2009. Der Wert der Dinge: Güter im Prestigediskurs: "Formen von Prestige in Kulturen des Altertums": Graduiertenkolleg der DFG an der Ludwig-Maximilians-Universität Munich. Munich: Utz.

Hill, G. F. 1903. Coins of Ancient Sicily. Westminster: A. Constable & Co.

Hinz, V. 1998. Kult von Demeter und Kore auf Sizilien und in der Magna Graecia. Palilia 4. Wiesbaden: Ludwig Reichert.

Hitzl, K. 1996. Die Gewichte griechischer Zeit aus Olympia. Berlin: De Gruyter.

Hoffmann, A., and M. H. Sayar. 2007. "Vorbericht zu den in rien Jahren 2003 bis 2005 auf dem Berg Karasis (bei Kozan/Adana) und in seiner Umgebung durchgeführten Untersuchungen." Istanbuler Mitteilungen 57: 365–468.

Hogan, A. 2019. "The Auction of Pharaoh Revisited." In New Approaches in Demotic Studies: Acts of the 13th International Conference of Demotic Studies, edited by F. Naether, 107–22. Berlin: De Gruyter.

Holloway, R. R. 1960. "Numismatic Notes from Morgantina II: Half Coins of Hieron II in the Monetary System of Roman Sicily." American Numismatic Society Museum Notes 9: 65–73.

Holloway, R. R. 1962. "Eagle and Fulmen of the Coins of Syracuse." Revue belge de numismatique 108: 5–28.

Holloway, R. R. 1965. "Monetary Circulation in Central Sicily to the Reign of Augustus as Documented by the Morgantina Excavations." In Atti del Congresso internazionale di numismatica, Roma, 11–16 settembre 1961, 135–50. Rome: Istituto italiano di numismatica.

Holloway, R. R. 1979. "The Bronze Coinage of Agathocles." In Greek Numismatics and Archeology: Essays in the Honor of Margaret Thompson, edited by O. Mørkholm and N. M. Waggoner, 87–95. Wetteren: Editions NR.

Holm, A. 1898. Geschichte Siciliens im Alterthum. Leipzig: Engelmann.

Holm, A. 1906. Storia della Sicilia nell'antichità. Vol. 3, pt. 2. Translated by G. Kirner. Turin: C. Clausen.

Hopkins, K. 1980. "Taxes and Trade in the Roman Empire (200 B.C.–A.D. 400)." Journal of Roman Studies 70: 101–25.

Horden, P., and N. Purcell. 2000. *The Corrupting Sea: A Study of Mediterranean History.* Malden, MA: Wiley-Blackwell.

Houghton, A. 2004. "Seleucid Coinage and Monetary Policy of the 2nd c. B.C.: Reflections on the Monetization of the Seleucid Economy." *Topoi. Orient-Occident* 6: 49–79.

Houghton, A., and C. Lorber. 2002. *Seleucid Coins: A Comprehensive Catalogue.* Part 1: *Seleucus I through Antiochus III.* New York: American Numismatic Society.

Hoyos, B. D. 1985. "The Rise of Hiero II: Chronology and Campaigns 275–264 BC." *Antichthon* 19: 32–56.

Hoyos, B. D. 2011. "The Outbreak of War." In *A Companion to the Punic Wars,* edited by B. D. Hoyos, 131–48. Malden, MA: Wiley-Blackwell.

Hoyos, D. 2015. *Mastering the West: Rome and Carthage at War.* Ancient Warfare and Civilization. Oxford: Oxford University Press.

Hultsch, F. 1882. *Griechische und römische Metrologie.* 2nd ed. Berlin: Weidmannsche Buchhandlung.

Hunter, R. L. 1996. *Theocritus and the Archaeology of Greek Poetry.* Cambridge: Cambridge University Press.

Hyde, W. W. 1903. *De Olympionicarum statuis a Pausania commemoratis.* Halle: M. Niemeyer.

Ialongo, N., A. Vacca, and A. Vanzetti. 2018. "Indeterminacy and Approximation in Mediterranean Weight Systems in the Third and Second Millennia BC." In *Gifts, Goods and Money: Comparing Currency and Circulation Systems in Past Societies,* edited by D. Brandherm, E. Heymans, and D. Hofmann, 9–44. Oxford: Archaeopress.

Ierardi, M. 1995–6. "The Tetradrachms of Agathocles of Syracuse: A Preliminary Study." *American Journal of Numismatics* 7–8: 1–73.

Iwahashi, M. 2004. "The Institutional Framework of the Tokugawa Economy." In *Emergence of Economic Society in Japan, 1600–1859,* edited by A. Hayami, O. Saito, and R. P. Toby, 85–104. Oxford: Oxford University Press.

Jeannin, P. 1972. *Merchants of the 16th Century.* New York: Harper & Row.

Jenkins, G. K., and R. W. B. Lewis. 1963. *Carthaginian Gold and Electrum Coins.* London: Royal Numismatic Society.

Jeppesen, K. 1958. *Paradeigmata: Three Mid-Fourth Century Main Works of Hellenic Architecture Reconsidered.* Aarhus: Aarhus University Press.

Jones, D. E. 2020. "Hieron II, Ptolemy, and the 'Ptolemies': Numismatic Imitation and Bronze Coinage in Hellenistic Sicily." *Revue Belge de Numismatique et de Sigillographie* 166: 198–226.

Judson, S. 1963. "Stream Changes during Historic Time in East-Central Sicily." *American Journal of Archaeology* 67: 287–9.

Jursa, M., and J. García. 2015. "The Ancient Near East and Egypt." In *Fiscal Regimes and the Political Economy of Premodern States,* edited by A. Monson and W. Scheidel, 115–66. Cambridge: Cambridge University Press.

Kallet, L. 2001. *Money and the Corrosion of Power in Thucydides: The Sicilian Expedition and Its Aftermath.* Berkeley: University of California Press.

Karlsson, L. 1992. *Fortification Towers and Masonry Techniques in the Hegemony of Syracuse: 405–211 B.C.* Göteborg: Åströms Förl.

Karlsson, L. 1993. "Did the Romans Allow the Sicilian Greeks to Fortify Their Cities in the Third Century BC?" In *Aspects of Hellenism in Italy: Towards a Cultural Unity?,* edited by P. G. Bilde, I. Nielsen, and M. Nielsen, 31–51. Copenhagen: Museum Tusculanum Press.

Karlsson, L. 1997. "The Altar of Hieron at Syracuse: A Discussion of Its Function." *Opuscula Romana* 21: 83–7.

Kaye, N. 2018. "Taxation in the Greco-Roman World: The Hellenistic East." In *Oxford Handbooks Online in Classics.* DOI: 10.1093/oxfordhb/9780199935390.013.36.

Kehoe, D. P. 2007. *Law and the Rural Economy in the Roman Empire.* Ann Arbor: University of Michigan Press.

Kehoe, D. P. 2015. "Contracts, Agency, and Transaction Costs in the Roman Economy." In *Law and Transaction Costs in the Ancient*

Economy, edited by D. P. Kehoe, D. M. Ratzan, and U. Yiftach, 231–52. Ann Arbor: University of Michigan Press.

Kemp, B. J. 1986. "Large Middle Kingdom Granary Buildings." *Zeitschrift für Ägyptische Sprache und Altertumskunde* 113: 130–46.

Kingsley, S. 2001. "The Economic Impact of the Palestinian Wine Trade in Late Antiquity." In *Economy and Exchange in the East Mediterranean during Late Antiquity: Proceedings of a Conference at Somerville College*, edited by S. Kingsley and M. Decker, 44–68. Oxford: Oxbow.

Kiser, E. 1994. "Markets and Hierarchies in Early Modern Tax Systems: A Principal-Agent Analysis." *Politics & Society* 22: 284–315.

Kiser, E., and D. Kane. 2007. "The Perils of Privatization: How the Characteristics of Principals Affected Tax Farming in the Roman Republic and Empire." *Social Science History* 31: 191–212.

Kleyman, I. B. 1989. *Arkheologicheskiye pamyatniki stepey Podnestrovya i Podunavya*. Kiev: Naukova Dumka.

Knorr, W. 1978. "Archimedes and the Elements: Proposal for a Revised Chronological Ordering of the Archimedean Corpus." *Archive for History of Exact Sciences* 19: 211–90.

Konuk, K. 2004. "The Ptolemaic Coins in the Bodrum Underwater Archaeology Museum." In *The Salmakis Inscription and Hellenistic Halikarnassos*, edited by S. Isager and P. Pedersen, 204–23. Odensee: University Press of Southern Denmark.

Kosmin, P. J. 2014. *The Land of the Elephant Kings: Space, Territory, and Ideology in the Seleucid Empire*. Cambridge, MA: Harvard University Press.

Kosmin, P. J. 2018. *Time and Its Adversaries in the Seleucid Empire*. Cambridge, MA: Belknap Press of Harvard University Press.

Kramer, S. N. 1950. "'Inanna's Descent to the Nether World' Continued and Revised." *Journal of Cuneiform Studies* 4: 199–214.

Kremydi, S. 2011. "Coinage and Finance." In *Brill's Companion to Ancient Macedon*, edited by R. J. Lane Fox, 159–78. Leiden: Brill.

Kroll, J. H. 1997. "Coinage as an Index of Romanization." In *The Romanization of Athens: Proceedings of an International Conference Held at Lincoln, Nebraska (April 1996)*, edited by M. C. Hoff and S. I. Rotroff, 135–50. Oxford: Oxbow.

Kroll, J. H. 2007. "The Emergence of the Ruler Portraiture on Early Hellenistic Coins: The Importance of Being Divine." In *Early Hellenistic Portraiture: Image, Style, Context*, edited by P. Schultz and R. von den Hoff, 113–22. Cambridge: Cambridge University Press.

Kroll, J. H. 2009. "What about Coinage?" In *Interpreting the Athenian Empire*, edited by J. Ma, N. Papazarkadas, and R. Parker, 195–209. London: Bristol Classical Press.

Kroll, J. H. 2011. "The Reminting of Athenian Silver Coinage, 353 B.C." *Hesperia: The Journal of the American School of Classical Studies at Athens* 80: 229–59.

Kroll, J. H., and A. S. Walker. 1993. *The Greek Coins*. Princeton, NJ: American School of Classical Studies at Athens.

Kuhlmann, P. 2010. "Die Maecenas-Rede bei Cassius Dio: Anachronismen und intertextuelle Bezüge." In *Stimmen der Geschichte: Funktionen von Reden in der antiken Historiographie*, edited by D. Pausch, 109–21. Berlin: De Gruyter.

Kula, W. 1986. *Measures and Men*. Princeton, NJ: Princeton University Press.

Kunze, E., and F. Eckstein. 1958. *Bericht über die Ausgrabungen in Olympia*. Vol. 6: *1953–1954 und 1954–1955*. Berlin: De Gruyter.

Kushnir-Stein, A. 2001. "Was Late Hellenistic Silver Coinage Minted for Propaganda Purposes?" *The Numismatic Chronicle (1966–)* 161: 41–52.

Kyrieleis, H. 1975. *Bildnisse der Ptolemäer*. Berlin: Mann.

La Bua, V. 1960. "Agrigento dalla morte di Agatocle alla conquista romana." *Kokalos* 6: 98–109.

La Bua, V. 1966. *Filino-Polibio, Sileno-Diodoro: Il problema delle fonti dalla morte di Agatocle alla guerra mercenaria in Africa*. Palermo: Flaccovio.

La Bua, V. 1968. "Finzia, la fondazione di Finziade e la Sicilia dal 289 al 279 a.C." *Atti* dell'*Accademia di Scienze, Lettere e Arti di Palermo* 27: 117–60.

La Bua, V. 1980. "La spedizione di Pirro in Sicilia." *Miscellanea greca e romana* 7: 179–254.

La Torre, G. F., and F. Mollo, eds. 2013. *Finziade I. Scavi sul Monte S. Angelo di Licata (2003–2005)*. Rome: L'Erma di Bretschneider.

La'da, C. A. 2002. *Prosopographia Ptolemaica*. Vol. 10: *Foreign Ethnics in Hellenistic Egypt*. Leuven: Peeters.

Lagos, C. 1996. "A Hoard of the Chremonidean War." *The Numismatic Chronicle* 156: 272–8.

Lang, M. 1952. "A New Inscription from Thasos: Specifications for a Measure." *Bulletin de correspondance hellénique* 76: 18–31.

Lang, M., and Crosby, M. 1964. *The Athenian Agora*. Vol. 10: *Weights, Measures, and Tokens*. Princeton, NJ: American School of Classical Studies at Athens.

Larsen, J. A. O. 1968. *Greek Federal States: Their Institutions and History*. Oxford: Clarendon Press.

Lawrence, A. W. 1946. "Archimedes and the Design of Euryalus Fort." *Journal of Hellenic Studies* 66: 99–107.

Le Rider, G. 1986. "Les Alexandres d'argent en Asie Mineure et dans l'Orient Séleucide au IIIe siècle av. J.-C. (c. 275–c. 225): Remarques sur le système monétaire des Séleucides et Ptolémées." *Journal des Savants* 1: 3–57.

Lehmler, C. 2005. *Syrakus unter Agathokles und Hieron II: Die Verbindung von Kultur und Macht in einer hellenistischen Metropole*. Frankfurt am Main: Verlag Antike.

Leighton, R., ed. 2012. *Prehistoric Houses at Morgantina: Excavations on the Cittadella of Morgantina in Sicily, 1989–2004*. Specialist Studies on Italy 15. London: Accordia Research Institute, University of London.

Lenschau, T. 1913. "Hieron." In *Paulys Realencyclopädie der classischen Altertumswissenschaft*, Vol. 8.2, 1503–1511. Stuttgart: Metzler Verlag.

Lentini, M. C. 2002. "Testimonianze della prima metà del IV secolo a.C. a Naxos." In *La Sicilia dei due Dionisî*, edited by N. Bonacasa, L. Braccesi, and E. De Miro, 223–42. Rome: L'Erma di Bretschneider.

Leventhal, M. 2017. "Eratothenes' Letter to Ptolemy: The Literary Mechanics of Empire." *American Journal of Philology* 138: 43–84.

Lévêque, P. 1957. *Pyrrhos*. Paris: E. de Boccard.

Levi, M. 1988. *Of Rule and Revenue*. Berkeley: University of California Press.

Levi, M. A. 1970. "Zeus Olimpico e le statue di Ierone II a Olimpia." *Acme* 23: 153–6.

Levinson, R. A. 2007. *The Early Dated Coins of Europe 1234–1500*. Clifton, NJ: Coin and Currency Institute.

Lewis, S. 2000. "The Tyrant's Myth." In *Sicily from Aeneas to Augustus: New Approaches in Archaeology and History*, edited by C. J. Smith and J. Serrati, 97–106. Edinburgh: Edinburgh University Press.

Lewis, S. 2009. *Greek Tyranny*. Exeter: Bristol Phoenix Press.

Lo Cascio, E. 2006. "The Role of the State in the Roman Economy: Making Use of the New Institutional Economics." In *Ancient Economies, Modern Methodologies: Archaeology, Comparative History, Models and Institutions*, edited by P. F. Bang, M. Ikeguchi, and H. Ziche, 215–34. Bari: Edipuglia.

Lo Cascio, E. 2007. "The Early Roman Empire: The State and the Economy." In *Cambridge Economic History of the Greco-Roman World*, edited by I. Morris, R. P. Saller, and W. Scheidel, 619–47. Cambridge: Cambridge University Press.

Lombardo, M. 1982. "Il sinecismo di Entella." *Annali della Scuola Normale Superiore di Pisa* series III, 12: 849–86.

Lorber, C. 2012a. "Egyptian Hoards Relating to the Abandonment of the Attic Standard by Ptolemy I." In *I ritrovamenti monetali e i processi storico-economici nel mondo antico*, edited by M. Asolati and G. Gorini, 33–47. Padua: Esedra.

Lorber, C. 2012b. "The Coinage of the Ptolemies." In *The Oxford Handbook of Greek and Roman Coinage*, edited by W. E. Metcalf, 211–34. Oxford: Oxford University Press.

Lorber, C. 2018. "The Currency Reforms and Character of Ptolemy I Soter." In *Ptolemy I Soter: A Self-Made Man*, edited by T. Howe, 60–87. Oxford: Oxbow.

Lorenzen, E. 1964. *The Arsenal at Piraeus, Designed by Philo and Reconstructed after His Description*. Copenhagen: Gads Forlag.

Lucchelli, T. M., and G. Di Stefano. 2004. *Monete dall'agorà di Camarina: Campagne di scavo 1983–1995*. Milan: CUEM.

Lucore, S. K. 2009. "Archimedes, the North Baths at Morgantina, and Early Developments in Vaulted Construction." In *The Nature and Function of Water, Baths, and Bathing and Hygiene from Antiquity through the Renaissance*, edited by C. Kosso and A. Scott, 43–59. Leiden: Brill.

Lucore, S. K. 2013. "Bathing in Hieronian Sicily." In *Greek Baths and Bathing Culture: New Discoveries and Approaches*, edited by S. K. Lucore and M. Trümper, 151–79. *BABesch* Supplement 23. Leuven: Peeters.

Lucore, S. K. 2015. "Le terme sud di Morgantina: Impianti idrico e di riscaldamento." In *Morgantina duemilaquindici: La ricerca archeologica a sessant'anni dall'avvio degli scavi*, edited by L. Maniscalco, 92–101. Palermo: Regione siciliana.

Lupi. A. M. 1734. *Dissertatio et animadversiones ad nuper inventum Severae Martyris epitaphium illustratum*. Palermo: Ex typographia Stephanus Amato.

Luraghi, N. 1994. *Tirannidi arcaiche in Sicilia e Magna Grecia: Da Panezio di Leontini alla caduta dei Dinomenidi*. Florence: Olschki.

Lyttkens, C. H. 2013. *Economic Analysis of Institutional Change in Ancient Greece: Politics, Taxation and Rational Behaviour*. Abingdon: Routledge.

Ma, J. 2000. *Antiochos III and the Cities of Western Asia Minor*. Oxford: Oxford University Press.

Ma, J. 2003. "Peer Polity Interaction in the Hellenistic Age." *Past and Present* 180: 9–39.

Ma, J. 2013. "Hellenistic Empires." In *The Oxford Handbook of the State in the Ancient Near East and Mediterranean*, edited by P. F. Bang and W. Scheidel, 324–57. Oxford: Oxford University Press.

MacDonald, G. 1899. *Catalogue of Greek Coins in the Hunterian Collection*. Vol. 1. Glasgow: University of Glasgow.

Mackil, E. M. 2016. *Creating a Common Polity: Religion, Economy, and Politics in the Making of the Greek Koinon*. Berkeley: University of California Press.

Mafodda, G. 1979. "Aspetti e problemi di storia siceliota dalla morte di Agatocle all'insediamento mamertino in Messana." *Kokalos* 25: 197–204.

Malay, H. 1983. "A Royal Document from Aigai in Aiolis." *Greek, Roman and Byzantine Studies* 24: 349–53.

Manenti, A. M. 2015. "Monili e oggetti di ornamento rinvenuti a Morgantina." In *Morgantina duemilaequindici: La ricerca archeologica a sessant'anni dall'avvio degli scavi*, edited by L. Maniscalco, 167–71. Palermo: Regione siciliana.

Manganaro, G. 1963. "Tauromenitana." *Archeologia Classica* 15: 13–31.

Manganaro, G. 1964. "Iscrizioni latine e greche dal nuovo edificio termale di Taormina." *Cronache di archeologia e storia dell'arte* 3: 38–68.

Manganaro, G. 1965. "Una epistola di Gerone II ai Siracusani." *Athenaeum* 43: 312–20.

Manganaro, G. 1977. "Per la storia dei culti nella Sicilia greca." *Cronache di archeologia e storia dell'arte* 16: 148–64.

Manganaro, G. 1979. "L'età greca." In *La Sicilia nella storiografia dell'ultimo ventennio: Atti del Congresso di Mazara*, edited by G. Di Stefano, 3–22. Vallo di Mazara: Istituto di Storia.

Manganaro, G. 1981–2. "Un ripostiglio siciliano del 214–211 a.C. e la datazione del *denarius*." *Jahrbuch für Numismatik und Geldgeschichte* 31–2: 37–54.

Manganaro, G. 1988. "La Sicilia da Sesto Pompeo a Diocleziano." In *Aufstieg und Niedergang der römischen Welt*, edited by H. Temporini and W. Haase, 2.11.1, 3–89. Berlin: De Gruyter.

Manganaro, G. 1989. "Movimento di uomini tra Egitto e Sicilia (III–I sec. a.C.)." In *Egitto e storia antica dall'ellenismo all'eta araba: Bilancio di un confronto. Atti del colloquio internazionale, Bologna, 31 agosto–2 settembre 1987*, edited by L. Criscuolo and G. Geraci, 513–53. Bologna: CLUEB.

Manganaro, G. 1996. "Per una storia della chora Katanaia." In *Catania antica: Atti del convegno della Società italiana per lo studio dell'antichità classica, Catania 23–24 maggio 1992*, edited by

B. Gentili, 19–59. Pisa: Istituti editoriali e poligrafici internazionali.

Manganaro, G. 1999a. *Sikelika: Studi di antichità e di epigrafia della Sicilia greca.* Rome: Edizioni dell'Ateneo.

Manganaro, G. 1999b. "Dall'obolo alla litra e il problema del '*Damareteion*.'" In *Travaux de numismatique grecque offerts à Georges le Rider*, edited by M. Amandry and S. Hurter, 239–55. London: Spink.

Manganaro, G. 2001. "Byzantina Siciliae." *Minima Epigraphica et Papyrologica* 5: 131–78.

Manganaro, G. 2005. "La stele in pietra scura (*IG* XIV 7) con l'epistola di Gerone II ai Siracusani." *Zeitschrift für Papyrologie und Epigraphik* 152: 141–51.

Manganaro, G. 2012. *Pace e guerra nella Sicilia tardo-ellenistica e romana (215 a.C.–14 d.C.): Ricerche storiche e numismatiche.* Bonn: Habelt.

Mann, C., and P. Scholz, eds. 2012. *"Demokratie" im Hellenismus: Von der Herrschaft des Volkes zur Herrschaft der Honoratioren?* Mainz: Verlage Antike.

Manni, E. 1981. *Geografia fisica e politica della Sicilia antica.* Rome: Bretschneider.

Manning, J. G. 2003. *Land and Power in Ptolemaic Egypt: The Structure of Land Tenure 332–30 BCE.* Cambridge: Cambridge University Press.

Manning, J. G. 2007. "The Ptolemaic Economy." In *The Cambridge Economic History of the Graeco-Roman World*, edited by I. Morris, R. Saller, and W. Scheidel, 434–59. Cambridge: Cambridge University Press.

Manning, J. G. 2008. "Coinage as 'Code' in Ptolemaic Egypt." In *The Monetary Systems of the Greeks and Romans*, edited by W. V. Harris, 84–111. Oxford: Oxford University Press.

Manning, J. G. 2010. *The Last Pharaohs: Egypt under the Ptolemies, 305–30 BC.* Princeton, NJ: Princeton University Press.

Manning, J. G. 2018. *The Open Sea: The Economic Life of the Ancient Mediterranean World from the Iron Age to the Rise of Rome.* Princeton, NJ: Princeton University Press.

Manning, J. G., and W. Scheidel. 2010. Review of *Counting the People in Hellenistic Egypt. Volume 1: Population Registers (P. Count). Volume 2: Historical Studies*, by W. Clarysse

and D. J. Thompson. *The Bulletin of the American Society of Papyrologists* 47: 267–73.

Manning, W. H. 1975. "Roman Military Timber Granaries in Britain." *Saalburg-Jahrbuch* 32: 105–29.

Marcellesi, M.-C. 2010. "Adoption et diffusion de la monnaie de bronze dans le monde égéen: Une évolution économique et institutionnelle." *Studi ellenistici* 24: 255–71.

Marchetti, P. 1993. "Numismatique romaine et histoire." *Cahiers du Centre Gustave Glotz* 4: 25–65.

Marconi, C. 2007. "Acrolithic and Pseudo-Acrolithic Sculpture in Archaic and Classical Greece and the Provenance of the Getty Goddess." In *Cult Statue of a Goddess: Summary of Proceedings from a Workshop Held at the Getty Villa May 9, 2007*, 4–13. Los Angeles: J. Paul Getty Trust.

Marconi, C. 2012. "Between Performance and Identity: The Social and Cultural Context of Theaters in Late Classical and Hellenistic Sicily." In *Theater outside Athens: Drama in Greek Sicily and South Italy*, edited by K. Bosher, 175–207. Cambridge: Cambridge University Press.

Marino, R. 1988. *La Sicilia dai 241 al 210 a.C.* Rome: G. Bretschneider.

Marston, J. M. 2017. *Agricultural Sustainability and Environmental Change at Ancient Gordion.* Philadelphia: University of Pennsylvania Museum of Archaeology and Anthropology.

Martin, S., ed. 2019. *Rural Granaries in Northern Gaul (Sixth Century BCE–Fourth Century CE).* Leiden: Brill.

Martin, T. R. 1985. *Sovereignty and Coinage in Classical Greece.* Princeton, NJ: Princeton University Press.

Martin, T. R. 1991. "Silver Coins and Public Slaves in the Athenian Law of 375/4 B.C." In *Mnemata: Papers in Memory of Nancy M. Waggoner*, edited by W. E. Metcalf, 21–47. New York: American Numismatic Society.

Martin, R., and G. Vallet. 1980. "L'architettura monumentale religiosa e civile." In *La Sicilia antica.* Vol. 1, pt. 2: *Le città greche di Sicilia*, edited by E. Gabba and G. Vallet, 271–314. Naples: A. Lombardi.

Mathews, D. 1992. *The Norman Kingdom of Sicily.* Cambridge: Cambridge University Press.

Mattingly, H. B. 1996. *The Athenian Empire Restored.* Epigraphic and Historical Studies. Ann Arbor: University of Michigan Press.

Mattingly, H. 2000. "Methodology and History in Third Century Sicilian Numismatics." *Schweizerische Numismatische Rundschau* 79: 35–48.

Mattioli, M. 1995. "Camarina in età ellenistico–romana." *Kokalos* 41: 229–70.

Mayerson, P. 1998. "The Sack (σακκος) Is the *Artaba* Writ Large." *Zeitschrift für Papyrologie und Epigraphik* 122: 189–94.

Mayerson, P. 2000. "Standardization of Wine Measures at Oxyrhynchus in the Third Century A.D. and its Extension to the Fayum." *The Bulletin of the American Society of Papyrologists* 37: 105–9.

McArdle, F. 1978. *Altopascio: A Study in Tuscan Rural Society 1587–1784.* Cambridge: Cambridge University Press.

McInerney, J. 2010. *The Cattle of the Sun: Cows and Culture in the World of the Ancient Greeks.* Princeton, NJ: Princeton University Press.

Meadows, A. 2001. "Money, Freedom and Empire in the Hellenistic World." In *Money and Its Uses in the Ancient Greek World*, edited by A. Meadows and K. Shipton, 53–63. Oxford: Oxford University Press.

Meadows, A. 2013. "The Ptolemaic League of Islanders." In *The Ptolemies, the Sea and the Nile: Studies in Waterborne Power*, edited by K. Buraselis, M. Stefanou, and D. Thompson, 19–38. Cambridge: Cambridge University Press.

Meadows, A. 2014. "The Spread of Coins in the Hellenistic World." In *Explaining Monetary and Financial Innovation: A Historical Analysis*, edited by P. Bernholz and R. Vaubel, 169–95. Cham: Springer International.

Mège, F. 2014. "Features of Hellenistic Housing at Megara Hyblaia: Insights into Recent Works on Early Excavations." In *Hellenistische Häuser und ihre Funktionen, Internationale Tagung Kiel, 4. bis 6. April 2013*, edited by A. Haug and D. Steuernagel, 163–76. Bonn: Verlag Dr. Rudolf Habel.

Meiggs, R., and D. M. Lewis. 1969. *A Selection of Greek Historical Inscriptions to the End of the Fifth Century B.C.* Oxford: Clarendon Press.

Meister, K. 1984. "Agathocles." In *The Cambridge Ancient History.* 2nd ed. Vol. 7, pt. 1: *The Hellenistic World*, edited by F. W. Walbank, A. E. Astin, M. W. Frederiksen, and R. M. Ogilvie, 384–411. Cambridge: Cambridge University Press.

Meritt, B. D. 1946a. "Greek Inscriptions." *Hesperia: The Journal of the American School of Classical Studies at Athens* 15: 169–253.

Meritt, B. D. 1946b. "The Athenian Alliances with Rhegion and Leontinoi." *The Classical Quarterly* 40: 85–91.

Messina, E. 2009. "Lo scavo di Via Zappalà (Siracusa)." *Kokalos* 47–48: 807–819.

Metcalf, D. M. 1998. *An Atlas of Anglo-Saxon and Norman Coin Finds, c. 973–1086.* London: Royal Numismatic Society.

Meyer, H.-C., and A. Moreno. 2004. "A Greek Metrological *Koine*: A Lead Weight from the Western Black Sea Region in the Ashmolean Museum, Oxford." *Oxford Journal of Archaeology* 23: 209–16.

Migeotte, L. 1991. "Le pain quotidien dans les cités hellénistiques: À propos des fonds permanents pour l'approvisionnement en grain." *Cahiers du Centre Gustave Glotz* 2: 19–41.

Migeotte, L. 2009. *The Economy of the Greek Cities: From the Archaic Period to the Early Roman Empire.* Berkeley: University of California Press.

Militello, E. 1961. "Troina: Scavi effettuati dall'Istituto di Archeologia dell'Università di Catania negli anni 1958 e 1960." *Notizie degli scavi di antichità* 15: 322–404.

Millar, F. 1964. *A Study of Cassius Dio.* Oxford: Clarendon Press.

Millino, G. 2003. "Ierone II, Roma e L'Adriatico." In *Roma, l'Adriatico e il mondo ellenistico: Atti dell'incontro di studio. Venezia 2001. 7 marzo.*, edited by L. Braccesi, 105–27. Rome: L'Erma di Bretschneider.

Mirone, S. 1919. "Micone, figlio di Nicerato, statuario siracusano." *Rivista italiana di numismatica e scienze affini* 2: 53–72.

Molev, Y. A. 2003. "Kyrta." In *Ancient Greek Colonies in the Black Sea*, edited by D. V. Grammenos and E. K. Petropoulos, 841–94. Thessaloniki: Archaeological Institute of Northern Greece.

Monson, A. 2007. "Rule and Revenue in Egypt and Rome: Political Stability and Fiscal Institutions." *Historical Social Research (Historische Sozialforschung)* 32: 252–74.

Monson, A. 2012. *Agriculture and Taxation in Early Ptolemaic Egypt: Demotic Land Surveys and Accounts (P. Agri)*. Papyrologische Texte und Abhandlungen 46. Bonn: Habelt Verlag.

Monson, A. 2015. "Hellenistic Empires." In *Fiscal Regimes and the Political Economy of Premodern States*, edited by A. Monson and W. Scheidel, 169–207. Cambridge: Cambridge University Press.

Moore, J. D. 1996. *Architecture and Power in the Ancient Andes: The Archaeology of Public Buildings*. Cambridge: Cambridge University Press.

Morakis, A. 2015. "The *Gamoroi* and the History of Archaic Syracuse: A New Examination." *Studi di Antichità* 13: 33–50.

Moreno, A. 2003. "Athenian Bread-Baskets: The Grain-Tax Law of 374/3 B.C. Re-Interpreted." *Zeitschrift für Papyrologie und Epigraphik* 145: 97–106.

Moreno, A. 2007. *Feeding the Democracy: The Athenian Grain Supply in the Fifth and Fourth Centuries B.C.* Oxford: Oxford University Press.

Moreschini, D. 1992. "Montagna di Marzo." In *Bibliografia topografica della colonizzazione greca in Italia e nelle isole tirreniche*, edited by G. Nenci, G. Vallet, and G. Panessa, 10: 229–35. Pisa: Scuola Normale Superiore; Rome: École française de Rome.

Morley, N. 1996. *Metropolis and Hinterland: The City of Rome and the Italian Economy 200 B.C.–A.D. 200*. Cambridge: Cambridge University Press.

Mørkholm, O. 1991. *Early Hellenistic Coinage: From the Accession of Alexander to the Peace of Apamea (336–188 B.C.)*. Cambridge: Cambridge University Press.

Morris, I. 2009. "The Greater Athenian State." In *The Dynamics of Ancient Empires: State Power from Assyria to Byzantium*, edited by I. Morris and W. Scheidel, 99–177. Oxford: Oxford University Press.

Morris, I., and B. R. Weingast. 2004. "Views and Comments on Institutions, Economics and the Ancient Mediterranean World: Introduction." *Journal of Institutional and Theoretical Economics (JITE)/Zeitschrift für die Gesamte Staatswissenschaft* 160: 702–8.

Muggia, A. 1997. *L'area di rispetto nelle colonie magno-greche e siceliote: Studio di antropologia della forma urbana*. Palermo: Sellerio.

Muhs, B. P. 2005. *Tax Receipts, Taxpayers, and Taxes in Early Ptolemaic Thebes*. Chicago: Oriental Institute of the University of Chicago.

Muhs, B. P. 2016. *The Ancient Egyptian Economy, 3000–30 BCE*. Cambridge: Cambridge University Press.

Mussa, V. 2017. "La sitonia nell'Atene del IV secolo a.C." *Historika* 6: 36–60.

Mussinano, L. 1966. "Montagna di Marzo: Relazione preliminare." *Cronache di archeologia* 5: 55–66.

Nabers, N. 1967. "Macella: A Study in Roman Archaeology." PhD diss., Princeton University.

Nenci, G. 1993. "Agrigento e la Sicilia nel quadro dei rifornimenti granari del mondo greco." *Annali della Scuola Normale Superiore di Pisa* series 3, 23: 1–7.

Netz, R. 2003. "The Goal of Archimedes' *Sand-Reckoner*." *Apeiron* 36: 251–90.

Netz, R. 2009. *Ludic Proof: Greek Mathematics and the Alexandrian Aesthetic*. Cambridge: Cambridge University Press.

North, D. C. 1979. "A Framework for Analyzing the State in Economic History." *Explorations in Economic History* 16: 249–59.

North, D. C. 1990. *Institutions, Institutional Change and Economic Performance*. Cambridge: Cambridge University Press.

North, D. C. 1991. "Institutions." *The Journal of Economic Perspectives* 5, no. 1: 97–112.

North, D. C. 1992. *Transaction Costs, Institutions, and Economic Performance*. San Francisco, CA: International Center for Economic Growth.

North, D. C. 1993. "The New Institutional Economics and Development." Economic

History 9309002, University Library of Munich, Germany.

Ober, J. 2015a. *The Rise and Fall of Classical Greece*. Princeton, NJ: Princeton University Press.

Ober, J. 2015b. "Access, Fairness, and Transaction Costs: Nikophon's Law on Silver Coinage (Athens, 375/4 BCE)." In *Law and Transaction Costs in the Ancient Economy*, edited by D. P. Kehoe, D. M. Ratzan, and U. Yiftach, 51–79. Ann Arbor: University of Michigan Press.

Oliver, G. 2001. "The Politics of Coinage: Athens and Antigonos Gonatas." In *Money and Its Uses in the Ancient Greek World*, edited by A. Meadows and K. Shipton, 35–52. Oxford: Oxford University Press.

Oliver, G. J. 2007. *War, Food, and Politics in Early Hellenistic Athens*. Oxford: Oxford University Press.

Oost, S. I. 1976. "The Tyrant Kings of Syracuse." *Classical Philology: A Journal Devoted to Research in Classical Antiquity* 71: 224–36.

Orsi, P. 1909. "Barrafranca: Tesoretto di piccolo bronzi sicelioti e romani." *Notizie degli scavi di antichità* 6: 67–8.

Orsi, P. 1915. "Scavi in Siracusa." *Notizie degli scavi di antichità* 1915: 185–208.

Orsi, P. 1925. "Siracusa." *Notizie degli scavi di antichità* 1925: 176–208.

Orsi, P. 1930. "Tesoretto di bronzi greci, sicelioti e romani da Piazza Armerina." *Atti e Memorie dell'Istituto Italiano di Numismatica* 6: 105–16.

Osborne, J. F. 2014. "Monuments and Monumentality." In *Approaching Monumentality in Archaeology*, edited by J. F. Osborne, 1–19. Albany: SUNY Press.

Osborne, P. J., and R. Rhodes. 2003. *Greek Historical Inscriptions: 404–323 BC*. Oxford: Oxford University Press.

Packman, Z. M. 1968. *The Taxes in Grain in Ptolemaic Egypt: Granary Receipts from Diospolis Magna, 164–88 B.C.* Toronto: American Society of Papyrologists.

Pais, E. 1921. *Ricerche sulla storia e sul diritto pubblico di Roma*. 4 vols. Rome: Loescher.

Panagopoulou, K. 2016. "Gold in Ptolemaic Egypt: Exchange Practices in Light of *P.Cair.Zen.* I 59021." *Zeitschrift für Papyrologie und Epigraphik* 197: 179–90.

Papi, E., and F. Martorella. 2007. "Il grano della Tingitana." In *Supplying Rome and the Empire*, edited by E. Papi, 85–96. JRA Supplementary Series 69. Portsmouth, RI: Journal of Roman Archaeology.

Parise, N. F. 1979. "Il sistema della litra nella Sicilia antica tra V e IV secolo a.C." In *Le origini della monetazione di bronzo in Sicilia e in Magna Grecia: Atti del 6. convegno del Centro internazionale di studi numismatici, Napoli 17–22 aprile 1977*, 293–304. Rome: Istituto italiano di numismatica.

Parisi Presicce, C. 2004. "Ecatombi nell'area dell'altare di Ierone II a Siracusa." In *Nuove prospettive della ricerca sulla Sicilia del III sec. a.C. Archeologia, numismatica, storia. Atti dell'incontro di studio (Messina 4–5 luglio 2002)*, edited by M. Caccamo Caltabiano, L. Campagna, and A. Pinzone, 213–28. Messina: Dipartimento di Scienze dell'Antichità dell'Università degli Studi di Messina.

Patanè, R. P. A. 1997. "'Il Castello della Principessa': Un centro indigeno ellenizzato nella campagna di Gagliano Castelferrato." *Cronache di archeologia* 36: 9–33.

Paton, W. R., trans. 1923. *Polybius: The Histories*, 6 vols., vol. 3, Loeb Classical Library 138. London: Heinemann.

Pearson, L. 1987. *The Greek Historians of the West: Timaeus and His Predecessors*. Atlanta, GA: Scholars Press.

Pelagatti, P. 1970. "Akrai (Siracusa), ricerche nel territorio." *Notizie degli scavi di antichità* 24: 436–99.

Pelagatti, P. 1984–5. "Ricerche nel quartiere orientale di Naxos e nell'agorà di Camarina." *Kokalos* 30–1: 679–94.

Pelagatti, P. 2001. "Ripostigli di età ellenistica da Camarina." *Annali dell'Istituto italiano di numismatica* 48: 259–66.

Pellegrino, V. 2017. "Granai e spazi per lo stoccaggio e per il trattamento dei cereali nelle villae rusticae vesuviane." *Mélanges de l'École française de Rome – Antiquité* 129-2. https://doi.org/10.4000/mefra.4506.

Perkins, P. 2007. "*Aliud in Sicilia?* Cultural Development in Rome's First Province." In

Articulating Local Cultures: Power and Identity under the Expanding Roman Empire, edited by P. van Dommelen and N. Terrenato, 35–53. JRA Supplementary Series 63. Portsmouth, RI: Journal of Roman Archaeology.

Petculescu, L. 1987. "Roman Military Granaries in Dacia." *Saalburg-Jahrbuch. Bericht des Saalburg-Museums* 43: 66–76.

Pfuntner, L. 2019. *Urbanism and Empire in Roman Sicily*. Austin: University of Texas Press.

Phillips, K. M. 1960. "Subject and Technique in Hellenistic-Roman Mosaics: A Ganymede Mosaic from Sicily." *The Art Bulletin* 42: 243–62.

Pinzone, A. 1999. "*Maiorum sapientia e lex Hieronica*: Roma e l'organizzazione della provincia Sicilia da Gaio Flaminio a Cicerone." In *Provincia Sicilia: Ricerche di storia della Sicilia romana da Gaio Flaminio a Gregorio Magno*, edited by A. Pinzone, 1–37. Catania: Edizioni del Prisma.

Pisani, M. 2008. *Camarina: Le terrecotte figurate e la ceramica da una fornace di V e IV secolo a.C.* Rome: L'Erma di Bretschneider.

Pisani, M. 2011. "Una testa fittile d'influenza alessandrina dall'area antistante le mura urbiche meridionali di Camarina." *Bollettino d'arte* 96: 1–16.

Pittia, S. 2007. "Les données chiffrées dans le *De Frumento* de Cicéron." In *Sicilia Nutrix Plebis Romanae: Rhetoric, Law, and Taxation in Cicero's Verrines*, edited by J. R. W. Prag, 49–80. Bulletin of the Institute of Classical Studies Supplement 97. London: Institute of Classical Studies.

Polacco, L., and C. Anti. 1981. *Il teatro antico di Siracusa*. Rimini: Maggioli.

Pollock, S. 1999. *Ancient Mesopotamia*. Cambridge: Cambridge University Press.

Portale, E. C. 1995. "Problemi del mosaico ellenistico in Sicilia: Rapporti con Alessandria." In *La Sicilia tra l'Egitto e Roma: La monetazione siracusana dell'età di Ierone II. Atti del seminario di studi, Messina 2–4 dicembre 1993*, edited by M. Caccamo Caltabiano, 157–79. Messina: Accademia Peloritana dei Pericolanti.

Portale, E. C. 2004. "*Euergetikotatos . . . kai philodoxotatos eis tous Hellenas*. Riflessioni sui rapporti fra Ierone II e il mondo greco." In *Nuove prospettive della ricerca sulla Sicilia del III sec. a.C. Archeologia, numismatica, storia. Atti dell'incontro di studio (Messina 4–5 luglio 2002)*, edited by M. Caccamo Caltabiano, L. Campagna, and A. Pinzone, 229–64. Messina: Dipartimento di Scienze dell'Antichità dell'Università degli Studi di Messina.

Portale, E. C. 2013. "La cultura artistica sotto Ierone II." In *Archimede: Arte e scienza dell'invenzione*, edited by G. Di Pasquale and C. Parisi Presicce, 54–9. Florence: Giunti Editore.

Porten, B. 2011. *The Elephantine Papyri in English: Three Millennia of Cross-Cultural Continuity and Change*. Atlanta, GA: Society of Biblical Literature.

Porter, T. 1995. *Trust in Numbers*. Princeton, NJ: Princeton University Press.

Pounder, R. L. 1983. "A Hellenistic Arsenal in Athens." *Hesperia: The Journal of the American School of Classical Studies at Athens* 52: 233–56.

Prag, J. R. W., ed. 2007. *Sicilia Nutrix Plebis Romanae: Rhetoric, Law, and Taxation in Cicero's Verrines*. Bulletin of the Institute of Classical Studies Supplement 97. London: Institute of Classical Studies.

Prag, J. R. W. 2013. "Sicily and Sardinia-Corsica: The First Provinces." In *A Companion to Roman Imperialism*, edited by B. D. Hoyos, 53–65. Leiden: Brill.

Prag, J. R. W. 2015. "Cities and civic life in late Hellenistic Roman Sicily (with an appendix on Cicero, *in Verrem* 3.12–13 and the Status of Cities in Sicily after 210 BC." *Cahiers du Centre Gustave Glotz* 25 (2014): 165–208.

Prag, J. R. W., and J. C. Quinn, eds. 2013. *The Hellenistic West: Rethinking the Ancient Mediterranean*. Cambridge: Cambridge University Press.

Préaux, C. 1939. *L'économie royale des Lagides*. Brussels: Édition de la Fondation égyptologique Reine Élisabeth.

Prestianni Giallombardo, A. M. 2004. "Cinte murarie fortificate, granai e altri problemi nella Sicilia dell'età di Ierone II." In *Nuove prospettive della ricerca sulla Sicilia del III sec. a.C. Archeologia, numismatica, storia. Atti dell'incontro di studio (Messina 4–5 luglio 2002)*, edited by M. Caccamo Caltabiano, L. Campagna, and A. Pinzone, 99–123. Messina: Dipartimento di Scienze dell'Antichità dell'Università degli Studi di Messina.

Prestianni Giallombardo, A. M. 2006. "Il ruolo dei mercenari nelle dinamiche di guerra e di pace in Sicilia tra fine V e metà III sec. a.C." In *Guerra e pace in Sicilia e nel Mediterraneo antico (VIII–III sec. a.C.): Arte, prassi e teoria della pace e della guerra*, edited by M. A. Vaggioli, 107–29. Pisa: Edizioni della Normale.

Price, M. J. 1991. *The Coinage in the Name of Alexander the Great and Philip Arrhidaeus*. London: British Museum Press.

Pritchard, R. T. 1970. "Cicero and the 'Lex Hieronica.'" *Historia: Zeitschrift für Alte Geschichte* 19: 352–68.

Pritchard, R. T. 1971. "Gaius Verres and the Sicilian Farmers." *Historia: Zeitschrift für Alte Geschichte* 20: 224–38.

Privitera, F. 1988–9. "Valverde: Saggi di scavo in contrada Casalrosato." *Sicilia* 9–10: 80–3.

Privitera, S. 2014. "Long-Term Grain Storage and Political Economy in Bronze Age Crete: Contextualizing Ayia Triada's Silo Complexes." *American Journal of Archaeology* 118: 429–49.

Psoma, S. E. 2009. "*Tas sitarchias kai tous misthous* ([Arist.], *Oec.* 1351b). Bronze Currencies and Cash-Allowances in Mainland Greece, Thrace and the Kingdom of Macedonia." *Revue belge de numismatique et de sigillographie* 145: 3–38.

Psoma, S. E. 2015a. "Did the So-Called Thraco-Macedonian Standard Exist?" In *ΚΑΙΡΟΣ: Contributions to Numismatics in Honor of Basil Demetriadi*, edited by U. Wartenberg and M. Amandry, 167–90. New York: American Numismatic Society.

Psoma, S. E. 2015b. "Choosing and Changing Monetary Standards in the Greek World During the Archaic and the Classical Periods." In *The Ancient Greek Economy: Markets, Households and City-States*, edited by E. M. Harris and D. M. Lewis, 90–115. Cambridge: Cambridge University Press.

Puglisi, M. 2004. "La circolazione monetale in Sicilia nell'età di Ierone II." In *Nuove prospettive della ricerca sulla Sicilia del III sec. a.C. Archeologia, numismatica, storia. Atti dell'incontro di studio (Messina 4–5 luglio 2002)*, edited by M. Caccamo Caltabiano, L. Campagna, and A. Pinzone, 305–27. Messina: Dipartimento di Scienze dell'Antichità dell'Università degli Studi di Messina.

Puglisi, M. 2005. "Distribuzione e funzione della moneta bronzea in Sicilia dalla metà del V sec. a.C. all'età ellenistica." In *Atti del XIII congresso internazionale di numismatica, Madrid, 15–18 settembre 2003*, edited by C. Alfaro, C. Marcos, and P. Otero, 285–94. Madrid: Ministerio de Cultura.

Puglisi, M. 2009. *La Sicilia da Dionisio I a Sesto Pompeo: Circolazione e funzione della moneta*. Messina: Dipartimento di Scienze dell'Antichità dell'Università degli Studi di Messina.

Puglisi, M. 2011. "Coin Circulation Data in Sicily as a Source for Quantifying Monetary Supplies?" In *Quantifying Monetary Supplies in Greco-Roman Times*, edited by F. De Callataÿ, 181–97. Bari: Edipuglia.

Queyrel, F. 2003. *Les portraits des Attalides: Fonction et représentation*. Athènes: École française d'Athènes.

Quinn, J. C. 2017. "Translating Empire from Carthage to Rome." *Classical Philology* 112: 312–31.

Radt, T. 2011. "The Ruins on Mount Karasis in Cilicia." In *From Pella to Gandhara: Hybridisation and Identity in the Art and Architecture of the Hellenistic East*, edited by A. Kouremenos, S. Chandrasekaran, and R. Rossi, 49–64. Oxford: Oxford University Press.

Radt, T. 2016. "Fortified Palaces and Residences in Hellenistic Times." In *Focus on Fortifications: New Research on Fortifications in the Ancient Mediterranean and the Near East*, edited by R. Frederiksen, S. Müth, P. I. Schneider, and M. Schnelle, 263–76. Oxford: Oxbow.

Radt, W. 1999. *Pergamon: Geschichte und Bauten einer antiken Metropole*. Darmstadt: Primus Verlag.

Rampling, D. 2011. "The Cut Pence of Medieval Scotland." *Journal of the Numismatic Association of Australia* 21: 49–72.

Rathbone, D. 1983. "The Weight and Measurement of Egyptian Grains." *Zeitschrift für Papyrologie und Epigraphik* 53: 265–75.

Rathbone, D., and S. von Reden. 2015. "Mediterranean Grain Prices in Classical Antiquity." In *History of Market Performance: From Ancient Babylonia to the Modern World*, edited by R. J. van der Spek, B. van Leeuwen, and J. L. van Zanden, 149–235. London: Routledge.

Reger, G. 1994. *Regionalism and Change in the Economy of Independent Delos, 314–167 B.C.* Berkeley: University of California Press.

Reger, G. 2003. "The Economy." In *A Companion to the Hellenistic World*, edited by A. Erskine, 331–353. Oxford: Blackwell.

Rempe, M. 2018. "From Swing to Swamp? Considering Landscape Change in Kamarina between Greek and Roman Times." In *Römisches Sizilien: Stadt und Land zwischen Monumentalisierung und Ökonomie, Krise und Entwicklung/La Sicilia Romana: Città e Territorio tra monumentalizzazione ed economia, crisi e sviluppo*, edited by O. Belvedere and J. Bergemann, 47–60. Palermo: Palermo University Press.

Rhodes, P. J., and R. Osborne, eds. 2003. *Greek Historical Inscriptions: 404–323 BC*. New York: Oxford University Press.

Richter, H.-D. 1992. "Verwaltungswiderstand gegen ein Prostagma Ptolemaios II Philadelphos? (*P. Cairo Zen.* 59021)." *Tyche* 7: 172–86.

Rickman, G. E. 1971. *Roman Granaries and Store Buildings*. Oxford: Oxford University Press.

Ridgway, B. S. 1987. "Ancient Greek Women and Art: The Material Evidence." *American Journal of Archaeology* 91: 399–409.

Riggsby, A. 2019. *Mosaics of Knowledge: Representing Information in the Roman World*. Oxford: Oxford University Press.

Rigsby, K. J. 1996. *Asylia: Territorial Inviolability in the Hellenistic World*. Berkeley: University of California Press.

Rizzo, G. E. 1923. *Il teatro greco di Siracusa*. Milan: Bestetti e Tumminelli.

Robert, J., and L. Robert. 1953. "Bulletin épigraphique." *Revue des Études Grecques* 66: 113–212.

Roberts, W. M., trans. 1905. Livy, *History of Rome*. London: J. M. Dent & Sons.

Robinson, E. 2011. *Democracy beyond Athens: Popular Government in the Greek Classical Age*. Cambridge: Cambridge University Press.

Roesch, P. 1982. *Etudes béotiennes*. Paris: E. de Boccard.

Rostovtzeff, M. I. 1902. "Geschichte der Staatspacht in der romischen Kaiserzeit bis Diokletian." *Philologus Erganzungsband* 9: 331–512.

Rostovtzeff, M. I. 1910. *Studien zur Geschichte des römischen Kolonates*. Leipzig: B. G. Teubner.

Rostovzeff, M. I. 1941. *The Social and Economic History of the Hellenistic World*. Oxford: Clarendon Press.

Roussel, D. 1970. *Les siciliens: Entre les Romains et les Carthaginois*. Besançon: Presses universitaires de Franche-Comté, DL.

Rowan, C. 2014. "The Value of Coinage in the Second Punic War and After." In *Embodying Value: The Transformation of Objects in and from the Ancient World*, edited by C. Rowan and A. Bokern, 77–88. Oxford: BAR Publishing.

Runciman, S. 1958. *The Sicilian Vespers*. New York: Cambridge University Press.

Rutter, K. 1986. "Sicily and South Italy: The Background to Thucydides Books 6 and 7." *Greece & Rome* 33: 142–55.

Rutter, N. K. 1993. "The Myth of the 'Damareteion.'" *Chiron* 23: 171–88.

Rutter, N. K., and A. Burnett, eds. 2001. *Historia Numorum: Italy*. London: British Museum Press.

Sadori, L., and B. Narcisi. 2001. "The Postglacial Record of Environmental History from Lago di Pergusa, Sicily." *The Holocene* 11: 655–71.

Sadori, L., E. Ortu, O. Peyron, G. Zanchetta, B. Vannière, M. Desmet, and M. Magny. 2013. "The Last 7 Millennia of Vegetation and Climate Changes at Lago di Pergusa (Central Sicily, Italy)." *Climate of the Past* 9: 1969–84.

Salido Domínguez, P. J. 2008. "La investigación sobre los 'horrea' de época romana: Balance historiográfico y perspectivas de futuro."

Cuadernos de Prehistoria y Arqueología 34: 105–24.

Salido Domínguez, P. J. 2009. "Los graneros romanos militares de Hispania." In *Limes XX: XX Congreso International de Estudios sobre la Frontera Romana*, edited by A. M. Cerdán, N. Hanel, and E. Martín Hernández, 2: 679–92. Madrid: Polifemo.

Salido Domínguez, P. J. 2017. *Arquitectura rural romana: Graneros y almacenes en el Occidente del Imperio.* Archéologie et histoire romaine 35. Autun: Éd. M. Mergoil.

Salido Domínguez, P. J. 2019. "Is It Possible to Quantify the Roman Agrarian Economy?" In *Rural Granaries in Northern Gaul (6th Century BCE–4th Century CE): From Archaeology to Economic History*, edited by S. Martin, 23–32. Leiden: Brill.

Salinas, A. 1883. "Selinunte." *Notizie degli scavi di antichità*, 287–314.

Salinas, A. 1889. "Selinunte: Nuove cretule selinuntine." *Notizie degli scavi di antichità*, 224.

Samuel, A. E. 1993. "The Ptolemies and the Ideology of Kingship." In *Hellenistic History and Culture*, edited by P. Green, 168–210. Berkeley: University of California Press.

Santagati, E. 2016. *Pirro e la Sicilia.* Messina: DICAM.

Sargent, T. J., and F. R. Velde. 2002. *The Big Problem of Small Change.* Princeton, NJ: Princeton University Press.

Särström, M. 1940. *A Study in the Coinage of the Mamertines.* Lund: Gleerup.

Şaul, M. 1986. "Development of the Grain Market and Merchants in Burkina Faso." *The Journal of Modern African Studies* 24: 127–53.

Şaul, M. 1987. "The Organization of a West African Grain Market." *American Anthropologist* 89: 74–95.

Sayar, M. H. 1995. "Eine neuentdeckte seleukidische Bergfestung im ostkilikischen Taurus." *Antike Welt* 26: 279–82.

Scalisi, S. 2007. "Il ciclo del grano: Dall'aratura alla panificazione." In *Il ciclo del grano nella terra di Demetra*, edited by C. Paterno and S. Scalisi, 63–82. Enna: Società Rocca di Cerere.

Schenk von Stauffenberg, A. 1933. *König Hieron der Zweite von Syrakus.* Stuttgart: Kohlhammer.

Schirmer, C., D. A. Walthall, A. Tharler, E. Wueste, B. Crowther, R. Souza, J. Benton, and J. Millar. 2021. "Preliminary Report on the 2018 Field Season of the American Excavations at Morgantina: Contrada Agnese Project (CAP)." *Fasti Online Documents & Research* 500: 1–24. www.fastionline.org/docs/FOLDER-it-2021-500.pdf.

Schmitt, H. H. 1974. "Polybios und das Gleichgewicht der Mächte." *Entretiens sur antiquité classique (Fondation Hardt)* 20: 67–93.

Scholten, J. 2000. *The Politics of Plunder: Aitolians and Their Koinon in the Early Hellenistic Era, 279–217 B.C.* Berkeley: University of California Press.

Schubert, T. 2016. *"Pars Fructuaria": Studie zu Nebengebäuden mit Speicherfunktion auf römerzeitlichen Villae im Tagebaugebiet Hambacher Forst. Mit Vergleichen aus den germanischen und britannischen Provinzen.* Hamburg: Tredition.

Schulten, A. 1927. *Die Lager des Scipio.* Munich: Bruckmann.

Scott, J. C. 1998. *Seeing like a State: How Certain Schemes to Improve the Human Condition Have Failed.* New Haven, CT: Yale University Press.

Scramuzza, V. M. 1937. "Roman Sicily." In *An Economic Survey of the Roman Empire*, edited by T. Frank, 3: 225–377. Baltimore: Johns Hopkins University Press.

Seibert, J. 1967. *Historische Beiträge zu den dynastischen Verbindungen in hellenistischer Zeit.* Historia Einzelschriften 10. Wiesbaden: F. Steiner Verlag.

Serrati, J. 2000. "Garrisons and Grain: Sicily between the Punic Wars." In *Sicily from Aeneas to Augustus: New Approaches in Archaeology and History*, edited by C. J. Smith and J. Serrati, 115–33. Edinburgh: Edinburgh University Press.

Serrati, J. 2007. "Warfare and the State." In *The Cambridge History of Greek and Roman Warfare*, edited by P. Sabin, H. van Wees, and L. M. Whitby, 461–97. Cambridge: Cambridge University Press.

Serrati, J. 2008. "A Syracusan Private Altar and the Development of Ruler-Cult in Hellenistic Sicily." *Historia* 57, no. 1: 80–91.

Seyrig, H. 1951. "Antiquités syriennes." *Syria: Archéologie, Art et histoire* 28, nos. 3–4: 191–228.

Seyrig, H. 1963. "Monnaies hellénistiques." *Revue numismatique* 6, no. 5: 7–64.

Sharp, H. K. 2015. "Nuove ricerche sul *macellum* di Morgantina. Funzioni pratiche e metaforiche." In *Morgantina duemilaequindici: La ricerca archeologica a sessant'anni dall'avvio degli scavi*, edited by L. Maniscalco, 172–8. Palermo: Regione siciliana.

Shelton, J. 1977. "Artabs and Choinices." *Zeitschrift für Papyrologie und Epigraphik* 24: 55–67.

Shipley, G. 2000. *The Greek World after Alexander, 323–30 BC*. London: Routledge.

Siedentopf, H. B. 1968. *Das hellenistische Reiterdenkmal*. Waldsassen: Stiftland-Verlag.

Sigaut, F. 1988. "A Method for Identifying Grain Storage Techniques and Its Application for European Agricultural History." *Tools and Tillage* 6, no. 1: 3–32.

Sjöqvist, E. 1958a. "Excavations at Serra Orlando (Morgantina) Preliminary Report II." *American Journal of Archaeology* 62, no. 2: 155–64.

Sjöqvist, E. 1958b. "Timoleonte e Morgantina." *Kokalos* 4: 3–14.

Sjöqvist, E. 1959. "Morgantina: Hellenistic Inkstands." *American Journal of Archaeology* 63, no. 3: 275–77.

Sjöqvist, E. 1960a. "Excavations at Morgantina (Serra Orlando) 1959: Preliminary Report IV." *American Journal of Archaeology* 64, no. 2: 125–35.

Sjöqvist, E. 1960b. "Numismatic Notes from Morgantina I: The Sikeliotan Coinage." *American Numismatic Society Museum Notes* 9: 53–63.

Sjöqvist, E. 1962. "Excavations at Morgantina (Serra Orlando) 1961 Preliminary Report VI." *American Journal of Archaeology* 66, no. 2: 135–43.

Sladen, D. B. W. 1907. *Sicily, the New Winter Resort: An Encyclopaedia of Sicily*. New York: E. P. Dutton.

Smarczyk, B. 2015. "The Hellenic Leagues of Late Classical and Hellenistic Times and Their Place in the History of Greek Federalism." In *Federalism in Greek Antiquity*, edited by H. Beck and P. Funke, 452–70. Cambridge: Cambridge University Press.

Smith, R. R. R. 1988. *Hellenistic Royal Portraits*. Oxford: Clarendon Press.

Soraci, C. 2011. *Sicilia frumentaria: Il grano siciliano e l'annona di Roma, V a.C.–V d.C.* Saggi di storia antica 32. Rome: L'Erma di Bretschneider.

Sorg, T. 2015. "Agyrrhios beyond Attica: Tax-Farming and Imperial Recovery in the Second Athenian League." *Historia: Zeitschrift für Alte Geschichte* 64: 49–76.

Souza, R., D. A. Walthall, J. Benton, E. Wueste, A. Tharler, B. Crowther, C. Schirmer, and J. Huemoeller. 2019. "Preliminary Report on the 2016 Field Season of the American Excavations at Morgantina: Contrada Agnese Project (CAP)." *Fasti On Line Documents & Research* 450: 1–25. fastionline.org/docs/FOLDER-it-2019-450.pdf.

Spadea, R. 1987. "Produzioni ellenistiche sullo Stretto." In *Lo stretto crocevia di culture: Atti del XXVI convegno di studi sulla Magna Grecia, Taranto – Reggio Calabria 9–14 ottobre 1986*, edited by G. Pugliese Carratelli, 337–60. Taranto: Istituto per la storia e l'archeologia della Magna Grecia.

Spanò Giammellaro, A., F. Spatafora, and P. van Dommelen. 2008. "Sicily and Malta: Between Sea and Countryside." In *Rural Landscapes of the Punic World*, edited by P. van Dommelen and C. Gómez Bellard, 129–58. Monographs in Mediterranean Archaeology 11. London: Equinox.

Spigo, U. 2003. "Un ventennio di ricerche a Francavilla di Sicilia." In *Archeologia del Mediterraneo: Studi in onore di Ernesto De Miro*, edited by G. Fiorentini, E. De Miro, A. Calderone, and M. Caccamo Caltabiano, 643–63. *Biblioteca archeologica* 35. Rome: L'Erma di Bretschneider.

Spigo, U., and M. C. Rizzo. 1993–4. "Ricerche a Francavilla di Sicilia 1989–1991." *Kokalos* 39–40: 1039–57.

Squillace, G. 2013. "Alexander the Great, Ptolemy I and the Offering of Arms to Athena Lindia." In *After Alexander: The Time of the Diadochi (323–81 BC)*, edited by V. A. Troncoso and E. M. Anson, 215–24. Oxford: Oxbow.

Stahl, A. M. 2000. *Zecca: The Mint of Venice in the Middle Ages*. Baltimore: Johns Hopkins University Press in association with the American Numismatic Society, New York.

Stannard, C. 2011. "Weight Adjustment *al marco* in Antiquity, and the Athenian Decadrachm." In *Proceedings of the XIVth International Numismatic Congress, Glasgow 2009*, edited by N. Holmes, 427–34. London: Spink & Son.

Stannard, C. 2018. "The Crisis of Small Change in Central Italy of the Second and First Centuries BC, and the Function of Overstriking." *Revue belge de Numismatique et de Sigillographie* 164: 97–170.

Steel, C. 2007. "The Rhetoric of the *De Frumento*." In *Sicilia Nutrix Plebis Romanae: Rhetoric, Law, and Taxation in Cicero's Verrines*, edited by J. R. W. Prag, 37–48. Bulletin of the Institute of Classical Studies Supplement 97. London: Institute of Classical Studies.

Stewart, A. F. 1993. *Faces of Power: Alexander's Image and Hellenistic Politics*. Hellenistic Culture and Society 11. Berkeley: University of California Press.

Stillwell, R. 1961. "Excavations at Serra Orlando (Morgantina) 1960 Preliminary Report V." *American Journal of Archaeology* 65, no. 3: 277–81.

Stillwell, R. 1963. "Excavations at Morgantina (Serra Orlando) 1962: Preliminary Report VII." *American Journal of Archaeology* 67, no. 2: 163–71.

Stillwell, R. 1964–5. "The Theater of Morgantina." *Kokalos* 10–11: 579–88.

Stillwell, R., and E. Sjöqvist. 1957. "Excavations at Serra Orlando: Preliminary Report." *American Journal of Archaeology* 61, no. 2: 151–9.

Stone, S. C. 1983. "Sextus Pompey, Octavian and Sicily." *American Journal of Archaeology* 87, no. 1: 11–22.

Stone, S. C. 2014. *Morgantina Studies, vol. 6: The Hellenistic and Roman Fine Pottery*. Princeton, NJ: Princeton University Press.

Storaci, E., and A. M. Manenti. 2013. "Un nuovo ripostiglio di Filistide a Siracusa." *Annali dell'Istituto italiano di numismatica* 59: 217–23.

Strootman, R. 2005. "Kings against Celts: Deliverance from Barbarians as a Theme in Hellenistic Royal Propaganda." In *The Manipulative Mode: Political Propaganda in Antiquity: A Collection of Case Studies*, edited by K. E. Enenkel and I. L. Pfeijffer, 101–41. Mnemosyne Supplementum 0261. Leiden: Brill.

Strootman, R. 2007. "The Hellenistic Royal Court, Court Culture, Ceremonial and Ideology in Greece, Egypt and the Near East, 336–30 BCE." PhD diss., Utrecht University.

Strootman, R. 2011. "Kings and Cities in the Hellenistic Age." In *Political Culture in the Greek City after the Classical Age*, edited by R. Alston, O. van Nijf, and C. Williamson, 141–53. Groningen-Royal Holloway Studies on the Greek City after the Classical Age 2. Leuven: Peeters.

Stroud, R. S. 1974. "An Athenian Law on Silver Coinage." *Hesperia: The Journal of the American School of Classical Studies at Athens* 43, no. 2: 157–88.

Stroud, R. S. 1998. *The Athenian Grain-Tax Law of 374/3 B.C.* Hesperia Supplements 29. Princeton, NJ: American School of Classical Studies at Athens.

Svoronos, J. N. 1904. *Ta Nomismata tou Kratous tōn Ptolemaiōn*. Athens: P. D. Sakellarios.

Tan, J. 2017. *Power and Public Finance at Rome, 264–49 BCE*. New York: Oxford University Press.

Tarn, W. W. 1969. Reprint. *Antigonos Gonatas*. Chicago: Argonaut. Original edition, 1913.

Temin, P. 2013. *The Roman Market Economy*. Princeton, NJ: Princeton University Press.

Terpstra, T. 2013. *Trading Communities in the Roman World: A Micro-Economic and Institutional Perspective*. Columbia Studies in the Classical Tradition 37. Leiden: Brill.

Terpstra, T. 2019. *Trade in the Ancient Mediterranean: Private Order and Public Institutions*. Princeton, NJ: Princeton University Press.

Tharler, A., D. A. Walthall, E. Wueste, C. Schirmer, B. Crowther, R. Souza, J. Benton, and K. P. D. Huemoeller. 2020. "Preliminary Report on the 2017 Field Season of the American Excavations at Morgantina: Contrada Agnese Project (CAP)." *Fasti Online Documents & Research* 487: 1–23. www.fastionline.org/docs/FOLDER-it-2020-487.pdf.

Thompson, D. J. 1983. "Nile Grain Transport under the Ptolemies." In *Trade in the Ancient Economy*, edited by P. Garnsey, K. Hopkins, C. J. Whittaker, 64–75. Berkeley: University of California Press.

Thompson, S. M. 1999. "A Central Sicilian Landscape: Settlement and Society in the Territory of Ancient Morgantina (5000 BC–AD 50)." PhD diss., University of Virginia.

Thompson, S. M. 2002. "The Metapontino and Morgantina Archaeological Survey Projects (Basilicata and Sicily)." In *New Developments in Italian Landscape Archaeology: Theory and Methodology of Field Survey, Land Evaluation, and Landscape Perception, Pottery Production and Distribution. Proceedings of a Three-Day Conference Held at the University of Groningen, April 13–15, 2000*, edited by P. Attema, G.-J. Burgers, E. van Joolen, M. van Leusen, and B. Mater, 76–82. BAR International Series 1091. Oxford: BAR Publishing.

Thonemann, P. 2013. "The Attalid State, 188–133 BC." In *Attalid Asia Minor: Money, International Relations, and the State*, edited by P. Thonemann, 1–48. Oxford: Oxford University Press.

Thonemann, P. 2015. *The Hellenistic World: Using Coins as Sources*. Cambridge: Cambridge University Press.

Thorne, J. A. 2001. "Warfare and Agriculture: The Economic Impact of Devastation in Classical Greece." *Greek, Roman, and Byzantine Studies* 42, no. 3: 225–53.

Thorpe, B. 1840. *Ancient Laws and Institutes of England: Comprising Laws Enacted under the Anglo-Saxon Kings from Aethelbirht to Cnut: With an English Translation of the Saxon; The Laws Called Edward the Confessor's, the Laws of William the Conqueror and Those Ascribed to Henry the First; Also, Monumenta ecclesiastica Anglicana from the Seventh to the Tenth Century, and the Ancient Latin Version of the Anglo-Saxon Laws*. 2 vols. London: Eyre & Spottiswoode.

Tigano, G., and R. Burgio. 2019. "Messana (Mylai) e Alesa: L'uso del mattone nell'edilizia pubblica e private." In *Alle origini del laterizio romano: Nascita e diffusione del mattone cotto nel Mediterraneo tra IV e I secolo a.C.*, edited by J. Bonetto, É. Bukowiecki, and R. Volpe, 233–52. Rome: Edizioni Quasar.

Toscano Raffa, A., M. Venuti, M. Papale, and M. Miano. 2015. "Nuovi dati dall'abitato ellenistico-romano di Finziade sul Monte S. Angelo di Licata (AG): Gli scavi dei Settori H (2012–2013), F (2014) e J (2014)." *Quaderni di archeologia* 5: 63–82.

Treister, M. J., and Y. G. Vinogradov. 1993. "Archaeology on the Northern Coast of the Black Sea." *American Journal of Archaeology* 97, no. 3: 521–63.

Trendall, A. D. 1960. "Archaeology in South Italy and Sicily, 1958–1960." *Archaeological Reports* 7: 36–53.

Tréziny, H. 2018. *Mégara Hyblaea*. Vol. 7: *La Ville Classique, Hellenistic et Romaine. Chronique des activités archéologiques de l'École française de Rome*. Rome: École Française de Rome.

Trigger, B. G. 1990. "Monumental Architecture: A Thermodynamic Explanation of Symbolic Behavior." *World Archaeology* 22, no. 2: 119–32.

Trigger, B. G. 2003. *Understanding Early Civilizations: A Comparative Study*. Cambridge: Cambridge University Press.

Trümper, M. 2017. "Morgantina under Roman rule: Recent Research in the Contrada Agnese Quarter." In *Römisches Sizilien: Stadt und Land zwischen Monumentalisierung und Ökonomie, Krise und Entwicklung, Seminar für die Alumni des Double Degree Göttingen – Palermo mit finnanzieller Förderung des Deutschen Akademischen Austauschdienstes, Archäologisches Institut, Universität Göttingen, 25.–27. November 2017*, edited by O. Belvedere and J. Bergemann, 369–386. Palermo: Palermo University Press.

Trümper, M. 2018. "Gymnasia in Eastern Sicily of the Hellenistic and Roman Period." In

Development of Gymnasia and Graeco-Roman Cityscapes, edited by U. Mania and M. Trümper, 43–73. Berlin Studies of the Ancient World 58. Berlin: Edition Topoi.

Trümper, M. 2019. "Crisis and Decline in Morgantina under Roman Rule: A Reassessment." In *Collapse or Survival? Micro-Dynamics of Crisis, Change and Socio-Political Endurance in the Late Prehistoric and Early Roman Central Mediterranean*, edited by E. Perego, R. Scopacasa, and S. R. Amicone, 97–138. Oxford: Oxbow Books.

Tsakirgis, B. 1984. "The Domestic Architecture of Morgantina in the Hellenistic and Roman Periods." PhD diss., Princeton University.

Tsakirgis, B. 1989. "The Decorated Pavements of Morgantina I: The Mosaics." *American Journal of Archaeology* 93, no. 3: 395–416.

Tsakirgis, B. 1995. "Morgantina: A Greek Town in Central Sicily." In *Ancient Sicily*, edited by T. Fischer-Hansen, 123–47. Acta Hyperborea 6. Copenhagen: Museum Tusculanum Press.

Turfa, J. M., and A. G. Steinmayer Jr. 1999. "The *Syracusia* as a Giant Cargo Vessel." *The International Journal of Nautical Archaeology* 28, no. 2: 105–25.

Turner, E. G. 1984. "Ptolemaic Egypt." In *Cambridge Ancient History*. Vol. 7, pt. 1: *The Hellenistic World*, edited by F. W. Walbank, A. E. Astin, M. W. Frederiksen, and R. M. Ogilvie, 118–74. 2nd ed. Cambridge: Cambridge University Press.

Twohig, D., and W. W. Abbot, eds. 1993. *The Papers of George Washington. Presidential Series.* Vol. 4: *8 September 1789–15 January 1790.* Charlottesville: University Press of Virginia.

Uggeri, G. 2015. *Camarina: Storia e topografia di una colonia greca di Sicilia e del suo territorio.* Rivista di Topografia Antica 8. Galatina: Mario Congedo Editore.

Uguzzoni, A., and F. Ghinatti. 1968. *Le tavole greche di Heraclea.* Pubblicazioni dell'Istituto di Storia Antica 7. Rome: L'Erma di Bretschneider.

Vallet, G., and F. Villard. 1966. *Mégara Hyblaea.* Vol. 4: *Le temple du IVe siècle.* Mélanges de l'École française de Rome 1. Paris: E. de Boccard.

Vallone, A. 1955. "I Mamertini in Sicilia." *Kokalos* 1: 22–61.

van Bremen, R. 1996. *The Limits of Participation: Women and Civic Life in the Greek East in the Hellenistic and Roman Periods.* Dutch Monographs on Ancient History and Archaeology 15. Amsterdam: J. C. Gieben.

van der Spek, R. J., J. L. van Zanden, and B. van Leeuwen. 2015. *History of Market Performance: From Ancient Babylonia to the Modern World.* Routledge Explorations in Economic History 68. London: Routledge.

Vanderpool, E., J. R. McCredie, and A. Steinberg. 1962. "Koroni: A Ptolemaic Camp on the East Coast of Attica." *Hesperia: The Journal of the American School of Classical Studies at Athens* 31, no. 1: 26–61.

Vartsos, J. A. 1970. "Osservazioni sulla campagna di Pirro in Sicilia." *Kokalos* 16: 89–97.

Vassallo, S. 1988–9. "Montagna dei Cavalli." *Archivio Storico Siciliano* 14–15: 313–23.

Vassallo, S. 1997. "Montagna dei Cavalli: Hippana." In *Archeologia e territorio*, edited by C. A. Di Stefano, 275–306. Palermo: G. B. Palumbo.

Vats, M. S. 1974. *Excavations at Harappā: Being an Account of Archaeological Excavations at Harappā Carried Out between the Years 1920–21 and 1933–34.* 2 vols. Varanasi: Bhartiya Publishing House.

Veit, C. 2008. "Zur Kulturpolitik Hierons II in Syrakus." In *Stadtbilder im Hellenismus*, edited by A. Matthaei and M. Zimmermann, 365–79. Die hellenistische Polis als Lebensform 1. Berlin: Verlag Antike.

Veit, C. 2013. "Hellenistic Kingship in Sicily: Patronage and Politics under Agathokles and Hieron II." In *Sicily: Art and Invention between Greece and Rome*, edited by C. L. Lyons, M. Bennett, and C. Marconi, 27–37. Los Angeles: J. Paul Getty Museum.

Vera, H. 2008. "Economic Rationalization, Money and Measures: A Weberian Perspective." In *Max Weber Matters: Interweaving Past and Present*, edited by D. Chalcraft, F. Howell, M. Lopez Menendez, and H. Vera, 135–47. London: Routledge.

Vera, H. 2011. "The Social Life of Measures: Metrication in the United States and Mexico, 1789–2004." PhD diss., New School.

Verity, A., and R. L. Hunter. 2002. *Theocritus: Idylls*. Oxford: Oxford University Press.

Vester, M. 2004. "The Political Autonomy of a Tax Farm: The Nice-Piedmont Gabelle of the Dukes of Savoy, 1535–1580." *The Journal of Modern History* 76, no. 4: 745–92.

Virlouvet, C. 2015. "Les métiers du port: Les saccarii, dockers du monde romain antique – Elena Martelli, *Sulle spalle dei saccarii. Le rappresentazioni di facchini e il trasporto di derrate nel porto di ostia in epoca imperiale* (BAR International Series 2467; Archaeopress, Oxford 2013). Pp. 140, tav/pls. XIII. ISBN 978 1 4073 1078 7." *Journal of Roman Archaeology* 28: 673–83.

von Reden, S. 2001. "The Politics of Monetization in Third-Century BC Egypt." In *Money and Its Uses in the Ancient Greek World*, edited by A. Meadows and K. Shipton, 65–76. Oxford: Oxford University Press.

von Reden, S. 2002. "Money in the Ancient Economy: A Survey of Recent Research." *Klio* 84, no. 1: 141–74.

von Reden, S. 2007. *Money in Ptolemaic Egypt: From the Macedonian Conquest to the End of the Third Century BC*. Cambridge: Cambridge University Press.

von Sydow, W. 1984. "Die hellenistischen Gebälke in Sizilien." *Mitteilungen des Deutschen Archäologischen Instituts (Römische Abteilung)* 91: 239–358.

von Szalay, A., and E. Boehringer. 1937. *Die hellenistischen Arsenale: Garten der Königin*. Altertümer von Pergamon 10. Berlin: De Gruyter.

Voza, G. 1968–9. "L'attività della Soprintendenza alle Antichità della Sicilia Orientale fra il 1965 e il 1968." *Kokalos* 14–15: 360–2.

Voza, G. 1973. "Eloro." In *Archeologia nella Sicilia Sud-Orientale*, edited by P. Pelagatti and G. Voza, 117–26. Naples: Centre Jean Bérard.

Voza, G. 1976–7. "L'attività della Soprintendenza alle Antichità della Sicilia Orientale. Parte II." *Kokalos* 22–3: 551–85.

Voza, G. 1984–5. "L'Attività nel territorio della Soprintendenza alle antichità di Siracusa nel quadriennio 1980–1984." *Kokalos* 30–1: 657–78.

Voza, G. 1999. *Nel segno dell'antico: Archeologia nel territorio di Siracusa*. Palermo: Lombardi.

Voza, G. 2007. "Teatro greco di Siracusa: Stato delle conoscenze." In *Teatri antichi nell'area del Mediterraneo: Conservazione programmata e fruizione sostenibile. Contributi analitici alla carta del rischio; atti del II convegno internazionale di studi La materia e i segni della storia, Siracusa 13–17 ottobre 2004*, edited by D. La Manna and E. Lentini, 72–80. Quaderni di Palazzo Montalbo 9. Palermo: Regione siciliana.

Walbank, F. W. 1957. *A Historical Commentary on Polybius*. Vol. 1: *Commentary on Books I–VI*. Oxford: Clarendon Press.

Walbank, F. W. 1981. *The Hellenistic World*. Sussex: Harvester Press; Atlantic Highlands, NJ: Humanities Press.

Walbank, F. W. 1984. "Monarchy and Monarchical Ideas." In *The Hellenistic World*, edited by F. W. Walbank, A. E. Astin, M. W. Ferderiksen, and R. M. Ogelvie, 62–100. *CAH* 7, pt. 1. 2nd ed. Cambridge: Cambridge University Press.

Walthall, D. A. 2011. "Magistrate Stamps on Grain Measures in Early Hellenistic Sicily." *Zeitschrift für Papyrologie und Epigraphik* 179: 159–69.

Walthall, D. A. 2013a. "Becoming Kings: Spartan *Basileia* in the Hellenistic Period." In *The Splendors and Miseries of Ruling Alone: Encounters with Monarchy from Archaic Greece to the Hellenistic Mediterranean*, edited by N. Luraghi, 129–63. Studies in Ancient Monarchies 1. Stuttgart: Franz Steiner.

Walthall, D. A. 2013b. "Figure 11. Map of the Syracusan kingdom under Hieron II." In *Sicily: Art and Invention between Greece and Rome*, edited by C. L. Lyons, M. Bennett, and C. Marconi, 25. Los Angeles: J. Paul Getty Museum.

Walthall, D. A. 2013c. "A Measured Harvest: Grain, Tithes, and Territories in Hellenistic and Roman Sicily (276–31 BCE)." PhD diss., Princeton University.

Walthall, D. A. 2015. "Recenti scavi nei granai monumentali a Morgantina." In *Morgantina duemilaequindici: La ricerca archeologica a sessant'anni dall'avvio degli scavi*, edited by

L. Maniscalco, 82–91. Palermo: Regione siciliana.

Walthall, D. A. 2017. "Numismatic Material from Late Third-Century Contexts at Morgantina, Sicily." *American Journal of Numismatics* 29: 101–24.

Walthall, D. A. 2020a. "Three Unpublished Early Hellenistic Hoards from the Contrada Agnese Quarter at Morgantina (Sicily)." *Numismatica e antichità classiche* 49: 119–40.

Walthall, D. A. 2020b. "Agriculture in Magna Graecia (Iron Age to Hellenistic)." In *A Companion to Ancient Agriculture*, edited by D. Hollander and T. Howe, 317–41. Hoboken, NJ: Wiley-Blackwell.

Walthall, D. A. 2021. "The Hellenistic House in Motion: Reflections on the CAP Excavations at Morgantina (2014–2019)." In *Trinacria, "an Island Outside of Time": International Archaeology in Sicily*, edited by C. Prescott et al., 55–68. Oxford: Oxbow.

Walthall, D. A. 2023. "Weights and Standards at Hellenistic and Roman Morgantina." In *Un marché commun dans l'Antiquité? Unités de mesure et instruments commerciaux dans le bassin égéen (et au-delà) à la basse époque hellénistique, Université de Fribourg, 25–26 janvier 2018*, edited by C. Doyen and N. Badoud. Basel: Schwabe Verlag.

Walthall, D. A., J. Benton, and R. Souza. 2016. "Preliminary Report on the 2014 Field Season of the American Excavations at Morgantina: Contrada Agnese Project (CAP)." *Fasti On Line Documents & Research* 364: 1–23. www.fastionline.org/docs/FOLDER-it-2016-364.pdf.

Walthall, D. A., R. Souza, J. Benton, and J. F. Huemoeller. 2014. "Preliminary Report on the 2013 Field Season of the American Excavations at Morgantina: Contrada Agnese Project (CAP)." *Fasti On Line Documents & Research* 322: 1–15. www.fastionline.org/docs/FOLDER-it-2014-322.pdf.

Walthall, D. A., R. Souza, J. Benton, E. Wueste, and A. Tharler. 2018. "Preliminary Report on the 2015 Field Season of the American Excavations at Morgantina: Contrada Agnese Project (CAP)." *Fasti On Line Documents &*

Research 408: 1–23. www.fastionline.org/docs/FOLDER-it-2018-408.pdf.

Walton, F. R., trans. 1957. *Diodorus Siculus: Library of History*. Vol. 11: *Books 21–32*. Loeb Classical Library 409. Cambridge, MA: Harvard University Press.

Warden, L. A. 2015. "Centralized Taxation during the Old Kingdom." In *Towards a New History for the Egyptian Old Kingdom: Perspectives on the Pyramid Age*, edited by P. D. Manuelian and T. Schneider, 470–95. Harvard Egyptological Studies 1. Leiden: Brill.

Weber, M. 1947. *The Theory of Social and Economic Organization*. Edited by T. Parsons. Translated by A. M. Henderson and T. Parsons. New York: Oxford University Press.

Weber, M. 1978. *Economy and Society: An Outline of Interpretive Sociology*. 2 vols. Edited by G. Roth and C. Wittich. Translated by E. Fischoff, H. Gerth, C.W. Mills, F. Kolegar, A. M. Henderson, T. Parsons, E. Shills, and M. Rheinstein. Berkeley: University of California Press.

Welles, C. B. 1934. *Royal Correspondence in the Hellenistic Period: A Study in Greek Epigraphy*. New Haven, CT: Yale University Press.

Welles, C. B. 1938. "New Texts from the Chancery of Philip V of Macedonia and the Problem of the 'Diagramma.'" *American Journal of Archaeology* 42, no. 2: 245–60.

Wescoat, B. D., ed. 1989. *Syracuse, the Fairest Greek City: Ancient Art from the Museo Archaeologico Regionale "Paolo Orsi."* Atlanta, GA: Emory University Museum of Art and Archaeology.

Westall, R. 2011. "Rome and Ptolemaic Egypt: Initial Contacts." In *Aegyptiaca et Coptica: Studi in onore di Sergio Pernigotti*, edited by P. Buzi, D. Picchi, and M. Zecchi, 349–60. BAR International Series 2264. Oxford: BAR Publishing.

Westermark, U. 1961. *Das Bildnis des Philetairos von Pergamon Corpus der Münzprägung*. Acta Universitatis Stockholmiensis. Stockholm Studies in Classical Archaeology, 1. Stockholm: Almqvist & Wiksell.

Westlake, H. D. 1960. "Athenian Aims in Sicily, 427–424 B.C.: A Study in Thucydidean Motivation." *Historia* 9, no. 4: 385–402.

White, D. 1964. "Demeter's Sicilian Cult as a Political Instrument." *Greek, Roman, and Byzantine Studies* 5, no. 4: 261–79.

Whitehead, D. 2016. *Philo Mechanicus: On Sieges. Translated with Introduction and Commentary.* Historia – Einzelschriften 243. Stuttgart: Franz Steiner Verlag.

Wick, T. E. 1976. "Athens' Alliances with Rhegion and Leontinoi." *Historia* 25, no. 3: 288–304.

Więcek, T. 2018. "The Coin of Akrai: La primavera." In *On the Borders of Syracuse: Multidisciplinary Studies on the Ancient Town of Akrai/Acrae, Sicily,* edited by R. Chowaniec, 271–330. Warsaw: Institute of Archaeology, University of Warsaw.

Wiegand, T. 2015. Reprint. *Bericht über die Ausgrabungen in Pergamon 1927.* Abhandlungen der Preussischen Akademie der Wissenschaften 1928 no. 3. Berlin: De Gruyter. Original edition, 1928.

Wilhelm, A. 1900. "Inschrift aus Syrakus." *Jahreshefte des Österreichischen Archäologischen Institutes in Wien* 3: 162–71.

Wilkinson, T. A. H. 2000. *Royal Annals of Ancient Egypt: The Palermo Stone and Its Associated Fragments.* London: Kegan Paul International.

Will, E. 1966. *Histoire politique du monde hellenistique (323–30 av. J.-C.).* Vol. 1: *De la mort d'Alexandre aux avenements d'Antiochos III et de Phillippe V.* Nancy: Faculté des Lettres et des Sciences humaines de l'Université de Nancy.

Wilson, R. J. A. 1985. "Changes in the Pattern of Urban Settlement in Roman, Byzantine and Arab Sicily." In *Papers in Italian Archaeology IV: The Cambridge Conference. Pt. 1: The Human Landscape* edited by C. Malone and S. Stoddart, 313–44. BAR International Series 243. Oxford: BAR Publishing.

Wilson, R. J. A. 1990. *Sicily under the Roman Empire: The Archaeology of a Roman Province, 36 BC–AD 535.* Warminster: Aris and Phillips.

Wilson, R. J. A. 1995–6. "Archaeology in Sicily 1988–95." *Archaeological Reports* 42: 59–123.

Wilson, R. J. A. 2000. "Aqueducts and Water Supply in Greek and Roman Sicily: The Present *Status Quaestionis.*" In *Cura Aquarum in Sicilia: Proceedings of the Tenth International Congress on the History of Water Management and Hydraulic Engineering in the Mediterranean Region. Syracuse, May 16–22, 1998,* edited by G. C. M. Jansen, 5–36. *BABesch* Supplement 6. Leuven: Peeters.

Wilson, R. J. A. 2012. "*Agorai* and *fora* in Hellenistic and Roman Sicily: An Overview of the Current *Status Quaestionis.*" In *Agora greca e agorai di Sicilia,* edited by C. Ampolo, 245–67. Seminari e Convegni 28. Pisa: Edizioni della Normale.

Wilson, R. J. A. 2013. "Hellenistic Sicily, c. 270–100 BC." In *The Hellenistic West: Rethinking the Ancient Mediterranean,* edited by J. R. W. Prag and J. C. Quinn, 79–119. Cambridge: Cambridge University Press.

Wilson, R. J. A. 2015. "UBC Excavations of the Roman Villa at Gerace (EN), Sicily: Results of the 2013 Season." *Mouseion: Journal of the Classical Association of Canada* 12, no. 2: 175–230.

Wilson, R. J. A., and J. Ramsay. 2017. "UBC Excavations of the Roman Villa at Gerace, Sicily: Results of the 2015 Season." *Mouseion: Journal of the Classical Association of Canada* 14: 253–316.

Winter, F. E. 2006. *Studies in Hellenistic Architecture.* Phoenix 42. Toronto: University of Toronto Press.

Wolf, D. 2013. "A Metrological Survey of Ptolemaic Bronze Coinage." *American Journal of Numismatics* 25: 49–118.

Wolf, D. 2017. "The Bronze Coinage Reform of Ptolemy II." In *XV International Numismatic Congress Taormina 2015 Proceedings,* Vol. 1, edited by M. Caccamo Caltabiano, B. Carroccio, D. Castrizio, M. Puglisi, and G. Salamone, 540–5. Rome: Arbor Sapientiae.

Wolf, D. 2022. "The Sicilian Ptolemaic Bronzes and the Coinage of Hieron II of Syracuse." *Revue belge de Numismatique et de Sigillographie* 168: 113–131.

Wolf, D., and C. Lorber. 2011. "The 'Galatian Shield without Σ' Series of Ptolemaic Bronze Coins." *The Numismatic Chronicle* 171: 7–53.

Wolf, M. 2016. *Hellenistische Heiligtümer in Sizilien: Studien zur Sakralarchitektur innerhalb und außerhalb des Reiches König Hierons II.* Sonderschriften 20. Wiesbaden: Reichert Verlag.

Wörrle, M., and P. Zanker. 1995. *Stadtbild und Bürgerbild im Hellenismus: Kolloquium, München, 24. bis 26. Juni 1993.* München: Beck.

Wynne-Jones, S., and J. Fleisher. 2012. "Coins in Context: Local Economy, Value and Practice on the East African Swahili Coast." *Cambridge Archaeological Journal* 22: 19–36.

Yardley, J. C., trans. 1994. *Justin, Epitome of the Philippic History of Pompeius Trogus.* With Introduction and Explanatory Notes by R. Develin. American Philological Association. Classical Resources Series, 3. Atlanta, GA: Scholars Press.

Yonge, C. D., ed. and trans. 1903. *The Orations of Marcus Tullius Cicero.* London: George Bell and Sons.

Youtie, H. C. 1950. "Greek Ostraca from Egypt." *Transactions and Proceedings of the American Philological Association* 81: 99–116.

Zahrnt, M. 2000. "Die Gesellschaft des hellenistischen Syrakus nach dem ende der Monarchie." In *Politics, Administration and Society in the Hellenistic and Roman World: Proceedings of the International Colloquium, Bertinoro 19–24 July 1997,* edited by L. Mooren, 489–514. Studia Hellenistica 36. Leuven: Peeters.

Zambon, E. 2000. "Finzia, i Mamertini e la seconda distruzione di Gela." In *Hesperìa: Studi sulla grecità di occidente,* vol. 12, edited by L. Braccesi, 303–8. Rome: L'Erma di Bretschneider.

Zambon, E. 2006. "From Agathocles to Hieron II: The Birth and Development of *Basileia* in Hellenistic Sicily." In *Ancient Tyranny,* edited by S. Lewis, 77–94. Edinburgh: Edinburgh University Press.

Zambon, E. 2008. *Tradition and Innovation: Sicily between Hellenism and Rome.* Historia Einzelschriften 205. Stuttgart: Franz Steiner Verlag.

Zancan, P. 1934. *Il monarcato ellenistico nel suoi elementi federativi.* Pubblicazioni della Facoltà di Lettere e Filosofia, Università di Padova 7. Padua: Casa Editrice Dott. Antonio Milani.

Zecchino, M. R. 2017. "Weights and Measures in the Norman-Swabian Kingdom of Sicily." In *People, Texts and Artefacts: Cultural Transmission in the Medieval Norman Worlds,* edited by D. Bates et al., 253–66. London: University of London Press.

Zevi, F., and B. Zevi. 1991. "L'Atrium Regium." *Archeologia Classica* 43: 475–87.

Zoppi, C. 1996. "Le cretule di Selinunte." In *Archives et sceaux du monde Hellénistique/archivi e sigilli nel mondo ellenistico: Torino, Villa Gualino, 13–16 gennaio 1993,* edited by M.-F. Boussac and A. Invernizzi, 327–40. Bulletin de correspondance hellénique Supplement 29. Paris: E. de Boccard.

Zupko, R. E. 1981. *Italian Weights and Measures from the Middle Ages to the Nineteenth Century.* Philadelphia: American Philosophical Society.

INDEX LOCORUM

INDEX